Ouidah

Western African Studies

Ouidah

The Social History
of a West African Slaving 'Port'
1727–1892

ROBIN LAW
Professor of African History
University of Stirling

Ohio University Press
ATHENS

James Currey
OXFORD

James Currey
73 Botley Road
Oxford OX2 0BS

Ohio University Press
Scott Quadrangle
Athens, Ohio 45701

British Library Cataloguing in Publication Data
Law, Robin
    Ouidah : the social history of a West African slaving
    'port', 1727-1892. - (West African studies)
    1. Slave trade - Africa, West - History - 18th century
    2. Slave trade - Africa, West - History - 19th century
    3. Ouidah (Benin) - History - 18th century 4. Ouidah (Benin)
    - History - 19th century
    I. Title
    966.8'3

ISBN 0-85255-498-2 (James Currey cloth)
ISBN 0-85255-497-4 (James Currey paper)

Library of Congress Cataloging-in-Publication Data
available on request

ISBN 0-8214-1571-9 (Ohio University Press cloth)
ISBN 0-8214-1572-7 (Ohio University Press paper)

Typeset in 10½/11½ pt Monotype Ehrhardt
by Long House Publishing Services, Cumbria, UK
Printed in Great Britain
by Woolnough, Irthlingborough

To the memory of
the more than one million enslaved Africans
who passed through Ouidah
on their way to slavery in the Americas
or death in the Middle Passage

Contents

Contents

8

From Dahomian to French Rule

List of Maps & Tables

Maps

Tables

Acknowledgements

*Illustrations on chapter openings: based on an appliqué cloth
representing the history of Ouidah,
Historical Museum at Ouidah*

The project of writing a history of Ouidah was initially conceived in 1991 and took on more concrete shape in a visit to the Republic of Bénin in January 1992. That it has finally come to fruition is the result of generous assistance received from numerous institutions and individuals, for which acknowledgement is gratefully made.

Among the many institutions that have contributed to the realization of the project, thanks are due first to the University of Stirling, not only for maintaining me in gainful employment, but more particularly for the grant of sabbatical leave in the autumn semester of 2001, when much of the final work of writing was done. During the academic session 2000/01 I held a visiting position at the Hebrew University of Jerusalem, when much of my time was likewise devoted to this work; my thanks to the Lady Davis Fellowship Trust and the Harry S. Truman Research Institute of the Hebrew University for their support in this period. Other institutions that in various ways have supported and assisted the research, especially by the promotion of collaborative networks for the exchange of ideas and information, from which it has benefited enormously, are the Nigerian Hinterland Project at York University, Toronto (and, through its funding of this project, the Social Sciences and Humanities Research Council of Canada), and the UNESCO Slave Route Project.

Research was undertaken in several archives and libraries, to whose staff grateful thanks are recorded: notably the libraries of the University of Stirling and the School of Oriental and African Studies, London; the Public Record Office, London; the Archives Nationales, Section d'Outre-Mer, Aix-en-Provence; the Centre de Documentation de la Faculté des Arts et Sciences Humaines of the Université Nationale du Bénin, Abomey-Calavi, and the Archives Nationales, Porto-Novo, in Bénin. Although the research has been mainly based on work in archives overseas, it also critically depended on several visits to Bénin, not only to work in local archives but also to collect oral information in Ouidah and more generally for discussions with local scholars; my gratitude is due therefore to those institutions that gave financial support for some of these visits, notably the Faculty of Arts and the Department of

Acknowledgements

History of the University of Stirling, for visits in 1992, 1996 and 2001, and UNESCO, for a visit in 1994.

The individuals who have contributed to this work are too numerous for all to be acknowledged here by name, but there are some to whom my debts are so great as to require explicit mention. First, I must make clear my indebtedness to earlier researchers in the field, upon whose work I have depended even when my own conclusions have sometimes differed: especially important has been the work of Ouidah's leading local historian, Casimir Agbo, while among modern academic scholars, particular acknowledgement is due to Ade Akinjogbin, Edna Bay, Patrick Manning, John Reid, David Ross, Elisée Soumonni and Jerry Michael Turner. For their generosity in supplying ideas, material and information, special mention should be made of Edna Bay, Suzanne Preston Blier, Alberto da Costa e Silva, Léopold David-Gnahoui, Félix Iroko, Adam Jones, Kristin Mann and Elisée Soumonni; for assistance in tracking down and verifying particular references, I thank Olatunji Ojo and Silke Strickrodt; and for reading and commenting on a preliminary draft of this work, Ella Keren, Paul Lovejoy, Martin Lynn and David Richardson. For her assistance as guide and interpreter in several visits to Ouidah, as well as for sharing her profound local knowledge, my thanks to Martine de Souza. For their generous hospitality and other practical assistance in Bénin, I am deeply grateful to Elisée and Maria Soumonni and Obarè and Maryamou Bagodo.

This book is not offered with any pretensions to represent the final word on the history of Ouidah. There is space, and indeed need, for much further work, especially (although certainly not exclusively) in areas and periods where my own firsthand research has been restricted, including French archival sources for the nineteenth century, Portuguese and Brazilian sources more generally and the period of Ouidah's transition from Dahomian to French rule in the late nineteenth and early twentieth centuries. I hope that those who work on Ouidah in future will enjoy the experience, and especially working in the town itself, as much as myself.

Abbreviations

Africa (London) Africa, Journal of the International African Institute
Africa (Rome)   Africa, Rivista trimestrale di studi e documentazione dell'Istituto
          Italo-Africano
ANB   Archives Nationales du Bénin, Porto-Novo
ANF   Archives Nationales de la France, Aix-en-Provence
BIFAN   *Bulletin de l'Institut Français/ Fondamental d'Afrique Noire*
CEA   *Cahiers d'Études Africaines*
CJAS   *Canadian Journal of African Studies*
ED   *Études Dahoméennes*
GLL   Le Grand Livre Lolamè (Aného, Togo)
HA   *History in Africa*
IJAHS   *International Journal of African Historical Studies*
JAH   *Journal of African History*
PP   Parliamentary Papers, United Kingdom
JHSN   *Journal of the Historical Society of Nigeria*
PRO   Public Record Office, London
RC   *Revue Coloniale*
RGCG   *Royal Gold Coast Gazette and Commercial Advertiser*
RMC   *Revue Maritime et Coloniale*
S&A   *Slavery and Abolition*
UGDO   Union Générale pour le Développement de Ouidah
UNB   Université Nationale du Bénin
WMMS   Wesleyan Methodist Missionary Society Archives, London
WMQ   *William and Mary Quarterly*

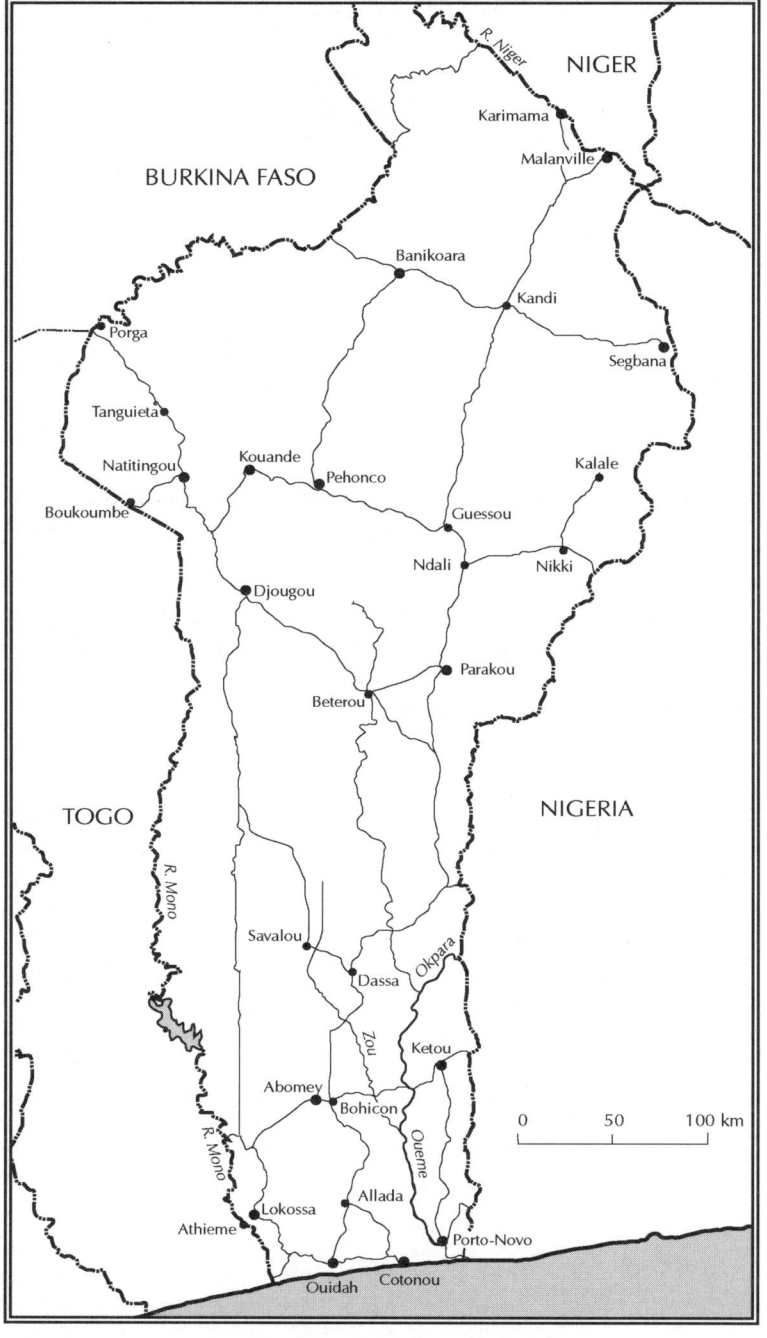

Map 1 The Republic of Bénin

Introduction

Ouidah is situated in the coastal area (in the Department of Atlantique) of the modern Republic of Bénin (formerly the French colony of Dahomey) in West Africa.[1] In origin, it is an indigenous African town, which had existed long before the French colonial occupation in 1892. In the pre-colonial period, it had belonged successively to two African states, first the kingdom of Hueda (whence the name 'Ouidah') and from 1727 that of Dahomey, from which the French colony took its name;[2] and the first language of its inhabitants today remains Fon, the language of Dahomey, with French inherited from the colonial period as the superimposed official language of administration and education. Today, Ouidah has a population of around 25,000, which by modern standards is quite modest, and it is dwarfed by the two leading cities of southern Bénin: the official capital Porto-Novo, 60 km to the east (with a population probably around 200,000), and the commercial centre and international port of Cotonou, 40 km to the east (perhaps approaching 1,000,000).

In the precolonial period, however, Ouidah was the principal commercial centre in the region and the second town of the Dahomey kingdom, exceeded in size only by the capital Abomey, 100 km inland. In particular, it served as a major outlet for the export of slaves for the trans-Atlantic trade. The section of the African coast on which Ouidah is situated, in geographical terms the Bight (or Gulf) of Benin, was known to Europeans between the seventeenth and nineteenth centuries as the 'Slave Coast', from its prominence as a source of supply for the Atlantic slave trade; and within this region Ouidah was by far the most important point of embarkation for slaves, far outshadowing its nearest rival, Lagos, 150 km to the east (in modern Nigeria). Ouidah was a leading slaving port for almost two

---

[1] The French colony became the independent Republic of Dahomey in 1960, the change of name to Bénin occurring in 1975. The Republic of Bénin should be distinguished from the kingdom of Benin, situated in what is today Nigeria.

[2] In the present work, to avoid confusion, the name Dahomey is used only with reference to the pre-colonial kingdom, the modern territory being referred to as Bénin.

centuries, from the 1670s to the 1860s. During this period, the Bight of Benin is thought to have accounted for around 22 per cent of all slaves exported to the Americas, and Ouidah for around 51 per cent of exports from the Bight.[3] Given the current consensual estimate of between 10 and 11 million slaves exported from Africa in this period, this suggests that Ouidah supplied well over a million slaves, making it the second most important point of embarkation of slaves in the whole of Africa (behind only Luanda, in Angola).[4]

This prominence of Ouidah in the Atlantic slave trade is reflected in the occurrence of versions of its name in various contexts in the African diaspora in the Americas. For example, there is a village called 'Widah' in Jamaica, originally a sugar plantation, presumably so named through being settled with slaves imported from Ouidah. In Haiti, one of the principal deities of the Afro-American *vaudou* religion, the goddess Ezili, is distinguished in one of her forms as Ezili-Freda-Dahomi, 'Ezili [of] Ouidah [in] Dahomey';[5] although one modern account has argued that Ezili is a purely Haitian creation, without African antecedents, there is in fact in Ouidah to the present day a shrine of Azili (*sic*), a female river spirit, who is evidently the prototype of the Haitian goddess.[6] The name of the town was also commemorated in that of the ship of the pirate Sam Bellamy, the *Whydah*, wrecked off Cape Cod in what is now the USA in 1717, but located and excavated by marine archaeologists, to become the subject of a museum exhibition in the 1990s, this ship having been originally, prior to its capture and appropriation by pirates, engaged in the slave trade and named after the West African town.[7] Ouidah's prominence in European commerce is also reflected in the application of the name Whidah-bird to a genus of the weaver-bird that is in fact common throughout tropical Africa but became familiar to the wider world through Ouidah; in English usage, the name was commonly corrupted into 'widow-bird' (whence, rather than directly from the name Ouidah, its zoological name, *Vidua*), under which form it was celebrated in a poem by Shelley.

In more recent times, Ouidah has figured in a historical novel dealing with the slave trade, by Bruce Chatwin, based on the career of the Brazilian slave-trader Francisco Felix de Souza, who settled permanently in the town in the 1820s.[8] In the 1990s a systematic attempt was made to exploit Ouidah's historical role in the Atlantic slave trade for its promotion as a centre of 'cultural tourism', with the development of monuments to the slave trade and its victims along the road from the town to the beach where slaves were embarked, now designated 'the slaves'

---

[3] David Eltis & David Richardson, 'West Africa and the transatlantic slave trade: new evidence of long-run trends', *S&A*, 18 (1997), 16–35; David Eltis et al., 'Slave-trading ports: towards an Atlantic-wide perspective', in Robin Law & Silke Strickrodt (eds), *Ports of the Slave Trade* (Stirling, 1999), 12–34.

[4] These figures relate to the period 1650–1870. Perhaps a further 1 million slaves were exported before 1650; the Bight of Benin would have contributed a much smaller proportion of this earlier trade, and Ouidah very little.

[5] Alfred Métraux, *Le Vaudou haïtien* (Paris, 1958), 22.

[6] Joan Dayan, *Haiti, History and the Gods* (Berkeley, 1998), 58; for Azili in Ouidah, see Chapter 3.

[7] Barry Clifford, *Expedition Whydah* (New York, 1999).

[8] Bruce Chatwin, *The Viceroy of Ouidah* (London, 1980). For de Souza, see below, Chapters 5–6.

route [la route des esclaves]'.[9] This also led to the town featuring in television programmes dealing with the slave trade, including a BBC 'Timewatch' pro-gramme in 1997 and an episode of the African travels of Henry Louis Gates, Jr, in 1999.[10] What has hitherto remained lacking, however, is any study based on detailed research of the town's history in general, or of its role in the Atlantic slave trade in particular: a deficiency which this volume seeks to redress.

Situating Ouidah's history

The present work represents, at one level, a continuation of my earlier research on the history of the Slave Coast, and in particular its role as a source of supply for the Atlantic slave trade.[11] A central concern of the present book, as of this earlier work, remains the organization of the African end of the slave trade, and the impact of participation in this trade on the historical development of the African societies involved. The present work, however, is informed by a significantly different perspective. My earlier analysis was very much written from the viewpoint of the Dahomian monarchy, in effect of the inland capital city of Abomey; and this focus is shared by other earlier work on the history of Dahomey, including the major published studies by Ade Akinjogbin (1967) and Edna Bay (1998), and the unpublished doctoral theses of David Ross (1967) and John Reid (1986).[12] This more recent research, on the other hand, in focusing on the coastal commercial centre of Ouidah, represents, if not quite a view from below, nevertheless a perspective from what was, in political terms, the periphery rather than the centre. It therefore foregrounds rather different aspects of the operation of the slave trade, including especially the evolution of the merchant community in Ouidah, and in particular the growth of a group of private traders that was distinct from the official political establishment, and whose relations with the Dahomian monarchy grew increasingly problematic over time.[13]

[9] For slave trade commemoration in Ouidah, see Thereza A. Singleton, 'The slave trade remembered on the former Gold and Slave Coasts', S&A, 20 (1999), 150-69; Roberta Cafuri, 'Silenzi della memoria: la tratta degli schiavi', Africa (Rome), 55/2 (2000), 244-60; Robin Law, 'Memory, oblivion and return in commemoration of the Atlantic slave trade in Ouidah', Republic of Bénin, in Ralph Austen (ed.), The Atlantic Slave Trade in African and Diaspora Memory (forthcoming, Durham, N.C.). See also the official Bénin government publication, Nouréini Tidjani-Serpos & Patrick Écoutin, Ouidah, La Route des esclaves (English version, Ouidah, The Slave Route) (Cotonou, n.d.); and two local tourist guide-books: Martine de Souza & Mère Jah Evejah, Bienvenue à Ouidah au Bénin/Welcome to Ouidah in Benin (Ouidah, [1998]); Martine de Souza, Regard sur Ouidah/A Bit of History (Ouidah, 2000).

[10] 'The African Trade', BBC 2, 1998; 'The Slave Kingdoms', episode in the series 'Into Africa with Henry Louis Gates, Jr', BBC 2, 1999.

[11] Esp. Robin Law, The Slave Coast of West Africa, 1550–1750 (Oxford, 1991).

[12] I.A. Akinjogbin, Dahomey and its Neighbours 1708–1818 (Cambridge, 1967); Edna G. Bay, Wives of the Leopard: Gender, Politics and Culture in the Kingdom of Dahomey (Charlottesville, 1998); David A. Ross, 'The autonomous kingdom of Dahomey 1818–1894' (PhD thesis, University of London, 1967); John Reid, 'Warrior aristocrats in crisis: the political effects of the transition from the slave trade to palm oil commerce in the nineteenth-century kingdom of Dahomey' (PhD thesis, University of Stirling, 1986).

[13] For a preliminary treatment, see Robin Law, 'The origins and evolution of the merchant community in Ouidah', in Law & Strickrodt, Ports of the Slave Trade, 55–70.

Introduction

African coastal entrepôts such as Ouidah played a critical role in the operation of the Atlantic slave trade, by helping to coordinate exchanges between hinterland suppliers and European ships, thereby accelerating their turn-round, and also by supplying them with provisions to feed the slaves on their voyage.[14] In addition to extending and deepening understanding of the working of the slave trade, a study of Ouidah also represents a contribution to a second area of growing interest recently within African historical studies, urban history. Studies of urban history in Africa have tended to concentrate on the growth of towns during the colonial and post-colonial periods;[15] but in West Africa especially, substantial towns existed already in the pre-colonial period, and Ouidah offers an exceptionally well-documented case-study of this earlier tradition of urbanism.[16] Within southern Bénin, Ouidah provides the premier example of the 'second generation' of pre-colonial towns, which served as centres for European maritime trade: what have been termed, although somewhat infelicitously, 'fort towns [*villes-forts*]', in distinction from the 'first generation' of 'palace-cities [*cités-palais*]', which served as capitals of indigenous African states, such as Abomey.[17]

The study of African coastal communities such as Ouidah also has a relevance for the currently fashionable project of 'Atlantic history', i.e. the attempt to treat the Atlantic as a historical unit, stressing interactions among the various states and communities that participated in the construction and operation of the trans-Atlantic trading system.[18] Although proponents of Atlantic history have tended to concentrate on links between Europe and the Americas, it needs to be recognized that African societies were also active participants in the making of the Atlantic world.[19] If there was an 'Atlantic community', the African coastal towns which served as embarkation points for the trans-Atlantic slave trade were part of it, their commercial and ruling elites being involved in political, social and cultural networks, as well as purely business linkages, which spanned the ocean.[20] The study of such African towns, moreover, adds an important comparative dimension to our

---

[14] A.G. Hopkins, *An Economic History of West Africa* (London, 1973), 106–7.

[15] J.D.Y. Peel, 'Urbanization and urban history in West Africa', *JAH*, 21 (1980), 269–77.

[16] See David M. Anderson & Richard Rathbone (eds), *Africa's Urban Past* (Oxford, 2000). This includes a preliminary treatment of the case of Ouidah: Robin Law, 'Ouidah: a pre-colonial urban centre in coastal West Africa, 1727–1892', 85–97.

[17] For this classification, see Alfred Comlan Mondjannagni, *Campagnes et villes au sud de la République Populaire du Bénin* (Paris, 1977), 295–341; the 'third generation' being towns that served as administrative or commercial centres within the colonial system, and the 'fourth generation' the unique case of Cotonou as the modern economic and de facto political capital of Bénin. These 'generations', it should be stressed, are not to be understood necessarily as distinguishing among different groups of towns, since they may represent successive periods in the history of a single town: for example, Ouidah itself originated as a town of the 'second generation' but then developed as a colonial town of the 'third generation'. The term '*villes-forts*' seems unfortunate since, as Mondjannagni acknowledges (309–10), the European commercial establishments in them were not necessarily (and for example in Ouidah were not originally) fortified.

[18] E.g. Bernard Bailyn, 'The idea of Atlantic history', *Itinerario*, 20/1 (1996), 38–44.

[19] See John Thornton, *Africa and Africans in the Making of the Atlantic World, 1400–1680* (Cambridge, 1992).

[20] Robin Law & Kristin Mann, 'West Africa in the Atlantic community: the case of the Slave Coast', *WMQ*, 56/2 (1999), 307–34; also Robin Law, 'The port of Ouidah in the Atlantic community', in Horst Pietschmann (ed.), *Atlantic History: History of the Atlantic System 1580–1830* (Göttingen, 2002), 349–64.

understanding of the growth and functioning of port cities in the Atlantic world in the era of the slave trade, since previous studies of Atlantic port towns in this period have concentrated on ports in the Americas.[21] But such American ports were European colonial creations, which functioned as enclaves or centres of European power, a model that is not applicable to Atlantic ports in Africa, which remained under indigenous sovereignty (apart from the exceptional case of Luanda in Angola, which uniquely had already become a Portuguese colony in the sixteenth century).

There have been a number of studies of particular West African coastal 'port' communities in the pre-colonial period, which have served to delineate a number of general issues in their history: the organization of overseas commerce, the relationships between ports and their hinterlands, the effects of their involvement in Atlantic commerce on their political and social structures and demographic growth, and the problems posed for them by the transition from the slave trade to exports of agricultural produce such as palm oil in the nineteenth century.[22] Much of this work, however, has dealt with the general history of the states or communities in which ports were situated, rather than with the specific history of the port towns themselves. Examples are, within the Slave Coast, studies of two coastal communities west of Ouidah, the Gen kingdom (which included the port of Little Popo, modern Aného) by Nicoué Gayibor, and the Anlo confederacy (including the port of Keta) by Sandra Greene.[23] Those studies which have focused on the history of coastal towns specifically have generally related to communities which were 'city-states', in the sense of being independent of outside political authority: examples being, on the eastern Slave Coast, the study of Badagry by Caroline Sorensen-Gilmour; and beyond the Slave Coast, in the Bight of Biafra to the east, those of Bonny by Susan Hargreaves, of New Calabar by Waibinte Wariboko, Old Calabar by John Latham, and Douala by Ralph Austen and Jonathan Derrick.[24] In consequence, these have a rather different and more diffuse focus than the present work, which seeks to highlight especially the development and functioning of Ouidah as an urban community. The work which comes closest to my own concerns among earlier studies of West African port communities is Harvey Feinberg's study of Elmina, on the Gold Coast (modern Ghana), to the west.[25] But Elmina was a very different sort of place from Ouidah, not only in being

[21] E.g. Franklin W. Knight & Peggy K. Liss (eds), *Atlantic Port Cities* (Princeton, 1991).

[22] See the studies collected in Law & Strickrodt, *Ports of the Slave Trade*.

[23] Nicoué L. Gayibor, *Le Genyi* (Lomé, 1990); Sandra E. Greene, *Gender, Ethnicity and Social Change on the Upper Slave Coast: A History of the Anlo-Ewe* (London, 1996). See also Silke Strickrodt, 'Afro-European trade relations on the western Slave Coast, 16th to 19th centuries' (PhD thesis, University of Stirling, 2003).

[24] Caroline Sorensen-Gilmour, 'Badagry 1784–1863' (PhD thesis, University of Stirling, 1995); Susan M. Hargreaves, 'The political economy of nineteenth-century Bonny' (PhD thesis, University of Birmingham, 1987); W.E. Wariboko, 'New Calabar and the forces of change, c. 1850–1945' (PhD thesis, University of Birmingham, 1991); A.J.H. Latham, *Old Calabar 1600–1891* (Oxford, 1973); Ralph A. Austen & Jonathan Derrick, *Middlemen of the Cameroons Rivers: The Duala and their Hinterland, c. 1600–c. 1960* (Cambridge, 1999).

[25] Harvey Feinberg, *Africans and Europeans in West Africa: Elminans and Dutchmen on the Gold Coast during the Eighteenth Century* (Philadelphia, 1989).

a 'city-state', but also in the preponderant influence exercised there by a European power, in the form of the Dutch West India Company, so that its history, in relation to that of Ouidah, is illuminating as much by way of contrasts as of similarities.

The case of Ouidah may also serve to refine or qualify some of the conventional conceptual categories that have been applied to West African 'port' communities. In the most general terms, Ouidah can be interpreted as a 'middleman' community: this term being understood, as Austen and Derrick propose for the case of Douala, not only in relation to the exchange of commodities, but also with reference to the role of such coastal communities as intermediaries in the transmission of cultural influences, and in the longer term in mediating the accommodation of African societies to European economic and political dominance.[26] However, the more specific categories that have been developed in order to elucidate the interstitial position of African coastal 'middleman' communities seem more problematic. The concept of an 'enclave-entrepôt', applied to Elmina by Feinberg, for example, does not fit the case of Ouidah, where European power was much more limited, and which in this was a more typical case.[27] That of a neutral 'port of trade', propounded by economic anthropologists of the 'substantivist' school, such as Karl Polanyi, although elaborated with reference to the specific case of Ouidah, is not in fact sustained by the detailed empirical evidence relating to the operation of the Atlantic trade there.[28]

Chronologically, this study concentrates on the period of Dahomian rule over Ouidah, after 1727, although an introductory chapter deals with the town's origins, including its earlier history under the Hueda kingdom. The justification for this emphasis relates basically to the nature of the available source material, which is much more abundant for the Dahomian period. This, however, also reflects the fact that Ouidah became much more important under Dahomian rule, not only as a commercial centre, but also now as a centre of provincial administration. The study effectively concludes with the French occupation in 1892, although with a brief epilogue treating the fate of the town under colonial rule. This has been done with some hesitation, since in general there is a strong case for downplaying the conventional perception of the establishment of colonial rule as a watershed, and for tracing continuities and transformations in the 'middleman' role into the colonial period, as was illuminatingly done by Austen and Derrick for the case of Douala.[29] However, whereas in the cases of ports that remained prominent into the colonial period – such as Accra in Ghana, and Lagos in Nigeria, as well as Douala in Cameroun – the reality of continuity is transparent, this is less true of Ouidah,

---

[26] Austen & Derrick, *Middlemen*, 1–4.

[27] Feinberg, *Africans and Europeans*, 1–6, 155–8.

[28] Rosemary Arnold, 'A port of trade: Whydah on the Guinea Coast', in Karl Polanyi et al. (eds), *Trade and Market in the Early Empires* (New York, 1957), 154–76; Karl Polanyi, *Dahomey and the Slave Trade* (Seattle, 1966), 96–139.

[29] See also the emphasis on pre-colonial antecedents by John Parker, *Making the Town: Ga State and Society in Early Colonial Accra* (Oxford, 2000), xviii–xix; although the study itself focuses on the period of colonial rule.

where the imposition of colonial rule represented more of a historical break. The experience of Ouidah under colonialism was essentially of economic and political marginalization; although this process had begun already in the second half of the nineteenth century, and was only intensified and accelerated by the changed conditions of colonial rule.

Reconstructing Ouidah's history

Apart from its intrinsic interest as one of the leading African slave-trading ports, the case of Ouidah also warrants study because the documentation available for its history is exceptionally rich, and serves to pose or illustrate some significant methodological issues of more general relevance in the field of pre-colonial African history, especially in the possibilities of combination of information from different categories of material: basically, as between foreign (European) contemporary and local traditional sources.[30]

The greatest mass of detailed documentation for the history of Ouidah derives from the European commercial presence, although the most useful sources are not in fact those deriving directly and specifically from the conduct of European trade. The most informative sources for the eighteenth century are the records of the permanently organized fortified factories which the three leading European nations involved – the French, English and Portuguese – maintained in Ouidah;[31] among which, the best preserved are those of the English.[32] These provide detailed documentation of the forts' day-to-day activities and interactions with the rest of the community, and thus constitute a rich source for the social and political, as well as the narrowly economic history of the town. With the legal abolition of the slave trade in the early nineteenth century, these forts were abandoned, leaving something of a hiatus in the evidence until the 1840s. In the middle decades of the nineteenth century, documentation on the town's history is provided above all by the records of the British government, relating to its campaign to suppress the now illegal slave trade, which included the maintenance of a vice-consulate in Ouidah between 1849 and 1852. The French government also intervened in Dahomey, to defend France's commercial interests, from the 1850s, and likewise maintained a vice-consulate in Ouidah from 1863. Some material is also provided by Christian missions that operated in the town: British Methodists in 1854–67, and French Catholics in 1861–71 and again from 1884. There are also a number of detailed

---

[30] On this, this study represents a more optimistic perspective than that of Ralph A. Austen, 'The slave trade as history and memory: confrontations of slaving voyage documents and communal traditions', *WMQ*, 58 (2001), 229–44.

[31] Only the French fort has been the subject of detailed study: Simone Berbain, *Le Comptoir français de Juda (Ouidah) au XVIIIe siècle* (Paris, 1942).

[32] Since the original foundation of this factory, in the 1680s, predated the Union of England and Scotland (1707), it is properly called 'English' in its earliest phase. Strictly, it later became 'British', but insistence on this distinction can tend towards pedantry, especially as the word for 'British' in Fon (as also in French) is in fact 'English [Glensi]'; I have therefore continued to refer to the 'English fort' in conformity with local usage.

published accounts by European visitors to Ouidah in this period, among which the most informative are those of the Scottish explorer John Duncan in 1845, the British naval officer (engaged in the anti-slaving squadron) Frederick Forbes in 1849–50, and the British consul (and pioneer anthropologist) Richard Burton in 1863–4.[33]

Source material of local provenance also includes some contemporary written material, deriving from the community of settlers from Brazil that was established in the town in the nineteenth century. Occasional items of correspondence from or addressed to Brazilian traders resident in Ouidah are preserved in overseas archives, especially in Britain among papers seized from illegal slave ships intercepted by the British navy. Little comparable material seems to have been preserved in Ouidah itself, although it is frequently claimed that written records which once existed were destroyed by fire or other hazards. A few items do, however, survive in local possession (or at least did so until recently), notably a letter-book of the Brazilian trader José Francisco dos Santos, containing correspondence from 1844–7 and 1862–71;[34] and the will of Antonio d'Almeida, an African-born freed slave who had returned from Brazil to resettle in Africa, made out at Ouidah in 1864.[35]

More substantial, as well as of greater chronological depth, is the information provided by local traditions. Much of this material also exists already in written form. Two surveys of Ouidah traditions were made by French colonial officials, Marcel Gavoy in 1913 and Reynier in 1917; the purpose of the collection of this material was explicitly to understand the existing political system, in order to inform administrative arrangements under French colonial rule.[36] Although these were published only many years later, they evidently circulated in Ouidah in typescript earlier, and have exercised considerable influence on local perceptions of history.

There is also a substantial tradition of local historical writing by African authors. Among such works by local writers, the earliest was a study of Ouidah 'origins' published in a Roman Catholic church journal in 1925–6, by Paul Hazoumé, a leading figure in the literary history of Bénin, who was in origin from Porto-Novo rather than Ouidah, but had worked for several years as a schoolmaster in the latter town.[37] The most substantial local history (and an indispensable source and guide

---

[33] John Duncan, *Travels in Western Africa* (London, 1847); Frederick E. Forbes, *Dahomey and the Dahomans* (London, 1851); Richard F. Burton, *A Mission to Gelele, King of Dahome* (London, 1864).

[34] Published in French translation by Pierre Verger, 'Cent-douze lettres de Alfaiate', in Verger et al., *Les Afro-américains* (Dakar, 1952), 53–99 (cited hereafter as 'Dos Santos correspondence'). Recent enquiries in Ouidah failed to confirm the continued existence of this letter-book in the dos Santos household there; it may be in the possession of a family member resident outside the town.

[35] Ibid., 21–3; with original Portuguese text in Pierre Verger, *Os libertos: sete caminhos na liberdade de escravos da Bahia no século XIX* (Salvador, Bahia, 1992), 121–4.

[36] 'Note historique sur Ouidah par l'Administrateur Gavoy (1913)', *ED*, 13 (1955), 45–70; ANB, 1E14₆, 'Recherches sur l'organisation intérieure du commandement indigène', by Reynier, Ouidah, 1 Dec. 1917, published as 'Ouidah: organisation du commandement', *Mémoire du Bénin*, 2 (1993), 30–68.

[37] Paul Hazoumé, 'Aperçu historique sur les origines de Ouidah', in 6 parts (apparently incomplete), in *La Reconnaissance africaine*, nos 4–5, 7–8, 10–11 (1925–6).

for the modern historian) is a book by Casimir Agbo, published in 1959.[38] There are also a number of histories of particular Ouidah families. Traditions of the de Souza family, descended from the Francisco Felix de Souza mentioned above, were published by Norberto Francisco de Souza, a grandson of the founder and successor to the headship of the family, in 1955; and a more extended compilation of material from various sources was published by Simone de Souza, a Frenchwoman married into the family, in 1992.[39] Substantial histories also exist of the Dagba family, descended from a man who served as Yovogan, or Dahomian governor, of Ouidah for an exceptionally long period in the nineteenth century (1823–1870s); and of the Quénum family, who were the most prominent indigenous Dahomian merchants in the town in the second half of the nineteenth century.[40] This material available already in written form has been supplemented by local fieldwork undertaken by myself, during several visits to Ouidah between 1992–2001. Besides interviewing informants in the town, this has involved extensive conversations with experts in local history, including members of the staff of the Historical Museum of Ouidah: especially Martine de Souza, one of the museum guides (and a great-great-great-granddaughter of the original de Souza).

Something may be said here of the character of historical 'tradition' in Ouidah. First, it should be stressed that it is not exclusively 'oral'; not only has much of it been recorded in writing, as has been seen, since the early twentieth century, but it has also evolved in interaction with written sources. Gavoy's survey of 1913 already represents an attempt to combine local traditions with information derived from contemporary European sources; and this conflation of written and oral material has remained characteristic of local history writing in Ouidah ever since. Agbo's *Histoire*, for example, cites the earlier studies of Gavoy and Reynier, together with published sources, as well as additional material of his own; the latter including reminiscences of persons with direct personal experience of the late pre-colonial period, as well as more strictly 'traditional' material relating to earlier times. In Ouidah, as in coastal West Africa more generally, the 'traditions' current nowadays in oral form are regularly subject to the influence of 'feedback' from written sources, including now especially Agbo's own work.[41]

It should also be noted that local traditions provide relatively little in the way of a narrative of the history of the community as a whole, apart from certain major events, such as the original foundation of the town, the arrival of the first European traders, the Dahomian conquest in the 1720s, and the establishment in the town of Francisco Felix de Souza in the nineteenth century. Local historical

---

[38] Casimir Agbo, *Histoire de Ouidah* (Avignon, 1959). Other examples of the genre are Venance S. Quénum, *Ouidah, cité historique des "Houeda"* (Ouidah, [1982]); Dominique Avimagbogbênou Quénum, *L'Histoire de Glexwe (Ouidah)* (Dakar, 1999).

[39] Norberto Francisco de Souza, 'Contribution à l'histoire de la famille de Souza', *ED*, 13 (1955), 17–21; Simone de Souza, *La Famille de Souza du Bénin-Togo* (Cotonou, 1992).

[40] Léon-Pierre Ghézowounmè-Djomalia Dagba, *La Collectivité familiale Yovogan Hounnon Dagba de ses origines à nos jours* (Porto-Novo, 1982); Maximilien Quénum, *Les Ancêtres de la famille Quénum* (Langres, 1981). See also a shorter version of the Quénum family history: Faustin Possi-Berry Quénum, *Généalogie de la dynastie Houéhoun à la collectivité familiale Azanmado Houénou-Quénum* (Cotonou, 1993).

[41] On 'feedback', see David Henige, *Oral Historiography* (London, 1982), 81-7.

memory is in general more focused on the component elements that make up the town. As it existed by the end of the nineteenth century, Ouidah comprised twelve quarters, each with its own distinct origins and history. These were: first, Tové, the original settlement, which predated European contact, on the east of the town; second, three quarters associated with the European forts which were established in the town in the late seventeenth and early eighteenth centuries – from west to east (which is also the chronological order of their establishment) Ahouandjigo (French), Sogbadji (English) and Docomè (Portuguese); third, two quarters on the north of the town, which represent the Dahomian administrative establishment installed after the conquest of the 1720s – Fonsaramè, the 'Fon [i.e. Dahomian] quarter' (the location of the residence of the Dahomian viceroy), and Cahosaramè, 'Caho's quarter' (originally the site of the Dahomian military garrison, whose commander had the title Caho); and finally, six further quarters were added in the nineteenth century, all on the western side of the town, and all founded by individual merchants – Ganvè, founded by the Afro-French trader Nicolas d'Oliveira; three quarters associated with the Brazilian Francisco Felix de Souza, called Blézin, or in French Brésil (i.e. Brazil), Maro and Zomaï, and two established by indigenous African traders, Boya and Quénum quarters.[42] Gavoy's survey thus follows a sketch of the history of the town by separate notes on its various quarters, while Reynier's is wholly organized around the distinctive histories of the twelve quarters, and indeed most of its material relates to the origins and history of individual families within them; and a large section of Agbo's later *Histoire* reproduces this framework (along with most of Reynier's detailed information). In addition, as noted above, some prominent Ouidah families have published their own histories; and my own fieldwork has also related mainly to the history of particular families and compounds in the town.

The focus of local tradition on individual families is paralleled by the mass of detailed documentation in contemporary sources, which record the names or titles of many individuals in Ouidah with whom the various European agencies had dealings. In many cases, the same persons figure in both traditional and contemporary sources; in fact, my own interest in the possibility of a study of the town's social history was initially stimulated by the realization, in my first visits to Ouidah in the 1980s, that many of the names of families still living in the town were already familiar to me from the contemporary documentation of the pre-colonial period. The combination of traditional and contemporary sources often permits a quite detailed confrontation between the two, in which each can serve both as a control over and to elucidate obscurities in the other; and the history of particular families can

---

[42] The 12 quarters were listed by Reynier in 1917, although by then Boya and Ganvè were regarded as sub-divisions of a single quarter. Subsequent amalgamations reduced the number of recognized quarters to six: by the 1930s, these were Tové, Ahouandjigo, Sogbadji-Docomè (amalgamated in 1936), Fonsaramè (now including Cahosaramè), Boya-Ganvè and Brésil (incorporating Maro, Zomaï and Quénum quarters). On the other hand, some subsections of the original 12 quarters have subsequently claimed autonomous status: e.g. the compound of the Hodonou family, formerly part of Fonsaramè, is nowadays regarded as a separate quarter, Hodonousaramè.

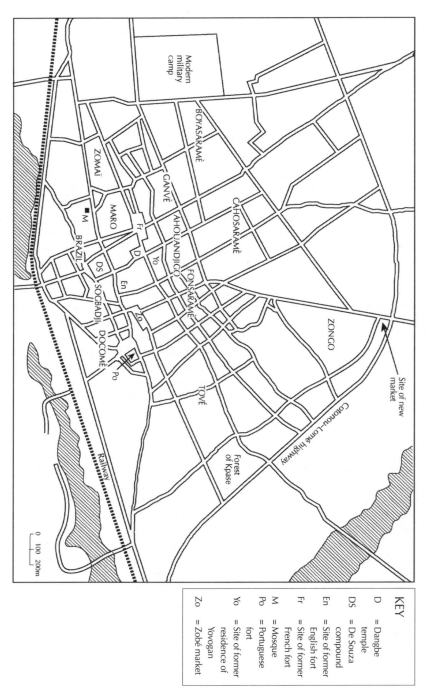

Map 2 Ouidah, showing the quarters and major historical sites

KEY

D = Dangbe temple

DS = De Souza compound

En = Site of former English fort

Fr = Site of former French fort

M = Mosque

Po = Portuguese fort

Yo = Site of former residence of Yovogan

Zo = Zobè market

be traced over several generations, in some cases back into the eighteenth century.

A further important 'source' for the history of Ouidah is the town itself, as it survives to the present. One consequence of Ouidah's marginalization in the twentieth century was that it was not subject to radical redevelopment. There were some important changes: notably the elimination of the office of the Dahomian viceroy, together with his official residence, whose site was given for the construction of the Roman Catholic cathedral in 1901, and the demolition of the French fort (now a public square) in 1908. But the basic layout of the town as it existed in the second half of the nineteenth century was preserved; the major colonial developments were added on to the town, as an extension of it (to the north-west), rather than disturbing the character of its historical centre. It is thus quite possible to use the walking tour of the town in Richard Burton's account from the 1860s to find one's way around and identify the major monuments even today.[43] Moreover, a detailed survey of the town's architectural heritage was undertaken as a joint project of the Bénin government with the French Organization for Overseas Research in 1990–91, and provides invaluable information on the town's history.[44]

The problem of perspective: Ouidah and the slave trade

Any study of an African 'middleman' community such as Ouidah in the pre-colonial period necessarily emphasizes the role of specifically 'African agency' in the operation of the Atlantic slave trade.[45] I am very conscious, in part through some of the responses to earlier presentations of my own work, that this is a controversial issue, in so far as there is a widespread disposition to regard any emphasis on the voluntary cooperation of Africans in the slave trade as, by implication, an attempt to deny or minimize the culpability of Europeans in it.[46] My own motive and purpose are quite other: it is because my starting point is within the history of Africa rather than of the slave trade as such, that I approach the latter from the perspective of its mode of operation and effects within Africa. Nor do I personally subscribe to the view that the involvement of some Africans in the operation of the slave trade serves to exonerate either the European societies or the individual Europeans who engaged in it. In part, this is because it implicitly assumes a sort of moral calculus, positing a fixed quantum of responsibility available for distribution, which would seem bizarre if applied in other contexts – in a case of murder, for example, where contributory responsibility assigned to others would not, I think, normally be thought to cancel or even diminish the guilt

---

[43] Burton, *Mission*, i, 58–116, chapter IV, 'A walk round Whydah'.

[44] Alain Sinou & Bernardin Agbo (eds), *Ouidah et son patrimoine* (Paris/Cotonou, 1991); see also the coffee-table spin-off, Alain Sinou, *Le Comptoir de Ouidah, une ville africaine singulière* (Paris, 1995).

[45] For the recent trend to emphasize the role of African agency in the slave trade, see, for example, David Eltis, *The Rise of African Slavery in the Americas* (Cambridge, 2000), ch. 7.

[46] E.g. Lansiné Kaba, 'The Atlantic slave trade was *not* a "black-on-black holocaust"', *African Studies Review*, 44/1 (2001), 1–20.

of the murderer. Beyond this, in the tradition of Leopold von Ranke,[47] I am in general sceptical about the enterprise of assigning guilt retrospectively, where this runs the risk of applying standards of moral or legal judgement in an ahistorical manner, as in the case of the slave trade, which, although nowadays consensually stigmatized as a 'crime against humanity', was for most of its history legal under both European and African law.[48] The historian is more properly concerned with issues of causation than of moral judgement of past events. Here, the view that the Atlantic slave trade was driven by supply conditions within Africa rather than by demand in the Americas seems to me perverse.[49] Even in narrowly economic terms, it is difficult to square with the statistics of the trade, which were characterized, at least from the late seventeenth century onwards, by a combination of increasing volume of exports with rising prices, implying that this expansion was demand-driven.[50] Beyond this, at a more basic level, it was after all not Africans who turned up in ships at ports in Europe or America offering cargoes of slaves for sale. As King Glele of Dahomey said in 1863, to a British mission urging him to abolish the trade, 'He did not send slaves away in his own ships, but "white men" came to him for them ... if they did not come, he would not sell'.[51]

It may also be said that, in stressing African agency in the slave trade, this work is consistent with the perceptions of the people of Ouidah themselves, who are of course in many cases descendants of the slave merchants prominent in the town's earlier history. It is sometimes suggested that Africans are nowadays reluctant to admit the 'complicity' of their ancestors in the slave trade.[52] In Ouidah, however, there has been little disposition to deny this aspect of the community's history. The local historian Casimir Agbo, for example, explicitly invokes the partnership that operated between European slave-traders and the local African authorities: 'The Europeans were very accommodating in their relations with the Hueda kings ... and the latter benefited from the situation ... [this] secured large resources to the throne'; likewise, when Ouidah was brought under the rule of the kings of Dahomey after 1727, 'all these judicious arrangements [for the administration of the town] and above all the slave trade enriched the kings and their representatives'.[53] When the French authorities demolished the former French fort in Ouidah in 1908, this provoked protests from the community that it was a valued monument

---

[47] Van Ranke's famous dictum about telling history *wie es eigentlich gewesen* was not, as it is commonly misunderstood, a claim that the historian can determine 'objective' truth, but rather a repudiation of the view that the historian should or could act as a judge.

[48] Although in the last period of the slave trade (in Ouidah, effectively from 1815) it was illegal under European law, though still legal in African systems of law.

[49] See William Gervase Clarence-Smith, 'The dynamics of the African slave trade', *Africa* (London), 64 (1994), 275–86.

[50] Patrick Manning, *Slavery and African Life* (Cambridge, 1990), 92–9.

[51] PP, Despatches from Commodore Wilmot respecting his Visit to the King of Dahomey (1863), no. 1, 29 Jan. 1863.

[52] This was alleged, for example, by African-Americans resident in Ghana, in connection with controversies over the representation of the slave trade in a historical exhibition at Cape Coast Castle in the 1990s: Christine Mueller Kreamer, 'Contested terrain: cultural negotiations and Ghana's Cape Coast Castle exhibition, "Crossroads of People, Crossroads of Trade"', in Austen, *Atlantic Slave Trade*.

[53] Agbo, *Histoire*, 34, 50.

of local history, and in particular of its long association with France.[54] Why the French demolished the fort is not clear, though many people in the town nowadays believe that it was out of feelings of shame at France's earlier role in the slave trade; if this is so, it is ironic, since local people evidently did not have any such feelings of shame.

There has been, at least until very recently, a local consensus that the slave trade was a good thing for Ouidah. Burton in the 1860s found that Kpate, the man who according to tradition welcomed the first European traders to Ouidah (and thereby inaugurated the town's participation in the slave trade) was 'worshipped as a benefactor to mankind';[55] and the cult of Kpate continues to the present. Under French colonial rule, when Ouidah, although now commercially marginalized, remained a leading centre of French education and literate culture, the emphasis in celebration of Kpate shifted from the material benefits of the slave trade to its role in the penetration of European influence: in the 1930s, it was noted that Kpate was venerated as 'the hero of the importation of European civilization'.[56]

This perspective evidently focuses on the implications of the slave trade for the local community, those who benefited directly or indirectly from the sale of slaves, rather than for the victims of the trade. The experience of the slaves themselves does not appear to have figured largely in local understandings of the trade. Attitudes to the slave trade in Ouidah have also, however, been affected by the fact that some of those exported as slaves returned to resettle in West Africa. One quarter of Ouidah, Maro, in the south-west of the town, was settled by former slaves returning from Brazil, beginning in the 1830s. Casimir Agbo, while acknowledging the brutalities involved in their original enslavement and transportation, nevertheless maintains, on the authority of some of these returned ex-slaves, that slaves 'were quite well treated in the Americas', and in particular that 'almost all' gained their freedom and 'most' returned home to Africa (whereas, in fact, only a very small minority of those exported into slavery were able to return). Again, he stresses their role in the dissemination of European culture: their enslavement in America enabled them to get 'a taste of civilization' and by their return they 'contributed to the civilization of their country of origin by the modern habits which they transmitted to their descendants and relatives'.[57]

In more recent projects of historical commemoration in Ouidah, emphasis has continued to be placed upon the cultural interactions deriving from the slave trade, though now with increasing interest in the town's role in transmitting the African religious traditions visible in America, especially the *vaudou* religion of Haiti, Brazilian *candomblé* and Cuban *santería*, as well as in the Brazilian influence in West Africa. Reciprocal cultural influences between Brazil and Bénin are thus central to the representation of the history of Ouidah in the exhibition in the Historical Museum established in the 1960s;[58] while the transmission of African religion to

[54] Ibid., 25.
[55] Burton, *Mission*, ii, 297.
[56] Christian Merlo, 'Hiérarchie fétichiste de Ouidah', *BIFAN*, Série B, 2/1–2 (1940), 7.
[57] Agbo, *Histoire*, 52–3.
[58] See the original version of the museum guidebook: Pierre Verger & Clément da Cruz, *Musée historique de*

the Americas was celebrated in the UNESCO-sponsored 'Ouidah '92' conference (actually held in January 1993), which took the form of a 'world festival of *vodun* arts and cultures'. It can be argued that this emphasis on the cultural consequences of the slave trade serves implicitly to silence the sufferings of its victims.[59] However, the victims of the trade were also commemorated in monuments constructed in connection with the 'Ouidah '92' conference along the 'slaves' route' from the town to the sea, notably the 'Door of No Return [La Porte du Non-Retour]' at the embarkation point on the beach. And in 1998 an explicit 'ceremony of repentance' was instituted in Ouidah, held annually in January, at which speeches are made requesting forgiveness from the descendants of enslaved Africans in the diaspora for the community's historical role in their forcible transportation.

In writing the history of Ouidah, there is no doubt that part of the problem of perspective arises, in my own case, from the experience of courteous welcome and generous assistance received in the course of my research from members of the Ouidah community nowadays, and a perhaps inevitable tendency to read this friendliness back into the historical representation of their ancestors. It is difficult in any case to attempt to reconstruct the history of a community from within without historical empathy sliding into a degree of emotional sympathy. However, the most important dimension of the problem relates to the more basic technical problem of the nature of the sources. Not only does this study depend mainly on European rather than African sources, but even the African sources available reflect the perspective of local beneficiaries of the slave trade – Dahomian administrators and local merchants, or persons providing ancillary services (such as porters and canoemen) – rather than of its victims. Moreover, in so far as local traditions principally represent the collective memories of particular families, they inevitably recall slave-traders such as Francisco Felix de Souza in relation to their descendants, as benevolent founding ancestors, rather than in relation to the slaves whom they sold, as exploiters of their fellow-humans.

Local tradition does give some access to the experience of enslavement, to the extent that many slaves were retained within Ouidah, rather than being sold into export; and such slaves also have descendants, who may preserve some memory of their lives. Martine de Souza, for example, is descended not only from the slave-trader Francisco Felix de Souza, but also, in the maternal line, from a slave; one of her great-grandmothers, Marie Lima, being in origin a captive taken, at the age of 15, by the Dahomian army in an attack on the town of Meko to the east, in modern Nigeria (in 1882), and sold in Ouidah to a prominent Brazilian trader, Joaquim João Dias Lima, who took her as his wife.[60] But those retained in local slavery were, in

---

[58] (cont.) *Ouidah* (Porto-Novo, 1969). This emphasis is less prominent in a more recent version: Romain-Philippe Ekanyé Assogba, *Le Musée d'histoire de Ouidah: Découverte de la Côte des Esclaves* (Cotonou, 1990). However, the exhibition itself remains substantially unchanged.

[59] Peter Sutherland, 'In memory of the slaves: an African view of the Diaspora in the Americas', in Jean Muteba Rahier (ed.), *Representations of Blackness and the Performance of Identities* (Westport, 1999), 195–211.

[60] Fieldwork, de Souza compound, Eulalie Dagba (Martine de Souza's mother, and grand-daughter of Marie Lima); Lima compound, both 9 Dec. 2001. Joaquim Lima died in 1915, his wife Marie in 1948.

comparative terms, the fortunate ones, in escaping the brutality of the middle passage and the harsher exploitation that was generally the fate of those taken into slavery in the Americas; indeed, it is recalled that, when Marie Lima's mother visited Ouidah, in an attempt to secure her daughter's liberation and return home (probably after the French conquest of Dahomey in 1892), she declined to leave. Partly in recognition of this, the descendants of slaves in Ouidah tend to maintain an identification as clients with those of their ancestors' owners, even when not actually absorbed into the family through intermarriage.

The experience of those who were transported into trans-Atlantic slavery is in comparison very poorly represented in the surviving documentation. A few of those sold into export, as noted above, were able to return to Africa, and some of the families founded by repatriated former slaves in Ouidah preserve some recollection of the circumstances of their original enslavement in Africa. Joaquim Lima, for example, was himself descended from an ex-slave from Brazil, and tradition in his family recalls that its founder, who was probably his grandfather, was originally from Mahi, north of Dahomey, and had been seized as a slave when he went to Abomey in an attempt to redeem his brother, who had earlier been taken captive by the Dahomian army.[61] But firsthand accounts by victims of the Atlantic slave trade are very rare. Of over a million slaves who were exported through Ouidah, only two appear to have left any sort of personal record. One of these, Mahommah Gardo Baquaqua, was exported through Ouidah to Brazil in 1845, and published his autobiography in the USA in 1854.[62] A second, Kazoola, alias Cudjo Lewis, was taken from Ouidah to Alabama, USA, in 1860; his story was recorded over 50 years later, when he was a very old man.[63]

Given that their sufferings and exploitation were the basis of the prosperity of Ouidah, as well as of the much greater opulence of the slave-owning European colonial societies in the Americas and of slaving ports in Europe, the slaves themselves arguably ought to occupy centre-place in an analysis of the history of the town during its period as a port of the Atlantic slave trade. But, although an attempt has been made in what follows to give attention to what the slave trade meant for the slaves who passed through Ouidah in transit to the Americas, as well as for the permanent inhabitants of the town, it cannot be claimed that proportionally, in terms of the amount of space their experience is accorded, they are adequately represented. The dedication of this book to their memory is offered as a compensatory gesture of acknowledgement of this inevitable failure.

---

[61] Reynier, 'Ouidah', 42. Joaquim Lima was probably a son of Joaquim de Cerqueira Lima, attested at Ouidah in the 1860s, whose father was an 'emigrant' from Brazil, formerly resident in Lagos: Burton, *Mission*, ii, 8–9.

[62] *Biography of Mahommah G. Baquaqua* (ed. Samuel Moore, Detroit, 1854); see also the modern edition, Robin Law & Paul E. Lovejoy (eds), *The Biography of Mahommah Gardo Baquaqua* (Princeton, 2001).

[63] He was interviewed on several occasions, including by Zora Neale Hurston, 'Cudjo's own story of the last African slaver', *Journal of Negro History*, 12 (1927), 648–63; see also Natalie Suzette Robertson, 'The African Ancestry of the Founders of Africatown, Alabama' (PhD thesis, University of Iowa, 1996). The date of his transportation is commonly given as 1859, but was more probably 1860.

Note on spelling

The spelling of local words and names in this study presents considerable difficulty. The Fon language can be transcribed in a variety of ways. Most accurately, a phonetic script is employed, which includes some letters additional to (or with different values from) the standard Latin alphabet. This script is not widely used in writing, however, Fon words and names being more commonly spelled in the standard Latin alphabet, thereby losing some of the distinctions made in the phonetic script. Very often, moreover, spelling follows French conventions, offering for example 'ou' for 'u', 'dj' for 'j', 'c' for 'k'. As an illustrative example, the name of the kingdom from which that of the town of Ouidah is derived may be written 'Xweđa' in the phonetic script, 'Hueda' in the Latin alphabet, or 'Houéda' in the French spelling.

The conventions adopted in this work are a compromise among the conflicting demands of accuracy, consistency and recognizability. For ordinary Fon words, titles and common personal names and for the names of pre-colonial kingdoms and ethnic groups, the quasi-phonetic transcription in the standard Latin alphabet is generally employed: as, for example, 'Hueda'. For the names of towns, and of families that still exist in Ouidah, however, it seemed proper to use the forms that are currently in use, which are generally in the French form: for example, the names of two villages to the south of Ouidah are given as 'Zoungbodji' and 'Djegbadji' (which is what a visitor will find on local signposts), rather than 'Zungboji' and 'Jegbaji'; and those of three of the major merchant families of the town as 'Adjovi', 'Codjia' and 'Gnahoui' (which is how family members nowadays spell these names), rather than 'Ajovi', 'Kojia' and 'Nyawi'. Spelling conventions were, of course, not standardized until recently, so that early written sources employ spellings that are inconsistent with each other, as well as being inaccurate by modern standards. In general, such deviant forms are employed in this work only in direct quotations from sources; otherwise modern spellings are preferred. In a few cases, however, corrupt early forms of local toponyms have become sanctioned by usage, and remain in general use today, and these are retained here, examples being the names of the kingdom 'Dahomey' and its capital 'Abomey' (rather than the more strictly correct 'Danhomé', 'Agbomé'). A special problem is posed by the case of Ouidah itself, whose name is commonly given in Anglophone literature (including earlier work of my own) in the form 'Whydah', which was the usual English spelling in the pre-colonial period. But here considerations of familiarity have to yield to the usage of the community itself, in which 'Ouidah' is the spelling in current and official use.

1

Origins

Ouidah Before the Dahomian Conquest

The history of Ouidah is intelligible only by reference to its geographical situation, which has however often been misunderstood and misrepresented in accounts of the operation of European trade in West Africa. It is commonly referred to as a 'port', but this is strictly inaccurate, indeed positively misleading.[1] Although it became an important centre for European maritime trade from the seventeenth century onwards, it is not in fact situated on the coast, but some 4 km inland, actually to the north of the lagoon which in this area runs parallel to the coast, and so separates Ouidah from the seashore. The slaves and other commodities exported through Ouidah had therefore to be taken overland and across the lagoon to the beach, rather than being embarked directly into European ships. At the coast itself, moreover, there is no 'port' in the sense of a sheltered harbour, but only an open roadstead. Indeed, heavy surf along the beach, and on sandbars parallel to it, makes it impossible for large vessels to approach close to the shore. European ships trading at Ouidah had therefore to stand 2–3 km off, and to communicate with the shore through smaller vessels, for which purpose African canoes were normally employed. The town's relative isolation from the sea, combined with its proximity to the coastal lagoon, played a critical role in shaping its historical development, during as well as prior to its involvement in the trans-Atlantic trade.

Although 'Ouidah' is the spelling of the town's name current nowadays, it occurs in European sources between the seventeenth and nineteenth centuries in various other forms: in English most commonly 'Whydah', in Dutch 'Fida', in French 'Juda', and in Portuguese 'Ajudá'. All these are attempts to render an indigenous name that would be more correctly written, by modern conventions, as 'Hueda' (or in a dialect variant 'Peda'). Strictly and originally, Hueda was not the name of the town nowadays called Ouidah, but rather of the kingdom to which it belonged in the late seventeenth and early eighteenth centuries, whose capital was

---

[1] Finn Fuglestad, 'La questionnement du "port" de Ouidah', in Oystein Rian et al. (eds), *Revolusjon og Resonnement* (Oslo, 1995), 125–36.

Savi, 11 km further north.[2] The people of Hueda belonged to the same linguistic group as the Fon of Dahomey, although historically distinct from them; this language family is nowadays generally called by scholars 'Gbe' (but formerly commonly 'Ewe' or 'Adja', and in French colonial usage 'Djedji').[3] In contemporary sources, the name Hueda may have been noted first by Spanish missionaries visiting the kingdom of Allada to the north-east in 1660, who recorded it (apparently) in the form 'Jura' or 'Iura';[4] more certainly, it enters the historical record in 1671 (as 'Juda'), when the French first established a trading factory there.[5] In 1727 the Hueda kingdom was conquered by the inland kingdom of Dahomey. As a political unit, it thereafter survived only in the form of a minor successor-state, formed by refugees from the Dahomian conquest, on the western shore of Lake Ahémé (Hen), about 20 km west of Ouidah, this relocated kingdom being distinguished as Hueda-Henji, 'Hueda on [Lake] Hen'.[6] However, the name Hueda (in its various European misspellings) continued to be applied to the coastal town, now subject to Dahomey. In the present work, to avoid confusion, the form 'Hueda' is used only to refer to the pre-1727 kingdom, and after 1727 to the successor kingdom-in-exile established to the west, while the modern form 'Ouidah' is used of the town.

Strictly, although the town could properly be described as '[in] Hueda', the use of this name to designate the town specifically is in origin a foreign, European terminology; and in local usage even today 'Ouidah' remains its normal name only in French. The correct indigenous name of the town, which is still usually used by its inhabitants when speaking in the local language, Fon, is Glehue (in French spelling, 'Gléhoué'). This name also regularly occurs in contemporary European sources from the seventeenth century onwards. The earliest extant document written from Ouidah, a letter from an English trader in 1681, is dated, quite correctly, at 'Agriffie in Whidaw', i.e. Glehue in Hueda.[7] Later, Europeans used versions of the name Glehue interchangeably with, although less commonly than, Ouidah: for example, in English 'Grigue', 'Griwhee' or 'Grewhe'; in French sometimes 'Glégoué' or 'Grégoué', but most commonly 'Gregoy'.[8]

---

[2] For the history of the Hueda kingdom, see esp. Robin Law, '"The common people were divided": monarchy, aristocracy and political factionalism in the kingdom of Whydah, 1671–1727', *IJAHS*, 23 (1990), 201–29; Gilles Raoul Soglo, 'Les Xweda: de la formation du royaume de Sayi (Saxe) à la dispersion, XVe–XVIIIe siècle' (Mémoire de maîtrise, UNB, 1994/5).

[3] Ewe and Adja are properly the names of particular subgroups of the linguistic family (in eastern Ghana and Togo), while Djedji derives from the name given to speakers of these languages in Brazil; 'Gbe' is a neologism, derived from the word for 'tongue' (and hence 'language') in these languages.

[4] Basilio de Zamora, 'Cosmographia, o descripcion del mundo' (MS of 1675, in Bibliotheca Publica do Estado, Toledo, Collecçion de MSS Bornon-Lorenzo, no. 244), 47; Joseph de Naxara, *Espejo mistico, en que el hombre interior se mira prácticamente illustrado* (Madrid, 1672), 278.

[5] As related retrospectively (1688) by Jean Barbot: Paul Hair et al. (eds), *Barbot on Guinea: The Writings of Jean Barbot on West Africa, 1678–1712* (London, 1992), ii, 635–6.

[6] This Hueda successor-state has been little studied; but see Soglo, 'Les Xweda', 70–78.

[7] Robin Law (ed.), *The English in West Africa 1681–83: The Local Correspondence of the Royal African Company of England 1681–99, Part 1* (London, 1997: hereafter cited as *English in West Africa*, i), no.476: John Thorne, Glehue, 24 May 1681.

[8] The suggestion of Burton, *Mission*, i, 61–2, that the name 'Glehue' was given to the town only after the Dahomian conquest in 1727 is clearly incorrect.

The French trader Jean Barbot, who visited the Hueda kingdom in 1682, gives the coastal village that served as its commercial centre a further different name, 'Pelleau'.[9] This name does not occur independently in reference to Ouidah in any later source, and Richard Burton, who enquired about it at Ouidah in the 1860s, found it 'now unknown'.[10] What seem to be versions of this name do occur, however, in European sources earlier in the seventeenth century, applied to a place on the coast between Popo (nowadays Grand-Popo, 30 km west of Ouidah) and Allada (whose principal coastal trading outlet was at Godomey, 30 km to the east): 'Fulao' and 'Foulaen'.[11] From the situation indicated, this was presumably also identical with the later Glehue/Ouidah. The names 'Pelleau', 'Fulao' and 'Foulaen' probably represent Hula, or in an alternative form Pla, which is the name of an ethnic group (whose language belongs, like Fon and Hueda, to the Gbe family) which according to tradition originated in Grand-Popo (whose correct indigenous name is, in fact, Hula) and migrated east to settle at various places along the coast, including in particular Jakin (modern Godomey).[12] 'Offra', the name given by Europeans to their principal place of trade in Allada during the second half of the seventeenth century (which was situated close to, though distinct from, Jakin), is clearly another variant of this name. The application of this name to Ouidah presumably reflects the fact that an important, perhaps originally the dominant, element in its population was Hula rather than Hueda.

The foundation of Ouidah

Stories of the foundation of Ouidah are in fact contradictory. The original settlement, which predated European contact, is generally identified today with the quarter called Tové, on the north-eastern side of the town; and this is consistent with a report of the early eighteenth century that the indigenous village of Glehue was situated to the east of the French and English forts there.[13] There is also, however, a compound called 'Glehue Daho', i.e. 'Great Glehue', to the west of Tové (nowadays considered to fall within Fonsaramè, the Dahomian quarter of the town); although now occupied by a Dahomian family, Nassara, this is also sometimes claimed to represent the original pre-Dahomian settlement, as its name implies.[14]

---

[9] Barbot, *On Guinea*, ii, 635.

[10] Burton, *Mission*, i, 108.

[11] 'Fulao', e.g. in Alonso de Sandoval, *Naturaleza, policia sagrada i profana, costumbres i ritos, disciplina i catechismo evangelico de todos Etiopes* (Seville, 1627), 51; 'Foulaen', in Olfert Dapper, *Naukeurige Beschrijvinge der Afrikaensche Gewesten* (2nd edn, Amsterdam, 1676), 2nd pagination, 115.

[12] For the Hula, see esp. A. Félix Iroko, *Les Hula du XIVe au XIXe siècle* (Cotonou, 2001), which concentrates on the original Hula homeland to the west. For traditions of Hula migrations to settle at Godomey and other places to the east, see Thomas Mouléro, 'Histoire et légendes des Djêkens', *ED*, ns, 3 (1964), 51–76.

[13] Jean-Baptiste Labat, *Voyage du Chevalier des Marchais en Guinée, isles voisines et à Cayenne* (2nd edn, Amsterdam, 1731), ii, 34. Here as often, the published version of this work includes material not in the original manuscript: 'Journal du voiage de Guinée et Cayenne, par le Chevalier des Marchais' (Bibliothèque Nationale, Paris: fonds français, 24223).

[14] Fieldwork, Glehue Daho compound, 3 Dec. 2001; Sinou & Agbo, *Ouidah*, 225.

The founder of Ouidah is regularly named in local tradition as Kpase (in French spelling, 'Passè'), who is in consequence the subject of a cult in the town to the present. After his death, he is said to have metamorphosed into a tree that still survives as the focus of his shrine, in what is known as Kpasezun, 'Kpase's Forest', located in Tové quarter, or, rather, originally in the bush beyond Tové, but nowadays absorbed within the town.[15] In contemporary sources, however, the earliest reference to the story of Kpase and his cult in Ouidah is only from the 1840s.[16] The inhabitants of Tové are said to have been dispersed in the Dahomian conquest of 1727, but subsequently resettled there under Dahomian rule; they were led in this resettlement by a nephew of Kpase called Tchiakpé, who founded a family that still exists in the quarter.[17] The dominant family in Tové in recent times, which also controls Kpase's shrine, called Adjovi, rose to prominence only in the nineteenth century, but claims descent from Kpase (although this claim is disputed by others in the town).[18]

Kpase is normally supposed to have been a king of Hueda,[19] usually identified as its second ruler, son and successor to the founder of the kingdom, who is named as Haholo.[20] While this has become the canonical version, however, a different account of the origins of Ouidah is given in the traditions of the Hula kingdom of Jakin, whose capital was originally Godomey but was removed, after the destruction of that town by the Dahomians in 1732, further east to Ekpè, and subsequently (after the destruction of the latter in turn in 1782) to Kétonou. These recount the migration of the Hula founder-king, called Kposi ('Possi'), from Grand-Popo to settle at Glehue, which by implication he founded. This account envisages a period when Glehue was independent of the Hueda king at Savi, with whom Kposi is said to have delimited a frontier. However, subsequently the Savi king is said to have made war on Kposi, driving him to move east to settle at Godomey.[21] Although the traditions state that this displacement occurred in the reign of Hufon (Houffon), the last Hueda king before the Dahomian conquest (reigned 1708–27),[22] it is clear that if historical it must in fact have been earlier; Glehue was evidently already

---

[15] Described in Sinou & Agbo, *Ouidah*, 223.

[16] Brue, 'Voyage fait en 1843, dans le royaume de Dahomey', *RC*, 7 (1845), 55 (giving the name as 'Passi').

[17] Reynier, 'Ouidah', 47–8.

[18] Ibid., 47; but see, for example, Agbo, *Histoire*, 203, who describes the claim as 'hazardous'.

[19] This version first in Gavoy, 'Note historique', 48. But the other early recension of local tradition, by Reynier, 'Ouidah', 47, is vaguer: Kpase merely 'belonged to the Pedah [Hueda] family of which the head was the King of Savi'. The earliest recorded reference to Kpase, in the 1840s, presents him as a purely local figure, 'cabocir [chief] of a small hamlet in the vicinity of Grégoué [Glehue]': Brue, 'Voyage', 55.

[20] So Gavoy, 'Note historique', 52, and later sources deriving from him, which list only five kings down to and including Hufon (1708–27). However, other versions of the Hueda king list include several additional names: one lists 13 kings of whom Kpase is the eighth, another 14 with Kpase the fourth; for discussion, see Soglo, 'Les Xweda', 47–51. Some of the additional kings listed (Yé, Amiton) appear in fact to be persons who ruled over sections of the Hueda in exile after the Dahomian conquest of the kingdom.

[21] Mouléro 'Histoire', 43–4; also Reynier, 'Ouidah', 51–2.

[22] Hufon's attack on Kposi is linked by tradition to his war against King Agaja of Dahomey (in 1727), but accounts differ in detail: Mouléro says that Hufon attacked Kposi because he refused to assist him against Agaja, but Reynier says that Hufon's attack on Kposi came first, and Kposi incited Agaja to attack Hufon in revenge.

subject to Savi by 1671, when the French established their trading factory there, since they negotiated with the Hueda king for permission to settle it.[23]

The names 'Kpase' and 'Kposi' are sufficiently similar to raise suspicions that they might be variants of a single name, and I suggested earlier that Kpase/Kposi was originally a figure in Hula tradition, whose co-option into the list of Hueda kings is spurious.[24] But the two names are understood locally to be philologically distinct. At the very least, however, some degree of confusion (or conflation) between the two figures is indicated by traditional stories relating to the arrival of the first European traders in Ouidah. These agree in attributing the first contact with Europeans to a man called Kpate ('Patè'), who is said to have been collecting crabs on the seashore when a European ship was passing, and raised a cloth on a pole as a makeshift flag to attract their attention;[25] in contemporary sources, Kpate's name and story were first recorded in the 1860s.[26] Like Kpase, Kpate is worshipped as a deified hero. The office of priest of Kpate, or Kpatenon, remains hereditary within a family that claims descent from him, resident in Docomè, the quarter of the Portuguese fort. In different versions of his story, Kpate is associated either with Kpase, the Hueda king at Savi (to whom he allegedly introduced the European traders), or with Kposi, the Hula king settled locally (in whose entourage he originally arrived in Ouidah).[27] The former version, it may be noted, implies that Europeans were hitherto unknown; whereas the latter explicitly states that Kposi and Kpate were familiar with them already, from earlier experience at Grand-Popo. There is also a parallel (and evidently related) ambiguity about Kpate's own ethnic affiliation. Some versions claim that he was, like Kpase, a member of the Hueda royal family;[28] current tradition in the Kpatenon family denies this, but agrees that Kpate was Hueda.[29] But other accounts state that he was Hula.[30] These two traditions, of foundation by the Hueda Kpase and the Hula Kposi, may perhaps be regarded as complementary rather than contradictory, since Ouidah clearly included both a Hueda and a Hula element: the different stories may therefore relate to the origins of different elements within Ouidah, rather than strictly representing alternative traditions of the foundation of the town as a whole.

The Hula element in Ouidah is represented today most visibly by the cult of Hu, the *vodun* (god) of the sea, who was in origin the national deity of the Hula people. The priest of the cult, the Hunon (Hounon), nowadays has his compound in Sogbadji, the quarter of the English fort, which was established only in the 1680s;[31] and one of the oldest-established Hueda families in this quarter, called

---

[23] Barbot, *On Guinea*, ii, 636.

[24] Robin Law, *The Kingdom of Allada* (Leiden, 1997), 42.

[25] E.g. Gavoy, 'Note historique', 48–9; Reynier, 'Ouidah', 38.

[26] Burton, *Mission*, i, 146. An earlier (1840s) version of the tradition of the arrival of the first Europeans mentions only Kpase, not Kpate: Brue, 'Voyage', 55.

[27] For the former version, see Gavoy, 'Note historique', 48–9; for the latter, Reynier, 'Ouidah', 51–2.

[28] Reynier, 'Ouidah', 38, 47.

[29] Fieldwork, Kpatenon compound, 3 Dec. 2001. This version claims that Kpate was settled in Ouidah even before Kpase, and gave him land to settle there.

[30] E.g. Merlo, 'Hiérarchie fétichiste', 6.

[31] The Hunon's compound in Sogbadji is described Sinou & Agbo, *Ouidah*, 201.

Déhoué, claims to have invited the first Hunon to settle there, implying Hueda priority of settlement.[32] However, the traditions of the Hunon priesthood itself claim that Déhoué was instrumental, not in the Hunon's original settlement in Ouidah, but in his resettlement there after fleeing from the Dahomian conquest in the 1720s.[33] In any case, there is an older shrine of Hu, located in the area called Adamé, which is now included within the Maro quarter of Ouidah, but before the nineteenth century was beyond the south-western limits of the town; and it is this earlier shrine which is said to have been established by the Hula founder-hero Kposi. The cult was certainly established locally already in the seventeenth century, since European accounts of the Hueda kingdom in the 1690s refer to the worship of the sea, to whom offerings were made for calm weather to facilitate the operation of the European trade.[34] Hu's importance was presumably enhanced, as these accounts imply, by the development of the trans-Atlantic trade, but he functioned as patron of watery spaces more generally, including the coastal lagoon; among lesser deities associated with him (and represented as his children) was the goddess Tokpodun, who was linked with the lagoon (and identified with the crocodile).[35] The Hula identity was in fact defined by their occupation of the lagoon environment, rather than by their connections with the sea as such. Certainly, the traditions of the Hunon priesthood claim that it was established in Ouidah already before the arrival of the first European traders, and insist that Ouidah was in origin a Hula settlement, in distinction from the Hueda town of Savi.

The question of priority of settlement as between the Hueda and Hula is difficult to resolve, but Hula claims to precedence are supported by evidence relating to the hierarchy of status among the gods worshipped in Ouidah. The national deity of the Hueda was Dangbe, the royal python, originally associated with agricultural fertility, who was incarnated in actual snakes that were maintained in his shrines.[36] Dangbe remains today one of the most important *vodun* of Ouidah, with his principal shrine located in the centre of the town.[37] Local tradition nowadays asserts that the cult was instituted in Ouidah from its beginnings by the Hueda founder-hero Kpase.[38] In the Hueda kingdom as a whole, as reported in the 1690s, first rank among the gods was held by Dangbe, to whom the sea-god Hu was considered a 'younger brother'.[39] The principal shrine of Dangbe at this

---

[32] Reynier, 'Ouidah', 36; fieldwork, Déhoué compound, 9 Jan. 1996. Another account claims that the Hunon settled in Sogbadji only during the reign of King Glele of Dahomey (1858–89): K. Fall et al., 'Typologie des cultes vodoun', in Sinou & Agbo, *Ouidah*, 72.

[33] Fieldwork, Dagbo Hounon compound, 18 Jan. 1996.

[34] Thomas Phillips, 'A Journal of a Voyage made in the *Hannibal* of London', in Awnsham Churchill & John Churchill, *Collection of Voyages and Travels* (London, 1732), vi, 226; William Bosman, *A New and Accurate Description of the Coast of Guinea* (London, 1705), 383.

[35] Melville J. Herskovits, *Dahomey* (New York, 1938), ii, 155. The worship of the crocodile was also noted in the 1690s, and the name Tokpodun first recorded in the 1860s: Phillips, 'Journal', 223; Burton, *Mission*, ii, 148.

[36] For the Dangbe cult, see esp. Christian Merlo & Pierre Vidaud, 'Dangbe et le peuplement houeda', in François de Medeiros (ed.), *Peuples du Golfe du Bénin* (Paris, 1984), 269–304.

[37] Described in Sinou & Agbo, *Ouidah*, 195–7.

[38] E.g. Agbo, *Histoire*, 15–16, who says that Kpase 'consecrated his town to the fetish Dangbe'.

[39] Bosman, *Description*, 368a, 383.

period, however, was located at the Hueda capital Savi, rather than in Ouidah; its relocation in Ouidah being a consequence of the destruction of Savi in the Dahomian conquest in the 1720s.[40] In Ouidah itself in recent times, it is in fact Hu rather than Dangbe who has been regarded as first in status among local *vodun*; in contemporary sources, the primacy of the Hunon within the priesthood of Ouidah was first recorded in the 1860s.[41] In local tradition, this reordered ranking of the *vodun* is linked to the Dahomian conquest in the 1720s, the Hunon then being given 'a special delegation of the royal authority of Abomey' over the priests of the other cults, including that of Dangbe.[42] It seems likely, however, that in this the Dahomians were merely recognizing and confirming the pre-existing local hierarchy, the point of their edict being probably to maintain the local primacy of the Hunon, in spite of the removal of Dangbe's principal shrine into the town.

The Hula connection might also help to resolve a puzzle about the name of the town, Glehue, commonly explained as meaning 'Farmhouse'.[43] It has been argued that the form of this name is linguistically Fon, rather than Hueda; and this has led to the suggestion that it represents a Fon 'translation' of a hypothetical original Hueda name, Single.[44] This, however, seems improbable, since, as has been seen, the name Glehue was already in use before the Dahomian conquest, being attested in contemporary European sources from the 1680s onwards; and it is difficult to understand why Europeans should have adopted a Dahomian form of the name, rather than the one current locally. Possibly the name was originally Hula rather than Fon, since names of this form also occur in Hula country;[45] however, even if Ouidah was not a Hula settlement, the Europeans, approaching it from the sea and therefore via the Hula, might have employed a Hula version of its name.

The principal local history of Ouidah, by Casimir Agbo, dates the foundation of the town by Kpase to 'around 1550'.[46] This date is evidently based upon an earlier suggestion, by the French administrator Gavoy, that the encounter of Kpase and Kpate with the first Europeans to visit Ouidah occurred around 1580, with an allowance added for Kpase's rule prior to this event.[47] The traditions of the priest-

---

[40] The main Dangbe shrine was in fact located outside Savi, according to European accounts of the early 18th century ¾ or ½ a league (1½–2 miles/2–3 km) away: 'Relation du royaume de Judas en Guinée' (MS. of *c*. 1715, ANF, Dépôt des Fortifications des Colonies, Côtes d'Afrique 104), 60; Labat, *Voyage*, ii, 154. However, an earlier (1690s) source gives a much greater distance, about 2 [Dutch] miles (= 8 English miles/12 km), perhaps a different site: Bosman, *Description*, 370. Some versions of local tradition maintain that the earliest shrine of Dangbe was in a forest outside Ouidah to the north, near the modern Roman Catholic seminary, which might be the location indicated: Sinou & Agbo, *Ouidah*, 195.

[41] Burton, *Mission*, ii, 141.

[42] Merlo, 'Hiérarchie fétichiste', 4. Other local accounts claim that the primacy of the Hunon was established only during the colonial period: Fall et al., 'Typologie', 72, n. 31. But this is refuted by Burton's earlier evidence.

[43] An alternative etymology, however, posits a founder called Gle: I. Akibode, 'De la traite à la colonisation', in Sinou & Agbo, *Ouidah*, 31.

[44] Hazoumé, 'Aperçu historique', 2nd part, no. 5 (19 Nov. 1925), 8–9. Tradition in Zoungbodji recalls the original Hueda name of the town as 'Glesinme': fieldwork, Zoungbodji, 11 Dec. 2001.

[45] For examples, see Iroko, *Les Hula*, 56–8.

[46] Agbo, *Histoire*, 15.

hood of Kpate, however, give an alternative and earlier date for his encounter with the Europeans, 1548.[48] It may also be noted that the traditions of the Hunon priesthood give a list of eight predecessors in the title prior to the present incumbent, for whom dates of tenure are supplied which indicate that the first took office in 1452; but since this involves an improbably long average tenure of over 50 years each (and a term of office for the first Hunon of over 120 years, 1452–1581), this should evidently be taken symbolically, as an assertion of antiquity (and by implication, priority) of establishment, rather than literally.[49] There is no reason to suppose, however, that any of these dates have any firm basis. Gavoy's date of *c*. 1580, for example, although sanctified by frequent repetition, was by his own account merely a speculative estimate made on the basis that the last king of Hueda, Hufon, displaced by the Dahomian conquest of 1727, was the third successor to (and great-grandson of) Kpase, on the assumption of an average length of reign/generation of 30 years (though the mathematical calculation is bungled).[50] However, it is known from contemporary sources that the king of Hueda recalled in local tradition as the son and immediate successor of Kpase, Agbangla, was reigning from the 1680s, dying in 1703.[51] This might be held to suggest that Kpase and his foundation of Ouidah belong rather to the middle of the seventeenth century. But this is surely to take too literalistic a view of traditional history, and in particular of the remembered royal genealogy, which may well be telescoped, even if not in part fictitious.[52] All that can be said with confidence is that the settlement at Ouidah predated the beginnings of European trade there in the seventeenth century.

In the long run, it may be hoped that archaeology will provide more concrete evidence on the early history of settlement in Ouidah. But to date no excavation has been undertaken in the town, apart from limited exploratory work within the courtyard of the former Portuguese fort during reconstruction works there in 1992;[53] more systematic excavation was concentrated at Savi, the former capital of the Hueda kingdom, rather than at Ouidah itself.[54]

---

[47] Gavoy, 'Note historique', 48–50.

[48] This date is given on painted and appliqué cloths commemorating the event kept in the Kpatenon compound, as observed in fieldwork, 3 Dec. 2001.

[49] These dates are painted on a wall in the Hounon compound, observed in fieldwork, 18 Jan. 1996.

[50] In fact, 120 years (four reigns at 30 years each) backwards from the end of Hufon's reign in 1727 would indicate a date for the beginning of Kpase's reign of *c*. 1610, rather than *c*. 1580.

[51] See esp. ANF, C6/25, Du Colombier, 10 Aug. 1714 (giving the name in the form 'Bangala').

[52] For variant versions of the Hueda king list, see n. 20 above.

[53] Alexis Adandé, 'Buried heritage, surface heritage: the Portuguese fort of São João Baptista de Ajudá', in Claude Daniel Ardouin & Emmanuel Arinze (eds), *Museums and History in West Africa* (Oxford, 2000), 127–31.

[54] Kenneth G. Kelly, 'Transformation and continuity in Savi, a West African trade town: an archaeological investigation of culture change on the coast of Bénin during the 17th and 18th centuries' (PhD thesis, University of California at Los Angeles, 1995); idem, 'Using historically informed archaeology: seventeenth and eighteenth century Hueda/European interaction on the coast of Bénin', *Journal of Archaeological Method & Theory*, 4 (1997), 353–66.

Environment and economy

The name Glehue, 'Farmhouse', is usually explained in local tradition as reflecting the fact that the town was originally established by Kpase as a farm.[55] Although this story may be no more than an inference from the name, the suggestion that Ouidah was originally an agricultural settlement is consistent with its location, some distance north of the coastal lagoon, on permanently dry and therefore cultivable ground. However, Ouidah's proximity to the coastal lagoon clearly also played an important role in its early development, and it is likely that the settlement was sited with this also in mind.

The configuration of the lagoon system is complex and varies seasonally with the level of the water, becoming more extensive during the rainy seasons (April to July and October/November). It has very probably also changed over time, through processes of silting and erosion. In recent times, the only permanently continuous waterway in the Ouidah area has been the lagoon immediately behind the coast, called locally Djesin ('Salt water'). Early European sources, however, speak of two major 'rivers' in the Hueda kingdom. The second (called by Europeans 'Euphrates'), to the north of the capital Savi, is evidently the more northerly 'lagoon' called locally Toho, which runs south-eastwards by Savi before turning east into Lake Nokoué; this is nowadays for most of its length no more than a marshy depression, but was presumably a more substantial watercourse in earlier times.[56] In addition, the area between Ouidah and the coastal lagoon is low-lying and swampy and subject to seasonal flooding, temporarily creating additional watercourses. The only significant area of cultivable land south of Ouidah is around the village of Zoungbodji, halfway towards the beach. Tradition suggests that Zoungbodji is of comparable antiquity to Ouidah itself, attributing its foundation to a man called Zingbo (or Zoungbo), who is regularly linked with Kpate in the story of the arrival of the first Europeans; in the usual version, Zingbo fled in fright at their approach, leaving Kpate to make the first contact.[57] In contemporary sources, however, the settlement of Zoungbodji is not documented until after the Dahomian conquest in the 1720s, when it became important as the location of a Dahomian military garrison. The only other substantial settlement is Djegbadji, situated on a group of islands in the lagoon to the south-west of Zoungbodji. This was in origin a settlement of the Hula people, although Hueda and later (after the Dahomian conquest of Hueda in the 1720s) Fon elements also settled there subsequently.[58]

---

[55] This explanation first in Gavoy, 'Note historique', 48.

[56] See esp. des Marchais, 'Journal', 40v; Labat, *Voyage*, ii, 10–11. Des Marchais describes this river as running by the Allada capital, evidently conflating the Toho with a watercourse that runs into it further east.

[57] However, a variant recorded in Zoungbodji itself claims that it was Kpase who accompanied Kpate to the shore and fled, and that Kpate then took the Europeans to meet Zingbo at Zoungbodji. These discrepancies evidently relate to disputes about seniority/primacy; the Zoungbodji version also claims that Zingbo was the first settler in the area, and gave land to both Kpase and Kpate. Fieldwork: Zoungbodji, 11 Dec. 2001.

[58] Sinou & Agbo, *Ouidah*, 173.

In recent times, the lagoon has been an important source of fish, which are caught in static traps, as well as with lines and nets both from the shore and from canoes.[59] In the nineteenth century, it was noted that fish, rather than meat, formed the staple diet of most of the inhabitants of Ouidah; and dried fish was also traded from the coast into the interior, as far as the Dahomian capital Abomey.[60] In the late seventeenth century European visitors already noted that the 'rivers' in Hueda produced large quantities of fish;[61] and there is no reason to suppose that this tradition of fishing did not date back earlier, before the arrival of the Europeans. Although the main centre of fishing in the area was presumably Djegbadji, families in Ouidah itself were also involved: the Déhoué family of Sogbadji, who claim to have been settled there prior to the establishment of the English fort in the quarter (in the 1680s), were traditionally canoemen and fishermen.[62] One early eighteenth-century account also noted the existence to the south of Ouidah of salt-works, at which salt was obtained by boiling sea water in jars and was traded into the interior.[63] This evidently refers to Djegbadji, which remains a centre of salt production to the present day (as reflected in its name, meaning 'On the salt marsh'). The reference to the boiling of sea water is inexact since later accounts make clear that salt was extracted in this area from the water of the lagoon.[64] Concentrations of salt are formed through the evaporation of shallow pools at the borders of the lagoon by the heat of the sun; earth is collected from these, the salt leached out by straining water through it, and it is the resulting highly saline water which is then boiled to produce the salt.

Although Ouidah's main commercial function in early times was probably in retailing the produce of the lagoon, fish and salt, overland into the interior, it probably also acted as an intermediary in trade conducted by the lagoon itself, which offered a medium of lateral communication and trade along the coast. In recent times, the lagoon has normally been navigable by canoe as far as Porto-Seguro (Agbodrafo), in modern Togo, 70 km west of Ouidah, while to the east it is navigable as far as Godomey, where a brief overland portage can be made to Lake Nokoué, from where navigation continues further east to Lagos and beyond, in modern Nigeria. Some nineteenth-century sources claim that the navigation along the lagoon to the east was originally continuous from Ouidah into Lake Nokoué, the interruption at Godomey being due to recent silting.[65] However, it was reported

[59] For the fishing techniques employed in recent times by Hueda displaced by the Dahomian conquest of their kingdom in 1727, on Lake Ahémé to the west, see R. Grivot, 'La pêche chez les Pedah du lac Ahémé', *BIFAN*, Série B, 11/1–2 (1949), 106–28.

[60] Burton, *Mission*, i, 33, says that 'many' preferred fish to meat; cf. 136–7, where he states that only the rich ate meat. For dried fish in the Abomey market, see ii, 243.

[61] Phillips, 'Journal', 214, 221; Bosman, *Description*, 362a.

[62] Fieldwork, Déhoué compound, 9 Jan. 1996.

[63] 'Relation du royaume de Judas', 2, 75.

[64] E.g. Duncan, *Travels*, i, 190-1. For salt production in modern times, including reference to Djedgbadji, see Josette Rivallain, 'Le sel dans les villages côtiers et lagunaires du Bas Dahomey', *Annales de l'Université d'Abidjan*, série I (Histoire), 8 (1980), 81–127; also A. Félix Iroko, 'Le sel marin de la Côte des Esclaves durant la période précoloniale', *Africa* (Rome), 46 (1981), 520-40.

[65] E.g. Pierre Bouche, *Sept ans en Afrique occidentale* (Paris, 1885), 8, 320.

already in the seventeenth century that the lagoon was 'lost in the earth' at Jakin (Godomey);[66] recollections of uninterrupted travel by canoe eastwards seem to relate to an artificial clearing of the northern branch of the lagoon, the Toho, which was only temporarily effective.

It is not strictly accurate to describe Ouidah as a 'lagoonside port', any more than as an 'Atlantic port',[67] since it is in fact situated over 3 km north of the permanently navigable waterway. Although the width of the lagoon varied both seasonally and from year to year, and in times of very heavy rainfall (as happened, for example, in 1686) the intervening land might be flooded, permitting canoes to carry goods over part of the distance to the town, this was clearly exceptional.[68] Nevertheless, Ouidah was sufficiently close to the lagoon to be able to benefit from the canoe-borne traffic along it: in the 1680s, for example, an English trader at Ouidah noted that trade could be done with Little Popo to the west for slaves, locally made beads and corn, communication being 'by the river', i.e. the lagoon.[69] Slaves were also supplied to Ouidah from Offra to the east, although it is not specified that these were brought by canoe.[70] In the nineteenth century, communication between Ouidah and Godomey was more usually on foot, although the journey was sometimes made by canoe along the lagoon.[71] Beyond Godomey, Lake Nokoué and the lagoons further east provided a continuous navigable waterway, which was regularly used for trade. For example, in the mid-seventeenth century salt manufactured in the coastal area of Allada was being taken by canoe to Lagos, and thereby to 'Lukumi', or the Yoruba interior, from which locally made cloth was brought in exchange; and later Yoruba cloth was also taken further west to Ouidah.[72] Very probably, such trade had also existed prior to the arrival of the Europeans, although its scale was certainly increased by their presence, Europeans purchasing African-made cloth and beads (both for resale on the Gold Coast to the west) and corn (for the provisioning of slave ships), brought along the lagoon, as well as slaves.[73]

---

[66] Barbot, *On Guinea*, ii, 621.

[67] As suggested in Law & Strickrodt, 'Introduction', in *Ports of the Slave Trade*, 3.

[68] Robin Law (ed.), *The English in West Africa, 1685–88: The local correspondence of the Royal African Company of England, 1681–1699, Part 2* (London, 2001; hereafter *English in West Africa*, ii), no. 817: John Carter, Ouidah, 7 June 1686. On this occasion the level of the water had risen '4 or 5 feet higher than ever I saw them, and flooded the dry ground about a mile in breadth'.

[69] Law, *English in West Africa*, i, no. 495: Petley Wyburne, Ouidah, 26 June 1683.

[70] Robin Law (ed.), *Correspondence from the Royal African Company's Factories at Offra and Whydah on the Slave Coast of West Africa in the Public Record Office, London, 1678-93* (Edinburgh, 1990), no. 7: William Cross, Offra, 13 June 1681; Law, *English in West Africa*, i, no. 490: Timothy Armitage, Ouidah, 5 Dec. 1682.

[71] PRO, FO2/886, Louis Fraser, Journal, Ouidah, 30 July 1851: 'messengers go from here to Godomey by land, the rest of the route by canoe as far as Lagos'. But for an instance of travel by canoe from Ouidah to Godomey, see WMMS, William West, Cape Coast, 6 June 1859.

[72] Dapper, *Naukeurige Beschrijvinge*, 2/118–19. The English fort at Ouidah in 1723 reported explicitly that the 'Whydah cloths' purchased by Europeans were not made locally, but in 'Lucamee': PRO, T70/7, Baldwyn, Mabyn & Barlow, Ouidah, 9 Aug. 1723.

[73] For the impact of the European trade in stimulating the expansion of the lagoon traffic, see more generally Robin Law, 'Between the sea and the lagoons: the interaction of maritime and inland navigation on the pre-colonial Slave Coast', *CEA*, 29 (1989), 220–4.

The importance of trade along the lagoon also afforded opportunities and temptations for piracy, although here again this would presumably have become more profitable after the initiation of the European maritime trade and the stimulus it gave to the lagoon traffic. Burton in the 1860s was told that Ouidah had been 'originally a den of water-thieves and pirates'.[74] This is corroborated by a contemporary account of the mid-seventeenth century, relating to 'Foulaen', which as noted earlier seems to be identical with Ouidah, which reports that it was accustomed to send 'robbers' to raid the coastal towns of Allada to the east.[75]

In contrast to the lagoon, the sea beyond it can have played only a marginal material (as opposed to religious) role in the life of early Ouidah. Unlike on the Gold Coast to the west, the inhabitants of the Slave Coast did not venture onto the sea prior to the arrival of the European traders. This was evidently due, on the one hand, to the greater difficulty of navigation on the sea in this region, due to the heavy surf and dangerous sand bars noted earlier, and, on the other, to the availability of the much easier facility for fishing and canoe-borne communication afforded by the lagoon. Indeed, the local people largely continued this avoidance of the sea even after the initiation of the European maritime trade; as will be seen hereafter, European ships trading at Ouidah had to bring both canoes and canoemen with them from the Gold Coast to the west, in order to communicate with the shore. Even after this introduction of seagoing canoes, little or no fishing in the sea was done at Ouidah, the canoes being employed only in servicing the overseas trade.[76] It has sometimes been suggested that African merchants from the Gold Coast may have conducted a canoe-borne maritime trade with the Slave Coast even before the arrival of the Europeans; but there is no evidence for such a trade before the mid-seventeenth century, and it is more likely that such contacts were initiated by the Europeans, and only subsequently imitated by the Gold Coast merchants.[77] Earlier, interest in the sea was probably restricted to foraging along the shore, for crabs, as recalled in the traditional story of Kpate's meeting with the first European visitors cited above.

Both the role and the importance of Ouidah were, however, transformed by the arrival of the Europeans and the initiation of maritime trade, which until the mid-nineteenth century was primarily in slaves. The Portuguese first explored along the Bight of Benin in 1472, and a regular trade began during the second half of the sixteenth century; from the 1630s the Portuguese monopoly of this trade was challenged by the Dutch, joined in the 1640s by the English and in the 1670s by the French. European trade was initially located at Grand-Popo, west of Ouidah;

---

[74] Burton, *Mission*, i, 62. Burton assumed this tradition to refer to the period prior to the rise of Ouidah as a centre for the European trade in the seventeenth century, but this may have been a misunderstanding on his part, since an account by the Roman Catholic missionary Francesco Borghero, who was one of Burton's principal informants, recorded stories of Hueda piracy along the lagoons in relation to a later period, after the Dahomian conquest in 1727, when the section of the Hueda people now in exile to the west recurrently raided Ouidah itself: 'Relation sur l'établissement des missions dans le Vicariat de apostolique de Dahomé', 3 Dec. 1863, in *Journal de Francesco Borghero, premier missionnaire du Dahomey, 1861–1865* (ed. Renzo Mandirola & Yves Morel, Paris, 1997), 240.

[75] Dapper, *Naukeurige Beschrijvinge*, 2/120.

[76] 'Relation du royaume de Judas', 17; des Marchais, 'Journal', 60v; Labat, *Voyage*, ii, 20.

[77] For discussion, see Law, 'Between the sea and the lagoons', 229–31.

but by the beginning of the seventeenth century had shifted east to the kingdom of Allada, where the principal centre of the trade, and the site of the European factories, was initially at Offra.[78] In 1671, however, the French West Indies Company transferred its factory from Offra to Ouidah, initiating the latter's rise to become the pre-eminent slave port within the region.

The French establishment at Ouidah in 1671 is often assumed to mark the beginnings of European trade there.[79] However, it should be noted that King Hufon of Hueda in 1720 said that the Portuguese had been the first Europeans to trade in his kingdom.[80] Local tradition in Ouidah also generally identifies the first European traders welcomed by Kpate and Kpase as Portuguese, while the French are said to have arrived only subsequently. According to one (no doubt apocryphal) story, the first Portuguese in Ouidah buried an inscribed stone to commemorate their visit; and when they returned, to find the French now in residence, they were able to disinter it to establish their claim to precedence.[81] The dates of 1580 or 1548 assigned locally for the arrival of the first Portuguese, as noted earlier, are merely speculative, but it must have occurred sometime during the late sixteenth or early seventeenth century. There are, indeed, a couple of earlier references, in the 1620s, to Portuguese trade at 'Fulao', which as noted earlier was probably an alternative name for Ouidah.[82] But it is likely that any such early contact was not sustained, and that therefore the French establishment in 1671 remains significant as marking the beginnings of continuous European trade at Ouidah.

The French move from Allada to Hueda was soon followed by the other principal European nations engaged in the trade, the English and Portuguese in the 1680s and the Dutch in the 1690s, leaving Ouidah as the dominant 'port' in the region by the end of the seventeenth century. The slave trade through Ouidah had reached a volume of probably around 10,000 slaves per year by the 1690s, and attained its all-time peak in the years 1700–13, when probably around 15,000 slaves annually were passing through the town;[83] at this period, indeed, Ouidah may have been accounting for around half of all trans-Atlantic exports of African slaves.[84]

---

[78] Law, *Slave Coast*, 118–27.

[79] E.g. Akinjogbin, *Dahomey*, 31.

[80] King of Hueda to viceroy of Brazil, 26 Oct. 1720, in Pierre Verger, *Flux et reflux de la traite des nègres entre le Golfe de Bénin et Bahia de Todos os Santos du XVIIe au XIXe siècle* (Paris, 1968), 132.

[81] Gavoy, 'Note historique', 49–51. However, one recorded version of the story of Kpate's encounter with the first Europeans identifies them as French rather than Portuguese: Reynier, 'Ouidah', 51–2.

[82] De Sandoval, *Naturaleza*, 51. In 1625 Dutch pirates took a Portuguese ship at 'Fulao': Beatrix Heintze (ed.), *Fontes para a história de Angola de seculo XVII* (Wiesbaden, 1985–8), ii, no. 53, Fernão de Souza, n.d. [*c*. 25 March 1625].

[83] These figures are derived from Eltis, *Rise of African Slavery*, 166 (Table 7.1). See. also the earlier estimates of Patrick Manning, 'The slave trade in the Bight of Benin, 1640–1890', in Henry A. Gemery & Jan S. Hogendorn (eds), *The Uncommon Market: Essays in the Economic History of the Atlantic Slave Trade* (New York, 1979), 107–41, who gives a slightly higher figure for the 1700s; and also contemporary estimates cited in Law, *Slave Coast*, 163–5 (which are somewhat higher again). The estimates of Eltis and Manning relate to the Bight of Benin as a whole, but in this period slave exports from the Bight were almost entirely through Ouidah. Exports from the Bight continued at a comparable (or slightly lower) level in the 1710s, but from 1714 a significant proportion of the trade was diverted through rival ports to the east and west of Ouidah.

[84] Eltis, *Rise of African Slavery*, 182.

The European forts

As far as the record goes, the first permanent European trading post in Ouidah (or indeed, anywhere in the Hueda kingdom) was established by Henri Carolof (Heinrich Caerlof), a German in the service of the French West Indies Company, as has been seen in 1671.[85] One version of local tradition claims that even before this, in 1623, a Frenchman called Nicolas Olivier had settled in Ouidah, and founded the quarter of the town called Ganvè, to the west of the site of the French fort.[86] But this story is certainly spurious: contemporary sources do not support the suggestion of any French activity at Ouidah before the 1670s. The Olivier (or d'Oliveira) family of Ganvè is in fact descended from a man who was director of the French fort in Ouidah at a much later date (1775–86); the attempt of the d'Oliveiras to claim priority of settlement may derive from rivalries for the leadership of the 'French' community in Ouidah in the nineteenth century.

The French factory was abandoned when it was destroyed in a local war in 1692; a French captain who visited the Hueda kingdom in 1701 requested its re-establishment, but the king was initially willing only to allow the French a lodge in his capital Savi.[87] However, in 1704 a visiting French expedition secured permission not only for the re-establishment of a lodge nearer the coast, but also for its fortification; the Hueda king supplied over 400 men and women for the construction.[88] It subsequently became known officially as 'Fort Saint-Louis de Gregoy [i.e. Glehue]'. The local traditions nowadays current of the establishment of the French fort, which attribute it to the reign of the fourth king of Hueda, Ayohuan (or Hayehoin), clearly relate to this subsequent refoundation, rather than to the original settlement in 1671, since Ayohuan is evidently to be identified with the king known to contemporary Europeans as 'Aisan' or 'Amar', who reigned in 1703–8.[89] The French fort was owned by a succession of trading companies until 1767, when it passed into the authority of the French crown. It was abandoned in 1797, but reoccupied by private French merchants (of the firm of Régis of Marseille) from 1842. The building, however, no longer survives, having been

---

[85] The date is commonly given in local sources inexactly as 1670. Local 'tradition' (here as often, manifestly conflated with material from published contemporary sources) also attributes the founding of the Ouidah factory to Delbée: first in Gavoy, 'Note historique', 50. This is a confusion: Delbée had served in the expedition that established the original French factory at Offra in 1670, but did not accompany Carolof on the second expedition that transferred the factory to Ouidah in the following year.

[86] This story first in Gavoy, 'Note historique', 50, 66.

[87] 'Relation du voyage d'Issyny fait en 1701 par le Chevalier Damon', in Paul Roussier (ed.), *L'Établissement d'Issigny 1687–1702* (Paris, 1935), 106 (where 'Janire' is clearly a miscopying of 'Savire', i.e. Savi).

[88] *Journal du corsaire Jean Doublet de Honfleur* (ed. Charles Bréard, Paris, 1883), 253–6.

[89] Gavoy, 'Note historique', 50–1. Gavoy himself assumed that the tradition related to the original establishment in 1671, with consequent distortion of his chronology of the Hueda kings. Agbo, *Histoire*, 40, supposed that 'Amar' was a distinct person from Ayohuan, and his immediate successor, and this is generally followed by subsequent writers. But since Ayohuan is described as son and successor to Agbangla, who is known from contemporary sources to have died in 1703 (and these also make clear that there was no other king intervening between Amar and Hufon, the last Hueda king, who succeeded in 1708), it is clear that the two are identical.

demolished in 1908; its site is now a public square, which is still however called 'La Place du Fort français'.[90]

Assuming that the fort built in 1704 was on the same site as the earlier French factory, at the time of its original foundation in 1671 the latter must have been physically separate from the indigenous settlement of Tové, since the later fort was on the opposite (west) side of the town from Tové, the intervening space being occupied by the quarter of the English factory, Sogbadji, which was established later. This is consistent with the account of Barbot in 1682, which describes the French and English factories at Ouidah as situated 'near to', rather than actually in, the indigenous village.[91] This arrangement was seemingly also paralleled in the kingdom of Allada earlier, where the original site of the European factories, Offra, was distinct from although close to the town of Jakin, although Offra eventually developed into a substantial and autonomous indigenous settlement also.[92] This suggests the policy widely attested elsewhere in West Africa of segregating foreign traders in distinct quarters, on the outskirts of the indigenous towns. This practice is most familiar from the colonial period, when in Nigeria, for example, southern immigrants in northern cities were regularly segregated into 'new towns' (*sabon gari*), while in the south northern merchants settled in separate quarters called '*zongos*'.[93] (There is, in fact, a Zongo quarter in Ouidah itself, on the north-east of the town, which dates from the period of French colonial rule after 1892.) But in this colonial practice clearly followed indigenous pre-colonial precedents: in towns in the Borgu region in the north of modern Bénin, inland from Dahomey, for example, foreign Muslim merchants likewise formed their own quarters, such as the Maro quarter of Nikki and the Wangara quarter of Djougou.[94] This arrangement probably also accounts for the location of the principal market in Ouidah, called Zobé, which is still today situated south-west of Tové quarter, and between it and the quarters of the former English and French forts to the west.[95]

The second of the European factories to be established was the English. The Royal African Company, which held a legal monopoly of English trade in West Africa at this time, first projected a factory at Ouidah in April 1681; but this was abortive, the factor left there being recalled four months later to take over the company's factory at Offra to the east.[96] Later in 1681 a factory was established in Ouidah by an English trader called Petley Wyburne, who was not an agent of the

---

[90] Description of the site in Sinou & Agbo, *Ouidah*, 127–9.

[91] Barbot, *On Guinea*, ii, 635.

[92] Law, *Kingdom of Allada*, 18–19.

[93] Akin L. Mabogunje, *Urbanization in Nigeria* (London, 1968), 118, 205, 283; Abner Cohen, *Custom and Politics in Urban Africa: A study of Hausa Migrants in Yoruba Towns* (London, 1969). Hausa quarters in Yoruba towns are generally called *sabo*, but in Ghana they are called *zongo*: see Nehemiah Levtzion, *Muslims and Chiefs in West Africa* (Oxford, 1968), 23.

[94] Denise Brégand, *Commerce caravanier et relations sociales au Bénin: les Wangara du Borgou* (Paris, 1998), 81–96.

[95] Local tradition maintains that the location of the Zobé market predates the Dahomian conquest of Ouidah in the 1720s: Agbo, *Histoire*, 105–6.

[96] Law, *English in West Africa*, i, nos 476–8: John Thorne, Glehue, 24 May 1681; William Cross, Offra, 18 Aug. 1681; Thorne, Offra, 19 Aug. 1681.

Royal African Company but an 'interloper', that is, a trader operating independently of the company and in breach of its monopoly, and this was maintained until Wyburne was forcibly removed by agents of the Royal African Company in 1686.[97] The company itself had meanwhile established a factory in the Hueda kingdom, at a second attempt, in July 1682; but this was located not at Ouidah, but at the capital Savi.[98] In April and May 1684, however, this factory suffered two serious fires, which evidently effectively destroyed it, since later in 1684 the local chief factor reported that he was 'busied about building a house';[99] and the new factory now built was evidently situated at Ouidah.[100] The English factory was situated east of the French factory (at least, east of where the later French fort was established in 1704), between it and the indigenous settlement of Tové. It was fortified with earthworks, mounted with cannon, for defence against its French neighbour, in 1692, and a moat was added in 1694;[101] it was later known as 'William's Fort, Whydah', alluding to King William III (1689–1703), the English monarch in whose reign it was fortified.

From the Royal African Company William's Fort passed into the possession of the Company of Merchants Trading to Africa, which replaced it in 1752, but it was abandoned in 1812, following the legal abolition of the British slave trade. It was reoccupied by a private British merchant, Thomas Hutton, operating from the Gold Coast to the west, from 1838, and was later occupied by a British vice-consulate (1851–2), by a British Methodist mission (1856–67), and again by a different British trading firm (F. & A. Swanzy, also of the Gold Coast) in the 1870s. It was sold off to a German firm (C. Goedelt, of Hamburg) in the 1880s, but was confiscated as enemy property by the French colonial authorities in the First World War and passed back into the hands of another British firm, John Walkden of Manchester, who remained in occupation until 1963 and with whose name it is still locally associated. Redevelopment had destroyed its appearance as a fortification by 1890, when the building occupied by Goedelt was described as 'an ordinary house'; the moat was filled in in 1908.[102] The only material remains of the earlier fort visible today are a few cannon scattered around its courtyard.[103] In local usage, the area nevertheless remains 'Le Fort anglais'.

---

[97] Ibid., no. 479: Thorne, Offra, 4 Dec. 1681. In 1686 Wyburne was arrested and taken prisoner to the Royal African Company's headquarters at Cape Coast Castle on the Gold Coast, and from there shipped back to England: PRO, T70/11, Henry Nurse et al., Cape Coast, 19 March 1686; T70/12, Edwyn Steede & Stephen Gascoyne, Barbados, 27 April 1686. For the location of Wyburne's factory, in 'the Lower Town', i.e. Glehue, as opposed to the royal capital Savi, see Law, *English in West Africa*, i, no.487: Timothy Armitage, Ouidah, 24 Oct. 1682. The English factory in Ouidah noted by Barbot in April 1682 was evidently Wyburne's: Barbot, *On Guinea*, ii, 635.

[98] Law, *English in West Africa*, i, no. 492: Thorne, Offra, 28 Jan. 1683; also enc. 2 in no. 487: Accounts of John Winder, Hueda, July–Oct. 1682. The location of this factory at Savi is implied in a reference to the removal of goods from it 'to the Lower Town', i.e. Ouidah: ibid., no. 487: Armitage, Ouidah, 24 Oct. 1682.

[99] Law, *Correspondence from Offra and Whydah*, nos 16, 18: Carter, Hueda/Ouidah, 26 May & 11 Dec. 1684.

[100] In 1685 the factor referred to having gone 'up to the king's town', i.e. Savi: Law, *English in West Africa*, ii, no. 812: Carter, Ouidah, 19 Sept. 1685.

[101] Robin Law (ed.), *Further Correspondence of the Royal African Company of England Relating to the 'Slave Coast', 1681–1699* (Madison, 1992), no. 63: John Wortley, Ouidah, 5 Jan. 1692; Phillips, 'Journal', 215.

[102] Édouard Foà, *Le Dahomey* (Paris, 1895), 417; Gavoy, 'Note historique', 30.

[103] Description of site in Sinou & Agbo, *Ouidah*, 133.

The third and last of the European forts in Ouidah was the Portuguese. Some accounts date the foundation of the Portuguese fort to 1680;[104] but although a Portuguese factory was indeed established in the Hueda kingdom around this time, it appears that this was at the capital Savi rather than at Ouidah, and in any case was ephemeral, or at least not continuously occupied.[105] The Portuguese fort in Ouidah was in fact built in 1721;[106] it was later known as 'Fort São João Baptista de Ajudá [= Hueda]'. It was situated east again from the English factory, and adjoining Tové quarter on the south; a contemporary account of its establishment indicates that, unlike the earlier factories, it was constructed within an already built-up part of the town, which had to be demolished in order to clear the site, the construction employing over 500 persons for 30 days.[107] Unlike the other two forts, the Portuguese was from the first a possession of the Portuguese crown, and under the immediate authority of the viceroy of Brazil at Salvador, Bahia; and later (after the Brazilian capital was removed to Rio de Janeiro in 1763) under the provincial governor of Bahia. It was abandoned after the legal abolition of the Portuguese slave trade north of the equator in 1815, but the Portuguese claim to it was maintained. It was reoccupied by the Portuguese government in 1844, this time administered from the local Portuguese headquarters on the island of São Tomé, off the West African coast. This renewed Portuguese presence was at first tenuous and intermittent, and possession of the fort was briefly usurped by Roman Catholic missionaries of the French Société des Missions Africaines in 1861–5. But it was definitively reoccupied by Portugal in 1865, and remained an anomalous Portuguese enclave within the French colony of Dahomey throughout the colonial period, its evacuation being forced by the newly independent Republic of Dahomey only in 1961. Alone of the three European forts the Portuguese retains its character as a fortification, though the present layout of the buildings appears to date from the reoccupation of 1865 rather than from the original period of occupation in the eighteenth century.[108] It now houses the Historical Museum of Ouidah.

Local tradition speaks of the existence of Dutch and Danish forts also in Ouidah, and even indicates their supposed sites.[109] Memory of a Dutch fort that had allegedly existed earlier is already attested in Ouidah in the 1860s, when it was said to have been on the site occupied since the 1820s by the Brazilian slave-trader Francisco Felix de Souza, which remains today the de Souza family compound.[110] But the existence of such a Dutch fort is not corroborated by earlier contemporary evidence. The Dutch West India Company did contemplate establishing a factory in Ouidah, after their existing factory at Offra was destroyed in the war of 1692, when the Hueda authorities offered them the factory formerly occupied by the

[104] Augusto Sarmento, *Portugal no Dahomé* (Lisbon, 1891), 52; Agbo, *Histoire*, 30.

[105] Law, *Slave Coast*, 134–6.

[106] A.F.C. Ryder, 'The re-establishment of Portuguese factories on the Costa da Mina to the mid-eighteenth century', *JHSN*, 1/3 (1958)', 160–1; Verger, *Flux et reflux*, 132–9.

[107] Verger, *Flux et reflux*, 136–9.

[108] Description in Sinou & Agbo, *Ouidah*, 139–47.

[109] Agbo, *Histoire*, 31–2; Sinou & Agbo, *Ouidah*, 148–9.

[110] Borghero, *Journal*, 44 [20 April 1861]; also Burton, *Mission*, i, 67 (who probably had the information orally from Borghero). More recent tradition, however, has moved the site further west, to the area called Adamé.

English interloper Wyburne.[111] Although the Dutch factors were in the event evacuated, some of the company's African employees apparently remained behind; in 1694 it was noted that there was a settlement of 'Mina' people (i.e. from Elmina, the Dutch headquarters on the Gold Coast), half a mile from the English factory at Ouidah, who assisted Dutch ships trading there.[112] But it does not appear that this establishment was maintained. A Dutch fort is mentioned at Ouidah, alongside the French and English, in one source of the early eighteenth century; but this seems to be a simply a mistake.[113] The West India Company did maintain a factory (which was not fortified) in the Hueda kingdom between 1703 and 1727, but this was situated at the capital Savi, rather than Ouidah.[114] Although the company's local chief factor in 1726 obtained permission to build a lodge 'where the other nations have their forts', i.e. in Ouidah, this was not in fact carried out;[115] and after the destruction of Savi, including the European factories there, in the Dahomian conquest of 1727, the Dutch company no longer maintained any establishment in the area. Although it is of course possible that some later individual Dutch trader maintained a factory in Ouidah, this can only have been ephemeral, and the authenticity of the 'traditional' site is suspect.

The idea of a Danish fort in Ouidah seems to have arisen from a misreading of the same early eighteenth-century account that wrongly mentioned a Dutch fort there.[116] Contemporary sources, again, do not corroborate this; the factor of a Danish ship that traded at Ouidah in 1784–5 lodged in the English fort.[117] Recent tradition asserts that the Danish fort was on the site occupied in the late nineteenth century by the French firm of Cyprien Fabre, immediately east of the English fort, but this is probably a confusion; contemporary evidence suggests that the former occupant of this building was the British trader Hutton, who after relinquishing the English fort to the British vice-consulate in 1852 occupied premises east of the fort, which after his death (in 1856) passed into the possession of a Spanish merchant, and by the mid-1860s into the hands of the Dahomian crown.[118]

---

[111] Law, *Further Correspondence*, no. 63: Wortley, Ouidah, 5 Jan. 1692.

[112] Phillips, 'Journal', 228.

[113] Charles Davenant, *Reflections upon the Condition and Management of the Trade to Africa* (1709), reproduced in *The Political and Commercial Works of Charles d'Avenant* (London, 1771), v, 226. Also repeated in the English version (published 1732) of Jean Barbot's work (see *On Guinea*, ii, 644), and from Barbot by Burton, *Mission*, i, 84.

[114] ANF, C6/25, 'Mémoire de l'estat du pays de Juda et de son négoce', 1716; des Marchais, 'Journal', 29; Labat, *Voyage*, ii, 35.

[115] Albert Van Dantzig (ed.), *The Dutch and the Guinea Coast 1674–1742: A Collection of Documents from the General State Archive at The Hague* (Accra, 1978), no. 250: Agreement with the King and Grandees of Hueda, 12 Nov. 1726.

[116] First in Burton, *Mission*, i, 84, citing Barbot (in turn repeating Davenant), but the Danish fort mentioned by the latter was clearly at Accra, not Ouidah: see Barbot, *On Guinea*, ii, 644. Burton makes clear that in the 1860s there was no local recollection of this supposed Danish fort, which was 'now quite forgotten'; very probably, the later 'tradition' derives from his work.

[117] Paul Erdman Isert, *Letters on West Africa and the Slave Trade* (trans. Selena Axelrod Winsnes, London, 1992), 96; see discussion in Klavs Randsborg, et al., 'Subterranean structures: archaeology in Bénin, West Africa', *Acta Archeologica*, 69 (1998), 219.

[118] Burton, *Mission*, i, 83.

The European forts were distinctive within Ouidah by being built, in part, in two storeys, being consequently known locally as *singbo* (or *singbome*), 'great houses'.[119] Nevertheless, it should be stressed that the Ouidah forts were structures of much less military strength than the better-known examples on the Gold Coast. Unlike the latter, those at Ouidah were built in local materials – in mud rather than in brick or stone, which left them subject to rapid dilapidation if not regularly maintained, and with thatched rather than tiled roofs, which made them more vulnerable to fire. Their relative weakness is demonstrated by the fact that the Dahomians were able to capture and/or destroy forts in Ouidah on three occasions, the Portuguese in 1727, the French in 1728 and the Portuguese again in 1743; on the latter two occasions at least, the destruction of the forts was due to the buildings catching fire and causing the explosion of stores of gunpowder. Moreover, the Ouidah forts were located a considerable distance from the sea, and therefore their cannon could not, like those on the Gold Coast, command the landing-places for their own supplies; in consequence, as Europeans explicitly recognized, even if they could defeat direct attack they could be starved into surrender.[120] In the early eighteenth century, both the English and the Dutch pressed for permission to build forts at the seaside, but the Hueda king, Hufon, refused, precisely because he was aware of the power that English and Dutch forts exercised on the Gold Coast, and feared that the erection of such a fort at the shore would make the Europeans 'masters of his port'. When the trade at Ouidah was disrupted by the activities of European pirates in 1719–20, Hufon did authorize the construction of a stone fort on the beach by the French, in order to protect ships trading in his dominions, but, again, the idea was not pursued.[121]

The forts in Ouidah operated as secure places of storage for goods and slaves, rather than exercising any serious military power over the local community. The concept of an 'enclave-entrepôt', which has been applied to coastal towns on the Gold Coast in which Europeans settled, such as Elmina, does not seem applicable to Ouidah, which was in no sense an enclave of European authority, or even of their informal predominating influence.[122] In Ouidah, there was never any question that the European establishments were in the final analysis subject to local control, rather than representing independent centres of European power.[123] This was explicitly expressed in the policy of the Hueda kings of forbidding fighting among Europeans in the kingdom, even when their nations were at war in Europe, which was formalized in 1703, when the king obliged the local agents of the Dutch,

---

[119] Agbo, *Histoire*, 32–3; Forbes, *Dahomey*. i, 224; Burton, *Mission*, i, 156. However, Agbo's statement that the Ouidah forts were the first 'storey houses [*maisons à l'étage*]' on the Slave Coast is not accurate, since already in 1670 part of the royal palace at Allada was 'raised in two storeys': 'Journal du voyage du Sieur Delbée', in J. de Clodoré (ed.), *Relation de ce qui s'est passé dans les isles et terre-ferme de l'Amérique pendant la dernière guerre avec l'Angleterre* (Paris, 1671), 418–19.

[120] 'Relation du royaume de Judas', 67; William Snelgrave, *A New Account of Some Parts of Guinea, and the Slave Trade* (London, 1734), 128.

[121] ANF, C6/25, 'Mémoire concernant la Colonie de Juda', 1722.

[122] For Elmina, see Feinberg, *Africans and Europeans*.

[123] Robin Law, '"Here is no resisting the country": the realities of power in Afro-European relations on the West African "Slave Coast"', *Itinerario*, 18 (1994), 50–64.

English and French companies to sign a treaty prohibiting hostilities in the Ouidah roadstead, or within sight of the shore, on pain of payment of damages to the value of eight slaves;[124] one chief of the English fort was deported in 1714, after a fracas with his French counterpart, which was deemed to be a breach of this treaty.[125]

Each of the three European forts in Ouidah became the centre of a quarter of the town, occupied by persons in the service of the forts. These were commonly called the French, English and Portuguese quarters (or, in contemporary European sources of the eighteenth and nineteenth centuries, 'towns', 'villages' or 'camps'), or in local parlance Zojage-ko, Glensi-ko and Aguda-ko (ko meaning 'quarter').[126] Of these names, 'Glensi' is merely a local version of the name 'English', but the others call for further comment. 'Zojage' is explained as meaning 'Fire has come to earth', which is said to have been an exclamation of wonder uttered by Zingbo, the companion of Kpate, upon sight of the first Europeans to land at Ouidah (alluding to their 'red' skin colour, which was thought to resemble fire).[127] This story implies that it was originally applied to Europeans in general (these first visitors being in fact Portuguese), but it was subsequently restricted to the French in particular; when first documented in a contemporary source, in a vocabulary collected in Brazil among African slaves from the Dahomey area, it already designated the French specifically.[128] 'Aguda' is a term of uncertain etymology, which is commonly understood nowadays to mean 'Brazilian', and when first attested, in the same vocabulary, was applied specifically to Bahia, as opposed to Portugal; but in West Africa in the nineteenth century its reference was national rather than geographical, applied to 'Portuguese' in general, including Brazilians, rather than to Brazilians as distinct from Portuguese.[129]

In recent times, the three 'European' quarters of Ouidah have more commonly been known by other names, that of the French fort being called Ahouandjigo, that of the English Sogbadji, and the Portuguese Docomè, these names being first attested in the contemporary record in the 1860s.[130] The name 'Ahouandjigo' is translated as 'where war cannot come', and is usually explained by tradition as recording an undertaking by the Hueda king Ayohuan not to make war on the French fort there;[131] it seems more likely, however, that it alluded to the policy of the Hueda kings of forbidding fighting among Europeans at Ouidah, which was reaffirmed in the treaty signed in 1703, the year before the establishment of the

---

[124] Van Dantzig, Dutch and the Guinea Coast, no. 115: W. de la Palma, Elmina, 10 Oct. 1703, with no. 121, copy of agreement, 25 Apr. 1703; text of the treaty also in des Marchais, 'Journal', 29–30v; Labat, Voyage, ii, 88–91. The date given in the latter, 8 Sept. 1704, is that of a subsequent renewal of the treaty.

[125] ANF, C6/25, Du Colombier, Hueda, 4 Feb. 1715; PRO, C113/276, Randle Logan, 20 Feb. 1715.

[126] Agbo, Histoire, 41.

[127] Gavoy, 'Note historique', 49.

[128] Obra nova de lingua geral de Mina de António da Costa Peixoto (ed. Luís Silveira & Edmundo Correia Lopes, Lisbon, 1945), 20 (giving the term in the form 'sujaquem').

[129] Burton, Mission, i, 65, n. The suggestion sometimes made that 'Aguda' derives from 'Ajudá', the Portuguese version of the name Hueda, is unlikely on both linguistic and historical grounds.

[130] First in ibid., i, 64–5.

[131] Gavoy, 'Note historique', 50–51.

French fort. That of 'Sogbadji' for the English quarter refers to So, the *vodun* of thunder, meaning 'So's enclosure'; it is said to have been the place where the bodies of persons killed by lightning were taken, from which they could be redeemed for burial only on payment of a fine.[132] The etymology of the name 'Docomè', 'Do quarter', is uncertain.[133]

Although their origins are understood at one level to be connected with the establishment of the European forts, it is noteworthy that all three of these quarters celebrate indigenous Hueda persons rather than Europeans as their actual founders; by implication, these were already settled locally before the arrival of the various European groups whom they welcomed. Ahouandjigo claims to have been founded by a prince of the Hueda royal family called Agbamu (in French 'Agbamou'); a prominent family in the quarter, that of Agbo, claims descent from him.[134] Docomè is said to have been founded by a man called Ahohunbakla ('Ahohounbacla'), who belonged to the same family as Kpate, the hero who welcomed the first Europeans, who is also sometimes said to have belonged to Hueda royalty.[135] Both Agbamu and Ahohunbakla are also said to have survived to lead their quarters in resistance to the Dahomian conquest of the town in the 1720s–40s. The details of these traditions are suspect. The claim in both cases that the founder of the ward was also its leader against the Dahomians, although chronologically possible (at any rate, if Agbamu is assumed to have been associated with the building of the French fort in 1704, rather than the original establishment in 1671), may be doubted; it seems more likely that Agbamu and Ahohunbakla are composite or symbolic figures, into whose careers as recorded in the traditions events from different epochs have been telescoped. Indeed, as will be seen in the next chapter, it is clear that the historical Agbamu cannot have been either the founder of Ahouandjigo or its leader against the Dahomians, since he was in fact a king of the Hueda in exile, two generations after the Dahomian conquest. It may also be suspected that the name 'Ahohunbakla' is a variant or corruption of that of Agbangla, the Hueda king who died in 1703 and who is said by tradition to be buried in Docomè quarter.[136] The appropriation of such founding ancestors from among Hueda royalty is, however, significant as a claim of indigenous legitimacy, which was probably asserted against Dahomian overlordship, as well as and probably more than against European primacy. In Sogbadji, however, the claimed indigenous founder is of non-royal Hueda stock. The founder is usually named as Zossoungbo, said to have been a hammock-bearer to the Hueda king at Savi, whose descendants claim the hereditary headship of the

---

[132] Fall et al., 'Typologie', 66; also fieldwork, Zossoungbo compound, 9 Jan. 1996.

[133] Local informants offer derivations from *doko*, a form of bean cake supposedly sold in the area, or from the male personal name Dosu, supposedly a member of the founding family. These look like imaginative speculations.

[134] Reynier, 'Ouidah', 32–3; also fieldwork, Agbamou compound, 11 Dec. 2001.

[135] Reynier, 'Ouidah', 38–9; cf. Gavoy, 'Note historique', 66; also fieldwork, Sebastien Amoua, 11 Dec. 2001. The name is alternatively spelt 'Ahomblaca' or 'Baclahahoun'. Reynier says that Ahohunbakla was a nephew (son of a sister) of Kpate, but Sebastien Amoua says that Kpate was his son.

[136] Merlo, 'Hiérarchie fétichiste', 16–17, who gives the name in the form 'Ahoho Agbangla' (*ahoho* meaning apparently 'old king'); however, this identification is not recognized in local tradition.

quarter; but another Hueda family in Sogbadji, that of Déhoué, disputes priority of settlement with the Zossoungbos.[137]

The personnel of the 'European' forts was in fact predominantly African. The English fort in the 1700s, for example, was manned by only 20 white men, with 100 'gromettoes', or African slaves.[138] The 'European' quarters also included free Africans who were either in place before the establishment of the European factories or were attracted into their service subsequently. To the present day, these quarters are largely occupied by descendants of persons associated with the forts, including some Europeans who fathered families by local women, but mainly free African employees and slaves. Some of these families claim to be descended from persons employed in the forts before the Dahomian conquest in 1727, although most of those in place today seem to have arrived later, in the period of Dahomian rule. In addition to indigenous Hueda (and Hula) families, the populations of the 'European' quarters also included a large non-indigenous African element. Many of the fort slaves employed in Ouidah were from the Gold Coast to the west: in 1694 it was noted that 'most' of the slaves employed in the English fort were 'Gold Coast negroes', who were considered superior soldiers to the local Huedas; likewise in 1716 the slaves of the English fort at Ouidah (and also of the Dutch factory at Savi) were 'almost all inhabitants of the Gold Coast, or Minas'.[139] Conversely, it may be noted, slaves purchased in Ouidah and Allada were commonly employed by Europeans in their factories on the Gold Coast;[140] this being reflected to the present day in the existence of 'Alata [i.e. Allada]' quarters in the Dutch and English sections of Accra.[141] The logic of employing such 'foreign' Africans was, explicitly, that such outsiders were less liable to run away than slaves recruited locally, whose homelands were more accessible. Other fort slaves employed in Ouidah were imported from the interior; in effect, a portion of those purchased for export through the town was retained for local use. The slaves of the French fort in the eighteenth century were generally called 'Acqueras', a usage already established by the 1710s, and this was in origin the name of a specific ethnic group, reported to be located in the far interior, from which presumably many of the French fort slaves were derived.[142] In 1723 the French fort reported that it had purchased 'Chamba [Tchamba]' slaves, this being another ethnicity in the interior (in northern Togo).[143]

---

[137] Gavoy, 'Note historique', 67; Reynier, 'Ouidah', 35; fieldwork, Zossoungbo compound, 9 Jan. 1996; Déhoué compound, 9 Jan. 1996.

[138] Davenant, *Reflections*, in *Works*, v, 226.

[139] Phillips, 'Journal', 228; ANF, C6/25, 'Mémoire de l'estat du pays de Juda', 1716. The term 'Minas', although in origin referring specifically to Elmina (originally 'A Mina', 'The Mine' in Portuguese), the Dutch headquarters on the Gold Coast, was frequently used in a wider sense, of persons from the Gold Coast (called the 'Costa da Mina' in Portuguese usage) in general.

[140] Law, *Kingdom of Allada*, 90–1; cf. Eltis, *Rise of African Slavery*, 226.

[141] Parker, *Making the Town*, 10–14.

[142] Already in the earliest documents surviving from the French fort: ANF, C6/25, 'Estat ou mémoire de la dépense nécessaire pour relever le fort de Juda et pour l'entretien du directeur et des employés', enc. to Du Colombier, 10 Aug. 1714. For 'Acqueras' as an ethnonym, see Law, *Slave Coast*, 189–90.

[143] ANF, C6/25, Levesque, 4 April 1723. One early eighteenth-century account refers to the slaves of the

Other African foreigners settled in Ouidah as free immigrants, attracted there by the opportunities for employment in the European trade. The most prominently visible category among such incomers were canoemen from the Gold Coast. As noted earlier, the indigenous people of Ouidah, although using canoes on the inland lagoons, had no tradition of navigation on the sea, whereas on the Gold Coast the inhabitants had employed canoes for sea-fishing and coastwise communication even before the arrival of the Europeans. Since at Ouidah (and elsewhere on the Slave Coast) European ships were unable to approach close to the shore (owing to the dangerous bars and surf), they regularly bought canoes and hired crews of canoemen on the Gold Coast on their way down the coast, in order to land goods and embark slaves.[144] During the second half of the seventeenth century, indigenous Gold Coast merchants also began to travel to the Bight of Benin by canoe, to trade independently of (and in competition with) the Europeans, for cloth and other goods for resale on the Gold Coast: in 1688, for example, it was noted of the trade in African cloth at Ouidah that 'the Blacks come with canoes there to trade in them, and carry them off continuously'.[145]

Most of the canoemen who came to Ouidah from the Gold Coast returned home on completion of their contracts, but some settled permanently in Ouidah. At the end of the seventeenth century, Cape Coast, the English headquarters on the Gold Coast, was said to be visibly depopulated because of the recruitment from there of canoemen by English ships trading at Ouidah, 'after which they liking the place, live there, and seldom remember to come home again'.[146] Some of these immigrant canoemen entered the service of the European factories in Ouidah on a long-term basis, as free employees, while other canoemen were recruited as pawns (bound to work while paying off debts) or slaves. In the 1710s, it was noted that the English and Dutch factories enjoyed the services of canoemen recruited respectively from Cape Coast and Elmina, whereas the French, having no Gold Coast establishments of their own, were at a disadvantage in this respect, and French ships had to hire canoemen on their voyage down the coast.[147] By the mid-eighteenth century, however, the French fort also had its own corps of canoemen, who in this case were slaves.[148]

The cosmopolitan character of Ouidah, arising from its coastwise connections with the Gold Coast, is illustrated by an incident in 1686, when one Gold Coast

---

[143] (cont.) French fort in Ouidah as 'Bambaras', which is a name usually given to slaves from the interior of Senegambia; but this is presumably used here in a generic sense, transferred from Senegambian usage, for slaves employed as soldiers: Labat, *Voyage*, ii, 34.

[144] See, for example, Barbot, *On Guinea*, ii, 529; Phillips, 'Journal', 210, 228–9.

[145] 'Relation du voyage de Guynée fait en 1687 sur la frégate "La Tempeste" par le Sieur Du Casse', in Roussier, *L'Etablissement d'Issigny*, 15.

[146] Bosman, *Description*, 50–51.

[147] ANF, C6/25, Du Colombier, 10 Aug. 1714. This disadvantage of the French is mentioned in several later documents, and was an argument regularly used in support of proposals for the French to acquire a fort on the Gold Coast.

[148] ANF, C6/25, Pruneau & Guestard, 'Mémoire pour servir à l'intelligence du commerce de Juda', 18 March 1750.

man, described as from Kormantin but 'an ancient inhabitant here', was murdered by another, from Elmina, the latter having been sent to collect a debt owed by the first man to a third party in Elmina.[149] Some of these Gold Coast immigrants became prominent people in the local system: in the 1690s the official who served as interpreter to the English factory in Ouidah, who was also a substantial trader in slaves, called 'Captain Tom', was in origin from the Gold Coast.[150] This Gold Coast element in the population is reflected in the currency of local versions of the personal names used in the Akan languages of the Gold Coast which allude to the day of the week on which a person was born: as for example, Kwadwo, Kwamina, Kwaku and Kofi (given to boys born respectively on Monday, Tuesday, Wednesday and Friday), which occur in Ouidah in the forms Codjo, Comlan, Cocou and Coffi.

Early Ouidah

By the 1720s, Ouidah was thus made up of the combination of Tové, the original Hueda village, with the three quarters associated with the European forts, Ahouandjigo, Sogbadji and Docomè. The size of the settlement, along what was presumably its longest axis, from the French to the Portuguese fort, was only around 1 km in length. In comparison, the Hueda capital Savi was larger, being estimated in the 1720s to have a circuit of over 4 miles, or 6 km; while the Allada capital was said to have a circuit of 3–4 Dutch miles, that is 12–16 English miles, or around 18–24 km.[151]

The population of Ouidah at this time is a matter for speculation. The combined personnel of the European forts cannot have been more than a few hundred. In the 1710s the French fort had a total of 160 African slaves, including children as well as adults; by the 1770s this had grown only slightly to between 180–200, who were said to comprise 50 separate 'families', each living in its own 'hut [*caze*]' near the fort. The 'European' quarters also included free families whose members were employed by or provided services for the forts, who were perhaps roughly as numerous as the fort slaves; by *c.* 1789, when the French fort was reported to have 207 slaves, the total population of the French 'village', including free persons outside the fort, was thought to be nearly 500.[152] The only scrap of evidence for the population of the settlement as a whole is an account of the establishment of the Portuguese fort in 1721, which refers to its location as being in a 'quarter' containing 300 households ('hearths'), all the inhabitants of which were employed in the service of foreigners trading in the town.[153] This high figure seems likely to refer to the town as a whole rather than the two pre-existing 'European' quarters

---

[149] Law, *English in West Africa*, ii, no. 819: Carter, Ouidah, 22 Nov. 1686.

[150] Phillips, 'Journal', 219; Bosman, *Description*, 375.

[151] William Smith, *A New Voyage to Guinea* (London, 1744), 192; Dapper, *Naukeurige Beschrijvinge*, 2/115.

[152] ANF, C6/25, 'Le Fort de Juda, Côte de Guinée', n.d. [1714?]; C6/26, Baud-Duchiron, 'Exploration et construction du comptoir de Juda', 1 Sept. 1778; C6/27, Gourg, 'Mémoire pour servir d'instruction au Directeur qui me succédera au comptoir de Juda', 1791.

[153] Verger, *Flux et reflux*, 136.

only, and suggests (on the analogy of 200 persons in 50 'families' reported for the French quarter in the 1770s) a population of between 1,000-1,500; the addition of Docomè quarter with the construction of the Portuguese fort would have raised this figure, but the total population of the town is still unlikely to have reached as high as 2,000. In comparison, while no figures are available for Savi, the Allada capital in 1660 was thought to have 30,000 inhabitants.[154]

In addition, there was a substantial transient population, in the form of African officials and merchants from Savi, as well as Europeans from visiting ships, and especially slaves in transit to embarkation from the shore. The total number of slaves annually passing through Ouidah, which peaked at around 15,000 in the early eighteenth century, was in fact substantially higher than that of the resident population. Although many of these slaves passed through the town rapidly, significant numbers might be held for some time locally, in the European factories: the English factory in 1687 was said to have space to lodge between 600 and 800 slaves.[155]

In its spatial organization, Ouidah clearly differed radically from towns further inland that served as capitals of states, such as Savi and Allada (and later, Abomey), which were centred around the royal palace.[156] Ouidah was multi-centred, focused on the three European forts; in so far as it had a single centre, this was perhaps the Zobè market.[157] However, to what extent Ouidah yet formed a coherent community, rather than an assemblage of discrete settlements, is doubtful. In the early eighteenth century, the indigenous 'village of Grégoué' (i.e. Tové quarter) was still described as separate from the French and English forts, which were 'a very short distance' away.[158] The establishment of the Portuguese fort in 1721, immediately south of Tové and east of the English fort and Sogbadji quarter, produced greater contiguity of settlement, grouped around the market of Zobé; but the French fort with Ahouandjigo to the north-west remained physically distinct. In fact, it is not clear whether, within the Hueda kingdom, the town was administered as a unit or, perhaps more likely, the three European forts were individually responsible to the king of Hueda, and separately from the local indigenous authorities. There was a Hueda chief called 'Prince Bibe' or 'Captain Bibe', who is named along with the king as negotiating to permit the establishment of the French at Ouidah in 1671 and who in 1682 seems to have been residing at Ouidah, rather than at the capital Savi.[159] In the early eighteenth century, a list of Hueda chiefs who served as 'governors' of 'provinces' within the kingdom includes one entitled 'Gregoué Zonto', who was presumably the governor of Glehue;[160] and maybe this is the title

---

[154] Law, *Kingdom of Allada*, 14.

[155] Law, *English in West Africa*, ii, no. 822: Carter, Ouidah, 6 Jan. 1687.

[156] For Abomey, see Sylvain C. Anignikin, 'Etude sur l'évolution historique sociale et spatiale de la ville d'Abomey' (Ministère de l'Equipement et des Transports, République Populaire du Bénin, 1986).

[157] Although it should be noted that there is no reference to a market in Ouidah (as opposed to the capital Savi) in contemporary sources prior to the Dahomian conquest.

[158] Labat, *Voyage*, ii, 33.

[159] Barbot, *On Guinea*, ii, 635, 642.

[160] Des Marchais, 'Journal', 41v; Labat, *Voyage*, ii, 12. The second element in the title seems to be a generic term for provincial governors, given in the form 'onto' in another source: 'Relation du royaume de Judas', 27. Perhaps 'zonto' is a miscopying of 'honto', i.e. *hunto*, which meant in origin 'ship's captain' (*hun* =

which 'Prince Bibe' held.[161] But whether he had overall administrative responsibility for the town, including the European forts, is doubtful; more probably, he was governor of the indigenous 'village' only.

The operation of the European trade in the Hueda kingdom gave rise to a number of new official positions. Most important was that of 'Captain of the White Men', as Europeans correctly translated the indigenous title Yovogan, or Yevogan, which is already attested in the 1680s,[162] and from the 1690s was held by a man called 'Carter'.[163] There was also an assistant to the Yovogan called 'Agou', and separate 'captains' for the European nations with factories in Hueda: the French (whose captain was called 'Assou'), English (served in the 1690s by 'Captain Tom'), Dutch and Portuguese.[164] But these officials who dealt with European traders did not, like their counterparts under Dahomian rule later, form a local administration for Ouidah; in fact, there is no evidence that they even resided there. In 1718 the Yovogan Carter was reported to be building a new house outside the capital Savi, where he was in consequence now expected to attend less regularly, but this residence was not at Ouidah; a later map of the Hueda kingdom shows Carter's village situated to the east of Savi, while that of the 'French captain' Assou was even further from Ouidah, to the north-west of the capital.[165]

Ouidah in this period did not engross the conduct of the European trade, since much of the business of European traders had to be transacted at the capital Savi. The emphasis in some modern accounts on the 'separation of the political and commercial capitals' as a feature of the organization of the slave trade in Hueda is in fact misconceived – or, more precisely, it incorrectly reads back into the period of the Hueda kingdom a distinction that emerged only after the Dahomian conquest.[166] When the English Royal African Company first sent a ship to trade in Hueda, in 1681, its chief factor 'bought slaves at Sabba [Savi], the king's town', while his assistant was ordered to 'Agriffie [Glehue], the lower town [i.e. Ouidah]', where he presumably managed the landing of goods.[167] This pattern continued even when permanent factories were established in Ouidah. The French trader Barbot in 1682 thus noted that 'it is with the king that you do the trade', i.e. at the capital Savi, while the goods were 'brought from the vessel to the lodge' at Ouidah; and the chief of the English factory at Ouidah in 1685 reported that he 'went up to

---

[160] (cont.) 'boat') but, at least by the nineteenth century, was also applied to indigenous officials: see Burton, *Mission*, i, 121, n.

[161] This now seems to me more likely than that he held the title Yovogan, as suggested in Law, *Slave Coast*, 214.

[162] Law, *English in West Africa*, i, no. 478, enc., Accounts of Thorne, Glehue, 20 April 1681, giving the title in the form 'Captain Blanko' (from Portuguese *branco*, 'white'). The indigenous title is given (as 'Lievauga') in 'Relation du royaume de Judas', 27.

[163] Bosman, *Description*, 359.

[164] See Law, *Slave Coast*, 207.

[165] Van Dantzig, *Dutch and the Guinea Coast*, no. 234: Diary of Ph. Eytzen, 22 April 1718; map of the Hueda kingdom in Labat, *Voyage*, ii; des Marchais, 'Journal', 40.

[166] Polanyi, *Dahomey*, 118, 123, 126.

[167] Law, *English in West Africa*, i, no. 476: Thorne, Glehue, 24 May 1681; see Thorne's accounts in the 'warehouse' in 'Agriffie', in no. 478, enc.

the king's town' to buy slaves for an English ship trading there.[168] It has been suggested that, although this was the practice earlier, by the first decade of the eighteenth century the trade had been localized at Ouidah, rather than Savi; but there is no basis for this in the contemporary evidence.[169] In 1716, for example, it was still explicitly noted that slaves brought for sale were lodged in prisons 'in the place where they are traded, this place is Xavier [Savi], the king keeps his residence there'.[170] At this period the Dutch West India Company, as noted earlier, actually maintained its factory at Savi rather than at Ouidah. By 1716 the English and French companies, in addition to their forts in Ouidah, also maintained lodges at Savi; in fact, the local French and English directors normally resided in Savi, leaving the forts at Ouidah under subordinate officers.[171] When the Portuguese established their fort at Ouidah in 1721, they also maintained a subsidiary lodge in Savi.[172] The factories at Ouidah served only as storehouses for goods and for slaves in transit to and from Savi; an English trader in 1694 noted that the factory at Ouidah 'proved very beneficial to us, by housing our goods which came ashore late, and could not arrive at the king's town (where I kept my warehouse) ere it was dark', and also when slaves could not be embarked owing to bad weather.[173]

European activities in Ouidah provided economic opportunities for the local inhabitants mainly in the form of employment in ancillary services, such as the supply of provisions and firewood, and especially as porters and canoemen. It has been argued that European trade in Africa, even at the height of the Atlantic slave trade in the late eighteenth century, was simply too small in scale, measured by per capita export earnings, to have had any major impact on indigenous societies.[174] While this may have some a priori plausibility for West Africa as a whole and for many particular societies in its interior, it is clearly not applicable to coastal communities such as Ouidah which were heavily involved in the trade. The value of slave exports through Ouidah by the end of the seventeenth century was enormous, in relation to the population of the town; 10,000 slaves per year in the 1690s, when the price of an adult male slave in the local currency of cowry shells was 10 'grand cabess [large heads]' (40,000 shells), equivalent to £12.10s. (£12.50), would have represented (allowing for lower prices paid for women and children) the value of around 320 million cowries (£100,000), at a time when the wage for a porter per journey (in effect, per day) in Ouidah was 3 'tockies', or 120 cowries (9 pre-decimal pence, £0.03¾).[175] But most of the income from this trade would have accrued to

---

[168] Barbot, *On Guinea*, ii, 637; Law, *English in West Africa*, ii, no. 812: Carter, Ouidah, 19 Sept. 1685.

[169] Polanyi, *Dahomey*, 123.

[170] ANF, C6/25, 'Mémoire de l'estat du pays de Juda', 1716.

[171] Des Marchais, 'Journal', 28v, 40v; Labat, *Voyage*, ii, 34–5.

[172] There was a Portuguese factory at Savi by 1727, when it was destroyed in the Dahomian conquest: Smith, *New Voyage*, 190.

[173] Phillips, 'Journal', 215–16.

[174] As argued notably by David Eltis: e.g. 'Precolonial western Africa and the Atlantic economy', in Barbara L. Solow (ed.), *Slavery and the Rise of the Atlantic System* (Cambridge, 1991), 97–119.

[175] For slave prices, see Law, *Slave Coast*, 178; the average price is assumed to be 80% of that for adult males. For wage rates, see Robin Law, 'Posthumous questions for Karl Polanyi: price inflation in pre-colonial Dahomey', *JAH*, 33 (1992), 415–16.

officials and merchants in the capital Savi (and beyond, to the officials and merchants of states in the interior from where many of the slaves were purchased), rather than to the inhabitants of Ouidah. It is difficult to estimate what sums would have been expended on goods and services in Ouidah itself, but some indication is provided by the statement of Barbot in 1682 that every ship had to pay the value of five to six slaves for the carriage of goods from the shore to the factory in Ouidah, and the same again for the canoes that landed goods and embarked slaves at the beach.[176] In the case of the canoemen, since many of these were hired from the Gold Coast rather than permanently resident in Ouidah, these earnings were partly, indeed perhaps predominantly, repatriated to the Gold Coast, rather than being expended or retained locally.[177] But, assuming 40 ships per year, and the price of a slave to be that of an adult male, payments for porters alone at this rate would have amounted to around 8.8 million cowries (£2,750) a year, representing wages for over 73,000 person-days, or, assuming that workers took one day of rest in each four-day 'week', continuous year-round employment for around 270 porters.

Porterage and other services for the European trade, of course, represented only one of the major sources of income for people in Ouidah, along with fishing, salt-making and agricultural production. The continuing importance of fishing, in particular, is attested by a European account of the town in the early eighteenth century, which observes that its wealth derived as much from the fact that its inhabitants were 'all fishermen and canoemen' as from the presence of European factories.[178] There is little basis on which to estimate the relative importance of the European trade in comparison with other sectors of the local economy. One stray figure recorded in the 1690s is that the revenue derived by the king of Hueda from a toll levied on fishing was the value of 100 slaves, presumably annually, from each of the two principal 'rivers' in the kingdom.[179] This was not far short of the revenue from the royal duty on slave exports, levied at 5 'galinas' of cowries (1,000 shells) per slave, which would have yielded (on exports of 10,000 slaves per year) the value of 250 slaves annually, although the king's total revenue from the slave trade, including 'customs' (in contemporary parlance, payments for permission to trade) and the proceeds of his own sales of slaves, was much higher than this, estimated in this period at around 30 slaves' value per ship.[180] It is not specified at what rate the toll on fish was levied, but if it was comparable to that levied generally on sales in the kingdom, which was one-tenth,[181] this would suggest a total output for the fishing industry of the value of 2,000 slaves annually, which was around a fifth of slave exports through Ouidah in the 1690s. It was also very substantially greater than the total paid for portering, as calculated earlier (and, if incomes from fishing

---

[176] Barbot, *On Guinea*, ii, 637.

[177] Canoemen hired from the Gold Coast were paid half of their wages in advance on recruitment, in gold, and the remainder at the termination of their employment, in goods, which they would presumably carry back with them to the Gold Coast: Phillips, 'Journal', 229.

[178] Labat, *Voyage*, ii, 33.

[179] Bosman, *Description*, 362a.

[180] For the latter estimate, see ibid. (given in the original in the form $1,500 per ship, around £375); see also analysis (with slightly different calculations) in Law, *Slave Coast*, 213.

[181] Des Marchais, 'Journal', 49; Labat, *Voyage*, ii, 81.

were comparable to the wages paid to porters, would suggest that fishing employed around 2,400 persons). Although this figure for fish production is for the Hueda kingdom as a whole, rather than for Ouidah alone, any reasonable assumption of the share to be assigned to Ouidah would still leave fishing as a larger sector of its economy than portering.

The rise and fall of the Hueda kingdom

In a recent study, David Eltis suggested that, despite considerable research on the history of Hueda, 'the question of why this small African state was so dominant in the slave trade still has no answer'.[182] This seems an unduly pessimistic assessment of previous research. It is true that Ouidah had no obvious geographical advantage over other ports in the region, either in terms of coastal harbour facilities (of which, in common with its rivals, it had none) or of access to inland waterways (for which it was no better positioned than its competitors to west and east). As regards its geographical situation, the principal advantage possessed by Ouidah was its proximity to and accessibility from the powerful kingdoms in the immediate interior which were the principal suppliers of slaves to the coast, initially Allada (and, after 1727, Dahomey). This advantage, of course, was equally shared by Offra to the east, which in fact preceded Ouidah as the main outlet for Allada's slave trade. The story of Offra's displacement by Ouidah in the 1670s, however, is straightforward (and well-known). The initial diversion of trade from Offra to Ouidah in 1671 was due to a rebellion by Offra against Allada's authority, which closed the paths between the two; and difficulties in relations between Allada and Offra recurred through the following two decades, culminating in the war in which Offra was destroyed in 1692, an event that decisively confirmed the commercial supremacy of Ouidah. In the early eighteenth century the kings of Allada sought to redivert trade away from Ouidah through a 'port' under their own control, now Jakin, which inherited the commercial role of Offra, and initially with some success. But this process was overtaken by the Dahomian conquest of both Allada and Hueda in the 1720s, which served to remove obstacles to the passage of trade to Ouidah; and, even more critically, by the subsequent Dahomian destruction of Jakin in 1732, which reconfirmed the concentration of trade at Ouidah.[183]

A second factor in the shift from Offra to Ouidah is implied in a letter from the English Royal African Company to the king of Hueda in 1701, which states that the English had moved there because of the 'ill treatment' which they had received in Allada.[184] One aspect of the better treatment offered at Ouidah was that the Hueda kings accepted lower levels of 'customs' for permission to trade. In the 1680s the French at Ouidah were paying the value of 25 slaves per ship for customs, whereas at Offra they had paid 50; total charges, including the hire of porters and canoemen, came to between 32 and 35 slaves per ship at the former, but between 70 and

[182] Eltis, *Rise of African Slavery*, 184.

[183] Law, *Slave Coast*, 127–41.

[184] PRO, T70/51, Royal African Company to King of Hueda, 12 Aug. 1701.

80 at the latter.[185] By the 1690s, the rate of customs at Ouidah had fallen further, to only 8 slaves, 6 to the king and 2 to the 'caboceers', or chiefs.[186] A second aspect was the problem of theft, and the failure of the Allada authorities to repress it; another observer in 1701 explained that no trade was done any longer at Allada, because of the reputation of its people for 'cheating and stealing'.[187] Correspondence from the English company's Offra factory in the early 1680s also alludes to problems in recovering debts.[188]

To the extent that the greater attractiveness of Ouidah over Offra related to the policies pursued by their rulers, these were subject to change over time. By the 1710s the differential in customs between Ouidah and its rivals had been substantially reduced, although not entirely eliminated; the charges for permission to trade at Jakin, now the principal port of Allada, being only 12 slaves in all (6 to the king, 4 to the governor of Jakin, one each to two other chiefs), doubtless driven down by the need to compete with Ouidah.[189] By the 1690s also, Ouidah itself had acquired a reputation for the prevalence of petty theft, both by porters carrying goods up from the beach and from the European warehouses, the people of Ouidah being considered worse thieves than those of the Gold Coast.[190] There is no record, however, of problems at Ouidah over issues of credit: an account of trading in the 1690s stresses rather the meticulousness of the African merchants there in the prompt settlement of their debts.[191]

That the trade nevertheless remained concentrated at Ouidah was in part due, as noted earlier, to the political history of the region, as this affected relations between Allada (and later Dahomey) in the interior and Ouidah and Jakin at the coast. But in addition, it seems likely that Ouidah's continued dominance reflected in large part the forces of inertia. It is noteworthy that the pattern of concentration of the slave trade at a single port within the Bight of Benin is paralleled in other regions of western Africa, as for example the dominance of Bonny in the Bight of Biafra; and indeed it also mirrors the situation in Europe, where a single port was likewise commonly dominant within the slave trade of each European nation, for example Liverpool in England and Nantes in France. As a recent analysis co-authored by Eltis himself has suggested, this pattern of concentration probably reflects, in both Europe and Africa, cost savings arising from access to market information in established ports.[192] On the

---

[185] Barbot, *On Guinea*, ii, 636–7, 658. Barbot actually says that the French in 1671 had paid 100 slaves in 'customs' at Offra, but this figure was for two ships, the rate per ship being 50: see Delbée, 'Journal', 439–40.

[186] Phillips, 'Journal', 227. The term 'caboceer' (Portuguese *cabeceiro*, 'headman') was commonly applied to African officials.

[187] Damon, 'Relation du voyage d'Issyny', 107.

[188] Law, *Correspondence from Offra and Whydah*, esp. nos 4, 6, John Mildmay, Offra, 13 Oct. 1680 (referring to the possibility of recovering 'your old debts from [the King] and some of the chief captains'); William Cross, Offra, Feb. 1681 (an unsuccessful attempt to refuse further credit to the governor of Offra).

[189] Law, *Kingdom of Allada*, 96–7.

[190] Bosman, *Description*, 348–9; cf. Phillips, 'Journal', 225–6.

[191] Albert Van Danztig, 'English Bosman and Dutch Bosman: a comparison of texts – VI', *HA*, 7 (1980), 284 [passage omitted in the English translation of Bosman's work].

[192] Eltis et al., 'Slave-trading ports'.

Bight of Benin itself, on the European side of the trade, existing investment in the forts in Ouidah also operated to discourage relocation elsewhere.

Karl Polanyi linked the concentration of the slave trade at Ouidah to its status as a 'port of trade', which was politically 'neutral' and militarily 'weak', and therefore acceptable to traders of the different nationalities involved.[193] This idea of a 'neutral' place of trade does, indeed, have considerable plausibility, not only in abstract theory but also in the documented history of this particular region: in the later eighteenth century, the lagoonside port of Abomey-Calavi, on the shore of Lake Nokoué, east of Ouidah, was described as a 'neutral place', which functioned as 'a sort of free fair, where the different nations go to trade'.[194] It is doubtful, however, whether this analysis has any bearing upon the rise of Ouidah as an Atlantic port in the late seventeenth century. Ouidah was indeed maintained by the Hueda kings as a 'neutral' port as regards traders of different European nations, as decreed in the treaty of 1703 forbidding hostilities among Europeans, and this policy was clearly among the factors that attracted European traders there: as the director of the French fort noted in 1716, it was 'the only place of neutrality where the vessels of every nation are bound to find a secure retreat in time of [intra-European] war'.[195] This, however, was a neutrality imposed upon Europeans by the strength of the Hueda state, rather than a reflection of the latter's 'weakness'; and Hueda was not in any sense recognized as a 'neutral' area by its African neighbours. Although Hueda was certainly a small and therefore relatively weak power in relation to the interior state of Allada, which was its principal supplier of slaves, its independence of Allada was sustained in the face of systematic opposition from the latter (including an actual military invasion in 1692), rather than accepted as serving its convenience.[196]

Eltis also observes that 'the question of why, with all the income from its Atlantic trade and a significant military capacity, Whydah was unable to maintain its independence or, indeed, become a major power has yet to be addressed', and suggests that this might indicate that 'the transatlantic slave trade was not the central event shaping African economic and political developments'.[197] This also seems an idiosyncratic reading of the literature. Hueda did, in fact, develop as a significant regional 'power' in the coastal area in the late seventeenth century, extending its authority at least briefly over Grand-Popo to the west and disputing control of Offra with Allada to the east;[198] and contemporary Europeans, at least, thought that its military power was enhanced by the wealth it derived from the Atlantic trade, although it is noteworthy that the factor they stressed was not Hueda's ability to import European firearms but the financial resources that

---

[193] Polanyi, *Dahomey*, ch. 7; see also Arnold, 'Port of trade'. For a critique of Polanyi's analysis with reference to market centres in the West African interior, see Paul E. Lovejoy, 'Polanyi's "ports of trade": Salaga and Kano in the nineteenth century', *CJAS*, 16 (1982), 245–77.

[194] De Chenevert & Bullet, 'Réflexions sur Juda' (MS of 1776, in ANF, Dépôt des Fortifications des Colonies, Côtes d'Afrique 111), 5.

[195] ANF, C6/25, Levesque, mémoire (responding to a proposal to abandon the Ouidah fort), 6 July 1716.

[196] For details, see Law, *Slave Coast*, 238–42, 245–7, 252–60; idem, *Kingdom of Allada*, 52–61.

[197] Eltis, *Rise of African Slavery*, 184.

[198] Law, *Slave Coast*, 243–4, 247, 249.

enabled it to hire mercenary soldiers from other African communities for its wars.[199] In relation to the dominant hinterland state of Allada, however, its potential power was limited by sheer demographic weight: it was estimated (probably with some exaggeration) that Allada had twenty times the population of Hueda, a disproportion beyond what could be offset by greater financial resources.[200] Also, Hueda's potential power was compromised in the early eighteenth century by chronic internal divisions, which may well have been exacerbated by competition over revenues from the Atlantic trade, although this was certainly not their only cause.[201]

The ultimate fall of Hueda to conquest by Dahomey in 1727 on the face of it also presents no mystery. In addition to Hueda's persisting internal divisions, which critically undermined its efforts at self-defence on this occasion, the Dahomian forces were decisively superior qualitatively, Dahomey having developed both a superior military organization and a more systematic military ethos than any other state in the region. This does not, however, demonstrate the irrelevance of the Atlantic slave trade to questions of military power, since the militarization of Dahomey was itself a consequence of the impact of that trade, Dahomey having been a major supplier of slaves for sale at the coast since at least the 1680s and its forces being by the 1720s equipped with imported European firearms obtained in exchange for such slave exports. The imbalance of military power between Hueda and Dahomey reflected the division of labour that operated within the African section of the slave trade, in which coastal communities such as Hueda operated mainly as middlemen, while the actual process of violent enslavement was left to military states in the interior such as Dahomey.[202] The Dahomian conquest of Hueda is thus an illustration, rather than a refutation, of the importance of the Atlantic slave trade in shaping local economic and political developments.

[199] 'Relation du royaume de Judas', 13.
[200] N****, *Voyages aux Côtes de Guinée et en Amérique* (Amsterdam, 1719), 121; see also Bosman, *Description*, 396.
[201] Law, '"The common people were divided"'.
[202] Robin Law, 'Warfare on the West African Slave Coast, 1650–1850', in R. Brian Ferguson & Neil L. Whitehead (eds), *War in the Tribal Zone* (Santa Fé, 1992), 103–26.

2

The Dahomian Conquest
of Ouidah

The political and commercial situation on the Slave Coast was transformed by the rise of Dahomey, under its king Agaja (died 1740), who conquered Allada in 1724 and Hueda in 1727. This profoundly affected Ouidah, which became subject to Dahomey from 1727 and was left as its exclusive outlet for trade with the Europeans after the Dahomians destroyed the rival 'port' of Jakin in 1732.[1] The origins of the Hueda–Dahomey war of 1727 have been treated at length elsewhere, and detailed rehearsal would be out of place here; it need only be stated that the general view of contemporary European observers – that Agaja sought control of Ouidah principally in order to secure more effective and unrestricted access to the European trade – remains persuasive.[2] For present purposes, it is the consequences rather than the causes of the war that are of central importance.

The Dahomian forces invaded Hueda in March 1727, and quickly overran it.[3] The capital Savi was taken on 9 March[4] and destroyed; the European factories there, which had survived the initial sack of the town, were burned down by the Dahomians a few days later.[5] Many thousands of the inhabitants of the kingdom were killed or enslaved and sold, and others fled, settling in communities along the coast to both east and west of Ouidah, where the lagoon and other inland waterways afforded a degree of protection against the land-based forces of Dahomey.

---

[1] For the Dahomian conquest of the coast, see Akinjogbin, *Dahomey*, 64–100; Law, *Slave Coast*, 278–97.

[2] See discussion in Law, *Slave Coast*, 300–08; as against the view of Akinjogbin, *Dahomey*, 73–81, that Agaja's original intention was to bring the slave trade to an end.

[3] For the campaign, see esp. Robin Law, 'A neglected account of the Dahomian conquest of Whydah (1727): the "Relation de la Guerre de Juda" of the Sieur Ringard of Nantes', *HA*, 15 (1988), 321–8; Snelgrave, *New Account*, 9–18.

[4] So according to the Gregorian (or New Style) calendar, but 26 Feb. by contemporary English (Julian, or Old Style) reckoning. The date is regularly given in local sources as 7 Feb. 1727: first in A. Le Herissé, *L'Ancien Royaume du Dahomey* (Paris, 1911), 297, n. The source of this date is unclear, but it is certainly incorrect.

[5] Francisco Pereyra Mendes, Ouidah, 4 April 1727, in Verger, *Flux et reflux*, 145; Smith, *New Voyage*, 190–91.

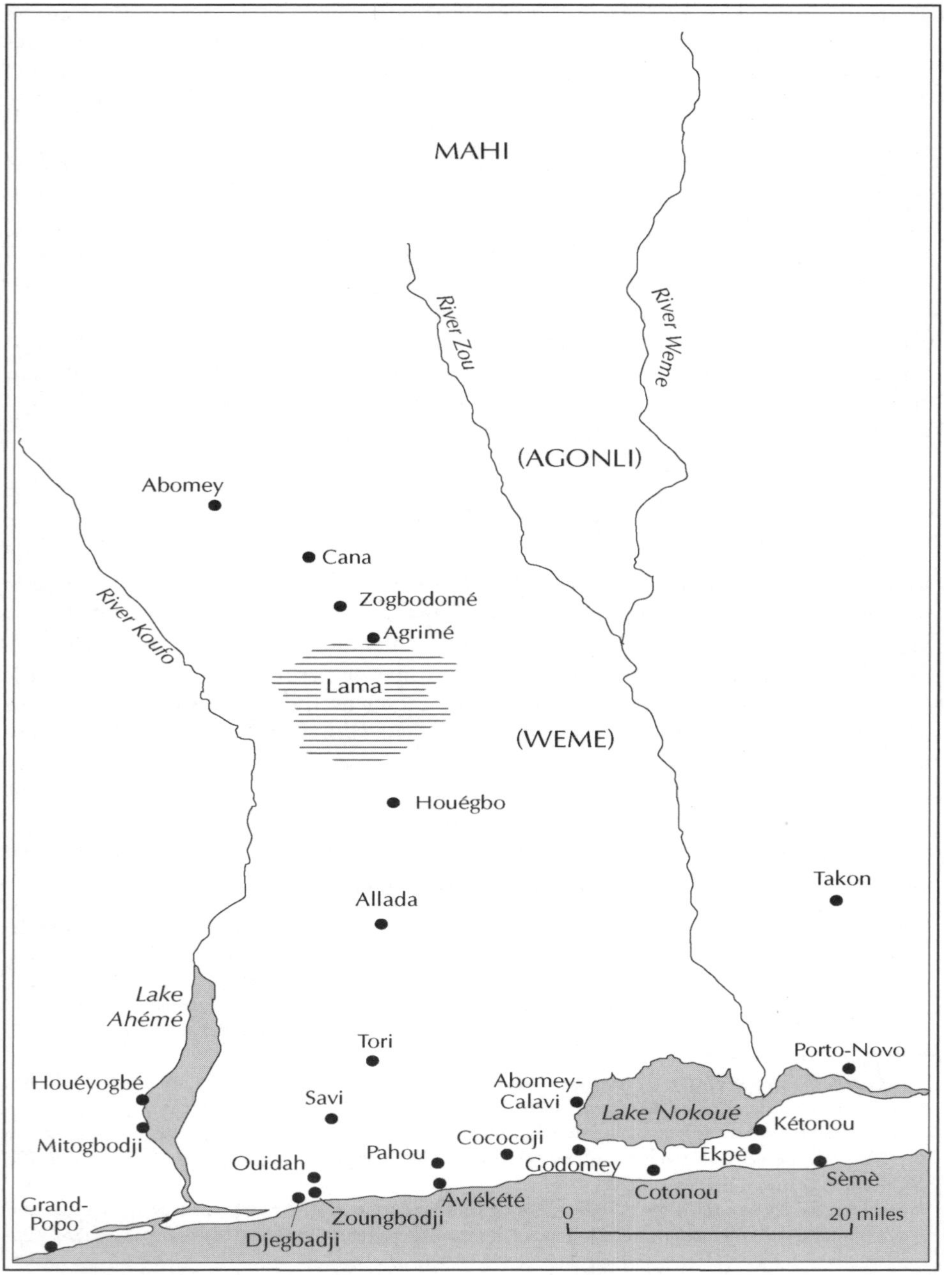

MAHI

River Zou

River Weme

(AGONLI)

Abomey

River Koufo

Cana

Zogbodomé

Agrimé

Lama

(WEME)

Houégbo

Takon

Allada

Lake
Ahémé

Tori

Porto-Novo

Houéyogbé

Savi

Abomey-
Calavi

Lake Nokoué

Kétonou

Mitogbodji

Cococoji

Ekpè

Ouidah

Pahou

Godomey

Cotonou

Sèmè

Grand-
Popo

Avlékété

Zoungbodji

Djegbadji

0

20 miles

Map 3 Dahomey and its immediate neighbours

51

There is thus a Hueda quarter, Houédakomè, in Porto-Novo, to the east, and a significant Hueda element also settled in Badagry, further east again.[6] The Hueda king Hufon, together with many of his subjects, however, fled westwards, to found the kingdom later known as Hueda-Henji. They first took refuge, as reported immediately after the conquest, on 'an island on the sea coast ... lying near [Grand-] Popoe'.[7] In early 1728 the place where Hufon was residing was named as 'Topoy', which may represent 'Tokpa', a generic toponym meaning 'on the waterside';[8] but 'Topoy' was attacked and destroyed by the Dahomians soon after, and Hufon evidently removed to a less accessible site. Hueda tradition indicates that the initial settlement of the exiles was at Mitogbodji, an island in the south-west of Lake Ahémé; but Hufon subsequently moved his capital to Houéyogbé, further north, on the western shore of the lake.[9] Presumably, this exiled Hueda community was originally subject to Grand-Popo, in whose territory it was settled, but relations with their hosts quickly deteriorated, leading to war in 1731, after which the new Hueda state presumably became independent.[10]

The conquest of Ouidah, 1727–33

After the fall of Savi on 9 March 1727, the victorious Dahomian army, pursuing the retreating Hueda, pressed on south to Ouidah, where it attacked and captured the Portuguese fort and laid siege to the French and English forts; the Portuguese fort was 'demolished to the ground' and its cannon carried off into the interior.[11] The Dahomians did not, however, press their attack on the other forts; the siege was lifted after a few days, and Agaja sent to assure the Europeans of his good intentions towards them and issued a proclamation threatening death to 'anyone who came near the [French] fort or harmed the whites'.[12] The main body of the Dahomian army was then withdrawn from the Hueda kingdom, leaving only a garrison at Savi.[13] Ouidah itself was neither garrisoned nor subjected to any form of Dahomian administration, being by implication left under the authority of the European forts.

[6] A. Akindélé & C. Aguessy, *Contribution à l'étude de l'histoire de l'ancien royaume de Porto-Novo* (Dakar, 1953), 153; Robin Law, 'A lagoonside port on the eighteenth-century Slave Coast: the early history of Badagri', *CJAS*, 28 (1994), 38–41. Three of the 8 quarters of Badagry are of Hueda origin (one of them having the same name as one of the quarters of Ouidah, Awhanjigo [= Ahouandjigo]); the senior chief of Hueda origin, the Wawu of Ahoviko quarter, claims descent from the royal family of the old Hueda kingdom.

[7] Snelgrave, *New Account*, 14–15.

[8] ANF, C6/25, unsigned letter [Dupetitval], Ouidah, 20 May 1728.

[9] Soglo, 'Les Xweda', 72–3. The name Mitogbodji, 'ancestral dwelling', was evidently given retrospectively, after its abandonment (Houéyogbé meaning, in contrast, 'new home'). A contemporary account of the 1770s gives the name of the settlement of the exiled Hueda as 'Ouessou', which is not identifiable: de Chenevert & Bullet, 'Réflexions', 40.

[10] Van Dantzig, *Dutch and the Guinea Coast*, no. 303: Hertog, Jakin, 26 June 1731. In 1733 the Hueda even made an unsuccessful attempt to seize control of Grand-Popo, burning half of the town before they were repelled: ANF, C6/25, Levet, Ouidah, 26 Aug. 1733 (lettre de nouvelles).

[11] Van Dantzig, *Dutch and the Guinea Coast*, no. 252: Hertog, Jakin, 18 March 1727.

[12] Francisco Pereyra Mendes, Ouidah, 4 April 1727, in Verger, *Flux et reflux*, 145.

[13] Snelgrave, *New Account*, 115.

Local tradition in Ouidah, it may be noted, claims that Agaja visited the town in person. A story is told that he paused under a tree, either in the pursuit of the defeated Hufon or after the conquest, in order to take his first drink of imported European gin, although this story is attached in different versions to two different trees, one immediately south of the town (called the 'Captains' Tree') and one in the village of Zoungbodji, halfway to the beach.[14] The contemporary evidence, however, makes clear that Agaja did not personally accompany the army that invaded Hueda in 1727;[15] and there is no suggestion in the contemporary record that he did so on any subsequent occasion either.

The Dahomian conquest of 1727 was not definitive, since the displaced Hueda now established to the west continued to dispute possession of the country and enlisted the assistance of the Yoruba kingdom of Oyo, in the interior to the north-east, whose forces launched a series of invasions of Dahomey during 1728-30. In January 1728 Agaja was in negotiation with Hufon at 'Topoy', offering to allow him to re-establish himself in his capital Savi and to give him a share of the 'customs' levied from European ships; but Hufon, believing that the support of Oyo would secure his restoration in complete independence, rejected the overture.[16] In February, a force commanded by Assou, the former 'French Captain' in the Hueda kingdom, encamped on the beach south of Ouidah;[17] effective control was established, to the extent of intercepting the customs paid by European ships, and Dahomian messengers who came to Ouidah were assaulted.[18] Subsequently, while Dahomey was distracted by an Oyo invasion, which presumably caused the withdrawal of the garrison from Savi, the Hueda even began to rebuild their capital. At the end of April, however, a Dahomian army reappeared in the area, destroyed the buildings which the Hueda had erected at Savi, and encamped north of Ouidah; at its approach the Hueda there fled, most of them back to Grand-Popo, but Assou and others taking refuge in the French fort. A detachment of the Dahomian army therefore proceeded, on 1 May, to attack the French fort, but it was repulsed after four hours' fighting, with some assistance from the artillery of the neighbouring English fort.[19] The Dahomians now withdrew from Ouidah, leaving the town for the moment in the control of Assou and the Hueda forces, and moved westwards to attack Hufon's base at 'Topoy'. However, they returned to Ouidah on 14 May and evidently reasserted their control there. Despite the earlier involvement of the French and English forts in the fighting against them, the Dahomian commanders again offered assurances to the Europeans that they had no

[14] Sinou & Agbo, *Ouidah*, 115, 161.

[15] Agaja was clearly not with the Dahomian army when it took Savi, since the Europeans taken prisoner there were taken to the king at Allada: Snelgrave, *New Account*, 17.

[16] ANF, C6/25, [Dupetitval], Ouidah, 20 May 1728.

[17] Van Dantzig, *Dutch and the Guinea Coast*, no. 274: Hertog, Jakin, 16 Feb. 1728, in Minutes of Council, Elmina, 23 March 1728. Assou's involvement appears from ANF, C6/25, [Dupetitval], 20 May 1728.

[18] Robin Law (ed.), *Correspondence of the Royal African Company's Chief Factors at Cabo Corso Castle with William's Fort, Whydah and the Little Popo Factory, 1727–8* (Madison, 1991), no. 15: Thomas Wilson, Ouidah, 24 Feb. 1728.

[19] ANF, C6/25, [Dupetitval], Ouidah, 20 May 1728; Law, *Correspondence with William's Fort*, no. 19: Wilson, Ouidah, 29 April 1728.

hostile intentions against them but only against the Hueda; and also undertook 'to spare the people belonging to the crooms [i.e. villages] near the forts [i.e. the three quarters of Ahouandjigo, Sogbadji and Docomè], for cargadoers [i.e. porters] and servants to the whites'. At the same time, they gave out that they did not intend any further action against the Hueda, but this turned out to be merely a ruse to catch the latter off guard, since a few days later they again attacked 'Topoy', which they destroyed on 16 May, although Hufon himself escaped. The Dahomians then, however, once again withdrew their forces from Ouidah, leaving only a detachment encamped at Savi, 'to protect the King of Dahomy's trade'.[20]

Dahomian control of Ouidah was now threatened from another quarter, when in July an army from Little Popo arrived on the beach to the south; this was engaged in independent banditry, rather than supporting the Hueda against the Dahomians, intending 'to help neither but to rob both'. It was understood to intend to march on Ouidah itself, where the French fort put itself in a state of defence against the anticipated attack. However, the attack on Ouidah never materialized, and the raiders withdrew after only three weeks, on the approach of a Dahomian army.[21] Following the departure of this Popo force in mid-August, the Director of the French fort, Houdoyer Dupetitval, in view of the recent demonstration of Dahomian military dominance, resolved on a policy of conciliation with Dahomey, sending one of his subordinate officers on a mission to Agaja in his capital Abomey, to offer him assurances of friendship and to dissociate the French from the Hueda–Oyo alliance.[22] Agaja for his part thought again of consolidating his conquest through the resettlement of at least part of the Hueda people. In August he was reported to have concluded an agreement with a son of Hufon, then at Jakin to the east, to install him as king of Hueda; and at the beginning of October he issued a proclamation encouraging the Hueda to reoccupy their former homes.[23]

This attempt at a peaceful settlement once again broke down, however. Although Assou again led a party of the exiled Hueda to reoccupy Ouidah, he refused a demand from Agaja for his formal submission, and in consequence, in December 1728, a Dahomian army was dispatched against him. On its approach Assou and his troops again withdrew to the French fort, where the director Dupetitval, despite his earlier undertakings of support for the Dahomians, granted them refuge. The Dahomians therefore again assaulted the fort, and this time were assisted by the circumstance that the roofs of buildings within the fort took fire, threatening to ignite gunpowder stored in the magazine. The European personnel thereupon abandoned the fort, taking refuge in the English fort; but over 1,000 of the Hueda were killed in the subsequent explosion of the magazine, although Assou himself was also able to escape to the English fort. The Dahomians were

---

[20] ANF, C6/25, [Dupetitval], Ouidah, 20 May 1728; Law, *Correspondence with William's Fort*, nos 19, 22: Wilson, 29 April (PS of 3 May), 12 July 1728.

[21] Law, *Correspondence with William's Fort*, no. 22: Wilson, 12 July 1728, PS of 19 July; ANF, C6/25, Minutes of Conseil de Direction, Fort Saint-Louis de Gregoy, 11 Aug. 1728.

[22] See account of negotiations in ANF, C6/25, Minutes of Conseil de Direction, 26 Aug.–3 Oct. 1728.

[23] ANF, C6/25, Dayrie, Jakin, 18 Aug. 1728, in Minutes of Conseil de Direction, 15 Aug. 1728; Dupetitval, Ouidah, 4 Oct. 1728.

repelled from the English fort by cannon fire, but were left in occupation of the French fort. Once again, however, the Dahomian army then withdrew, allowing the French to recover possession of their fort.[24]

Although the campaigns of 1728 appeared to have decisively confirmed Dahomian military control over Ouidah, still no move was yet made towards setting up any permanent Dahomian presence in the town. In September 1728 Agaja took the first step towards establishing an administrative structure for Ouidah when he appointed three 'captains', one each for the three European forts, in imitation of the system that had operated in the Hueda kingdom earlier.[25] These officials levied customs, each from the European nation assigned to him, and also conducted the king's own trade. However, they do not seem to have resided permanently in Ouidah but only went there when there was specific business to transact.[26] For most practical purposes, both of defence and of day-to-day administration, the town remained for the moment under the control of the directors of the European forts. The campaigns of 1728 had a decisive but contradictory impact on the attitudes of the Europeans in Ouidah. The English, on the one hand, concluded that the continuation of Dahomian control of Ouidah would be ruinous to trade; Charles Testefole, who became governor of the English fort in July 1729, actively encouraged the exiled Hueda to continue their attempts to recover their country.[27] In contrast, the French director Dupetitval, having suffered the weight of Dahomian military power in two attacks on his fort, resolved to align the French with what now appeared to be the winning side. When Hufon from exile sought European assistance for a further attempt to repossess his kingdom, whereas the English and Portuguese forts promised support, Dupetitval refused.[28]

In 1729, under cover of another Oyo invasion of Dahomey and encouraged by Testefole, the Hueda made a further and more serious attempt to reoccupy Ouidah. They were reinforced by allies from Grand-Popo and led this time by Hufon in person, although with Assou again as a subordinate commander. The Dahomian garrison at Savi had been withdrawn to reinforce the national army facing the Oyo, and the Hueda-Popo force seems to have encountered no initial opposition, entering Ouidah on 4 May, and remaining in occupation of the town for over two months. But, once the Dahomians had seen off the Oyo, they dispatched an army to Ouidah, where it arrived on 16 July. Although Assou and the Popos made a stand, the bulk of the Hueda forces again fled without offering to fight; Hufon himself took refuge in the English fort and was later smuggled out

---

[24] Snelgrave, *New Account*, 115–20; for the date, see ANF, C6/10, Dupetitval, 17 March 1729, summarized in Robert Harms, *The Diligent* (New York, 2002), 217–19. This reconstruction of the sequence of events amends that in Law, *Slave Coast*, 288–9, which assumed that Snelgrave's account of the destruction of the French fort related to the Dahomian attack on 1 May 1728; also that of Akinjogbin, *Dahomey*, 84, that the second attack which destroyed the fort, occurred later in the same month.

[25] ANF, C6/25, Delisle, Dahomey, 7 Sept. 1728, in Minutes of Conseil de Direction, 13 Sept. 1728.

[26] This is clear from the fact that the Dahomians were unaware of the reoccupation of Ouidah by the exiled Hueda in 1729, until Agaja 'sent down some of his traders, with slaves' to the European forts there: Snelgrave, *New Account*, 125.

[27] Ibid., 123.

[28] ANF, C6/25, 'Mémoire de la Compagnie des Indes contre le Sr Galot', 8 Nov. 1730.

of the country back to his retreat to the west.[29] Although the English director Testefole actively assisted the Hueda on this occasion, the latter evidently felt that the other two European forts in Ouidah had not been equally supportive, and took reprisals against their personnel. During their occupation of Ouidah, they seized and killed an official of the Portuguese fort, on the allegation that he had helped the Dahomians.[30] The French director Dupetitval was also kidnapped, on 29 July, and taken prisoner to the Hueda refuge in Grand-Popo, where he subsequently died, presumed to have been executed on Hufon's order.[31] Contrariwise, the English director Testefole, even after the withdrawal of the Hueda, continued to offer provocations to the Dahomians, eventually administering a flogging to one of their officials who visited the English fort. He was seized when he imprudently ventured outside the fort, held prisoner for some time at Savi and eventually tortured and executed.[32] Presumably in connection with this incident, the Dahomians also attacked the English fort, in an engagement which lasted six hours.[33]

Early in 1730 the Oyo again invaded Dahomey, and Hufon from his place of exile in the west gave notice to the Europeans at Ouidah that he intended to make a further attempt to repossess his kingdom, but on this occasion it does not appear that this materialized.[34] In fact, Agaja now opened negotiations with the king of Oyo, through the mediation of the director of the Portuguese fort at Ouidah, João Basilio, and Oyo made peace, abandoning the exiled Hueda to their fate. During 1730–31 attempts were made to arrange peace between Dahomey and the exiled Hueda also, on the basis of Hufon agreeing to become a tributary of Agaja, first by the governor of the English fort and then by the Portuguese director Basilio, but these came to nothing.[35] The Hueda continued to mount raids on the beach to the south of Ouidah, severely disrupting trade there: in May and again in July 1731, for example, they plundered the European traders' tents on the beach, on the second occasion killing six Europeans whom they caught there.[36] By 1733 the Hueda seem to have established effective control over the beach, since 'boys' belonging to Captain Assou were then reported to be 'serving' in the tents set up on shore by two Portuguese ships trading there, and other Hueda were established in the Portuguese and English quarters of Ouidah itself. There is even some hint that Hueda control was formally recognized by Dahomey, the director of the French fort claiming credit with Assou for having interceded with

[29] Snelgrave, *New Account*, 123–8; for the dates, see PRO, T70/7, Charles Testefole, Ouidah, 30 Oct. 1729, which says that the Hueda occupied Ouidah from 23 April to 5 July [Old Style: = 4 May to 16 July, New Style].

[30] Viceroy of Brazil, 28 July 1729, in Verger, *Flux et reflux*, 149 (the fort storekeeper, Simão Cordoso).

[31] ANF, C6/25, 'Mémoire de la Compagnie des Indes', 8 Nov. 1730.

[32] Snelgrave, *New Account*, 130–34.

[33] PRO, T70/395, Sundry Accounts, William's Fort, 30 June–31 Oct. 1729.

[34] PRO, T70/1466, Diary of Edward Deane, Ouidah, 30 Dec. 1729 & 21 Feb. 1730.

[35] PRO, T70/7, Brathwaite, Ouidah, 1 June & 16 Aug. 1730; João Basilio, Ouidah, 20 May 1731, in Verger, *Flux et reflux*, 153.

[36] Basilio, Ouidah, 20 May 1731, in Verger, *Flux et reflux*, 153–4; Van Dantzig, *Dutch and the Guinea Coast*, no. 305: Hertog, Jakin, 2 Aug. 1731; Harms, *The Diligent*, 151, 202–4, 234.

Agaja on his behalf, seemingly to protect his interests in controlling the beach.[37]

At the same time, the rudimentary administration of the European trade at Ouidah which Agaja had established was in some disarray. In 1732 the 'English Caboceer' at Ouidah was executed by Agaja, for reasons which the English were unable to discover but which were presumed to reflect internal tensions on the Dahomian side.[38] Relations between the Dahomian officials and the European forts were also bad; the 'captain' for the Portuguese, in unexplained circumstances, even made an attempt to seize the French fort. In 1733, however, Agaja decided to assert his control over Ouidah more effectively. As a first step, in January he summoned the directors of the three European forts to attend his 'Annual Customs' at Abomey; this attendance, which became an annual obligation thereafter, being probably intended to assert their status as holding office under Dahomian sovereignty. The Directors took the opportunity to complain against the three existing Dahomian 'captains', and Agaja in response replaced them with a single official, called 'Tegan'.[39] This was evidently a title, rather than a personal name, being held apparently by three successive persons, down to 1745.[40] This new official was clearly concerned with more than just the conduct of trade, being referred to by the French, soon after his appointment, as 'Governor of Gregoy [Glehue]', implying that he exercised a more general administrative authority.[41] His position therefore corresponded to the later office of Yovogan, 'Chief of the Whites', commonly described by Europeans as the 'Viceroy' of Ouidah, although the actual title of Yovogan does not appear to have been used for the Dahomian administrator of Ouidah until the late 1740s.[42] The Yovogan's residence was later to the north of the English fort and east of the French fort, on the site occupied nowadays by the Roman Catholic cathedral, the northern section of the town in which it is situated being still called Fonsaramè, 'the Fon [i.e. Dahomian] quarter' and being populated to the present by the descendants of Dahomian officials and merchants. The appointment of the Tegan probably marks the beginning of this Fon quarter in Ouidah.[43]

---

[37] ANF, C6/25, Levet, Ouidah, 26 Aug. 1733 (lettre de nouvelles): on a visit to Assou in his place of refuge in Popo, Levet reminded him of 'what I did for him, with Dada [= Agaja], when the English Director wished to furnish canoes to all nations'.

[38] Snelgrave, *New Account*, 154.

[39] ANF, C6/25, Levet, Juda, 26 Aug. 1733 (nouvelles).

[40] One European account, written in the 1770s, Robert Norris, *Memoirs of the Reign of Bossa Ahadee, King of Dahomy* (London, 1789), 40–48, treats it as a personal name; and this is followed by Akinjogbin, *Dahomey*, 102–3. But after the original Tegan (or, more probably, his successor) was executed in 1743, his successor was also called Tegan: ANF, C6/25, Levet, 20 Aug. 1743. It may represent *togan*, a generic term for provincial governors.

[41] ANF, C6/25, Levet, Juda, 26 Aug. 1733 (nouvelles).

[42] Norris, *Memoirs*, 36–8, 40, uses the title Yovogan for the viceroys of Ouidah before 1745; and this is followed, for example, by Akinjogbin, *Dahomey*, 102–3, 119–20. But, in fact, this is clearly an anachronism. In records of the English fort, the title Tegan was used down to Sept. 1745, while that of Yovogan ('Evegah') first appears in Jan. 1746: PRO, T70/703–4, Sundry Accounts, William's Fort, Sept.–Dec. 1745, Jan–April 1746. Dahomian tradition asserts that the title of Yovogan was created by Agaja, but local tradition in Ouidah says by his successor Tegbesu: Le Herissé, *L'Ancien Royaume*, 42; Reynier, 'Ouidah', 51.

[43] But note that local tradition attributes the foundation of Fonsaramè to the first Yovogan, Dasu, appointed under Tegbesu in the 1740s: Reynier, 'Ouidah', 51.

In records of the English fort in the following year the Tegan is described as 'a Chief Captain of War deputed by the King of Dahomey to reside among the Forts', and as 'the Viceroy or Commanding Officer for Dahomey residing among the Forts', indicating he also had command of troops stationed permanently in Ouidah.[44] The installation of a military garrison seems to have occurred not at the time of the Tegan's original appointment, but a few months later. In June 1733, in a decisive assertion of control over Ouidah, the Dahomians arrested about 80 Hueda in the Portuguese and English quarters of the town, and the next day a force of 400–500 Dahomian troops arrived 'at the beach' to the south and encamped there, seizing 40 'boys' belonging to Assou who were employed by Portuguese ships trading there, all those taken prisoner being then carried off to Dahomian capital inland.[45] This report of the setting up of a military camp on 'the beach' probably relates to the establishment of a Dahomian garrison at Zoungbodji, actually mid-way between Ouidah and the beach; local tradition recalls the establishment of this garrison after the Dahomian conquest, to oversee the arrival of European traders, under a chief with the title of Kakanaku (or, in its usual French form, Cakana-cou).[46] In contemporary sources, the Cakanacou is first attested in 1747, when the existing incumbent was killed in action and a replacement sent from Dahomey: his function is described as 'General of War for the Beach'.[47] Zoungbodji was generally referred to by Europeans in the eighteenth century as 'Cakanacou's village'.[48]

This assertion of Dahomian military control over Ouidah was complemented by efforts to conciliate and incorporate the exiled Hueda. As has been seen, Agaja had contemplated re-establishing the Hueda monarchy earlier: during 1728, he had first offered to permit Hufon to reoccupy his capital Savi and then to appoint a son of Hufon as king of Hueda. In the abortive negotiations with Hufon in 1731, Agaja again offered to accept him as a tributary, though whether the intention on this occasion was for him to be reinstalled in Savi or recognized as king over the Hueda in exile is not clear. However, Hufon died still in exile around the end of August 1733, and the succession to his kingship was disputed between two of his sons. One of the contenders, although able to occupy the royal capital, found himself besieged there by his opponent and contrived to send word to Agaja to offer his submission in return for Dahomian support. A Dahomian force marched to his relief, and he then went in person to Allada, where Agaja was currently residing, to pay homage to him, and received permission to reoccupy the old Hueda capital Savi, on

---

[44] PRO, T70/402, Castle Charges at Whydah, 12 July–31 Oct. 1734.

[45] ANF, C6/25, Levet, Juda, 26 Aug. 1733 (nouvelles).

[46] Agbo, *Histoire*, 112–14. Agbo says that the title was created by Tegbesu in the 1740s, but other accounts say by Agaja earlier: e.g. Sinou & Agbo, *Ouidah*, 161. The title of Cakanacou still survives as that of the chief of Zoungbodji; nowadays he claims the status of king (and is sometimes even represented to be 'king of Ouidah').

[47] PRO, T70/423, Sundry Accounts, William's Fort, May–Aug. 1747 ['Cockracoe']

[48] E.g. ANF, C6/27, Gourg, 'Mémoire pour servir d'instruction au Directeur', 1791 ['un poste appelé Cakeracou']; John M'Leod, *A Voyage to Africa* (London, 1820), 102 ['Kakeraken's croom']. The name Zoungbodji was first recorded in 1797: Vicente Ferreira Pires, *Viagem de Africa em o reino de Dahomé* (ed. Clado Ribeiro de Lessa, São Paulo, 1957), 28 ['Zambugi'].

condition of becoming tributary to Dahomey.[49] This settlement was accompanied by a return of some of the exiled Hueda to Ouidah, around 500–600 of whom resettled there, according to a later account, 'under the protection of the Portuguese fort', meaning evidently in Tové, the indigenous Hueda quarter of the town, immediately north of the fort.[50] Hueda tradition names the son of Hufon who succeeded him as king and submitted to Dahomian authority as Akamu.[51] Local tradition in Ouidah also recalls the submission of the exiled Hueda to Agaja and their return to reoccupy their home country;[52] the name of Akamu is also remembered there as having assisted in the resettlement of Tové quarter after the Dahomian conquest, and the Adjovi family traces its descent from Hueda royalty through him.[53]

The Hueda–Dahomey wars, 1743–75

The settlement of 1733 was not in fact the end of the matter, since the attempt to reconstitute the Hueda kingdom as a dependency of Dahomey was not in the long run successful. The new king appointed by Agaja was not accepted as legitimate by most Hueda, and he eventually withdrew to Dahomey, where he died 'universally despised'.[54] Agaja's successor Tegbesu (1740–74) seems to have continued or revived the attempt to maintain a Hueda puppet monarchy under Dahomian suzerainty, since the records of the English fort at Ouidah report that in 1756 he appointed a 'King of the Whydahs' and sent him down to Ouidah, and in 1769 he proclaimed a new 'King of the Whydahs', named 'Bangra' (i.e. Agbangla, also the name of one of the pre-Dahomian Hueda kings), and sent him to Ouidah to be introduced to the European forts there.[55] Where these 'kings of the Whydahs' were ruling is not made clear; but a context is suggested by traditions among the exiled Hueda which record that, in the second generation after Hufon, the royal dynasty split, when a dissident prince called Amiton, who had gone to Dahomey to secure recognition as king but was rejected by the people, established a rival dynasty at Séhoumi, to the north of Houéyogbé.[56] The main body of the exiled Hueda at Houéyogbé, however, evidently remained hostile to Dahomey.

From the 1740s the exiled Hueda resumed their attempts to repossess their homeland by military force, and they continued to present a serious threat to Dahomian control of Ouidah down at least to the early 1760s. Their hopes of

---

[49] ANF, C6/25, Levet, Ouidah, 21 Nov. 1733; cf. the later account of Norris, *Memoirs*, 27–9 (who, however, misdates this campaign to 1741). Norris suggests that it was originally intended that this king should rule in the Hueda place of refuge to the west, but the contemporary account indicates that he was set up as king in the Hueda homeland, at Savi.

[50] Norris, *Memoirs*, 29–30.

[51] Assogba, *Découverte de la Côte des Esclaves*, 18.

[52] Gavoy, 'Note historique', 56.

[53] Reynier, 'Ouidah', 47; Merlo, 'Hiérarchie fétichiste', 17.

[54] Norris, *Memoirs*, 35.

[55] PRO, T70/1158, 1160, Day Book, William's Fort, May–June 1756, 10 Aug. 1769.

[56] Soglo, 'Les Xweda', 76–7. However, these traditions do not mention any king called Agbangla.

recovering possession of it were revived when Dahomey became involved in hostilities with the rising power of Gen or 'Little Popo', on the coast to the west, under its ruler Ashangmo, from 1737 onwards.[57] The Hueda soon established a close alliance with Little Popo, and perhaps became politically subject to it.[58] Dahomey's position was further weakened by a renewed outbreak of war with Oyo in 1742–8. In 1743, when an Oyo army invaded Dahomey and the main Dahomian forces in Ouidah were withdrawn to meet this threat, the Hueda exiles, supported by allied forces from 'Popo' (meaning now, presumably, Little Popo rather than Grand-Popo), seized the opportunity to attack Ouidah, where they defeated the small Dahomian garrison remaining, pillaged and burned the town and blockaded the European forts. They occupied the country for more than three months before the Dahomians again drove them out. The Dahomian viceroy and the commander of the local garrison are both said to have been killed in this campaign, referring presumably to the Tegan and the Cakanacou.[59]

The Dahomians believed that the European forts in Ouidah had again assisted the Hueda, and after the restoration of their authority there proceeded to take reprisals. The director of the French fort was seized and deported, on the allegation that he had refused to grant refuge in his fort to Dahomians remaining in Ouidah during the Hueda invasion.[60] Later in the same year, in June, the director of the Portuguese fort, Basilio, was also arrested, on the charge that he was in negotiation with the exiled Hueda and was harbouring Hueda emissaries within his fort; and at the same time the Gau, the commander-in-chief of the Dahomian army, laid siege to the Portuguese fort. Basilio was held prisoner for some time and released only to be deported from the country. Meanwhile, during his imprisonment, the Dahomian force attacked the Portuguese fort, on 21 July 1743; as had happened with the French fort in 1728, the roofs took fire and caused the powder magazine to explode, after which the Dahomians were able to enter the fort and massacre its inhabitants, including the returned exiled Hueda who had taken refuge in it; the African 'head servant' of the fort, who had led the defence in Basilio's absence, blew himself up with gunpowder rather than surrender.[61] Local tradition names the African leader of the defence of the Portuguese fort on this occasion as Amoua, though he is said to have been captured and killed by the Dahomians, rather than dying in the fighting.[62] The demonstration of Dahomian

[57] Law, *Slave Coast*, 316–18; Gayibor, *Le Genyi*, 104–13.

[58] Norris, *Memoirs*, 26, says that the Hueda were 'incorporated' with the 'Popoes', so that the two became effectively 'one nation'. Although often, as here, European observers referred to 'the Popoes', without specifying whether Grand- or Little Popo was meant, it is presumed that from the 1740s onwards references to 'Popo' as allied to the Hueda relate to Little Popo, rather than (as earlier) to Grand-Popo.

[59] Norris, *Memoirs*, 36–9. This account (recorded a generation after the event) actually gives the titles of the Dahomian leaders killed as Yovogan and Caho, but this is presumed to be an anachronism, as these titles are not attested at Ouidah in the contemporary record until later in the 1740s.

[60] ANF, C6/25, Levet, Ouidah, 20 Aug. 1743.

[61] Ibid.; also Norris, *Memoirs*, 30–33 (who, however, misdates this incident, placing the capture of the Portuguese fort on 1 Nov. 1741).

[62] Gavoy, 'Note historique', 57; Reynier, 'Ouidah', 39. The traditions may conflate two persons: Norris, *Memoirs*, 33, says that the second-in-command in the fort's defence was captured and executed.

power on this occasion was seemingly decisive for the future attitude of the European forts, which never afterwards ventured to support challenges to Dahomian authority.

Although Dahomian military control of Ouidah was thus decisively reasserted, Dahomian administration of the town was now undermined by serious internal divisions, which were part of a wider crisis of royal authority within Dahomey in the early years of Tegbesu's reign.[63] The new Tegan appointed after the Hueda invasion in 1743 antagonized the governors of the European forts, and was arrested and executed by Tegbesu, upon their complaints, in July of the same year.[64] His successor as Tegan also alienated the European governors by his 'oppressive conduct' and, when they set out to the capital to complain about his behaviour, ordered their arrest and forcible return to Ouidah. Subsequently, it was alleged that he plotted to set himself up as an independent king in Ouidah, to which end he tried to seize the English fort in August 1745, but its governor was forewarned and refused him entry – although conceivably this was a false allegation contrived by the Europeans, as a means of revenge. However this may be, Tegbesu declared the Tegan an outlaw and dispatched military forces, which besieged him in his residence in Ouidah. The Tegan attempted to escape, but was killed in a second attempt to enter the English fort.[65] In the aftermath of this revolt, the title of Tegan was evidently suppressed, his successor in office being given the title Yovogan, 'Chief of the White Men', which then remained the normal title of the governors of Ouidah throughout the period of Dahomian rule. This title had existed in the Hueda kingdom earlier, but the office there had had purely commercial functions, dealing with the Europeans as traders; the 'Chief of the White Men' in Dahomey, in contrast, exercised political authority in Ouidah, including over the European forts.

Despite their defeat in 1743, the exiled Hueda also continued to pose a military threat. Later in the same year they raided the beach south of Ouidah, destroying the tents of European traders there; and at the beginning of 1744 there were rumours of a further attempt to reoccupy their homeland, although it is unclear whether in the event this took place.[66] Subsequently, further raids were mounted on Ouidah by forces from Little Popo, presumably operating in support of the exiled Hueda; and the Dahomians in response progressively strengthened their garrison in the town. In August 1747 a party of 'Blacks from Accra' (referring evidently to Little Popo, which had been founded in the 1680s by refugees from Accra) raided the beach south of Ouidah, killing most of the Dahomian forces posted there, including their commander the Cakanacou, but was then beaten off by the main garrison from Ouidah. Shortly afterwards, on a report that Ashangmo himself was marching to attack the town, the Dahomians sent down 'another General of War Cockavo', with instructions 'to remain here to protect this place'; and later in the year the garrison was further reinforced, when the king sent down

[63] For this wider context, see Law, *Slave Coast*, 324–8.
[64] ANF, C6/25, Levet, Ouidah, 20 Aug. 1743.
[65] Norris, *Memoirs*, 40–47.
[66] ANF, C6/25, Levet, Ouidah, 20 Aug. 1743, 31 Jan. 1744.

'another General of War Joehena for this place and Bunjam, another General of War for the Beach'.[67]

Of the additional 'generals' mentioned, 'Cockavo' is evidently identical with 'Caukaow' or 'Cakaow', given later in the eighteenth century as the title of 'the military officer who commands in Whydah'.[68] In the nineteenth century this title is recorded in a shorter form, Kao, nowadays generally rendered locally in a French form, 'Caho'.[69] Dahomian tradition identifies the Caho as the general who commanded in Agaja's conquest of Hueda in 1727;[70] and local tradition in Ouidah also associates the appointment of the first Caho with the original Dahomian conquest.[71] The wording of the contemporary report, however, implies that it was an office newly created, or at least newly assigned to Ouidah, in 1747. Initially, the Caho seems to have been posted to Ouidah on a seasonal basis, rather than residing there permanently, since the English fort records down to 1755 refer to him as recurrently 'sent down to take care of the country'.[72] But, in the longer run, the office became localized in Ouidah. Unlike the Cakanacou, the Caho resided in Ouidah itself; his encampment is shown in a map of 1776 as close to but separate from the town, to the north-west;[73] the site is nowadays incorporated within the town, but still bears the name of Cahosaramè, 'Caho's quarter'. The significance of the appointment may have been not only reinforcement of the existing garrison at Ouidah, but also to remove operational command of it from the Yovogan. Of the officers sent to Ouidah later in 1747, the 'Bunjam' is referred to again in the following year, when the first holder of the title was replaced, and is then described more precisely as '2^d General of War for the Beach'.[74] This indicates that this officer served as deputy to the Cakanacou in command of the garrison at Zoungbodji; his appointment therefore presumably represented a strengthening of this garrison. 'Bunjam' in these documents is probably a miscopying of 'Dunjam', and represents the title Dognon, which is recalled in local tradition as that of the Cakanacou's deputy.[75] The third name 'Joehena', however, represents 'Zoheino', which is recorded later as the title of one of the four leading officers of the main Dahomian field army.[76] His posting to Ouidah was evidently only temporary; in the

---

[67] PRO, T70/423, Sundry Accounts, William's Fort, May–Aug. & Sept.–Dec. 1747.

[68] Norris, *Memoirs*, 36; cf. Archibald Dalzel, *The History of Dahomy. An Inland Kingdom of Africa* (London, 1793), 194.

[69] Burton, *Mission*, i, 52 ['Kawo'].

[70] Le Herissé, *L'Ancien Royaume*, 296. Burton in the 1860s was told that the office had existed even earlier: *Mission*, i, 52.

[71] Gavoy, 'Note historique', 67; Reynier, 'Ouidah', 61. The former says that the first Caho was appointed by Tegbesu (by implication, in 1743), but the latter by Agaja (suggesting 1733).

[72] PRO, T70/1158, Day Book, William's Fort, 1752–5.

[73] ANF, C6/27bis, map of Abbé Bullet, 1776.

[74] PRO, T70/424A, Sundry Journals, William's Fort, Jan–June 1748.

[75] Agbo, *Histoire*, 113. There was also an official at Ouidah entitled Boya, sometimes rendered 'Bunio' in later sources, and it is conceivable that the 1747 report relates to the creation of this office (as assumed by Akinjogbin, *Dahomey*, 119). But the Boya was a commercial rather than a military official (as discussed more fully in the following chapter).

[76] Dalzel, *History*, 167.

following year, the Caho and the 'Zoheino' were summoned back to the capital, and the Caho alone (together with the replacement Dognan) returned to Ouidah.[77]

Although Dahomey was able to make peace with Oyo in 1748, at the price of becoming its tributary, fighting against the exiled Hueda, supported by Ashangmo of Little Popo, continued. In January 1752 the Hueda again raided the beach south of Ouidah, but were 'repulsed' by the local Dahomian garrison; and shortly afterwards 'Aproga General of War' was 'sent down to take care of the land', the reference being to the Aplogan, the provincial governor of Allada to the north, from where forces were evidently sent temporarily to support the Ouidah garrison. In July or August 1755 they apparently attacked Ouidah itself, but were driven off by the local Dahomian forces.[78] In October of the same year the Hueda, this time assisted by the Popos, again raided the beach, where they seized several Europeans, and remained for two and a half days, defeating the local Dahomian forces and inflicting severe casualties, including 'an army General, 3 Captains of War, several of the principal merchants, and many soldiers'; those killed on the Dahomian side on this occasion included the Caho, commander-in-chief of the Ouidah garrison, and the Boya, one of the king's merchants. Ouidah itself was again attacked, or at least threatened, since the English fort recorded that its African personnel had been afraid to go out to buy provisions until reinforcements for the garrison arrived; once again the Aplogan came 'down from Arda [Allada] on the first alarm', this time followed shortly afterwards by the main Dahomian army under the command of the Gau.[79] The nervousness arising from this raid was still apparent at the beginning of the following year, when Europeans returning from attending the 'Annual Customs' at the capital were escorted from Allada to Ouidah by forces supplied by the Aplogan, 'on account of the Whydahs'. Later in the year, in September or October, there was a further raid by the Popos (the Hueda this time not being explicitly mentioned), once more causing the Aplogan to be summoned down from Allada, followed again by the main army under the Gau.[80]

The most serious attack in the series came on 12 July 1763, when a combined force of Hueda and Popo, commanded by a son of Ashangmo called Foli ('Affurey' in contemporary reports), crossed to the north of the lagoon and attacked the town of Ouidah itself. The Yovogan was wounded in the action and took refuge in the French fort. The town was abandoned to the invaders, who 'set the suburbs on fire' and were 'preparing to burn the vice-roy's quarters', when they were checked by artillery fire from the English fort. The Dahomian forces then rallied and repelled the invaders, with great slaughter; 30 of 32 generals of the attacking army were killed in the action and its commander Foli committed suicide in his disgrace, the main Dahomian army under the Gau this time arriving only after the fighting was

---

[77] PRO, T70/424A, Sundry Accounts, William's Fort, Jan.–June 1748.

[78] PRO, T70/1158, Day Book, William's Fort, May–June 1752, July–Aug. 1755 (the latter recording an attack on 'this place', meaning presumably the town of Ouidah, rather than the beach south of the lagoon).

[79] ANF, C6/25, Guestard, 25 Nov. 1755; PRO, T70/1158, Day Book, William's Fort, Sept.-Oct. and Nov.–Dec. 1755. The former mentions only the Hueda ('Judaiques') as involved, but the latter refers to 'the Popoes & Whydahs'.

[80] PRO, T70/1158, Day Book, William's Fort, Jan.–Feb. & Sept.–Oct. 1756.

over.[81] The tree under which Foli shot himself continued to be identified into the nineteenth century, and even beyond.[82]

The war of 1763 did not mark the end of Hueda–Popo raids, but nevertheless represented a decisive defeat of the exiled Hueda and their allies, who were no longer able to present any serious threat to Dahomian control of Ouidah. After 1763, they gave up the attempt to dispute possession of the town, contenting themselves with raiding the beach to the south in order to disrupt the operation of the European trade, though they may have calculated that the destruction of the town's commercial value would eventually persuade the Dahomians to abandon it.[83] In April 1767, for example, a party of Popos raided the beach and plundered goods landed from European ships which they found there, but did not advance any further; there was another raid in February 1768, and further attacks were feared, raising apprehensions for the security of the European forts at Ouidah.[84] In 1769 Tegbesu announced that he was 'at peace with the Popoes', but this was evidently only short-lived.[85] Between July and September 1770, the Hueda–Popo forces made no fewer than five raids on the beach, plundering goods and burning the Europeans' tents and canoes. On a final raid they stayed four days, 16–20 September, provoking fears that they might attack Ouidah itself, where the French fort put itself in readiness against such an event; but no such attack materialized, the Hueda retiring upon the approach of a reinforcing Dahomian force, commanded this time by the Mehu, the second most senior chief of Dahomey.[86] Early in 1772 the Popos again seized control of the beach and interrupted communication between Ouidah and the shipping for an entire month, causing the main Dahomian army under the Gau again to be sent down to protect the town.[87]

Later in 1772, Tegbesu enlisted the governor of the English fort, Lionel Abson, to negotiate peace with Little Popo; and in July the Mehu was sent down to Ouidah, invested with full powers 'to settle all differences with the Popos'.[88] The exiled Hueda are not explicitly mentioned as parties to these negotiations, which suggests that they had been abandoned by their erstwhile allies. King Kpengla, who succeeded to the Dahomian throne in 1774, was able to go over on to the offensive against the Hueda. His opportunity was provided, as for Agaja in 1733, by a disputed succession to the Hueda kingship. Following the death of the reign-

---

[81] Norris, *Memoirs*, 56–9; Pruneau de Pommegorge, *Description de la Nigritie* (Amsterdam, 1789), 223–35; PRO, T70/1159, Day Book, William's Fort, 12 & 17 July, 2 & 30 Aug. 1763.

[82] Burton, *Mission*, i, 112–14; cf. Gavoy, 'Note historique', 57.

[83] Norris, *Memoirs*, 59–60; Akinjogbin, *Dahomey*, 148–50.

[84] PRO, T70/31, Archibald Dalzel, Ouidah, n.d. & 17 March 1768, cited in Gilbert Petrie, Cape Coast Castle, 6 Nov. 1767, 15 May 1768.

[85] PRO, T70/1160, Day Book, William's Fort, 23 Nov. 1769.

[86] ANF, C6/26, Guestard, 15 Oct. 1770; PRO, T70/31, Lionel Abson, Ouidah, 24 Oct. 1770; T70/1160, Day Book, William's Fort, 17 Aug., 22 & 23 Sept. 1770. The French account attributes the raids to 'les nègres Judaiques du Grand-Popo', but the English to 'the Popoes'.

[87] See the retrospective reference to this raid in ANF, C6/26, Baud-Duchiron, 'Mémoire d'observations sur ceux faits par le Sr Baud-Duchiron, pour les nouveaux établissemens à faire à la Côte de Guinée', 28 Oct. 1777; for the Gau's arrival, see PRO, T70/1161, Day Book, William's Fort, 10 March 1772.

[88] PRO, T70/1161, Day Book, William's Fort, 29 April, 13 July 1772; cf. Norris, *Memoirs*, 60.

ing king, the throne was contested between two princes, Agbamu and Yé (these names being given as 'Agbavou' and 'Eyee' in a contemporary report). Agbamu initially seized control and drove out his rival, but the latter then appealed for assistance to Kpengla. Dahomian forces invaded the Hueda country and besieged Agbamu on an 'island', into which they eventually forced entry by building a causeway across the lagoon. Agbamu surrendered and was taken captive to Dahomey, where he was executed, his head being exhibited to a visiting European in the following year.[89]

In Hueda tradition, the defeat and death of Agbamu in 1775 are recognized as marking the end of the kingdom's independence and 'the end of the resistance'.[90] In fact, it does not appear that the exiled Hueda community became formally subject to Dahomey. Although Yé was enthroned as their king, he was deposed in an internal coup soon afterwards, without the Dahomians attempting further intervention in his support;[91] and in 1776 the Hueda were described as preserving 'neutrality', implying that they remained beyond formal Dahomian rule.[92] Their military power, however, had been decisively curbed, and the regular raids they had mounted against Ouidah now came to an end; subsequent hostilities involved rather Dahomian raids on the Hueda in their place of exile, as on several occasions during the 1780s.[93] Little Popo to the west remained a threat for several years longer. In 1777 the king of Popo sent to Ouidah to give notice of the termination of the peace with Dahomey.[94] In 1778 and 1780 there were reports that the Popos intended to attack, causing the Europeans to bring their canoes north of the lagoon for safety; in 1781 the main Dahomian army under the Gau was posted to Savi as a precaution against an invasion, and in 1784 there were again rumours of an impending attack.[95] But, in the event, no attacks materialized. In 1789 there were fears that the Popos might attack Ouidah itself, causing the Posu, the second-in-command of the metropolitan army, to be sent down to defend the town, but again the reports proved false.[96] The threat from Little Popo was finally brought to a definitive end in 1795, when Dahomey allied with Grand-Popo to inflict a crushing defeat upon it.[97]

No serious threat to Dahomian possession of Ouidah seems ever to have been offered from any other quarter. In 1787–8 there were reports that forces from

---

[89] Norris, *Memoirs*, 130–35; PRO, T70/1161, Day Book, William's Fort, 4, 7 & 9 Oct. 1775; also Dahomian traditions of this campaign, in Le Herissé, *L'Ancien Royaume*, 305–6.

[90] Assogba, *Découverte de la Côte des Esclaves*, 18; the latter phrase was used by Tobias Agbo, interviewed at Agbamou compound, 11 Dec. 2001.

[91] Le Herissé, *L'Ancien Royaume*, 306.

[92] De Chenevert & Bullet, 'Réflexions', 17, 40.

[93] PRO, T70/1162–3, Day Book, William's Fort, 6 June 1781, 13 May 1782, 27 July 1788, 27 Oct. 1789; Dalzel, *History*, 197, 225.

[94] ANF, C6/26, Baud-Duchiron, 'Mémoire pour servir à faire de nouveaux établissemens à la Côte de Guinée, depuis de Cap de Monte jusqu'à la Rivière du Benin', 23 July 1777.

[95] PRO, T70/1161–2, Day Book, William's Fort, 23 Sept. 1778, 20 March, 1 June 1780, 27 June 1781, 16 Oct. 1784.

[96] ANF, C6/26, Gourg, 27 Jan. 1789; cf. Dalzel, *History*, 201.

[97] Akinjogbin, *Dahomey*, 181; Gayibor, *Le Genyi*, 115–16.

Porto-Novo and Badagry, to the east, planned to attack Ouidah, but no attack in fact occurred.[98] Again, in 1803, there were fears of an attack on the town by enemy forces in the neighbourhood, and a false alarm caused the Yovogan to take refuge in the English fort, but no attack materialized, and a Dahomian force was despatched to chase off the raiders; although the attackers on this occasion are not identified in the contemporary report, they were probably also from Badagry.[99] Thereafter, no challenge to Dahomian control of Ouidah occurred for the remainder of the nineteenth century until the war with France in the 1890s.

The Dahomian conquest in local tradition

In the traditions of Ouidah, as recorded in the twentieth century, it is the campaign of 1743 under Tegbesu, rather than the original invasion of the Hueda kingdom by Agaja in 1727, which is regarded as representing the definitive Dahomian conquest of the town, although this campaign is commonly given the incorrect date of 1741, derived from published European sources.[100] The Ouidah traditions, however, present a distorted account of the Dahomian conquest, which in particular telescopes events that in fact occurred over several years into a single campaign. Although unreliable as a source for the actual events of the Dahomian conquest, these stories are illuminating of the way in which the Ouidah community viewed its historical relationship both to the pre–1727 Hueda monarchy and to the Dahomian state that replaced it, and therefore warrant extended treatment here.

Some brief accounts of local traditions concerning the Dahomian conquest were already recorded by European visitors to Ouidah in the 1860s.[101] More extended accounts were recorded by French administrators in the early years of colonial rule, first by Gavoy in 1913, with supplementary material, from the perspective of the individual quarters of Ouidah, added by Reynier in 1917. The more elaborate account of the local historian Casimir Agbo published in 1959, which has become canonical, reproduces most of their material, but also supplements and revises it in significant ways.[102]

One interesting, though unsurprising, aspect of these traditions is that they present a much more heroic account of Hueda resistance to the Dahomian conquest in 1727 than the contemporary accounts suggest. In the story as told in the traditions, Hufon is in fact alleged to have twice defeated the Dahomian forces sent against him by Agaja, mainly by virtue of his possession of cannon but also because he had arranged for the removal of the hammers from muskets he had earlier supplied to the Dahomians. Agaja is said to have been successful only at a

---

[98] Dalzel, *History*, 197–8.
[99] M'Leod, *Voyage*, 44–6. The same campaign seems to be alluded to in G.A. Robertson, *Notes on Africa* (London, 1819), 270, who identifies the enemy as Badagry.
[100] Ultimately from Norris, *Memoirs*, 27, 33.
[101] Esp. Borghero, 'Relation', in *Journal*, 240–41; WMMS, T.B. Freeman, 'West Africa' (typescript of c.1860), 209–13.
[102] Gavoy, 'Note historique', 53–8; Reynier, 'Ouidah', 32, 35, 38–9, 47; Agbo, *Histoire*, 36–46.

third attempt, and then through treachery, employing agents in Ouidah to discover and send on the missing hammers for the muskets and to render Hufon's cannon ineffective by pouring water on their supplies of gunpowder. These measures to undermine the Hueda forces are usually credited to a daughter of Agaja, called Na-Geze, whom he married to Hufon for this purpose. A variant story, however, credits the neutralization of Hufon's cannon rather to Zossoungbo, the head of Sogbadji quarter of Ouidah, who, when summoned by the king to join the muster of the Hueda forces against the Dahomians, instructed his men to carry out this sabotage.[103] The tale of the Dahomian princess Na-Geze is a version of a wide-spread traditional stereotype, in which women given or taken in marriage betray the secret (material or spiritual) of a king's power, and is more illuminating about general perceptions of the ambiguous position of women, subject to divided loyalties between their natal and marital families, than about the circumstances of the fall of Hueda; if it relates at all to Ouidah's historical experience, it may reflect conditions under Dahomian rule, when royal women married to local officials and merchants were commonly perceived to act as spies for the king.[104] But the alternative story blaming the Hueda Zossoungbo may well represent a genuine recollection of the role of internal treachery, as recorded in contemporary sources. The emphasis on the decisive role played by imported artillery and firearms in these stories, on the other hand, evidently also serves purposes of local pride, by implication underlining the importance of Ouidah and its trade in supporting Dahomian military power after the conquest.

The Ouidah traditions also distinguish, more starkly than the contemporary accounts, between the original conquest of the Hueda kingdom in 1727 and the extension of Dahomian control over Ouidah, which is presented as being effected only after several years of further struggle. It is claimed that after 1727 the Dahomians, although now occupying the Hueda capital Savi, were initially unable to establish control over Ouidah, because the inhabitants of the latter were supported by the European forts with their cannon, so that possession of the town remained contested between the Dahomians and the Hueda – a representation which, as has been seen, although simplified and exaggerated, has some basis in events as recorded in the contemporary sources. Eventually, however, in the course of a clash in which the Hueda had been initially the victors, the tables were turned when the Hueda alienated the Europeans by firing on the English fort and killing its governor's wife, provoking the European forts to turn their artillery on the Hueda, and the Dahomians were then able to conquer the town, in the process attacking and destroying the Portuguese fort. According to Gavoy's version, the Hueda were led in this war by a chief called Foli, while the Portuguese fort was defended by Amoua, both of whom were captured and executed by the victorious Dahomians. Reynier adds that the forces of Ahouandjigo and Docomè quarters were led against the Dahomians by their respective founders, the royal princes Agbamu and Ahohunbakla, with Amoua merely a lieutenant of the latter; Agbamu as well as

---

[103] Reynier, 'Ouidah', 35.
[104] See Bay, *Wives of the Leopard*, 59–63, 247–8.

Amoua was killed, but Ahohunbakla survived to transfer his service to the Dahomians after the conquest. Agbo, however, synthesizes the traditional stories to rather different effect, presenting Agbamu as 'king' rather than merely chief of a quarter, with Foli as his subordinate military commander, implying that Agbamu was the successor to the Hueda kingship, who had set himself up as king in Ouidah after the fall of Savi.[105] In this version, therefore, it is the supposed overthrow of Agbamu in Ouidah in 1743, rather than that of Hufon in Savi sixteen years earlier, which is presented as representing the end of the Hueda monarchy.

These accounts, however, clearly represent a conflation of the campaign of 1743 with subsequent fighting against the exiled Hueda established to the west. 'Foli', as seen earlier, was actually the commander of the Little Popo forces who joined the exiled Hueda in their initially successful attack on Ouidah in 1763; and the story of the Hueda provoking retaliation from the English fort by killing the governor's wife also belongs to this later campaign.[106] The displacement of the latter incident to the original conquest in local narratives was already noted in the 1860s.[107] Agbamu, on the other hand, was the name of the king of the Hueda in exile who was killed by the Dahomians in 1775. The traditional account thus runs together a number of originally discrete episodes, each of which was in its way decisive: the campaign of 1743 was the last occasion when the Hueda had been able temporarily to reoccupy Ouidah, that of 1763 was the defeat of their last attempt to repossess the town and that of 1775 marked the definitive subjugation of the Hueda community in exile. Together, they could reasonably be taken to represent the consolidation of Dahomian control over Ouidah, through the destruction of the independent power of the Hueda.

This representation also has the important implication of stressing continuity between the pre-1727 Hueda kingdom and the post-1727 Ouidah community and therefore the status of the latter as a victim of foreign conquest. Already in the 1860s, it was noted that the Dahomian conquest of Ouidah remained vivid in local memory and was recounted in terms that appropriated the leaders of post-1727 Hueda raids on the town as defenders of local independence, and even represented the Hueda invasion of 1763 as a local rebellion against Dahomian rule.[108] The sense of subjection to the Dahomians as foreign conquerors was evidently central to the self-image of Ouidah, despite the reality that, demographically, it became a predominantly Dahomian town.

---

[105] Agbo, *Histoire*, 42–4.

[106] The account of this campaign in Norris, *Memoirs*, 58–9, records the role of the English fort, but not the detail of the killing of the governor's wife. The latter appears first in accounts recorded in the 1860s, e.g. Borghero, 'Relation', in *Journal*, 240–41; WMMS, Freeman, 'West Africa', 210–11.

[107] Burton, *Mission*, i, 112–14, tells the story of the defeat of Foli, including the shooting of the English governor's wife, and correctly assigns it to the campaign of 1763, but adds in a footnote that 'Some indeed … referred it to the first capture of Whydah by the Dahomians'.

[108] Borghero, 'Relation', in *Journal*, 240–41; PP, Despatches from Commodore Wilmot, no. 2, 10 Feb. 1863.

The repeopling of Ouidah

Ouidah suffered considerable destruction in the Dahomian wars of conquest between 1727 and 1743. Local tradition recalls that Tegbesu, in the campaign of 1743, 'completely razed the town'.[109] This is confirmed and elaborated by traditions relating to particular quarters: Docomè, the quarter of the Portuguese fort, was 'pillaged and burned' by the Dahomians and its inhabitants were killed or taken captive or fled to the west, while in Ahouandjigo, the quarter of the French fort, the inhabitants were 'almost all massacred'.[110] Only Sogbadji, the quarter of the English fort, is said to have escaped relatively unscathed, because Agaja gave orders for it to be 'spared', in return for the assistance which Zossoungbo, the head of the quarter, had allegedly given in the campaign against Hufon.[111]

When Dahomian control of Ouidah had been firmly established, however, measures were taken to reconstitute the town. Tradition in Sogbadji recalls that Agaja charged Zossoungbo to invite those who had fled to return to the town. The traditions of other quarters also recall the repeopling of the town under Dahomian rule. In Ahouandjigo, it is said that the French complained to Agaja that the depopulation of the quarter by war had left them short of labourers, in response to which he sent them a new batch of 100 male and 100 female captives; the family that later held the headship of the quarter, Atchada, claims descent from the head of this new batch of fort slaves.[112] Other families in Ahouandjigo, however, claim origins antecedent to the Dahomian conquest, notably that of Agbo, hereditary servants in the French fort, which claims descent from the Hueda king Agbamu. In Docomè and Tové also, tradition stresses continuity with the pre-Dahomian community, despite the disruption of the Dahomian conquest. In Docomè, it is claimed that Ahohunbakla, the commander of the quarter's forces against the Dahomians, survived the defeat and was invited by the Dahomians to continue to serve as intermediary in their dealings with the Europeans; Ahohunbakla in turn requested that a son of Amoua, his deputy commander, who had been killed in the war, should be associated with him in this role, and the headship of the quarter subsequently remained in the Amoua family.[113] In Tové, following the defeat of Hufon, a man called Sale, who was married to a woman of the Kpase family, made his submission to Agaja, who charged him with recalling those who had fled from the quarter; Sale received from the Dahomian king the surname Tchiakpé, which is still borne by the family of his descendants in the quarter.[114] Although there may be an element of fiction in the claiming of specifically royal descent, there seems no reason to question the Hueda antecedents of these families. Other families in

---

[109] Gavoy, 'Note historique', 58.

[110] Reynier, 'Ouidah', 32; Agbo, *Histoire*, 189.

[111] Reynier, 'Ouidah', 35.

[112] Ibid., 32.

[113] Ibid., 39. In contemporary sources, an Amoua is first documented as head of Docomè quarter in 1861, when he welcomed the French missionaries who then took up residence in the Portuguese fort: Borghero, *Journal*, 47 [6 May 1861] etc.

[114] Reynier, 'Ouidah', 47.

Ouidah that claim to derive from the time of the Hueda monarchy and to have returned to resettle there after initially fleeing from the Dahomian conquest include those of the priests of several important *vodun*, notably of the sea-god Hu in Sogbadji and the earth-god Hwesi in Ahouandjigo.[115] This survival of a substantial Hueda element in the population of Dahomian Ouidah, recalled in local tradition, is confirmed by a contemporary report of 1780s that 'there are still at Juda many of the former inhabitants or their descendants', who were recognizable by their distinctive facial marks.[116]

The Dahomian conquest also, however, involved the introduction of new settlers and the extension of the town by the foundation of new quarters, thereby transforming the ethnic composition of the community. The principal new quarter established was Fonsaramè, which included the residence of the Dahomian viceroy, the Yovogan. This may have been created in part through the appropriation of land from existing quarters, since local tradition claims that the Yovogan's palace occupies the site of the former residence of Agbamu, the supposed founder of Ahouandjigo quarter.[117] But mainly it represented an extension of the town to the north. The second quarter associated with the Dahomian conquest was Cahosaramè, taking its name from the title of the commander of the Dahomian military garrison, which is said by tradition to date to the time of either Agaja or Tegbesu. This was originally, as noted earlier, a separate encampment outside the town, but it was later absorbed within the town as it expanded, presumably in the nineteenth century. The other six quarters of the town (Ganvè, Boya, Brazil, Maro, Zomaï and Quénum) were not founded until the nineteenth century.[118]

In the long run, at least, the Dahomian element was not restricted to the new Fon and Caho quarters, since individual Dahomians also settled in older quarters of the town. Families of Dahomian origin include, for example, the Adanle family in Sogbadji, related to Hwanjile, the official 'Queen Mother' of Tegbesu, under whose auspices its founder settled in the town.[119] Overall, it was the Fon rather than the Hueda element which came to predominate in the town, though this presumably owed something to assimilation over time as well as to the original ethnicity of settlers: in the 1930s it was reckoned that persons who considered themselves Fon outnumbered Hueda by a ratio of nearly 2 : 1.[120] That the Ouidah community nevertheless continued to see itself as distinct from Dahomey and, by implication as a conquered people, subject to Dahomian rule as a foreign administration, reflected its problematic relationship with the Dahomian monarchy, rather than its biological origins.

[115] Fieldwork, Dagbo Hounon compound, 18 Jan. 1996; Reynier, 'Ouidah', 34, 36.

[116] ANF, C6/27, Gourg, 'Mémoire pour servir d'instruction au Directeur', 1791.

[117] Reynier, 'Ouidah', 32.

[118] Some accounts suggest that Boyasaramè, named after a leading Dahomian commercial official, was also established in the 1740s: e.g. Gavoy, 'Note historique', 63, 67. But, although the title of Boya certainly existed in Ouidah from the mid-eighteenth century, it is clear that a separate Boya quarter was established only in the nineteenth century.

[119] Reynier, 'Ouidah', 37.

[120] Merlo, 'Hiérarchie fétichiste', 29.

3

Dahomian Ouidah

Under Dahomian rule, Ouidah remained a major centre of the Atlantic slave trade, albeit at a lower level of exports than under the Hueda kings. In other respects, the town's commercial importance was enhanced by the Dahomian conquest; in particular, whereas earlier most of the actual business of trading had been transacted at the Hueda capital Savi, with Ouidah serving merely as a place of storage for slaves and goods in transit to and from the coast, the conduct of the trade was now concentrated wholly at Ouidah. One consequence of this is that the documentation of events and conditions in Ouidah from European records becomes much more substantial and detailed for the period of Dahomian rule, enabling a more solidly documented and rounded presentation of the life of the community. Moreover, although Ouidah remained subordinate, now to the kings of Dahomey at Abomey, its political importance was also greatly enhanced. With the appointment of a viceroy from 1733, it became the seat of Dahomian provincial administration and of the principal military garrison in the coastal area; in effect, it now replaced Savi as the political centre of its local region. Dahomian Ouidah was thus a much more important (and larger) town than it had been under Hueda rule.

The town and its inhabitants

Ouidah in the second half of the eighteenth century consisted of six quarters: the original Hueda settlement of Tové on the east; the three quarters linked with the European forts, Docomè, Sogbadji and Ahouandjigo; the newly established Dahomian administrative quarter of Fonsaramè, on the north; and the military garrison, commanded by the Caho, to the north-west. In this period, for the first time, we begin to get some detailed sense of the town's physical layout and size. Its layout is depicted in a map of 1776, which shows the French, English and Portuguese quarters as still distinct settlements around the periphery of the main conurbation, and the garrison under the Caho in a separate encampment in the

71

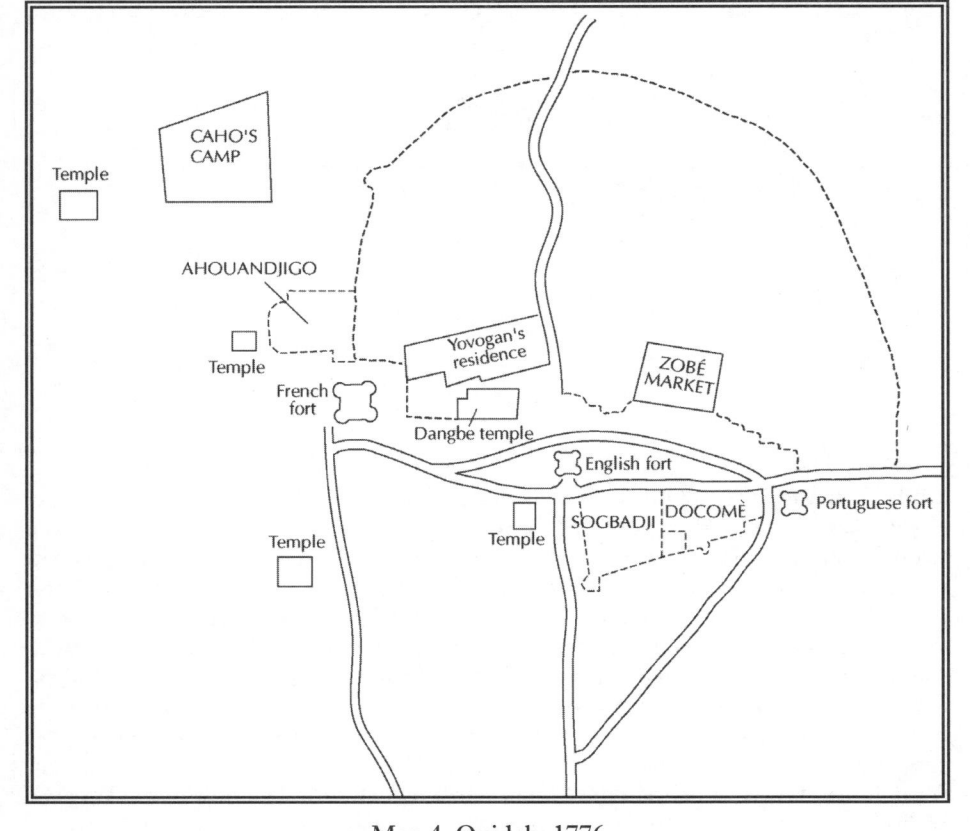

Map 4 Ouidah, 1776
(Adapted from a map in the Archives Nationales de la France, C6/27bis.)

countryside (see Map 4). With the extension of the town to the north, through the creation of Fonsaramè, the physical as well as the political centre of the town was now the residence of the Dahomian viceroy, the Yovogan, called the 'Agore' (more correctly, Agoli).[1] The square in front of the Yovogan's residence, still today called 'Place Agore', became the ceremonial centre of the town, where public religious festivals began. Facing it across the square was one of the principal religious shrines of Ouidah, that of the python–deity Dangbe.

Unlike the capital Abomey, which was surrounded by a defensive ditch and enterable only through gates under military guard, Ouidah was not fortified.[2] Its

---

[1] The name was first recorded in contemporary sources in the 1860s: Burton, *Mission*, i, 101.

[2] As noted by Burton, ibid., i, 60. However, the assumption of Mondjannagni, *Campagnes et villes*, 298–300, that fortification was one of the defining features of royal capitals ('*cités-palais*'), as opposed to coastal commercial towns ('*villes-forts*'), is doubtful. For example, in Allada in the seventeenth century, the coastal centre of Jakin was defended by an earth wall, whereas the capital inland was described as 'open', although the royal

boundaries were, however, formally defined by customs posts (*denu*) placed on major roads at the approaches to the town, to levy tolls on goods entering, passage being barred by a rope that was lowered upon payment.[3] The circuit of the town was estimated in the 1780s at 1½ Dutch miles (6 English miles, around 9 km), substantially larger than its pre-Dahomian size.[4] During the period of Dahomian rule, several European visitors offered figures for the population of Ouidah. Although these are problematic, since they evidently represent impressionistic estimates rather than actual counts and are not entirely consistent among themselves, they are nevertheless usefully suggestive of the general order of the town's size (see Table 3.1). The estimates of about 8,000 in 1772 and between 6,000 and 7,000 in 1793 can be taken as giving the scale of its normal size in this period. The low figure of under 2,000 in 1776 reflected a temporary decline, due to a period of neglect and disruption in the last years of the reign of Tegbesu; but that of 20,000 suggested for 1803 is aberrant and should be discounted. In the nineteenth century, the population was to grow significantly larger, with a peak of perhaps 18,000–20,000 in the 1850s.

In 1772, Ouidah was reckoned to be only the third largest town in Dahomey, exceeded by Cana, which was a seasonal royal residence (whose population was put at 15,000), as well as the capital Abomey (24,000).[5] By the nineteenth century, however, it was generally accounted the second town in the kingdom, exceeded only by Abomey.[6] Ouidah in the eighteenth century was smaller than the largest port towns on the Gold Coast to the west; the population of Elmina in this period, for example, has been estimated at between 12,000 and 15,000.[7] On the other hand, it was larger than other coastal towns on the Slave Coast: in the 1790s, for example, Lagos was thought to have only 5,000 inhabitants, although in the nineteenth century, when Lagos replaced Ouidah as the region's principal port, it also grew larger, to around 20,000 by the 1850s.[8] In comparison with the American ports to which they supplied slaves, West African ports were within the same range as the smaller of these, as for example Cap-Français and Port-au-Prince in French Saint-Domingue (15,000 and 6,200 respectively in the 1780s), although smaller than the largest, such as Salvador, Bahia (over 30,000).[9]

Demographically, the population of Ouidah was extremely heterogeneous, including indigenous (Hula and Hueda) and Dahomian as well as European elements.

---

2 (cont.) palace within it was surrounded by a wall: Dapper, *Naukeurige Beschrijvinge*, 2/115–16. Likewise, there were walls in the Hueda capital Savi, but these seem to have enclosed the palace area rather than the town as a whole: Kelly, 'Using historically informed archaeology', 360–2.

3 Burton, *Mission*, i, 65; for the nature of the barrier (described at Savi, rather than Ouidah), see i, 141–3.

4 Isert, *Letters*, 100.

5 Norris, *Memoirs*, 82, 92.

6 E.g. Dr Repin, 'Voyage au Dahomey', *Le Tour du monde*, 1 (1863), 70; PP, Despatches from Commodore Wilmot, no. 2, 10 Feb. 1863.

7 Feinberg, *Africans and Europeans*, 83–5.

8 John Adams, *Remarks on the Country Extending from Cape Palmas to the River Ganges* (London, 1823), 100. For the later growth of Lagos, see Robin Law, 'Towards a history of urbanization in pre-colonial Yorubaland', in Christopher Fyfe (ed.), *African Historical Demography* (Edinburgh, 1977), 266.

9 Jacob Price, 'Summation', in Knight & Liss, *Atlantic Port Cities*, 263.

Table 3.1 Estimated Population of Ouidah, 1772–1890[5]

1772	about	8,000
1776	under	2,000
1793		6,000–7,000
1803	about	20,000
1841	about	10,000
1851		25,000–30,000
1854–6		18,000–20,000
1856		20,000–25,000[6]
1858		25,000–30,000
1862/3	about	12,000
1863	over	15,000
1863/4		12,000[7]
1865		18,000–20,000
1866	about	15,000
1866–8		20,000–25,000
1871		10,000
1890		15,000

Sources: 1772: Norris, *Memoirs*, 62; 1776: De Chenevert & Bullet, 'Réflexions', 19; 1793: John Adams, *Remarks on the Country Extending from Cape Palmas to the River Congo* (London, 1823), 50; 1803: M'Leod, *Voyage*, 13; 1841: PP, Select Committee on the West Coast of Africa, 1842, Minutes of Evidence, § 3685, letter of Capt. Lawrence, Sierra Leone, 4 June 1841; 1851: Auguste Bouet, 'Le royaume de Dahomey', *L'Illustration*, 20 (1852), 40; 1854–6: WMMS, T.B. Freeman, 20 July 1855 [18,000], and 'West Africa', 202 [18,000–20,000]; 1856: A. Vallon, 'Le royaume de Dahomey', 2 parts, *RMC*, 1–2 (1860–1), 1/333, 343; 1858: Guillevin, 'Voyage dans l'intérieur du royaume de Dahomey', *Nouvelles annales des voyages*, 8e série, 2 (1862), 270; 1862/3: PP, Despatches from Commodore Wilmot, no. 2, 10 Feb. 1863: Borghero, 'Relation', in *Journal*, 254; 1863/4: Burton, *Mission*, i, 61; 1865: Carlos Eugenio Corrêa da Silva, *Uma viagem ao estabelecimento portuguez de S. João Baptista de Ajudá* (Lisbon, 1866), 33; 1866: M. Béraud, 'Note sur le Dahomé', *Bulletin de la Société de la Géographie*, 12 (1866), 372; 1866/8: Bouche, *Sept ans*, 323; 1871: J.A. Skertchly, *Dahomey As It Is* (London, 1874), 45; 1890: Foà, *Le Dahomey*, 419.

Note, however, that another member of the same French mission thought that this figure should be reduced by a third, i.e. between 13,333 and 16,667: Dr Repin, 'Voyage au Dahomey', *Le Tour du monde*, 1 (1863), 70.

Note, however, that Burton gives this figure on the authority of the French Catholic mission, whose own head Borghero gave an estimate of over 15,000 around the same time.

The heterogeneity was greater, indeed, than apparent at first sight, since the 'Dahomian' element was itself heterogeneous in its remoter ancestries, including families that traced their origins from outside Dahomey or from originally distinct communities absorbed within it by recent conquest. Several prominent Dahomian families in Ouidah (Gnahoui, Hodonou, Quénum) claim ultimate origins from the kingdom of Weme, south-east of Dahomey, by which it was conquered in the early eighteenth century, while the Boya family traces its origins to Savalou, north of Dahomey, and the Adanle family to Adja-Tado, to the west (in modern Togo).[10] The personnel of the European forts also reflected this diversification, with Dahomian elements recruited into their service after the 1720s. For example, one family of Sogbadji who acknowledge to have been former 'servants' to the English fort, Midjrokan, identify themselves as Fon, although their ultimate origins are from Adja-Tado; the founder of this family is identifiable in the fort records as 'Majerican', appointed as 'linguist' in 1767.[11] There was also still a Gold Coast

[10] Reynier, 'Ouidah', 37, 51, 53, 58; Quénum, *Les Ancêtres*, 20–48; fieldwork, Adanle compound, 11 Jan. 1996.

[11] Fieldwork, Midjrokan compound, 9 Jan. 1996; Reynier, 'Ouidah', 36. For the ancestor, see PRO, T70/1160, Day Book, William's Fort, 1 July 1767, etc.

element in the personnel of the forts, represented by canoemen who continued to be recruited from there. All three 'European' quarters nowadays contain a family of Gold Coast origin descended from ancestors who were canoemen in the service of European shipping: Kocou in Sogbadji, Cotia in Ahouandjigo and Agbessikpé in Docomè.[12] The first of these is also traceable in eighteenth-century records: although 'Kocou' is a common name (being the local version of the Akan name Kwaku, for one born on a Wednesday), it is likely that the family ancestor is to be identified with a 'Quacoe' who was recruited as a canoeman by the English fort from Cape Coast in 1776 and promoted to 'boatswain' or head canoeman in 1781.[13] Others from the Gold Coast came to Ouidah as independent traders, such as the founder of the Gbeti family of Sogbadji, who was from Accra.[14]

This ethnic diversity was further compounded by the incorporation of numerous slaves. The slaves sold into export through Ouidah were mainly from immediately neighbouring peoples raided by the Dahomian army, especially the Mahi to the north and the Nago (Yoruba) to the north-east, and presumably those retained locally had similar origins. In the nineteenth century, when Dahomian military operations were successfully directed mainly against western Yoruba towns, the element of enslaved Yoruba became more prominent. Some of the slaves in Ouidah, however, originated from the remoter interior. Two families in Ahouandjigo descended from slaves of the French fort, Soloté and Oundasso, recall that their founding ancestors came from the Bariba (i.e. Borgu) country, in the north of modern Bénin.[15] When the French Catholic mission in Ouidah purchased slaves for local use in 1862, from among a batch of captives recently taken by the Dahomians in an attack on the Yoruba town of Ishaga, they found that these included some foreigners who had the misfortune to be caught in the town, including some who were Hausa (from what is today northern Nigeria).[16]

Given this heterogeneity of origins, Ouidah must have been a multilingual community. Although those from Adja, Weme, Savalou and Mahi spoke languages closely enough related to Fon and Hueda to be mutually intelligible, Fante, spoken by the Gold Coast immigrants (or Ga in the case of those from Accra), and Yoruba were only remotely related, and Baatonu (the main language of Borgu) and Hausa not at all. Presumably such elements became linguistically assimilated over time, although many people in Ouidah were probably bilingual. Knowledge of European languages also spread within the town. Some Europeans who resided in Ouidah learned Fon; notably Lionel Abson, the longest-serving director of the English fort, who lived in the town for 36 years until his death in 1803 and became fluent in the local language.[17] But this was exceptional; normally, communication depended on local people learning European languages. Some knowledge of the latter spread

---

[12] Reynier, 'Ouidah', 34, 36, 39 (giving the first name as 'Kodjia'); fieldwork, Kocou compound, 9 Jan. 1996.
[13] PRO, T70/1161–2, Day Book, William's Fort, 1 Oct. 1776, 1 Jan. 1781. A 'Cotia' is also listed among the slave canoemen of the French fort c. 1789: ANF, C6/27, 'Liste des nègres captifs du Roi au fort de Juda', appendix to Gourg, 'Mémoire pour servir d'instruction au Directeur', 1791.
[14] Reynier, 'Ouidah', 36; fieldwork, Gbeti compound, 9 Jan. 1996.
[15] Reynier, 'Ouidah', 33; Agbo, Histoire, 185–6.
[16] Borghero, Journal, 114 [1 Sept. 1862].
[17] Dalzel, History, vi–vii; Adams, Remarks, 52.

quite widely within Ouidah; in the 1780s it was noted that it was common in passing through the town to be saluted in three different European languages at once, everybody knowing at least enough to offer greetings in the language of the fort they served.[18] In the nineteenth century, Portuguese became the dominant lingua franca, reflecting both the predominance of trade with Brazil and the settlement of numerous Brazilians in the town.

On the age and gender composition of the town there is little hard information, but one substantial sample is provided by a list of slaves of the French fort in c. 1789. There were then said to be a total of 207 fort slaves, but only 194 (including 8 'mulattoes', or persons of mixed African/European descent) are named in a list of those receiving wages; presumably the 13 omitted were infants too young for work. Those listed comprise 127 adults to 67 children and 87 males to 107 females. The family relationships among them are not indicated, although a slightly earlier document states that the fort slaves, then estimated to number between 180 and 200, comprised 50 separate households.[19] It is debatable, however, whether the balance of generations and sexes among such fort slaves was typical of the Ouidah population as a whole. In fact, the 1789 list distinguishes between those who received regular payment and those paid only occasionally, when actually working, and these two groups have quite different profiles, the latter containing a higher proportion both of children (44 out of 115, as compared with 23 out of 79 in the first group) and of women (75 of 115, as against 32 of 79). It seems likely that the second group would have been those established in self-supporting households and was perhaps more representative of the population at large.

At any rate, it seems certain that the population of Ouidah, like other comparable coastal communities, was predominantly female.[20] This contrasts with the situation in the colonial period, when towns tended to have a majority of male inhabitants, owing to the predominance of men in migration into urban centres;[21] this pattern was already evident in Lagos under British rule in the second half of the nineteenth century, which had more men than women residents by the 1880s.[22] Pre-colonial towns also grew by in-migration, at times very rapidly, but this mainly took the form of the purchase of slaves, and the principal demand for slaves within the domestic economy was for females, with a majority of enslaved males sold into the trans-Atlantic trade.[23] Women were employed not only within the household, but also very widely outside it. They were especially prominent in retail trade: as was noted in the 1780s, although the slave trade was dominated by men, otherwise 'trading of all kinds is left to the women'.[24] Likewise in the 1850s, traders in the

---

[18] Isert, *Letters*, 100.

[19] ANF, C6/27, Gourg, 'Liste des nègres captifs du Roi au fort de Juda', 1791; C6/26. Baud-Duchiron, 'Exploration et construction du comptoir de Juda', 1 Sept. 1778.

[20] As noted, for example, for Accra by Parker, *Making the Town*, xxiii; cf. 170, with 190 n. 78.

[21] Emmanuel Akyeampong, '"*O pe tam won pe ba*"/"*You like cloth but you don't want children*": urbanization, individualism and gender relations in colonial Ghana, *c*. 1900–1939', in Anderson & Rathbone, *Africa's Urban Past*, 222–4; Mabogunje, *Urbanization in Nigeria*, 133–4.

[22] C.W. Newbury, *The Western Slave Coast and its Rulers* (Oxford, 1961), 80.

[23] Paul E. Lovejoy, *Transformations in Slavery: A History of Slavery in Africa* (Cambridge, 1983), 62–5.

[24] Isert, *Letters*, 101. See the similar observation about the Hueda kingdom in the 1720s: Labat, *Voyage*, ii, 166.

market were said to be 'only' or 'mostly' women.[25] Women were also extensively employed as porters; Frederick Forbes in 1849–50, for journeys from Ouidah to Abomey, hired more female than male porters.[26] In agriculture, although men did the initial clearing and planting, the subsequent tending and harvesting of the crop was done by women.[27] Fishing was done by men (although the catch was marketed by their wives), but most of the work of salt-making by women.[28] Although the slave trade was a male business, therefore, the infrastructure that supported it in Ouidah depended upon the exploitation of female labour.

Ouidah was also predominantly a community of slaves. In addition to the African personnel of the European forts, the households of indigenous officials and merchants also included many slaves. Illustrative examples are available only for persons who, although partially or wholly of African descent, formed part of the 'European' community, but there is no reason to suppose that these were atypical of the wider population. In 1850, for example, Madiki Lemon of Sogbadji, grandson of a soldier in the English fort, owned ten slaves. The African-born Brazilian ex-slave Antonio d'Almeida in his will in 1864 bequeathed nine slaves to various members of his family and provided for the continuation of two senior slaves in their positions within his household, giving a total of 11 slaves apparently in his urban establishment, as well as 24 working on his farm.[29] In the nineteenth century, European observers gained the impression that the population of Ouidah consisted mainly of slaves, although their accounts sometimes suffer from conceptual imprecision, including pawns (whose labour was pledged for the security of debts) and even free clients within their definition of 'slave'. Forbes in 1850 believed that nine-tenths of the population of Dahomey were slaves; another observer in 1866 estimated two-thirds.[30] These figures seem too high for Dahomey as a whole: a modern scholar suggests that at the end of the nineteenth century slaves may have accounted for between a quarter and a third of the population.[31] It seems likely, however, that these high estimates were based on the specific case of Ouidah, with which Europeans were most familiar; another visitor in 1871 thought that four-fifths of the population of Ouidah were 'slaves or [introducing the conceptual ambiguity] dependent upon the caboceers and merchants in the place'.[32] In this, Ouidah was comparable to other coastal towns of the region; for example, the population of Lagos in the 1850s was reported to be 90 per cent slaves.[33] Although the scale of domestic slavery was probably larger in the nineteenth century than earlier (owing to the changed economic conditions of the transition from the slave trade to trade in palm produce), a substantial proportion of the population was certainly of

---

[25] Auguste Bouet, 'Le royaume de Dahomey', *L'Illustration*, 20 (1852), 40; Repin, 'Voyage', 73.

[26] Forbes, *Dahomey*, i, 51–2; ii, 80.

[27] A. Vallon, 'Le royaume de Dahomey', 2 parts, *PMC*, 1 (1860), 358.

[28] Grivot, 'La pêche', 123; Rivallain, 'Le sel', 112–13.

[29] Forbes, *Dahomey*, i, 129; text of d'Almeida's will in Verger, *Os libertos*, 121–4.

[30] Forbes, *Dahomey*, i, 14; M. Béraud, 'Note sur le Dahomé', *Bulletin de la Societé de la Geographie*, 12 (1866), 380.

[31] Patrick Manning, *Slavery, Colonialism and Economic Growth in Dahomey, 1640–1960* (Cambridge, 1982), 192.

[32] J.A. Skertchly, *Dahomey As It Is* (London, 1874), 45.

[33] PP, Slave Trade 1858–9, Class B, no. 11, Consul Campbell, Lagos, 28 March 1858.

servile status or descent already in the eighteenth century. In Ouidah, as throughout West Africa, the growth of internal slavery was closely linked to that of the
export trade in slaves, the same mechanisms of enslavement serving both markets.[34]

Slaves held within the local community were, it should be stressed, in principle
distinct from those sold into export. Dahomian law prohibited the sale overseas of
anyone born in Dahomey, and this included slaves as well as free-born. This
applied even to slaves held by the European forts in Ouidah; as the French fort
complained, its slaves were 'protected by the King of the Dahomians', and so were
'not at all in the position of being bought by the private captains or being
transported to America, at least unless it is punishment of a very serious offence'.[35]
Moreover, slaves in Dahomey enjoyed legal protection against ill-treatment: 'the
government protects the slave who can, if he is mistreated, appeal to the authorities
who can oblige a master to fulfill his duties better or take away the slave'.[36] Many
slaves in urban centres such as Ouidah also had a measure of economic independence. In the 1840s it was said to be 'general practice' for masters to allow slaves 'to
prosecute their own affairs, and to receive in exchange for this concession of their
time, a stipulated monthly sum derived from their labour', and under such
arrangements slaves were sometimes able to accumulate sufficient funds to purchase their freedom, for which the value of two slaves was generally demanded.[37]
Freed slaves and their descendants, however, normally remained clients of the
families of their former owners.

In its physical appearance, despite the long-established European presence,
Ouidah remained an essentially African town. Before the nineteenth century, the
European forts remained the only structures built (in part) in two storeys, and also,
as Burton still noted in the 1860s, the only buildings with European-style windows,
others deriving light only through doorways.[38] The generality of buildings, including the forts, were constructed of mud and roofed with thatch; only in the nineteenth century were some of the buildings in the forts, and a few private residences
of wealthy foreign merchants beginning to be built in brick and roofed with tiles.
The construction of a house, as witnessed by Forbes in 1850, involved the cutting
of timber from the countryside to make a frame, the mixing of clay with water and
straw for the walls, thatching with straw, and finally whitewashing the walls with
lime obtained by burning oysters from the lagoon.[39] Individual properties consisted
of 'compounds', enclosing a variable number of buildings and courtyards; buildings
were mostly rectangular, although a few (mainly religious establishments) were
circular in form, perhaps preserving an older style.[40] As Forbes noted, apart from

---

[34] See Lovejoy, *Transformations in Slavery*, 115–22.

[35] ANF, C6/27, 'Mémoire sur le Fort de Juda', n.d. [post–1763].

[36] Borghero, 'Relation', in *Journal*, 247.

[37] PP, Copy of Despatches from the Lieutenant-Governor of the Gold Coast, giving an account of Missions to
the King of Ashantee and Dahomey (1849), Report by B. Cruickshank, of his Mission to the King of
Dahomey, 9 Nov. 1848, 15; see also PRO, FO84/886, Louis Fraser, Copy of rough notes from daily journal, 5
Aug. 1851.

[38] Burton, *Mission*, i, 67.

[39] Forbes, *Dahomey*, i, 129.

[40] E.g. the Dangbe temple, as noted by Duncan, *Travels*, i, 126.

the European forts, all buildings were similar in appearance, except in size; in Ouidah, there was nothing as distinctive as the royal palace in Abomey, even the residence of the Yovogan being 'a mere enclosure of huts'.[41]

European visitors to Ouidah in the late eighteenth century described it as 'a large straggling town', with open spaces 'scattered here and there throughout the town', which were planted with crops; likewise in the 1860s, Burton observed that 'the houses are scattered' and 'except round the principal market-place, there is far more bush than building'.[42] This spacing of buildings was deliberate, intended to minimize the danger of fire spreading from one to another. The thatched roofs were vulnerable to fire, especially in the dry season, making the danger of fire a prominent feature of urban life, in Ouidah as in other towns of the region.[43] Recurrent fires are recorded in the European forts during the eighteenth century, the most serious being one that destroyed the French fort in 1728. Likewise in 1764 the English fort suffered a fire, which 'consumed all but the [outer] wall and swish walls [of the buildings]', destroying 100 oz. [£400] worth of goods; and there were further fires in 1770, 1773 and 1775, which required assistance from people from the French and Portuguese forts to extinguish.[44] Local tradition recalls a devastating fire that occurred during the first half of the nineteenth century, called 'Gudamiro's fire', after a Yoruba slave who was alleged to have started it, when a fire by which he was roasting cashew nuts ignited the thatched roof of a building in Zomaï quarter, on the west of the town, belonging to the Brazilian trader Francisco Felix de Souza. From Zomaï, the fire spread eastward through the town, lasting three days; the town was 'entirely destroyed', with 'several' human fatalities and 'incalculable' losses in goods. This may refer to a fire reported in *c.* 1838, in which de Souza lost considerable property.[45] Again in 1852 a fire destroyed 60 houses, including the Yovogan's residence and a 'fetish house' with sacred snakes inside it (evidently a building in the nearby Dangbe temple); the French fort to the west was also set alight, but the fire there was successfully put out.[46] Illustration of 'continual fears of fires' as an aspect of life in Ouidah is also provided by the journal of the Roman Catholic missionary Francesco Borghero in the 1860s. During 1861, in the night of 10/11 August there was a fire in Docomè in which 'the entire quarter was burned', with over 150 houses destroyed, although the Portuguese fort in which the Catholic mission was resident escaped unscathed; and, on 11 September, 'again a great fire near us', and 'a good number of houses were burned'. Borghero also noted that fires were commonly the occasion for thefts from the damaged

[41] Forbes, *Dahomey*, i, 54, 106, 110–11.

[42] Norris, *Memoirs*, 62; Isert, *Letters*, 100; Burton, *Mission*, i, 60.

[43] See A. Félix Iroko, 'Les hommes et les incendies à la Côte des Esclaves durant la période précoloniale', *Africa* (Rome), 48 (1993), 396–423; and, for the specific case of Lagos, Spencer H. Brown, 'A history of the people of Lagos, 1852–1886' (PhD thesis, Northwestern University, 1964), 75–9, 373–81; C. Onyeka Nwanunobi, 'Incendiarism and other fires in nineteenth-century Lagos (1863–1886)', *Africa* (London), 60/1 (1990), 111–20.

[44] ANF, C6/25, [Dupetitval], 20 May 1728; PRO, T70/31, William Goodson, Ouidah, 10 Nov. 1764; T70/1160, Day Book, William's Fort, 12 Feb. 1770, 1 June 1773, 6 Feb. 1775.

[45] Agbo, *Histoire*, 115–17; see PRO, CO96/12, Thomas Hutton, 17 March 1847.

[46] PRO, FO84/886, Louis Fraser, 'Occurrences, gossip &c. at Whydah', 16 March 1852.

buildings. Again in 1863, on 1 April lightning struck the fort, causing a fire that destroyed the priests' living quarters.[47] The most destructive fire, however, occurred in 1864, beginning on 17 February in the east of the town (close to the Portuguese fort) and spreading westwards, with renewed outbreaks recurring over the next three days. Two-thirds of the town was destroyed, including Zobé market, the French fort and the de Souza compound; up to 80 people were killed and 200 injured, and the French fort lost property to the value of $40,000.[48]

Given this constant threat from fire, arson in Ouidah was treated as a major crime, subject to the severest penalties. A British trader in 1772 witnessed the public execution by beheading of a woman who had accidentally caused a fire in the market.[49] After Gudamiro's fire in the 1830s, 1,000 slaves from Zomaï who were held responsible were sold overseas; and likewise, after the fire of 1864, the owners of the houses where it started were arrested, but on this occasion were found not to be culpable.[50] People also invoked supernatural protection, fire (*zo*) being regarded as a *vodun*; Burton noted the practice of hanging buildings with ropes with leaves attached, sacred to Zo, as a prophylactic, a practice that became 'almost universal' in the aftermath of a fire.[51]

Like other towns in West Africa in this period, the urban environment of Ouidah also posed particular problems of public health.[52] A European visitor described it as 'very filthy and unhealthy', from the practice of digging holes to obtain mud for construction, which were then left to fill up with stagnant water and refuse.[53] Health problems were also compounded by the holding of large numbers of slaves awaiting embarkation on European ships, in crowded and insanitary conditions. Europeans regularly suffered high mortality in Ouidah, mainly from malarial fever and dysentery, including the especially virulent form of amoebic dysentery known as the 'bloody flux'.[54] Of these, the prevalence of malaria was related to the town's lagoonside situation, being carried by mosquitoes, which throve in the neighbouring swampy ground; but dysentery was more a function of urban conditions, caused by contamination of water-supplies through poor sanitation. Malaria was a greater problem for Europeans than for local people, who had some immunity to it. Forbes noted that the European and indigenous inhabitants of Ouidah were liable to mortality at different seasons of the year, the former being most vulnerable in June and July, at the end of the main rains, when the danger from mosquito-borne malaria was greatest, while the indigenous population, on the contrary, were suffering 'much sickness' in March, at the end of the dry season.[55] Local people, however, were equally subject to diseases arising from contaminated water. Tradition in Ouidah recalls a catastrophic outbreak of a disease, retrospectively

---

[47] Borghero, *Journal*, 52–3 [10–11 August 1861], 53–4 [10 Sept. 1861]; 129–32 [1 April 1863].

[48] Ibid., 145–9 [17–26 Feb. 1864]; WMMS, Bernasko, Ouidah, 4 March 1864; Burton, *Mission*, ii, 302–5.

[49] Norris, *Memoirs*, 63–6.

[50] Agbo, *Histoire*, 116–17; Burton, *Mission*, ii, 304–5.

[51] Burton, *Mission*, i, 79.

[52] For a comparative case: Spencer H. Brown, 'Public health in Lagos, 1850–1900', *IJAHS*, 25 (1992), 337–60.

[53] Bouet, 'Le royaume de Dahomey', 40.

[54] E.g. Barbot, *On Guinea*, ii, 634.

[55] Forbes, *Dahomey*, i, 120–1.

identified as cholera, around 1820, the dead from which were buried at the site called Kindji, in Brazil quarter, which was consequently thought to be haunted.[56]

The concentration of population also facilitated the transmission of contagious diseases, especially smallpox. In the Hueda kingdom in the early eighteenth century, it was noted that smallpox caused great mortality;[57] and it seems significant that Hwesi, the *vodun* of the earth, who was believed to cause smallpox, as well as the fire-*vodun* Zo, was among the deities who according to tradition were established in Ouidah before the Dahomian conquest. By the 1770s European traders buying slaves at Ouidah were inoculating them against smallpox; but it is not clear whether inoculation was ever practised in Dahomey itself.[58] Certainly, smallpox remained a major scourge. In 1861, for example, there was a major epidemic, which in particular decimated the Dahomian army on campaign, and the disease also spread into Ouidah, where 'many' died of it; and there was a further outbreak in 1864, with again 'many' mortalities in Ouidah.[59] Venereal disease was likewise reportedly 'very common' in Ouidah and consequently a source of concern for European slave-traders, who tried to avoid buying infected persons, the reference being apparently not to syphilis, which was probably introduced from America, but to yaws, an indigenous and less virulent disease, often confused with venereal syphilis.[60]

The character of urban life

In Dahomey, as elsewhere in West Africa, there was an explicit conceptual opposition in local thought between town and country, *to* (or *tome*) and *gleta*, the latter often translated as 'bush' but strictly meaning cultivated land (from *gle*, 'farm').[61] The term translated as 'town' in fact applies to settlements of all sizes, including small villages. It also, however, means more generally 'country' or 'locality'; governors of provinces of the Dahomey kingdom, for example, were called *togan*, 'chiefs of *to*'. The implication is that urbanity was defined not (or not only) by size and concentration of population, but by political autonomy and the role of the town as a seat of administration.[62] Towns, and the character of urban life, were also defined by their possession of markets (*ahi*). The existence of markets was, indeed, linked with the role of towns as centres of political authority, since the local government guaranteed security and order in the market, while

---

[56] Agbo, *Histoire*, 109.

[57] 'Relation du royaume de Judas', 38.

[58] Norris, *Memoirs*, 117–18. Inoculation was practised in West Africa by the eighteenth century, but no evidence from Dahomey or immediately neighbouring areas is cited in the survey by Eugenia W. Herbert, 'Smallpox inoculation in Africa', *JAH*, 16 (1975), 539–59.

[59] WMMS, Henry Wharton, Cape Coast, 13 June 1861; Bernasko, Ouidah, 2 Dec. 1861, 4 March 1864.

[60] Phillips, 'Journal', 218; 'Relation du royaume de Judas', 47.

[61] These terms were recorded in a vocabulary collected in 1849–50: Forbes, *Dahomey*, i, 223–4 ['toh', 'gree tah', translated as 'city or town', 'field']. For the town/country opposition elsewhere, see for Accra, Parker, *Making the Town*, 6–8; and for the Yoruba, Eva Krapf-Askari, *Yoruba Towns and Cities* (Oxford, 1969), 23.

[62] So also among the Yoruba: Krapf-Askari, *Yoruba Towns*, 25.

conversely the concentration of exchanges in the market-place facilitated their regulation and taxation. John Duncan in 1845 noted that the market in Ouidah was 'superintended by a chief constable', responsible to the Yovogan, who 'attends to its cleanliness and regularity', as well as levying a sales tax.[63]

The market in Ouidah was frequently described by European visitors.[64] It was clearly in the same place as the town's main market nowadays, called Zobé, or Zobémi, this name being first recorded (as 'Zobeme') by Burton in 1863/4. Duncan described it as 'formed of several streets of low huts, built square, and generally joining one another', the floors of the huts being 'composed of well-worked clay, ... very hard and smooth ... raised about a foot above the streets, passing between the huts or stalls, consequently the latter are always dry'; it covered 'about three-fourths of an acre, or an acre'. Dahomey operated a four-day market cycle, and some accounts state that this applied to the Ouidah market: thus, in 1784–5, 'every fourth day is the weekly market to which foreigners may bring their wares', and in 1825, 'there is a regular market every four days'. However, other accounts (including Duncan) report explicitly that the market was held daily; probably the resolution of this contradiction is that it was attended every fourth day by outsiders, while on other days it handled only local exchanges. Attendance was at its height, according to Burton, in the late afternoon, around 4 p.m. As Forbes noted, all exchange was concentrated in the market: 'As there are no shops, all trade is carried on here.' Transactions were for cash, rather than by barter, in the local currency of cowry shells, which came ultimately from the Maldive Islands in the Indian Ocean and were imported into the Slave Coast by the European trade.[65] The cowry currency was especially well adapted to small-scale transactions, being valued from the 1720s at £1 sterling to the 'grand cabess' of 4,000, making a single shell equivalent to around 1/17 of a pre-decimal penny.[66] In the Ouidah market in 1850, for example, an orange cost 3 cowries, an egg 10.[67]

Europeans were regularly impressed with the size of the Ouidah market and the range of goods on sale: Duncan thought it 'superior to any I have seen on the coast, and ... better supplied even than Sierra Leone [i.e. Freetown]', and Forbes likewise called it 'the finest I have seen in Africa; well supplied with every luxury and many useful goods'. Forbes noted that the market was 'divided into appropriate proportions for each description of article'; meat, fish, corn, flour, vegetables, fruit and 'foreign goods' all having their own 'separate markets'. The fullest account of the range of goods on sale is that given by Duncan:

[63] Duncan, *Travels*, i, 120, 124.

[64] E.g. de Chenevert & Bullet, 'Refléxions', 20 (referring to 1776); Isert, *Letters*, 101 (1784–5); PRO, ADM55/11, Hugh Clapperton, Journal, 16 Nov. 1825; Duncan, *Travels*, i, 120–22; Forbes, *Dahomey*, i, 109–10; Burton, *Mission*, i, 76–8.

[65] See in general Jan Hogendorn & Marion Johnson, *The Shell Money of the Slave Trade* (Cambridge, 1986).

[66] This is according to their 'trade' value, i.e. their exchange value in Africa, rather than 'prime cost', or purchase price in Europe, conventionally reckoned at 50% of the 'trade' value, by which the grand cabess was worth only 10 shillings (£0.50). On interpretation of local prices, see Robin Law, 'Computing domestic prices in pre-colonial West Africa: a methodological exercise from the Slave Coast', *HA*, 18 (1991), 239–57.

[67] Forbes, *Dahomey*, i, 110.

It is well supplied with every article of native consumption, as well as medicinal plants, and many articles of European manufacture. Among other articles generally exposed for sale are the following: – Pork, beef, mutton; cotton cloth, native and English; thread, beads, gun-flints, tobacco-pipes, iron, pepper, elu (a composition to destroy mosquitoes), chuchume, bill-hooks, Badagry pipes, flints and steel, raw native cotton; tancacam, a medical root resembling ginger; goora [*golo*, i.e. bitter kola] and kolla nuts; eyo-nuts, used in playing the game of 'adjito' [a board game]; skins of the alligator [i.e. crocodile], deer, bush-pig, and cat; dried rats and mice; raw and dried fish; fish cooked in palm-oil; kootataffue, a root resembling onion, but very bitter; cocoa [i.e. coconut] and dego-nuts [? = shea-nuts], for making oil; boiled and raw Indian corn; country pots and calabashes; lime, made from oyster-shell; grass bags and baskets; porcupine quills, craw-fish, palm-oil, tomato, shallots, and occro [okra]; water-cresses, salt, farina [i.e. cassava flour], ground nut; atoo, or quashie-root [used for medicinal purposes]; sakwadee, a root similar to ginger having a taste resembling manioc-root; palm-nuts; bodya, a root used as a decoction to expedite labour in child-birth; agwbaja [*agbaja*], used for cartridge-boxes; gun-flints, stones for grinding corn, brought from Abomey; dookwa [*doko*], ball[s] made from beans ground with palm-oil and pepper; kahoma [Hausa *kanwa*], akaowo (native name) [*akanmu*], saltpetre in its original state.

Although most of these items were of local provenance, they included some brought by long-distance trade from the interior (e.g. bitter kola, from Asante in modern Ghana; and 'saltpetre', actually natron, from Borno in north-eastern Nigeria) as well as European imports. All accounts stress that foodstuffs were extensively sold in the market, much in already cooked form; Burton thought that 'half the shops contain either raw or cooked provisions'.

The prominence of foodstuffs in the market reflected in part the division of labour within the community, between the farming population and those involved in other occupations. Pre-colonial towns in West Africa are commonly assumed to have been predominantly agricultural communities (this agrarian character being often taken to put in question their 'urban' status);[68] but this does not apply to coastal commercial centres, where a large and indeed the major proportion of the population was involved in non-agricultural activities, including fishing and salt-making as well as the European trade.[69] The farming and non-agricultural sectors were not entirely distinct, since some persons divided their time between the two. Even the slaves employed in the European forts did some farming: as was noted of the French fort, each family had its own grounds near the fort, on which they cultivated food crops.[70] But it is clear that many of the inhabitants of Ouidah did not produce their own food. The division of labour might operate within a household, rather than through the market, slaves employed in non-agricultural work by their owners being subsisted from the produce of their farms.[71] Slaves of the European forts, however, regularly received payment in cowries, and employees

[68] E.g. Krapf-Askari, *Yoruba Towns*, 223–4.
[69] Cf., for example, Accra, where only about 5% of the population in 1891 were farmers: Parker, *Making the Town*, 7. In Lagos in 1881, under 1% of the population was engaged in agriculture: Newbury, *Western Slave Coast*, 81.
[70] ANF, C6/26, Bauduchiron, 'Exploration et construction du comptoir de Juda', 1 Sept. 1778; C6/27, Gourg, 'Mémoire pour servir d'instruction au Directeur', 1791.
[71] Forbes, *Dahomey*, i, 129; ii, 200.

of European traders more generally, if not paid daily, received 'subsistence' (at a standard rate of 80 cowries per day), implying that they bought their food in the market.[72] As Burton observed, in Ouidah 'many a "working man" breakfasts and dines in the alley [of the market]'.[73]

But even beyond this specialization of function within the town, Ouidah itself, at least prior to the nineteenth century, had only a limited agricultural hinterland. In 1776 it was noted that the land around the town was planted with maize, but only for a distance of around three-quarters of a league (3.5 km). A visitor to Dahomey in 1803 observed that cultivation was done only 'in the immediate neighbourhood of their towns'; and although presented in general terms, it seems likely that this also was based on the case of Ouidah, which was the only Dahomian town this observer knew at first hand.[74] The implication is that, like other coastal towns such as Lagos, Ouidah was not self-sufficient in basic foods, but depended upon importing them from elsewhere.[75] In 1772 it was noted that agricultural produce – yams, sweet potatoes, beans and corn – cultivated at Savi was taken for sale at Ouidah, and also that 'great quantities' of palm oil were traded there from Allada, although some of this oil was probably intended for export rather than local consumption. Likewise, in 1850, traders from Ouidah were observed going to the market at Tori, between Savi and Allada, to buy foodstuffs – corn, pepper, fruit and vegetables, and livestock – as well as palm oil and locally made cloth, which they paid for with salt, fish and imported commodities – 'foreign cloths', rum and tobacco.[76]

The supply of labour in Ouidah was also to some degree commercialized, not only through the purchase of slaves but also by the hiring of free workers. The accounts of the English fort list payments, separately from those to the 'Castle slaves', also for 'free canoemen and labourers' hire', freemen being regularly employed to carry messages and to assist in delivering supplies and in repair of the fort buildings.[77] The canoemen and porters employed by European ships were likewise paid, and presumably recruited, individually, the standard rate for porters being 120 cowries per day. In the nineteenth century, there was also a system of fixed long-term contracts: in 1850 it was noted that canoemen in Ouidah were hired by English traders by the month, for which they were paid 4,000 cowries, plus 80 cowries per day subsistence, but by the Portuguese for terms of two years, receiving 16,000 cowries on recruitment and goods to the value of 20,000 cowries and $10 in cash at the end of their service, and 80 cowries daily subsistence during the contract.[78] Some of these 'free' workers may in fact have been slaves, but allowed by their owners to work independently, under the arrangements noted earlier. Free labour in Ouidah, however, was clearly in limited supply. An alternative mechanism for obtaining workers was through the system of pawning, whereby a

---

[72] For subsistence rates in Ouidah, see Law, 'Posthumous questions', 412–14.

[73] Burton, *Mission*, i, 77.

[74] De Chenevert & Bullet, 'Réflexions', 19; M'Leod, *Voyage*, 17–18.

[75] For Lagos, which imported food not only from agricultural communities on the north bank of the lagoon but also from Abeokuta in the interior, see Brown, 'History of the people of Lagos', 73–5.

[76] Norris, *Memoirs*, 66, 71; Forbes, *Dahomey*, i, 114.

[77] PRO, T70/1158–63, Day Books, William's Fort, 1752–1812.

[78] Forbes, *Dahomey*, i, 122.

person who took out a loan was bound to work for the creditor until the debt was cleared.[79] In the nineteenth century, Europeans adapted this practice to evade the legal prohibition of slave-holding, buying slaves who were then treated as pawns. The French Roman Catholic mission in the 1860s found that it was 'impossible to find free workers' for necessary building and repair work – 'it was necessary either to possess slaves or to borrow them'; in 1862, it resorted to 'redeeming' slaves, who were then bound to serve the mission until they had worked off the cost of their purchase. Likewise, the British Methodist mission in 1864 purchased slaves, at $60 each, on the basis that the cost of their 'redemption' would be deducted from their wages at the rate of $2 per month, so that they would pay off their debt over 30 months.[80] Slaves could also be hired out by their masters; Forbes in 1850, finding himself short of porters, hired slaves belonging to a Dahomian merchant, Gnahoui, who appropriated their wages.[81]

By the nineteenth century at least, there was also a market in urban property. In Dahomian law all land belonged to the king, and residential sites in Ouidah were in the first instance acquired by royal grants, as tradition recalls in the cases of Nicolas d'Oliveira, the founder of Ganvè quarter, Francisco Felix de Souza and other settlers in the nineteenth century.[82] Strictly, such grants did not confer ownership, occupants enjoying only rights of usufruct; as expressed by Burton, in European legal terminology, land was held in 'fee-simple'.[83] However, those who received land from the king could in turn grant use of it to others – d'Oliveira in Ganvè is remembered to have '[given] portions of his property to a large number of new-comers'.[84] In the European sector, at least, such transfers were partially commercialized. Temporary accommodation was available for rent, in return for money payment: Forbes in 1850 opted not to lodge in the English fort, but rented a house from Madiki Lemon; and another observer in 1851 noted that individual 'houses' within large compounds were commonly 'let separately to tenants at so many cowries per week', mainly to Africans from the Gold Coast and Sierra Leone.[85] Properties were also occasionally sold. In 1852 the British merchant Thomas Hutton, having to relinquish the English fort to the British vice-consulate, purchased a house from a locally resident Portuguese merchant, Jacinto Joaquim Rodrigues, for $750; and around the same time the leading Brazilian merchant, Domingos José Martins, also put his house with its furniture and other properties on the market, for an asking price of $1,500, although he did not in the event leave Ouidah. The status of such sales, however, was doubtful under Dahomian law; Rodrigues was subsequently fined $200 for selling his house without royal permission.[86]

[79] Robin Law, 'On pawning and enslavement for debt in the pre-colonial Slave Coast', in Toyin Falola & Paul E. Lovejoy (eds), *Pawnship in Africa* (Boulder, 1994), 55–69.

[80] Borghero, *Journal*, 95, 113–14 [1 Feb. & 1 Sept. 1862]; WMMS, William West, Cape Coast, 9 Oct. 1866.

[81] Forbes, *Dahomey*, ii, 200.

[82] Reynier, 'Ouidah', 41, 44, 58.

[83] Burton, *Mission*, ii, 248.

[84] Reynier, 'Ouidah', 59.

[85] Burton, *Mission*., i, 97, 129–30; PRO, FO84/886, Fraser, Daily journal, 5 Aug. 1851.

[86] PRO, FO84/886, Fraser, *Daily Journal*, Appendix on 'The Fort'; 'Occurrences', 6 March 1852; Bill of sale between Hutton & Rodrigues, 21 Jan. 1852.

The commercialization of domestic services extended to the provision of sex, as well as food and accommodation. In the Hueda kingdom in the 1690s it was noted that there was 'a very great plenty' of prostitutes, who operated from huts along 'the great roads throughout the whole country', some of whom were slaves purchased for this purpose by wealthy women.[87] Although this report implies that their customers were mainly local men, presumably they also served visiting Europeans. A similar system existed in Ouidah under Dahomian rule. Tradition in Docomè quarter recalls that a female slave taken as a wife by a member of the Agbessikpé family (canoemen in the service of the Portuguese fort) also served as concubine to a European, and with the money she obtained from this relationship she invested in the purchase of girl slaves for the establishment of a 'public house'; the Dahomian authorities seized her household, to the number of 480 men and women, leaving her with only 6 girls, on whose earnings she had to pay an annual tax. Another Docomè household, called Avloko, was founded by a woman who originally supplied her daughters as concubines to Europeans and ultimately established a brothel with 333 girls.[88]

Despite the centrality of exchange in the life of Ouidah, Karl Polanyi argued that this was not a truly 'market' economy, since he believed that prices were set administratively, in accordance with traditional notions of equity, rather than determined by supply and demand.[89] However, although prices were indeed regulated by the local authorities, it is clear that they were subject to short-term fluctuations, reflecting shifts in supply and demand, and that over the longer run they tended to rise. The price of a chicken, for example, rose from 50–67 cowries in 1694 to 96 by the end of the 1690s, 160 in 1721, and between 267 and 333 by the 1750s, although it then remained stable for a century, being still cited at 280 cowries in 1850, while the charge made by prostitutes rose from 3 to 20 cowries per session. This inflation probably reflected an oversupply of cowrie shells, through the expansion of the European trade for slaves. Wages, however, were more effectively controlled, those for porters remaining at 120 cowries per day down to the 1850s, this nominal stability, in the face of price inflation, representing a substantial reduction of their real value.[90] This erosion of real wages was a factor in the growth of theft in the European sector of the economy; already in the late 1690s, in the early stages of price inflation, porters were justifying their pilfering as a legitimate supplement to inadequate earnings; 'they have assurance enough to ask us, whether we can imagine that they would work so hard, as they do, for such small wages, without the liberty of stealing?'[91] The operation of the market economy tended to accentuate disparities of wealth, generating poverty for many alongside affluence for a few. Inequalities existed in consumption of basic foods and services, as well as in access to imported luxuries: Burton observed that meals offered to guests in Dahomey seldom included meat – 'a chicken, a fowl, or a goat denote a rich man' –

[87] Bosman, *Description*, 214–15.
[88] Reynier, 'Ouidah', 39–40; Bay, *Wives of the Leopard*, 210–11.
[89] Polanyi, *Dahomey and the Slave Trade*, 81–95.
[90] Law, 'Posthumous questions': see 403–11 for prices, 414–17 for wages.
[91] Bosman, *Description*, 349.

and that in Ouidah some houses were constructed of matting, rather than mud, these being those of 'the poorer classes'.[92]

In Dahomey, as elsewhere in pre-colonial West Africa, the town/country dichotomy carried implications of differential value; the term *gletanu*, 'country-man', in Fon has pejorative connotations, suggesting lack of sophistication and even stupidity, as the conventional translation 'bushman' implies.[93] A proverb illustrates the naïvety of the *gletanu* by his amazement at seeing a European child, 'Are there little ones too?';[94] in Ouidah, the term *Savinu*, 'person from Savi', is often substituted for 'countryman' in such remarks. The low status attached to farming was reinforced in Dahomey by the military ethos of its ruling elite; as King Adandozan (1797–1818) is remembered to have said, when the king of Oyo urged him to generate wealth (in order to enable him to pay tribute) by cultivating the soil, 'Our fathers ... cultivated not with hoes but with guns, the kings of Dahomey cultivate only war.'[95] It was also compounded by the fact that free men, being regarded as primarily soldiers, took little part in farming, most agricultural work devolving upon women, or else upon male slaves: as Burton observed, 'agriculture is despised, because slaves are employed in it'.[96] The Dahomian military ethos looked down upon commerce, as well as agriculture; as was noted in the 1780s, although the kings of Dahomey sold the war captives taken by their armies, 'trade' in the sense of purchasing slaves for resale was a profession they had 'always regarded as ignoble' and consequently traditionally left to their 'caboceers'.[97] In Ouidah, however, even under Dahomian rule, these values were inverted; as was noted in the 1770s, there 'the status of merchant is the first'.[98]

European visitors to Dahomey, while noting the distinctive ethos of Ouidah, from its character as a cosmopolitan and commercial centre, tended to project upon it their own cultural preconceptions, regarding towns (and especially port towns) as morally corrupt in comparison with the countryside. Forbes, for example, observed that:

> At Whydah, the Dahoman port, the personal depravity of the [European and American] slave merchants has destroyed the inborn honesty and chastity of the natives, and the meretricious gaze of the females and debauched and stealthy appearance of the men, are strongly and painfully contrasted with the modesty of the former and the honesty and openness of the latter, as the traveller nears the capital of the Dahoman kingdom.[99]

Metropolitan Dahomians thought similarly: Ouidah was proverbial as a site of sexual and moral corruption.[100] But in Ouidah itself there was a feeling rather of

[92] Burton, *Mission*, i, 136–7, 66.
[93] The term first recorded by Burton, ibid., i, 61, n. For this negative valuation of rural life elsewhere in West Africa, see Parker, *Making the Town*, 7; Krapf-Askari, *Yoruba Towns*, 25.
[94] Pamphile Boco, *Proverbes de la sagesse fon* (Cotonou, 1995–2000), i, no. 349.
[95] Le Herissé, *L'Ancien Royaume*, 313.
[96] Burton, *Mission*, ii, 248
[97] Dalzel, *History*, 213.
[98] De Chenevert & Bullet, 'Réflexions', 8, 48.
[99] Forbes, *Dahomey*, i, 13–14.
[100] Boco, *Proverbes*, iv, no. 1658: 'A porter meets a woman in Glehue, "Would I succeed in remaining clean in her company?"'

cultural superiority. As Burton in the 1860s observed, the Chodaton, deputy to the Yovogan of Ouidah, regarded even a leading member of the royal court, the king's principal diviner-adviser, 'with supreme contempt ... as an ancient bushman who knows nothing of the whites'.[101]

Religious life

Ouidah today has a reputation as a centre of the indigenous religion of *vodun*, expressed in the 1990s in the promotion of the ceremony at Ouidah for the sea-god Hu as the premier *vodun* festival, and the self-representation of the priest of the sea cult, the Hunon, as the 'Pope' of *vodun*.[102] This perception has been informed by awareness of the town's role, through the Atlantic slave trade, in the transmission of African religious traditions to the Americas – whence the modern touristic slogan of Bénin, and more particularly Ouidah, as 'the cradle of *vodun* [*le berceau du vodun*]'. But it is also a claim to local religious primacy in Africa.

European observers in the pre-colonial period, in apparent congruence with local tradition, also frequently stressed the strongly religious character of life in Ouidah. What they referred to most often was the large number of publicly visible 'idols' or 'fetishes'. In the Hueda kingdom in the 1680s, Barbot observed an 'infinite number' of 'fetishes', placed 'in special places on the roads', made of wood or clay and 'shaped like puppets'; and this was echoed in many subsequent accounts of Dahomian Ouidah.[103] The clay figures, which were commonly placed outside houses and at the entrances to the town, were of the *vodun* Legba.[104] Legba was a 'trickster' god, held responsible for misfortune and consequently worshipped to secure good luck; a similar *vodun*, called Aïzan, presided over the Zobé market.[105] The wooden images were those called *bocyo*, which were also protective in character, providing insurance against evil magic.[106] These practices were universal, or at least very widespread, among the population, and essentially individual, rather than collective. This was basically true also of the practice of divination by casting palm-kernels or cowries, associated with the *vodun* Fa, which was less often noticed by European observers but is also attested from the early eighteenth century onwards.[107] This was done by specialist diviners, who were consulted by individuals wanting advice about the future.

Europeans also sometimes noted the ancestral cults practised in individual households. Barbot in the 1680s found that the dead were usually buried within their own houses, and this practice remained standard through the Dahomian

---

[101] Burton, *Mission*, i, 311.

[102] For which, see Sutherland, 'In memory of the slaves'.

[103] Barbot, *On Guinea*, ii, 638; for clay images, see, for example, Duncan, *Travels*, i, 124–5; Forbes, *Dahomey*, i, 109.

[104] For the identification of the clay images as of Legba, see Burton, *Mission*, i, 81–3.

[105] Agbo, *Histoire*, 106–8.

[106] For *bocyo*, see Suzannne Preston Blier, *African Vodun* (Chicago, 1995).

[107] First noted by 'Relation du royaume de Judas', 56–7.

period, and indeed to some degree even to the present. The tombs remained the focus of commemorative rites for the dead; as Duncan noted, 'anniversary offerings are made by all who can afford them, to commemorate the death of their parents', involving the sacrifice of sheep, goats and fowls, and the eating of their meat.[108] These ancestral ceremonies were called *huetanu*, 'year-head-thing', from being celebrated at the end ('head') of the year, which corresponded in the local as well as the European calendar to around December/January.[109]

When local people speak of Ouidah's special religious status, however, they are generally referring to something rather different: the organized cults of the *vodun*. These were collective rather than individual, sometimes concerning particular families, but more often congregations of initiates that transcended lineage affiliation. At the level of active participation (as opposed to subjective belief), people normally belong to only one cult. Rather than thinking of *vodun* as a single religion worshipping a pantheon of many gods, it is better conceptualized as comprising a number of distinct and separate 'churches'.[110] What distinguishes Ouidah above all is the sheer number of different *vodun* worshipped in the town. A European visitor in 1784–5 reported that the town contained more than 30 'public fetish temples', but this was certainly an underestimate; a survey in 1937 counted a total of 104 *vodun* 'temples', and the quarters of the town that already existed in the eighteenth century – Tové, Ahouandjigo, Sogbadji, Docomè and Fonsaramè – accounted for the great majority of these, no fewer than 79.[111] The total of *vodun* worshipped is greater since, although some *vodun* have more than one temple, several different *vodun* are normally worshipped within each temple.

This diversity reflects the history of the development of the town and the composite character of its population, with different cults associated with the successive elements that settled in it. Local tradition distinguishes cults that date from the rule of the Hueda kings before 1727 from those introduced under Dahomian rule subsequently. The principal pre-Dahomian cults are those of Hu, the sea, Dangbe, the python, Hwesi, the *vodun* of smallpox, and Zo, the *vodun* of fire, the seniority of these four having been formally recognized by the Dahomian authorities after their conquest of the Hueda kingdom in the 1720s.[112] European accounts of Hueda religious practice prior to the conquest, although they do not relate specifically to Ouidah, attest the existence of some of the cults later prominent in the latter, including not only Dangbe and Hu, but also the worship of 'some lofty high trees', associated with healing (referring probably to Loko, the African teak), and of thunder, whose bolts were believed to punish thieves (i.e. the *vodun* So, who gave his name to Sogbadji quarter).[113] Other Hueda cults in Ouidah

---

[108] Barbot, *On Guinea*, i, 640; Duncan, *Travels*, i, 125.

[109] The 'Annual Customs' at Abomey, for deceased kings of the royal dynasty, were also called *huetanu*, as noted by Burton, *Mission*, i, 345; however, his translation as 'yearly head thing', with the implication that this referred to the sacrifice of human victims (by decapitation) in the Abomey ceremonies, is misconceived. Human sacrifice was rarely practised in Ouidah.

[110] Herskovits, *Dahomey*, ii, 170.

[111] Isert, *Letters*, 105; Merlo, 'Hiérarchie fétichiste'.

[112] Merlo, 'Hiérarchie fétichiste', 4.

[113] Bosman, *Description*, 368, 383; 'Relation du royaume de Judas', 53.

relate to deified heroes of the pre-Dahomian period: notably the founder of the town, Kpase, and the initiator of contact with European traders, Kpate; but also other kings of pre-Dahomian Hueda: Agbangla, Ayohuan and Hufon.[114] The pre-Dahomian origin of these cults is confirmed by the fact that their principal shrines are located in the quarters of the town whose origins likewise predate the Dahomian conquest: several in Tové, the original Hueda quarter, but others in those of the European forts, Hu and So in Sogbadji, Kpate in Docomè and Hwesi in Ahouandjigo.

Even these 'indigenous' cults are in fact, according to tradition, of disparate origins. Among the four senior gods, for example, the sea-god Hu, as seen in an earlier chapter, was in origin a Hula deity, derived ultimately from Grand-Popo, while Hwesi is also said to have been introduced from the west (from the Lake Ahémé region) by King Agbangla. The thunder-god So was associated with the Aïzo people, in the area of the Allada kingdom, as indicated by his common appellation Hevioso, 'So of Hévié', a village about 20 km north-east of Ouidah. Likewise, it may be noted that the *vodun* of smallpox exists in Ouidah in two forms: Hwesi, the original local version, and Sakpata, the latter acknowledged to have originated in the interior, from Dassa, north of Dahomey, although it is nevertheless insisted in Ouidah that his cult was already established locally under the Hueda kings.[115] The divination cult of Fa was of Yoruba origin, the diviners being mostly Yoruba.[116]

Cults of Dahomian origin include those connected with worship of ancestors of the royal dynasty, notably Nesuhwe (in Fonsaramè, the Dahomian quarter). Nesuhwe is thought to have been an innovation of the nineteenth century;[117] consistently with this hypothesis, in Ouidah it is associated with the Dagba family, descended from a Yovogan of Ouidah appointed in the 1820s.[118] Another important cult of Dahomian origin is that of Mawu (in Sogbadji), goddess of the heavens (and creator of the world), which is said to have originated from Adja-Tado, whence it was introduced into Dahomey by Hwanjile, the 'Queen Mother' of Tegbesu; in Ouidah it is associated with the Adanle family, whose founder was related to Hwanjile and settled in the town under her patronage.[119] The Dahomian families of Weme origin (Gnahoui, Quénum, etc.) worship a *vodun* of specifically Weme provenance, Mase, the spirit of the River Weme.[120] Other cults were introduced into Ouidah by slaves from the interior who were retained for local service rather than sold into export. An example is Azili, a female water-spirit (the prototype of the Haitian Ezili), whose shrine (in Tové quarter) is said to have been founded by an enslaved woman from Agonli-Houegbo, north-east of Dahomey, who was captured by the Dahomian army and brought to Ouidah under Agaja.[121] Also

[114] Merlo, 'Hiérarchie fétichiste', 15–16.
[115] Ibid., 19–20.
[116] As noted by 'Relation du royaume de Judas', 58.
[117] Bay, *Wives of the Leopard*, 250–51.
[118] Merlo, 'Hiérarchie fétichiste', 43; see Dagba, *La Collectivité familiale*, 57.
[119] Merlo, 'Hiérarchie fétichiste', 8; also Reynier, 'Ouidah', 37.
[120] Merlo, 'Hiérarchie fétichiste', 23, 39; Quénum, *Les Ancêtres*, 35, with n. 2.
[121] Fieldwork, Azilinon compound, 14 Sept. 2000.

prominent in Ouidah are various forms of Dan, the serpent-deity (distinct from Dangbe, and unlike him not considered to be incarnated in actual snakes), who is acknowledged to be in origin from Mahi, north of Dahomey. The Dan cults were perhaps also introduced under Dahomian rule, since they are mainly concentrated in the Dahomian quarters of the town, Fonsaramè and Boyasaramè, and also in the Brazil quarter settled by immigrants from Brazil (including returned African-born ex-slaves) in the nineteenth century. One form of Dan, the rainbow-serpent Aïdohuedo, famous from his prominence in Afro-American religion in Haiti, is also present in Ouidah. There are also cults of Nago (Yoruba) origin, for example of Chango (Shango, the Yoruba version of the god of thunder) and Yalode (the Yoruba counterpart of the indigenous Tokpodun, and like her identified with the crocodile).[122] Cults associated with slaves from the north-western interior that occur in coastal towns to the west, such as 'Tchamba' (the name of an ethnic group in northern Togo) and 'Goro' (from *golo*, kola), do not seem to have developed in Ouidah; the latter does nowadays exist in the town, but was introduced only in the twentieth century, and from the west rather than directly from the interior.[123] A *vodun* called Adjigo is associated with families of Gold Coast origin, who were generally free immigrants rather than slaves, including that of Dossou-Yovo, an offshoot of the Kocou family of Sogbadji, descended (as noted earlier) from a Gold Coast canoeman recruited by the English fort in the eighteenth century.[124]

Notably absent from the repertoire of cults introduced into Ouidah from the interior, prior to the nineteenth century, is Islam; this contrasts with Porto-Novo to the east, where Islam was introduced by Yoruba immigrants in the second half of the eighteenth century.[125] Muslims had been among the merchants who brought slaves to the Hueda kingdom in the early eighteenth century, but after the Dahomian conquest traders from the interior were not permitted to come to the coast; although Europeans occasionally met Muslims in the capital Abomey, therefore, they were no longer seen in Ouidah.[126] There must have been Muslims among the slaves sold into export through Ouidah, and indeed it is likely that some were retained in slavery locally;[127] but there was no organized Islamic worship in the eighteenth century. Islam was established in Ouidah only in the 1830s, and then not directly from the interior, but by returned ex-slaves from Brazil who settled in Maro quarter.

Emphasis on the heterogeneity of religious practice in Ouidah should not be taken to imply that alien elements of the population were not assimilated. As Sandra Barnes has argued for another coastal community, Lagos, although the continuing practice of ethnically specific ancestral cults served at one level to maintain

---

[122] Merlo, 'Hiérarchie fetichiste', 12–13, 26–7.

[123] Ibid., 28; for the Tchamba and Goro cults in coastal towns of Togo and south-eastern Ghana, see Judy Rosenthal, *Possession, Ecstasy and Law in Ewe Voodoo* (Charlottesville, 1998); Tobias Wendl, 'The Tchamba cult among the Mina in Togo', in Heike Behrend & Ute Luig (eds), *Spirit Possession* (Oxford, 1999), 111–23.

[124] Merlo, 'Hiérarchie fétichiste', 28.

[125] Akindélé & Aguessy, *Contribution à l'histoire de Porto-Novo*, 131.

[126] Robin Law, 'Islam in Dahomey', *Scottish Journal of Religious Studies*, 7/2 (1986), esp. 97–106.

[127] Two slaves of the French fort in 1787 were called 'Aly' and 'Boulaly', which may represent the Muslim names Ali and Bilali: ANF, C6/27, case of Joseph Le Beau, interrogation of Dahou, 10 Oct. 1787.

a sense of cultural difference, to the extent that these cults involved public ceremonies in which the generality of the population took part, their operation also served to express the incorporation of foreign elements into the local community.[128]

The heterogeneous character of religious practice in Ouidah involved not only the juxtaposition of cults of different origin, but also a measure of religious syncretism within individual cults. As noted above, most temples in Ouidah venerate a multiplicity of *vodun*, and, while in some cases these are groups of related deities, in others they combine gods that were originally distinct. An example is the thunder-*vodun* So, or Hevioso, whose cult is controlled by the priest of the sea-god Hu, the Hunon, and whose principal shrine is located within the Hunon's compound in Sogbadji. This aggregation of the sea- and thunder-deities was not unique to Ouidah, also occurring in the Dahomian capital Abomey, although there it is Hevioso who is superior in status and Hu subordinate. On the other hand, it does not appear in the form of the *vodun* religious tradition which was transmitted by the slave trade to Haiti, where the sea- and thunder-deities remain distinct, which arguably suggests that the combination occurred in Africa relatively recently, only after the diffusion of these cults to the Caribbean.[129] Whether the combination originated in Ouidah and was diffused from there to Abomey or the borrowing was in the opposite direction is a matter for speculation. Its occurrence in Dahomey is of great interest, since such combinations of originally distinct deities within a single temple are characteristic of other Afro–American religious traditions, such as Brazilian *candomblé*. It is very likely that Dahomian practice provided a precedent and source for such composite cults in Brazil, as argued by Luís Nicolau;[130] although conceivably also the two cases may represent parallel but independent responses to a similar situation of demographic heterogeneity bringing together different religious traditions within a single community and even within individual households.

It is difficult to test the traditional account of Ouidah religion against contemporary sources of the pre-colonial period, that are generally not very illuminating on the religious life of the town. The one element that attracted regular notice and commentary was the cult of the 'snake-god' Dangbe, described by virtually every European visitor to Ouidah. This was generally recognized as deriving from pre-Dahomian days, although Dangbe's shrine in Ouidah, in the main square across from the residence of the Yovogan, was a new foundation. Tradition recalls that there was originally one sacred python regarded as chief of the others, called Ahwanba, who however became 'invisible' during the colonial period; nineteenth-century sources confirm that this chief serpent then still existed and was paraded on ceremonial occasions.[131] Dangbe was the most popular,

---

[128] Sandra Barnes, 'The organization of cultural diversity in pre-colonial coastal communities of West Africa', paper presented at the Annual Meeting of the African Studies Association, 1991.

[129] Guérin Montilus, *Dieux en diaspora: Les loa haïtiens et les vaudou du royaume d'Allada* (Niamey, 1988), 84–5.

[130] Luís Nicolau Parés, 'Transformations of the sea and thunder voduns in the Gbe-speaking area and the Bahian Jeje Candomblé', in José Curto & Renée Soulodre-La France (eds), *Africa in the Americas: Interconnections during the Slave Trade* (New Brunswick, N.J., 2003).

[131] Merlo, 'Hiérarchie fétichiste', 10; Bouche, *Sept Ans*, 395–6.

although not the highest-ranking, *vodun* in Ouidah; Burton in the 1860s estimated that he had 1,000 initiated followers, or 'wives' (a term applied to male as well as female devotees), whereas the formally senior sea-god Hu had only 500.[132] The map of 1776 shows the location of a number of 'fetish' shrines, although without specifying the *vodun* worshipped. Within the town, one shrine specified as the 'fetish of the Yovogan' is clearly, from its location, immediately south of the Yovogan's palace, that of Dangbe. Two others are distinguished as belonging to the English and French forts. Another eighteenth-century source names the cult house situated within the grounds of the English fort as that of 'Nabbakou, the titular god of the place', while a nineteenth-century account refers to a shrine of 'the King's fetish *mawoo*', located in 'the back yard of the fort'.[133] These names represent Nana-Buruku and Mawu, both forms of the supreme creator-deity, the former conventionally regarded as parent to the latter, and the reference is clearly to the Mawu cult practised in Sogbadji quarter, as mentioned earlier. The 'fetish' of the French fort probably alludes to some 'sacred trees' near the fort, which are mentioned in another eighteenth-century source, and may be identified with *Huntin* (silk-cotton) trees still visible at the site, although no longer the object of any active cult.[134] Other shrines are shown on the 1776 map outside the built-up area of the town; one of these, towards the south-west, corresponds at least roughly in its location to the oldest shrine of the sea-god Hu, in what is nowadays Maro quarter. Otherwise, there are only fragmentary references, and few even of these before the nineteenth century. An account of 1776 refers to the god of thunder, i.e. Hevioso, and more vaguely the veneration of trees and rivers; the god of smallpox (Hwesi or Sakpata) is mentioned incidentally in the records of the English fort in 1812; and the founder-hero Kpase is mentioned for the first time in the 1840s.[135] For anything approaching a comprehensive account we have to wait until the 1860s, in the account of Burton, although even this is not very clear in distinguishing religious practice at Ouidah and elsewhere in Dahomey. This provides, for example, the earliest clear allusion to the generic serpent-deity Dan, as distinct from Dangbe, and his particular form as the rainbow, Aïdohuedo, and the first references of any sort to the Nesuhwe cult (although with reference to the capital Abomey, rather than Ouidah), and to more purely local Ouidah deities such as Kpate and Aïzan.[136]

The principal public festivals for *vodun* took place at the beginning of the year, following the ancestral rites of the *huetanu* (and after the public version of these, celebrated at the capital Abomey for deceased kings, known to Europeans as the 'Annual Customs'); Burton referred to the 'Whydah fetish fêtes' as taking place 'in December and January'.[137] These festivities began with sacrifices at the shrine of

[132] Burton, *Mission*, ii, 139, 141.

[133] Norris, *Memoirs*, 42; WMMS, Joseph Dawson, Ouidah, 4 Jan. 1865.

[134] ANF, C6/27, Gourg, 'Mémoire pour servir d'instruction au Directeur', 1791; cf. Justin Fakambi, *La Route des esclaves au Bénin* (Cotonou, n.d. [1992]), 17–18.

[135] De Chenevert & Bullet, 'Réflexions', 14, 74; PRO, T70/1163, Day Book, William's Fort, Jan.–Feb. 1812 (recording payments to 'the fetishmen as usual making their Grand Custom for the smallpox and other diseases'); for Kpase, see Brue, 'Voyage', 55.

[136] Burton, *Mission*, ii, 135–48.

[137] Ibid., i, 88.

Kpate, whose precedence is traditionally explained as due to his role as the initiator of trade with the Europeans and thereby in the introduction of imported brandy, which is regularly used in the rites for other gods. The main ceremonies were processions called *gozin* ('water jars'), so named because they involved the collection of water in jars from sacred rivers near the town. Recent tradition recalls that these involved public rites for four deities - Dangbe, Hu, Kpase and Zo, although when they were revived, after many years of neglect, in 1948, only processions for Dangbe and Hu were conducted.[138] No contemporary source records these ceremonies in full, but there are occasional allusions. Annual processions for Dangbe were held in the Hueda kingdom, at the capital Savi, prior to the Dahomian conquest, and these were evidently now transposed to Ouidah, although perhaps in an attenuated form. European observers under Dahomian rule noted the performance of an annual procession by Dangbe devotees to collect water from the lagoon to the south, referring evidently to the *gozin* ceremony in January.[139] Tradition in Ouidah recalls that there were also formerly two other public ceremonies for Dangbe, which were 'suppressed' under French rule: one called *adi mime* ('ordeal by burning'), in which persons who had offended the deity were confined in a hut, which was set on fire, and the offenders were pursued and stoned in their flight from there to the sacred river south of the town; and another when the senior sacred python Ahwanba was carried around the town in a hammock, during which members of the general public had to remain indoors and Dangbe's devotees could seize any animals found in the streets.[140] These ceremonies are also attested (although evidently not fully understood) in accounts of the pre-colonial period. Duncan, for example, in May 1845 witnessed a case of persons accused of killing sacred snakes being required to run the gauntlet from a burning hut to 'the nearest running water', although he interpreted this as an ad hoc punishment rather than an annual ceremony; and he was also told that this would be followed 13 days later by a day during which all dogs, pigs and fowl found in the streets were killed and eaten, alluding evidently to the ceremonial parading of Ahwanba, but which he understood to be a 'custom or holiday ... for the deceased snakes'; and Forbes in May 1850 reported a ceremony performed overnight, when Europeans were told that they and their servants should not go out or even look out of the window, again clearly Ahwanba's annual outing. The latter ceremony, however, seems to have been in decline already in the nineteenth century: Catholic missionaries in the 1860s heard that the parading of the sacred python, although an annual event in earlier times, was now held only 'every three years', one instance of its celebration being in 1868.[141]

The ceremony for Hu as revived in 1948 also involved a procession to collect water from a river south of the town. Tradition also recalls a distinct ceremony called *huta yiyi*, 'going to the beach', when water was collected from the sea itself, which is said to have been performed originally every seven years (although much

[138] Agbo, *Histoire*, 132; with description of the 1948 ceremonies, 133–6, 138–43.
[139] Pruneau, *Description*, 196–7; Bouche, *Sept ans*, 394–6.
[140] Agbo, *Histoire*, 136–8.
[141] Duncan, *Travels*, i, 195–7; Forbes, *Dahomey*, ii, 4; Bouche, *Sept ans*, 391–3, 395.

less frequently in the twentieth century);[142] it is the latter which was revived and elaborated in the 1990s as the principal festival of *vodun*, now held annually. Pre-colonial accounts do not clearly make this distinction, and this suggests that the nature of the ceremonies has changed over time. An eighteenth-century source refers to an annual festival for the god of sea, to attract European commerce to Ouidah, which involved rites at the beach, where two human sacrifices were thrown into the sea. Burton in the 1860s, however, describes the priest of Hu as processing to the sea to offer sacrifices 'at stated times' (perhaps implying that this ceremony was no longer performed every year), and specifies the offerings made as 'rice and corn, oil and beans, cloth, cowries, and other valuables', with no mention of human sacrifices.[143] Additionally, King Gezo (1818–58) instituted a 'custom' at the capital Abomey, known to Europeans as 'firing to Ouidah', which involved soldiers stationed at intervals along the road south to Ouidah beach firing muskets in succession (and back again), and it appears that this was also connected with the worship of the sea; at least, one observer understood that it involved 'some cere-mony about a bottle of sea water, going to the King'.[144]

Some of the *vodun* cults maintained establishments (nowadays called 'convents') in which devotees, especially young girls, were required to spend several months receiving ritual instruction.[145] The system served both as a source of income for the priesthood, since the girls were released back to their families only upon payment of a fee, and to secure control of their labour during their confinement. European sources generally describe this practice in relation to the cult of Dangbe. In Hueda before the Dahomian conquest, Dangbe's devotees used to range the streets of Savi overnight to seize girls from their homes for the cult's convents; but Burton reported that such 'excesses' were no longer practised under Dahomian rule.[146]

One striking feature of accounts of religious practice in pre-colonial Ouidah is a silence: the lack of reference to masquerades associated with 'secret societies'. Such masquerades were prominently visible in other coastal towns in the region, where they played a significant political as well as religious role: notably Zangbeto in Porto-Novo and Badagry, which patrolled the streets against thieves at night.[147] Zangbeto has existed in Ouidah in recent times, but is almost certainly a recent importation.[148] Likewise Egungun, a masquerade representing spirits of the dead (and known in Fon as Kutito, 'ghosts'), which is of Yoruba origin and is practised by persons of Yoruba descent in Ouidah, is probably of recent emergence; another Yoruba masquerade, Gelede, is explicitly said to have been initiated in Ouidah only

---

[142] Sinou & Agbo, *Ouidah*, 77, described on the basis of ceremonies performed in 1987.

[143] Pruneau, *Description*, 199; Burton, *Mission*, ii, 141.

[144] PRO, FO84/886, Fraser, Daily memoranda, 10 Nov. 1851. Forbes also understood that the firing to Ouidah was 'a salute to the Fetish of the Great Waters, or God of Foreign Trade': Forbes, *Dahomey*, i, 18.

[145] E.g. Adams, *Remarks*, 70–4; Burton, *Mission*, ii, 151–3.

[146] Bosman, *Description*, 371–2; Burton, *Mission*, i, 99.

[147] B.F. Houssou, 'Histoire et civilisation: le Zangbeto à Xogbonu (Porto-Novo) des origines à nos jours' (Mémoire de maîtrise, UNB, 1985); Adefioye Oyesakin, 'Preliminary notes on Zangbeto: the masked vigi-lante group among the Ogu in Badagry', in G.O. Ogunremi et al. (eds), *Badagry* (Ibadan, 1994), 165–73; Sorensen-Gilmour, 'Badagry', 123–5.

[148] Described by Herskovits, *Dahomey*, i, 249.

in 1913.[149] The Dahomian monarchy appears to have forbidden such masquerades, presumably because they represented an independent source of power that might threaten royal authority.[150] The night-watch in Ouidah, as noted later, was maintained instead by the central authorities, by soldiers of the local garrison. Also notable is the absence of any institutionalized system for the detection and execution of witches, such as existed for example in Badagry.[151] It is not that witchcraft or sorcery (the distinction is not clearly made in local usage, which refers unspecifically to 'black magic', *aze*) was not a cause of concern, but it was countered by individual investment in apotropaic charms, rather than by collective action. This too may reflect the concern of the Dahomian monarchy to suppress institutions that might form the basis of an autonomous power. At the same time, the social function of witchcraft accusations in expressing commercial and political competition, as suggested for other coastal trading communities such as Old Calabar,[152] was filled in Dahomey by the mechanism of denunciation to the king.

The religious system of Ouidah reflected not only the historical origins of its heterogeneous population, but also the particular character of its urban way of life. This is most obvious in the prominence of the sea-deities, which reflected the importance of maritime commerce (and lagoon fishing) in the local economy. More generally, the Dan cults are associated with wealth, and thus appropriate to a commercial centre. This applied especially to the rainbow-serpent Aïdohuedo, who is linked with the 'Popo' (or 'aggrey') beads regarded as symbolic of wealth (and thought to derive from the serpent's excrement): as Burton noted, he 'makes the Popo beads and confers wealth upon man'.[153] It has also been suggested that the prevalence of *bocyo* charms in Dahomey reflects a state of insecurity and disempowerment created by the Atlantic slave trade.[154] However, it is not clear that this analysis could apply to Ouidah, whose inhabitants were beneficiaries rather than victims of the slave trade; although certainly not exempt from the threat of enslavement and sale overseas (in judicial punishment), they were less vulnerable to it than the populations in the interior that were the victims of Dahomian raids. Feelings of insecurity in Ouidah might have derived from the perceived arbitrary nature of the Dahomian state and the undependability of preferment received from it, or perhaps from the uncertainties of the market economy in general, rather than from the slave trade in particular.

The provision of religious, as well as other services in Ouidah was partially commercialized, or at least monetized. Begging for cowries, in return for benedictions, was a feature of religious festivals and merchants entering the town were expected to make donations at shrines which clustered for this purpose close to the royal

---

[149] Fall et al., 'Typologie', 80–81 (for Egungun); Joseph Adandé, 'Le *gelede* à Ouidah: mieux vaut tard que jamais', in Alexis Adandé (ed.), *Ouidah à travers ses fêtes et patrimoines familiaux* (Cotonou, 1995), 65–82.

[150] Bay, *Wives of the Leopard*, 24.

[151] Sorensen-Gilmour, 'Badagry', 130–4.

[152] A.J.H. Latham, 'Witchcraft accusations and economic tension in pre-colonial Old Calabar', *JAH*, 13 (1972), 249–60.

[153] Burton, *Mission*, ii, 148.

[154] Blier, *African Vodun*, ch. 1, 'Vodun art, social history and the slave trade'.

customs-posts.[155] Such religious mendicancy did not serve for the relief of poverty but to enrich the priesthood; as Forbes observed, 'they who are initiated have great power, and exact much in return', citing a proverb that 'the poor are not initiated'.[156] The practice of seizing girls for *vodun* 'convents' was even conceptually assimilated to the slave trade, their redemption by their families being referred to as 'selling slaves' (*kannumonsisa*).[157]

The highly syncretistic religious system of Dahomian Ouidah did not grow up altogether haphazardly, but reflected in some measure the policy of the Dahomian state. Tradition recalls that the Dahomian kings pursued a systematic policy, when conquests were made, of 'purchasing' the local religious cults, among specific instances cited being those of Dangbe, purchased by Agaja after his conquest of Hueda, and Hu, acquired subsequently by Tegbesu.[158] Although this policy is explained as a means of securing the support of the *vodun* appropriated, presumably it also served to secure the allegiance of their human followers. This aspect of the matter was explicitly perceived by contemporary European observers, one of whom in the 1770s attributed Dahomey's success in reconciling and assimilating conquered peoples to Agaja's policy of 'tolerating his new subjects with the free exercise of their various superstitions', referring specifically to the cult of Dangbe at Ouidah: 'The remnant of the Whydahs who had escaped the edge of [Agaja's] sword were abundantly thankful to him, for permitting them to continue in the enjoyment of their snake-worship.'[159]

The Dahomian authorities also intervened to regulate and modify the local hierarchy of deities. They did not seek, however, to promote a uniform Dahomian pantheon but adjusted their policies to the local situation. In Ouidah, as noted earlier, they recognized the seniority of the existing deities Hu, Dangbe, Hwesi and Zo, and the primacy of Hu among these four. Other cults, including those introduced under Dahomian rule, were assigned to the authority of their priests, each of whom 'had a jurisdiction given by Abomey over other fetishes';[160] for example, Mawu in Ouidah fell under the authority of the Hunon and Mase under that of the Zonon. Religious activity was also subject to day-to-day regulation. In 1897 it was recalled that 'during the Dahomian occupation, the fetishers were placed under an active supervision of the king's agents'; after the French takeover these restraints were removed, and the 'fetishers' were initially able to perpetrate serious abuses on the population, including 'arrests, confiscations, rapes', this last referring probably to the seizure of girls for *vodun* 'convents'.[161] According to tradition, supervision of religious cults in Dahomey was among the functions of the Ajaho, a senior official of the royal palace (head of the king's eunuchs); in Ouidah, this is confirmed by a contemporary reference, in 1810, to a visit by the Ajaho to

[155] Forbes, *Dahomey*, ii, 4; Burton, *Mission*, i, 65.
[156] Forbes, *Dahomey*, i, 32.
[157] Herskovits, *Dahomey*, ii, 180.
[158] Le Herissé, *L'Ancien Royaume*, 102–3, 110, 243.
[159] Norris, *Memoirs*, 2, 105 n.
[160] Merlo, 'Hiérarchie fétichiste', 4.
[161] ANB, 1E14/6₁, Rapport politique du mois d'août 1897, Ouidah.

'superintend' a religious ceremony.[162] The principal cults also received royal patronage. In the 1770s it was noted that the king provided clothing for two leading *vodunnon* (priests) in Ouidah (presumably those of Hu and Dangbe), and allowed them the sum of 80 *livres* (i.e. 32,000 cowries) for each European ship that traded there.[163] Tradition recalls that the king also 'authorized' the sacrifice annually of a bull to Hu and to Hwesi; and Burton confirms that the temple of Dangbe was visited annually, after the 'Annual Customs' at Abomey, by the Yovogan, who gave a bullock and other animals to the priest, who in return offered prayers 'for the King, the country, and the crops'.[164] Burton also reported that the king 'at times' sent a human sacrifice to Hu, who was taken out in a canoe and thrown into the sea; one such occasion specifically recorded was in 1860, as part of the funeral ceremonies for Gezo.[165]

The European presence in Ouidah compounded the town's religious pluralism by introducing the '*vodun* of the whites', in the form of Christianity; the French and Portuguese forts normally included a Roman Catholic priest among their personnel, although the Protestant English did not maintain any religious establishment. These priests, however, existed to serve the European community, rather than making any attempt to evangelize local people. In the nineteenth century, when the chapel within the Portuguese fort alone remained functional as a centre of Christian worship, the kings of Dahomey recognized Christianity along with the African cults, transmitting through the Yovogan a gift of oil and rum to the chapel every year on the feast of St John the Baptist (patron of the fort), 24 June, but there is no documentation of this practice in the eighteenth century.[166]

Administration

Within Dahomey, responsibility for administration, under the king, was shared by the two principal 'chiefs', the Migan (or, in eighteenth-century sources, 'Temigan') and the Mehu. Of these, it was the Migan who was senior in status and consequently usually referred to by Europeans as the 'prime minister'. The Mehu, however, had responsibility for finance and commerce, and it was therefore he who was primarily concerned with matters relating to European trade and hence with Ouidah. This was reflected in arrangements for provincial administration. Tradition recalls that Tegbesu divided responsibility for the newly conquered territories to the south between the Migan and the Mehu, giving the former charge of the former kingdom of Allada and the latter of Hueda; and this arrangement is confirmed by an account of the 1770s, which describes the provincial governor of Allada, the Aplogan, as the 'second' of the Migan, and the Yovogan of Ouidah as

---

[162] Maurice Ahanhanzo Glélé, *Le Danxome* (Paris, 1974), 75; PRO, T70/1163, Day Book, William's Fort, 5 June 1810.

[163] De Chenevert & Bullet, 'Réflexions', 75.

[164] Merlo, 'Hiérarchie fétichiste', 6, 19; Burton, *Mission*, i, 99.

[165] Burton, *Mission*, ii, 141; WMMS, Bernasko, Ouidah, 29 Nov. 1860.

[166] Borghero, 'Relation', in *Journal*, 257; Burton, *Mission*, i, 63.

'second' of the Mehu.[167] The Yovogan was not only responsible to, but actually appointed by the Mehu, subject to confirmation by the king.[168] Europeans sometimes described the Yovogan as the third person in the kingdom (under the king), ranking immediately after the Migan and Mehu;[169] but this must be a misunderstanding, due to the fact that the Yovogan was the official with whom Europeans dealt, since logically the Aplogan, as the 'second' to the Migan, would rank third, and the Yovogan only fourth.

No Dahomian king (with the possible exception of Agaja, in the original conquest) ever visited Ouidah; indeed, Europeans understood that the king was forbidden by a religious taboo from seeing the sea.[170] Even visits by the Mehu were infrequent. The records of the English fort in the second half of the eighteenth century mention only six occasions when the Mehu came to Ouidah: in 1756, to install a new Yovogan; in 1770 to aid against attack from Little Popo; in 1772, to negotiate peace with Popo; in 1778, to transmit a complaint from the king about the lack of ships coming to trade; and in 1780 and 1784, on business unspecified.[171] Day-to-day administration was therefore left to the locally resident viceroy, the Yovogan. As seen in the last chapter, a 'viceroy' for Ouidah was first appointed by Agaja in 1733, but the indigenous title of the first three incumbents, down to 1745, was Tegan. The last of these was killed in a rebellion against Tegbesu, a circumstance that probably accounts for the suppression of the title. The title of Yovogan is first recorded as held by this man's successor, appointed apparently in late 1745; it remained standard thereafter, except that that of Tegan was revived for one very short-lived viceroy, during 1755.[172]

Local tradition records the name of the first Yovogan as Dasu (Dassou); since this man is said to have been appointed by Tegbesu, this must refer not to the first viceroy appointed, with the title Tegan, in 1733, but to the first to hold the specific title of Yovogan, who held office in 1745–55. Tradition recalls the names of only four subsequent Yovogan who held office prior to the accession of Gezo in 1818: Gbédélé, Sékplon, Basso and Adjossogbé, of whom the last is to be identified with the Yovogan whose death was noted in a contemporary report in 1823. However, it is explicit that this is not a complete list but records only those who held office for a significant length of time.[173] Contemporary sources show that a much larger number of persons held the title of Yovogan (or, as noted above, in one case, Tegan):

[167] Le Herissé, *L'Ancien Royaume*, 40–41; de Chenevert & Bullet, 'Réflexions', 52.

[168] Vallon, 'Le royaume de Dahomey', 1/355; Burton, *Mission*, i, 100.

[169] M'Leod, *Voyage*, 41; Burton, *Mission*, i, 100, 225–6.

[170] Pruneau, *Description*, 161; Béraud, 'Note sur le Dahomé', 377.

[171] PRO, T70/1158, 1160–62, Day Book, William's Fort, May–June 1756, 17 Aug. 1772, 13 July 1772, 12 Nov. 1778, 12 Dec. 1780, 12 Sept. 1784.

[172] This man held office for only a few months: PRO, T70/1158, Day Book, William's Fort, March–April & May–June 1755, referring to 'the new Tegan or Viceroy, the King having killed the old Eubegah [Yovogan] or Viceroy'; but shortly afterwards to 'the new Eubegah or Viceroy, the King having killed the Tegan'.

[173] Reynier, 'Ouidah', 51; *RGCG*, 11 Feb. 1823. Comparison with contemporary records (summarized later in this chapter) suggest that Gbédélé and Sékplon might be identified with the Yovogan who held office in 1761–8 and 1771–6, both of whom exceptionally died in office of natural causes; while Basso may be the Yovogan appointed in 1784.

no fewer than 13 down to the 1780s, many of whom held office only very briefly. However, they record the names of only two of these: 'Bocco Bambia', who held office briefly in 1755, and 'Honnou', serving in 1761–8, and neither of these are recalled in the traditions.[174]

The Yovogan administered Ouidah in conjunction with subordinate officials, the senior among whom formed a sort of governing council: one European observer described the town as governed by a 'senate'.[175] From the 1740s, the administrative structure was elaborated through the creation of further offices, a process that by implication involved the separation of functions earlier combined in the hands of the viceroy. This policy may have been a response to the rebellion of the third Tegan in 1745, which illustrated the danger of allowing too much power to be exercised by a single person. Around the beginning of 1746, perhaps as part of the reconstruction of the administration in the aftermath of this rebellion, Tegbesu carried out a purge of existing merchants at Ouidah and reorganized the conduct of trade there. This important event is best described in the words of a contemporary European report:

> The King of the Dahomets has had all the black merchants left here with whom anything could be done beheaded, firstly to seize their effects, and in second place in order to do all the trade himself, through the medium of Temigan and Mehou, his two principal ministers, who each have two or three boys here, through whose hands everything passes, and who do not dare to devote themselves to their own account, in fear of suffering the same fate as those who were trading before them, so that the result of all this is that, apart from Temigan's and Mehou's people, who alone do the trade, there remains only a troop of thieves and brigands, who live only from plunder, and nibble at us every day ... in short if you have goods to sell, you must give them at the price they wish, or else resolve to keep them, since you can no longer sell except to his merchants alone.[176]

The precise significance of this reorganization is open to debate. Akinjogbin suggested that those executed were private merchants who had infringed the king's monopoly of trade;[177] but the wording of the report implies that they were rather royal officials who had engaged in illicit private trade. In either case, Tegbesu's intention to reassert royal monopoly control of trade is clear. The statement that the new traders were appointed by the Migan and Mehu jointly may be a misunderstanding, or alternatively the arrangement was subsequently revised, since by the 1770s the king's traders were understood to be under the authority of the Mehu alone.[178] What is not in doubt is that the group of royal traders created in 1746 remained in place thereafter, into the nineteenth century. An account relating to the 1750s–60s observed that the king of Dahomey maintained four or five traders at Ouidah who sold only his slaves; they were still recognisable in 1850, when

---

[174] PRO, T70/1158, Day Book, William's Fort, May–June 1755; Norris, *Memoirs*, 57. 'Honnou' may in fact represent the honorific title Hunnon, 'master of ships', which was held by at least one later Yovogan (Dagba, in the nineteenth century): Dagba, *La Collectivité familiale*, 38.

[175] Robertson, *Notes*, 261.

[176] ANF, C6/26, Levet, Ouidah, 1 Feb. 1746.

[177] Akinjogbin, *Dahomey*, 127.

[178] De Chenevert & Bullet, 'Réflexions', 8.

Forbes referred to 'six traders or superintendants of trade appointed by the king'.[179]

The membership of this group of royal merchants is only partly known, and evidently changed over time. A French account of the 1770s names two of them, listing the officials at Ouidah who were second and third in rank after the Yovogan as 'Cocq, 1st King's merchant' and 'Bouillon, also King's merchant'.[180] The first of these titles is more commonly given in English sources as 'Coke' or 'Coki'. In the records of the English fort, it is first documented in 1746, when it was probably newly created, and when the Coke is described as 'a King's Councillor and his special trader'; in later references he is called 'first councillor' and 'second caboceer' to the Yovogan.[181] Other contemporary references confirm the Coke's rank as second 'caboceer' of Ouidah;[182] a Portuguese missionary in 1797 named the 'second caboceer' as 'Tuli', but since this source does not mention the Coke, this was perhaps the current Coke's personal name.[183] Consistently with this status, the Coke is reported as deputizing for the Yovogan when the latter was absent from Ouidah;[184] and on at least three occasions, when the Yovogan died or was removed, it was the Coke who was promoted to succeed him.[185] The office of Coke survived into the early nineteenth century, being regularly referred to in the records of the English fort until its abandonment in 1812. It is not documented later, however; when Burton asked after it in the 1860s, he was unable to find it,[186] and it is not recalled in tradition nowadays. It was probably suppressed in a reorganization of commercial administration at Ouidah at the beginning of the reign of Gezo.

The title of the second of the 'king's merchants' is commonly given as 'Bonio' or 'Bunio' in English records. It is first documented in 1755, when a 'new Bonio' was appointed.[187] A later reference confirms his status as 'third caboceer' of Ouidah; and on at least one occasion, when the Coke was executed, the 'Bonio' was promoted to succeed him.[188] In records of the French fort in the 1780s, it is this official who is described as 'second caboceer of Juda', the Coke not being mentioned;[189] the reason for this discrepancy is unclear, although a possible explanation is that the 'Bonio' had now been assigned to deal with the French fort specifically, whereas

---

[179] Pruneau, *Description*, 209; Forbes, *Dahomey*, i, 111.

[180] De Chenevert & Bullet, 'Réflexions', 19.

[181] PRO, T70/704, Sundry Accounts, William's Fort, Jan.–Apr. 1746; T70/1158–9, Day Book, William's Fort, March–April 1755, 27 March 1765.

[182] ANF, C6/26, Cuillié, Ouidah, 1 Aug. 1764 ['Cocq second gouverneur des nègres']; Dalzel, *History*, 194.

[183] Pires, *Viagem*, 30.

[184] E.g. M'Leod, *Voyage*, 68: 'the Coke ... who, in the absence of the Yavougah, was the next caboceer'.

[185] PRO, T70/1160, 6 July 1768, 'Caboceer Cook, now made Eubegah or Viceroy'; T70/1161, 28 Feb. 1771, 'Caboceer Coke who arrived to supercede [sic] his predecessor the Viceroy'. In 1778 the Yovogan was executed on the basis of accusations from his subordinate officers, the Coke and the 'Fooey', and was succeeded by 'one of his accusers', presumably Coke: Dalzel, *History*, 163.

[186] Burton, *Mission*, i, 99 n.

[187] PRO, T70/1158, Day Book, William's Fort, May–June 1755, reporting the arrival of a 'a new Bonio, he being made Cabboceer in the room of Bocco Bambia who is new Viceroy'. Bocco Bambia (evidently a personal name) arrived in earlier in the same year, together with new appointees to the offices of Viceroy and Coke.

[188] PRO, T70/1160, Day Book, 27 March 1765; T70/1158, Day Book, July–Aug. 1757, 'the new Bonio the other being chosen Coke'.

[189] ANF, C6/27, Gourg, 'Mémoire pour servir d'instruction au Directeur', 1791 ['Bourion'].

the Coke continued to handle relations with the English. In another French record it is likewise this officer, rather than the Coke, who is described as 'commanding in the Yovogan's absence', although this may have been because the Coke was also then absent from Ouidah.[190] Unlike that of Coke, the office of 'Bonio' survived through the nineteenth century, being identifiable with the title Boya, recalled in local tradition. Tradition confirms that this office dates from the reign of Tegbesu, but also indicates that its importance was enhanced under Gezo after 1818: 'From the time of King Ghezo a Boya had a tight hand over all the slaves, and was in charge of overseeing embarkation operations.'[191] The implication is that under Gezo the Boya replaced the Coke as the head of the royal traders. The office does not seem to have remained important in the second half of the nineteenth century, but the title was perpetuated in the name of a family descended from the Boya who held office under Gezo, and also of a quarter of the town which this man founded, Boyasaramè, 'Boya's Quarter', of which the family held the hereditary headship.[192]

A third 'king's merchant' is named in records of the French fort in 1789, when he was held responsible for the deportation of the fort's director Gourg and even physically assaulted Gourg in the process of his forcible embarkation, 'Tinion'; and this name also appears (as 'Teneu') in the Portuguese account of 1797, which describes him rather than the Boya as being the 'third caboceer' of Ouidah.[193] An English account names the man who assaulted Gourg as 'Alindehoo'; from comparison with the other reports, this is presumably a miscopying of 'Atindehoo', which is in fact the name of a family that still exists in Ouidah, Atindéhou, descended from a man whom its traditions confirm was 'a former functionary of King Tegbesu, assistant to a Yovogan'.[194] In 1803 one of the 'king's traders' was 'Johatoo', who in this capacity presided over a judicial hearing into allegations against a British merchant, but this name is not otherwise recorded.[195] Another subordinate official in the Ouidah administration documented in the late eighteenth century (first in the 1770s) was 'Fooey', although he is not specifically described as one of the 'king's merchants'.[196]

The others who served as 'king's traders' in this period cannot be identified in the contemporary record, although it is likely that some of them are mentioned in it, among Dahomians named as selling slaves to Europeans, but without being explicitly distinguished as trading for the king. Recent tradition suggests that one of those who served as a 'king's merchant' in the eighteenth century was the founder of the Bahini family, who is said to have been 'a trader on the account of King Agonglo [1789–97]'; but this name is not recorded in contemporary accounts

---

[190] ANF, C6/26, Gourg, Ouidah, 2 Feb. 1789 ['Bouuion']. It appears from Dalzel, *History*, 201, that at this time the Coke, together with the Yovogan, was engaged in a military campaign in the interior. The title is also recorded, in the form 'Boião', in the Portuguese account of 1797, though without any indication of his ranking within the Ouidah administration: Pires, *Viagem*, 30.

[191] Gavoy, 'Note historique', 62, 67.

[192] Reynier, 'Ouidah', 58.

[193] ANF, C6/27, Gourg, 'Mémoire pour servir d'instruction au Directeur', 1791; Pires, *Viagem*, 30.

[194] Dalzel, *History*, 227; Reynier, 'Ouidah', 53.

[195] M'Leod, *Voyage*, 111.

[196] Dalzel, *History*, 158, referring to 'the Coke and Fooey, two subordinate officers'.

before the nineteenth century.[197] In 1850 all six 'traders appointed by the king' are named by Forbes; they still included the Boya, but only two of the other five are identifiable with titles or family names still current: Aklassato and Tokpo, which are the names of two Ouidah families, the first descended from a man who is said to have been an 'assistant' to the first Yovogan appointed by Tegbesu, and the latter from a merchant who settled in Ouidah under Gezo.[198] Forbes elsewhere in his account names Atindéhou and Bahini, but these were evidently no longer counted among the 'king's traders'.[199]

The precise division of responsibilities between the Yovogan and the 'king's traders' is not clearly explained in the sources. The assumption that after 1746 the latter took over responsibility for the conduct of the king's trade, leaving the Yovogan merely as the 'political Governor' of Ouidah, is logical but perhaps over-schematic.[200] The Yovogan as well as the 'king's traders' in fact continued to figure as a supplier of slaves to Europeans, and, although some of this trade may have been done on his personal account, on some occasions he was clearly delivering slaves on the king's behalf.[201] The explanation may be that, although the actual trade was now conducted by the royal traders, slaves belonging to the king might be lodged in the Yovogan's residence while awaiting sale or shipment. The Yovogan also remained responsible for the collection of duties on the export of slaves, the goods received in payment being likewise stored in his residence, prior to being sent up to the capital.[202]

Under the Yovogan, there were junior officials posted to the European forts to collect these duties. Between 1728 and 1733 Agaja had maintained separate 'captains' for the three forts in Ouidah, those originally appointed being 'Ouroakaye' for the English, 'Bagba' for the Portuguese and Alidji ('Alliguy') for the French, but by 1733 Yansu ('Nançou') was serving as English 'captain' and 'Zonglar' for the Portuguese.[203] Although the contemporary account of the appointment of the first Tegan as viceroy of Ouidah in 1733 implies that this office superseded rather than supplemented the separate 'captains' for different European nations, later evidence shows that a form of the latter system was later revived. The records of the English fort in 1747 refer to an 'English Cabboceer', who assisted in securing the release of

---

[197] Reynier, 'Ouidah', 49.

[198] Ibid., 55. Forbes gives these names as 'Boh-ee-ah', 'Oh-klah-foh-to' [presumably miscopied for 'Oh-klah-soh-toh'], 'Toh-poh'; the other three, which are not identifiable or attested in any other source, are 'Ah-boo-veh-mah', 'Goo-vah-moo' and 'Ah-hah-doh-moh-toh'.

[199] Atindéhou is mentioned in 1849 as 'caboceer' for Fonsaramè quarter (discussed below). 'Baa-hee-nee' is listed, following the Yovogan and other Ouidah dignitaries, among recipients of royal bounty at the Annual Customs in 1850: Forbes, *Dahomey*, ii, 246.

[200] Robin Law, 'Royal monopoly and private enterprise in the Atlantic trade: the case of Dahomey', *JAH*, 18 (1977), 563–4; Law, *Slave Coast*, 337.

[201] See, most explicitly, dos Santos correspondence, nos 43, 52, 59 [28 Dec. 1846; 19 Feb. & 13 April 1847], recording 30 slaves bought from the king, for which payment was made to the Yovogan, and which were collected from the Yovogan's house.

[202] As noted in the 1840s: Duncan, *Travels*, i, 123–4.

[203] ANF, C6/25, Delisle, Dahomey, 7 Sept. 1728; Levet, Ouidah, 26 Aug. 1733. These appear to be titles rather than personal names (as assumed by Akinjogbin, *Dahomey*, 101, n.2), since after the first Alidji was executed in 1732 his successor was also so called.

British citizens taken prisoner by the Dahomian army; moreover, this man had the same name or title, Yansu, as the one who had served as 'captain' of the English prior to 1733, though whether this means he was the same man (or perhaps his son) or merely the successor to his title is a matter for speculation.[204] In the mid-nineteenth century, the position of 'caboceer of the British fort' was held by Hechili, which is the name of a family that formerly lived in Fonsaramè quarter; its traditions claim that its founder was an official in Ouidah from the time of the original conquest under Agaja, even before the appointment of the first Yovogan, but if so the functions attached to the title evidently changed over time.[205]

Some information on the other 'national' officials in the mid-nineteenth century is given by Forbes, who listed the 'caboceers' who had 'superintendence' over various quarters of Ouidah: in addition to Hechili for 'English Town' (Sogbadji), he understood that Ahouandjigo ('French Town') was under the Yovogan, Docomè ('Portuguese Town') under Boya, de Souza's Brazil quarter ('Chacha Town') under Noudofinin, 'Viceroy's Town' (Fonsaramè) under Atindéhou, and 'Market Town' (i.e. Zobé market) under 'Ah-poo-dehnoo'.[206] Although his wording implies that these were administrative heads of these quarters, this must represent either imprecision or misunderstanding on Forbes's part; more probably, they were intermediaries between these quarters and the central authorities. The statement that the French fort was directly under the Yovogan is perhaps also a misunderstanding, since all such officials would be under the overall authority of the Yovogan. Forbes does not convey a clear impression of the functions of these officials. An obvious inference is that they collected duties on trade conducted at the particular factories assigned to them (or, in the case of 'Ah-poo-dehnoo', on transactions in the market); and tradition in Ouidah does recall the existence of a group of officials with this function, who had the title *ganhonto*, 'chiefs at the gates [i.e. of the factories]'.[207] However, whereas the traditions imply that the *ganhonto* were distinct from those who conducted the king's trade, Forbes understood that it was in fact the king's traders who collected taxes on trade: 'one or the other of these must be present at all sales to take the royal duty'.[208] The Boya, listed as 'caboceer' for Docomè, was indeed currently also head of the king's traders, but otherwise the names do not correspond with those in Forbes's own listing of the latter, although an earlier Atindéhou had been one of the 'king's traders' in the 1780s. Of the others, Noudofinin is the name of a family in Brazil quarter; its traditions confirm the founder's role as an agent in royal tax collection, claiming that his name

---

[204] PRO, T70/423, Sundry Accounts, William's Fort, May–Aug. 1747 ['Lansue'].

[205] PP, Slave Trade 1850–51, Class A, enc.2 in no. 220, Forbes, Journal, 29 May 1850; PRO, FO84/886, Fraser, Daily memoranda, 8 Nov. 1852 etc. ['Heecheelee', 'At-chil-lee']; Reynier, 'Ouidah', 48. Current tradition in the Hechili family does not recall any connection specifically with the English fort: fieldwork, 13 June 1997.

[206] PP, Slave Trade 1849–50, Forbes, Journal, 7 Oct. 1849; Forbes, *Dahomey*, i, 105, giving the first 4 names as 'Schecheeler/Hie-chee-lee', 'Borgnon/Boognon', 'Gnodeferch', 'Ahtinderhood [= Ahtinderhooh]'. The post of 'governor' of Sogbadji was later held by 'Nyonun' but was vacant by 1863: Burton, *Mission*, i, 64–5.

[207] Paul Marty, 'Etudes sur l'Islam au Dahomey, Livre 1: Le Bas Dahomey', 2 parts, *Revue du monde musulman*, 61 (1926), 2/100. Note also that although the name/title 'Ahpoodehnoo' is not identified, it clearly includes the term *denu*, 'customs house'.

[208] Forbes, *Dahomey*, i, 111.

(explained as meaning 'There is something there!') records his services to Gezo in uncovering wealth concealed from royal attention, although the story is told in relation to the levying of inheritance tax on the Adjovi family of Tové rather than with reference to Brazil quarter.[209] It must be admitted that contemporary accounts give an impression of imprecision and confusion in the division of responsibilities among various officials of the Ouidah administration. This may not be due merely to imperfect understanding on the part of European observers, since it is very likely that both the overlapping of functions and their recurrent redefinition represented a deliberate policy of the Dahomian monarchy, designed to prevent excessive concentration of power in any single official.

Alongside these 'caboceers' of the various European nations, there were also officials who served as interpreters. The English fort records of 1747 refer, in addition to the 'English caboceer' Yansu, to a second 'caboceer' called 'Adomo'. This man seems likely to be identical with a 'Captain Tom', alias 'Adomo Tomo', who had been employed in the English factory at Jakin, but was taken captive by the Dahomians at their conquest of Allada in 1724 and subsequently served as interpreter to a Dahomian embassy to England in 1731-2; probably therefore in 1747 he was also serving as interpreter.[210] Later, the post of official English interpreter was held by a man called Gnahoui, who according to family tradition learned English in Ouidah, and 'was designated by the King of Abomey to accompany the Englishmen who went up to the royal residence, and served as interpreter'; the death of this man, 'Yowee, the king's linguist', was reported in 1823.[211] His son inherited the position and is recorded as serving as interpreter to various British missions to Dahomey in the 1840s and 1850s: as Forbes explained, 'This man's father was a servant in the British fort at Whydah [sic: though he was actually rather a Dahomian official, who dealt with the fort], and his son by birthright has his place.'[212] The Gnahoui family is nowadays resident in Fonsaramè but may originally have lived in Sogbadji; at least, the younger Gnahoui in 1843 was understood by a British visitor whom he served as interpreter to be a 'native' of 'the English town'.[213] Likewise, in records of the French fort in the 1780s, reference is made to a person called 'Baupé', who was 'French interpreter for the Dahomians'; this name evidently represents Bokpé, which is that of a family in Ahouandjigo whose traditions confirm that it served the kings of Dahomey as interpreters in French.[214]

Not much is known of the system of appointment to the Ouidah administration. The office of Yovogan was clearly a non-hereditary appointment, as well as being a very insecure one (with the great majority of incumbents down to the 1770s dismissed from office, and most of these executed, as noted hereafter). The Tegan

---

[209] Reynier, 'Ouidah', 42.

[210] Robin Law, 'King Agaja of Dahomey, the Slave Trade, and the question of West African plantations: the mission of Bulfinch Lambe and Adomo Tomo to England, 1726–32', *Journal of Imperial and Commonwealth History*, 19 (1991), 137–63.

[211] Reynier, 'Ouidah', 51; *RGCG*, 11 Feb. 1823.

[212] Forbes, *Dahomey*, i, 53; ii, 175.

[213] T.B. Freeman, *Journal of Various Visits to the Kingdoms of Ashanti, Aku and Dahomi* (London, 1844), 250.

[214] ANF, C6/27, Gourg, 'Mémoire pour servir d'instruction au Directeur', 1791; Reynier, 'Ouidah', 33–4.

of 1743–5 was a eunuch of the royal palace, in origin a captive taken by the Dahomian army, but this was probably exceptional.[215] Contrariwise, the Yovogan appointed in 1823, called Dagba, was a member of the Dahomian aristocracy, but this also was probably a new departure. What is clear is that Dahomian officials in Ouidah were regularly appointed from outside the town, rather than from local families. Forbes in 1850 observed the bodies of two recently deceased 'caboceers', from Ouidah and Godomey, being taken up to Abomey, and commented that 'it is the custom of Dahomey that all the bodies of officers that die shall be sent for interment to Abomey', explaining that 'the official positions are mostly held by Abomey people, and all have ancestral houses in the city, in which there is invariably a family tomb'. In Ouidah, even Dagba, who held office as Yovogan for the unprecedented term of around 50 years, and founded a family that still exists in the town, was buried in his ancestral home in Abomey.[216]

However, it appears, as noted earlier, that appointment to the highest offices in Ouidah was often by promotion from within the local administration, the offices of Yovogan, Coke and Boya forming a sort of promotional ladder, with the Coke succeeding to the office of Yovogan, and the Boya to that of Coke. This implies that one of the qualifications for office was considered to be prior acquaintance with the operation of the European trade. In the late eighteenth century, at least one of those who served as Yovogan was a person of great experience and consequent linguistic competence. The man appointed in 1784 spoke all three European languages in local use, French, English and Portuguese; although convention nevertheless required him to speak to Europeans through an interpreter, he would correct the latter when he mistranslated. Likewise, the Yovogan in office in 1803 (who was possibly the same person) was fluent in English, French and Portuguese, it being explained that this was from his 'having resided from his birth chiefly in the vicinity of the forts, and in his younger days been much connected with them officially, as a linguist'.[217]

Although European observers tended to stress the role of the Yovogan and other officials at Ouidah in the conduct of overseas trade, their functions extended beyond this to the management of the affairs of the town more generally. They included, first, the collection of taxes, especially in the commercial sector of the economy. Taxes were levied, not only on the export trade (as described more fully in the following chapter) but on the movement and exchange of goods more generally. In Zobé and other markets in Ouidah, as described in the nineteenth century, sellers of goods had to pay a duty, which was collected by an officer of the Yovogan. Other collectors were stationed to levy tolls 'on all public roads leading from one district to another, and on the lagoon on each side of Whydah'. Taxes are said to have been 'farmed to collectors', but this probably means only that the officials who collected them were entitled to retain a proportion of what they received as remuneration.[218]

[215] Norris, *Memoirs*, 41, 47.

[216] Forbes, *Dahomey*, ii, 199; Dagba, *La Collectivité familiale*, 51, 54.

[217] Isert, *Letters*, 102–3; M'Leod, *Voyage*, 34–6.

[218] Duncan, *Travels*, i, 120, 122, 124; Forbes, *Dahomey*, i, 35.

But the critical function of government in local conceptions was the administration of justice.[219] The autonomy of the local administration in this respect was, however, severely circumscribed. An early nineteenth-century source reports that the local authorities in Ouidah could settle only 'ordinary disputes', while those 'of greater consequence' were referred to the capital, and even in the case of 'minor affairs' the parties involved could appeal to the 'supreme court' at the capital.[220] Other accounts note more specifically that cases liable to capital punishment had to be referred to the king at the capital.[221] When a British trader in 1772 witnessed the Yovogan superintending the execution of a woman in the market-place of Ouidah, it was explained to him that 'the King himself had considered the offence, and decreed the sentence'.[222] Apart from execution (and sale into slavery), the normal forms of punishment inflicted in Dahomian courts included fines and imprisonment. As noted by Duncan, prisoners were detained in shackles in the Yovogan's house. Although Duncan says that imprisonment was both 'for life, and for limited periods', this is probably a misunderstanding; more probably, incarceration was normally short-term, as a means of enforcing payment of fines.[223] Judicial administration included the arbitration of disputes, as well as the application of criminal justice. Burton, for example, refers to the Ouidah 'dignitaries' as 'settling small cases, such as petty debts and the disobedience of wives and slaves', and to the Yovogan adjudicating financial disputes between foreigners.[224]

Under the Yovogan, the component quarters of the town enjoyed a measure of autonomy. The quarter head, according to a nineteenth-century account, 'judges ordinary affairs, he is in some sense a judge and guardian of the peace'.[225] Presumably, quarter heads were in the first instance responsible for the maintenance of order and the adjudication of disputes within their own quarters, with serious or disputed cases being referred upwards to the Yovogan. Within this system, the directors of the three European forts operated as heads of their respective quarters, responsible to the king for their good behaviour. The directors were evidently treated as Dahomian chiefs; in particular, they were required to attend the 'Annual Customs' at the end of the year, and to bring tribute (or, as they preferred to see it, 'gifts') for the king. During the eighteenth century, European directors were from time to time dismissed, and sometimes even their successors appointed by the king. In the case of the director who served longest, Lionel Abson of the English fort (1770–1803), on his death the king seized his estate, including his children, as was normal for a Dahomian chief.[226]

In Elmina on the Gold Coast it appears that the Dutch enjoyed rights of 'extra-territoriality', the personnel of the Dutch fort being tried and punished by its own

[219] See Law, *Slave Coast*, 89–91.
[220] Robertson, *Notes*, 261, 271–2. See also Forbes, *Dahomey*, i, 26: 'the caboceers, headed by the Eavogan [Yovogan] form a court, of which the decision is subject to royal confirmation'.
[221] Repin, 'Voyage', 102; Burton, *Mission*, i, 100.
[222] Norris, *Memoirs*, 63–4.
[223] Duncan, *Travels*, i, 124.
[224] Burton, *Mission*, i, 54, 211.
[225] Bouche, *Sept ans*, 347.
[226] Akinjogbin, *Dahomey*, 190.

officials rather than the indigenous authorities.[227] But, beyond the fact that the director as ward head would have handled purely internal or minor matters, this does not appear to have been the case in Ouidah. In 1788 a slave of the English fort who burgled the house of one of the king's wives was executed, without any reference to the fort's governor; and in the following year another of the fort's slaves, together with two freemen of Sogbadji ward and one of Docomè, was arrested, for having 'debauched' the wife of one of the Yovogan's officers.[228] In the 1780s a substantial woman trader who acted as agent for the director of the French fort, called Kposi ('Paussie'), was seized and her property confiscated by the Dahomian authorities, on the allegation that she had illicitly dealt in coral, legally a royal monopoly.[229] Even Europeans were clearly subject to local jurisdiction. An interesting case occurred in the 1840s, when one of the Portuguese residents in Ouidah murdered another. The culprit was arrested and taken to Abomey; but the European merchants, fearing that the execution of a white man by the indigenous authorities would set a dangerous precedent, 'bought him off', and he was still at large in Ouidah in 1850. In 1852, when a British trader at Ouidah was arrested and fined by the Yovogan for having accidentally injured a child, the British vice-consul (now occupying the English fort) protested that the matter should have been handled through himself, but the Yovogan brushed this aside, declaring that 'he did not care if I, or any other person was in Whydah, as the English representative, he should continue to imprison and fine Englishmen as he thought fit'.[230]

Ouidah was also the location of a military garrison, commanded by the Caho. At the time of the Hueda-Popo attack on Ouidah in 1763, the local garrison numbered between 800 and 900 troops, but by 1776 this had fallen to around 300, and in the 1860s it was even lower, about 200.[231] The local military forces were divided between two main encampments, the Caho's on the north-west of Ouidah, and a detachment under the Cakanacou, at Zoungbodji on the road to the beach. In the eighteenth century, when the main military threat to Ouidah was represented by the exiled Hueda and Popo, who normally approached by canoe along the lagoon, the principal strength of the garrison was located at Zoungbodji. In the 1770s it was noted that 6 or 7 soldiers were posted at the beach, to oversee the European traders' tents there, while there were 225 in the Cakanacou's camp, as against only about 40 in the Caho's; but the Zoungbodji garrison was probably less substantial in the nineteenth century.[232] According to one account, these 'standing or perma-nent troops' stationed in Ouidah were condemned to this service in punishment for offences, such as adultery.[233] There was also, however, in Ouidah as in Dahomey

[227] Feinberg, *Africans and Europeans*, 32.
[228] PRO, T70/1163, Day Book, William's Fort, 24 Sept. 1788, 2 April 1789.
[229] Dalzel, *History*, 208–10.
[230] Forbes, *Dahomey*, ii, 202–4; PRO, FO84/886, Fraser, Ouidah, 2 March 1852.
[231] Pruneau, *Description*, 224; de Chenevert & Bullet, 'Refléxions', 4; Burton, *Mission*, i, 100. The statement in the second source, that 7–8 years earlier (*c.* 1768/9) the garrison had numbered 8,000–10,000 is improbable; although forces of this size may have been posted to Ouidah temporarily, in response to Hueda–Popo raids.
[232] ANF, C6/27bis, notes to map by Bullet. But Burton's account of Zoungbodji in the 1860s does not register the presence of any substantial military garrison: *Mission*, i, 36–9.
[233] Duncan, *Travels*, i, 140–41.

generally, an obligation of military service, which might be invoked for major campaigns, which in principle fell upon the entire adult male population but in practice normally involved each 'caboceer' supplying a quota of troops; the total military strength which Ouidah could be called upon to supply was reported in the 1850s to be nearly 2,000.[234]

The main function of the Ouidah garrison was defence of the town and the beach to the south against outside threats, especially the raids of the exiled Hueda and Popo down to the 1770s. But the troops were also sometimes employed in offensive operations outside Ouidah. In 1787, for example, a Dahomian raid on Porto-Novo to the east was carried out by the Coke and the Caho from Ouidah, and later in the same year troops from Ouidah joined a force sent down from Abomey in an expedition against the exiled Hueda to the west.[235] In 1890 also, as will be seen in a later chapter, it was the Ouidah forces, commanded by the Caho, who undertook an attack on the French at Cotonou. On other occasions, forces from Ouidah joined the main Dahomian army on more distant campaigns. In 1789, for example, the Yovogan, Coke and Caho were called up from Ouidah for a campaign against Ketu, in the interior to the north-east; and persons from Ouidah also took part in (and were captured in) an attack on Abeokuta, to the east, in 1864.[236] Troops of the Ouidah garrison also carried out police functions within the town, the Caho having charge of the 'constabulary', who maintained a watch during the night.[237]

Under Dahomian rule, Ouidah became a centre of provincial administration in the coastal area. As nineteenth-century sources specify, the Yovogan was governor not only of Ouidah but of 'all the part of Dahomey neighbouring the sea'; and likewise the Caho was commander of 'the war captains of all the maritime regions'.[238] The chief of Savi, the former capital of the Hueda kingdom, was now subordinate to the Yovogan of Ouidah.[239] Ouidah's jurisdiction extended beyond the boundaries of the old Hueda kingdom, to include neighbouring towns that prior to the Dahomian conquest had been belonged to Allada, such as Tori, inland from Savi.[240] On the coast, when Godomey and Cotonou to the east were developed as outlets for Dahomey's trade in the nineteenth century, their chiefs, who also had the title of Yovogan, were likewise subordinate to the Yovogan of Ouidah; as was the lagoonside port of Abomey-Calavi.[241]

In general, Dahomian administration was effective, judged by Europeans to maintain a framework of reasonable order. This is not to deny that there were pervasive problems of theft in the European trade sector, as there had been under the Hueda kings before the Dahomian conquest. The Dahomian authorities after 1727 proclaimed their intention to suppress such abuses: Agaja told a British trader

[234] Vallon, 'Le royaume de Dahomey', 1/344.

[235] Dalzel, *History*, 194, 197.

[236] Ibid., 201; Borghero, *Journal*, 159–61 [21 April 1864].

[237] Burton, *Mission*, i, 55–6.

[238] Béraud, 'Note sur le Dahomé', 378; Burton, *Mission*, i, 32.

[239] Burton, *Mission*, i, 132.

[240] Herskovits, *Dahomey*, ii, 25.

[241] Foà, *Le Dahomey*, 272; Le Herissé, *L'Ancien Royaume*, 42.

that 'I might depend upon it, he would prevent all impositions, and thievery, and protect the Europeans that came to his country'.[242] In 1763, after complaints from the European forts of the theft of goods in transit from the beach, Tegbesu summoned the Yovogan to Abomey to deliver a 'personal reprimand'; and after further complaints, he issued a proclamation at Ouidah that 'whoever stole the value of even a single cowrie the King was determined to punish with death'. The proclamation was repeated in identical terms by Kpengla in 1777, and again in 1781, 'that if any body is detected stealing white men's property they would be killed'.[243] The very frequency of such proclamations implies, however, that they were ineffective. Testimony on this is contradictory. One European merchant in the early nineteenth century observed that 'an existing law to punish theft with death, prevents mischievous acts of that nature ... The Evo Gaw [Yovogan] regulates all grievances complained of, without delay.'[244] But others continued to complain of the theft of goods by porters. Duncan in 1845 thought that the severity of punishment was actually counter-productive, 'the [European] merchants being too humane to urge the king's interference, for they are aware that if he were requested to take cognizance of any case of robbery of a white man, the robber would certainly lose his head'. Burton in the 1860s, however, suggested that Europeans' reluctance to pursue cases of theft in the Yovogan's court was due to the heavy fees payable there and that they preferred rather to 'take their own measures', including private violence.[245]

Even so, a British merchant in the 1860s compared Ouidah favourably with Lagos, recently brought under British rule: 'property, as regards theft, is quite as safe, if not more so, at Whydah' – where, moreover, taxes were lower.[246] As regards more serious crime, European judgements of Ouidah (and of Dahomey more generally) were more uniformly positive. Burton remarked that, despite the prevalence of petty theft, crimes of violence were 'exceedingly rare', murder almost unknown and burglary 'almost impossible', except after a fire.[247] Murders of Europeans were evidently very rare; the killing of a German merchant, on a canoe journey from Ouidah westwards to Popo in 1843, created something of a sensation, the culprits being executed and their bodies exposed at the lagoonside as an example.[248] Likewise tradition in Ouidah recalls that Dahomian administration was effective in 'watching over the security of the people, educating and disciplining them, averting evil spirits and in short repressing evil by punishing very severely evildoers [and] criminals', and in particular in 'habitually inflicting the death penalty on murderers, no attempt was pardoned'.[249] Given the generally negative

[242] Snelgrave, *New Account*, 64.

[243] PRO, T70/1159–61, Day Book, William's Fort, 17, 21 & 28 March, 22 & 27 Nov., 5 Dec. 1763, 18 Nov. 1777, 8 Sept. 1781.

[244] Robertson, *Notes*, 264.

[245] Adams, *Remarks*, 239–40; Duncan, *Travels*, i, 197–8; Burton, *Mission*, i, 211.

[246] PP, Report from the Select Committee on the State of the British Settlements on the Western Coast of Africa, 1865, Minutes of Evidence, § 5458, Capt. James Croft.

[247] Burton, *Mission*, i, 56.

[248] PRO, CO96/12, Hutton, Cape Coast, 17 March 1847; Duncan, *Travels*, i, 113.

[249] Agbo, *Histoire*, 55.

representation of Dahomian rule in local tradition, stressing its oppressive and exploitative character, this seems eloquent testimony in its favour.

The emergence of a private merchant sector

In early scholarly literature on the slave trade in Dahomey, in the 1960s, it was supposed that it was operated as a royal monopoly; but the detailed contemporary evidence shows that this was not so.[250] First, Dahomian chiefs other than the king also engaged in the trade: the English fort in 1782 listed the Migan, the Mehu and the Ajaho, as well as the Yovogan, among persons owing slaves;[251] and other records refer in the 1770s to a 'trading man' of the Yovogan, called Dosugan ('Dosu senior') and in the 1780s to a man called 'Seignion', who was 'merchant' of the Ajaho.[252] But there were also private merchants, outside the Dahomian administrative hierarchy.

The key to understanding the combination of state and private enterprise in the Atlantic trade is the distinction between the sale of Dahomey's own war captives and the middleman trade in slaves brought from the farther interior.[253] The disorders arising from the Dahomian conquest of the coastal area in the 1720s disrupted the supply of slaves from the interior, and for several years afterwards the Dahomian authorities showed no interest in reviving the middleman trade. Tegbesu from the 1740s, however, consciously sought to revive the supply of slaves from the interior, to supplement that derived from Dahomey's own military operations: in 1746 he issued a proclamation declaring 'the paths open and free to all traders' to come to Ouidah, and this policy was reaffirmed in subsequent proclamations notified to Ouidah, for example in 1769 to declare 'the king's intention to open all the paths and for the future to live in amity with all his neighbours'.[254] In principle, the king had a monopoly of the disposal of captives taken by the Dahomian army, which had to be surrendered to him in exchange for payment in cowries at the end of the campaign, although some of these captives were then distributed as gifts from the king to favoured officials and courtiers. But, as Dahomian tradition makes clear, slaves obtained by purchase from neighbouring countries were handled by independent merchants, rather than royal officials.[255] The revival of the middleman trade from the 1740s, therefore, implied the emergence of a private sector in the slave trade at Ouidah.

---

[250] The assumption of a royal monopoly of overseas trade is central, for example, to the analyses of Polanyi, *Dahomey*; Akinjogbin, *Dahomey*; Georg Elwert, *Wirtschaft und Herrschaft von 'Daxome' (Dahomey) im 18 Jahrhundert* (Munich, 1973). For critiques, see Law, 'Royal monopoly'; Werner Peukert, *Der atlantische Sklavenhandel von Dahomey 1740–1797* (Wiesbaden, 1978).

[251] PRO, T70/1545, Lionel Abson, Ouidah, 14 Dec. 1782.

[252] Dalzel, *History*, 162 ['Dossugah']; ANF, C6/26, Interrogatoire de Joseph Le Beau, 8 Sept. 1787.

[253] Robin Law, 'Slave-traders and middlemen, monopolists and free-traders: the supply of slaves for the Atlantic trade in Dahomey, *c*. 1715–*c*. 1850', *JAH*, 20 (1989), 45–68; for a different interpretation, see David Ross, 'The Dahomean middleman system, 1727–*c*. 1818', *JAH*, 28 (1987), 357–75.

[254] PRO, T70/704, Sundry Accounts, William's Fort, Jan–April 1746; T70/1160, Day Book, William's Fort, 23 Nov. 1769.

[255] Le Herissé, *L'Ancien Royaume*, 52–3.

In the contemporary record, the existence of a group of private merchants distinct from the king's official traders was first noted in the account cited earlier relating to the 1750s/60s, which distinguished between the agents whom the king maintained at Ouidah to trade for him and 'the other merchants', who 'sell the captives which are brought to them from several parts of Africa, on commission or for their own account'.[256] It is also clear in an account of an attempt of Kpengla in the 1780s to establish a 'monopoly of trade'. Whether his policy strictly involved a state 'monopoly', in the sense of excluding all private participation in the slave trade, is doubtful. But Kpengla certainly reversed earlier royal policy by himself entering the middleman trade; he decreed fixed prices, below the current market rate, for the purchase of slaves from the interior, and 'himself commenced trader, and began to buy slaves on his own account', setting his agents to buy up slaves for resale at the coast, and when traders proved reluctant to sell at the official price, he resorted to compulsory purchase, decreeing 'that every trader, possessing two slaves, should relinquish one, and the best of them, to him; and if three, two were to be the king's'. These measures provoked fierce opposition from the Dahomian trading community, however, and Kpengla's successor Agonglo, on his accession in 1789, was obliged to repudiate his policy, allowing traders once more 'full liberty to trade'.[257]

There is little evidence on the balance between royal and private enterprise in the slave trade in Dahomey, which probably in any case varied over time. In 1848 when a British mission was attempting to persuade Gezo to accept the abolition of the slave trade, and there was some discussion of payment of compensation for the financial losses that this would involve, the Dahomians supplied an estimate of royal income from the trade that was based on the assumption of 8,000 slaves exported annually (certainly an exaggeration), of which 3,000 were sold by the king; given the context in which it was given, it seems remarkable that the share of trade claimed to be done by the king (37.5 per cent) was so low. In 1850 another British mission was told by the Mehu and the Yovogan that 'if one trade-ship arrived in Whydah, the king claimed half the trade; if three, he monopolised two', which the British understood to imply that 'whatever was offered in subsidy, one half only became the property of the king; the other of the traders'; if their interpretation was correct, contrariwise, it is notable that the share which they claimed for non-royal enterprise (33–50 per cent) was so low.[258] Given these contradictory biases, it may be believed that in the mid-nineteenth century the king's share of trade was somewhere close to a half.

For the eighteenth century, on the face of it, the best evidence for the balance between royal and private enterprise in the slave trade in Dahomey is provided by the accounts of two ships trading there, the French ship *Le Dahomet* in 1773 and the English ship *The Swallow* in 1792–3, which exceptionally provide details of the purchase of each individual slave or batch of slaves, including the names of the

---

[256] Pruneau, *Description*, 208–9.
[257] Dalzel, *History*, 213–15, 223–4.
[258] PP, Missions to Ashantee and Dahomey, Cruickshank Report, 15–16; Forbes, *Dahomey*, ii, 184–5.

persons from whom they were bought.[259] These records, however, present great problems of interpretation. One complication is that some of the slaves (in the case of the *Dahomet*, the majority) were bought from Europeans resident in Ouidah, rather than directly from Africans. The king himself is mentioned only in relation to slaves supplied in symbolic exchange for payments of 'customs', at the opening of trade. The remaining sales by presumed Africans involve a large number of individuals, 44 in 1773 and 36 in 1792–3, but for most of these there is no way of determining their status as between officials and private traders. The difficulty of identifying them is compounded by the fact that in many cases they are clearly referred to by their personal names, rather than family names or titles, and some of these are so common (e.g. Amusu, Capo, Dosu) as to make any attempt at individuation futile. One interesting point is that only a handful of names are common to the two lists, though whether this reflects the gap in time between the two voyages, or the fact that they involved ships of two different European nationalities is uncertain.[260]

The principal previous attempt to analyse the details of transactions in these journals, by Werner Peukert, identified only three state officials (Yovogan, Coke and Boya) among the sellers of slaves in 1773, and only two (Yovogan and Coke) in 1792–3, together selling only 23 out of 184 slaves sold by presumed Africans on the first occasion and 12 out of 129 on the second; on which basis he estimated that the 'state sector' accounted for only about 13 per cent of the total trade in 1773 and 9 per cent in 1792–3.[261] Even within its own terms, the logic of this inference seems questionable, since some at least of the unidentified sellers of slaves must surely have been state traders or officials also. In fact, several of those whom Peukert failed to identify can be identified, and some of these were also officials. The Boya ('Bonyo'), for example, sold slaves to the *Swallow* as well as to the *Dahomet*, and a third 'king's merchant', Atindéhou ('Atinue'), also appears among the sellers in 1792–3, while another of the Ouidah 'caboceers', the one called 'Fooey' in other sources, is perhaps listed among those selling slaves to the French ship (as 'Vouy') and certainly among those supplying the English ship ('Capuseer Fohy'). Moreover, officials may well have been involved in more sales than those for which they are specifically named, operating through subordinate agents. In fact, one of those recorded as selling a single slave to the *Swallow* is explicitly said to have done so on behalf of the Coke;[262] while the 'Desouga' or 'Dasouga' recorded as selling 8 slaves to the *Dahomet* in 1773, is probably to be identified with the Dosugan documented in other evidence as the 'trading man' of the Yovogan at this time, and a 'Senes' who sold 2 slaves in 1792–3 may be miscopied for 'Seneo', representing the

[259] Accounts of *Le Dahomet* in Berbain, *Le Comptoir français de Juda*, 99–125; accounts of *The Swallow* in George Plimpton (ed.), 'The Journal of an African slaver, 1789–1792', *Proceedings of the American Antiquarian Society*, 39/2 (1930), 379–465.

[260] Apart from the official titles Yovogan, Coke, Boya and probably 'Vouy'/'Fohy', the only names that appear in both lists are 'Boucaud'/'Boko', the largest African supplier on both occasions, and 'Capoe', this last being too common a name to be sure that it is the same person.

[261] Peukert, *Der atlantische Sklavenhandel*, 122–5, 333–7.

[262] Accounts of the *Swallow*, 23 March 1793, recording the seller as 'Conrequire', but with the interlinear note, 'this is Cock['s] slave'.

'Seignion' who traded for the Ajaho. Adding in these additional sales would raise the share of state officials to 32 slaves in 1773 and 24 in 1792–3, around 17 per cent and 19 per cent respectively; and these must be regarded as minimum figures, since some slaves were presumably sold by 'king's merchants' who remain unidentified, or by others on their behalf in cases where this is not specifically noted. Moreover, some slaves were sold by other persons who, although not 'king's merchants', held official positions: the king's French interpreter Bokpé ('Beaupré') sold 8 slaves to the *Dahomet*, and his English interpreter Gnahoui ('Yawe') sold 5 slaves (and also some ivory) to the *Swallow*. The latter ship also received 3 slaves each from a 'Donio' and a 'Semong', who are probably to be identified with local military officers: Dognon being deputy commander of the garrison at Zoungboji, while Chimon was the name of a subordinate of the Caho in the garrison at Ouidah itself.[263] If these are also considered to belong to the 'state sector', the latter's minimum share would rise to 22 per cent (40 slaves) in 1773 and 28 per cent (36) in 1792–3. It is possible, however, that, despite their status as officials, these men were selling slaves on their own account.

It is nevertherless clear that a large proportion, indeed the majority, of the slaves sold to these two ships must have been supplied by private merchants. The largest supplier seems to have been the same person on both occasions, called 'Boucaud' in the records of the *Dahomet* and 'Boko' in those of the *Swallow*, who sold no less than 51 out of the 184 slaves sold by Africans (28 per cent) to the former ship, and 13 out of 129 (10 per cent) to the latter. This man's pre-eminence is confirmed by a reference in the records of the French fort in 1787, which describes him as 'Great Boucaud [i.e. Boucaud senior], first merchant of the country'.[264] 'Boco' is a common personal name, but nobody so called seems to be recalled in traditions in Ouidah relating to this period, and it may well be that his family did not remain prominent in the town subsequently. But given that no contemporary evidence suggests that this Boco held any official position, it is a reasonable presumption that he was a private merchant.

In principle, it ought to be possible to identify some of the private merchants active in Ouidah at this period from local traditions. The merchant families that survived into the twentieth century include some which trace their origins or their settlement in Ouidah to the eighteenth century: three (Hodonou, Kossou–Naèton, Zobatié) to the reign of Tegbesu (1740–74), one (Ahidasso) to that of Kpengla (1774–89) and three (Bahini, Codjia, Déguénon) to that of Agonglo (1789–97).[265] Some of these, however, may have been originally royal rather than private traders: the first Bahini, as noted earlier, is said to have traded 'for the account' of Agonglo. Others are remembered to have worked for women of the royal palace: the first Kossou-Naèton was a brother of Hwanjile, the 'Queen Mother' of Tegbesu, and traded at Ouidah on her behalf, and the first Hodonou was his nephew (son of a

---

[263] Peukert read the second name as 'Donco' rather than 'Donio'; 3 other slaves were bought from 'Dones', which may be a miscopying of the same name. For the Chimon family, which provided the heads of the Caho quarter in the early years of French colonial rule, see Reynier, 'Ouidah', 61.

[264] ANF, C6/26, Interrogatoire de Joseph Le Beau, 8 Oct. 1787.

[265] Reynier, 'Ouidah', 42, 49, 53–5.

brother of Hwanjile) and associated with him in his trading activities, while the first Codjia was the brother of a wife of Agonglo and traded for her.[266] However, few if any of these individuals can be traced in the contemporary record. Déguénon may appear among those who supplied slaves to the *Swallow* in 1792–3 ('Dekeneuo'), selling 9 slaves, and these also included a Kossou ('Caussue'), who might be Kossou-Naèton, and a Sossou ('Saussue'), which was the personal name of the second-generation head of the Hodonou family, selling 4 slaves each.

A further difficulty in interpreting the contemporary evidence relating to the division between state and private enterprise is that the distinction between royal and private merchants is not very clearly recollected in traditions nowadays current in Ouidah. Local informants generally use the term *ahisinon* (or *ahinon*) to refer to the leading merchants of Ouidah in the pre-colonial period. Ancestors of a number of particular merchant families are remembered to have held this rank, including some already in the eighteenth century: thus the founders of the Hodonou and Zobatié families are said to have been appointed *ahisinon* by Tegbesu, that of the Ahidasso family by Kpengla and those of the Abodooui, Tchibozo, Tokpo and Quénum (Houénou) families by Gezo (1818–58).[267] Quénum family tradition lists the other *ahisinon* of Ouidah in the mid-nineteenth century as Adjovi, Bahini, Boya, Codjia, Dossou-Yovo, Gnahoui and Hodonou.[268] Linguistically, *ahisinon* means merely 'merchant' generically (literally 'market-wife-mother', apparently with the connotation of 'regular customer'); but in Dahomey it evidently had a technical meaning for a status conferred by royal authority, although the precise functions attached to this status are difficult to determine. In contemporary sources, the term was recorded only once (as 'akhi'sino'), by Burton in the 1860s, who explained it, unhelpfully, as denoting 'the great traders, who pay over duties to the King'.[269] In the traditions, the *ahisinon* are said to have been distinguished from the generality of lesser traders by the privilege of being authorized to trade beyond the frontiers of Dahomian jurisdiction.[270] They were distinct from the royal officials who collected duties from European factories (the *ganhonto*), but are described as selling slaves on the king's behalf, as well as trading on their own account.[271]

The traditions thus describe a situation in which the categories of royal and private traders were overlapping rather than distinct. Some holders of royal offices were able simultaneously to develop a substantial independent trade, as in the cases of Boya and Gnahoui; while conversely, some who began as private traders were subsequently appointed as agents for royal trade, as happened most clearly (and is discussed in a later chapter) in the case of Houénou. The traditions evidently describe the system as it operated in the nineteenth century, and it would be hazardous to extrapolate these arrangements back into the eighteenth century, since

---

[266] For nineteenth-century instances, see Bay, *Wives of the Leopard*, 212–13.

[267] Reynier, 'Ouidah', 50, 53–55, 63.

[268] Quénum, *Les Ancêtres*, 63, n. 9.

[269] Burton, *Mission*, i, 226.

[270] Maximilien Quénum, *Au pays des Fons* (3rd edn, Paris, 1983), 134.

[271] Marty, 'Etudes sur l'Islam', 2/100. But see Anselme Guézo, 'Commerce extérieur et evolution économique au Dahomey' (Mémoire de maîtrise, UNB, 1978), 38–9, who suggests that the *ahisinu* traded for Dahomian officials, rather than for the king.

commercial organization in Ouidah was certainly subject to significant change in the intervening period. In particular, it is clear there were originally restrictions on royal officials engaging in private trade, but these were subsequently relaxed. In the early years of Dahomian rule at Ouidah, under Agaja, royal officials were forbidden to trade on their own account and, although this rule was breached in practice, detected violations were rigorously repressed: in 1733, for example, the king's 'chief gaoler' (i.e. the official in charge of his captives) was executed for having illicitly sold slaves on his own account.[272] The principle was reasserted in Tegbesu's liquidation of existing merchants at Ouidah in 1746, after which it was noted (as quoted earlier) that the officials who replaced them did not dare to trade on their own account. By the nineteenth century, however, this rigorous prohibition was no longer operative: Forbes found that the six 'traders ... appointed by the king', including the Boya, were not paid, but instead had 'the advantage of trading at the royal price, or ten per cent under the market', by implication evidently on their own account.[273] When and how this relaxation of regulations occurred is unclear; although a likely context is at the beginning of the reign of Gezo, when, as argued hereafter, other evidence suggests that the commercial community in Ouidah acquired greater autonomy.

It should also be stressed that even 'private' merchants in Dahomey were, in a sense, officials in that they were authorized to trade by royal authority. As was noted in the 1780s, 'the negotiators [= traders] must have a proper licence from the king'.[274] Moreover, in 1779 Kpengla is recorded to have granted 'the black traders' permission 'to sit upon chairs: a privilege that, heretofore, they had not been permitted to enjoy'.[275] The significance of this act is clarified by later sources, which specify that a chair was part of the insignia of a Dahomian 'caboceer' or chief, a status that was conferred upon several prominent merchants; the king granted this rank to wealthy men in return for lavish gifts, the system serving in effect as a source of revenue through the sale of honours.[276] This status of 'caboceer' was not purely honorary, as it carried an obligation to provide military forces: Forbes noted that the leading merchants in Ouidah 'have to supply whole regiments' for the Dahomian army.[277]

Given the problematic nature of the evidence, the composition of the private merchant community in Ouidah in the eighteenth century is difficult to grasp. On general grounds, it would be expected that the conditions of wholesale trading, requiring access to substantial capital and credit, would favour the dominance of a small number of large-scale entrepreneurs.[278] In Ouidah, there were certainly substantial merchants, such as Boco, who sold many slaves to both the *Dahomet* in 1773 and the *Swallow* in 1792/3. But the accounts of these ships show that around

[272] ANF, C6/25, Levet, Juda, 26 Aug. 1733.

[273] Forbes, *Dahomey*, i, 111.

[274] Isert, *Letters*, 98.

[275] Dalzel, *History*, 170.

[276] Burton, *Mission*, i, 73; Béraud, 'Note sur le Dahomé', 378–9.

[277] Forbes, *Dahomey*, i, 113.

[278] Hopkins, *Economic History*, 86, 120; Herbert S. Klein, *The Atlantic Slave Trade* (Cambridge, 1999), 121.

a fifth of the slaves purchased from Africans on both occasions (42 of 184 by the former, 24 of 129 by the latter) were sold by persons who were involved in only a single transaction, for only one or two slaves, which has been cited as indicating a significant role for 'small-scale traders'.[279] However, even someone selling a single slave was operating on a relatively large scale; the selling price of an adult male slave in 1773, 11 'ounces' or 44 grand cabess of cowries, was equivalent to the wages of a porter for over five years.[280] The substantial merchants were clearly overwhelmingly male: as was explicitly noted in the 1780s, in contrast to local trade which was conducted by women, the slave trade was 'the province of men'.[281] An exception was the woman merchant Kposi arrested in the 1780s, although it is not specified that she traded in slaves; however, she is described as 'follow[ing] her husband, who was also a considerable trader' to do business at Abomey, implying that she operated in partnership with him, rather than having risen independently from the ranks of the female petty traders.[282]

In the nineteenth century, the Ouidah merchant community incorporated a number of persons of foreign origin who settled permanently in the town, such as Francisco Felix de Souza. Some of the longer-serving directors of the European forts in the eighteenth century, such as Lionel Abson of the English fort, might be regarded in the same light, as having become effectively naturalized Dahomians and often trading on their own account. A more precise parallel and precedent was 'Irookoo', alias Dom Jeronimo (died 1790), who was in origin a prince of the Dahomian royal family, sold into slavery in Brazil by Tegbesu, but redeemed and returned to Dahomey by Kpengla, who became a prominent slave-dealer at Ouidah in the 1780s. He, however, enjoyed the honorific title of 'the king's friend', which suggests that he functioned as a royal agent (as did de Souza later), rather than a strictly independent merchant, and he remained basically part of the Dahomian ruling establishment, even presenting himself as a candidate for the royal succession in 1789.[283]

Private merchant enterprise under Dahomian rule suffered competitive disadvantages in relation to the state. As described more fully in the next chapter, the kings of Dahomey enforced a right to sell their slaves first, before anyone else could trade, and to receive higher prices. Private merchants were also subject to heavy taxation. Transit duties were levied on slaves, as well as other commodities, at various points along the road from Abomey south to Ouidah.[284] The Hueda kings earlier had also levied an export tax, at a rate of 5 galinas (1,000 cowries) per slave (2.5 per cent of their current selling price), collected from the African sellers rather

---

[279] Marion Johnson, 'The Atlantic slave trade and the economy of West Africa', in Roger Anstey & P.E.H. Hair (eds), *Liverpool, the African Slave Trade and Abolition* (Liverpool, 1976), 24–5.

[280] Assuming that a porter worked and was paid (at 120 cowries per day) for only three days of the four-day 'week'; 44 grand cabess (176,000 cowries) represented wages for over 1,400 person/days.

[281] Isert, *Letters*, 100.

[282] Dalzel, *History*, 208.

[283] PRO, T70/1545, Lionel Abson, Ouidah, 14 Dec. 1782; T70/1162, Day Book, William's Fort, 13 Jan. 1784, 19 Jan. 1785; Dalzel, *History*, 222–3, 225.

[284] PP, Missions to Ashantee and Dahomey, Cruickshank Report, 16; Vallon, 'Le royaume de Dahomey', 2/336.

than the European purchasers.[285] Under Dahomian rule, a reference in the 1770s to the levying of duties 'at the gate of the forts' may allude to a similar tax. More explicitly, it was noted in the 1840s that all exports, including palm oil and ivory as well as slaves, were subject to a tax, levied on the Dahomian sellers and collected by the Yovogan, the duty on slaves being 'very high', charged 'according to the number of slaves shipped on board' and usually paid in rum or tobacco; another source gives the rate of this duty as $5 (10,000 cowries) per slave, equivalent to 6.25 per cent of the current selling price.[286]

The profits left to private merchants after these impositions were taxed further, through a levy on merchant incomes. In 1772 it was noted that the Annual Customs at the capital were attended by 'the black merchants, or trading men, and indeed every head of a family', who were obliged to bring 'a quantity of cowries, proportioned to their circumstances'.[287] Tradition indicates that this tax on merchant incomes was regarded as the counterpart of the taxes levied in kind on farmers and craftsmen, the same term, *kuzu*, being applied to both; one nineteenth-century source, however, gives the local name of the income tax paid in cowries as 'head-money' (*takwe*).[288] Dahomian tradition describes the annual tax in cowries as levied on all adult males at a flat rate (which in the late nineteenth century was 4,000 cowries per head).[289] But presumably this was a minimum figure, and those with substantial monetary incomes paid more. Other contemporary sources certainly confirm that the tax was graduated: two accounts of the 1840s, for example, report that chiefs paid according to their status and merchants 'proportionately to the extent of their commerce' and that taxes were levied 'according to rank, reputation, and income'.[290] The taxing of merchant incomes was based on an informed assessment, rather than a conventional figure: the king posted one of his own daughters and two officers in the household of each of his 'ministers', to 'superintend the minister's trade, on which he pays tribute according to their report'.[291] The rate of the tax in the early nineteenth century was one-third of income.[292]

Merchant wealth was also subject to an inheritance tax. It was noted in the late eighteenth century that 'The King of Dahomy ... is heir to all his subjects. On the death of any of his officers, their whole effects, of which their wives and children are considered to be a part, go to the King'. This royal right of inheritance is also recorded in the nineteenth century, one account for example reporting that 'at the decease of any caboceer, the whole of his property is considered as belonging to the King'.[293] Local tradition in Ouidah likewise recalls that on the death of a chief, 'all

[285] 'Relation du Royaume de Judas', 76–7; Labat, *Voyage*, ii, 80; des Marchais, 'Journal', 49.

[286] De Chenevert & Bullet, 'Réflexions', 7; Duncan, *Travels*, i, 122–3; PP, Missions to Ashantee and Dahomey, Cruickshank Report, 16. In the 1860s, the duty is given as $4 per slave: PP, Slave Trade 1863, Class B, no. 21, Consul Freeman, Lagos, 1 July 1863; PP, Despatches from Commodore Wilmot, no. 1, 29 Jan. 1863.

[287] Norris, *Memoirs*, 87.

[288] Quénum, *Au pays des Fons*, 24; Duncan, *Travels*, i, 122–3.

[289] Le Herissé, *L'Ancien Royaume*, 83–4.

[290] Brue, 'Voyage', 65; Duncan, *Travels*, i, 122–3.

[291] Forbes, *Dahomey*, i, 33–4.

[292] Robertson, *Notes*, 271: 'one third of the property of every individual is collected annually'.

[293] Ibid.; Duncan, *Travels*, ii, 264.

the goods forming the inheritance, including their wives and children, are held at the disposition of the king, who decides their fate'.[294] As one contemporary observer, Burton, grasped, the deceased's estate was in fact normally restored to his family, on payment of a death duty.[295] Dahomian tradition maintains that the royal right of inheritance was merely 'fictitious', since only limited sums were taken in tax.[296] But the contemporary evidence indicates that, at least in the case of merchant estates in Ouidah, the inheritance tax was heavy. Two nineteenth-century accounts thus assert that 'the greater part of the property of every individual reverts to the crown at his demise', the heir receiving back only 'a very small portion of the estate'.[297] Ouidah tradition indicates that, at least in the nineteenth century, the tax was levied at a rate of three-quarters of the estate, while also recalling that efforts were regularly made to conceal movable property, including slaves, in order to evade payment.[298]

Ouidah within Dahomey

Karl Polanyi argued that Ouidah was never fully integrated into the Dahomian state. Rather, the Dahomian kings contented themselves with a 'remote control', which kept Ouidah deliberately 'isolated from the core of the country'; in this way, it is suggested, the supposed earlier status of Ouidah as a politically neutral 'port of trade' was effectively perpetuated, albeit in a changed form, under Dahomian rule.[299] In this, Polanyi seems to have been influenced by an observation of Burton that Ouidah was 'a "white man's town", and under the direct supervision of the King, who rarely interferes with the administration', though Burton went on to qualify this by noting that 'If any evil report reaches the capital a royal messenger comes down, and the [local] authorities tremble.'[300] A contrary view is propounded by Elisée Soumonni, that the administration of Ouidah under Dahomian rule was rather 'organized within the framework of a province integrated into the rest of the kingdom', and this seems to offer a better fit with the evidence.[301] The autonomy of the Dahomian officials based locally in Ouidah was severely circumscribed, important matters being referred to the authority of the king in the capital. These officials also, and indeed the directors of the European forts and also visiting European traders, regularly travelled to the capital to consult with the king, while conversely officials and royal messengers from the capital were sent to Ouidah to inspect conditions and to transmit and enforce royal orders.

[294] Agbo, *Histoire*, 54.
[295] Burton, *Mission*, i, 367.
[296] Le Herissé, *L'Ancien Royaume*, 84–5.
[297] Robertson, *Notes*, 271; PP, Missions to Ashantee and Dahomey, Cruickshank Report, 16.
[298] Foà, *Le Dahomey*, 26; de Souza, *La Famille de Souza*, 22, 59–60. But at one point de Souza gives the rate as ⅔: ibid., 43.
[299] Polanyi, *Dahomey*, 131–9.
[300] Burton, *Mission*, i, 56–7.
[301] E.A. Soumonni, 'The administration of a port of the slave trade: Ouidah in the nineteenth century', in Law & Strickrodt, *Ports of the Slave Trade*, 48–54.

Nevertheless, Edna Bay's study of Dahomian political culture notes the 'great distance ... both psychologically and culturally' which persisted between Abomey and Ouidah. From the perspective of the Dahomian ruling elite, she suggests, Ouidah remained 'something alien, ... an entity which could not be wholly controlled'; the belt of marshland (called the Lama) that separated the original heartland of Dahomey from Allada and Ouidah remained a cultural and psychological as well as a physical barrier, even after the political incorporation of the southern kingdoms.[302] Europeans noted that people travelling from Ouidah inland to the capital Abomey talked of going 'to Dahomey', as if it were a different country.[303] Recent Ouidah tradition represents the period of Dahomian rule between 1727 and 1892 in terms of an alien and exploitative, effectively colonial, regime; local historian Casimir Agbo, for example, speaks of the 'Fon domination' or 'Dahomian occupation'.[304] This idea of Dahomian rule as a foreign conquest was supported, as has been seen, by the appropriation, in local tradition, of the history of the pre-Dahomian Hueda kingdom as that of the urban community of Dahomian Ouidah. This perspective may reflect mainly recollections of the nineteenth century, when relations between Ouidah and the Dahomian monarchy became increasingly difficult, especially during the second half of the century after the ending of the Atlantic slave trade. But there was clearly tension already in the eighteenth century. In the 1780s it was suggested that the reason why the king never came to Ouidah was 'because he fears for his life', in consequence of local resentment of the 'extreme despotism' of his rule.[305]

The problematic nature of the relationship between Ouidah and Dahomey in the eighteenth century is dramatically illustrated by the insecurity of tenure of officials in the town. The frequency of executions and dismissals of senior officials during the first half-century of Dahomian administration is truly astonishing. As seen earlier, the second viceroy, appointed in 1743 with the title Tegan, was executed after only a few months in office, and the third Tegan was killed in a rebellion in 1745. This was probably the occasion for the suppression of the title of Tegan and its replacement by that of Yovogan; and probably in connection with this reorganization Tegbesu around the beginning of 1746 also executed and replaced the existing royal traders at Ouidah. The turnover of officials can subsequently be followed in detail in the records of the English fort from 1752 onwards.[306] In January 1752 the Caho, commander of the local garrison, was executed. In May or June 1754 a senior official from Abomey, the Tokpo (to be distinguished from the Ouidah merchant family of this name), was sent down to Ouidah to 'seize some great men's effects near this place', and in July or August the Coke, head of the king's traders, was killed. In March or April 1755 both the Yovogan and the Coke

[302] Bay, *Wives of the Leopard*, 107–8.

[303] PRO, FO84/886, Louis Fraser, Daily journal, 23 July 1851; Bouche, *Sept ans*, 347.

[304] Agbo, *Histoire*, 12, 45.

[305] Isert, *Letters*, 102.

[306] PRO, T70/1158–63, Day Books, William's Fort, 1752–1812. The record becomes more fragmentary, with some years' accounts missing and others compiled only perfunctorily, from the 1790s onwards. For the execution of the Yovogan in Nov. 1755, see also ANF, C6/25, Guestard, 25 Nov. 1755.

were executed; in May or June the Yovogan's successor (who held the title Tegan, rather than Yovogan) was likewise executed; and the succeeding viceroy (now again entitled Yovogan), named Bocco Bambia, was executed in his turn in November. In May or June 1756 the Yovogan was summoned to Abomey and either dismissed or executed, his replacement being installed at Ouidah by the Mehu in person. The Boya, second to the Coke among the king's traders, was killed in September or October 1756, and the Coke himself in September or October 1759. In April 1760 the Yovogan was 'recalled from the post'; his successor held office for only twelve days (28 April to 10 May) before being summoned back to Abomey and killed, and the new appointee in turn was 'displaced' in October 1761. The Yovogan appointed on this occasion (named 'Honnou' in other sources) died a natural death while still in office in June 1768, seemingly the first holder of the title to achieve this distinction. In March 1770 the Coke was 'degraded' and replaced, and in February 1771 the Yovogan was 'superseded'. The new Yovogan then appointed died in July 1776, again apparently of natural causes, but his successor was executed in March 1778. Continuing tensions are suggested by the fact that twice, in March 1778 and May 1779, the Yovogan and other officials of Ouidah were ordered to assemble in order to swear loyalty to the king. The Yovogan appointed in 1778, however, survived six years, a new incumbent being appointed in June 1784. In these records, these executions and dismissals are reported as bald facts, without explanation. Only very occasionally is more detail available from other sources. The execution of the Yovogan in 1778, for example, was due to allegedly false accusations made by his subordinates, the Coke and 'Fooey', that he had usurped the royal prerogatives of wearing sandals and using a 'white man's umbrella'; his replacement is said to have gone insane, so presumably was removed on grounds of incapacity.[307]

After the 1770s the frequency of executions of officials diminished, though whether this reflected the monarchy's success in suppressing opposition or that of the officials in placing restraints upon royal power is uncertain. Tensions between Ouidah and Dahomey persisted but now took a different form, involving confrontations between the monarchy and the local merchant community. Although merchants had been given official recognition as 'caboceers' in the 1770s, they were still not altogether socially respectable. The heavy scale of taxation of merchant wealth, it may be suggested, reflected not only the royal appetite for revenue, but also a conviction that commercial wealth required to be restrained for sociopolitical reasons, since the accumulation of riches in private hands was thought to pose a threat to the dominance of the martial values with which the Dahomian monarchy was identified: as Forbes perceived, enterprise was 'not encouraged' because 'the king is aware that, if the enjoyment of home, and the luxuries of health and happiness, were once obtained, he would fail in volunteers for the annual slave-hunt'.[308] A major clash was provoked, as noted earlier, by Kpengla's attempt to enter the middleman trade in slaves purchased from the interior in the 1780s, which roused such fierce opposition from the merchant community that it was abandoned by his successor Agonglo. However, there were further clashes under

---

[307] Dalzel, *History*, 158–63 (misdating the execution of the Yovogan to 1775).
[308] Forbes, *Dahomey*, i, 21.

Agonglo's successor Adandozan (1797–1818), when one leading Ouidah merchant, Déguénon, is said to have suffered confiscation of his property on two separate occasions, on one of which he lost no fewer than 380 slaves; and around the same time another, Sossou Hodonou, was imprisoned and presumably also had his property confiscated, since the family fortunes had to be rebuilt by his brother and successor Dovonou.[309] Most famously, as will be seen in a later chapter, the locally resident Brazilian trader Francisco Felix de Souza also quarrelled with Adandozan, over unpaid royal debts, which led to his imprisonment at Abomey, in consequence of which de Souza gave his support to the coup d'etat that overthrew Adanzozan in favour of his brother Gezo in 1818. The revolution of 1818 thus represented, in one of its aspects, an assertion of the interests of private merchant enterprise against the centralizing authority of the Dahomian monarchy.

[309] Reynier, 'Ouidah', 53–4.

4

The Operation of the Atlantic Slave Trade

Ouidah under Dahomian rule was more than simply a site of European trade. Even in narrowly economic terms, it was also a centre for fishing and salt production, as well as for local trade, especially along the coastal lagoon. It also served, as has been seen, as a seat of Dahomian provincial administration and as a military garrison town. Nevertheless, its central function was in trade with Europeans; this is not just a Eurocentric perception, it was shared by the Dahomians themselves, as reflected in the title of the administrator of the town, Yovogan, 'Chief of the white men'. Ouidah was a 'white man's town', not in the sense of being under European control but in that its principal function was as the site of trade with Europeans.

The Dahomian kings continued the policy of the earlier Hueda kings, of maintaining Ouidah as a neutral port where hostilities among Europeans were prohibited. In 1755, for example, Tegbesu sent to Ouidah to remind the directors of the European forts that 'the road should be free and nobody should be molested while at anchor there'; in 1762, when British ships fired on a canoe delivering supplies to the French fort, he again sent to protest and to 'desire all white men to live in friendship and let all palavers drop'. In 1791, when war with France was again threatening, the British were still confident that Ouidah would remain a safe haven, since 'the king of Dahomey is so absolute a monarch there as never to suffer any Europeans settled in his dominions to have any controversies of any hostile nature whatever'.[1] The policy began to break down only after 1794, when the French revolutionary government, having ended its own slave trade and thus no longer having any interest in the security of the Ouidah 'port', began a systematic campaign of piracy against British and Portuguese shipping at Ouidah and elsewhere on the Bight of Benin.[2] As late as 1803, however, after a British ship had taken a French vessel off Ouidah, the Dahomian authorities were still seeking to

[1] PRO, T70/1158–9, Day Book, William's Fort, Nov.–Dec. 1755, 2 & 6 Oct. 1762; T70/1563, Governor & Council, Cape Coast, 1 March 1791.
[2] Akinjogbin, *Dahomey*, 183.

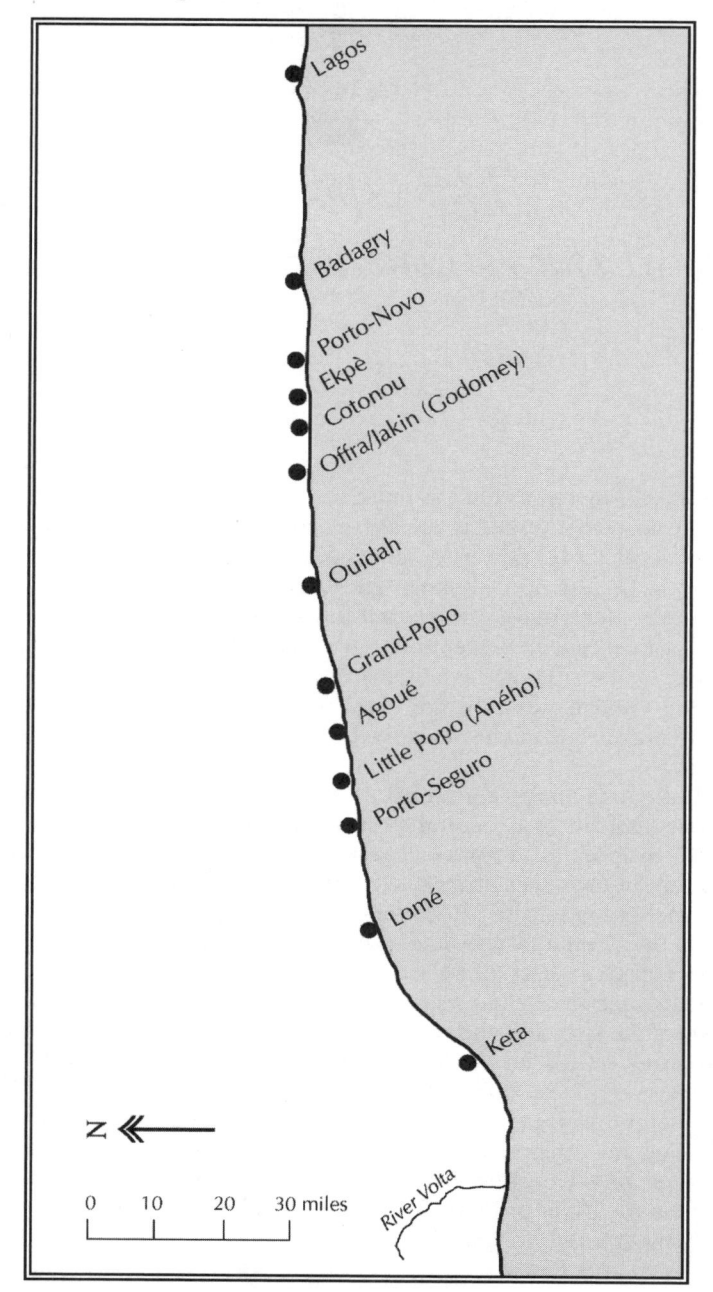

Map 5 The 'ports' of the slave trade

uphold the principle, arresting a British factor on shore on suspicion of complicity in the attack.[3]

Until the second quarter of the nineteenth century the European trade was still overwhelmingly in slaves. Although significant trade was also made at Ouidah for gold during the first half of the eighteenth century, this was not a local product but a re-export, brought from Brazil by Portuguese traders to exchange for slaves.[4] When the French fort at Ouidah was abandoned in 1797, following the ending of the French slave trade, its former director suggested the possibility of alternative trade in ivory, cotton, locally manufactured cloth and palm oil, and a British trader at Ouidah in 1803 reported that the trade there included ivory and palm oil, as well as slaves.[5] Ivory, however, was sold only in very small quantities; the British ship *Swallow* in 1792–3, for example, purchased ivory to the value of only 70 ounces (£280), representing under 2 per cent of the value of the 422 slaves obtained. Cloth was exported principally to Brazil, the demand coming from the population of African origin there, but this was manufactured in Yorubaland and went mainly through more easterly ports, such as Porto-Novo and Lagos.[6] Palm oil was in growing demand in Britain as an industrial raw material (mainly in soap-making), and by the 1780s 'large quantities' were already being exported through Ouidah for the British market;[7] but the real take-off of the palm-oil trade occurred later, in the 1840s. These other commodities were as yet of trivial importance in comparison with the slave trade, which remained the mainstay of Ouidah's business throughout the eighteenth century.

After the destruction of Jakin in 1732, Ouidah was left as the sole outlet for Dahomey's export trade; a project to reopen Jakin as a slaving port in 1776-7 came to nothing.[8] Nevertheless, under Dahomian rule the volume of the slave trade through Ouidah was lower than earlier. Total exports from the Bight of Benin as a whole tended to be lower after the 1730s; and within this total Ouidah suffered increasing competition from rival ports in the region: Grand-Popo and Little Popo to the west, and Badagry, Ekpè, Porto-Novo (from the 1750s) and Lagos (from the 1760s) to the east. Ouidah, however, remained the largest port in the region down to the end of the eighteenth century, still accounting for between a third and a half of all exports from the Bight of Benin. In 1750, Ouidah was estimated to be exporting between 8,000 and 9,000 slaves annually, which must have represented the great majority of exports from the Bight. In 1765, however, when exports from the entire coast from the Volta to Benin were put at 12,100 slaves annually, Ouidah was contributing only 5,000 of these, although this was well ahead of its nearest rival Grand-Popo, with exports of 2,000 annually, and Porto-Novo and Benin (meaning Warri, rather than the kingdom of Benin itself), each with 1,200; in 1788,

[3] PRO, T70/1163, Day Book, William's Fort, 5 Aug. 1803; M'Leod, *Voyage*, 113–14.
[4] Robin Law, 'The gold trade of Whydah in the seventeenth and eighteenth centuries', in David Henige & T.C. McCaskie (eds), *West African Economic and Social History* (Madison, 1990), 105–18.
[5] ANF, C6/27, mémoire enc. in Denyau de la Garenne, Paris, 25 nivôse, Year VII; M'Leod, *Voyage*, 14.
[6] Adams, *Remarks*, 97.
[7] Norris, *Memoirs*, 146.
[8] Akinjogbin, *Dahomey*, 156–8.

total exports from the Bight of Benin were estimated at 12,500 annually, of which Ouidah accounted for 4,500, while Porto-Novo and Badagry together supplied 3,500, and Lagos and Benin a further 3,500.[9]

The diversion of trade to ports east of Ouidah mainly reflected the rising importance of the kingdom of Oyo, in the interior to the north-east, as a supplier of slaves; by the 1770s Oyo was reported to be the source of most of the slaves sold at the coast. Some of the trade from Oyo went through Ouidah; Abomey-Calavi on the western shore of Lake Nokoué served as a frontier market for the purchase of slaves from Oyo traders.[10] But in the longer run, the Oyo preferred to take their slaves to eastern ports beyond Dahomian jurisdiction. Dahomey attempted to eliminate the competition of the eastern ports by military action, raiding Ekpè in 1747 and Porto-Novo in 1763. Subsequently, the Dahomians allied with Porto-Novo to attack and destroy Ekpè in 1782, and Badagry in 1784, and, after this alliance had broken down, they again raided Porto-Novo in 1787, 1791 and 1804. This Dahomian pressure on Badagry and Porto-Novo, however, was ineffective in the long run, to the extent that it drove the trade of Oyo further east to Lagos, which was beyond the effective reach of Dahomian military operations.[11]

In the second half of the eighteenth century, the slaves exported through Ouidah went mainly to Brazil and to French Caribbean colonies, especially Saint-Domingue (the future Haiti). Over the entire history of the Atlantic trade, around 60 per cent of slaves exported from the Bight of Benin are estimated to have gone to Brazil, as against 20 per cent to the French Caribbean and only 10 per cent to British colonies. The relative importance of different markets varied over time, however, with the British taking the majority of exports in the late seventeenth century but declining in importance after 1700, as British slaving increasingly focused on the Bight of Biafra and Angola, while the French trade grew to rival that to Brazil in the second half of the eighteenth century, until the market in Saint-Domingue was closed down by the slave insurrection there in 1791.[12]

The conduct of the European trade

Details of the mode of operation of European trade at Ouidah are documented by a number of descriptions of trading procedures, for example in a French source of 1750, and in Danish and British accounts relating to the 1780s.[13] Also illuminating

---

[9] ANF, C6/25, Pruneau & Guestard, 'Mémoire pour servir à l'intelligence du commerce de Juda', 18 March 1750; K. David Patterson, 'A note on slave exports from the Costa da Mina, 1760–1770', *BIFAN*, série B, 33/2 (1971), 255; evidence of Robert Norris to the Select Committee of the Privy Council on the Slave Trade, 1789, in Elizabeth Donnan (ed.), *Documents Illustrative of the History of the Slave Trade to America* (Washington, 1930–5), ii, 598.

[10] De Chenevert & Bullet, 'Réflexions', 5.

[11] See Law, 'Lagoonside port', 47–53; for the rise of Lagos, see also Robin Law, 'Trade and politics behind the Slave Coast: the lagoon traffic and the rise of Lagos, 1500–1800', *JAH*, 24 (1983), 321–48.

[12] Eltis & Richardson, 'West Africa and the transatlantic slave trade', 20–21.

[13] ANF, C6/25, Pruneau & Guestard, 'Mémoire', 18 March 1750; Isert, *Letters*, 97–9; 'Account of the Expences attending the Purchase of a Cargoe of Slaves at Whydah', in evidence of Archibald Dalzel to the Committee

are the accounts of the two ships already mentioned in the preceding chapter, the French *Dahomet* in 1773 and the British *Swallow* in 1792–3.[14]

The European trade at Ouidah under Dahomian rule was closely regulated by the state. In general, the Dahomians continued the system that had operated under the Hueda kings before 1727, although with some modifications.[15] The most obvious change was that European traders now normally did the initial business of opening the trade with the Yovogan at Ouidah rather than with the king in the capital. European ships' captains did sometimes travel to Abomey to see the king, but only when they had some specific problem or dispute to resolve with him. Also, Dahomey enforced more rigorously than Allada and Hueda earlier its position as middleman in the slave trade, requiring traders from the interior to sell to Dahomian merchants rather than being able to deal directly with Europeans; this was a principal reason for the preference of the Oyo to take their slaves to the eastern ports of Ekpè, Porto-Novo and Badagry, where 'they are allowed to come to trade at the coast'.[16]

Under Dahomian rule, Europeans continued to have to pay 'customs' for permission to trade, now delivered to the Yovogan at Ouidah; it was stressed that the payment of customs 'ought to be done as soon as possible, for the traders dare not receive goods till the King has got his dues'.[17] Under the Hueda kings immediately prior to the Dahomian conquest the customs consisted of goods to the value of 6 slaves to the king and 2 to the 'caboceers', one each to those most involved in the European trade, the Yovogan and the Agou.[18] Under Dahomian rule, the rate was higher and seemingly paid only to the king, although collected on his behalf by the Yovogan. The French fort at Ouidah in 1750 complained that customs at Ouidah were 'heavier than at any other place on the Coast', consisting of the value of 10 slaves paid to the king, plus one further paid 'for the opening of trade'; in 1752 the Yovogan attempted to raise the customs to 20½ slaves, but on appeal to the king the rate was reduced to the normal 11.[19] Later, the system was refined, with payments graduated according to the size of the ship, measured by the number of its masts. The change may possibly have been introduced in 1777, when a Portuguese trader requested to be allowed to pay 'only half custom' and the king sent to consult the directors of the forts at Ouidah as to 'whether the white men would look upon it as a precedent for the future'; although the size of the ship involved is not explicitly mentioned as the issue, it seems a likely basis for requesting a lower rate.[20] In 1784–5 the rate was given as the value of 12 slaves for a

[13] (cont.) of the Privy Council, 1789, in Donnan, *Documents*, ii, 596–7; see also 'State of the Customs which the ships that make their whole trade at Whydah pay to the King of Dahomey' (undated, but apparently of the 1770s–80s), in Gomer Williams, *History of the Liverpool Privateers* (London, 1897), 550–53.

[14] See also the account, based mainly on the case of the *Dahomet*, in Berbain, *Le Comptoir français de Juda*, 69–71.

[15] See further Law, 'Royal monopoly'.

[16] De Chenevert & Bullet, 'Réflexions', 5.

[17] 'Account of Expences', in Donnan, *Documents*, ii, 596.

[18] Law, *Slave Coast*, 209.

[19] ANF, C6/25, Pruneau & Guestard, 'Mémoire', 18 March 1750; Guestard, 22 Nov. 1752.

[20] PRO, T70/1161, Day Book, William's Fort, 9 March 1777.

ship of three masts, but only 7 for a two-master; but a few years later it was cited as 14½ slaves for a ship, 7 for a snow or brig (i.e. with two masts) and 3½ for a sloop (with one mast); and by 1803 it had risen to 21 slaves for a ship of three masts, 14 for a brig or schooner, and 7 for a cutter or sloop, a rate of 7 slaves per mast.[21] Europeans sometimes sought to reduce the rate to which they were subject by dismantling one of the ship's masts prior to arrival at Ouidah. A British ship in 1803, which obtained most of its slaves at Lagos but some also at Ouidah, evaded the higher rate by posting a cutter to trade at Ouidah and conveying the slaves purchased from there to the main ship at Lagos, so as to pay customs only on the smaller ship, although when the ruse was detected this involved the factor posted on shore in a dispute with the local authorities for tax fraud.[22]

Slaves for the purpose of payment of customs, it should be noted, were valued under Dahomian rule not at the current market price, but at a fixed rate. In 1750, for example, customs at Ouidah were calculated on the value of 20 grand cabess of cowries, 40 iron bars, 40 pieces of linen cloth or 25 guns per slave, whereas the current market price for male slaves was 33 grand cabess, 45 iron bars, 70 linen pieces or 40 guns; and in the 1780s customs payments were still calculated on a rate of 5 'ounces' (equivalent to 20 grand cabess of cowries, 40 iron bars, etc.) per slave, although the price of a male slave was now up to 13 ounces.[23] The price used in customs calculations probably represents the market rate at the time of the Dahomian conquest in 1727, when the level of customs was presumably reset by the new local authorities. In consequence, although the rate of the customs in numbers of 'slaves' had increased, relative to the current price of slaves it had actually declined.

Following the abolition of the British slave trade in 1807 and the abandonment of the English fort at Ouidah in 1812, it was reported that the system of charging according to the number of a ship's masts had been suspended and the charge reduced 'from a desire to encourage Europeans to settle here', the rate of customs now being 'settled by agreement' and only 'trivial' in value.[24] But this concession was evidently only temporary, presumably abandoned when the slave trade revived. By 1850, slave merchants at Ouidah were again paying a 'very heavy King's duty', said to be $800 per ship (equivalent to the value of ten slaves at current prices), although the British merchant Hutton, who was trading in palm oil, was paying only goods to the value of $180 per ship.[25] The system of charging according the number of a ship's masts was also reinstated: in the early 1870s, when the trade had shifted wholly into palm produce, customs were cited as around £45 [= $180] for a two-masted ship, but 'much more' for one of three masts, and by 1875 the rate had risen to between £50 and £60 for a brig, and between £75 and £90 for a barque.[26]

[21] Isert, *Letters*, 97; 'Account of Expences', in Donnan, *Documents*, ii, 596; M'Leod, *Voyage*, 10–11.
[22] M'Leod, *Voyage*, 10–11, 113–15.
[23] 'Account of Expences', in Donnan, *Documents*, ii, 596.
[24] Robertson, *Notes*, 264.
[25] PP, Slave Trade 1850–1, Class A, enc. 3 in no. 198, Forbes, 6 April 1850.
[26] A. Swanzy, 'On the trade in Western Africa', *Journal of the Society of Arts*, 22 (1874), 481; PRO, FO84/1465, Governor Strahan, Cape Coast, 22 Nov. 1875.

In Hueda before the Dahomian conquest, the king had also exercised a right to sell his slaves first, before anybody else could trade.[27] The earliest accounts are explicit that Europeans were obliged to take as many slaves as the king had to offer, or else to agree on the number they would take. By the 1720s, however, they were obliged to purchase only a fixed number, three from the king and two each from the Yovogan, Agou and the 'captain' for the European nation involved (in the French case, Assou), a total of nine in all.[28] This restricted form of the system was continued under Dahomian rule: the French fort in 1733 referred to 'the four customary captives which you are obliged to take from the King'; and in 1750 to a requirement to purchase 4 boys of 9–10 years of age, before the formal opening of trade, which had to be paid for at adult rates.[29] By the 1770s, however, although the king was still supplying 2 young boys (or girls) prior to the opening of trade, these were given in symbolic exchange for the payment of customs, rather than as a separate transaction. However, both the *Dahomet* in 1773 and the *Swallow* in 1792 opened their actual trade with the purchase of 2 further children from the Yovogan, who were presumably sold on the king's behalf. The royal right of first sale was evidently maintained in the illegal trade of the nineteenth century, when the Brazilian Francisco Felix de Souza, in his capacity as agent to Gezo, is explicitly recorded to have enjoyed the right to 'command refusal of all articles offered for sale'.[30] Although limited in scale, this right of first sale served to enable the king to insist upon his choice of the merchandise on offer. The practice also continued in the palm produce trade of the nineteenth century; in the 1860s it was noted that 'no other trader can trade with you until the king has made his selection of the cargo', and in the 1870s that 'the king's trader selects from fresh importations such goods as he deems suitable to his master'.[31]

In Hueda before 1727, prices were settled with the king, at the beginning of trade, rather than being negotiated separately with each individual African supplier.[32] This did not mean that prices were invariant, as was inferred by Karl Polanyi, since in fact slave prices at Ouidah rose substantially, from 9 grand cabess of cowries (36,000 shells, 90 lb. by weight) in the 1680s to 18–20 cabess (72,000–80,000 cowries, 180–200 lb.) by the 1720s.[33] A similar practice of administered prices operated under Dahomian rule, although the detailed mechanisms were different. One innovation was that prices were now regularly denominated in terms of the 'ounce', which had in origin represented the value in goods of an ounce of gold (value £4 sterling), which was subject to some variation according to the state of the market but which by the 1770s had become a conventional unit of account,

[27] Barbot, *On Guinea*, ii, 637; Phillips, 'Journal', 218; Bosman, *Description*, 363a; Van Danztig, *Dutch and the Guinea Coast*, no. 128, J. van den Broecke, 10 Nov. 1705; John Atkins, *A Voyage to Guinea, Brasil, and the West Indies* (London, 1735), 172.

[28] Labat, *Voyage*, ii, 93; des Marchais, 'Journal', 32.

[29] ANF, C6/25, Levet, 26 Aug. 1733; Pruneau & Guestard, 'Mémoire', 18 March 1750.

[30] Burton, *Mission*, i, 104.

[31] PP, 1865 Select Committee, § 5329, James Aspinall Tobin; Swanzy, 'On the trade', 481.

[32] Barbot, *On Guinea*, ii, 637; Phillips, 'Journal', 217.

[33] Polanyi, *Dahomey*, 150–51; for prices, see Law, *Slave Coast*, 177–80.

Table 4.1 Prices of (adult male) slaves at Ouidah, 1725–93

	Cowries (grand cabess)	Ounces
1725	18–20	
1731		7
1733	29	7
1743	30–32	
1750	33	[6][a]
1764	40	10
1773	40–44	10–11
1776	44	11
1787	52	13
1792–3	52–60	13–15

Sources: 1725: Labat, *Voyage*, ii, 92; des Marchais, 'Journal', 31v; 1731: Harms, *The Diligent*, 152; 1733: ANF, C6/25, Levet, 26 Aug. 1733; 1743: ANF, C6/25, Levet, 14 June 1743; 1750: ANF, C6/25, Pruneau & Guestard, 'Mémoire', 8 March 1750; 1765: ANF, C6/25, Cuillié, 21 Nov. 1764; 1773: accounts of *Le Dahomet*; 1776: De Chenevert & Bullet, 'Réflexions', 48; 1787: ANF, C6/26, Interrogatoire de Joseph Le Beau, 8 Sept. 1787; 1792/3: accounts of the *Swallow*.

[a] This price is evidently given according to the market price of cowries (currently 20,000 to the oz. of gold), rather than the conventional rate of 16,000 to the oz.

equivalent to, for example, 16,000 cowries (4 grand cabess, 40 lb. by weight), 4 iron bars, 5 guns, 1 roll (80 lb. weight) of Brazilian tobacco or 8 pieces of linen cloth.[34] This served to facilitate payment for slaves in an assortment of different goods, rather than in a single sort of goods for each slave, as had been the normal practice earlier.[35] An account of the 1770s states that the price of slaves was 'fixed', at a certain number of ounces; and it was still reported by Forbes in 1850, when the trade included palm oil as well as slaves, that prices were 'laid down by law'.[36] This wording seems to imply a longer-term stability of prices than had existed under the Hueda kings, but although they may no longer have been renegotiated from one ship to the next they were still subject to change over time. In fact the price of slaves continued to rise under Dahomian rule, from 7 ounces per male slave in the 1730s to 13 ounces by the 1790s (see Table 4.1). Changes in the ruling price were now decreed by the king from the capital rather than settled in local negotiations with the Yovogan at Ouidah; in 1767, for example, the king sent messengers to the European forts to give notice of 'his intention to raise the price of slaves'. The value of the ounce in goods could also be varied by royal decree; in 1783, following complaints that European traders were giving goods of poor quality and/or short measure, the king temporarily doubled the quantity of certain goods (including

[34] Marion Johnson, 'The ounce in eighteenth-century West African trade', *JAH*, 7 (1966), 197–214; with some refinements in Law, 'Gold trade', 112–15.
[35] Karl Polanyi, 'Sortings and "ounce trade" in the West African slave trade', *JAH*, 5 (1964), 154–69.
[36] De Chenevert & Bullet, 'Réflexions', 48; Forbes, *Dahomey*, i, 111.

tobacco and linen) reckoned to the ounce.[37] Differential prices were paid for men and women and for adults and children. The *Dahomet* in 1773, for example, at the beginning of its trade paid 10 ounces for adult men, but only 7 ounces for women and boys and 6 for girls; the *Swallow* in 1792 paid 13 ounces for men and 11 for boys, but 10 for women and 8 for girls. The age of children was apparently estimated by their height; an account of the 1780s records that the trader went to purchase slaves 'with his measuring stick in hand'.[38]

The system of 'fixed' prices was not entirely inflexible, even within the course of the trade of any single ship. Under the Hueda kings in the 1690s, it was noted that European captains sometimes competed for the slaves on offer, 'out-bidding each other, whereby they enhance the prices'; but this apparently alludes to bargaining over which goods (or what combination of different goods) should be paid, rather than over the price in any particular sort of goods.[39] Under Dahomian rule, however, there was evidently also some flexibility in relation to the price as set in ounces, as is shown by the accounts of the *Dahomet* and the *Swallow*. The first began paying 10 ounces for a man and 7 for a woman, but raised its price to 11 and 8 ounces respectively after less than two weeks' trading; the latter did most of its trade at 13 ounces for men and 10 for women, but paid 15 and 13 ounces during its last week of trading. This is consistent with evidence from elsewhere in West Africa, that ships tended to pay higher prices towards the end of their trade, in order to expedite their departure.[40] How this relates to the regime of supposedly fixed prices at Ouidah is not clear; possibly the 'fixed' price was in practice a minimum, which Europeans could exceed if they wished. Forbes in 1850 also suggests some flexibility around the fixed price, noting that the legally established price was 'subject to [the king's agent's] alteration, if concurred in by the viceroy and six traders or superintendants [sic] of trade appointed by the king'.[41]

The Hueda kings before the Dahomian conquest also received higher prices than other sellers of slaves; according to the Dutch trader Willem Bosman in the 1690s, for example, slaves purchased from the king cost 'commonly one third or one fourth higher than ordinary'.[42] It is not clear whether this practice was initially continued under Dahomian rule. No eighteenth-century source explicitly refers to it, and the accounts of the *Dahomet* and the *Swallow* do not suggest any such price differential, except that the former (but not the latter) paid for the two children purchased from the Yovogan at the opening of trade at adult prices.[43] Otherwise, African suppliers were generally all paid at the same rate; the only systematic distinction was that higher prices were paid for slaves bought from Europeans, who

[37] PRO, T70/1160, Day Book, William's Fort, 17 Sept. 1767; T70/1545, Lionel Abson, Ouidah, 26 Sept. 1783.

[38] Isert, *Letters*, 98.

[39] Phillips, 'Journal', 218; see Bosman, *Description*, 364a.

[40] Klein, *Atlantic Slave Trade*, 104.

[41] Forbes, *Dahomey*, i, 111.

[42] Bosman, *Description*, 363a; see Atkins, *Voyage*, 172.

[43] The *Dahomet* paid 17 oz. for a boy and a girl, evidently representing the price of a man at 10 oz. and a woman at 7, but the *Swallow* only 19 oz., when prices were 13 for a man and 10 for a woman.

received one ounce per slave more than given to Africans, the difference presumably representing the European traders' commission on the sales. However, royal price differentials are again attested in the trade of the nineteenth century. Forbes in 1850 referred to the 'royal price' as being 'ten per cent under the market' (i.e. in terms of the prices for European goods), although he noted that officials such as the Boya were permitted to trade at the royal price, in lieu of salary. Likewise in the palm-produce trade in the 1870s, Europeans were 'compelled to sell goods to the king at lower rates than to his subjects, and thus we have two distinct trades, the king's trade and our ordinary business'; it was then also noted that women of the royal palace sometimes arranged for their own business to be done by the king's trader, in order to benefit from these preferential prices, although this was strictly irregular.[44]

After payment of customs, permission to trade with the ship was formally proclaimed by the official 'bell-ringer' or 'Captain Gong Gong [Fon *gangan*, bell]'. The actual business of trade was conducted through officially appointed inter-mediaries. The Yovogan designated two 'brokers' for the European trader, whose duty was to serve as agents in the purchase of slaves, 'to go to the [African] traders' houses and look for slaves and stand interpreter for the purchase'.[45] Under the Hueda kings, slaves had been brought to a central communal prison, or 'trunk', in the capital Savi, where Europeans went to buy them.[46] It does not appear, however, that there was any similar central point of sale in Ouidah under Dahomian rule. Nowadays, visitors to Ouidah are shown a site, by a tree south of the de Souza compound, which is described as the 'place of auction [la place des enchères]' where it is said slaves were sold. This was, indeed, formerly the site of a market, but slaves were not in fact sold in this or any other public market in Ouidah, but rather out of merchants' houses. An account of the 1780s describes how the Dahomian broker employed by a European trader 'criss-crosses the town every morning, going from one negotiator [i.e. trader] to another and asking if slaves have arrived'; when they did arrive, the factor 'goes into the houses of the black merchants to inspect the slaves and, if they please him, he buys them'. This remained the practice in the nineteenth century also: 'Slaves are never exposed in the market, but all sales are arranged privately in the houses of the dealers.'[47] Moreover, as has been seen, slaves destined for export were not, in fact, auctioned but sold at prices set in advance by the local authorities; recollections of auctions of slaves, if authentic, may relate to domestic slaves, forming part of the estates of deceased Europeans, which were indeed sold in Ouidah by public auction, at least occasionally.[48]

Prior to the nineteenth century, slaves were not usually held in large numbers against the arrival of ships, but were delivered as they became available; as Barbot noted in 1682, '[they] send their slaves on board, as soon as they arrive from the interior of the country'.[49] Later in the 1680s, the English factory in Ouidah was

---

[44] Forbes, *Dahomey*, i, 111; Swanzy, 'On the trade', 481–2.
[45] 'State of the customs', in Williams, *History*, 551; see Isert, *Letters*, 98
[46] Bosman, *Description*, 364.
[47] Isert, *Letters*, 98; PP, Slave Trade 1849–50, Class B. enc. 10 in no. 9, Forbes, 5 Nov. 1849.
[48] For an example, see Duncan, *Travels*, i, 112.
[49] Barbot, *On Guinea*, ii, 637.

instructed to stockpile slaves in order to expedite the loading of ships, but its local agent complained that it lacked sufficient stores of goods to do so.[50] Under Dahomian rule in the eighteenth century, the accounts of the *Dahomet* and the *Swallow* show that most of their slaves were purchased in small lots, only a few each day, which presumably reflects the pace of their delivery from the interior to Ouidah; the former, however, did buy some slaves in large batches, two of 66 and 55 from the English fort and three of 20, 23 and 14 from the French fort, which had probably been accumulated and held in advance of sale. Loading times were highly variable, depending on the number of ships competing for slaves as well as on the supply arriving from the interior. At the height of the trade under the Hueda kings, Ouidah had a reputation for rapid delivery: in the late 1690s, Bosman reckoned that it could supply a thousand slaves every month, if the paths from the interior were open, and that ships could be dispatched on average in less than a month.[51] Under Dahomian rule later, however, at any rate from the 1770s onwards, the supply of slaves for sale at Ouidah became less reliable, reflecting both the diversion of the trade from the interior to rival coastal ports and the patchy record of success of Dahomey's own military operations.[52] The European forts collectively complained to the king in 1774 of 'the badness of trade' and in 1780 of 'the scarcity of slaves'.[53] In consequence, the loading of a ship might now take considerable time: the *Dahomet* in 1773 took three and a half months to purchase 422 slaves (8 March to 25 May) and the *Swallow* in 1792–3 over five months (10 November to 25 April) to obtain only 153. Slow rates of loading were also a recurrent subject of complaint to the king and from the capital to Ouidah: in 1782, for example, the king sent a message to the officials and merchants there requiring them to dispatch a British captain within the month, 'otherwise they would incur his displeasure'.[54]

Slaves were not always delivered upon payment, goods sometimes being advanced on credit against their subsequent delivery.[55] Bosman in the 1690s noted that 'If there happen to be no stock of slaves, the [European] factor must then resolve to run the risk of trusting the inhabitants with goods to the value of one or two hundred slaves; which commodities they send into the inland countries, in order to buy with them slaves at all markets.'[56] Likewise, under Dahomian rule, in the 1780s 'the slave traders here … may often have a credit from the Europeans to the extent of a thousand or more thalers [dollars]', equivalent to the value of around 70 slaves; and in the palm-oil trade of the nineteenth century, in the 1870s it was reported that the king 'rarely pays ready cash or produce for his purchases' and was usually in debt to British merchants at Ouidah for between £200 and 400,

---

[50] Law, *English in West Africa*, i, no. 812, John Carter, Ouidah, 19 Sept. 1685; idem, *Correspondence from Offra and Whydah*, no. 29, John Carter, Ouidah, 13 Oct. 1685.

[51] Bosman, *Description*, 338, 343.

[52] Akinjogbin, *Dahomey*, 141–3.

[53] PRO, T70/1161–2, Day Book, William's Fort, 14 Oct. 1774, 12 Sept. 1780.

[54] PRO, T70/1162, Day Book, William's Fort, 10 June 1782.

[55] Robin Law, 'Finance and credit in pre-colonial Dahomey', in Endre Stiansen & Jane I. Guyer (eds), *Currencies, Credit and Culture* (Uppsala, 1999), 15–37.

[56] Bosman, *Description*, 363a.

equivalent to around 8–16 tons of palm oil.[57] Although the credit extended to African merchants was evidently short-term in intention, normally cleared during the course of a ship's trading, it was sometimes extended for longer periods. The accounts of the English factory at Savi in 1682, for example, listed among its assets 15 slaves 'standing out', which had been 'acknowledged before the King and assured to be paid off at the arrival of the next [Royal African] Company's ship'.[58] Moreover, in practice, debts were often left unpaid beyond the agreed term. The governor of the English fort in Ouidah in 1782 tried to refuse further credit, complaining of debts owed by several leading officials: the Migan owed him for 47 slaves, plus 150 oz. worth of goods supplied for ivory, the Mehu 6 slaves and over 39 oz. for ivory, the Ajaho owed for 8 slaves, the Brazilian returnee Dom Jeronimo 37, the current Yovogan 3, and there were debts of 12 slaves due from two previous Yovogan, which the king had undertaken to pay, besides which he was owed 500 oz. for cowries by 'the Black Traders, women &c'.[59] In 1781 presumably in response to European complaints, the king issued an edict 'forbidding his people getting into white men's debts'.[60] However, the practice continued and remained a feature of the illegal trade of the nineteenth century. The Brazilian trader José Francisco dos Santos in the 1840s, for example, complained that 'You have to give credit to the Blacks, and they pay late or never.'[61]

In some other West African coastal ports, such as Old Calabar and Douala, credit extended by European to African merchants was secured by the giving of persons as 'pawns', who could be taken as slaves in case of default on the delivery of the slaves for whose purchase goods had been advanced.[62] There is no evidence for this practice in the European trade at Ouidah, however, either under the Hueda kings before 1727 or under Dahomian rule later, although pawning was practised within the domestic economy. Under the Hueda kings, payment of debts could be enforced by 'panyarring' (from Portuguese *penhorár*, 'distrain'), seizing a person who might be sold to clear the debt, but this was no longer permitted under Dahomian rule.[63] In Dahomey, debts could only be pursued in the royal courts, which in principle could order the debtor and his family to be sold into slavery, although this sanction was rarely invoked.[64] This absence of private-order mechanisms for the recovery of debts in Ouidah evidently reflected both the effectiveness of the Dahomian state, which was strong enough to guarantee the policing of credit, and its concern to monopolize coercive power.

Credit was also extended in the opposite direction, from Africans to Europeans.

---

[57] Isert, *Letters*, 98; Swanzy, 'On the trade', 481.

[58] Law, *English in West Africa*, i, no. 488, receipt for goods, 24 Oct. 1682, enc. to Timothy Armitage, Ouidah, 28 Oct. 1682.

[59] PRO, T70/1545, Lionel Abson, Ouidah, 14 Dec. 1782.

[60] PRO, T70/1162, Day Book, William's Fort, 30 Nov. 1781.

[61] Dos Santos correspondence, no. 28 [3 March 1846].

[62] Paul E. Lovejoy & David Richardson, 'Trust, pawnship and Atlantic history: the institutional foundations of the Old Calabar slave trade', *American Historical Review*, 102 (1999), 333–55; idem, 'The business of slaving: pawnship in Africa, *c.* 1600–1810', *JAH*, 41 (2001), 67–89.

[63] Law, 'On pawning', 60–2, 64–5.

[64] As was noted in the 1870s: Swanzy, 'On the trade', 482.

Bosman recalled that in the 1690s when he had taken slaves on board but was unable to land goods to pay for them, owing to bad weather, the king and chiefs agreed to accept payment 'at the arrival of other ships', although in the event the weather improved and Bosman was able to pay them.[65] The Hueda traders accepted written 'notes' from European traders for the goods due to them.[66] Immediately after the Dahomian conquest, the king's traders, being unfamiliar with this practice, showed a marked lack of confidence in these notes, saying 'they did not like a bit of paper for their slaves, because the writing might vanish from it, or else the notes might be lost'.[67] But by the 1780s 'notes of credit' were again standard in the Ouidah trade; a British trader in 1803 noted that 'The black traders seldom receive payment for a slave, from the whites, at the time of delivery', but 'prefer promissory notes, or books as they call them', which were presented for payment 'at the winding up of accounts'.[68] Problems arose over default on debts owed by Europeans to Africans, as well as by Africans to Europeans. In 1786, for example, the king sent to complain about non-payment for slaves he had supplied on credit.[69]

The landing of goods and embarkation of slaves continued to be done by African canoes. It remained normal practice in the eighteenth and into the nineteenth century for European ships to bring canoes and canoemen with them from the Gold Coast on their way down to Ouidah, although alternatively, they could be hired locally from the European forts, which maintained their own staff of canoemen. The passage through the surf was extremely hazardous, with canoes frequently capsized, and crews and passengers at risk from man-eating sharks as well as from drowning. Bad weather could prevent canoes landing or embarking for several days at a time, with the worst conditions occurring during the rainy season, between April and July.[70]

Tents or huts were set up on the beach, for the temporary storage of goods, but these were occupied only during the daytime, European traders normally retiring to Ouidah itself overnight.[71] Goods had to be taken from the beach overland to Ouidah, employing the services of local porters, who were hired at the rate of 120 cowries per load or day. The cost of carriage of goods was a recurrent source of concern for Europeans trading at Ouidah, especially in pre-Dahomian times, when they had to be carried not just to Ouidah but from there on to Savi, where the actual purchasing of slaves was then done.[72] In 1713 the director of the English fort proposed the cutting of a canal from the sea to the town, to enable canoes to

---

[65] Bosman, in Van Dantzig, 'English Bosman and Dutch Bosman – VI', 284–5.
[66] Phillips, 'Journal', 218.
[67] Snelgrave, *New Account*, 87–8 (at Jakin, rather than Ouidah).
[68] Isert, *Letters*, 98; M'Leod, *Voyage*, 89.
[69] Akinjogbin, *Dahomey*, 145.
[70] E.g. Norris, *Memoirs*, 61–2; Adams, *Remarks*, 239; M'Leod, *Voyage*, 7–8; Forbes, *Dahomey*, i, 127–8; see also Law, 'Between the sea and the lagoons', 224–9.
[71] E.g. Isert, *Letters*, 97; Adams, *Remarks*, 239; Burton, *Mission*, i, 32.
[72] In 1682 the local factor of the Royal African Company advised against moving their factory from Offra to Hueda, on the grounds that 'the cheapness of carrying goods to the factory from the waterside was not so great': Law, *English in West Africa*, i, no. 493, John Winder, 15 March 1683.

transport goods directly to the town, but this project was rejected by the Hueda authorities as 'not natural'. In 1714 he alternatively suggested employing horses, in order to save the cost of hiring porters, but this too was not implemented, presumably because it was realized that horses did not thrive in the coastal environment. Although horses were known in Ouidah, they were very few and employed only for riding on ceremonial occasions by the Yovogan and other senior officials.[73] Goods were normally head-loaded to Ouidah, a standard load being 50–60 lb., equivalent for example to 2 iron bars, 5 gallons of rum or 20,000 cowries;[74] to deliver the price of a single slave would therefore take several porters (or journeys). Barrels of goods too large to be head-loaded were probably rolled along the ground; certainly the delivery of water to the beach for the ships was done by 'water-rollers', hired in gangs of six, who were paid 80 cowries per barrel delivered, plus 80 cowries daily for subsistence. The journey involved crossing the lagoon, which was normally forded on foot, although when the waters were high it might be done by canoe.[75] In 1776 the Dahomians constructed a 'bridge' (meaning probably a causeway) over the lagoon, in order to facilitate the movement of troops to the beach, but this is not mentioned subsequently, so presumably was either not completed or not maintained.[76]

Under the Hueda kings, there were two officials, a 'captain of the sand [i.e. of the beach]', who oversaw the security of goods delivered at the beach, and a 'captain of the slaves', who directed the delivery of slaves to the beach.[77] Under Dahomian rule, however, contemporary accounts in the eighteenth century refer to a single official, called the 'conductor', whose business it was 'to take care of goods coming from, and slaves going to the beach', and who was 'answerable for deficiency' and was paid a galina (200) of cowries for every time he conducted anything, plus a flask of brandy every Sunday.[78] Other references to a person posted on the north bank of the lagoon to monitor the movement of Europeans, who required the permission of the Yovogan to leave the country and were issued 'passes' for this purpose, may refer to the same official.[79] Recent tradition names the official who managed the embarkation of slaves as 'Gankpé' (or 'Yankpé').[80] This name also occurs occasionally in contemporary sources: as 'Gampe' in an account of 1797, described as a subordinate of the Cakanacou of Zoungbodji, having the responsibility of guarding the beach and sending advice to Ouidah of the arrival of European traders; and as 'Nar-o-pay' in 1851, who was said to own a house on the bank of the lagoon.[81]

---

[73] ANF, C6/25, Du Colombier, 14 Feb. 1715; PRO, T70/5, Joseph Blaney & Martin Hardrett, Ouidah, 4 Aug. 1714.

[74] Phillips, 'Journal', 227; Forbes, *Dahomey*, i, 51.

[75] Duncan refers to a 'ferry': *Travels*, i, 112; for an instance of crossing by canoe, see PRO, FO84/886, Louis Fraser, Daily journal, 22 July 1851.

[76] ANF, C6/26, Dewarel, 1 Oct. 1776.

[77] Phillips, 'Journal', 218–19. Another source refers to a 'conducteur des marchandises' and a 'conducteur des captifs': Labat, *Voyage*, ii, 92–3; des Marchais, 'Journal', 32.

[78] 'State of the customs', in Williams, *History*, 551.

[79] E.g. Duncan, *Travels*, i, 112.

[80] E.g. Fakambi, *La Route des esclaves*, 38.

[81] Pires, *Viagem*; PRO, FO84/886, Fraser, Daily journal, 30 July 1851.

This probably represents Gnahouikpe ('Gnahoui junior'), which is the name of a family in Ouidah whose founder is said to have been appointed as 'assistant' to the first Yovogan, in the 1740s.[82]

In the seventeenth and eighteenth centuries, slaves were normally embarked as and when they were purchased, although the process might be delayed by weather conditions. While awaiting an opportunity for embarkation, they were lodged in secure buildings called by Europeans 'trunks' (Dutch *troncken*; French *troncs*);[83] the Fon term was *ganho*, 'iron hut', referring to the shackles in which slaves were held.[84] Under the Hueda kings, when a communal 'trunk' was maintained at Savi by the local authorities, slaves were returned to this trunk after their purchase had been agreed, their subsistence thereafter being charged to their European purchasers; a 'Captain of the Trunk' was responsible for any losses through escape (but evidently not through death).[85] Alternatively, slaves could be lodged in the European forts at Ouidah. Under Dahomian rule, the system was some- what different. As reported in the 1780s, once the purchase had been concluded, 'the slave, if not a royal slave, is then delivered to the fort or factory in the evening. But if it is a royal slave, he must stay with the black negotiators until he can be brought directly to the ship.'[86] The reason for this distinction is not explained, but it may be because private traders did not have secure facilities for the holding of slaves; presumably the king's slaves were lodged in the prison in the Yovogan's residence.

In the illegal trade of the nineteenth century, when the three European forts were no longer functioning (and by the 1840s were taken over for 'legitimate' trade in palm oil), the leading foreign slave-traders resident in the town maintained their own prisons for slaves, now generally known as 'barracoons' (from the Spanish *barracón*). Duncan in 1845 reported seeing six 'large barracoons' at Ouidah.[87] Another account reported that the barracoons were situated near the residence of the leading slave merchant of the period, Francisco Felix de Souza.[88] Local 'tradi- tion' nowadays asserts that de Souza's barracoon was located in Zomaï quarter, on the west of the town;[89] the name Zomaï, 'Fire (or Light) prohibited', is commonly linked to its role as a barracoon – the usual explanation being that slaves were brought to the barracoon by night and kept there in darkness as a means of control. This story is doubtful, however, since earlier sources explain the name as alluding to the location of de Souza's stores of gunpowder in this area;[90] probably, an authentic tradition of a storehouse here has been embellished in the recent quest for 'sites of memory' connected to the slave trade. Likewise, recent 'tradition'

---

[82] Reynier, 'Ouidah', 53 (spelling the name as 'Niaouké'); Agbo, *Histoire*, 210.

[83] E.g. Barbot, *On Guinea*, ii, 637.

[84] Agbo, *Histoire*, 235 (in the praise-name of Gnahoui).

[85] Bosman, *Description*, 364a; Phillips, 'Journal', 234.

[86] Isert, *Letters*, 98.

[87] PP, Report from the Select Committee on the Slave Trade, 1848, Minutes of Evidence, § 3048–52.

[88] Sir Henry Huntley, *Seven Years' Service on the Slave Coast of Western Africa* (London, 1850), i, 117.

[89] Fakambi, *La Route des esclaves*, 30; Gilles Soglo, 'Notes sur la traite des esclaves à Glexhe (Ouidah)', in Elisée Soumonni et al. (eds), *Le Bénin et la Route de l'esclave* (Cotonou, 1994), 69.

[90] E.g. Burton, *Mission*, i, 107.

identifies a second place, also called Zomaï, situated in the village of Zoungbodji south of Ouidah, as the location of a barracoon in which slaves were lodged before their final departure for the beach; an adjoining site, which is believed to have been that of a communal grave for those who died prior to embarkation, was chosen in 1992 for the erection of a memorial for the victims of the slave trade (called 'Le Mémorial du souvenir'). Here again, although the story is not intrinsically implausible, the location of a barracoon at Zoungbodji is not corroborated in any contemporary source.

The experience of the victims

The above description follows convention in describing the operation of the trade from the point of view of the European purchasers. But what of the experience of the slaves themselves? This is more difficult to reconstruct from the available evidence. There are few descriptions of the embarkation of slaves in European sources; the only really detailed treatment is by Duncan, in 1845; and the only accounts by persons who had themselves experienced embarkation as slaves from Ouidah, by Mahommah Gardo Baquaqua and Cudjo Lewis, also relate to the mid-nineteenth century (1845 and 1860 respectively). By this time the slave trade was illegal, and this illegality, as will be seen in the following chapter, affected the conditions under which slaves were exported, in particular, encouraging their embarkation *en bloc* rather than, as earlier, in small parties as and when they were purchased and weather conditions permitted. Also, in the illegal trade, slaves were often not shipped directly from Ouidah, but were sent along the lagoon to other places for embarkation, as happened to Baquaqua, who was taken by boat on a journey of two nights and a day, to be embarked from a place whose name he did not remember but which was probably Little Popo.[91]

The slaves sold through Ouidah included some who had been enslaved through capture by the Dahomian army and others who were purchased from the interior; some of the latter, it was noted in the eighteenth century, might have been 'sold 7 or 8 times from market to market before arriving' at Ouidah.[92] Of the two whose narratives survive, Cudjo Lewis exemplifies the former and Baquaqua the latter pattern. Cudjo was captured in a Dahomian raid on his home town of 'Togo' or 'Tarkar', probably Takon, north of Porto-Novo;[93] while Baquaqua was from Djougou in northern Bénin, enslaved by kidnapping, and had been resold at least twice before arriving in Ouidah. His original captor took him to Tchamba (south-west of Djougou, in modern Togo), where he was sold to a woman, who took him on to 'Efau', i.e. Fon, referring apparently to a town in the north of Dahomey; there he was sold again to a 'very rich' man who lived locally, and it was presumably this man who subsequently took him south through Abomey to Ouidah, where

[91] Baquaqua, *Biography*, 41.
[92] Pruneau, *Description*, 209.
[93] The campaign seems to be identical with that recorded by Burton against 'Attako (Taccow), near Porto-Novo': *Mission*, i, 256.

'they took me to a white man's house', to whose owner he was presumably again sold.[94]

The distance which slaves had already travelled prior to their arrival at Ouidah affected their psychological state, as well as their physical condition. Those captured in Dahomian wars against neighbouring states might entertain hopes of escaping back home or of redemption by relatives, before they were sold into export. In one incident in 1803, following a Dahomian attack on a town in the interior, it transpired that a son of the town's ruler was among captives sold to a British trader at Ouidah; when the Dahomian authorities became aware of this, the Coke, head of the royal traders, came to the English fort to transmit an offer of restoration to his father's position, but when the young man identified himself, he was instead seized to be sacrificed at the Annual Customs.[95] Although in this instance the offer of liberation was a deceit, evidently this was only effective because the idea of last-minute rescue was considered plausible. The possibility of liberation in fact extended, exceptionally, even to slaves already embarked on European ships; in 1784 the king sent to Ouidah to redeem a slave who had been 'sold on board one of the ships in the road by mistake'.[96] Contrariwise, those brought from the remoter interior had already passed beyond any realistic prospect of redemption or escape. Baquaqua's account illustrates this; he recalls that on his passage south to the coast, he at first hoped that he might regain his freedom by escaping, or else that his mother might arrange to send money for his redemption. He explicitly indicates the point at which he lost hope of liberation, on his arrival in the Dahomian capital:

> When we arrived here I began to give up all hopes of ever getting back to my home again, but had entertained hopes until this time of being able to make my escape, and by some means or other of once more seeing my native place, but at last, hope gave way; the last ray seemed fading away, and my heart felt sad and weary within me, as I thought of my mother, whom I loved most tenderly, and the thought of never more beholding her, added very much to my perplexities. I felt sad and lonely.

Even as the prospect of redemption or escape faded, there remained the possibility of being retained in slavery locally rather than being sold on for export, the decision being outside the slaves' control and largely a matter of chance, although the fact that Europeans offered higher prices for male than for female slaves obviously encouraged the selling of males into export. Baquaqua records meeting a friend from Djougou, called Woru, who was already held as a slave in Ouidah and who 'seemed anxious that I should stay', but Baquaqua, as he says, 'was destined for other parts'.[97]

Slaves generally arrived in Ouidah overland from Abomey, via Allada, Tori and Savi, a journey of 100 km; Baquaqua recalled this journey as taking only a day and a half, although this seems an improbably rapid passage.[98] But some slaves arrived

---

[94] Baquaqua, *Biography*, 35–40.
[95] M'Leod, *Voyage*, 66–71.
[96] PRO, T70/1162, Day Book, William's Fort, 26 Feb. 1784.
[97] Baquaqua, *Biography*, 39–41.
[98] Ibid., 40.

in Ouidah from the east, from Oyo and other places, brought part of the way by canoe to the lagoonside ports of Abomey-Calavi or Jakin, from where they might be brought either overland or by canoe along the lagoon to Ouidah. Most probably arrived in small groups, as noted earlier. But when large numbers of slaves were taken in Dahomian campaigns, these might be delivered to Ouidah in bulk: in 1862, for example, a party of 400 slaves was awaited in Ouidah, apparently captives from a recent campaign against the town of Ishaga, to the east.[99]

Arrived in Ouidah, slaves might spend a variable amount of time in custody there, either before sale or while awaiting favourable weather conditions for embarkation. Baquaqua implies that he spent only a single night in Ouidah, being put on the morning after his arrival on a boat that took him along the lagoon to the place where he was embarked for the trans-Atlantic crossing, but this was surely exceptional; Cudjo Lewis was held in a 'stockade' for about three weeks before being sold.[100] The conditions under which slaves were held in Ouidah evidently anticipated the unhealthy conditions on board ship. In the 1690s a British trader remarked on the 'horrid stench of the Negroes' in the trunk at Savi, 'it being an old house where all the slaves are kept together, and evacuate nature where they lie, so that no jakes [i.e. latrine] can stink worse'; they were also poorly fed, subsisted at a minimal standard, 'like our [European] criminals, on bread and water', at a cost to their European owners of only 2 Dutch stuivers (about 30 cowries) per day.[101] Although Duncan in the 1840s painted a benign picture of conditions in the barracoons at Ouidah, maintaining that they were not overcrowded and the slaves held in them were well fed and taken out periodically for an 'airing', this was not the usual perception; another observer of the same period described the experience of those held while awaiting shipment as of 'filth, disease and famine'.[102] In these conditions, mortality among slaves prior to embarkation was clearly significant. The English fort at Ouidah in 1728 advised against purchasing slaves in advance of the arrival of ships on which to embark them, not only because of the cost of their subsistence but also because of 'the risk of mortality occasioned by the smallpox, flux, fevers and other distempers incident in this part of the country'.[103] This became a bigger problem in the illegal trade of the nineteenth century, when slaving operations were disrupted by the British navy's anti-slaving squadron, and slaves therefore often had to be kept locally for longer periods while awaiting an opportunity for embarkation. At the very end of the slave trade, in 1864, when the British blockade prevented the shipment of a cargo of slaves, smallpox 'wreaked … the most fearful ravages' among them; altogether 800 out of 2,000 died, from a combination of disease and starvation.[104]

In contrast to this neglect during their incarceration, slaves were prepared for sale so as to present the best possible appearance. Contemporary accounts report

---

[99] Borghero, *Journal*, 111 [Aug. 1862].

[100] Baquaqua, *Biography*, 40–41; Hurston, 'Cudjo's own story', 656.

[101] Phillips, 'Journal', 218; Bosman, *Description*, 364a.

[102] PP, 1848 Select Committee, § 3066–71; Duncan, *Travels*, i, 142; PRO, CO96/2, W.M. Hutton, 27 July 1843.

[103] Law, *Correspondence with William's Fort*, no. 22, Thomas Wilson, Ouidah, 12 July 1728.

[104] PP, Slave Trade 1864, Class A, no. 151, Commodore Wilmot, Ascension, 1 Dec. 1864.

that the African dealers closely shaved older male slaves, to conceal any grey hairs, and anointed their skin with palm oil;[105] and the shaving of the heads of older slaves prior to sale is also recalled in a Dahomian proverb.[106] One account says that female slaves were dressed up attractively when offered for sale, in multiple waist cloths, 'as if they were going to a dance'.[107] Slaves were examined by the ship's surgeon, to check their good health and verify their age, 'making them jump, stretch out their arms swiftly'; their age was estimated by examining their teeth, and Portuguese traders (who were particularly insistent on purchasing only adolescent males) even licked their faces with their tongues to check for stubble. There was an especial concern to check for venereal disease, for which purpose 'our surgeon is forc'd to examine the privities of both men and women with the nicest curiosity'; 'they are thoroughly examined, even to the smallest member, and that naked too both men and women, without the least distinction of modesty'.[108] Cudjo Lewis likewise recalled of the American captain who purchased him in 1860: 'He look and look. He look at our hands, and look at our feet. He feel our arms and legs, he open our mouths and look at our teeth. Then he point at those he want. And he point – like this – at Cudjo.'[109] In the 1780s it was noted that male slaves had their hands tied behind them during this examination, this being done 'by order of the king because a slave once bit a European terribly when he tried to inspect him'.[110]

What happened to the slaves who were rejected by European merchants is unclear. They may have been killed. The Dahomians are certainly reported to have adopted the practice of killing any captives who were old or wounded, or indeed too young, and therefore 'unmerchantable', for example in their campaigns against the Hueda in 1727–8, but this was normally done on the battlefield; as was noted in the 1830s, 'few of the old were so unfortunate [sic] as to reach the barracoon' at Ouidah.[111] One eighteenth-century account, however, records that infants who reached Ouidah with their mothers were commonly 'thrown to the wolves [i.e. hyenas]', meaning presumably that they were abandoned outside the town, because European traders were usually unwilling to buy them.[112] Alternatively, they may have been sold into the local market, although presumably old or sick slaves would have been difficult to dispose of there also. A Dahomian proverb recalls that slaves taken to market who failed to attract a purchaser might be beaten, this being a conventional paradigm of unjustified punishment.[113]

Slaves were branded at or after their sale. In the 1690s, this was done upon

---

[105] Phillips, 'Journal', 218; Labat, *Voyage*, ii, 106.

[106] 'An old slave has his head shaved and is asked to give his name, he says he is called "A few more days"': Jean-Norbert Vignondé, 'Esclaves et esclavage dans la parémologie fon du Bénin', in Doudou Diène (ed.), *La Chaîne et le lien: une vision de la traite négrière* (Paris, 1998), 349.

[107] Isert, *Letters*, 98.

[108] Phillips, 'Journal', 218; Bosman, *Description*, 364; also Labat, *Voyage*, ii, 106.

[109] James Saxon Childers, 'From jungle to slavery – and freedom', *Birmingham News-Age-Herald*, 2 Dec. 1934.

[110] Isert, *Letters*, 98.

[111] Smith, *New Voyage*, 192; Law, *Correspondence with William's Fort*, no. 22, Thomas Wilson, Ouidah, 12 July 1728; Huntley, *Seven Years' Service*, i, 117.

[112] Pruneau, *Description*, 209–12.

[113] Boco, *Proverbes*, i, no. 218.

purchase and prior to the return of the slaves for temporary lodging in the communal 'trunk' at Savi, and at Ouidah in the 1780s it was likewise done immediately after purchase, and prior to the delivery of the slaves to the European factories.[114] But in the illegal trade in the 1840s it was done at 'the beach' immediately prior to embarkation; the modern tradition that slaves were branded at Zoungbodji may, in this case, be an accurate recollection.[115] This marking of slaves was needed, in the system as it operated in the seventeenth and eighteenth centuries, when slaves remained in the custody of their sellers for some time after purchase, in order to prevent confusion between slaves owned by different parties, and also, as Bosman remarked in the 1690s, 'to prevent the Negroes exchanging them for others'.[116] It was still needed in the illegal trade in the nineteenth century, despite the delaying of the branding until immediately before departure, because it was normal practice in this period for several different merchants to embark slaves on any single ship; the correspondence of dos Santos in the 1840s, for example, meticulously transmits details of slaves' brands to their consignees in Brazil, in order to guarantee accurate identification.

The actual process of branding is described in several accounts by European slave-traders; an English captain in 1694, for example, reported that 'we mark'd the slaves in the breast, or shoulder, with a hot iron, having the letter of the ship's name on it, the place being before anointed with a little palm oil', reassuring his readers that this 'caused but little pain, the mark being usually well in four or five days, appearing very plain and white after'; and the Dutchman Bosman a few years later, recorded that 'a burning iron, with the arms and name of the Company's, lies in the fire, with which ours are marked on the breast', insisting that 'we yet take all possible care that they are not burned too hard, especially the women, who are more tender than the men'.[117] The process was also described by Duncan in the 1840s: 'the gang on each chain is in succession marched close to a fire previously kindled on the beach. Here marking-irons are heated, and when an iron is sufficiently hot, it is quickly dipped in palm-oil, in order to prevent its sticking to the flesh.'[118] We have the recollections of one victim of the process, in the account of Baquaqua, exported around the same time as Duncan's visit: '[a] man went round with a hot iron, and branded us, the same as they would the heads of barrels or any other inanimate goods or merchandize'.[119]

For the journey south from Ouidah to embarkation from the beach, slaves were marched in chains and some of them made to carry their provisions for the voyage. The passage of one batch was observed by Duncan in 1845:

> Knowing that a shipment of slaves was about to take place, I stationed myself on the road where I knew they would have to pass. The first party consisted of about seventy very strong athletic men, apparently from twenty to twenty-five years of age. These were followed by a number more, carrying pails or buckets for their food on the passage. About forty were

---

[114] Phillips, 'Journal', 218; Bosman, *Description*, 364; Isert, *Letters*, 98.

[115] Duncan, *Travels*, i, 143; Assogba, *Découverte de la Côte des Esclaves*, 30; Soglo, 'Notes sur la traite', 69.

[116] Bosman, *Description*, 364.

[117] Phillips, 'Journal', 218; Bosman, *Description*, 364–364a; see also Labat, *Voyage*, ii, 94.

[118] Duncan, *Travels*, i, 143.

[119] Baquaqua, *Biography*, 41.

children, varying from seven to ten years of age. These were not in chains; but marched with two slight grass cords, knotted at intervals of a yard. The two cords are put, one on each side of the neck, and another knot is made in front of the neck, leaving sufficient room, but so tight as to prevent the head from being slipped through. The others were all in chains, sometimes eight on one chain. At intervals of a yard are large circular links, which open to receive the neck, and which are secured by a padlock.[120]

In 1850 Forbes likewise saw slaves setting out from Zomaï, at the western end of Ouidah, for shipment from Popo, in a 'chain-gang'; and in 1863 the missionary Francesco Borghero saw slaves being marched from Ouidah eastwards to be embarked from Godomey, under armed guard, 'in detachments of 10 to 20, the men chained by the neck, the women tied by the neck with ropes', though children were carried by their mothers or led by the hand.[121] Cudjo Lewis also recalled that he and his fellow-slaves were marched to the beach, 'one chained behind the other', and Baquaqua too that 'we were all chained together, and tied with ropes round about our necks, and were thus drawn down to the sea shore'. The journey from Ouidah to the beach involved crossing the lagoon, which was done on foot: Cudjo recalled 'they had to wade, the water coming up to their necks'.[122]

Duncan observes that he was 'surprised to see with what cheerfulness they all bustled along as if going to a fair', although an explanation is in fact suggested by a remark which he himself makes elsewhere that when they were taken for shipment the slaves were 'taken out, as if for their usual airing ... without any intimation of their fate'.[123] Surprising as this may appear, the account of Baquaqua confirms that, until he was actually put on the ship, he was unaware that this was the intention: immediately prior to embarkation he and his fellow-slaves were given a hearty meal, of 'rice and other good things in abundance', of which he says 'I was not aware that it was to be my last feast in Africa, I did not know my destiny.'[124] Borghero, however, describes the slaves being taken to Godomey in 1863 as walking 'in the deepest silence', suggesting that these at least were aware of their fate.[125]

In a further brutality, prior to embarkation, slaves were stripped of their clothing. Bosman in the 1690s observed that 'their [African] masters strip them of all they have on their backs; so that they come on board stark-naked as well women as men', and the practice was still noted in the 1720s.[126] Although there is no explicit evidence for it during the first century of Dahomian rule, it evidently continued, since it is referred to again by Duncan in the 1840s: 'the little piece of cotton cloth tied round the loins of the slave is stripped off'.[127] Baquaqua also recalled that he and his fellow-slaves were put on board ship 'in a state of nudity', and Cudjo Lewis that 'as they stepped into the small boats which were to take them to the [ship] ... the Dahomians avariciously tore their garments from them, men and women alike

[120] Duncan, *Travels*, i, 201.
[121] Forbes, *Dahomey*. i, 117; Borghero, *Journal*, 139 [9 Oct. 1863].
[122] Hurston, 'Cudjo's own story', 657; Baquaqua, *Biography*, 41.
[123] Duncan, *Travels*, i, 201, 142–3.
[124] Baquaqua, *Biography*, 41.
[125] Borghero, *Journal*, 139 [9 Oct. 1863].
[126] Bosman, *Description*, 364a; Atkins, *Voyage*, 111, 180.
[127] Duncan, *Travels*, i, 143.

were left entirely nude', which he remembered, even after the passage of over 60 years, as 'a great humiliation'.[128] Likewise, when the French Catholic mission purchased slaves from the Yovogan for local use in 1862, it reported that he 'claimed back the wretched rags which they had to wrap themselves', so that the mission had to provide them with new clothes.[129]

A final ordeal (prior to the horrors of the trans-Atlantic crossing itself) was the embarkation through the surf and across the sandbars in the small canoes employed for this purpose. Even in the canoes, slaves might be shackled, in twos, to prevent rebellion or escape.[130] For those from the interior and who had no familiarity with the sea, who were presumably the great majority, the prospect must have been terrifying. Duncan in 1845, when embarking to leave Ouidah, took with him a seven year-old Mahi slave-girl whom he had received as a gift from Gezo. Although she was not destined for slavery in the Americas, her experience and feelings cannot have been all that different from those who were:

> [she] had never seen the sea, and consequently felt much alarm. She could scarcely be urged to get into the canoe, though I told her she was going back to her Abomey mother [i.e. her foster-mother in captivity in Dahomey], of whom she was very fond ... Unfortunately the sea was very high, and the surf heavy, and ... a sea passed completely over us from bow to stern, filling it ... The little girl, who was upon her knees in the bottom of the canoe, had certainly little cause to be pleased with a sea life, and is very likely to remember her first sea voyage for a long time. As soon as the little creature was able, for she was almost suffocated by the surf, she called out for her Abomey mother.[131]

The canoes were frequently overset, with loss of life by drowning or from the ubiquitous sharks, attracted to the area by the prospect of human prey. Baquaqua recalled that when he was embarked the first boatload of 30 persons was capsized, and everyone lost except for a single man (apparently a member of the crew, rather than one of the slaves).[132]

For some, however, death by drowning or sharks represented a release from the more terrible prospect of what awaited them in slavery across the Atlantic. In the 1690s, an English trader noted that slaves often jumped out of the canoes and dived under water in order to prevent their rescue, embracing death as a preferable alternative, 'they having a more dreadful apprehension of Barbadoes than we can have of hell'.[133]

The profits of the slave trade

The value of slave exports through Ouidah under Dahomian rule is easily enough calculated in aggregate, although of course it fluctuated substantially from year to

[128] Baquaqua, *Biography*, 42; Hurston, 'Cudjo's own story', 657.
[129] Borghero, *Journal*, 114 [1 Sept. 1862].
[130] Phillips, 'Journal', 219.
[131] Duncan, *Travels*, ii, 298–9.
[132] Baquaqua, *Biography*, 42.
[133] Phillips, 'Journal', 219.

year. The level of between 8,000 and 9,000 slaves annually reported in 1750, when male slaves were selling for 33 grand cabess (132,000) cowries, would have yielded (allowing for lower prices paid for females and children) a value of between 210,000 and 240,000 cabess, equivalent to £210,000 and 240,000.[134] Later in the eighteenth century, as has been seen, the volume of exports through Ouidah fell, but this was partly offset by an increase in prices. The export of 5,000 slaves annually in the 1760s, when the price of male slaves was 10 ounces, or 40 grand cabess, would have yielded around 40,000 ounces, equivalent to 160,000 grand cabess of cowries, or £160,000, while 4,500 slaves annually in the 1780s, at 13 oz. per male slave, represented around 50,000 ounces, 200,000 cabess, or £200,000.

But how much of this would have gone to people in Ouidah, as opposed to the royal court of Dahomey or suppliers of slaves further in the interior? On the price of slaves paid to suppliers in the interior, as opposed to those received from European purchasers at the coast, there is little evidence. In 1787 King Kpengla complained that slaves 'in the bush' were costing between 40 and 45 grand cabess, at a time when the price paid by Europeans was 13 ounces or 52 cabess for a man and 10 ounces/40 cabess for a woman, thus squeezing Dahomian profit margins severely; he subsequently tried to impose lower prices, decreeing that no more than 32 cabess should be paid for a man and 26 for a woman, but this had the effect merely of causing interior suppliers to divert their trade to rival ports east and west of Ouidah.[135] This suggests that a gross profit margin of 13 per cent was considered inadequate, but one of 38 per cent was, in current market conditions, unrealistic.

The only detailed analysis of the distribution of returns from the sale of slaves in Dahomey relates to the period of the illegal trade in the nineteenth century, when slave prices were normally denominated in dollars rather than 'ounces' (the dollar being conventionally taken as equivalent to the smaller 'head' of 2,000 cowries, making $8 to the ounce).[136] A British visitor in 1847 recorded that a slave cost $15 at Abomey and $5–6 more at the coast, plus the coastal agent's commission of $16, giving a total selling price of $36–37.[137] This account, however, is problematic, since other evidence gives selling prices for slaves during this same year of between $70–90, the higher price perhaps incorporating the agent's commission and other charges, and in the following year the 'average' price was cited as $80 (see Table 5.1). The rate of the agent's commission is confirmed as $16 in other evidence of this period,[138] but one or other of the other figures must be wrong, or at least aberrant – most probably (in comparison with prices for the 1780s), the initial purchase price at Abomey. If we assume a price of $80, the agent's commission of

---

[134] For a slightly different (and higher) calculation, see Akinjogbin, *Dahomey*, 134.

[135] ANF, C6/26, Gourg, journal, 17–28 Aug. 1787; Dalzel, *History*, 213–14.

[136] The dollar was conventionally valued at 5 shillings (£0.25) sterling; its equation with 2,000 cowries therefore followed the valuation in 'prime cost', by which the 'grand cabess' of 4,000 cowries was equivalent to 10s.(£0.50), rather than in 'trade' value, by which it was worth £1.

[137] Archibald Ridgway, 'Journal of a visit to Dahomey', *New Monthly Magazine*, 81 (1847), 414.

[138] PP, Papers relative to the Reduction of Lagos (1852), enc. in no. 8, Thomas Hutton, 7 Aug. 1850; T.B. Freeman, 'West Africa' (typescript of *c*. 1860, in WMMS), 251 (both referring to the commission received by the king's agent, Francisco Felix de Souza, in the 1840s).

$16 would represent 20 per cent of the selling price (or put in another way, a mark-up of 25 per cent). Although no more than a rough indication, this seems a reasonable figure to assume.

On this basis Ouidah merchants would have been earning in commission something between 32,000 and 48,000 grand cabess of cowries (£32,000–£48,000) annually in the second half of the eighteenth century. Assuming a population for Ouidah of around 7,000, this represented around 18,000–27,500 cowries per capita, equivalent to the standard subsistence rate (80 cowries per day) for 225–340 days. These calculations do not include earnings from the sale of provisions and other services to the European sector. Truly, whatever may have been the case for Dahomey as a whole, Ouidah lived by the slave trade.

The income from the European trade was not, of course, equally spread within Ouidah, but disproportionately enriched the wealthy merchant class. Little quantitative evidence is available on the scale of merchant wealth in Ouidah, but in the 1780s, when Kpengla's attempt to enter the middleman trade in slaves had the effect of forcing several private merchants into bankruptcy, these are said to have included some 'considerable traders' who owned property to the value of between 60 and 70 slaves; and the woman trader Kposi, who was arrested and expropriated in the same period, is also said to have 'acquired considerable property by trade, to the amount of seventy slaves, and upwards'.[139] Some evidence on the scale of merchant incomes in Ouidah is also offered for a later period, in the mid-nineteenth century, by figures for the income tax that leading traders paid, levied at the rate of one-third of income. In 1850 Houénou was reported to be paying tax of $3,500 annually, indicating an assessed annual income of $10,500, equivalent to the commission on the sale of around 650 slaves (or, by 1850, of palm oil to an equivalent value). Gezo himself, as reported by Forbes, claimed that Houénou, Gnahoui, Adjovi and other leading indigenous merchants were paying him $5,000 each annually in 'duties and presents [i.e. direct tax]'. Although Forbes himself thought this 'considerably exaggerated', the figure seems plausible; with export duties levied at $5 per slave, it implies trade of the order of 480–490 slaves annually apiece.[140] This level of taxation, and by implication of trade, was substantially less than that of the leading Brazilian merchant resident in Dahomey at this period, Domingos Martins, who in 1850 estimated his own 'expenses with the king' as no less than £5,000, or $20,000, annually.[141] But it was greater than that levied on senior chiefs of the capital, such as the Mehu, who was paying only 2,000 heads of cowries (equivalent to $2,000) annually, although this may mean that they were more heavily taxed, rather than that their incomes were greater.[142]

Not all of these earnings, of course, would have stayed in Ouidah, a substantial proportion being taken in taxes, and also in expenditure incurred in attendance at the royal court, as well as trading expenses incurred outside the town. In the mid-

[139] Dalzel, *History*, 208, 215.
[140] Blancheley, 'Au Dahomey', *Les missions catholiques*, 23 (1891), 576; PP, Slave Trade 1850–1, Class A, enc. 2 in no. 220, Forbes, Journal, 4 July 1850.
[141] PP, Slave Trade 1849–50, Class A, enc. 10 in no. 9, Forbes, 6 April 1850.
[142] Forbes, *Dahomey*, ii, 75.

nineteenth century returned former slaves from Brazil, many of whom were slave-traders, complained of being 'obliged to give up their trade, and attend the annual customs' in the capital, claiming that this involved 'spending, as they explained, their year's gains in the journey'.[143] But the fiscal exactions of the monarchy, although provoking persistent resentment and complaint, evidently left the Ouidah merchant community still in a position of considerable affluence.

The Atlantic trade and the domestic economy

Polanyi suggested that the European trade in eighteenth- and nineteenth-century Ouidah had no direct linkages to the local economy, since it was monopolized by the Dahomian state. European goods obtained through the sale of slaves thus did not generally enter the local market, and were available to the mass of people only in so far as they were distributed in largesse by the king, in the 'Annual Customs' at the capital. This supposed 'separateness of external trade from the market' was presented as a central feature of Dahomian economic organization.[144]

This picture is empirically unsustainable in several respects. As was seen in the previous chapter, the slave trade in Dahomey was not in fact a royal monopoly, slaves being supplied to Europeans by private merchants, operating on commission or on their own account, as well as by royal officials selling slaves on behalf of the king. It must be assumed that a significant proportion of their earnings, in the form of imported goods or money (cowrie shells), was expended within the local economy of Ouidah. Moreover, European traders also had to purchase goods and services in the local market, so that some of the imported goods went directly into the local economy. In the 1780s, for example, it was estimated that a ship would expend a total of around 100 ounces, mostly in cowries, over and above 'customs' and other duties to the king and other officials, in payment for various services, including 35 oz. for canoe hire, 20 paid to porters, 10 for water-rollers and 5 for laundry-women; 100 oz. representing a value of 1,600,000 cowries, or a standard subsistence rate (80 cowries per day) for 20,000 person/days.[145] The European forts, as well as visiting ships, also paid out substantial sums in wages and for services: the English fort between 1752 and 1811 expended on average in wages and other payments to fort slaves and free Africans the value of nearly 1,000 ounces, or 16 million cowries, annually.[146]

At the most basic level, the implication that imported goods did not go into the local market in significant quantities is demonstrably inaccurate. European descriptions of the main (Zobé) market in Ouidah consistently refer to the presence of stalls selling imported European commodities, as well as agricultural produce and

[143] Ibid., ii, 72.
[144] Polanyi, *Dahomey*, 94. See also Rosemary Arnold, 'Separation of trade and market', in Polanyi, et al., *Trade and Markets in the Early Empires*, 177–87.
[145] 'Account of expences', in Donnan, *Documents*, ii, 596–7.
[146] Derived from statistics in Peukert, *Der atlantische Slavenhandel*, 343–57 (assuming that these figures, which are in sterling, are calculated on the 'prime cost' valuation of £2 to the ounce of 16,000 cowries).

local manufactures. In 1776, for example, the market was described as dealing in 'foodstuffs and European and local goods'; in 1784–5, 'in the stalls one finds every possible kind of European as well as local trade goods'; in 1825, goods on sale in the market included 'a variety of Indian and English manufactures, beads, Brazil tobacco, etc.'; in 1845, it displayed 'many articles of European manufacture', including English cotton cloth and gun-flints; and in 1863 it was reported to include a 'gin palace' which sold 'Brazilian rum, and cheap French liqueurs'.[147] Likewise in 1850 it was noted that traders from Ouidah took 'foreign cloths', rum and tobacco, as well as salt and fish, to the market at Tori, to exchange for palm oil, foodstuffs and locally manufactured cloth.[148]

The lifestyle of Ouidah was clearly marked by widespread consumption of imported luxuries. Forbes noted that the 'general dress' in Dahomey included a large cloth worn over the shoulder, which might be either locally made or imported ('country or foreign'). He also observed that 'foreign liquors are scarce and expensive', the usual drink being local beer, but this, while perhaps true of the interior, was surely not the case in Ouidah; Duncan, on the contrary, refers to its (male) inhabitants as spending their leisure 'smoking and drinking rum'.[149] The impact of overseas trade on the domestic economy, however, penetrated even more deeply than this. The highly commercialized economy of Ouidah, which functioned essentially as a cash economy, was noted in the previous chapter. It was the European trade that provided the massive quantities of currency, in the form of imported cowry shells, which made possible this expansion of the exchange sector of the domestic economy. Even the purchase of basic foodstuffs was thus mediated by a commodity derived from the Atlantic trade.

Local understandings of the slave trade

It is difficult to reconstruct how local people understood the Atlantic slave trade at the time of its operation; and indeed even if the evidence were fuller it would present problems of generalization, since understanding of the trade presumably differed from one area to another and among different social groups within any geographical area. It is tempting to assume, in explanation (and by implication, extenuation) of the willingness of Africans to sell slaves into the Atlantic trade, that they were ignorant of what this involved. In Ouidah, however, and within the Dahomian ruling elite more generally, it seems clear that there must have been an informed understanding of where it was that slaves were sent and what fate awaited them when they got there. There were Dahomian officials who had been to America (and to Europe) on diplomatic missions and returned to tell the tale. Some had even themselves experienced slavery in the Americas. One example is Adomo Tomo, originally a linguist in the English factory at Jakin, who was sent by

[147] De Chenevert & Bullet, 'Réflexions', 20; Isert, *Letters*, 101; PRO, ADM 55/11, Clapperton Journal, 16 Nov. 1825; Duncan, *Travels*, i, 121; Burton, *Mission*, i, 77.
[148] Forbes, *Dahomey*, i, 55.
[149] Ibid., 27, 30; Duncan, *Travels*, i, 199.

Agaja as interpreter on a mission to England in 1726, but initially sold into slavery in Maryland, USA, where he spent around five years before being liberated to complete his journey to England and to return to Dahomey in 1732.[150] Another was the royal prince 'Irookoo', alias Dom Jeronimo, a leading figure in the commercial establishment of Ouidah in the 1780s, who had spent no fewer than 24 years as a slave in Brazil before being redeemed and repatriated to Dahomey.[151]

The slave trade was understood in Dahomey to raise moral issues, but only in relation to defining rules within which it should operate, especially in regard to whom it was considered acceptable to enslave and sell, rather than putting in question the legitimacy of the trade itself – in which, of course, Dahomian attitudes were essentially similar to those of Europeans, prior to the emergence of the abolitionist movement of the eighteenth century.[152] In Dahomian tradition, one of the fundamental laws attributed to the founder-king Wegbaja, in the seventeenth century, prohibited the sale as slaves of anyone born within the kingdom, contravention being a capital offence; in principle, this rule was enforced so rigorously as to prohibit the sale even of female captives who became pregnant while in transit through Dahomey.[153] The prohibition under Dahomian rule of the practice of 'panyarring' persons to enforce payment of debts, noted above, was evidently an expression of this principle, intended to eliminate the danger of Dahomians being wrongly sold into overseas slavery. Slaves in Dahomey were in principle foreigners, captives taken in war or purchased from outside the country; Dahomians should be enslaved only in punishment for some specific and serious offence. When kings of Dahomey, in default of sufficient supplies of foreign slaves, resorted to 'selling their own subjects', as was alleged both of Tegbesu in the last years of his reign and of Gezo in the early 1820s, this was considered aberrant and illegitimate, in effect an index of social breakdown.[154]

As long as the boundaries of what was considered legal enslavement were not transgressed, dealing in slaves does not appear to have raised moral scruples. Although the attitudes which local slave-traders had towards their business are not well documented, some insights are provided by the remembered praise-names of prominent slave-traders who were ancestors of families still resident in the town. References to the slave trade in these are sometimes, by the standards of modern susceptibilities, alarmingly callous. For example, the praise-name of the second head of the Gnahoui family, active in the 1830s–50s, contains the chilling lines: 'Weeping breaks out when the slaves see you visit the prison; the Portuguese man is sad at you selling him old slaves.'[155] The only hint of sympathy for the slaves, in the praise-name of the Brazilian Francisco Felix de Souza, is cast in terms of his

---

[150] Law, 'King Agaja of Dahomey'.

[151] PRO, T70/1545, Lionel Abson, Ouidah, 14 Dec. 1782.

[152] See generally, Robin Law, 'Legal and illegal enslavement in West Africa, in the context of the Atlantic slave trade', in Toyin Falola (ed.), *Ghana in Africa and the World* (Trenton NJ, 2003), 513–33.

[153] Le Herissé, *L'Ancien Royaume*, 55–6, 291.

[154] De Chenevert & Bullet, 'Réflexions', 3; PRO, ADM55/11, Clapperton, Journal, 16 Nov. 1825.

[155] Agbo, *Histoire*, 235–6. The second line also occurs in the praise-names of the d'Oliveira and Tchiakpé families: ibid., 223–4, 248–9.

benevolence rather than of the suffering of the slaves: '[he] on the spot buys the child, the mother, the husband, the wife, just for the asking', which may mean that de Souza, in purchasing slaves, out of the goodness of his heart, would not break up families, as was by implication normal.[156]

In recent times, de Souza family tradition has sought to justify the ancestor's participation in the slave trade by reference to the Dahomian practice of human sacrifice, arguing that those exported as slaves would otherwise have been put to death: it is even claimed, inaccurately, that prior to de Souza's time the Dahomians had killed all the captives whom they took in war, until he persuaded Gezo to sell them instead.[157] This rationalization in fact goes back to the time of de Souza himself; a British official visiting Ouidah in 1844 found that he 'considers himself a great philanthropist', on the grounds of having saved the lives of the slaves whom he purchased for export.[158] Likewise Forbes in 1850, on an abortive mission to persuade the Dahomian authorities to give up the slave trade, heard the same argument from the Yovogan of Ouidah: 'The King of Dahomey, not wishing to kill all his prisoners, would wish to sell a few; if he cannot sell them, what is he to do with them?'[159] Very probably, this argument was derived ultimately from European pro-slavery literature, in which the defence of the slave trade as saving persons from sacrifice in Africa was already standard in the eighteenth century.

The perceptions of the victims of the trade, as opposed to the African slave-traders, are even more difficult to document, but some indications may be derived from subsequent traditions, in so far as they reflect the perspective of communities and social groups that were vulnerable to seizure for enslavement and sale into export. In some other parts of West Africa, such as Sierra Leone and Cameroun, it has been suggested that modern beliefs about witches, who are envisaged either as inhabiting an invisible city where they consume both imported luxuries and human flesh, or as employing their zombified victims as labourers on remote plantations, may reflect memories of the operation of the Atlantic slave trade.[160] In Dahomey also, witches are believed sometimes to exhume their victims from their graves, to sell them 'into servitude in some far-away land'.[161] The implication is that the slave trade was understood in the idiom of witchcraft, European slave-traders (and also the African dealers who sold slaves to them) being equated with witches, who prospered through devouring or otherwise exploiting the souls of their fellow-humans. This interpretation must seem doubtful, however, in the case of Dahomey, where as has been seen people were well aware that America was a place in this world, from which some of those sold as slaves occasionally returned; Edna Bay,

---

[156] Ibid., 225. But an alternative reading might be that this is simply an illustration of de Souza's wealth: he could afford to buy up whole families, rather than individual slaves.

[157] Fieldwork, de Souza compound, Prosper de Souza, 18 Jan. 1996.

[158] PRO, CO96/4, Lieutenant-Governor Hill, Cape Coast Castle, 11 Nov. 1844.

[159] PP, Slave Trade 1850–51, Class A, enc. 1 in no. 198, Forbes, Journal, 15 March 1850.

[160] Rosalind Shaw, *Memories of the Slave Trade: Ritual and the Historical Imagination in Sierra Leone* (Chicago, 2002), ch. 8; Ralph A. Austen, 'Douala: slave trade and memory in the periphery of the Nigerian hinterland', in Law & Strickrodt, *Ports of the Slave Trade*, 79–80.

[161] Herskovits, *Dahomey*, ii, 243–4.

indeed, has argued that the slave trade was understood in Dahomey as a mechanism for the exile of political opponents.[162] But this is perhaps a question of different levels of understanding; what was well known in Ouidah and Abomey might have been unknown to the slaves themselves, especially if they did not speak a language in which they could communicate with their sellers.

The problem is basically one of evidence. While the equation of witchcraft with slave-trading in recent tradition is undeniable, this might represent a retrospective interpretation of witchcraft in terms of the slave trade, rather than a contemporaneous understanding of the slave trade as witchcraft. However, the latter hypothesis does have some support in the contemporary record, in recurrent reports that slaves believed that Europeans purchased them in order to eat them, this being perhaps better understood in terms of the spiritual cannibalism allegedly practised by witches, rather than in a literally culinary mode. Such beliefs were reported in Ouidah in the late seventeenth century. Barbot in the 1680s, for example, noted that 'all the slaves from [Ouidah and Offra] ... firmly believe that we have bought them to have them fattened in our own country, so that we will be better able to sell them when they are suitable to be eaten'; likewise, Bosman in the 1690s, 'We are sometimes sufficiently plagued with a parcel of slaves, which come from a far in-land country, who very innocently persuade one another, that we buy them only to fatten and afterwards eat them as a delicacy', and the belief was still reported at Ouidah in the 1720s.[163] It seems significant that Bosman refers to slaves specifically from the far interior, whose knowledge of the operation of the trade may be assumed to be have been more limited; and it is also noteworthy that this belief in European cannibalism is not reported from Ouidah itself in later periods, perhaps reflecting the diffusion of a more realistic understanding of the purpose of the trade. It evidently persisted, however, in the interior: in the 1820s it was still noted that slaves for sale in Borgu were terrified of being sold to the coast, as it was 'the universal belief that all those who are sold to the whites are eaten'. Likewise Baquaqua, who was from Djougou to the west of Borgu, claims, as noted earlier, to have had no knowledge of his intended destination prior to his embarkation for the trans-Atlantic passage, and initially understood his fate in religious terms, assuming that he was to be sacrificed: 'I had never seen a ship before, and my idea of it was, that it was some object of worship of the white man. I imagined that we were all to be slaughtered, and were being led there for that purpose.'[164]

A variant of the concept of slave-traders as cannibals that has been recorded in Dahomey relates that the cowry shells which were used locally as money were obtained by fishing with the corpses of slaves, who were killed and thrown into the sea, to be fed upon by the sea snails, and then hauled back out to retrieve the shells.[165]

---

[162] Edna G. Bay, 'Protection, political exile, and the Atlantic slave trade: history and collective memory in Dahomey', *S&A*, 22 (2001), 42–60.

[163] Barbot, *On Guinea*, ii, 639; Bosman, *Description*, 365; des Marchais, 'Journal', 38; Labat, *Voyage*, ii, 116.

[164] Hugh Clapperton, *Journal of a Second Expedition into the Interior of Africa* (London, 1829), 94; Baquaqua, *Biography*, 42.

[165] Elwert, *Wirtschaft und Herrschaft*, 90–92; A. Félix Iroko, 'Cauris et esclaves en Afrique occidentale entre le XVe et le XIXe siècles', in Serge Daget (ed.), *De la traite à l'esclavage* (Nantes, 1988), i, 199. In another

While this telescopes geography, since cowries were fished in the Indian Ocean rather than the Atlantic, it nicely expresses the moral truth that monetary wealth was obtained at the cost of the lives of the exported slaves.[166] Here again, however, whether this story dates back to the time of the slave trade or represents only a retrospective construction is uncertain.

A parallel belief is recorded in West/Central Africa, where the Kongo envisage the lands of the living and dead as separated by water, and the land of the dead is consequently identified with America (and/or Europe, the two continents being commonly conflated); within this framework also, the trans-Atlantic slave trade is understood as 'a form of witchcraft', involving the transportation of Africans to the Otherworld 'improperly and prematurely'.[167] In Dahomian belief likewise, the Land of the Dead, Kutomen, is located beyond a river, which the souls of the deceased have to cross by canoe; accordingly, a ceremony held some time after the actual burial, intended to secure their entry into the Otherworld, is called their 'embarkation' (*cyodohun*, 'putting the corpse in a boat').[168] Although Kutomen was thought to be underground, the river that had to be crossed to enter it was sometimes identified with actual rivers; Duncan in the 1840s understood it to be the Volta, to the west.[169] It was also, however, sometimes identified with the coastal lagoon, implying that the Land of the Dead lay in or beyond the Atlantic; this is one explanation offered for the name of Cotonou (Kutonun), the lagoonside port east of Ouidah, meaning 'At the mouth of the river of the dead'. However, no similar tradition seems to have been attached to Ouidah, and, indeed, even at Cotonou the story is not linked to the slave trade.[170] Moreover, existence in Kutomen was regarded positively; it was the souls who were unable to enter it (those 'not yet embarked') and were instead condemned to wander between the worlds of the living and the dead whose fate was pitied and feared and who might become victims of witchcraft. Evidently, for Dahomians the land of enslavement across the Atlantic was distinct from that of the properly buried dead.

In fact, liberation from slavery in America was often seen in terms of escape into the Land of the Dead back in Africa. One aspect of the experience and attitudes of the enslaved and transported Africans that is well attested in contemporary sources is the idea that when they died, their souls would return to Africa, which even caused some to commit suicide as a means of getting back home. Although this belief is mainly documented among African slave populations in the Americas, it was certainly current also in Africa among those

---

[165] (cont.) version, the story is transposed to America: Chatwin, *Viceroy of Ouidah*, 26.

[166] Ralph A. Austen, 'The moral economy of witchcraft', in Jean Comaroff & John Comaroff (eds), *Modernity and its Malcontents* (Chicago, 1993), 89–110.

[167] Wyatt MacGaffey, 'The West in Congolese experience', in Philip D. Curtin (ed.), *Africa and the West* (Madison, 1972), 49–74.

[168] Described by Barthélémy Adoukonou, *Jalons pour une théologie africaine: essai d'herméneutique chrétienne du vodun dahoméen* (Paris, 1980), ii, 1–12; Herskovits, *Dahomey*, i, 193–205.

[169] Duncan, *Travels*, i, 126.

[170] A. Félix Iroko, 'Le spectre de la mort à Cotonou des origines à nos jours', *Le Mois en Afrique*, 227–8 (1984/5), 133–44.

destined for export. An English captain shipping a cargo of slaves from Ouidah to Barbados in 1694 recorded that twelve of them committed suicide by drowning and others starved themselves to death, explaining that "tis their belief that when they die they return home to their own country and friends again'.[171] In the project of commemoration of the slave trade that developed at Ouidah in the 1990s, great emphasis was placed upon two alleged monuments of the trade: two trees on the route from the town south to the beach, along which slaves were taken to be embarked on ships for export across the Atlantic, the 'Tree of Forgetting [L'Arbre de l'oubli]' on the southern outskirts of Ouidah, and the 'Tree of Return [L'Arbre du retour]' in the village of Zoungbodji, halfway to the beach. As told nowadays, slaves were required to walk round the 'Tree of Forgetting' (men nine times, women seven) in order to make them lose their memories, the purpose of this practice being to prevent their spirits returning to trouble those who had enslaved and sold them. Contrariwise, they ran round the 'Tree of Return' (three times) in order in ensure the return of their spirits to Africa, this being done in order to give them hope for the future. These stories thus encapsulate two contradictory dimensions of the operation of the slave trade: its general tendency to obliterate the cultural identity of its victims and, on the other hand, the resistance of the slaves themselves to this process of deracination, while also suggesting some degree of bad conscience (or, at least, fear of retribution) on the part of African slave-dealers. They have been interpreted as suggesting a conscious policy on the part of the Dahomian kings, beginning with Agaja, who is sometimes credited with having planted both trees, to establish 'psycho-religious control' of the operation of the slave trade.[172]

It can be readily conceded that the stories of the Trees of Forgetting and Return are both emotionally appealing and intuitively plausible. But, unfortunately, they are probably spurious.[173] They are not supported by any contemporary account of the operation of the slave trade at Ouidah; in fact, they were seemingly not recorded prior to the 1990s. The more northerly of the two trees is recorded in contemporary accounts, under the alternative name of 'The Captains' Tree', but as the place where arriving European slave-traders were met by the Yovogan and other local authorities of Ouidah. Some accounts do mention a ceremony of circumambulation, but it was the Ouidah chiefs, rather than slaves, who circled the tree (three times), prior to formally greeting the Europeans.[174] The tree at Zoungbodji is not clearly referred to in any contemporary source of the period of the slave trade, and, when it was first recorded as a historical monument, it was explained as the place where Agaja, after his conquest of Ouidah, rested to take his first drink of European gin, rather than being connected with the embarkation of slaves;[175] the linking of the tree to slaves' spiritual return to Africa seems to have

---

[171] Phillips, 'Journal', 219.
[172] Soglo, 'Les Xweda', 101.
[173] For fuller discussion, see Law, 'Memory, oblivion and return'.
[174] ANF, C6/27, Gourg, 'Mémoire pour servir d'instruction au Directeur', 1791; PRO, FO84/886, Fraser, Journal, 23 July 1851; Burton, *Mission*, i, 39–45.
[175] Sinou & Agbo, *Ouidah*, 161.

been articulated only in the context of the project of commemoration of the slave trade connected with the 'Ouidah '92' conference. The validity of these monuments, it may be suggested, is as an expression of the need and desire of the modern inhabitants of Ouidah to come to terms with the town's slave-trading past, rather than as throwing light on how that trade was viewed by their ancestors who operated it.

5

De Souza's Ouidah
The Era of the Illegal Slave Trade
1815–39

In the first half of the nineteenth century, Ouidah was profoundly affected by the legal banning of the trans-Atlantic slave trade and the adjustments which this necessitated in the conduct of commerce, and by the related development of a substantial Brazilian community in the town.[1] In the early stages of both processes, the central figure was Francisco Felix de Souza, a Brazilian slave-trader who settled permanently in Ouidah in the 1820s. Unfortunately, this critical period in Ouidah's history is in many respects obscure, because of the deficiencies of the available evidence. The detailed documentation provided for the eighteenth century by the European forts ceased when these were abandoned in the early nineteenth century, and European visitors remained rare thereafter until the mid-1840s. For the 1820s and 1830s, the most informative contemporary material is to be found in the records of judicial proceedings relating to illegal slave-ships captured by the British navy; but these provide only fragmentary (and not always reliable) information on what was going on on shore. To a greater degree than either before or after, the internal history of Ouidah in this period has therefore to be reconstructed on the basis of local oral traditions.

The legal prohibition of the slave trade

The legal banning of the slave trade was a complex and protracted process. As far as it affected Ouidah, the first important move was the abolition of slavery in French colonies by the revolutionary government in 1794, which was itself a recognition of the reality of the destruction of slavery in the principal French colony of Saint-Domingue by the slave insurrection of 1791. Although slavery was relegalized by Napoleon in 1802, the attempt to restore the institution was not effective in Saint-Domingue, serving merely to provoke the proclamation of that

---

[1] See Robin Law, 'The evolution of the Brazilian community in Ouidah', *S&A*, 22 (2001), 22–41.

country's independence as the Republic of Haiti in 1804. Although French slaving revived after 1802, very few French ships seem to have called at Ouidah. The practical effect, therefore, was that what had lately been the principal market for slaves exported from Ouidah now disappeared.

Among other nations with an interest in the slave trade, the trade became illegal for citizens of Denmark from 1803, Britain and the USA from 1808 and the Netherlands from 1814, and France again banned the trade from 1818. None of these, however, were by the early nineteenth century very important in the slave trade specifically at Ouidah. The main market for slaves from Ouidah over the eighteenth century had been the Portuguese colony of Brazil, especially the province of Bahia, and this trade, although temporarily disrupted by the war in Europe, had revived even before the peace of 1815; in 1812 it was estimated that no fewer than 45 ships from Bahia traded at Ouidah.[2] By the 1820s, a substantial trade had also developed to the Spanish colony of Cuba. Portugal and Spain, however, resisted British pressure for abolition longer, and initially accepted only partial prohibition.[3] A first Anglo–Portuguese treaty in 1810 restricted the slave trade to Portuguese possessions in Africa, but these were explicitly stated to include the Portuguese fort at Ouidah, where the slave trade therefore (uniquely in West, as opposed to Central, Africa) remained legal for Portuguese subjects; however, in 1815 a second treaty banned Portuguese from slaving north of the equator, including therefore at Ouidah. The legal situation was complicated by the secession of Brazil from Portuguese rule in 1822, but in 1826 the newly independent government of Brazil accepted the banning of the slave trade north of the equator as the price of British recognition. Spain also accepted a treaty banning the trade north of the equator in 1817 and a total ban in 1820. By the 1820s, therefore, the slave trade in West Africa, including at Ouidah, was technically illegal for all interested European and American nations.

Legal prohibition, however, was by no means the same as effective abolition, since the banning of the slave trade proved difficult to enforce.[4] The policing of abolition in Africa fell mainly to Britain, although there was also some limited and intermittent action by France and the USA. From 1808 the British navy maintained patrols off the African coast, from its base at Freetown in Sierra Leone, in order to intercept illegal slave ships.[5] Initially, however, these patrols had no authority to arrest, or even inspect, ships of other nationalities. A supplementary Anglo–Portuguese treaty of 1817 conceded the right of search of suspected slave ships and this provision was also accepted by Brazil in 1826, and similar arrangements were agreed with Spain in 1818. However, the legal powers acquired by these treaties were limited in crucial respects, which compromised their effectiveness in practice. One difficulty was that Portugal and Brazil had initially accepted abolition only north of the equator; for Brazilian ships until 1831 and Portuguese

[2] Akinjogbin, *Dahomey*, 195.
[3] See further Leslie Bethell, *The Abolition of the Brazilian Slave Trade* (Cambridge, 1970); David R. Murray, *Odious Commerce: Britain, Spain and the Abolition of the Cuban Slave Trade* (Cambridge, 1980).
[4] See esp. David Eltis, *Economic Growth and the Ending of the Transatlantic Slave Trade* (New York, 1987).
[5] Christopher Lloyd, *The Navy and the Slave Trade* (London, 1949).

until 1836, the slave trade south of the equator remained legal. This loophole was exploited by slave-traders bound for Ouidah; as was noted in a British naval report of 1821, Portuguese ships trading there regularly carried papers authorizing them to trade for slaves south of the equator, at Malemba, Cabinda or Angola, and, once they had made the short passage south to the equator, they were effectively immune from seizure.[6] Even more critically, the treaties with Portugal, Spain and Brazil authorized the arrest of ships only if they actually had slaves on board, even though their intention to trade in slaves might be manifest. The British sought to close this loophole by negotiating new agreements to allow the arrest of ships equipped for the slave trade, even if they had no slaves on board. Such an 'equipment' clause was accepted by Spain in 1835, but this was of limited effectiveness, since it was evaded by the shift of Cuba-bound vessels into other national registrations, especially Portuguese. The British did not resolve this question until 1839 when, despairing of securing Portuguese concession of an equipment clause by negotiation, they unilaterally assumed the right to intercept suspected slave ships under Portuguese colours.

To the extent that the British naval campaign sometimes involved the seizure of slave ships at Ouidah itself, this also represented a violation of Dahomian national waters, but the British in general showed much less fastidiousness about encroachments upon African sovereignty.[7] In the case of Dahomey, such actions were also a challenge to the status of Ouidah as a neutral port, which Europeans had formerly been obliged to respect. The issue was raised by the Dahomian kings from time to time in their negotiations with the British. In 1845, for example, Gezo suggested that British warships should be instructed not to take any slave ships 'till they had entirely left the coast', and his successor Glele demanded in 1864 that they should not capture slavers 'near his beach'.[8] But the British do not seem to have understood the legal and historical basis of the Dahomian position or even to have registered it with any seriousness.

The main effect of the illegality of the trade, prior to 1839, was that it now became normal practice for slavers to lie off the coast while their cargoes were assembled on shore, and then to embark them *en masse*, in order to minimize the time in which they were subject to seizure. The speeding up of embarkation times was a frequently noted feature of the illegal trade: an officer of the British navy's anti-slaving squadron told the Parliamentary Select Committee on the West Coast of Africa in 1842, 'They can take in a cargo of 600 in about three hours.'[9] The implication for the slaves was that they now spent a shorter time on board ship, but a longer time held on shore. Some of the slaves in a cargo embarked from Ouidah in 1849, for example, had been reportedly detained in the town for no less than nine months, awaiting an opportunity for shipment.[10] This longer time waiting

[6] PRO, FO84/19, Sir George Collier, 'Report upon the Coasts and Settlements of Western Africa', 27 Dec. 1821, pp. 54–5, 106–7; see also Verger, *Flux et reflux*, 403–5.

[7] See generally Eltis, *Economic Growth*, 120–2.

[8] Duncan, *Travels*, ii, 263; Burton, *Mission*, i, 277.

[9] PP, Select Committee, Minutes of Evidence, § 1842, 2481, Commander Henry Broadhead.

[10] PP, Slave Trade 1849–50, Class B, no. 45, Vice-Consul Duncan, Ouidah, 21 Aug. 1849.

onshore necessarily meant increased mortality of slaves prior to embarkation. Several contemporary observers reported increased mortality on shore during the illegal trade: another witness to the 1842 Select Committee, for example, observed that, because slaves now needed to be held for long periods at Ouidah while waiting for an opportunity to embark them, 'perhaps the half of them may be dead before they can be shipped'.[11] Since, conversely, slaves now spent shorter periods on board the slave ships, it might be expected that this greater mortality on shore was counterbalanced by reduced mortality during the trans-Atlantic voyage, but it does not appear that this was the case. Contemporary observers, again, believed that the difficulties in shipping slaves encouraged overcrowding of ships, with consequently increased shipboard mortality. Duncan in the 1840s, for example, maintained that because the British navy's blockade restricted opportunities for shipping slaves, 'when these do occur, large numbers are put on board, which frequently causes a loss in the number before reaching their place of destination'.[12] Statistical evidence, although not clearly attesting an increase of physical crowding of slaves on board ship, does indicate that mortality was greater in the illegal trade of the nineteenth century than earlier;[13] the explanation may be that, because of their longer wait on shore, slaves were now in poorer health when they were embarked.

A second tactic adopted in this period, in order to evade the attentions of the British navy, was the dispersal of slave shipments from Ouidah to other ports to the east and west, to which slaves were sent by canoe along the coastal lagoon. Although such lagoon links were by no means new in the trade of Ouidah, they acquired an enhanced significance in the period of the illegal slave trade; moreover, whereas earlier the movement of slaves along the lagoon had normally been from other ports for shipment at Ouidah, now the direction was reversed. Given the notoriety of Ouidah itself as a slave port, it attracted the particular attention of the British, and slaves were therefore, even if originally bulked up at Ouidah, frequently moved along the lagoon for embarkation at other, less well-known places.[14] In particular, this period saw the development as a slave 'port' of Godomey, east of Ouidah. According to tradition, Godomey was the site of the former slave port of Jakin, which had been destroyed by the Dahomians in 1732. But it was re-established in this period, to serve as an outport of Ouidah. At least one recorded slave ship in 1830, after landing its cargo at Ouidah and purchasing its slaves from de Souza there, proceeded east to embark them from Jakin.[15] Its alternative name Godomey is first attested in the contemporary record in 1843, when de Souza was reported to have travelled there from Ouidah 'on business'.[16]

The slave trade at Ouidah in the early nineteenth century was disrupted not only by the difficulties created by the legal banning of the trade (and by the disruption of shipping due to the European war of 1793–1815), but also by internal

[11] PP, 1842 Select Committee, § 615, Francis Swanzy.

[12] Duncan, *Travels*, i, 115.

[13] Eltis, *Economic Growth*, 135–8.

[14] See, for example, on de Souza's operations in the 1830s, Huntley, *Seven Years' Service*, i, 115–16.

[15] PP, Slave Trade 1830, Class A, no. 33, & 1831, Class A, no. 24, case of the *Veloz Pasagera*.

[16] PRO, CO96/12, J.H. Akhurst, Agoué, 25 Sept. 1843.

The Era of the Illegal Slave Trade

Table 5.1 Slave prices at Ouidah in the illegal trade, 1834–64

	Price in $	Price in original form	Comments
1834	$72	12 oz. @ $6 per oz.	'All expenses paid'
1835	$85	520 slaves for $44,000	'When embarked'
1837	$66		
1841	$64	4 doubloons	Paid for a female slave
1842	$28–46	£6–10	Slaves 'very cheap'
1842	$48–64	3–4 doubloons	
1847 Feb.	$70–80		See sources
1847 Dec.	$75–90		See sources
1848	$80		+ $5 export duty
1849	$80–100		Price 'very high'
1850	$60		Slaves 'numerous'
1851	$40		'In the best conditions'
1857	$50–80		See sources
1858	$60–70		
1856–8	$100	500 fr.	'Increasing every day'
1861	$90		'On the beach'
1862	$80		+ $4 export duty
1861–3	$80	400 fr.	
1863/4	$75	£16.16s.	'Including the custom house fee'

Sources: 1834 and 1837: PP, Slave Trade 1840, Class A, no. 47, case of the *Jack Wilding*, receipt dated 18 Dec. 1838; 1835: PP, Slave Trade 1836, Class A, no. 47, case of the *El Esplorador*, Instruction for Capt. José da Inza, Havana, 14 April 1835; 1841: Slave Trade 1841, Class A, no. 126, case of the *Nova Fortuna*, letter from João Pereira Vianna, Bahia, to João Deus, Ouidah, n.d. [1841]; 1842: PP, 1842 Select Committee, § 776, Francis Swanzy, & 2519, Henry Broadhead; 1847: Dos Santos correspondence, nos 52 [19 Feb. 1847, stating that de Souza demands $80, whites pay $70 'outside' + duty, but dos Santos himself paid $3,000 for 43 slaves = $75 each], 80, 83 [1 & 22 Dec. 1847, giving current price as $90 'except at preference', but himself paid $75 each for 4 men, 2 women]; 1848, PP, Missions to Ashantee & Dahomey, Cruickshank Report, 16; 1849: PP, Slave Trade 1849–50, Class B, enc.10 in no. 9, Forbes, 5 Nov. 1849; 1850: PP, Slave Trade 1850–51, Class A, enc.3 in no. 198, Forbes, 6 April 1850; 1851: Auguste Bouet, in Jean-Claude Nardin, 'La reprise des relations franco-dahoméennes au XIXe siècle: la mission d'Auguste Bouet à la cour d'Abomey', *CEA*, 7/25 (1967), 118; 1857: PP Slave Trade 1857–8, Class B, no. 25, Consul Campbell, Lagos, 10 Aug. 1857; 1858: PP, Slave Trade 1858–9, Class A, no. 131, Commander Wise, 19 July 1858 [actually '$60–170', presumably miscopied]; 1856–8: Vallon, 'Le royaume de Dahomey', 1/357; 1861: PP Slave Trade 1861, Class A, enc.1 in no. 172, Commodore Edmonstone, 24 March 1861; 1862: PP, Slave Trade 1862, Class B, no. 34, Consul Freeman, Lagos, 1 July 1862, also PP, Despatches from Commodore Wilmot, no. 1, 29 Jan. 1863; 1861–3: Abbé Laffitte, *Le Dahomey* (Tours, 1874), 143; 1863/4: Burton, *Mission*, ii, 209–10. Conversions from French currency made at the conventional equivalence of $1 = 5 fr.; from sterling, although the dollar was conventionally equated with 5s. [£1 = $4], prices in 1842 seem to be based on the then official value of $1 = 4s.4d. [4⅓s.], and in 1863/4 on the actual current exchange rate of $1 = 4s.6d. [4½s.].

problems relating to the supply of slaves through Dahomey. As one European trader noted: 'Whydah … had, at one period, an extensive trade for slaves, but since the arbitrary measures of the government became troublesome to their neighbours, the trade for slaves has only been supported by [Dahomey's own] wars.'[17] Gezo, who came to the throne in 1818, sought to revive the middleman trade in slaves from the interior: when he sent a message to the British authorities at Cape Coast in 1820, urging them to reoccupy the recently abandoned English fort at Ouidah, he asserted that 'a new system of policy was established', permitting merchants from Oyo and other countries in the interior to 'trade there in common'.[18] This revival of

---

[17] Robertson, *Notes*, 260.

[18] PRO, CO2/11, G.A. Robertson, Cape Coast Castle, 2 Sept. 1820; cf. Law, 'Slave-raiders and middlemen', 57–8.

the middleman trade was compromised by the outbreak of war between Dahomey and Oyo in 1823, which led to a 'partial obstruction of trade'.[19] After Dahomey's victory, which ended the payment of tribute to Oyo, however, the supply of slaves generated by Dahomey's own wars increased substantially, as a result of a series of successful campaigns waged by Gezo, especially in the Mahi and Yoruba country to the north-east.

In these circumstances, the slave trade at Ouidah flourished, despite its illegality. In 1821 it was estimated that no fewer than 100 slave ships were calling annually at Ouidah and Lagos, though this figure was probably exaggerated.[20] In the Bight of Benin as a whole, slave exports recovered to high levels, estimated to have averaged around 12,000 per year in the 15 years immediately following the peace (1816–30), though falling to 9,000 per year in the 1830s; within this regional total, however, Ouidah's position of dominance was progressively eroded, principally through the development of Lagos to the east, which already accounted for more shipments than Ouidah in the 1820s and for almost twice as many in the 1830s.[21] This rise of Lagos to predominance was a consequence of the outbreak of a series of devastating of wars in southern Yorubaland from the 1820s, which created a large supply of captives in its immediate hinterland.

The continued buoyancy of the slave trade in its illegal phase can be measured by the prices paid for slaves (see Table 5.1). Comparison with the eighteenth century is complicated, because, although the 'ounce' continued to be current as a unit of account, prices were now more commonly denominated in dollars. The ounce was generally equated with $8, and the dollar therefore with the small 'head' of 2,000 cowries. But this seems to have been a conventional rate, and actual silver dollars (which were increasingly imported from the Americas to pay for slaves in Africa in this period) often passed at a premium; a receipt for goods paid for slaves signed by de Souza in the 1830s reckons only $6 to the ounce.[22] Even on this basis, slave prices were clearly lower in the 1830s and early 1840s than their peak of 13–15 oz. in the 1790s, although they rose somewhat later in the 1840s.

The abandonment of the European forts

Although it may have had little immediate effect in reducing the volume of slave exports, the legal banning of the slave trade had a significant impact on its mode of operation at Ouidah. The most obvious and immediate consequence was the abandonment of the three European forts in the town.

The first of the forts to be abandoned was the French, whose rationale was removed by the abolition of slavery in French colonies in 1794. The last officially appointed governor of the fort abandoned his post and embarked for France in

[19] *RGCG*, 21 Jan. 1823.
[20] PRO, FO84/19, Collier, 'Report', 27 Dec. 1821.
[21] Eltis, *Economic Growth*, 249–54 (Tables A.9 and A.10).
[22] PP, Slave Trade 1841, Class A, no. 109, case of the *Gratidão*, with, among papers found on board, 'Instructions respecting the trade between Popo and Onim'; 1840, Class A, no. 47, case of the *Jack Wilding*, receipt from de Souza, 18 Dec. 1838 (but relating to a transaction in 1834).

1797, entrusting its care to the storekeeper, a free 'mulatto' called Pierre Bonon. When slavery in French colonies was relegalized in 1802, there was some discussion of the possibility of reoccupying the Ouidah fort, as a base for renewed slave-trading, but nothing came of this. A French naval vessel that called at Ouidah to inspect the fort in 1803 found Bonon still in occupation, and delivered a certificate renewing his temporary appointment in charge of it.[23] Correspondence between the fort and France appears to have lapsed after 1806, but Bonon remained in residence; he was still there in 1829, when he wrote to the authorities in France asking for payment of arrears of pay due to him.[24]

By the 1820s the French fort was no longer serving specifically French trade; in 1825 it was being used as a warehouse by the Brazilian de Souza.[25] There was nevertheless some degree of continuity from the period of French occupation: a French naval officer who visited Ouidah in 1839 found French colours still displayed on the fort.[26] According to later testimony, the king, in order to maintain the French connection, appointed as 'temporary commandant' of the fort 'a mulatto deriving from the unions between the local women and the French who formerly lived in the fort'.[27] Local tradition identifies a family called Talon, which is still resident in Ahouandjigo ward, as having served as hereditary 'guardians' of the French fort, and this family claims descent from a European or 'mulatto' trader who served in the fort, whose name is recalled as 'Pierre Talon' or 'Pierre Bonnaud', and who is evidently to be identified with the Pierre Bonon left in charge in 1797.[28] In 1842 the fort was occupied by a French firm engaged in 'legitimate' trade for palm oil, Régis of Marseille, but Régis's agent in 1848 still alluded to a 'native mulatto' called Grimaud, who had formerly been 'commandant of the fort', prior to the arrival of the Marseille firm, who was presumably a son or more remote relative of Pierre Bonon.[29] In the 1860s and early 1870s the titular 'commandant' of the fort, under the French merchants in occupation, was a man called Titi, who was understood to be a son of the original indigenous commandant; and in 1890 the position was held by 'Talao [= Talon]', of the same family.[30]

The English fort likewise lost its purpose with the banning of the British slave trade in 1807. An official inquiry into the British possessions on the African coast in 1810 recommended that the fort at Ouidah should be abandoned, as it was now 'totally useless, being without any trade'. The last governor and other remaining

[23] ANF, C6/27, Denyau, Paris, to Minister of Marine, 25 Nivose, Year 7; Denyau, Paris, to Pierre Bonon, 20 Aug. 1797, & Capt. Arnoux to Bonon, 20 pluviose, Year XI , both enc. to Bonon, Ouidah, 10 vendémiaire, Year XII.

[24] Bernard Schnapper, *La Politique et le commerce français dans le Golfe de Guinée de 1838 à 1871* (Paris, 1961), 163.

[25] PRO, ADM55/11, Clapperton, Journal, 26 Nov. 1825.

[26] Report of Bouet, 3 May 1839, quoted in Robert Cornevin, *Histoire du Dahomey* (Paris, 1962), 274.

[27] Auguste Bouet, in Jean-Claude Nardin, 'La reprise des relations franco-dahoméennes au XIXe siècle: la mission d'Auguste Bouet à la cour d'Abomey', *CEA*, 7/25 (1967), 90.

[28] Reynier, 'Ouidah', 32, 36; Agbo, *Histoire*, 185.

[29] Blancheley, 'Au Dahomey', 536. 'Grimoin' is the name of a 'secondary branch' of the Talon-Bonnaud family: Reynier, 'Ouidah', 32.

[30] Bouche, *Sept ans*, 321; Foà, *Le Dahomey*, 418.

personnel were evacuated in 1812.[31] As in the case of the French fort, the Dahomian authorities took measures to maintain at least a nominal British presence. It was reported in 1825 that 'the King of Dahomey still keeps the English fort in some degree of repair, in the hope that the English might return and reoccupy it and bring a renewal of the slave trade'; and Gezo told Duncan in 1845 that 'he had always kept a temporary governor in the English fort, since our abandonment of the place'.[32] Duncan met this 'governor', who accompanied him to the capital, in order to introduce him to the king. He was still residing in the English fort, although since 1838 he had shared it with the agent of the British trader Hutton. According to Duncan this man was the son of a soldier of the former fort garrison.[33] Forbes in 1849–50 also found a 'Black Governor appointed by the king to the English fort', who served as one of his interpreters. Forbes names him as Mark, or in the Dahomian form of the name 'Madiki', Lemon and describes him as the grandson of a corporal of the fort garrison;[34] presumably this was a son of the man met by Duncan.[35] Madiki Lemon was still alive and associated with the English fort, now occupied by a British vice-consul, in 1851–2,[36] but he was evidently dead by 1859, when a son of his, called John Lemon or John Madiki, is recorded as 'Commandant, as he is called, of the English fort'; this man also served as interpreter to Richard Burton in 1863/4.[37]

This Lemon family, alternatively called Glessihounto ('English Captain'), also still exists, and remains resident in Sogbadji quarter. According to its own traditions, it is descended from an Englishman who married a local woman (from the Zossoungbo family, who claim to have been the first inhabitants of the quarter), the original 'Lemon' being either this Englishman or his son by his African wife.[38] The Englishman from whom the family is descended can, indeed, be identified in the contemporary record. Although modern tradition relates the name 'Lemon' to the citrus fruit, explaining it as a nickname given to the founding ancestor because of his sour disposition, it seems in fact to be an indigenized version of the name Raymond, and this was the first name of a soldier in the English fort at Ouidah, Raymond Cullie, who arrived there as a drummer (shortly afterwards promoted to the rank of gunner) in 1779.[39] This man was still listed as a member of the garrison when the fort was abandoned in 1812; whether he then left with the departing governor or stayed behind in Ouidah is unclear. Family tradition unfortunately

[31] Akinjogbin, *Dahomey*, 192–3.

[32] PRO, ADM55/11, Clapperton, Journal, 26 Nov. 1825; Duncan, *Travels*, ii, 269.

[33] Duncan, *Travels*, i, 140, 216–17. Duncan here describes him as having himself been formerly a corporal in the fort, but elsewhere says that he was 'the son of a serjeant' of the fort garrison: PP, 1848 Select Committee, § 3129.

[34] Forbes *Dahomey*, i, 48, 53–4, 129–30; ii, 176.

[35] A British visitor in 1843 was given as one of his 'guides and interpreters' a native of 'English Town' called 'Madaki', who is presumably Madiki Lemon, but he may then not yet have succeeded to the governorship of the fort: Freeman, *Journal*, 250.

[36] PRO, FO84/886, Fraser, Daily journal, 23 July 1851 etc.

[37] WMMS, William West, Cape Coast, 6 June 1859; Burton, *Mission*, i, 120–1.

[38] Reynier, 'Ouidah', 36; fieldwork, Lemon compound, 9 Jan. 1996.

[39] PRO, T70/1162, Day-Book, William's Fort, 1 May & 3 Aug. 1779.

preserves only a telescoped version of the genealogy and does not recollect either of the family heads documented by name in the contemporary record during the nineteenth century, Madiki Lemon and his son John.[40]

The case of the Portuguese fort was more complex. The last governor officially appointed to the fort, Jacinto José de Souza, was sent out from Brazil in 1804. He died soon after and command of the fort passed to his subordinate officials and eventually to his own brother, the famous Francisco Felix de Souza.[41] Communication between the Ouidah fort and Brazil was, however, disrupted by the Anglo-French war of 1803–15 and, by the time this ended, the situation was complicated by the legal restriction of the Portuguese slave trade. Technically, as seen earlier, the slave trade at Ouidah was outlawed by the Anglo–Portuguese treaty of 1815. In this context, there was some discussion in Brazil of closing the fort at Ouidah, though no formal decision seems to have been made.[42] By this time, Francisco Felix de Souza had abandoned the fort to set up as an independent trader and soon left Ouidah altogether, settling at Little Popo to the west. What happened to the fort in this period is unclear. A passport issued to de Souza by the Portuguese authorities in Brazil in 1821, shortly after he had returned to Ouidah, expressed official gratitude to him for his services in maintaining the fort over 'several years', but it is doubtful whether this should be taken to imply continuity of direction.[43] Other evidence shows that, even when he returned to Ouidah (*c.* 1820), de Souza did not take up residence in the Portuguese fort, which in 1825 was being used as a 'lodging house' for Portuguese captains.[44]

The abandonment of the European forts left a vacuum in the organization of trade at Ouidah, since they had served the function of facilitating contacts and organizing services for visiting traders and to some extent also of stockpiling slaves in anticipation of the arrival of ships. Such local agents were no less necessary in the illegal trade; indeed, they were needed even more since, as noted earlier, the threat from the British navy's anti-slaving squadron created pressures for the speeding up of embarkations, and this placed a premium on the bulking of slaves prior to shipment.[45] This gap was filled by unofficial resident agents settled on the coast. In Ouidah, the most important of these were the Afro-French merchant Nicolas d'Oliveira and the Brazilian Francisco Felix de Souza.

Nicolas d'Oliveira

Nicolas d'Oliveira was, according to tradition one of two sons (the other being called Jean-Baptiste) of a director of the French fort in Ouidah, called Joseph

---

[40] John Pita (Peter) Lemon, who was head of the family in 1917 (Reynier, 'Ouidah', 36) is now believed to have been the son of the founder.
[41] Verger, *Flux et reflux*, 240–1.
[42] Ibid., 299–300.
[43] Ibid., 462.
[44] PRO, ADM55/11, Clapperton, Journal, 26 Nov. 1825.
[45] See Eltis, *Economic Growth*, 153.

Ollivier, by a 'mulatto' woman called Sophia; some versions also recall a third son, Joseph, by a different mother.[46] The Portuguese form later adopted for the family name, d'Oliveira, reflects the family's subsequent absorption into the larger Brazilian community. The father is certainly identifiable as Joseph Ollivier de Montaguère, who was director of the French fort in 1778-86 and eventually left Ouidah in 1788;[47] his 'mulatto' wife Sophie (*sic*) is also referred to in the contemporary documentation, in records of an investigation held in 1787 into illegal private trading by her husband, to which she herself was allegedly a party.[48] According to tradition, on his departure from Ouidah, Ollivier entrusted Sophie to the care of the reigning Dahomian king Kpengla, on whose death (in 1789) she passed into the custody of his successor Agonglo: by both of which kings she had further children, her son by Agonglo, being called Ahokpe.[49] The traditional account may not be accurate in detail, since Sophie is presumably to be identified with a 'Miss Sophia', who sold a slave to the English ship *Swallow* in 1793, which implies that she was then still based in Ouidah, four years after Kpengla's death.[50] But there is no reason to doubt that she ended up in the royal harem. Portuguese missionaries who visited Abomey in 1797, at the time of Agonglo's death, received a message appealing for help from a 'mulatto' woman, whom they understood to be the daughter (*sic*) of a former governor of the French fort at Ouidah, who had given her to the king, and this woman is surely to be identified with Sophie Ollivier.[51] D'Oliveira family tradition, as will be seen, also recalls her presence within the royal palace during the reign of Agonglo's successor Adandozan (1797–1818).

Whatever may have been the case with their mother, the Ollivier sons initially remained in the French fort, all three of them being listed among the fort 'mulattoes', with the status of slaves, in *c*. 1789.[52] According to tradition, however, the eldest son Nicolas subsequently set up as an independent trader, who acquired sufficient wealth to establish his own quarter in Ouidah, immediately west of Ahouandjigo; this quarter was called Ganvè, which is said to derive from a praise-name of Nicolas d'Oliveira alluding to his commercial activities, meaning 'importer of iron'.[53] He subsequently, as will be seen below, played a critical role in assisting Francisco Felix de Souza in his establishment at Ouidah in 1820.

Nicolas d'Oliveira's career is poorly documented because it coincided with the hiatus in the contemporary documentation relating to Ouidah, due to the abandonment of the European forts there; in the contemporary record, he is not mentioned subsequently to his listing among the personnel of the French fort in 1789, when he can have been no more than 10–11 years old. Even his allegedly

[46] Reynier, 'Ouidah', 58–9; de Souza, *La Famille de Souza*, 18.
[47] The claim in some versions of tradition that the family ancestor settled in Ouidah as early as 1623 is certainly spurious.
[48] ANF, C6/26, Interrogatoire de Joseph le Beau, Sept.–Oct. 1787. Le Beau was a free 'mulatto' associated with the fort, who had acted as agent to Ollivier; he was arrested on 6 Aug. 1787 and died in prison on 20 Oct.
[49] Reynier, 'Ouidah', 58.
[50] Accounts of the *Swallow*, 23 March 1793.
[51] Pires, *Viagem*, 86.
[52] ANF, C6/27, Liste des nègres captifs du Roi au fort de Juda, 1791.
[53] Reynier, 'Ouidah', 58. His praise-name is quoted in full in Agbo, *Histoire*, 223–4.

critical role in the later installation of de Souza at Ouidah is not mentioned in any early source, the first allusion to his involvement being in traditions recorded in the 1890s.[54] His royal half-brother Prince Ahokpe is mentioned in contemporary sources, as a prominent member of the court of Gezo in 1849–50, but these contain no reference to Nicolas d'Oliveira (who was by then dead), or indeed any hint of Ahokpe's European connections.[55] Despite this obscurity, however, as the first private trader in Ouidah to found a quarter of the town, he was clearly a figure of great historical significance. His career prefigured that of the more eminent Francisco Felix de Souza and indeed paved the way for it.

Francisco Felix de Souza

The career of de Souza himself is much better known.[56] He was born in Brazil, in Bahia. He first came to West Africa in about 1792, staying three years before going back to Brazil, and returned to settle permanently probably in 1800.[57] His early activities were outside Ouidah, in the 1790s at Badagry to the east, and from 1800 at Little Popo, at both of which places he founded factories that he named Adjido.[58] But, when his commercial fortunes declined, he entered the service of the Portuguese fort at Ouidah, where he is attested serving as secretary to the storekeeper in 1803-6.[59] The last officially appointed governor of the fort, Jacinto José de Souza, sent from Bahia in 1804, was his brother, and later accounts indicate that Francisco procured his brother's appointment.[60] Jacinto de Souza died soon after his arrival, as did his immediate acting successor, and with the death of his superior officers Francisco assumed command of the fort. In the face of the breakdown of communications with Brazil at this time, however, he abandoned the fort to set up as a private trader in the still flourishing although now (from 1815) illegal, slave trade.[61]

De Souza seems initially to have continued to reside at Ouidah;[62] a slave ship partly owned by him, which was taken by the British navy in 1816, had taken its slaves there.[63] He subsequently became involved in a dispute with Adandozan, and in consequence supported the coup d'etat by which the latter was dethroned in

[54] First in Foà, *Le Dahomey*, 22.

[55] Forbes, *Dahomey*, i, 73; ii, 28, 93, 102, 130, 147, 213 ['Ah-hoh-peh'].

[56] See esp. David Ross, 'The first Chacha of Whydah: Francisco Felix de Souza', *Odu*, 2 (1969), 19–28; Robin Law, 'A carreira de Francisco Félix de Souza na África Ocidental', *Topoi*, 2 (2001), 9–39.

[57] PP, Papers relative to Lagos, enc. in no. 8: Hutton, Cape Coast, 7 Aug. 1850; Ridgway, 'Journal', 195.

[58] De Souza, 'Contribution', 17–18.

[59] Verger, *Flux et reflux*, 240–1, 460–1.

[60] *RGCG*, 15 April 1823; reflected in distorted form in later tradition, which says that Francisco appointed his brother (incorrectly named as Ignacio) to succeed him as governor of the fort when he himself left Ouidah: de Souza, 'Contribution', 2.

[61] Huntley, *Seven Years' Service*, i, 113.

[62] Freeman, 'West Africa', 170; see, for example, Reynier, 'Ouidah', 41. But other accounts state or imply that he moved to Little Popo.

[63] Verger, *Flux et reflux*, 638.

favour of his brother Gezo in 1818; although this story is fully told only in traditional accounts recorded after his death, there seems no reason to question its essential accuracy.[64] The dispute is usually said to have arisen from unpaid debts owed to de Souza by Adandozan; when de Souza went to Abomey to press for payment, he was imprisoned but escaped to Little Popo. The traditions of the d'Oliveira family maintain that Nicolas d'Oliveira played a key role in arranging his escape from Abomey, with the assistance of his mother Sophie, who was still alive in the royal harem.[65] From Popo, de Souza assisted Gezo with supplies of imported European goods, which the latter distributed to win support against the king. After his accession to the throne, Gezo sent d'Oliveira to Little Popo to invite de Souza to resettle at Ouidah. According to family tradition, de Souza moved back from Popo to Ouidah in September 1820, and this is consistent with the contemporary record, in which his presence there is first attested in 1821.[66]

It appears that de Souza did not initially intend to settle permanently in Ouidah, since in 1821 he obtained a passport to return to Brazil. Why he did not in the event return to Brazil is unclear. According to a story recorded after his death, he did in fact plan to leave for Brazil in a slave ship called the *Prince of Guinea*, but this was captured by the British navy; and a ship of this name was indeed taken by the British in 1826, when bound from Bahia for Ouidah, with a cargo consigned to de Souza.[67] But this does not explain why he did not repeat the attempt later. It may be that he was prevented from leaving by the Dahomian authorities: a British naval officer who met him in the 1830s understood that he was forbidden to leave Ouidah by Gezo, although he also suggested that this precaution was no longer necessary, since he was by then reconciled to continuing to live there.[68]

There may also have been legal or political obstacles to his returning to Brazil. The earliest contemporary account of his activities after his resettlement at Ouidah so far traced, in a British report of 1821, describes him as a 'renegado ... banished from the Brazils', and an account recorded shortly after his death states that he had been exiled from Brazil for 'some political crime'.[69] The circumstances of this banishment, however, are obscure. The illegal slave-trader Theophilus Conneau (alias Theodore Canot), who traded with de Souza at Ouidah in 1830, claimed that the latter had come to Africa after involvement in the Brazilian war of independence (1822–3), having initially enlisted in the nationalist forces at Rio de Janeiro but subsequently deserted.[70] This, however, cannot be true, since he had been resident in Africa since 1800, and in any case his 'banishment' was already reported in 1821, before the Brazilian secession. Perhaps the story of de Souza's

---

[64] First told (c. 1860) by Freeman, 'West Africa', 169–73; although Freeman met de Souza (first in 1843), he describes this story as 'traditionary information', which implies that he did not have it directly from the latter. For a synthesis of the traditional accounts, see Moussa Oumar Sy, 'Le Dahomey: le coup d'état de 1818', *Folia Orientalia*, 6 (1964), 205–38.

[65] Bay, *Wives of the Leopard*, 171.

[66] GLL, 'History of Francisco F. de Souza'.

[67] Freeman, 'West Africa', 255; PP, Slave Trade 1827, Class A, no. 49, case of the *Principe de Guiné*.

[68] Huntley, *Seven Years' Service*, i, 115.

[69] PRO, FO84/19, Collier, 'Report', 27 Dec. 1821; Forbes, *Dahomey*, i, 106–7.

[70] Theophilus Conneau, *A Slaver's Log Book* (London, 1977), 202.

'desertion' is a garbled allusion to his abandonment of his post at the Portuguese fort in Ouidah; alternatively, his status as an outlaw might have been due to his involvement in the now illegal slave trade. De Souza's legal position may also, however, have been complicated by the Brazilian rebellion. This had repercussions in Ouidah, where the title to the Portuguese fort was disputed between Portugal and Brazil but confirmed to the former in the agreement recognizing Brazilian independence in 1825;[71] a later account says that de Souza offered the fort to the Brazilian government but received no response.[72] A report of 1823 confirms at least a temporary breach between de Souza and the new government in Brazil, which had seized two of his ships with over 1,000 slaves.[73] It is also noteworthy that de Souza continued to assert his own status as a Portuguese national after 1822, and, although (as explained below) there were practical advantages in this in relation to his illegal slaving activities, it may also have represented a more positive statement of political and emotional allegiance. However this may be, de Souza did not return to Brazil; indeed, he appears never to have left Dahomey after 1820, his subsequent journeys outside Ouidah being only to the capital Abomey or to other coastal towns under Dahomian rule, such as Godomey to the east.

De Souza's position in Ouidah

According to the conventional view, when de Souza returned to Ouidah, this was not merely as a trader, since he was appointed by Gezo to an official position: in the formulation of David Ross, for example, he became 'a Dahomian chief ... [with] a special title ... the Chacha of Whydah'.[74] This, however, is certainly an over-simplification, since as has been seen he did not initially intend to settle permanently in Dahomey, but wanted to return to Brazil. Evidently, his evolution into a 'Dahomian chief' was not originally envisaged but took place over time; and certainly the appellation 'Chacha' was in origin a personal nickname, which was transformed into a title of office only retrospectively, when it was inherited by his sons after his death.[75]

The nature of de Souza's position at Ouidah is often misrepresented in local tradition as that of 'viceroy of Whydah, chief of the whites';[76] and this perception has been consolidated in the wider world through the historical novel by Bruce Chatwin, *The Viceroy of Ouidah*, which is based on the career of de Souza. The misrepresentation, however, goes back to his own lifetime. One of the British naval officers testifying before the 1842 Parliamentary Committee, for example, said that

---

[71] R.J. Hammond, *Portugal and Africa, 1815–1910* (Stanford, 1966), 69.
[72] Carlos Eugenio Corrêa da Silva, *Uma Viagem ao estabelecimento portuguez de S. João Baptista de Ajudá* (Lisbon, 1866), 59–60.
[73] *RGCG*, 15 April 1823.
[74] Ross, 'First Chacha', 20–21.
[75] Various etymologies of the name 'Chacha' are offered in the traditions; the most plausible is that it is from Fon *chacha*, 'quick', given him as nickname because he constantly used the word in urging his slaves to work.
[76] E.g. Foà, *Le Dahomey*, 22; Agbo, *Histoire*, 50.

'Mr De Souza is [the king's] viceroy, he has the power of life and death', and, although this was contradicted by another officer, who observed that the 'caboceer' of Ouidah was 'a native', he too opined that this governor was 'completely under' de Souza and implied that the latter had some sort of official position, since he could allegedly raise a large force of soldiers.[77] In fact, the position of 'viceroy' or Yovogan of Ouidah remained distinct and in the hands of a native Dahomian (from 1823, a man called Dagba). The Yovogan remained the paramount local authority, as is clear from the accounts of European visitors to Ouidah in de Souza's later years, in the 1840s, who upon arrival regularly visited the Yovogan to explain their business first and talked to de Souza only subsequently.[78] It is entirely likely that de Souza himself was formally appointed a 'caboceer' of Ouidah, which among other things involved an obligation to provide military forces; but this was not unique to him, but (as noted in an earlier chapter) was normal practice with regard to leading merchants of Ouidah. It is clear, in fact, that de Souza's position was essentially commercial rather than political, serving as the king's agent at Ouidah; Europeans tended to exaggerate his status in Dahomey because it was with him rather than directly with the king that they normally dealt. Even his commercial position was often misunderstood and exaggerated; although he was commonly represented as enjoying a 'monopoly' of trade, this is not strictly correct.[79] The reality was that, in his capacity as the king's agent, he enjoyed the royal privilege of first refusal of trade: as an account of 1839 explicitly noted, 'the other factors had only what he didn't want for himself'.[80] He also clearly traded extensively on his own account, as well as for the king, and thereby acquired, if not a formal monopoly, certainly an overwhelmingly predominant position in the trade of Ouidah, at least down to the late 1830s.

The contemporary sources also make clear that de Souza's position at Ouidah initially derived its legitimacy and authority, not from appointment by Gezo alone, but also from his claim to represent the Portuguese government. The passport he obtained from the Portuguese authorities in 1821 authorized him to bring with him to Brazil the slaves which he owned in Africa, and he seems to have represented this as authorization to continue trading in slaves until he returned to Brazil: a British report of 1823 noted that he 'confidently states that he has permission from the king of Portugal to realize his property in any way, either by shipping slaves or otherwise'.[81] He also reasserted his claim to be governor of the Portuguese fort at Ouidah and hence to official status as a representative of the Portuguese crown. Another British report of 1821 observed that he 'assumes the rights and privileges of a person in authority, granting papers and licences to all the slave traders, in all the form and confidence of one empowered to do so, by the Portuguese government'; the reference being to the common practice noted earlier, of issuing false passports authorizing ships to take slaves south of the equator, where the slave

[77] PP, 1842 Select Committee, § 4063, Lieutenant Reginald Levine; § 2461–4, Commander Henry Broadhead.
[78] E.g. Freeman, *Journal*, 239–40; Duncan, *Travels*, i, 117–19.
[79] See further Law, 'Royal monopoly', 567–8 .
[80] Broquant, *Esquisse commerciale de la Côte occidentale d'Afrique* (1839), quoted in Verger, *Flux et reflux*, 463.
[81] *RGCG*, 15 April 1823.

trade initially remained legal for Portuguese nationals.[82] He did not in fact take up residence in the Portuguese fort, establishing his household instead on the opposite (west) side of the town in what later became known as the 'Brazil' quarter. But he continued to claim to be its legal governor: it was still reported in the 1830s that he 'by no means disconnected himself from his position of a governor, whenever it became necessary to assume it upon any ground of policy with reference to natives or others'.[83]

This assertion by de Souza of his status as a Portuguese official was probably an attempt to secure for the slave-ships in which he had an interest the partial immunity from arrest by the British navy that Portuguese vessels enjoyed until 1839. In addition, an attempt was made to claim that, since Ouidah was a Portuguese possession, the British had no legal right to arrest ships there, within what were supposedly Portuguese national waters. In 1827, for example, when a Brazilian vessel was seized at Ouidah, its master protested that 'the said vessel and cargo are protected by the treaty or convention', because his ship had been 'brought to an anchor under the fort ... the said fort being in the possession of the Crown of Portugal', though the British authorities refused to acknowledge de Souza's occupation of the fort as having any official standing. Again, in 1839 when a ship under Portuguese colours was taken at Ouidah, its master, Joaquim Telles de Menezes (himself a resident of Ouidah and son-in-law to de Souza), protested 'on the ground that his vessel was Portuguese, and was improperly captured under the guns of the Portuguese fort at Whydah'.[84] De Souza's claim to be Governor of the Portuguese fort presumably ended in 1844, when it was officially reoccupied by Portugal, when he is said to have handed over the keys of the fort to the newly appointed Portuguese governor.[85] By then, the utility of claiming a Portuguese connection had in any case largely disappeared, with the British assertion of extended powers of arrest in 1839.

It is also clear that, again at least down to the end of the 1830s, de Souza operated in his commercial operations, not merely as the Dahomian king's local agent in Ouidah, but as an autonomous merchant whose business operations extended across the Atlantic. He regularly shipped slaves for sale in the Americas on his own account, rather than merely supplying them to ships in Africa; in Bahia, the merchant Andre Pinto da Silveira operated as his 'correspondent and agent' in such sales in the 1830s.[86] He also owned several ships employed in trans-Atlantic slaving. At least one of these was built to his order in America: the *Principe de Guiné* mentioned earlier, which was built at Philadelphia and sailed from there to Ouidah *en route* to Bahia in 1825, was, according to the testimony of its American master, the property of de Souza, who had supplied the money for its construction.[87] Others

---

82 PRO, FO84/19, Collier, 'Report', 27 Dec. 1821.
83 Huntley, *Seven Years' Service*, i, 114.
84 PP, Slave Trade 1827, Class A, no. 57, case of the *Trajano*; 1839–40, Class A, no. 77, case of the *Emprehendedor*.
85 Corrêa da Silva, *Viagem*, 79.
86 PP, Slave Trade 1835, Class B, no. 107, Mr Parkinson, Bahia, 10 Dec. 1834.
87 PP, Slave Trade 1826–7, Class A, no. 8, J.T. Williams, Sierra Leone, 30 March 1826. But when this ship turned up again on the coast in 1826, to trade with de Souza at Ouidah, its papers showed it to be owned by a

were purchased in West Africa: for example, the *George and James*, arrested off Ouidah in 1825, had originally been owned by the London firm of Mathew Forster & Co. and engaged in legal trade, but had been sold in West Africa to its mate, Mr Ramsay, who then took it on a voyage to Bahia and back; but the British held that the real owner was de Souza, who was believed to have given Ramsay the money for its purchase.[88] De Souza also purchased condemned and confiscated slave-ships for re-employment in the slave trade: in 1828 he had an agent in the British colony of Freetown, Sierra Leone, for this purpose.[89] Other ships taken by the British navy that were owned (or partly owned) by de Souza included the *Legitimo Africano*, captured in 1835 with a cargo of slaves bound for Bahia, and the appropriately named *Dom Francisco*, taken in 1837, the *Florida* also in 1837 and the *Fortuna* in 1839, these three all bound for Cuba.[90] Others, although not owned by de Souza at the time of their capture, had been his property earlier: the *Atrevido*, taken in 1834, had been purchased by its master from de Souza at Ouidah in 1831 for $2,000; and the *Emprehendedor*, mentioned earlier, taken in 1839, and then owned by de Souza's son-in-law Joaquim Telles de Menezes, had been purchased by him from his father-in-law in 1837 for $3,500.[91] Most of de Souza's ships seem to have been purchased in West Africa; the *Dom Francisco*, for example, had been bought from a French owner at Prince's Island for $12,000 and the *Florida* from an American owner at Ouidah; but the *Legitimo Africano* was said to have been built at Ouidah in 1834. This ownership of ships by merchants resident in Africa was a general pattern in the illegal trade, but de Souza appears to have been a pioneer in it, while the construction of ships on the African coast, either by assembly from imported prefabricated parts or from scratch from local materials, was likewise an occasional practice in this period.[92] De Souza's ships regularly called at Prince's Island to obtain passports from the Portuguese authorities there, and one of them, the *Fortuna*, carried a passport issued at Luanda, Angola.

Moreover, de Souza's slave-trading operations on the African coast in the 1820s and 1830s were not restricted to Ouidah or to places within Dahomian territory. Prior to returning to Ouidah *c.* 1820, as has been seen, his principal base had been at Little Popo, to the west. Despite his removal from Popo to Ouidah, he seems initially to have intended to maintain his influence in the former; in 1823 the leading trader there, George Lawson, was still described as 'agent to De Souza'.[93] In 1822–3 there was a civil war in Little Popo, in which Lawson challenged the authority of its chief Comlagan, who was driven out and settled with his followers at Agoué to the east, and tradition recalls that de Souza supported Lawson in this

---

[87] (cont.) Bahia merchant, Antonio Pedroso de Albuquerque: Slave Trade 1827, Class A, no. 49, case of the *Principe de Guiné*.

[88] PP, Slave Trade 1826–7, Class A, no. 38, George Randall, Sierra Leone, 30 March 1826.

[89] Christopher Fyfe, *A History of Sierra Leone* (London, 1962), 196.

[90] PP, Slave Trade 1835, Class A, no. 54, case of the *Legitimo Africano*; 1837, Further Series, no. 13, case of the *Dom Francisco*; no. 14, case of the *Florida* (owned jointly by de Souza and its master, Alexandre Balbino Proença of Havana); 1840, Class A, no. 61, case of the *Fortuna*.

[91] PP, Slave Trade 1835, Class A, no. 52, case of the *Atrevido*; 1839–40, Class A, no. 77, case of the *Emprehendedor*.

[92] Eltis, *Economic Growth*, 158, 182.

[93] *RGCG*, 11 Feb. 1823.

seizure of power.[94] Despite his ally's victory, however, it does not appear that de Souza maintained his factory at Popo; local tradition records that after his departure to Ouidah the house he had built there was neglected (indeed, 'fell down'), until it was reoccupied by his son Isidoro in 1840.[95] The reason for this abandonment is not explained, although it may be that communication between Ouidah and Popo was disrupted as a result of the civil war of 1822–3 and the settlement of the defeated faction at Agoué. The interruption of communications between Ouidah and Little Popo was not absolute, however. At least one ship in this period, in 1836, is reported to have purchased its slaves at Ouidah, but actually embarked them at Popo, whither they had been 'passed by land' (more probably, by the lagoon).[96]

In the 1820s and 1830s, de Souza was more active in ports to the east of Ouidah. His opening of a subsidiary port of slave embarkation at Godomey was noted earlier. But his activities also extended further east, to places beyond Dahomian territory. In particular, he re-established links with Badagry, in whose territory he had briefly maintained a factory earlier (at Adjido, actually a few miles east of Badagry town), during his first period of residence on the coast in the 1790s. According to de Souza family tradition, when his eldest son Isidoro returned from education in Brazil in 1822, he was sent by his father to trade at Badagry, from where he returned to Ouidah c. 1834.[97] Adjido is mentioned in records of the illegal slave trade in the 1820s, although these make no reference specifically to the de Souzas; one ship taken off Lagos in 1826 had earlier called at Adjid, to purchase provisions and other goods, and another was taken off Adjido itself with slaves on board in 1827.[98] The traditions explain the abandonment of the Adjido factory in the 1830s as due to losses incurred from fire and theft, and by implication attribute the failure to Isidoro's youth and inexperience. But it may be that broader geo-political factors were also involved; it is suggestive that Isidoro's installation at Badagry roughly coincided with the establishment there of Adele, the exiled king of Lagos further east, under whose rule the town achieved an enhanced commercial importance as the principal outlet for the trade of Oyo in the interior; but conversely the return of Adele to resume his throne at Lagos c. 1835 probably marked the end of this flourishing.[99] De Souza continued, however, to do some trade at Badagry; in 1836, for example, a ship from Bahia trading at Ouidah carried tobacco and other goods for de Souza to Porto-Novo and Badagry.[100] He also maintained connections further east along the coast with the rising port of Lagos: two of the ships that de Souza himself owned, the *Florida* in 1837 and the *Fortuna* in 1839, took in their slaves at Lagos.

[94] Gayibor, *Le Genyi*, 189–201; Strickrodt, 'Afro–European trade relations', 188–200.

[95] GLL: Memorandum of Judgement in the case of Kain versus Chico d'Almeida, Little Popo, 2 March 1893.

[96] PP, Slave Trade 1836, Class A, Supplement C, no. 11, case of the *Fenix*.

[97] De Souza, 'Contribution', 19. He then spent 6 years at Ouidah before being sent to Little Popo, which (on other evidence) was in 1840.

[98] PP, Slave Trade 1827, Class A, no. 51, case of the *Hiroina* (referring to 'Judo, a place between Badagry and Lagos'); also no. 54, case of the *Venus* ('Ajudo', identified in this document, wrongly, as Ouidah).

[99] Robin Law, 'The career of Adele at Lagos and Badagry, c. 1807–c. 1837', *JHSN*, 9/2 (1978), 35–59 (though this does not note the de Souza connection).

[100] PP, Slave Trade 1837, Class A, no. 39, case of the *Latona*.

Evidently de Souza in this period operated on an international scale, rather than as a specifically 'Dahomian' figure; the perception of him as essentially a 'Dahomian chief', it may be suggested, really applies only to his last years, in the 1840s, when the international dimensions of his activities became attenuated.

De Souza's associates in Ouidah

Although the traditions (and indeed, many of the contemporary accounts also) emphasize the individual role of de Souza and implicitly give the impression that he was the only significant trader in Ouidah, his career evidently depended upon the collaboration of a number of associates, both fellow-foreigners and indigenous Dahomians. In the early stage, his most important associate was the older-established merchant Nicolas d'Oliveira; as seen earlier, d'Oliveira is said to have assisted de Souza in his escape from imprisonment under Adandozan and was later delegated by Gezo to invite him back to Ouidah. Local tradition also states that on his return to Ouidah in 1820 de Souza initially lodged in d'Oliveira's Ganvè quarter, prior to setting up his own establishment.[101] De Souza family tradition claims that d'Oliveira was appointed as a sort of deputy to de Souza, with the status of 'second counsellor' to Gezo, but this is perhaps merely a rationalization.[102] Nicolas d'Oliveira seems to have died early in Gezo's reign, but the continuing importance of his family is indicated by the fact that his son Denis is said to have married his daughter to Gezo, the marriage being celebrated at Ouidah, with de Souza acting as proxy for the king.[103] However, Denis d'Oliveira also predeceased de Souza;[104] and the importance of the family evidently declined thereafter, at least to judge from the lack of any reference to it in contemporary sources through most of the nineteenth century.

Nicolas d'Oliveira does not appear anywhere in the contemporary records of illegal slaving at Ouidah during the 1820s and 1830s. These do, however, name several other persons who resided at Ouidah for purposes of trade, whether in association or competition with de Souza. Many of these names occur without sufficient context (or corroboratory reference in other material) to identify them or establish their precise role and importance. In two cases, however, such individuals emerge more clearly from the record. One was Joaquim Telles de Menezes, already mentioned, who settled in Ouidah around 1830 and married one of de Souza's daughters. He is first documented in 1835, as the owner of a ship taken by the British navy, the *Thereza*, bound with a cargo of slaves for Montevideo; and he is also documented as both master and owner of two slave-ships captured subsequently, the *Joven Carolina* bound for Cuba in 1836 and the *Emprehendedor* bound for Bahia in 1839. De Menezes himself, in the judicial proceedings relating to these captures, gave contradictory testimony about his origins, describing himself as

---

[101] Gavoy, 'Note historique', 60; Reynier, 'Ouidah', 59.

[102] De Souza, *La Famille de Souza*, 21.

[103] Adoukonou, *Jalons pour une théologie africaine*, i, 95; de Souza, *La Famille de Souza*, 23.

[104] See de Souza, *La Famille de Souza*, 59–60.

born either on Prince's Island or in Pernambuco, Brazil; but, like de Souza himself, he consistently asserted Portuguese nationality.[105] Like his father-in-law, his slaving activities extended beyond Ouidah; of his ships taken by the British, the *Thereza* in 1835, after calling at Ouidah, had taken in its slaves at Lagos, and the *Joven Carolina* in 1836 went even further afield, shipping its slaves at Old Calabar. His final appearance in the contemporary record was in 1841, when he was a passenger on a suspected slave-ship bound from Bahia to Prince's Island.[106] De Menezes presumably operated in partnership, or at least in cooperation, with his father-in-law; indeed, one of the ships he owned, the *Emprehendedor*, as seen earlier, had originally belonged to de Souza, who sold her to him. He is not remembered, however, in local tradition in Ouidah, presumably because he left no descendants there.

Another leading slave-dealer who settled in Ouidah in this period was Juan José Zangronis (or Sangron), the son of a prominent merchant of Havana, who supplied slaves for his father (and, later, for his brother) in Cuba. In the contemporary record, Zangronis is first attested at Ouidah, taking delivery of goods shipped from Cuba, in 1834. He is again documented there, serving as consignee of a cargo shipped by his father in 1835, as supplying slaves to two ships during 1836-7 and as consignee of part of a cargo shipped from Havana for Ouidah in 1839.[107] Whatever the circumstances of his original establishment in Ouidah, in the long run Zangronis clearly traded in association rather than in rivalry with de Souza; the ship *Emprehendedor* taken by the British in 1839, then owned by de Souza's son-in-law de Menezes, according to some testimony had previously been owned jointly by de Souza and Zangronis. The British missionary Freeman, who met Zangronis at Ouidah in 1843, described him as 'in rank and influence ... second only to De Souza'.[108] He died in February 1843, and was buried in 'the Portuguese burial-ground' (i.e. in the Portuguese fort).[109] Unlike de Menezes, Zangronis did leave descendants in Ouidah; a 'half-caste' son of his, Francisco Zangronis, is noted incidentally attending the royal court at Abomey in 1864.[110] Indeed, the family survives to the present, although its name is now given a Portuguese form, Sangrónio, and its founder (whose name is recalled as José Sangronio) is wrongly remembered as having been 'a Brazilian of Portuguese origin', rather than as Spanish from Cuba, this confusion evidently reflecting the family's absorption into the Brazilian community.[111]

[105] PP, Slave Trade 1836, Class A, no. 59, case of the *Thereza*; 1836, Class A, no. 69, case of the *Joven Carolina*; 1839–40, Class A, no. 77, case of the *Emprehendedor*. The first two accounts state that he had been resident at Ouidah for 5 years (i.e. since 1830/1); the third says for 18 years (since 1821), but perhaps this is a misprint for 8.

[106] PP, Slave Trade 1842, Class A, no. 79, case of the *Galliana*. Another passenger was 'José Telles de Souza, of Whydah', perhaps a relative; the British court identified him with the Chacha, but this was clearly a confusion.

[107] PP, Slave Trade 1836, Class A, no. 50, case of the *Mosca*; 1837, Class A, no. 39, case of the *Latona*; no. 41, case of the *Carlota*; 1840, Class A, no. 47, case of the *Jack Wilding*. Among papers found on the last ship, belonging to a passenger, Antonio Capo, was an account of goods delivered at Ouidah by the latter, when commander of the *General Manso* in 1834, to Zangronis and de Souza.

[108] Freeman, 'West Africa', 241.

[109] Freeman, *Journal*, 258.

[110] Burton, *Mission*, ii, 258 ['Francisco Zangrony'].

[111] De Souza, *La Famille de Souza*, 71.

De Souza also depended, and perhaps more critically, on his relations with indigenous African administrators and commercial partners in Ouidah. The supreme political authority in Ouidah, as noted earlier, continued to be the Dahomian governor, the Yovogan. A contemporary account reports that the Yovogan who had been in place at Gezo's accession died in 1823.[112] Tradition indicates that this was Adjossogbé, the man appointed to succeed him being Dagba.[113] Dagba was to occupy the office for an unprecedentedly long period (around 50 years); his name is recorded in several contemporary sources between the 1840s and 1860s.[114] His age was estimated in 1856 at between 55 and 60, which suggests that he was aged between 22 and 27 at his appointment in 1823 and over 70 at the time of his death in the 1870s.[115] As a consequence of this longevity in office, unusually among holders of the Yovogan title, he founded a family that exists in Ouidah to the present. The traditions of this family show that, again apparently unlike earlier occupants of the office, Dagba belonged to an aristocratic family, called Awesu, who were hereditary chiefs of Dokon, near Abomey, and indeed claimed to have exercised royal authority in the area before the rise of Dahomey. Dagba's original name, prior to his appointment to Ouidah, was Awesu Atokun; when he became Yovogan, he is said to have resigned the chiefship of Dokon to his brother, Awesu Ayaji.[116] This is corroborated by contemporary sources: Duncan in 1845, for example, who met 'Awassou, the caboceer of Doko', understood that he was a younger brother to Yovogan Dagba.[117] Tradition explains that Awesu/Dagba had been a partisan of Gezo in his coup d'etat of 1818 and was appointed as Yovogan at Ouidah in reward for his support.[118] The precise character of the relationship between the Yovogan Dagba and the Chacha de Souza is not very clearly explained in the traditions – for example, whether the Chacha was formally subject to the Yovogan's authority or directly and independently answerable to the king. The Yovogan's role as intermediary between the king and Europeans at Ouidah was evidently undermined by the Chacha's appointment, but he retained some responsibility in the management of European trade, notably in collecting 'customs' and in holding and delivering slaves on the king's behalf. Dagba family tradition insists that the relationship with the Chacha was cordial and cooperative: 'The two being friends of King Gezo it is easy to understand that solid bonds of friendship were quickly established between them.'[119]

De Souza also evidently depended upon African merchants to supply him with

---

[112] *RGCG*, 11 Feb. 1823.

[113] Reynier, 'Ouidah', 51; Agbo, *Histoire*, 56.

[114] E.g. Duncan, *Travels'*, i, 117–18 ['Dagbwa']; Forbes, *Dahomey*, i, 105, 127; ii, 72–3 ['Dagbah']; Vallon, 'Le royaume de Dahomey, 1/337–8 ['Dagba']; Burton, *Mission*, i, 100, n. ['Da-gba']; Treaty with France, 19 May 1868 ['Daba'], text in Edouard Aublet, *La Guerre au Dahomey 1888–1893* (Paris, 1894), 8.

[115] Vallon, 'Le royaume de Dahomey', 1/338.

[116] Dagba, *La Collectivité familiale*, 67.

[117] Duncan, *Travels*, ii, 259. See also Forbes, *Dahomey*, ii, 72–3.

[118] Dagba, *La Collectivité familiale*, 57. But note that the same source claims that he had, in fact, been designated for the office of Yovogan since childhood (supposedly by King Tegbesu), though the reason for the delay in his appointment is not explained.

[119] Ibid., 44.

slaves, whether as agents for the king or operating independently. The contemporary sources are uninformative on the identity of his African suppliers, but some light is thrown on these by local oral traditions. For example, one of de Souza's praise-names celebrates his generosity by referring to his gifts of cloth to various African merchants; of six names given, five can be identified: Boya, Codjia, Gnahoui, Adjovi and Houénou.[120] The sixth name, which cannot be identified, is Bewa; in comparison with other evidence, it ought perhaps to be the personal name of the head of the Hodonou family, which was also linked in this period to de Souza, although the name Bewa does not appear to be preserved in its traditions. Of the six Boya, as was seen in an earlier chapter, was the title of one of the king's traders at Ouidah. This title had existed since the mid-eighteenth century, but according to tradition in Ouidah it was conferred by Gezo on a partisan of his, called Boya-Cissé, who had assisted in organizing de Souza's escape from imprisonment at Abomey and was now installed at Ouidah to engage in the slave trade. This man originally resided in de Souza's 'Brazil' quarter, but later established his own quarter, Boyasaramè, 'Boya's quarter', on the north-west of the town; tradition says that his move out of 'Brazil' quarter was occasioned by frequent fires there, perhaps alluding to the great fire in *c*. 1838, in which de Souza lost a great deal of property.[121] In the eighteenth century the Boya had stood only second in rank among the royal traders, after the Coke, but the latter title is not recorded after the early nineteenth century and was presumably now suppressed, being superseded as head of the king's traders by the Boya. In the contemporary record, Forbes in 1850 noted the Boya as one of the 'six traders or superintendants [sic] of trade appointed by the king', though without indicating that he held any special position among them; but in the following year it was noted that the Boya served as 'acting Yovogan' in the absence of the latter.[122]

The other five (including Hodonou) seem to have been essentially private merchants, rather than royal officials (in so far as this distinction can be made in this period). None of them are attested as traders in contemporary sources during de Souza's lifetime, with the possible exception of Adjovi, whose name may have been given to a slave-ship from Bahia trading at Ouidah in 1846, called '*Adeovi*'.[123] However, all five were noted by Forbes in 1850, who listed them among recipients of the royal bounty at the Annual Customs in Abomey, immediately after the Yovogan.[124] Of these, the Codjia, Gnahoui and Hodonou families had already been established in Ouidah, as noted earlier, in the previous century. But the son of the first Codjia, called Agossukpé, became a friend of de Souza, and moved out of the

---

[120] Ayélé Marlène Tettekpoe, 'Portée socio-historique des louanges familiales au Bénin (cas de la famille de Souza de Ouidah)' (Mémoire de maîtrise, UNB, 1988–9), 96–7.

[121] Reynier, 'Ouidah', 58; cf. Agbo, *Histoire*, 216. Reynier actually says that Boya initially lived in the Quénum quarter, but the latter was originally part of Brazil quarter.

[122] Forbes, *Dahomey*, i, 111 ['Boo-ee-ah']; PRO, FO84/886, Louis Fraser, Daily Journal, 23 July 1851 ['Boayon'].

[123] Dos Santos correspondence, no. 44 [28 Dec. 1846].

[124] Forbes, *Dahomey*, ii, 243: listing 'Ah-quea-noo, Ah-joh-vee, Que-jah [for Quo-jah?], Hoo-doo-noo, Near-whey'; ii, 246: 'Quae-nung, Ah-joh-vee, Koh-jeh [= Koh-jah?], 'Nar-whey, Koh-doh-noo [= Hoh-doh-noo?]'.

Dahomian quarter of the town, Fonsaramè, to settle in de Souza's Brazil quarter, where the family still lives.[125] The first Gnahoui had died in 1823; the man who dealt with de Souza was his son, the second head of the family, recalled in tradition under the surname 'Dah Ahissigan'.[126] This man inherited his father's position as official interpreter for the English, serving in this capacity for various British visitors to Dahomey between 1843 and 1851.[127] But he also became a substantial merchant, described by Forbes in 1850 as 'as rich a merchant as exists in Dahomey, and as great a slave-trader'.[128] The Hodonou active at this time was the third head of the family, whose personal name was Dovonou, who is recalled to have rebuilt the fortunes of the family after the imprisonment and disgrace of his predecessor, his brother Sossou.[129] Family tradition recalls, in general terms, that Hodonou originally traded for the king but also on his own account, and that, when de Souza came to Ouidah, he became his friend and supplied slaves to him.[130] Although dealing with de Souza, Gnahoui and Hodonou seem to have maintained a relative independence of him; at any rate, unlike Codjia, their families remained resident in Fonsaramè, the Dahomian quarter of Ouidah.

Adjovi and Houénou, on the other hand, were newcomers to Ouidah, who arrived in the town as clients of de Souza. The founder of the Adjovi family is said to have been originally a palace musician in the Dahomian capital Abomey who was sent by Gezo to Ouidah to serve de Souza as guardian of slaves destined for export, but later moved out of de Souza's Brazil quarter, to set himself up in Tové, the quarter of the indigenous (pre-Dahomian) inhabitants of Ouidah, on the opposite (east) side of the town. The Adjovis nowadays claim descent from Kpase, the legendary founder of Ouidah, but this is contested by the de Souzas, who claim that the first Adjovi was in origin a slave, adopted into the Kpase family.[131] However this may be, Adjovi's rise to prominence was certainly based on his control of the shrine of Kpase, in Tové, as well as on his commercial wealth: Forbes in 1850 noted that he 'had a large fetish house, east of Whydah, situated in a pretty bosquet', referring evidently to the 'sacred forest' of Kpase.[132] The founder of the Houénou (or Quénum) family in Ouidah, Azanmado Houénou, is also claimed by the de Souzas to have been originally a slave who was given by Gezo to Francisco Felix de Souza.[133] But the Houénous themselves claim a more respectable origin, by descent from the kings of Weme, which was absorbed into Dahomey in the early eighteenth century; members of successive generations of the family are said to have served variously as officers in the Dahomian army, administrative officials and

[125] Fieldwork: Codjia compound, 13 June 1997.
[126] His praise-name is given by Agbo, *Histoire*, 235–6.
[127] Freeman, *Journal*, 250 ['Niawi']; Duncan, *Travels*, i, 119 ['Yamie']; Forbes, *Dahomey*, i, 53, ii, 175–6 etc. ['Narwhey']; PRO, FO84/886, Fraser, Journal, 15 Aug. 1851 etc. ['Narwhey'].
[128] Forbes, *Dahomey*, ii, 175.
[129] Reynier, 'Ouidah', 53.
[130] Fieldwork, Hodonou compound, 21 Sept. 2000.
[131] Reynier, 'Ouidah', 41, 47; de Souza, *La Famille de Souza*, 33–4.
[132] Forbes, *Dahomey*, i, 113.
[133] Personal communication, from Martine de Souza.

traders.[134] That the family had achieved distinction even before de Souza's time is supported by contemporary sources, which record a Houénou serving as a Dahomian military commander in the 1780s: as deputy to the Gau, the commander-in-chief of the Dahomian army, in the war against Badagry in 1784; and as 'one of the King's Generals of War' sent down to reinforce Ouidah against anticipated attack from Badagry in 1788.[135] Family tradition names the head of the family during the reign of Kpengla (1774–89) as Ahoglo, and does recall a visit by him to Ouidah, although as a trader (in slaves) rather than a military officer.[136] Ahoglo's son, Fadegnon, is said to have served as 'minister of finances' (meaning presumably Mehu) under Adandozan (1797–1818), and when Adandozan was overthrown by Gezo he was imprisoned as a partisan of the fallen monarch.[137] Azanmado Houénou was a nephew of Fadegnon. He is said to have served with distinction in Gezo's wars against the Mahi in the 1820s, but then retired to become a trader at Ouidah. He was initially associated with Nicolas d'Oliveira, who employed him in the purchase of slaves from the Mahi country; but was then taken up by Gezo, who gave him the rank of *ahisinon* and associated him with de Souza at Ouidah in selling slaves on the royal account.[138] The Houénou family property in Ouidah is situated immediately south of de Souza's Brazil quarter and is said originally to have formed part of it, but Azanmado Houénou eventually broke with de Souza, and was able to constitute his household as an independent quarter of the town, called after the family name, Quénum.

Another important associate of de Souza was Antonio Dossou-Yovo, who served as his interpreter in Portuguese and French. In origin this man belonged to the Kocou family of Sogbadji, descended from a canoeman from the Gold Coast employed by the English fort, but he now transferred to de Souza's service and took up residence in Brazil quarter.[139] The name Dossou-Yovo, 'the white man's Dosu', alludes to his employment by de Souza.[140] He is also said to have assisted in de Souza's escape from imprisonment at Abomey, and to have attended the subsequent swearing of a 'blood pact' between de Souza and the future king Gezo.[141] After Gezo's accession, he is said to have visited Brazil on an official embassy that attempted to locate and bring back Gezo's mother Agotime, who had been sold into slavery by his predecessor Adandozan.[142] In contemporary records, he is first mentioned in 1848, when he was described as de Souza's 'principal *moce* [Portuguese *môço*, boy] or domestic', and was seen in company with de Souza's son Ignacio at the royal court at Abomey; he was also noted by Forbes in 1850, in company with the Chacha (now Isidoro) and other members of the de Souza

---

[134] Quénum, *Les Ancêtres*.

[135] Dalzel, *History*, 184 ['Queenoh']; T70/1162, Day Book, William's Fort, 5 Dec. 1788 ['Weenoh'].

[136] Quénum, *Les Ancêtres*, 51–3.

[137] Reynier, 'Ouidah', 62; Quénum, *Les Ancêtres*, 54–6.

[138] Reynier, 'Ouidah', 63; cf. Quénum, *Les Ancêtres*, 59–60.

[139] Reynier, 'Ouidah', 42–3; fieldwork, Kocou compound, 9 Jan. 1996.

[140] So explained locally; the explanation offered by Burton, *Mission*, i, 151, n., that the surname alluded to his having been educated in Brazil, is presumably a misunderstanding.

[141] Gavoy, 'Note historique', 60; Paul Hazoumé, *Le Pacte de sang au Dahomey* (Paris, 1937), 29–31.

[142] Hazoumé, *Le Pacte de sang*, 31–2; see also Bay, *Wives of the Leopard*, 179–80.

family, at the Annual Customs at Abomey. He is recorded again in 1863, when he was ill with guinea-worm at Ouidah, but the British consul Burton was able to stay in his house at Tori on his way to Abomey.[143] He died, at a very advanced age, in 1887.[144] Dossou-Yovo also became a wealthy merchant, but this was perhaps after de Souza's death in 1849.[145]

Several other Ouidah merchant families claim descent from founder-ancestors who set up in Ouidah during the reign of Gezo: Akodé (who later, under Glele after 1858, received an official position, with the title Chodaton) and the ancestors of the Mahounon, Abodooui, Tchibozo and Tokpo families.[146] However, none of these is explicitly connected with de Souza, and they may have arrived in Ouidah in Gezo's last years, after de Souza's death. Two of them (Akodé, Mahounou) are said to have traded 'for the account' of Gezo; while the others (Abodooui, Tchibozo, Tokpo) are given the title of *ahisinon*, but whether this intends a distinction between royal and private traders is doubtful. The only one of them named in Forbes's account in 1850, Tokpo, is listed with the Boya among the official 'superintendants [sic] of trade appointed by the king'.

It is clear that a number of substantial commercial fortunes were made in Ouidah during this period. Although de Souza's wealth and influence were paramount, his success in not only building up a large household but also transmitting it to his descendants, thereby constituting a new quarter of the town, was not unique. He had been preceded by Nicolas d'Oliveira, and several of his African associates were similarly successful in creating hereditary estates, two of these, Boya and Houénou, also establishing their own quarters of the town. This successful accumulation was probably due to the political situation created by the coup d'etat of 1818. Gezo owed his success to the support, not of de Souza alone, but of the Ouidah merchant community, or at least a faction within it, more generally; as has been seen, Nicolas d'Oliveira and Antonio Dossou-Yovo were also party to the plot. Other partisans of Gezo, although they may not have had connections with Ouidah earlier, were appointed to positions there after his accession, as in the cases of Boya-Cissé and Yovogan Dagba. In these circumstances, it may reasonably be supposed, Gezo was disposed, if not constrained, to allow the Ouidah merchant community greater autonomy than it had hitherto enjoyed.

The accumulation of merchant wealth in Ouidah under Gezo was probably also facilitated by some relaxation of royal restrictions on trade, presumably in reward for services in his support. The granting of permission to the Boya, Tokpo and other official royal traders to trade also on their own account, first attested by Forbes in 1850, may well have originated with Gezo's accession. There is also some suggestion that the Ouidah merchant community benefited from a more liberal tax regime under Gezo, at least during the earlier part of his reign. Gezo himself told Duncan in 1845 that, although he was entitled to inherit his caboceers' estates on

---

[143] Blancheley, 'Au Dahomey', 536 ['Dosu Evo']; Forbes, *Dahomey*, ii, 245, 247 ['Dossoo-eea-noo', 'Dossoo-eea-voo']; Burton, *Mission*, i, 151 ['Antonio Dosu, known as Dosu Yevo'].

[144] Inscription on his grave, seen at the Dossou-Yovo compound, 11 Jan. 1996.

[145] Fieldwork, Kocou compound, 9 Jan. 1996.

[146] Reynier, 'Ouidah', 48, 49, 50, 54, 55.

their deaths, he in fact 'seldom exercise[d]' this right.[147] This is given some support by local tradition in Ouidah, which records that when Nicolas d'Oliveira died Francisco Felix de Souza interceded with Gezo to prevent the levying of the royal inheritance tax. However, this fiscal concession was evidently not maintained, since on the death of the second head of the family, Denis Nicolas d'Oliveira, the de Souzas are said to have connived in the concealing of some of his slaves in order to prevent their seizure by the king; one of the de Souza sons, Antonio 'Kokou', with whom the slaves were lodged, subsequently refused to surrender them but appropriated them for himself.[148] Moreover, when Francisco Felix de Souza himself died in 1849, Gezo claimed his customary share of the estate.[149] The reversal of this concession may have been due to the fiscal difficulties that the Dahomian monarchy faced from the 1840s, in consequence of the decline of the Atlantic slave trade.

The settlement of returned ex-slaves

In addition to the free Brazilians and others who settled in Ouidah as associates of de Souza, his prominence in the town also attracted the settlement of a large number of African-born former slaves. Individual former slaves had re-emigrated, from Brazil and elsewhere, to settle on the West African coast already in the eighteenth century: at Ouidah, an example was Dom Jeronimo, referred to in earlier chapters, an important slave-trader at Ouidah in the 1780s. The large-scale emigration of ex-slaves from Brazil to Africa seems to have begun, however, only after the great slave rebellion in Bahia in 1835, which the local authorities blamed upon the influence of the free black population, and which was followed by the deportation of many suspected of complicity in it; the re-emigration then continued on a more or less voluntary basis through the rest of the nineteenth century.[150] There was also a significant, but smaller, re-emigration of ex-slaves from Cuba, although in the long run such Cuban repatriates tended to be absorbed into the Brazilian community.[151] Brazilian ex-slaves settled at various ports along the coast, including Accra on the Gold Coast, but the most substantial repatriate communities were on the Bight of Benin, at Agoué to the west and Porto-Novo and Lagos to the east, as well as Ouidah itself.[152]

In the immediate aftermath of the rebellion, in 1835, one party of 200 free

---

[147] Duncan, *Travels*, ii, 264.

[148] De Souza, *La Famille de Souza*, 22, 59–60.

[149] Foà, *Le Dahomey*, 26; de Souza, *La Famille de Souza*, 43.

[150] On the Brazilian re-emigration to West Africa, see esp. Jerry Michael Turner, 'Les Brésiliens: The impact of former Brazilian slaves upon Dahomey' (PhD thesis, Boston University, 1975); Milton Guran, *Agudás: os "brasileiros" do Benim* (Rio de Janeiro, 1999).

[151] On which, see Rodolfo Sarracino, *Los que volvieron a Africa* (Havana, 1988).

[152] For the Brazilian community in Accra, see Parker, *Making the Town*, 14–16; for Agoué, Silke Strickrodt, 'Afro-Brazilians of the western Slave Coast', in José C. Curto & Paul E. Lovejoy (eds), *Enslaving Connections* (Amherst, N.Y., 2003), 213–44; for Lagos, Lisa A. Lindsay, '"To return to the bosom of their fatherland": Brazilian immigrants in nineteenth-century Lagos', *S&A*, 15 (1994), 22–50.

blacks was deported from Bahia on a ship that went specifically to Ouidah.[153] According to local tradition, Maro quarter of Ouidah, immediately west of de Souza's original Brazil quarter, was settled by a party of ex-slaves, who came in a ship to West Africa and were granted land by de Souza (or by the king, at de Souza's instance).[154] In contemporary sources, the Brazilian repatriate community in Ouidah was first noted by Duncan in 1845, who observed that, in addition to the 'real Portuguese' there were 'numerous' former slaves from Brazil, mainly of Fulani (i.e. Hausa) and Oyo (Yoruba) origin, who had obtained their freedom either by purchase or by returning as servants to slave-dealers. Duncan understood that 'many' of them had left Brazil after being 'concerned in an attempted revolution among the slaves there', referring evidently to the Bahia rising of 1835. Forbes in 1849–50 also alludes to 'liberated Africans' living in Ouidah, who he says originated from Yoruba and Borno, and who had purchased their freedom in Brazil, but had been unable to reach their home countries, 'many' of them being, according to him, themselves slave-dealers.[155] The name 'Maro' applied to these Brazilian ex-slaves was first recorded in 1851.[156]

One of the ex-slaves who were obliged to leave Bahia in the aftermath of the slave uprising was Luís Xavier de Jesus, who made out his will, prior to embarkation for Africa, in 1835. Either then or later, he settled in Ouidah. Some correspondence addressed to him there during 1841 survives, through being found on an illegal slave ship intercepted by the British navy. De Jesus claimed to be innocent of involvement in the 1835 rebellion, and in 1841 he was petitioning to be allowed to return to Brazil, but he died still in Africa c. 1851.[157] This man seems to have left no descendants in Ouidah, but other Brazilian re-emigrants did. One such was Antonio d'Almeida (died 1890), whose family lives in Ganvè quarter. He had been owned in Bahia by the prominent slave-trader Manoel Joaquim d'Almeida (who commanded the ship *Principe de Guiné*, consigned to de Souza but captured by the British in 1826), whose gratitude he earned, according to family tradition, by protecting him during a slave rebellion (referring presumably to 1835); having secured his freedom, he returned to Africa, settling first at Agoué but later moving to Ouidah, where he made out his will in 1864.[158] Not all of the ex-slaves who settled in Ouidah had left Brazil in connection with the 1835 rising, however. Sabino Vieyra, who founded a family in Sogbadji, came from Rio de Janeiro rather than Bahia; after obtaining his freedom he became a merchant in Brazil and originally returned to West Africa in the course of trade, but fell into poverty and settled in Ouidah as a client of de Souza.[159]

The main concentration of Brazilian settlement was in Maro quarter, where

---

[153] João José Reis, *Slave Rebellion in Brazil: The Muslim Rising of 1835 in Bahia* (Baltimore, 1993), 220.

[154] Gavoy, 'Note historique', 69–70; Reynier, 'Ouidah', 44. The dates given (1829 by Gavoy, 1812 by Reynier) are clearly speculative, and incorrect.

[155] Duncan, *Travels*, i, 138, 185, 201–2; Forbes, *Dahomey*, ii, 71–2.

[156] Bouet, in Nardin, 'La reprise des relations', 120 ['Malo'].

[157] Verger, *Os libertos*, 55–61, with text of will and other documents, 125–37.

[158] Ibid., 48–53, with text of will, 121–4; Turner, 'Les Brésiliens', 106–7; Agbo, *Histoire*, 219.

[159] Turner, 'Les Brésiliens', 117–20.

most of the families still in place acknowledge descent from returned ex-slaves, including Ahi, Dangana, da Matha, das Neves, Ode, Oguidan, Olougbon and Toubiaz; the last of these, although commonly classified as Brazilian, is sometimes said to have originated from Cuba rather than from Brazil.[160] Several other families founded by Brazilian ex-slaves can be found in other quarters of the town, however, such as Diogo in Brazil quarter, do Rego in Zomaï and Villaça in Boya quarter.[161] The date of arrival of their founders is in most cases uncertain and may have been later than the original party in 1835, but, for example, João Antonio do Rego was already established in Ouidah by 1840 and José Joaquim das Neves by 1847.[162] Several of these families remember not only their Brazilian origins, but also their ancestral African ethnicity, most being of Yoruba extraction. António d'Almeida, for example, was originally from the Yoruba town of Iseyin in modern Nigeria, and the family retains a Yoruba surname, Oloufadé.[163] Other Yoruba Brazilian families include Olougbon (whose founder was from the town of Ofa, also in Nigeria), Ahi (from Abeokuta), Villaça (who was Ijesha)[164] and Ode and da Matha (both from 'Boma', presumably Igbomina, a Yoruba subgroup). Others trace their origins from further in the interior, in what is today northern Nigeria: Sabino Vieyra and the founder of the Dangana family were Nupe ('Atakpa'), and Joaquim das Neves was Hausa, while João do Rego traced his origins to 'Kaniké', i.e. Borno.[165]

The Brazilian ex-slaves who settled in Ouidah were mainly Christian, having been baptized into the Roman Catholic Church in Brazil, and their settlement provided the basis for the establishment of organized Christian worship in the town, centred on the chapel in the Portuguese fort. When the fort was reoccupied in 1844, its personnel included a priest to act as chaplain.[166] Thereafter, the chapel in the Portuguese fort was maintained continuously throughout the nineteenth century, the clergy normally being supplied from São Tomé, apart from the years 1861–5, when possession of the fort was usurped by missionaries of the French Société des Missions Africaines. Forbes in 1849–50, for example, noted the Roman Catholic church in the Portuguese fort, patronized by the Bahia repatriates and staffed by black priests from São Tomé.[167] These clergy conducted weekly masses and performed baptisms and burial services (though not religious marriages, which were rare in Africa). The French missionaries in the 1860s were critical of the quality of the São Tomé clergy, whom they dismissed as having 'no knowledge beyond reading the mass and conducting religious ceremonies, and that in a

---

[160] Reynier, 'Ouidah', 44–6; Agbo, *Histoire*, 200–03; Germain Kadja, 'Les communaités de base de Ouidah', in [UGDO], *Les Voies de la renaissance de Ouidah* (Caen, 1985), 56–7.

[161] Reynier, 'Ouidah', 43, 56, 60; Agbo, *Histoire*, 198, 215–16.

[162] PP, Slave Trade 1841, Class A, case of the *Gratidão*, papers on board include a letter from Isidore José Marquis, Bahia, to João Antonio do Rego, at Ouidah, 6 Sept. 1840; Dos Santos correspondence, no. 64 [10 Aug. 1847], recording the transmission of $65 sent from Bahia to 'Mr Neves'.

[163] See the family praise-name, in Agbo, *Histoire*, 276–7.

[164] See the Villaça family praise-name, ibid., 295.

[165] For do Rego, see the family praise-name, ibid., 278–9.

[166] Sarmento, *Portugal no Dahomé*, 61; also contemporary notice, in De Monleon, 'Le Cap de Palmes, le Dahomey et l'Île du Prince en 1844', *RC*, 6 (1845), 72.

[167] Forbes, *Dahomey*, i, 93, 118–19.

wretched manner'. However, they acknowledged that they inherited from them a pre-existing Roman Catholic community in Ouidah, whose size they estimated at 600 persons.[168]

Not all of the repatriates were Christians, however. The 1835 rising in Bahia had involved specifically Muslim slaves and ex-slaves, and it must be presumed that Muslims were especially prominent among those deported in its aftermath. Local tradition confirms that a section of the Brazilian settlers in Maro quarter were Muslims, though one story distinguishes the original settlers from the specifically Muslim element that arrived later.[169] The name Maro applied to the quarter seems, indeed, to reflect this Muslim element, since it was the name applied to quarters of foreign Muslim merchants in towns in the interior north of Dahomey, notably Nikki in Borgu. Forbes in 1849–50 noted that the Muslims had a mosque in Ouidah.[170] Tradition identifies the earliest mosque in the town with one which still exists in Maro quarter;[171] the modern 'Great Mosque', also in Maro but further east, is a twentieth-century establishment. The first imam of Ouidah, Baba Oloug-bon, was one of the returned slaves from Brazil; although sometimes described as a Hausa in origin, he was in fact from the Yoruba town of Ofa. Later imams were Hausa or Yoruba or from Borno and presumably also from within the Brazilian community. The sixth imam, Ahmidou Soumaila, who came to office c. 1883 (and died in 1914), was the son of a Brazilian repatriate, Soumaila, who was originally from Ibadan in Yorubaland, had redeemed himself from slavery in Brazil and then lived successively in Borno, Sierra Leone and Agoué before settling in Ouidah, his son Ahmidou, who became imam, being born in Sierra Leone.[172] The imamate afterwards became hereditary in his family.

From the late 1830s, there was a parallel movement of re-emigration from the British colony of Freetown, Sierra Leone, by former slaves liberated from illegal slave ships by the British navy, known as 'Saros'.[173] These were also mainly Yoruba in origin, but were distinguished from the Brazilians by language and religion, speaking English rather than Portuguese and being mainly converts to Protestant versions of Christianity. Although the principal early focus of Saro settlement was Badagry to the east (and, from there, Abeokuta in the interior), some repatriates from Sierra Leone also settled in coastal towns of modern Bénin. There is a 'Salo [Saro]' quarter, as well as four quarters populated by Brazilian repatriates, in Agoué, for example.[174] There was also some Sierra Leonian settlement in Ouidah. When the British missionary Freeman visited Ouidah in 1843, he discovered a group of emigrants from Sierra Leone settled there, who attended a Christian

---

[168] Borghero, *Journal*, 45 [20 April 1861]; 'Relation', ibid., 252, 280.

[169] Gavoy, 'Note historique', 66, 70. This story claims that these people had originally been slaves in Ouidah, but were sold overseas on suspicion of complicity in a plotted slave revolt: perhaps a garbled recollection of the circumstances of their expulsion from Brazil.

[170] Forbes, *Dahomey*, i, 33, 176–7.

[171] Described in Sinou & Agbo, *Ouidah*, 244–5.

[172] Reynier, 'Ouidah', 44–5; Marty, 'Etudes sur l'Islam au Dahomey', 2/103–4.

[173] See esp. Jean Herskovits Kopytoff, *A Preface to Modern Nigeria: The 'Sierra Leonians' in Yoruba, 1830–1890* (Madison, 1965), though this work does not deal with 'Saro' settlement in Bénin.

[174] Strickrodt, 'Afro-Brazilians', 226.

service which he conducted in the English fort; he understood that they had arrived two or three years earlier, i.e. *c*. 1840/1. Duncan in 1845 confirms the presence of a 'few families' from Sierra Leone, who had built 'a small town' on land granted to them by the king of Dahomey; and Forbes in 1850 also refers to Sierra Leonian immigrants in Ouidah, who publicly affirmed their status as Christians by turning out on Sundays 'in all their finery', although they did not, like the Brazilians, have a church to attend.[175] However, this Sierra Leonean community seems to have disappeared by the mid-1850s (and is not recollected in local tradition); probably the Sierra Leonians in Ouidah had removed to Lagos after the establishment of British influence there from 1852.

De Souza's Ouidah

Local tradition credits de Souza with the transformation and extension of the town: 'he cleaned Ouidah and had streets traced, his slaves cleared the plots on which he built the quarters of Brésil, Quénum, Maro, a part of Zomaï and of Docomè'.[176] His activities led to a substantial extension of the town, towards the south-west. When he returned to Ouidah, as noted earlier, despite his continuing claim to be governor of the Portuguese fort, de Souza did not resume residence in the fort but constructed a new house of his own: in the 1830s he was reported to be living in 'a well constructed mansion, erected by himself'.[177] This was evidently on the site still occupied by the de Souza compound, on the south-west of the town. The building was called Adjido, in common with the factories de Souza had established earlier in Badagry and Little Popo;[178] it included a two-storey building, which was called, like the earlier European forts, *Singbome*, and was considered on a par with the forts.[179] This house became the centre of a quarter of the town, occupied to the present by the descendants of de Souza and his free clients and slaves. The quarter was originally called 'Chacha' ward, but subsequently became known as Blézin, i.e. 'Brazil'.[180] De Souza is also credited with the establishment of two other quarters, situated to the west of Brazil quarter. One of these, immediately west of Brazil, was Maro, settled, as has been seen, by returned ex-slaves from Brazil and dating probably from 1835. The other was Zomaï, further west again from Maro, which is still occupied mainly by descendants of slaves of the de Souza family; this is said to have been built by de Souza as a combined country retreat and storehouse for goods.[181] In contemporary sources, the existence of 'some large stores' on the western 'outskirts' of Ouidah belonging to de Souza (and

---

[175] Freeman, *Journal*, 242; Duncan, *Travels*, i, 117; Forbes, *Dahomey*, i, 33, 117–18. Another allusion to Sierra Leonians in Ouidah is in PRO, FO84/886, Fraser, Journal, 5 Aug. 1851.

[176] Gavoy, 'Note historique', 61.

[177] Huntley, *Seven Years' Service*, i, 116.

[178] This name first recorded in contemporary sources by Burton, *Mission*, i, 64.

[179] Gavoy, 'Note historique', 68; Burton, *Mission*, i, 67.

[180] Forbes, *Dahomey*, i, 105 ['Cha-cha town']; Burton, *Mission*, i, 64 ['Ajido, Chacha, or Brazilian Town'].

[181] Gavoy, 'Note historique', 65; Reynier, 'Ouidah', 56–7.

also including his billiard room) was first noted in 1847, and the actual name Zomaï in 1850.[182]

In addition to these three quarters directly founded by de Souza, two others, as has been seen, were founded by African associates of his, Boya and Quénum, respectively to the north-west and south of his own Brazil quarter. Five of the twelve quarters of Ouidah were thus created by de Souza or his associates. Together with Ganvè quarter, founded by his older contemporary Nicolas d'Oliveira, half of the town's quarters represent extensions in the nineteenth century, all to the west of its former area. Nineteenth-century Ouidah was thus a much larger town than in the previous century; Burton in the 1860s estimated that it was two miles long (north-west to south-east) by half a mile in depth.[183] The physical expansion of the town was also marked by the establishment of new market centres. Although Zobé in the east of the town remained the principal market, Burton noted that there were now also two markets in the new section of the town to the south-west: Adjido market, immediately south of the de Souza compound (in the area nowadays known as the 'Place du Chacha'), and another in Zomaï quarter.[184] The town was larger in population, as well as in extent. In 1825, shortly after de Souza's resettlement in Ouidah, it was thought to be 'not as populous as it was some years ago', although no figure was suggested.[185] But estimates of the population in the mid-nineteenth century suggest a significantly larger population than in the eighteenth: in 1841, it was already reckoned to be around 10,000 (see Table 3.1). In the 1850s it was even higher; but this probably reflected the growth of local slavery, with the decline of the slave trade and its replacement by 'legitimate' trade in palm produce, from the 1840s.

This nineteenth-century expansion also changed the demographic balance of the community by proportionately increasing the European element in it. The term 'European' or 'white man [*yovo*]' in local usage included descendants of Europeans by African women such as Madiki Lemon, hereditary 'governor' of the English fort in 1850, who was biologically only one-quarter 'white'.[186] Indeed, the term *yovo* was constructed in cultural rather than racial terms, returned ex-slaves from Brazil or Sierra Leone, although of purely African descent, being also counted as 'white men', who thus enjoyed the privileges of Europeans; for example, when attending the king at the capital, they were excused from the Dahomian practice of prostration and were permitted merely to bow. In effect, as the French Catholic mission in the 1860s noted, the term 'white man' was used to mean 'Christian'.[187] The 'European' community in Ouidah in this period also became, predominantly, specifically 'Brazilian'. In purely commercial terms, in the period of the illegal trade, Brazilian influence became overwhelmingly decisive, as the slave trade to Brazil continued while that of France and Britain was eliminated;

---

[182] Ridgway, 'Journal', 196; Forbes, *Dahomey*, i, 117.
[183] Burton, *Mission*, i, 60.
[184] Ibid., i, 49, 107.
[185] PRO, ADM55/11, Clapperton, Journal, 26 Nov. 1825.
[186] Forbes, *Dahomey*, i, 129.
[187] Ibid., i, 21; Borghero, 'Relation', in *Journal*, 251.

although from the 1820s Spanish Cuba rivalled Brazil as a destination for slaves exported, this trade was largely handled on the West African coast by established Brazilian merchants, including de Souza himself. The relative prosperity of the Brazilian section of the town was noted by Duncan in 1845: 'the Portuguese [*sic*] part of Whydah excels, in every sense of the word, both the English and French ... [they] live in comfort and plenty, and occupy good and well-furnished houses'.[188] The pre-eminence of the Brazilian commercial presence also resulted in the attraction of persons from the existing 'European' quarters into the service of de Souza and other Brazilian traders. The case of Antonio Dossou-Yovo, originally from the 'English' quarter of Sogbadji but recruited as an interpreter to de Souza, was noted above. Likewise Duncan observed that, despite the reoccupation of the French fort by the firm of Régis since 1842, only 'some few' of the inhabitants of Ahouandjigo had attached themselves to it, the people having 'chiefly turned over to the Portuguese'; and Forbes in 1850 found that Gnahoui, the king's official interpreter for the English language, actually spoke Portuguese better than English.[189]

In fact, the term 'Brazilians', although readily acknowledged retrospectively by the present-day descendants of immigrants from Brazil, is highly problematic, and the term 'Afro-Brazilians' favoured by historians even more so. Objectively, the 'Brazilian' community in Ouidah was not exclusively derived from Brazil, but included persons from Portuguese territories all around the Atlantic, including Madeira, São Tomé and Angola;[190] and in the long run it also absorbed elements of non-Lusophone origin, such as the Spanish-Cuban Zangronis and the Afro-French d'Oliveira families. Others who came to be considered as Brazilians were in fact Africans who had never been to Brazil but had assimilated Brazilian culture in Africa, for example, Pedro Felix d'Almeida, founder of a family in Ganvè quarter, who was originally from Little Popo but brought up in de Souza's household in Ouidah, where he learned to read and write Portuguese.[191] Subjectively, these people did not, in the nineteenth century, necessarily or even generally identify themselves as 'Brazilian'; even some of those whose origins were geographically from Brazil continued after Brazilian independence in 1822 to regard themselves as Portuguese nationals, including de Souza himself, as noted earlier. Contemporary sources more often refer to the community as 'Portuguese' than as 'Brazilian', and this usage probably reflects the self-identification of those concerned. Likewise, the indigenous Dahomian term 'Aguda' in the nineteenth century meant 'Portuguese' (including Brazilians), rather than 'Brazilians' (as distinct from Portuguese), and nobody in the nineteenth century, of course, would have called themselves 'Afro-Brazilians'.

The Portuguese–Brazilian community in the nineteenth century saw itself as belonging to a trans-Atlantic community, maintaining social as well as purely

---

[188] Duncan, *Travels*, i, 139,

[189] Ibid., i, 140; Forbes, *Dahomey*, ii, 175.

[190] The Aguidissou (originally da Silva) family in Docomè quarter traces its origins to São Tomé, and the Joaquim family of Boyasaramè to Angola: Reynier, 'Ouidah', 40, 58.

[191] Turner, 'Les Brésiliens', 108; de Souza, *La Famille de Souza*, 72.

business links with Brazil. Some members of it travelled backwards and forwards between Africa and America on trading voyages, or returned to Brazil after periods of residence in Africa, and even when such persons settled definitively in Africa, they commonly maintained family and other social ties with Brazil, and sometimes maintained households on both sides of the Atlantic.[192] De Souza sent his sons Isidoro and Antonio Kokou overseas for education, the former to Brazil and the latter to Portugal, and Antonio in turn had two of his sons educated in Brazil, from where they returned to Ouidah in 1851.[193] The leading Brazilian merchant of the following generation, Domingos José Martins, when he embarked from Brazil to settle definitively in Africa in 1845 (initially at Porto-Novo, rather than Ouidah), left a number of his children there in the care of friends, though his eldest son Rafael Domingos Martins later joined his father at Ouidah; and he continued to own property in Bahia, about whose maintenance and renting he corresponded with his business partner there, the leading banker Joaquim Pereira Marinho, although by the time of his death in Africa in 1864 it had fallen into neglect.[194] Another Brazilian merchant resident in Ouidah, José Francisco dos Santos, also maintained family links with the homeland, as documented in his surviving correspondence: in the 1840s both his mother and his young son, Jacinto da Costa Santos, were still in Bahia, and the correspondence refers to arrangements for their maintenance and for the son's baptism, while by the 1860s the son Jacinto was living with his father in Ouidah, but the mother was still in Bahia, and Jacinto travelled to Brazil to visit her in 1863. The dos Santos correspondence also documents the supply of everyday goods and services across the Atlantic: in 1862, for example, he sent his watch to Bahia for repair and his spectacles to be set in gold frames. He followed events in Brazil, expressing properly patriotic sentiments concerning the war against Paraguay in 1865.[195] Likewise Francisco Rodrigues da Silva, born into a Brazilian family in Ouidah in 1844, was sent to Bahia for education in 1856, and later spent periods in Portugal and after 1865 in Lagos, where he learnt English.[196]

The identity of the 'Brazilian' community was defined above all by its use of the Portuguese language, although this spread even beyond those of Portuguese-Brazilian origin, being now widely spoken by indigenous Dahomians. The French Roman Catholic mission, which arrived in the 1860s found itself obliged to preach and teach in Portuguese, in order to communicate with its congregation; when this practice was queried by its parent body in France, it pointed out that there were only six persons in Ouidah who spoke French, as against 3,000 who spoke Portuguese.[197] In addition to language, the Portuguese-Brazilian community was defined by religion, by its allegiance to the Roman Catholic church. The French missionaries in the 1860s regarded them, the descendants of 'whites' such as the de Souzas as well as the African-born returned ex-slaves, as no more than nominal

---

[192] Law & Mann, 'West Africa in the Atlantic community', 329–32; Law, 'Port of Ouidah', 359–61.

[193] De Souza, 'Contribution', 18; de Souza, *La Famille de Souza*, 42, 59; PRO, FO84/886, Fraser, Journal, 30 July 1851.

[194] Verger, *Flux et reflux*, 471–3, with text of will, 483–5; for the son Rafael, see Burton, *Mission*, i, 73–4.

[195] Dos Santos correspondence, *passim*.

[196] Rodrigues da Silva & Christophe da Silva, *Histoire de la famille Rodrigues da Silva* (Cotonou, 1992), 13.

[197] Turner, 'Les Brésiliens', 203.

Christians, who 'live exactly like pagans for the most part', practising polygamy and a syncretistic religion, 'a monstrous amalgam of paganism, Christian practices, and fetishist superstitions'. But this in no way compromised the central importance of Roman Catholic baptism as a marker of communal identity; as the French missionaries noted, also with disapproval, even Brazilian repatriates who were Muslim participated in rites of baptism.[198] Along with Catholic Christianity, the Portuguese–Brazilian community also retained associated ceremonies that continue to be practised in Ouidah today, notably the masquerade called *burian*, at which songs in Portuguese are still sung,[199] and they maintained distinctive food habits derived from Brazil, which likewise survive to the present.[200] They were also distinguished by their European-style dress: in Dahomian tradition, the 'mulattoes' and returned former slaves are distinguished as 'the men in jackets'; the Portuguese equivalent, *vestidos*, was also used of them.[201]

The Portuguese–Brazilian community was associated with a range of craft skills that made a significant contribution to the life and fabric of Ouidah. There was an influx of craftsmen from Brazil into West Africa, not only with skills of direct relevance to trade (such as coopers), but to serve the tastes of the Portuguese–Brazilian community more generally. José Francisco dos Santos, for example, prior to becoming a merchant, is said to have worked as a tailor, in the service of the de Souza family; and he kept the surname Alfaiate, 'The Tailor', in later life.[202] In the long run, Brazilian influence was especially significant in the sphere of architecture. In recent times, Ouidah, in common with other coastal towns in the region, has been marked by Brazilian influence on the architectural style of its wealthiest houses, this 'Afro–Brazilian' style being distinguished by shuttered windows, ornate mouldings, colonnades and verandahs.[203] Most of the 'Afro–Brazilian' houses visible in Ouidah today appear to have been built in the twentieth century, what is commonly considered the finest example of this style in the town, although now sadly dilapidated, the Villa Adjavon, for example, bearing the date 1922.[204] The origins of this style, however, certainly date back into the nineteenth century. It is not clear whether de Souza's 'Singbome' was built in Brazilian style, and Forbes's description of it in 1850 as 'a large ill-built erection of no particular form' suggests not; but Burton in 1863 noted that some of the associated tenements, perhaps added later, were built 'in the south of Europe style'.[205] Although the de Souza house was initially unique, in time others also built European-style houses. Forbes noted that de Souza's son Antonio Kokou had a 'Chinese-built house', in which he received visitors, while Madiki Lemon of Sogbadji had recently built a

---

[198] Borghero, *Journal*, 46 [21 April 1861]; 'Documents et considérations génerales' (1863), ibid., 285.

[199] Rachida Ayari de Souza, 'La danse de la mémoire: le *buriyan*', in Adandé, *Ouidah à travers ses fêtes*, 43–63.

[200] De Souza, *La Famille de Souza*, 105–6.

[201] Hazoumé, *Le Pacte de sang*, 33; for the term *vestidos*, see Emmanuel Karl-August, 'Pour une politique de recherche historique sur Ouidah et sa région', in [UGDO], *Les Voies de la renaissance de Ouidah*, 20–2.

[202] De Souza, *La Famille de Souza*, 51–3.

[203] M. da Cunha & M.C. da Cunha, *From Slave Quarters to Town Houses: Brazilian architecture in Nigeria and the People's Republic of Benin* (São Paulo, 1985).

[204] Described and illustrated in Sinou & Agbo, *Ouidah*, 347–51.

[205] Forbes, *Dahomey*, i, 105–6; Burton, *Mission*, i, 103.

'white man's house', with two verandahs, which Forbes rented from him. Domingos Martins also had a house in Ouidah by 1850, which Forbes considered 'the best building in the town'; as described by Burton later, this had a tiled roof and was built in part in two storeys.[206] In 1871 another prominent Brazilian trader, Francisco José de Medeiros, was building 'an extensive country-house' on the outskirts of Ouidah, to the north-west, which was expected, if completed, to be 'the finest building between Sierra Leone and Lagos'.[207] Antonio de Souza's 'Chinese' house was evidently imported prefabricated, but other buildings were constructed locally. In 1841, Luís Xavier de Jesus sent three slaves to Bahia to be trained as masons, and in 1864 a returned freedman from Brazil, Damião d'Oliveira (unrelated to the Afro-French d'Oliveira family) had the reputation of being 'the best mason at Whydah'.[208]

De Souza's Ouidah was also marked by the strength of Yoruba cultural influence. The Catholic mission in the 1860s listed 'Nago' (i.e. Yoruba), along with Fon ('Dahomian') and Portuguese, as the languages usually spoken in Ouidah. The prominence of Yoruba was in part due to the number of returned slaves from Brazil, who were mainly Yoruba in origin and who continued to speak their ancestral African language, as well as Portuguese.[209] But it also reflected an influx of Yoruba slaves directly from the interior, deriving from the successful expansionist wars of Gezo and his successor Glele (1858–89). The build-up of the population of enslaved Yoruba, and consequent Yoruba cultural influence, has been noted as an important development in this period in Dahomey generally.[210] It certainly applied to Ouidah, where many families of Yoruba origin descend from slaves introduced in the nineteenth century. One prominent example is the Alapini family of Zomaï quarter, whose founding ancestor was a slave sold to the first Chacha; the prominent local historian (and former curator of the Historical Museum) Justin Fakambi is likewise descended from a Yoruba slave purchased by the first Chacha's son Lino Felix de Souza and employed by him as a tailor.[211]

---

[206] Forbes, *Dahomey*, i, 108, 129, Burton, *Mission*, i, 72.

[207] Skertchly, *Dahomey As It Is*, 67.

[208] Letter of António Xavier de Jesus, Bahia, to Luís Xavier de Jesus, 30 Aug. 1841, in Verger, *Os libertos*, 132; Burton, *Mission*, i, 75, n.

[209] Borghero, *Journal*, 48 [10 May 1861]; 'Relation', ibid., 251.

[210] Bay, *Wives of the Leopard*, 187–92.

[211] Reynier, 'Ouidah', 56; fieldwork, Justin Fakambi, 3 Dec. 2001.

6

The Era of Transition

From Slaves to Palm Oil

1840–57

In contrast to the obscurity of the history of Ouidah during the first four decades of the nineteenth century, a relative abundance of documentation becomes available from the 1840s onwards. Principally, this comes from a series of foreign, mainly British, visitors, who left extended accounts, beginning with the missionary Thomas Birch Freeman in 1843 and including the explorer John Duncan in 1845. In addition, by the 1840s British and French merchants were engaged in trade in palm oil at Ouidah, some records of whose activities are preserved. This was followed by the involvement in Dahomian affairs of European governments, beginning with Portugal, which reoccupied its fort in Ouidah in 1844. British negotiations with the Dahomian authorities for the ending of the slave trade from 1847 involved a series of missions that passed through Ouidah and the mainte-nance of a vice-consulate in the town in 1849 and 1851–2; besides the official records of these contacts, one of those involved, the naval officer Frederick Forbes, published a lengthy account of his experiences in three visits to Ouidah in 1849–50. The French government, responding to the perceived threat of pre-emption by the British, also negotiated with Dahomey for commercial privileges, beginning with a treaty in 1851 and continuing in further diplomatic missions in 1856 and 1858. In addition, a British Methodist mission operated in Ouidah from 1854, which, although a failure in terms of its own agenda of evangelization, nevertheless provides useful documentation of its interactions with the local community. There is also an unprecedentedly detailed local source for this period, in the correspondence of the Brazilian trader José Francisco dos Santos, which survives for the years 1844–7. The papers of the Lawson family of Little Popo to the west likewise include correspondence from the period 1843–53, which makes frequent reference to links to Ouidah.[1]

Besides being relatively well documented, the 1840s and 1850s also comprise a critical period of transition in the history of Ouidah, with the decline of the

---

[1] Adam Jones, 'Little Popo and Agoué at the end of the Atlantic Slave Trade: glimpses from the Lawson correspondence and other sources', in Law and Strickrodt, *Ports of the Slave Trade*, 122–34.

Atlantic slave trade and the rise of an alternative export trade in palm oil.[2] This transition posed both difficulties and opportunities for the Ouidah merchant community, and was linked both to increasing tensions in its relationship with the Dahomian monarchy and to the beginnings of the decline of Ouidah from its status as the leading 'port' in the region.

The slave trade in difficulty: consequences of the Equipment Act of 1839

After flourishing through the 1820s and 1830s, the slave trade at Ouidah began to run into difficulties in the 1840s. A principal factor in this was a technical legal change: Lord Palmerston's Equipment Act of 1839, by which Britain assumed a right to arrest Portuguese slave ships, even if they had no slaves on board, and under pressure of which Portugal finally accepted a treaty conceding the right to arrest ships equipped for the slave trade in 1842. This not only curbed illegal slaving by Portuguese ships, but also ended the abuse of the Portuguese flag by ships of other nationalities. Merchants involved in the slave trade, both in Brazil and on the African coast, quickly recognized the threat this represented to their operations. In October 1839, a trader in Bahia wrote to a colleague at Ouidah to warn him that Portugal had concluded a treaty with Britain under which 'all vessels that shall hereafter be found on the coast of Africa under the Portuguese flag will be taken as pirates'. At Ouidah itself, someone on shore wrote to the captain of a Portuguese ship there to convey the news that 'to windward [west] they are taking all vessels with Portuguese colours, under a new Treaty which has recently come out from London'.[3] Although the references to a treaty were inaccurate (since the change was initially imposed by unilateral British action), the assessment of the difficulties that were posed was sound. A few years later, Britain also responded to the reluctance of Brazil to extend its concession of the right of search (which was now due to expire) by a second unilateral initiative, Lord Aberdeen's Act of 1845, which assumed the right to arrest Brazilian ships also.

The enhanced powers the British navy thus acquired to deal with illegal slave ships were combined with a more aggressive policy towards the bases of the trade on the African coast, beginning with the destruction of 'barracoons' at the River Gallinas, in Sierra Leone, in 1840. There was some reflection of this in the case of Ouidah also. In October 1841 a British warship at Ouidah, finding that warning of its presence had been communicated to an approaching slaver by signals from a flagstaff at the beach belonging to de Souza, fired on the flagstaff to force the lowering of the signal, the first of a number of naval bombardments of the town

---

[2] For this transition as it affected the Dahomian monarchy, see esp. Reid, 'Warrior aristocrats in crisis'; and more generally, Robin Law (ed.), *From Slave Trade to 'Legitimate' Commerce: The Commercial Transition in Nineteenth-century West Africa* (Cambridge, 1995).

[3] PP, Slave Trade 1840, Class A, no. 117, case of the *Sociedade Felix*, letter of Carlos de Souza Lopez, Bahia, to Manoel Jozé Teixeira, Ajuda [Ouidah], 20 Oct. 1839; no. 47, case of the *Jack Wilding*, letter of an unidentified person at Ouidah, to Antonio Capo, n.d.

that were to occur during the course of the nineteenth century.[4] The incident made a deep impression in Ouidah, where it was long remembered: thirteen years later Gezo cited the bombardment in his negotiations with the British, claiming that it had killed eight people and demanding an inquiry into the case; and in the 1860s it was reported that a cannon-ball from it was preserved and venerated as a 'fetish' in Ouidah.[5]

Although the effectiveness of naval action against the illegal slave trade in the long term is questionable, in the short term at least the new policy had a significant impact on trade at Ouidah. When the British Parliamentary Select Committee on the West Coast of Africa reviewed the state of the slave trade in 1842, several of the witnesses suggested that the trade at Ouidah had been significantly reduced. Of two British naval officers of the anti-slave trade squadron, one opined that the slave trade at Ouidah and other ports of the Bight of Benin was 'comparatively at an end', the Equipment Act having 'knocked the thing up completely'; and the other that the trade at Ouidah had within the last two years been 'much reduced' and 'very much broken up', mainly in consequence of the Act.[6] In further corroboration, one witness reported that in consequence of this disruption of trade slaves had become 'very cheap'; discrepant testimony was given on current prices at Ouidah, either around £6–10 ($28–46) or 3–4 doubloons ($48–64), but both were well below the levels of the 1830s.[7]

The evidence given to the Committee, however, also detailed the strategies slave-traders were adopting in response to the Equipment Act. The basic practical difference which the Act made was that slavers could no longer safely trade along the coast prior to taking on slaves, for example to purchase goods and provisions and to hire canoes on the Gold Coast, but now had to proceed direct to Ouidah, and, at Ouidah itself, they could no longer stand off shore while slave cargoes were assembled, but had to minimize their length of stay there. One new tactic reported in evidence to the Committee was to separate the outward and inward voyages; one ship would deliver the outward cargo and would not be identifiable as a slaver, while a second would come later to collect the slaves that had already been paid for.[8] A subsequent refinement was for the ship employed for the return voyage to be purchased locally in West Africa. Duncan refers to a shipment of slaves from Ouidah in 1845 in a US ship that had been bought by local slave-traders and manned from the crews of slavers who had been put on shore after the interception of their ships by the British navy, and observed that such selling of ships in Africa for use in the slave trade had lately become 'a favourite plan with the Yankees'.[9]

Alternatively, as the 1842 Committee was also informed, the slave ship might carry specie, in the form of silver dollars and gold doubloons, rather than goods;

---

[4] PP, 1842 Select Committee, Minutes of Evidence, § 2459–61, Henry Broadhead; § 3976, Reginald Levinge; Appendix No.3, Report of Her Majesty's Commissioner of Inquiry, 31 July 1841, pp. 25–7.

[5] PP, Slave Trade 1854–5, Class B, enc. 2 in no. 23, King of Dahomey, 18 Nov. 1854; Burton, *Mission*, i, 103.

[6] PP, 1842 Select Committee, § 2545, 2488, Henry Broadhead; 3964–5, Reginald Levinge.

[7] Ibid., § 769–76, Francis Swanzy; see Table 5.1.

[8] PP, 1842 Select Committee, § 2480–6, Henry Broadhead.

[9] Duncan, *Travels*, i, 200.

the ship would purchase its slaves with cash from a factor based on shore, the latter using the money to purchase goods from other shipping, which were then used to buy further slaves from the interior.[10] The importance of cash in the illegal trade in this period is illustrated in the dos Santos correspondence: in May 1845, for example, when Brazilian tobacco was out of demand, he asked for payment from Bahia to be made instead 'in coin, patacons [Brazilian silver coins], Mexican ounces [i.e. doubloons] or pesos [dollars], I don't care which'; in December 1845, he asked for the proceeds of slaves sold in Bahia on his account to be remitted in 'money of whatever sort except Spanish ounces'; in December 1846 he requested payment in 'Mexican ounces', in February 1847, 'in any sort of coin (gold or silver)', and in September 1847 in 'silver pesos'.[11] Considerable use was also made of letters of credit. Dos Santos during 1846–7 recorded drawing several bills against merchants of Bahia, in payment both for slaves and for goods which he purchased locally.[12] The advantage both of separating the delivery of goods from the collection of slaves and of paying in specie rather than goods was to accelerate the turn-round of the ship and thus minimize the danger of interception by the British navy. It may be, indeed, that the decline of the slave trade at Ouidah that witnesses reported to the Committee was to some degree illusory; although fewer slave vessels were visible, this was partly because they now spent only a very little time in port.

A further innovation of this period probably connected with the Equipment Act was the extension of cultivation around Ouidah. Whereas earlier visitors had emphasized the limited extent of farming in its immediate hinterland, Duncan in 1845 found that the country around the town was 'in many cases well cultivated' to a distance of 10–12 miles, much of this cultivation being undertaken by ex-slaves returned from Brazil. He also heard that the Yovogan had recently issued orders that 'all the spare land in and around the town Griwhee [Glehue] ... should be cultivated and planted with corn, or some other useful vegetables'. The chief crops raised on these farms were maize and cassava, of which the latter at least was used mainly to subsist slaves awaiting shipment and to provision slave ships.[13] The stimulus for this development was probably that 'equipment' for the slave trade as defined in the 1839 Act included the holding on board of food in excess of the needs of the crew, so that it now became dangerous for ships to take on provisions in advance of embarking the slaves; whereas earlier, therefore, provisions had often been purchased elsewhere on the coast, where they were generally cheaper than at Ouidah, now it made sense to take them in together with the slaves at Ouidah itself.

In addition to expediting the turn-round of ships, a further means of evading the attention of the British squadron was to send slaves from Ouidah along the lagoon for embarkation from lesser ports to the west and east. Although this tactic had been practised already in the 1820s and 1830s, it became more regular in

---

[10] PP, 1842 Select Committee, § 602–3, 735–45, Francis Swanzy.

[11] Dos Santos correspondence, nos 9, 25, 41, 54, 73 [25 May and 30 Dec. 1845, 28 Dec. 1846, 19 Feb. and 16 Sept. 1847].

[12] Ibid., nos 44 [28 Dec.1846], referring to 3 letters for $716, $1,192 and $2,000; 52–3 [19 Feb. 1847], 2 for $3,000 and $4,600, the former for slaves but the latter apparently for goods; 80 and 84 [1 and 22 Dec. 1847], 2 for $2,000 each.

[13] Duncan, *Travels*, i, 185, 192; ii, 268–9.

response to the new conditions following the 1839 Act. A naval officer told the 1842 Committee that, given the facility of communication along the lagoon, it was useless to blockade Ouidah without also blockading the coast for 20 miles either side of it, which was practically impossible.[14] The practice remained standard later: in 1848, for example, it was observed that it was 'frequent practice to convey [slaves] by the lagoon, either to the eastward [*sic*: = westward], as Little Popo, or the westward [= eastward], as Porto Nuovo'; likewise, Forbes explained in 1849 that 'from the numbers of slave-merchants residing at Whydah, that port is strictly watched by the cruizers … [but] by means of the lagoon the slaves can be shipped at either Porto Novo &c., to the eastward, or Popoe, &c. to the westward, with much greater safety'.[15]

In this dispersal of slave shipments from Ouidah, a leading role was taken by Francisco Felix de Souza. The first major instance of the policy was his re-establishment of links with Little Popo, to the west. After several years' neglect of this connection, he sent his eldest son Isidoro to reoccupy his former factory at Adjido, Little Popo; according to family tradition, this was in 1840,[16] and this is consistent with the contemporary record, in which Isidoro's presence at Popo is likewise first attested in that year.[17] The opening of the new port of Cotonou, on the southern shore of Lake Nokoué to the east, also belongs to this period. There was already a settlement at Cotonou in the eighteenth century, which is mentioned incidentally in 1787, but it was not then a centre for European trade.[18] Tradition generally credits the foundation of Cotonou to de Souza, whose association with the new port is confirmed by a phrase in his praise-name, which describes him as embarking slaves 'quickly, in a single day, at Cotonou'.[19] Gezo is said to have opened the new port on the advice of de Souza, who was seeking an alternative point of embarkation for slaves, less familiar to and therefore less subject to harassment by the British navy than Ouidah; this account also links his associate 'Sangronio', i.e. the Cuban Juan Zangronis (d. 1843), with the venture.[20] The implied date seems to be, here again, in the period following the Equipment Act of 1839, and this is supported by the fact that in contemporary sources the earliest allusion to trade at Cotonou seems to be in the evidence of a British naval officer to the 1842 Committee, who observed that slaves were sent from Ouidah for shipment instead at Ekpè ('Apee');[21] this probably alludes not to the Ekpè that had served as a

14 PP, 1842 Select Committee, § 3996–7, Reginald Levinge.
15 PP: Missions to Ashantee and Dahomey, Cruickshank Report, 16; Slave Trade 1849–50, enc. 10 in no. 9: Forbes, 5 Nov. 1849.
16 GLL, Memorandum of Judgement in the case of Kein versus Chico d'Almeida, Little Popo, 2 March 1893; de Souza, *La Famille de Souza*, 42.
17 PP, Slave Trade 1840, Class A, no. 85, case of the *Plant*. This ship, dispatched from Cuba in May 1840, was instructed to deliver its cargo at Popo to two other merchants or in their absence to 'Mr Yzidor Feliz Souza'.
18 Akinjogbin, *Dahomey*, 168, n. 5: the 'village of Cotony' was mentioned as a possible site for the establishment of a European fort, to defend Porto-Novo against attack from Dahomey.
19 Agbo, *Histoire*, 225–6.
20 Jacques Lombard, 'Cotonou, ville africaine', *ED*, 10 (1953), 30. For the role of Zangronis, cf. de Souza, *La Famille de Souza*, 71.
21 PP, 1842 Select Committee, § 3997, Reginald Levinge.

port of embarkation for slaves in the eighteenth century (until it was destroyed by the Dahomians in 1782), but to a place further west called in later sources 'Appi Vista', which was an alternative name for Cotonou.[22] The name 'Cotonou' first reappears in the contemporary record in 1852, three years after de Souza's death.[23] Like Godomey, Cotonou was an integral part of the Dahomian state, subject to the authority of the Yovogan of Ouidah. Local tradition records that de Souza 'had the lagoon and the Toho dredged, in order to allow canoes to go as far as Cotonou', referring to the northern branch of the coastal lagoon, which runs east of Ouidah; the opening of the passage in this period is confirmed by testimony recorded later in the nineteenth century, when Europeans recalled that in the past they had travelled by canoe non-stop from Ouidah to Porto-Novo.[24] However, the opening was evidently only temporary; by 1850, the Dahomians had reportedly built a barrier across the lagoon at Godomey, in order to prevent access by war canoes from Badagry.[25]

How this dispersal affected the profits of Ouidah-based merchants is unclear. Presumably, to the extent that it involved increased transport costs it reduced merchants' profit margins, and canoes passing along the lagoon to the west had also to pay a toll to the king of Grand-Popo.[26] This may have been offset by avoidance of the export duties paid on embarkations from Ouidah, but on this the evidence is contradictory. A report of 1848 maintained that the export duty on slaves (of $5 per head) had to be paid prior to their embarkation on the lagoon, so that the king's revenues were not affected.[27] This, however, may involve confusion between the export duty, properly speaking, and the transit duty levied on all goods leaving or entering Ouidah, whether by the lagoon or overland. In contrast, Forbes in 1849 reported that the king was 'jealous of his slaves being shipped without his kingdom', because he thereby lost the 'head-tax' due upon them (put by Forbes, anomalously, at $20 per slave).[28] The monarchy's loss, however, was presumably the merchants' gain, unless the latter had to pay equivalent duties to local authorities at the actual point of embarkation.

The reorganization of the slave trade

The 1840s also saw the entry of new merchants into the slave trade at Ouidah. In part, this was due to natural wastage, as the older generation of traders died off or retired. Of the two dominant figures in the 1830s, Zangronis died in 1843. Francisco Felix de Souza, although he lived on until 1849, had lost his dominant

[22] See, for example, PP, Slave Trade 1855–6, Class B, no. 28, Campbell, Lagos, 6 Jan. 1856 ('called in the Admiralty charts, Appi Vista, but … known on shore by its native name, Kootenoo').

[23] PRO, FO84/886, Fraser, 'Occurrences', 13 Feb. 1852, etc.

[24] Gavoy, 'Note historique', 61; Bouche, Sept ans, 8.

[25] PP, Slave Trade 1850–1, enc.1 in no. 198, Forbes, Journal, 29 March 1850. But in the published version of his journal, Forbes stated that the lagoon was interrupted at Godomey only 'in the dry season': Dahomey, i, 9.

[26] See, for example, Duncan, Travels, i, 109–11, 181–3.

[27] PP, Missions to Ashantee and Dahomey, Cruickshank Report, 16.

[28] PP, Slave Trade 1849–50, Class B, enc. 10 in no. 9, Forbes, 5 Nov. 1849.

position in the Ouidah trade before then. By 1845, as he told Duncan, he was doing 'very little [slave-trading] compared with what he formerly did'.[29] De Souza's declining importance was partly simply a consequence of his increasing age. As late as 1843, he was still travelling to Abomey to attend the Annual Customs, accompanying a French merchant in that year; but in 1845 Duncan found him bedridden with rheumatism and so unable to escort him to the capital.[30] The advancing age and ill-health of the head led to the passing of leadership in the de Souza family to the younger generation. His eldest son Isidoro (born in 1802), according to family tradition, had returned to Africa from education in Bahia in 1822. As seen earlier, he was employed initially in an out-factory at Badagry to the east, but was recalled to Ouidah after incurring heavy losses there; and in 1840 he was sent to re-establish the de Souza factory at Little Popo to the west. Isidoro's prominence at Popo is attested by several allusions to him in the correspondence of the Lawson family, from 1843 onwards;[31] he is also referred to in that of José dos Santos, resident at Ouidah but doing business also at Agoué and Popo, during 1844–7. In his new situation, Isidoro's commercial fortunes initially flourished; but in May 1849 his establishment at Little Popo was destroyed by fire, caused by gunfire during the ceremonies for his father's death; George Lawson (Jr) reported that 'the young man has lost a great deal and that will take him some few years more, before he can make it up again'.[32]

De Souza family tradition names several other sons whom the first Chacha authorized to establish themselves alongside Isidoro at Little Popo and to 'trade each on their own account': two Antonios (presumably those surnamed 'Kokou' and 'Agbakoun', who were the most prominent of four de Souza sons called Antonio), João, Manuel, Ignacio, Joseph and Francisco (called 'Chico', in distinction from his father).[33] Forbes in 1849, a few months after the founder's death, named three of his sons who were 'wealthy and slave-merchants': in addition to Isidoro at Little Popo, these were Antonio Kokou and Ignacio,[34] and the preeminence of these three is confirmed by the fact that it was they who competed for the succession to the father's title of Chacha in 1849–50 (and, indeed, held it successively after him). Antonio Kokou, although younger than Ignacio,[35] is the more prominent in contemporary records of the 1840s. His involvement in trade along the lagoon to the west is confirmed by the Lawson correspondence, which shows him supplying rum to Lawson at Little Popo in 1843 and buying cloth from a British trader at Agoué in 1848;[36] he was also active in trading at Ouidah by

[29] PP, 1848 Select Committee, § 3055.
[30] Brue, 'Voyage', 56; Duncan, *Travels*, i, 203.
[31] Jones, 'Little Popo and Agoué', 130.
[32] GLL, Lawson to Marmon, 10 May 1849. This fire is also recalled in de Souza family tradition: Foà, *Le Dahomey*, 27; de Souza, *La Famille de Souza*, 43.
[33] De Souza, 'Contribution', 20.
[34] PP, Slave Trade 1849–50, Class B, enc. 10 in no. 9, Forbes, 5 Nov. 1849.
[35] Ignacio was born in 1812, Antonio in 1814: de Souza, *La Famille de Souza*, 302–3; de Souza, 'Contribution', 18.
[36] Jones, 'Little Popo and Agoué', 131.

1846–7, supplying slaves to dos Santos.[37] He is also recorded as the owner of a suspected slave ship, the *Galliana*, arrested by the British off the African coast in early 1849 (but eventually released, for lack of conclusive evidence). The *Galliana* had been built to Antonio's order, at Oporto in Portugal, and sailed from there first to Bahia, where it was met by another of the de Souza brothers, Francisco Felix de Souza (i.e. 'Chico'), who served as supercargo on its journey to Africa.[38] Ignacio is not explicitly documented trading before his father's death, but is mentioned in 1848, attending the royal court at Abomey.[39]

More was involved in de Souza's decline, however, than his retirement through old age. By the 1840s his commercial operations had run into difficulties, and he was heavily in debt. At the time of his death in 1849, he was described as 'almost a pauper'; when the king sent his agents to take over his property they found 'neither money, nor goods, nor anything of value', only 'a little furniture and some plate' – though, very probably, his family would have removed or concealed any movable items, to avoid the royal inheritance tax. His son Ignacio was obliged to borrow money to pay for his father's funeral ceremonies. De Souza's debts were mainly to merchants in Brazil and Cuba; but he also owed $80,000 to Gezo, and a few days before his death had been obliged to send his silver coffin as a pawn for his debts to the king.[40] His financial difficulties were clearly due in large part to the losses which he incurred through the activities of the British anti-slaving squadron; he told a visiting British official in 1844 that the British had captured 36 of his ships and that the slave trade was 'now unprofitable'.[41] He also lost property to the value of 'some hundred thousand dollars' in a fire in Ouidah in *c*. 1838.[42] Some contemporary comment suggests, however, that his difficulties were compounded by his own extravagance and mismanagement, especially his reckless acceptance of goods on credit.[43] One account also refers to his 'having been over liberal in his presents' to the king.[44] Some versions of local tradition in Ouidah, in fact, place the principal blame for de Souza's ruin on Gezo, who is alleged to have become jealous of his great wealth and to have sought deliberately to ruin him by making excessive demands on his resources, including failing to pay for goods delivered on credit.[45] The contemporary evidence, however, lends no support to this allegation; indeed, as noted above, it shows that at his death de Souza owed money to Gezo, rather than vice versa.

Whatever the cause, de Souza's commercial difficulties prompted Gezo to

---

[37] The dos Santos correspondence refers to transactions with Antonio, involving letters of credit in the latter's favour for $2,000 in 1846, and two for $3,000 (for 43 slaves purchased from him) and $2,000 in 1847: nos 44, 52, 80 [28 Dec. 1846, 19 Feb. and 1 Dec. 1847].

[38] PP, Slave Trade 1849–50, Class A, no. 98, case of the *Galliana*.

[39] Blancheley, 'Au Dahomey', 536.

[40] PP, Slave Trade 1849–50, Class B, no. 7, Duncan, 22 Sept.1849; enc.10 in no. 9, Forbes, 5 Nov. 1849; Papers relative to Lagos, enc. in no. 8, Hutton, Cape Coast, 7 Aug. 1850.

[41] PRO, CO96/4, Hill, Cape Coast, 18 May 1844.

[42] PRO, CO96/12, Hutton, Cape Coast, 17 March 1847.

[43] PP, Papers relative to Lagos, enc. in no. 8, Hutton, 7 Aug. 1850.

[44] PP, Slave Trade 1849–50, Class B, enc. 10 in no. 9, Forbes, 5 Nov. 1849.

[45] Foà, *Le Dahomey*, 23; Hazoumé, *Le Pacte de sang*, 109.

reorganize the trade, depriving him of his position as sole royal agent. According to the British merchant Hutton (writing shortly after de Souza's death), following complaints to the king from de Souza's creditors in Brazil and Cuba, 'it was arranged that agents from the Havana and Brazils might settle at Whydah, and Da Souza should give up shipping slaves, but to receive a commission of a doubloon [$16] for every slave that was shipped'.[46] This account presents a number of difficulties, most obviously that no precise date is indicated; although an allusion to 'a more rigid law ... respecting the capture of slave-trading vessels' seems to point to the period after the Equipment Act of 1839. It might be objected that some other agents for the slave trade had been able to settle in Ouidah earlier than this, notably the Cuban Zangronis in the early 1830s; but he, as seen earlier, traded in association rather than in competition with de Souza. Conversely, de Souza was still shipping slaves as late as August 1839, when he is recorded as the owner of a slave ship taken by the British navy and owner and consignee of its cargo (although this ship did its trade at Lagos, rather than Ouidah).[47] More probably, therefore, the change occurred in the 1840s. The wording of Hutton's account of the new arrangements now introduced is also ambiguous, and open to different interpretations. David Ross read it to mean that de Souza ceased trading altogether, becoming instead 'a functionary levying a tax ... on every slave exported'.[48] But a more natural interpretation is that he would continue to supply slaves to other Brazilian and Cuban merchants in Ouidah, the payment of one doubloon per slave being his commission on such sales. A reference in the correspondence of dos Santos in 1847 to 'Don Francisco's embarkation duty' does not make its nature clear.[49] It is clear, however, that de Souza, as well as his sons, continued to sell slaves, at least occasionally. In 1844, for example, he was holding 800 slaves, recently captured by the Dahomian army, ready for shipping. As late as 1847 dos Santos complained of the high prices demanded for slaves bought from 'the old man', referring evidently to de Souza: 'he says he wants 80 pesos [dollars] apiece because the whites buy at 70 pesos outside and pay *caranquejo*', the meaning of this last word being obscure, but from the context perhaps referring to de Souza's 'commission' on slave sales.[50]

One of the new slave-traders who were able to set up in Ouidah under these new arrangements was dos Santos himself, who founded a family that still resides in Tové quarter.[51] According to tradition, dos Santos originally came to Ouidah in the service of the de Souza family, and indeed married Francisco Felix de Souza's eldest daughter.[52] This, however, was evidently at some period before 1844, when his surviving correspondence begins, since this contains no suggestion of any close relationship with the de Souza family; independence of the de Souzas is also suggested by his settlement in Tové, rather than in any of the de Souza quarters.

46 PP, Papers relative to Lagos, enc. in no. 8, Hutton, 7 Aug. 1850.
47 PP, Slave Trade 1840, Class A, no. 6, case of the *Fortuna*.
48 Ross, 'First Chacha', 25.
49 Dos Santos correspondence, no. 54 [19 Feb. 1847]. The sum paid, $10, was apparently for 2 slaves: see no. 45 [28 Dec. 1846].
50 PRO, CO96/2, Hill, 18 May 1844; Dos Santos correspondence, no. 52 [19 Feb. 1847].
51 Reynier, 'Ouidah', 48.
52 De Souza, *La Famille de Souza*, 51–3.

The first of his letters preserved, in August 1844, implies that he had only recently settled (or resettled) in Ouidah, after residing in or at least visiting Cuba, since he says that 'everything I possess is at Havana', and a later letter refers to the realization of his assets in Havana and remission of the proceeds via an associate in Bahia.[53] From 1844, however, he was operating as a merchant at Ouidah, supplying slaves to Brazil, mainly to Bahia but also to Rio de Janeiro (but not to Cuba), both on his account and as an agent for merchants in Brazil. He sometimes shipped slaves from Agoué and Little Popo to the west, as well as from Ouidah itself, and, in these operations along the lagoon to the west, he cooperated at least occasionally with Isidoro de Souza at Popo.[54] Within Ouidah, the correspondence is in general disappointingly reticent as regards from whom he purchased slaves, but occasional indications are given: in 1847, for example, he bought 43 slaves from Antonio de Souza, but in 1846 he bought 30 directly from the king, the latter being delivered locally by the Yovogan.[55] The correspondence shows that dos Santos shipped only part-cargoes of slaves, ranging from 5 to 95 on a single ship; he was also one of the local merchants who combined to purchase the American ship which Duncan reported as taking slaves from Ouidah in 1845.[56] Such pooling of resources was a common practice in the illegal trade as a means of spreading the risk. The volume of his trade grew over the period of the correspondence, from 20 slaves (in 3 separate shipments) in the last five months of 1844, to 79 (in 3 shipments) during 1845, 169 (5 shipments) in 1846, and 335 (7 shipments) in 1847, a total of 596 slaves, in 18 shipments.[57] Apparently only three of the ships in which he embarked slaves were intercepted by the British navy, one in 1844 and two in 1847, but the latter accounted for 140 of the slaves he shipped, nearly a quarter of the total (and 40 per cent of his shipments during 1847). The implication of lack of success in business is corroborated by Forbes, who met dos Santos in 1850 and observed that he 'is said to be in debt, owing to the uncertainty of his trade', commenting that 'having once embarked in the slave trade, he is still a gambler, and his speculations often bring him in a loser'.[58] He remained, however, a significant figure in the Ouidah merchant community. By 1855 had been appointed 'one of the Military Captains ... to command the forces that can be raised at Whydah and the neighbouring towns', i.e. to the official rank of 'caboceer', and in 1864 he received a wife from King Glele.[59]

[53] Dos Santos correspondence, nos 1 [20 Aug. 1844], and 8 [29 March 1845, addressed to João Antonio da Silva Chaves at Havana].

[54] Dos Santos is also mentioned in the correspondence of the Lawsons at Little Popo, though the two transactions with him recorded, both in 1848, do not relate to trade, but to gifts exchanged with him: Jones, 'Little Popo and Agoué', 130.

[55] Dos Santos correspondence, nos 43, 52, 59 [28 Dec. 1846, 19 Feb. and 13 April 1847].

[56] Ibid., no. 10 [25 May 1845], naming the ship as the *Americano*.

[57] These figures are offered tentatively, because references in the correspondence are difficult to interpret, with some figures apparently miscopied and some shipments mentioned on more than one occasion. Other scholars have computed differently: Newbury, *Western Slave Coast*, 40, n. 2, gives 27 slaves in 1844, 47 in 1845, 165 in 1846, 296 in 1847 (a total of 535); de Souza, *La Famille de Souza*, 53, gives a total of 609.

[58] Forbes, *Dahomey*, i, 114.

[59] PP, Slave Trade 1855–6, Class B, no. 11, Campbell, Lagos, 6 Sept. 1855; Burton, *Mission*, ii, 263.

Two others named by Forbes in 1849 among 'the number of Brazilian and Portuguese merchants' at Ouidah were 'Jacinta' and 'Jozé Joaquim', of whom the first was a native of Madeira and the latter a former soldier in Brazil.[60] The first is elsewhere given by Forbes the fuller name of 'Jacinta de Rodriguez', and is evidently to be identified with Jacinto Joaquim Rodrigues (d. 1882), who left a family in Maro quarter.[61] By his own later testimony, Rodrigues settled in Africa in 1844.[62] According to family tradition he originally settled in Ouidah 'with the support' of the Chacha de Souza, and this is consistent with the location of the family's household in Maro, within de Souza's section of the town. Duncan, who met Rodrigues in 1845, describes him as 'one of the most respectable slave-dealers in Whydah'.[63] Duncan then understood that Rodrigues had incurred considerable losses through British captures of slave ships and had in consequence given up slaving for the palm-oil trade. But he was certainly still (or again) involved in slaving in the following year, when he appears in the dos Santos correspondence in charge of the embarkation of a cargo of slaves: dos Santos blamed him for the loss of 3 slaves, as well as of letters, presumably through the overturning of a canoe.[64] Like dos Santos, Rodrigues had connections beyond Ouidah, along the lagoons, but in his case to the east rather than west of Ouidah: of his two sons, one was born in Lagos (Americo, 1847) and one in Porto-Novo (Candido, 1850).[65] The second person named by Forbes, 'Jozé Joaquim', is less easily identified, but a likely candidate is José Joaquim das Neves, a returned ex-slave from Brazil, founder of another family in Maro quarter.

More important than any of these, however, was Joaquim d'Almeida, who was in origin also a freed slave from Brazil, born in the Mahi country to the north of Dahomey, who had been owned in Brazil by the prominent slave-trader Manoel Joaquim d'Almeida, who was also the owner of Antonio d'Almeida.[66] One account links the breaking of de Souza's monopoly specifically with the entry into the trade of Joaquim d'Almeida, to whom Gezo granted 'the right to conduct wholesale trade at Whydah'.[67] D'Almeida's principal residence in later life was at Agoué to the west, rather than Ouidah. Local tradition in Agoué claims that he settled there in 1835,[68] and contemporary records show that he was trading at Agoué at least by 1840.[69] But he settled definitively in Africa, after returning to Brazil, only around

[60] PP, Slave Trade 1849–50, Class B, enc. 10 in no. 9, Forbes, 5 Nov. 1849.
[61] Forbes *Dahomey*, i, 92 ['Tacinta', clearly miscopied]; Reynier, 'Ouidah', 45; Turner, 'Les Brésiliens', 128–9.
[62] WMMS, William West, Cape Coast, 6 June 1859. Duncan in Feb. 1845 understood that Rodrigues had been at Ouidah for 2 years: *Travels*, i, 138.
[63] Duncan, ibid., referring to an unnamed merchant from Madeira; with the name 'Josinto' supplied in PP, 1848 Select Committee, § 3145.
[64] Dos Santos correspondence, no. 39 [28 Sept. 1846], referring to 'Jacinto José [= Joaquim] Rodrigues'.
[65] Turner, 'Les Brésiliens', 129.
[66] For whom, see esp. Verger, *Os libertos*, 43–8; also Turner, 'Les Brésiliens', 102–4.
[67] Foà, *Le Dahomey*, 23.
[68] This is the date given on his monument at Agoué: see photograph in Verger, *Flux et reflux*, plate 27.
[69] PP, Slave Trade 1841, Class A, no. 109, case of the *Gratidão* (taken by the British navy in Oct. 1840): papers found on this ship showed that a passenger on it, Tobiaz Barreto Brandão, had been involved in the slave trade over the previous 2 years and had traded at Agoué with d'Almeida among others.

the beginning of 1845.[70] It is possible that he settled in 1845 initially at Ouidah rather than Agoué; certainly, he established a business presence there. D'Almeida figures in the correspondence of dos Santos from 1845 onwards, but the earliest allusions do not make clear where he was based. However, by 1847, when he was involved together with dos Santos in a dispute with the Yovogan over payment of customs, he was clearly trading at Ouidah. Forbes in 1849 also described him as resident in Ouidah.[71] According to local tradition in Ouidah, d'Almeida's business associate there was Azanmado Houénou, formerly a client of de Souza but who now broke away to trade independently; by implication, he received slaves from Gezo through Houénou rather than the de Souzas. Indeed, in some accounts it is Houénou who is said to have persuaded Gezo to trade with d'Almeida, and to allow him to settle in Ouidah.[72] Consistently, d'Almeida's household in Ouidah was situated in Houénou's quarter of the town (Quénum quarter).[73] From Ouidah, d'Almeida sent slaves west along the lagoon for shipment; Forbes in 1850 witnessed a party of slaves belonging to him setting out for shipment at Popo from Zomaï, at the western end of Ouidah.[74]

Duncan in 1845 referred to two 'Portuguese' traders at Ouidah who were returned ex-slaves, and whom he describes as 'slaves' to de Souza, who paid 'head-money' (income tax) to the king of $2,500 and $1,500 per year.[75] It seems likely that the wealthier of these was Joaquim d'Almeida, while the second may possibly have been Joaquim das Neves. Although neither d'Almeida nor Neves had actually been a slave to de Souza, Duncan may have meant by this that they were clients (or former clients) of his or he may simply have been in error. The figures given for the tax paid by these two, since this was levied at one-third of income, indicate assessed annual incomes of $7,500 and $4,500, which on the basis of a standard commission of $16 per slave (as paid to de Souza in the 1840s) would be equivalent to the gross income on the sale of around 470 and 300 slaves respectively, a level of trade comparable to that of dos Santos. D'Almeida's business operations ultimately grew to a much higher level than this: in 1849 Forbes described him as 'the richest resident in Whydah'.[76] Like dos Santos, however, d'Almeida suffered losses through the operations of the British navy; a letter in the Lawson papers from January 1849 transmits regrets that d'Almeida had lately 'lost another vessel'.[77] In September 1849 Duncan, now British vice-consul at Ouidah, again referred to a man who was 'formerly himself a slave to old Da Souza', who had earlier been considered 'the richest merchant in Whydah', but who was 'now, from a succession

---

[70] He made out his will in Bahia, prior to embarkation to settle in Africa, in Dec.1844: text in Verger, *Os libertos*, 116–21.

[71] Dos Santos correspondence, no. 52 [19 Feb. 1847]; PP, Slave Trade 1849–50, Class B, enc. 10 in no. 9, Forbes, 5 Nov. 1849.

[72] Foà, *Le Dahomey*, 23; Reynier, 'Ouidah', 63; Quénum, *Les Ancêtres*, 60–1.

[73] Reynier, 'Ouidah', 66.

[74] Forbes, *Dahomey*, i, 117.

[75] Duncan, *Travels*, i, 122–3; PP, 1848 Select Committee, § 3184.

[76] PP, Slave Trade 1849–50, Class B, enc. 10 in no. 9, Forbes, 5 Nov. 1849.

[77] Jones, 'Little Popo and Agoué', 129.

of captures by our cruizers, reduced to nothing', and, here again, it seems likely that d'Almeida is meant.[78]

Even more important among the new generation of slave-traders was Domingos José Martins ('Domingo Martinez').[79] Martins had originally come to Africa c. 1834, as a member of the crew of a slave ship consigned to de Souza; the ship was captured and the crew put ashore at Ouidah, where Martins lived for some time 'upon the charity' of de Souza; but he then moved to Lagos, where he became the leading slave-merchant.[80] After a brief return home to Bahia, he came back to Africa in early 1846, and this time established himself at Porto-Novo.[81] Martins was the most important slave-trader in this period: Forbes in 1849 described him as 'the richest merchant in the Bights', noting that he was the only trader on the coast who would ship a whole slave cargo on his own, whereas others pooled their contributions to make up a cargo.[82] He settled in 1846 not in the capital of the kingdom of Porto-Novo (the modern city so called) to the north of the lagoon, but on the seashore to the south, at the village to which the name 'Porto-Novo' had originally been applied (modern Sèmè); this was in fact at this time under the effective control of the king of Dahomey rather than Porto-Novo, and it was to the former that Martins paid tribute.[83] He also received his main supply of slaves from Dahomey; towards the end of 1846 he visited Gezo at Abomey, taking 'splendid presents' which included 1,000 doubloons ($16,000) in cash, and assured him that 'he need not fear a demand ceasing for slaves; that he could take all that he, the king, could send him'.[84] This wording implies that Martins too traded directly with the king, rather than through the de Souzas. Probably much of this trade bypassed Ouidah altogether, slaves being taken overland (or down the River Weme) to Lake Nokoué, and then by canoe across the lake to Sèmè. But Martins also did some business through Ouidah; by 1849 he too had an establishment there.[85] This was situated on the east of the town, close to the Portuguese fort, again outside the de Souza quarters.[86]

The dismantling of de Souza's monopoly position involved not only the entry of rival Brazilian traders, but also the breakup of his own commercial organization, as some of his African employees and associates were able to set themselves up as independent traders. The clearest instance is the breach between Azanmado Houénou and de Souza, connected with the establishment of Joaquim d'Almeida in the Ouidah trade, as noted above. The breakaway of Adjovi and his removal from de Souza's Brazil quarter to set up in Tové on the other side of the town presumably belong to the same period. Forbes in 1850 noted the existence in Ouidah of

[78] PP, Slave Trade 1849–50, Class B, no. 7, Duncan, Ouidah, 22 Sept. 1849.
[79] For whom, see David A. Ross, 'The career of Domingo Martinez in the Bight of Benin, 1833–64', *JAH*, 6 (1965), 79–90; Verger, *Flux et reflux*, 467–74; Turner, 'Les Brésiliens', 100–2.
[80] PRO, CO96/12, Hutton, Cape Coast, 17 March 1847.
[81] Ibid.; see Dos Santos correspondence, no. 28 [3 March 1846].
[82] PP, Slave Trade 1849–50, Class B, enc. 10 in no. 9, Forbes, 5 Nov. 1849.
[83] PP, Slave Trade 1854–5, Class B, no. 21, Campbell, Badagry, 1 Nov. 1854.
[84] PRO, CO96/12, Hutton, 17 March 1847.
[85] PP, Slave Trade 1849–50, Class B, enc. 10 in no. 9, Forbes, 5 Nov. 1849.
[86] Burton, *Mission*, i, 72.

five 'native merchants' who were 'very rich': Houénou, Adjovi, Gnahoui and two others whose names he had forgotten. In fact, the missing names are identifiable elsewhere in his own account, in lists of recipients of royal bounty at the Annual Customs at Abomey, in which the same group of five persons occurs twice immediately after the Yovogan: the other two being Codjia and Hodonou.[87] Precisely the same five names are recalled in local tradition as the leading merchants of Ouidah, with the title of 'principal agents of trade', this last translating the indigenous title *ahisigan*, literally 'chief of merchants'.[88] Although the traditions are not explicit on this, it seems likely that the status of *ahisigan* was constituted in this period as a superior rank within the generality of merchants (*ahisinon*), in recognition of the presumably unprecedented wealth and importance of these five individuals. It was more than a merely honorific rank, as it involved political responsibilities: one traditional account describes the *ahisigan* as 'comparable to ministers of commerce', in that 'they periodically submitted a detailed report to the king on the general [economic] situation, suggested lines to follow, contributed to decisions of the royal council'.[89]

How effective the reorganization of the slave trade in the 1840s was in overcoming the problems posed by the Equipment Act is unclear. Duncan in 1845 thought that the slave trade at Ouidah and neighbouring ports had been 'much reduced' by a combination of British naval action and competition from British and French palm-oil traders. When he arrived back in Ouidah in 1849 he again reported 'the rapid decrease of the Slave Trade on this part of the coast', in comparison with 1845, and claimed that 'it is a well-known fact that the Slave Trade is very much reduced or nearly abolished'; but he seems to have inferred a decline in the slave trade from the expansion of the trade in palm oil, on the assumption that these two trades were incompatible, which was certainly (as will be seen below) a misunderstanding on his part.[90] Another observer in 1848, in contrast, estimated slave exports from Dahomey over the previous 12 years at nearly 8,000 annually.[91] This figure evidently relates not to Ouidah alone but to all shipments originating from Dahomey, including those embarked through minor ports to the east and west. Even so, it is probably an exaggeration; total slave exports from the entire Bight of Benin during the 1840s are thought to have averaged only around 10,000 annually, and within this total Lagos accounted for over half of all recorded shipments.[92]

[87] Forbes *Dahomey*, i, 113; ii, 243, 246.

[88] Agbo, *Histoire*, 50; for the title *ahisigan* applied to these five persons, see fieldwork, Hodonou compound, 21 Sept. 2000. The title is also claimed in the traditions of the Houénou and Codjia families and is applied to the second head of the Gnahoui family in his praise-name: Reynier, 'Ouidah', 63; Quénum, *Les Ancêtres*, 61, 71; fieldwork, Codjia compound, 13 June 1997; Gnahoui's praise-name in Agbo, *Histoire*, 235.

[89] Quénum, *Les Ancêtres*, 62–3. For a different interpretation of the *ahisigan*, as those merchants who traded for the king specifically, see Guézo, 'Commerce extérieur', 44.

[90] Duncan, *Travels*, i, 137–8; PP, Slave Trade 1849–50, Class B, nos 4, 7, Duncan, Ouidah, 17 Aug. and 22 Sept. 1849.

[91] PP, Missions to Ashantee and Dahomey, Cruickshank Report, 15.

[92] Eltis, *Economic Growth*, 251, 253; see also Manning, *Slavery, Colonialism and Economic Growth*, 332 (Appendix I), who suggests that only 4,100 slaves were exported annually in the 1840s from the entire area

The correspondence of dos Santos also gives some indication of the overall state of trade, as well as of his own individual operations. In 1845 he referred to the difficulty of disposing of goods – 'nothing from Brazil is worth anything, not even money' – and advised against shipping any more tobacco, since 'things here instead of improving get worse'. In 1846, he complained of a shortage of slaves, implicitly blaming the diversion of supplies to Porto-Novo: 'We are now going to be in a worse situation because Mr Domingo Martins has established himself at Porto-Novo.' In early 1847 slaves were coming in more freely, but he nevertheless noted that trade had not recovered the scale of de Souza's heyday – 'there hasn't yet arrived the great quantity which was customary for our old man' – and later in the year he again reported a scarcity: 'there are none to buy, those that appear are old'.[93] However, trading conditions that were bad for dos Santos, as a purchaser of slaves, were presumably good for the local sellers. The recovery of demand relative to the supply of slaves is attested by evidence on prices in this period, which recovered from the low levels reported to the 1842 Committee. Dos Santos himself during 1847 reported a range of prices between $70 and $90; in 1848 the current price was cited as $80 and in 1849 as between $80 and 100.[94]

The rise of the palm oil trade

The difficulties of the slave trade in the 1840s coincided with the development of an alternative 'legitimate' (i.e. non-slave) trade, principally in palm oil.[95] The export of palm oil through Ouidah was not wholly new. European ships had purchased palm oil for use as cooking and lamp oil throughout the history of the slave trade. The demand for industrial purposes in Britain had begun by the late eighteenth century and, although this trade was centred mainly at Old Calabar, Ouidah also made some contribution. A British observer, writing a few years after the abolition of the British slave trade in 1808, recorded the trade of Ouidah as being now 'very confined, consisting chiefly of a few elephants' teeth, some palm-oil, and cotton cloths'.[96] The wording, however, evidently implies only a limited scale of trade in oil. British traders continued to call at Ouidah after the legal abolition of the slave trade, and dealt there with de Souza among others. When the exploring expedition under Hugh Clapperton arrived on the coast in 1825, they met a British merchant, James Houtson, at Ouidah, although it is not specified what he was trading in.[97] During the 1830s several British merchants traded with

92 (cont.) of colonial 'Dahomey' (i.e. modern Bénin), which included the independent kingdom of Porto-Novo, as well as Dahomey.

93 Dos Santos correspondence, nos 13, 15, 28, 51, 78 [26 May and 17 June 1845, 3 March 1846, 19 Feb. and 1 Dec. 1847].

94 See Table 5.1.

95 See esp. Martin Lynn, *Commerce and Economic Change in West Africa: The Palm Oil Trade in the Nineteenth Century* (Cambridge, 1997).

96 Robertson, *Notes*, 264.

97 Richard Lander, *Records of Captain Clapperton's Last Expedition to Africa* (London, 1830), i, 41. Houtson also had a factory at Badagry, but he died in the following year.

de Souza at Ouidah. Their activities were criticized on the grounds that they were indirectly supporting the slave trade by supplying goods that were then employed to purchase slaves, a question that was a central concern of the Parliamentary Committee of 1842. The issue had come to a head in 1841, when a British captain, Robert Groves, was arrested by the British authorities on the Gold Coast after delivering wooden planks to de Souza at Ouidah, which were suspected of being intended for the construction of intermediate 'slave decks' on slave ships, although Groves insisted that they were merely for the construction of a house. Groves admitted that he had maintained a factory at Ouidah for the previous 10–12 years and had latterly employed a son of de Souza as his agent there, supplying guns, gunpowder and cloth to de Souza; but this trade was for cash ('hard dollars'), rather than for palm oil.[98] Of three other British traders who testified to the Committee that they had supplied goods to de Souza during the 1830s, one had been paid mainly in ivory (with 'a few dollars' in cash) and the others in specie ('dollars and doubloons').[99]

The principal pioneer of the British palm-oil trade at Ouidah was the Gold Coast-based merchant Thomas Hutton. Hutton began trading for oil east of the Gold Coast in the 1830s, initially mainly at Little Popo and Agoué, west of Ouidah.[100] In 1837, however, his agent at Popo, John Marmon, called at Ouidah to explore the possibility of opening trade there, and succeeded in obtaining 50–60 puncheons (about 20 tons) of palm oil.[101] In 1838 Hutton himself visited Ouidah, and established a factory in the abandoned English fort.[102] On a second visit in late 1839 or early 1840, he travelled to Abomey to visit Gezo and was appointed a 'caboceer', this probably representing his formal investiture as governor of the fort. In 1841, in reaction to the bombardment of Ouidah by a British warship noted earlier, Hutton's factory was 'broken up' and his agent was obliged to withdraw back to the Gold Coast. Early in 1842, however, Hutton was back at Ouidah, and succeeded in re-establishing his factory in the English fort.[103] The incumbent Dahomian 'governor' of the fort, Lemon, was not evicted, but was still resident in it, sharing it with Hutton's agent, when Duncan visited there in 1845. Hutton also inherited the services of other families connected with the fort: official British missions that passed through Ouidah to Abomey in 1847 and 1849 employed a man in charge of their porters called 'Mensarika' or 'Majelica', i.e. Midjrokan, evidently a descendant of the man of this name who served as 'linguist' for the fort in the eighteenth century. This man also asserted his hereditary right to the position of 'fort interpreter', serving Forbes in this capacity in 1850, although the latter remarked that, owing to the hiatus in the British presence, he was

---

[98] PP, 1842 Select Committee, Appendix No. 3, Report of Her Majesty's Commissioner, 31 July 1841, 25–7.

[99] Ibid., Minutes of Evidence, § 1617–20, 1751–7, John Arden Clegg; 2196–2204, Capt. Henry Dring; 2371–5, Capt. John Courtland.

[100] Strickrodt, 'Afro–European trade relations', 253–61.

[101] PP, 1842 Select Committee, § 2276–7, Capt. Henry Seward; 2459, Henry Broadhead.

[102] PRO, CO96/13, Hutton, Cape Coast, 22 Dec. 1847.

[103] PP, 1842 Select Committee, § 10257–61, 10329, William MacKintosh Hutton; 10267–8, citing letter of Topp, 12 May 1842.

'unaccustomed to the work, and, although a respectable man, was a bad interpreter'.[104]

The French firm of Régis of Marseille had also begun trading for palm oil at Ouidah from 1832. In 1842, with the permission of the French government, Régis reoccupied the French fort there to serve as his factory;[105] in the following year, his agent Brue visited Gezo in Abomey and was formally invested with command of the French fort.[106] Traders from Hamburg had also entered the palm-oil trade at Ouidah by the mid-1840s. One of these, Lorenz Diedrichsen, pioneered the importation of cowry shells direct from East Africa, utilizing cheaper supplies of shells from the coast opposite Zanzibar; although these were subject to some resistance locally, being larger than the cowries from the traditional source in the Maldive Islands, they soon became accepted.[107] There was also some trade in palm oil to Brazil, mainly for domestic consumption rather than industrial purposes, inaugurated in 1832.[108] The Brazil trade, however, was small in scale. Dos Santos was involved in this trade, alongside that in slaves, but only in trivial quantities, making a single shipment of palm oil to Bahia, in 1846, of only 10 'pipes', i.e. 1,200 gallons, less than 4 tons.[109]

There is little quantitative evidence on the aggregate scale of oil exports from Ouidah in this period. Two estimates of the volume of the trade c. 1836 (both offered retrospectively, several years later) give alternatively less than 100 puncheons (37.5 tons), or not more than 100 tons; by 1845–6, Duncan estimated that it had reached 1,000 tons annually, though this figure seems exaggerated.[110] The real take-off of palm oil exports occurred from 1846 onwards. Hutton at the end of that year observed that, although Ouidah was a more difficult place of trade than his main base at Agoué, nevertheless 'the legitimate trade is working wonders among the people there ... the supply of oil seems annually increasing, as well as the demand, and the number of legitimate traders that have sprung up for it'.[111] In 1848 exports of palm oil from Ouidah were estimated at 4,000 puncheons, equivalent to 1,500 tons, during the year. Duncan, returned to Ouidah in 1849, observed a 'very great increase of legitimate commerce' since his earlier visit; although not able to supply precise figures, he thought that the volume of exports had 'more than quadrupled' since 1846.[112]

[104] Ridgway, 'Journal', 300; Forbes, *Dahomey*, i, 86; ii, 177.

[105] Schnapper, *La Politique et le commerce français*, 163. On Régis, see also E.A. Soumonni, 'Trade and Politics in Dahomey 1841–92, with particular reference to the house of Régis' (PhD thesis, University of Ife, 1983). The date of the establishment of the French factory is commonly given as 1841, but this (Sept. 1841) was the date of the French government authorization; the actual establishment is reported, for example, in PP, 1842 Select Committee, § 10574, citing letters of George MacLean, Cape Coast, 31 March 1842; James Bannerman, Accra, 19 March 1842; Capt. Groves, Cape Coast, 30 March 1842.

[106] See his own account: Brue, 'Voyage'.

[107] Newbury, *Western Slave Coast*, 40; Hogendorn and Johnson, *Shell Money*, 74; see Dos Santos correspondence, nos 22, 49 [19 Dec. 1845, 20 Jan. 1847].

[108] Corrêa da Silva, *Viagem*, 125.

[109] Dos Santos correspondence, no. 30 [31 May 1846].

[110] PP, Missions to Ashantee and Dahomey, Cruickshank Report, 22; 1848 Select Committee, § 3195–6.

[111] PRO, CO96/12, Hutton, Agoué, 7 Dec. 1846.

[112] PP, Missions to Ashantee and Dahomey, Cruickshank Report, 23; Slave Trade 1849–50, Class B, no. 4, Duncan, Ouidah, 17 Aug. 1849.

The relationship between the continuing slave trade and the developing trade in palm oil has sometimes been misunderstood. Contemporary British observers commonly assumed that the established Portuguese and Brazilian slave-traders in Ouidah must have been opposed to the new trade in oil. This is given some support by the traditions of the Quénum family, which claim that the oil trade was pioneered by Azanmado Houénou, who persuaded Gezo to permit the new trade, against the opposition of Francisco Felix de Souza, who argued that this would divert provisions required by the Dahomian army.[113] (In a later elaboration, this is improved into the claim that Houénou persuaded Gezo to 'abolish the slave trade in favour of developing the cultivation of the oil palm').[114] But this story is of dubious authenticity. As told, it is certainly unreliable in detail, since it associates the new trade with a French trader called Béraud, who arrived in Ouidah only in the 1860s, long after de Souza's death, and, in fact, an earlier recorded version of the story attaches it to Azanmado's son Kpadonou Houénou, and refers to the initiation of trade specifically in palm kernels, which became an item of export only in the 1860s, rather than with the earlier development of the oil trade. This earlier version also describes the opposition to the proposal as coming from the Yovogan, rather than from de Souza.[115] The official traditions of the Dahomian monarchy, on the contrary, credit de Souza with advising the Dahomians of the commercial value of palm oil, and de Souza family traditions claim that he himself began cultivating oil-palms in the area of Ouidah shortly before his death.[116]

The contemporary evidence provides little support for the view that the Brazilians in general, or de Souza in particular, opposed the development of the new trade. Brazilian opposition to 'legitimate' trade has been inferred from a report of Duncan in 1845 that Gezo had prohibited the manufacture of shea-butter, except in small quantities for domestic consumption, allegedly at the urging of 'the Spanish and Portuguese slave-dealers' at Ouidah, who feared that the development of an export trade in shea-butter would divert energies from the slave trade.[117] It seems likely, however, that Duncan misunderstood the purpose of this ban, since a later account, in the 1850s, which records a parallel prohibition on the cultivation of groundnuts for export, says that this was intended rather to prevent the diversion of labour from the harvesting of palm oil.[118] Certainly, there was no official policy of discouragement of the palm-oil trade itself at this period; on the contrary, Gezo from 1843 onwards took measures to encourage the new trade, notably by prohibiting the felling of trees for the making of palm wine.[119] Other contemporary evidence suggests that de Souza himself was supportive of attempts to develop the new trade. When Hutton negotiated with Gezo in 1839/40, he

---

[113] Quénum, *Au pays des Fon*, 134; idem, *Les Ancêtres*, 63–4.

[114] Quénum, *L'Histoire de Glexwe*, 32, 40–1.

[115] Reynier, 'Ouidah', 63.

[116] Le Herissé, *L'Ancien Royaume*, 86, 327; Gavoy, 'Note historique', 61; Soumonni, 'Trade and politics', 52.

[117] Duncan, *Travels*, i, 285–6.

[118] Vallon, 'Le royaume de Dahomey', 1/352.

[119] E.A. Soumonni, 'Dahomean economic policy under Ghezo, 1818–1858: a reconsideration', *JHSN*, 10/2 (1980), 1–11; Reid, 'Warrior aristocrats in crisis', 163–8.

travelled to Abomey under de Souza's 'protection', and likewise in 1843 Régis's agent Brue went there in company with de Souza.[120] We should not read too much into these cases, since de Souza was notoriously hospitable to all European visitors, even including according to some accounts officers of the British navy's anti-slaving squadron, and it is more generally clear that social relations between slavers and 'legitimate' traders were normally cordial, Duncan himself noting that Hutton was 'a great favourite' with the Portuguese and Spanish merchants in Ouidah.[121] But on other occasions de Souza clearly did provide positive support: in 1837, for example, when Hutton's agent Marmon sought to open a factory for the palm-oil trade at Badagry, de Souza intervened to get him permission from Gezo. Moreover, de Souza and other slave-traders were at least on occasion willing to supply oil or facilitate its supply to 'legitimate' traders; in 1837 he reportedly offered himself to secure palm oil for Marmon 'because the slave trade was so bad'.[122] Again, in 1842, when Hutton had difficulty in completing a cargo of palm oil, de Souza and 'other extensive slave-traders' used their influence to obtain oil for him, in order to get in exchange his cargo of rum, which they themselves needed.[123] But these were evidently one-off ventures; there is no suggestion that de Souza was committed to personal participation in the oil trade in a more sustained way. This, however, reflected simply a commercial judgement of the limited profits to be made from the oil trade: in 1844, he told a visiting French officer that he 'despised' the palm-oil trade as being 'too insignificant to maintain the position which he had made for himself'.[124] Initially, the oil trade was evidently left in the hands of African traders: de Souza's eldest son Isidoro, when Hutton's agent suggested that he might supply palm oil, retorted indignantly, 'What! do you take me for a black man, that you think I deal in palm oil?'[125]

A significant move of Brazilian slave-traders into palm oil occurred, however, as part of the general expansion of the trade from 1846 onwards. Hutton observed with surprise that de Souza himself had entered the legitimate trade, having loaded five ships with oil in the course of that year; and in 1847 he even complained of the competition which 'the Portuguese' were offering in the oil trade.[126] Duncan in 1849 observed more generally that 'the whole of the merchants who during my last residence in this place in 1845 and 1846, were extensively engaged in the Slave Trade at that period, are now very extensively engaged in the palm-oil trade'.[127] Another example of this process was José dos Santos, who, as Forbes noted in 1850, 'although a slave-dealer, is also a palm-oil purchaser to a great extent'; Forbes found the yard of his premises 'filled with traders' bringing in oil.[128] This seems to

---

[120] PP, 1842 Select Committee, § 10329, W.M. Hutton, 22 July 1842; Brue, 'Voyage', 56.

[121] Duncan, *Travels*, i, 113–14.

[122] PP, 1842 Select Committee, § 2276–7, 2284, Henry Seward.

[123] PP, Slave Trade 1855–7, Class B, enc. in no. 43, Report on the Trade of the Bight of Benin for the year 1856 [Jan. 1857], referring to an episode 'fifteen years since'.

[124] De Monleon, 'Le Cap de Palmes', 74.

[125] PRO, FO84/886, Fraser, Daily memoranda, 13 Nov. 1852 (reporting an incident 'some years since').

[126] PRO, CO96/12, Hutton, 7 Dec. 1846, 17 March 1847.

[127] PP, Slave Trade 1849–50, Class B, no. 4, Duncan, 17 Aug. 1849.

[128] Forbes, *Dahomey*, i, 114.

imply more than the occasional small-scale shipments of oil which dos Santos had made to Brazil in the mid-1840s and suggests that he was now also supplying oil to European merchants (as he certainly did later, in the 1860s). Domingos Martins was also heavily involved in the palm oil trade, claiming to have made no less than $80,000 from it during the year 1849–50.[129]

This shift into palm oil in the late 1840s was clearly due, in large part, to its increasing profitability. Between 1844 and 1849 the price of palm oil at Ouidah rose from $4 to $5 per 18-gallon measure, and further to $7 per measure ($124, or £31, per ton) in 1849/50 and $8 per measure by 1851 (Table 6.1). This price rise was in part due, however, as Forbes noted in 1850, to the introduction of the cheaper Zanzibar cowries, which enabled European traders to bid up the cowry price of oil;[130] and this was soon offset by the consequent depreciation of cowries against the dollar.

Table 6.1 Price of palm oil at Ouidah, 1844–78

	Per ton (320 gal.)		Per measure (18 gal.)
1844	[$71]		$4
1849 Oct.	[$89]		$5
1850 Apr.	[$124]	£31	$7
1851	[$116–142]		$6.50–8
1852 Jan.	[$142–213]		$8–12
1853–4	[$71–107]		$4–6
1857	[$107]		$6
1876	[$115]	£24	[$6.50]
1878	[$115]	576 fr.	[$6.50]

Sources: 1844–50: PP, Slave Trade 1850–1, Class A, enc. 3 in no. 198, Forbes, 6 April 1850; 1851: PRO, FO2/7, Fraser, 15 May 1852; Jan. 1852: PRO FO84/886, Fraser, 17 Jan. 1852 [$8 per measure, raised to $12]; 1853–4: PP, Slave Trade 1854–5, Class B, no. 32, Campbell, Lagos, 7 Dec. 1854 [offered at 4½ gal. per $1, but lowered to 3 gal.]; 1857: FO2/20, George Williamson, 2 March 1857 [33,096 gal. valued at $11,032]; 1876: PRO, CO147/21, Lister, 11 May 1876 [500 large puncheons/80,000 gal. = £6,000]; 1878: Serval, 'Rapport sur une mission au Dahomey', RMC, 59 (1878), 191 [1.80 fr. per gallon, assuming $1=5 fr.]. For slightly different calculations, see Reid, 'Warrior aristocrats', 160. Interpretation of these prices is complicated by the fact that those down to 1852 appear to be in 'cowry dollars' (at the conventional rate of $1 = 2,000 cowries), but those for 1854–7 in actual silver dollars (which had appreciated against cowries): see Chapter 7 for further discussion. Also, whereas the 1850 price is converted to sterling in the original source at the conventional rate of $1=5s.[£1=$4], for the 1876 price the contemporary (since 1843) official value of $1 = 4s.2d. [£1 = $4.80] is assumed.

Some British observers, such as Duncan, assumed that the move into palm oil implied a move out of slaving; the expansion of the oil trade was therefore taken to be an index of the decline of the slave trade. But the reality was that the palm-oil trade was a supplement to rather than a substitute for the slave trade, and Ouidah merchants pursued both simultaneously.[131] As Forbes perceived in 1849, 'at this moment [there is] not one slave-merchant in Whydah but works both trades'.

[129] Ibid., ii, 85.
[130] PP, Slave Trade 1849–50, Class A, enc. 3 in no. 198, Forbes, 6 April 1850.
[131] See Elisée Soumonni, 'The compatibility of the slave and palm oil trades in Dahomey, 1818–1858', in Law, From Slave Trade to 'Legitimate' Commerce, 78–92.

Forbes himself thought that the oil trade served as a hedge against the uncertainty of the slave trade: 'each slave-merchant counteracts the chances of the losses in some degree, by embarking also in the palm-oil trade'.[132] But this was only part of the story. In fact, the two trades were complementary, rather than alternatives. One of the central problems for slave-traders in the illegal trade was getting the goods which they needed for the purchase of slaves. While they had ready access to Brazilian tobacco and rum, a wider supply of manufactured goods, especially British, was required. They could import British goods indirectly via Brazil, but this involved the cost of two freights (Europe to Brazil, and Brazil to Africa) and two sets of duties. Alternatively, and seemingly more commonly, they could purchase goods from European traders on the African coast, either in return for Brazilian goods or (as noted earlier) for specie, in the form of dollars and doubloons. These difficulties were compounded by the development of the palm-oil trade at Ouidah in the 1840s: Duncan in 1845 thought that the decline of the slave trade there was due not only to the activities of the British navy but also to the fact that the French and British legitimate traders could supply manufactured goods more cheaply than the Portuguese and Spanish slave-traders, so that the latter had to pay for their slaves in cash.[133] The move of the slave-traders into the palm-oil trade was clearly intended to solve this problem, by giving them better access to manufactured goods. As Hutton explicitly noted in 1847, 'they pursue the palm oil trade to induce ships to bring them out cargoes', which they then sold for slaves; likewise, Martins explained to Forbes in 1850 that 'the slave and palm oil trade helped each other'.[134]

Some of the oil exported through Ouidah was produced locally. Duncan, returning to Ouidah in 1849, reported that 'the whole of the land in the immediate neighbourhood of the settlement, which three years ago was occupied solely for the production of farinha [cassava flour] for slave subsistence, is now occupied for other purposes'.[135] But much of it was brought from further inland: in 1847 it was noted that some of the traders delivering oil to Hutton's factory in the English fort came from 'considerable distances'.[136] The French agent Brue, travelling inland in 1843, found the country between Ouidah and Tori 'studded with clumps of palm trees', while at Tori itself he saw an estimated 30 pipes (around 3,750 gallons) of oil on sale in the market and at Allada noted the cultivation of 'much oil, which is the subject of a quite extended trade'; likewise Forbes in 1850 saw traders from Ouidah going to Tori to purchase palm oil, along with provisions and locally made cloth.[137] The entry of Ouidah into production of palm oil for export qualified the 'middleman' role which it had occupied in the slave trade; but, to the extent that it also imported oil from places further inland, it continued to function as a middleman in the new trade also. A more critical implication of the transition was that it tied

---

[132] PP, Slave Trade 1849–50, Class B, enc. 10 in no. 9, Forbes, 5 Nov. 1849.

[133] Duncan, *Travels*, i, 138.

[134] PRO, CO96/12, Hutton, 17 March 1847; Forbes, *Dahomey*, ii, 85.

[135] PP, Slave Trade 1849–50, Class B, no. 4, Duncan, 7 Aug. 1849.

[136] Ridgway, 'Journal', 196.

[137] Brue, 'Voyage', 57; Forbes, *Dahomey*, i, 114–15 ('Forree', misprinted for 'Torree').

Ouidah more closely to its immediate hinterland, south of the Lama, where the oil was produced, rather than to the Dahomian capital further north, which had supplied it with slaves. This implied a weakening of the relationship of inter-dependence between the Ouidah merchant community and the Dahomian monarchy that had characterized the operation of the slave trade; and this increasing auton-omy no doubt tended to exacerbate the resentment they felt against the taxation and regulation of their trade imposed by the state.

The influential analysis of A.G. Hopkins suggested that the rise of 'legitimate' commerce in West Africa in the nineteenth century involved a significant dis-continuity in economic structures, since, whereas the slave-trade was dominated by a small number of large entrepreneurs, the production and marketing of agricul-tural produce such as palm oil were open to small-scale participation. Although he conceded that the transition had less impact on the organization of trade in coastal entrepôts such as Ouidah, since large wholesalers were still needed to bulk up the produce for sale to European merchants, he held that the new trade presented opportunities for the entry of new traders, because a greater number of inter-mediaries were needed to collect the palm oil from its original producers.[138] In the specific case of Dahomey, in contrast, Catherine Coquery-Vidrovitch argued that the same large-scale merchants who had controlled the slave trade continued to dominate the trade in palm produce.[139] On the face of it, the latter's insistence on continuity of commercial organization seems to be borne out in Ouidah, where both Brazilian slave-traders such as the de Souzas, Martins and dos Santos and indigenous merchants such as Houénou and Adjovi made the transition from dealing in slaves to selling palm oil. However, there is also evidence in support of Hopkins's thesis of the opening up of trade to small-scale participation. The combination of large-scale and small-scale enterprise was explicitly noted by Forbes in 1850, who reported seeing palm-oil traders arriving at the factory of dos Santos, 'some with only a gallon, others having slaves loaded with large calabashes of oil'.[140] The prominence of small-scale transactions in the oil trade is also indirectly attested by the importance of cowry shells among the goods exchanged for palm oil. Although cowries had of course been given in exchange for slaves earlier, in the slave trade they were paid in bulk (by weight or measure), whereas in the oil trade they were commonly counted out, implying smaller-scale transactions. Forbes noted that dozens of dos Santos's own slaves were employed in 'counting out cowries to pay for the produce', and similar observations occur in other accounts: for example, a visitor to Hutton's factory in 1847 saw 'a number of women who were occupied in counting out a cask of cowries', and the French factory in the 1850s also employed numerous people, mainly women and children, to count out cowries.[141] It

[138] Hopkins, *Economic History*, 125–6, 145–7.

[139] Catherine Coquery-Vidrovitch, 'De la traite des esclaves à l'exportation de l'huile de palme et des palmistes au Dahomey', in Claude Meillassoux (ed.), *The Development of Indigenous Trade and Markets in West Africa* (London, 1971), 107–23.

[140] Forbes, *Dahomey*, i, 114.

[141] Ridgway, 'Journal', 196; Forbes, *Dahomey*, i, 114; Vallon, 'Le royaume de Dahomey', 1/334; Repin, 'Voyage', 73.

is probable, indeed, that an additional factor in the take-off of palm-oil exports from the mid-1840s was the introduction of cheaper supplies of cowries from Zanzibar, mentioned above, which facilitated purchases from small-scale producers.[142]

It is clear, however, that much of the palm-oil production in the Ouidah area was done on large-scale plantations. These evidently involved the actual planting of oil-palms, as opposed to the harvesting of fruit from wild trees.[143] There was also a degree of technical innovation in the process of production. In the eighteenth century, in Dahomey as generally throughout West Africa, it is likely that the oil was squeezed out of the fruits by hand. In the Igbo country, in the hinterland of the Bight of Biafra, it appears that, with the rise of the export trade in palm oil, larger-scale methods of production were adopted, in which the palm fruits were placed to ferment in canoes or hollowed-out tree-trunks, and the oil trodden out in them.[144] A similar transition evidently occurred in the Ouidah area: a visitor in 1847 described a 'palm-oil manufactory' three miles from Ouidah, situated in 'a palm-tree plantation ... of some miles in extent', on which he observed gangs of men treading oil in large mud-walled troughs built for the purpose.[145] The labour on such large-scale plantations was clearly performed mainly by slaves; here as elsewhere in coastal West Africa, the rise of 'legitimate' trade created an increased local demand for slaves, which to some degree offset the decline of overseas sales.[146] It was already noted in 1844 that 'the inhabitants and black merchants' of Ouidah were beginning to retain slaves at home to produce palm oil, rather than selling them. In 1848 it was estimated that, in addition to 8,000 slaves exported annually, at least another 1,000 were being imported each year into 'the towns and villages upon the coast' for local use; although this report does not refer explicitly to palm-oil production, it seems reasonable to infer that this accounted for much of the internal demand for slaves.[147]

The rise of the export trade in palm oil had significant implications for gender relations in Ouidah and its hinterland, since whereas the slave trade had been dominated by men, a major role in the new trade was played by women.[148] In Dahomey, although the climbing of the palm trees to cut down the fruits was

---

[142] The connection between palm oil exports and the introduction of cowries as currency was noted on the Gold Coast in the 1830s: Brodie Cruickshank, *Eighteen Years on the Gold Coast of Africa* (London, 1853), ii, 43.

[143] Contemporary descriptions of oil 'plantations' are generally not explicit on whether these involved cultivation of palms, or merely exploitation of existing trees. However, a reference in 1850 to 'the native planters ... extending their plantations' seems to imply actual planting: PP, Slave Trade 1850–51, Class A, enc.3 in no. 198, Forbes, 6 April 1850. The French mission of 1856 refers more explicitly to 'newly planted young palms' and (at Cana) to 'rows of palm trees in straight lines', which must evidently have been deliberately planted: Vallon, 'Le royaume de Dahomey', 1/353, 357.

[144] Susan Martin, 'Slaves, Igbo women and palm oil in the nineteenth century', in Law, *From Slave Trade to 'Legitimate' Commerce*, 182–3.

[145] Ridgway, 'Journal', 412–13. Forbes in 1850 also referred to the treading out of oil in 'a large recess': *Dahomey*, i, 115–16.

[146] Lovejoy, *Transformations in Slavery*, 159–83.

[147] De Monleon, 'Le Cap de Palmes', 72; PP, Missions to Ashantee and Dahomey, Cruickshank Report, 15.

[148] Robin Law, '"Legitimate" trade and gender relations in Yorubaland and Dahomey', in Law, *From Slave Trade to 'Legitimate' Commerce*, 195–214.

normally done by men, the processing and marketing of the oil was considered women's work. The small-scale production of oil for export in the nineteenth century was therefore presumably dominated by women. Contemporary sources attest the prominence of women in the oil trade at Ouidah: a visitor to Hutton's factory in the English fort in 1847 observed 'a constant influx ... of women' bringing palm oil for sale; and a member of the French mission in 1856 even asserted that the oil trade was entirely in the hands of women, men seldom coming to Ouidah for this purpose unless they were accompanying their wives to help transport the cowries and merchandise received in exchange.[149] However, the slaves employed on large-scale plantations included men as well as women, as explicitly noted in the 1847 account cited earlier; likewise, Antonio d'Almeida's farm in 1864 was cultivated by 18 male and 6 female slaves, although it is not specified that this was producing palm oil.[150] More critically, these large-scale oil plantations were clearly owned mainly by men. The competition between small-scale and large-scale production in the oil trade thus took on a gender dimension. The consequent tensions may be relevant to the introduction into Ouidah of masquerade cults such as Zangbeto and Egungun, noted in an earlier chapter (although this may have occurred only after the French colonial occupation in 1892), since these cults were restricted to men, and functioned in part to control and discipline women, including especially those who were active in the commercial sector of the economy, whose independent earnings were explicitly perceived as a threat to male dominance.[151]

The large oil plantations now established in the Ouidah area were mainly owned by existing merchants, including both locally settled Brazilians and indigenous Dahomians. Forbes in 1850 noted that the Brazilian dos Santos had 'a plantation on which he manufactures oil'; and he visited two other plantations, one east of Ouidah, owned by the indigenous merchant Adjovi, described as 'a very extensive palm-oil plantation', on which were 'many establishments, slave villages, for the manufacture', and one three miles to the west (perhaps the same one described in 1847), owned by an unnamed returned ex-slave from Bahia, 'a splendid palm-oil plantation ... thickly set with palm trees'.[152] One implication of the rise of the palm oil trade, therefore, was that the Ouidah merchants became a class of commercial farmers and large-scale slave-owners, rather than merely traders. Forbes describes Adjovi, Houénou, Gnahoui and the other leading 'native merchants' as owning 'thousands of slaves'; Gnahoui alone having 'upwards of 1000 slaves' – though not all of these would have been employed in the production of oil for export, since he owned estates north of the Lama (at Abomey, Cana, Zogbodomé and Agrimé), beyond the current oil-producing area, as well as 'an extensive domain' at Ouidah, a 'large farm' at Tori and an estate at Houégbo, north of Allada.[153] The growth of palm oil cultivation was probably connected with the colonization of agricultural land to the east of Ouidah during this period, which is recalled in local tradition.

[149] Ridgway, 'Journal', 196; Vallon, 'Le royaume de Dahomey', 1/358.
[150] Verger, Os libertos, 123.
[151] For elaboration of this argument, see Law, '"Legitimate" trade', 208–10.
[152] Forbes, Dahomey, i, 114, 115, 123.
[153] Ibid., i, 113; ii, 175–6.

The head of the Hodonou family at this time, Dovonou, is said to have founded the village of Pahou, 15 km east of Ouidah; a reference by Forbes in 1850 to 'a new town lately built to the eastward' of Ouidah may allude to Pahou.[154] In the following generation, after the final end of the trans-Atlantic slave trade in the 1860s, the second head of the Houénou family, Kpadonou Houénou, is said to have settled the slaves who were now no longer exportable on oil-palm plantations, including estates east of Pahou, such as Cococodji, and at Godomey and Abomey-Calavi on the western shore of Lake Nokoué.[155]

This shift into commercial agriculture is encoded in the traditions of the Hodonou family that its head planted crops on his farms, which yielded a harvest of money, in the form of cowry shells.[156] This transition clearly affected the fortunes of individual merchants, some of whom found increased opportunities in the new trade. Adjovi, for example, who had earlier been employed by de Souza as warden of slaves awaiting export, is alleged by de Souza family tradition to have made his fortune by stealing some of the slaves under his care and putting them to work on oil-palm plantations.[157] The transition may have favoured indigenous merchants more generally, to the extent that they may have had readier access to farmland. But Brazilian merchants also obtained estates, as has been seen, presumably through grants from the king. Despite the extension of cultivation, there evidently remained sufficient land around Ouidah; as Burton still noted in the 1860s, 'when a man wants fresh ground he merely brings a little dash to the caboceer [i.e. the Yovogan]'.[158]

The transport of palm oil to Ouidah posed considerably greater difficulties and costs than the slave-trade, not only because slaves were self-transporting while oil had to be carried, but also because of the large quantities of oil that now had to be moved: as a rough equivalence, in the 1840s one slave commanded around the same price at the coast ($80) as 1 ton (320 gallons) of oil. Although oil could be transported laterally along the coast by canoe on the lagoons, its delivery to Ouidah from the interior could only be done by human porters, carrying it on their heads. A standard headload over long distances in Dahomey was only about 50–60 lb., although larger weights might be carried on shorter hauls. Palm oil was carried in containers with a capacity of between 5–12 gallons (weighing between 35–85 lb.): in earthenware pots, with a standard capacity of 5 gallons,[159] or calabashes, which contained 30–40 litres, c. 8–12 gallons, each.[160] At Ouidah itself, oil was commonly sold in measures of 18 gallons, but this quantity would have been too heavy to head-load over long distances. It would thus take between 30 and 60 porters to

---

[154] Reynier, 'Ouidah', 53; Forbes, *Dahomey*, i, 105.

[155] Reynier, 'Ouidah', 64. The later account of Quénum, *Les Ancêtres*, 65, attributes the foundation of these estates rather to Kpadonou's father Azanmado Houénou; probably they were established by Kpadonou during his father's lifetime.

[156] Fieldwork, Hodonou compound, 21 Sept. 2000.

[157] De Souza, *La Famille de Souza*, 33–4.

[158] Burton, *Mission*, i, 40.

[159] Ibid., i, 143, n.

[160] Vallon, 'Le royaume de Dahomey', 1/358. Cf. the earlier (1780s) account of the transportation of oil in 'large calabashes, containing from five to ten or twelve gallons each': Norris, *Memoirs*, 71.

move a ton of palm oil. Although delivered to Ouidah in small quantities, the oil was bulked up on arrival there. This is most explicitly stated in the account from 1847, which noted that upon delivery in the English fort, the oil was 'poured into casks and measured', prior to payment.[161] The standard barrel in which oil was exported was the 'puncheon'; this had a variable capacity on different parts of the African coast, but on the Slave Coast in the 1840s a puncheon of 120 gallons (⅗ of a ton) was in use.[162] After pouring into puncheons at Ouidah, the oil had still to be delivered to the beach over 3 km away. Puncheons were evidently too heavy to be head-loaded and were rolled along the ground. In the 1850s it was noted of the road between Ouidah and the beach that 'casks and puncheons of palm oil, cowries and other goods are daily rolled along it'; according to later testimony, this took two persons per puncheon.[163] In crossing the lagoon, palm oil being lighter than water, the puncheons could be floated on the water.[164]

In the early stages, the palm-oil trade remained in private hands, rather than being undertaken by state enterprise. A person who had visited Ouidah in 1843–5 noted that the king and his officials were uninvolved in the oil trade, except for taxing it.[165] The principal tax applied to the oil trade in the 1840s was an export tax levied on sales of palm oil, as first recorded by Duncan in 1845; according to later accounts, this was levied at the rate of one gallon in the measure of eighteen, which was physically ladled out in the European factories and sold on the king's behalf.[166] Although the method of payment was different (taken as a share of the commodity exported, rather than of goods imported), the rate of the duty was roughly comparable with that of the export tax on slaves ($5 per slave, on a standard price of $80 per slave). The complaint of Gezo to a British mission in 1848 that the oil trade 'brought only a very small amount of duties into his coffers' presumably reflects the low level of palm oil exports at that date, and perhaps also that the king as yet received no income directly from sales of palm oil, as he did from slaves.[167]

The reconstruction of the Brazilian community in Ouidah

The rise of the palm-oil trade coincided with significant changes in the composition and structure of the Brazilian merchant community in Ouidah. Francisco

[161] Ridgway, 'Journal', 196.

[162] E.g. PRO, CO96/2, J.H. Akhurst, 'Property destroyed at this factory by fire on Monday 2nd instant', Agoué, 7 Oct. 1843. However, there was also a 'large' puncheon of 160 gallons (half a ton).

[163] Freeman, 'West Africa', 201; Bertin, 'Renseignements sur le royaume de Porto-Novo et le Dahomey', *RMC*, 106 (1890), 393.

[164] Duncan, *Travels*, i, 119–20.

[165] PRO, FO84/1465, Anonymous letter to Editor of *African Times*, 23 June 1876, enc. to E. Fitzgerald to W.H. Wylde, 27 July 1876. The writer assumed that these conditions still applied in the 1870s, but this was certainly no longer the case.

[166] Duncan, *Travels*, i, 122; Forbes, *Dahomey*, i, 35–6, 111; FO2/7, Commercial Report, enc. to Fraser, 15 May 1852.

[167] PP, Missions to Ashantee and Dahomey, Cruickshank Report, 17.

Felix de Souza died on 8 May 1849.[168] Despite his partial loss of royal favour in his final years, he was given an official funeral appropriate to a major Dahomian chief; the ceremonies even included, despite the protests of his sons, the offering of human sacrifices, two being killed at the beach and two at his grave.[169] Although de Souza's dominant influence in Ouidah had been reduced by the time of his death, the succession to his position of Chacha remained an important issue. In the absence of the eldest son Isidoro, resident at Little Popo, the acting headship of the family seems to have devolved upon the next-born son, Ignacio; at least, it was he who took charge of the funeral ceremonies for the father.[170] The initial assumption in Ouidah was that Ignacio would also succeed to his father's position of Chacha. Gezo, however, at first offered the post to the now leading merchant, Domingos Martins, but the latter was unwilling to remove from Porto-Novo to Ouidah, and by late 1849 the general belief was that, in default of Martins the post would go to Isidoro.[171] The latter's willingness to move back to Ouidah was doubtless due to the destruction by fire of his property at Popo, noted earlier. In March 1850 Gezo summoned the de Souza family, together with the Yovogan, to Abomey, to appoint a new Chacha. Forbes observed that Isidoro was the wealthiest of the three brothers, but Ignacio was backed by Martins, and Antonio was 'the king's favourite', so that the issue was still in doubt; in the event, as Forbes found on returning to Ouidah in May, Isidoro was confirmed as Chacha, while Ignacio was made a 'caboceer' and Antonio given the honorific title of 'amigo–del–Rey' ('friend of the king', in Portuguese). It was understood that all three would pay a separate 'tribute' (i.e. 'head-money', or income tax) to the king, thus formalizing the dissolution of the family into autonomous segments.[172] According to later tradition, in fact, the de Souza property in Ouidah was also now partitioned between the three brothers, Isidoro occupying the main house of Singbome, while Ignacio took the nearby building of Kindji and Antonio occupied Zomaï at the western end of the town.[173]

The position to which Isidoro succeeded was of significantly less prestige and power than his father had enjoyed in his heyday. The financial liabilities bequeathed by the father were eased by a partial repudiation of his debts, Gezo decreeing that his heirs should 'pay the "legal" debts of his father, but not his debts to slave-dealers'; the meaning of this formula is not transparent, but probably the intention was that his debts to the king were safeguarded while others were discounted. The new Chacha also continued to enjoy the privileges that accrued to his position as agent for the king's trade, including royal rights of pre-emption, at least within Ouidah itself; as Forbes noted in 1850, the Chacha remained 'the principal agent to the king in all matters of trade; and to him must be subjected all commerce,

---

[168] PP, Slave Trade 1849–50, Class B. no. 6, Duncan, 22 Sept. 1849.
[169] Ibid., Class B, enc. 14 in no. 9, Duncan, 18 Sept. 1849.
[170] Ibid., Class B, no. 7, Duncan, 22 Sept. 1849.
[171] Ibid., Class B, no. 6, Duncan, 22 Sept. 1849 (referring to 'the second son', unnamed); enc. 10 in no. 9, Forbes, Ouidah, 6 Oct. 1849; Class A, enc.10 in no. 9, Forbes, 5 Nov. 1849.
[172] Forbes, *Dahomey*, i, 125; ii, 3.
[173] Foà, *Le Dahomey*, 26–7; Gavoy, 'Note historique', 68–9.

whether in slaves or palm-oil, that he may have the refusal'.[174] But Gezo no longer dealt through the Chacha alone. In 1850 he named four other persons who were also serving as his agents: his brothers Ignacio and Antonio de Souza, Martins at Porto-Novo and a Spanish trader called Joaquim Antonio, who was based at Grand-Popo to the west.[175]

Notably absent from this list of Gezo's agents is Joaquim d'Almeida. This probably reflects the fact that he had lately removed his residence from Ouidah; when Forbes returned there in April 1850 he found that d'Almeida was 'now' resident at Agoué,[176] and he remained at Agoué thereafter, until his death in 1857. The reason for this displacement is not recorded; perhaps it was linked to d'Almeida's financial difficulties arising from captures by the British navy, noted earlier, but possibly also it was connected with Isidoro's removal into Ouidah. D'Almeida continued to maintain a household in Ouidah, however; in 1863, six years after his death, it was noted that the family still had 'a large house' in the town and that several of his children were attending the school established by the French Roman Catholic mission there.[177] There is indeed still a d'Almeida household in Ouidah, in Quénum quarter, whose inhabitants seem to be descended from slaves of Joaquim d'Almeida, rather than himself.[178] While the removal of d'Almeida to Agoué tended to strengthen Isidoro de Souza's position within Ouidah, it was conversely undermined when Domingos Martins soon afterwards shifted the main focus of his activities from Porto-Novo into Ouidah. In 1851 the hostility of the king of Porto-Novo obliged Martins to abandon his establishment there, and soon after, in August 1851, he was appointed 'a caboceer, of his own place, at Whydah'. For a while he contemplated returning to Bahia, and even put his property in Ouidah up for sale, but in the event he did not leave, fearing that if he went to Brazil he might be prosecuted there for his illegal slaving activities.[179] This ousting of Martins from Porto-Novo was evidently only temporary, since he resumed trading there later. Nevertheless, the centre of gravity of his operations seems now to have shifted decisively towards Ouidah. Around the same time, he also formed a connection with the de Souzas, marrying one of the late Chacha's daughters.[180]

The composition of the merchant community in Ouidah was also indirectly affected by the British intervention at Lagos at the end of 1851, which ended the slave trade at that port and turned it into a quasi-protectorate of Britain.[181] This forced the relocation of several Brazilian slave-traders formerly resident there, some of whom ended up in Ouidah. One of the principal slave-dealers at Lagos, Carlos José de Souza Nobre, anticipated the British attack by withdrawing to Ouidah, reportedly in the hope of securing French or US counter-intervention; he

---

[174] Forbes, *Dahomey*, i, 106, 111.
[175] PP, Slave Trade 1850–1, Class A, enc. 2 in no. 220, Forbes, Journal, 4 July 1850.
[176] Ibid., Class A, enc. 3 in no. 198, Forbes, 6 April 1850.
[177] Borghero, *Journal*, 123 [4 Feb. 1863].
[178] Turner, 'Les Brésiliens', 105–6.
[179] PRO, FO84/886, Fraser, Journal, 30 July, 2 and 14 Aug. 1851.
[180] Their son was baptized in 1853: de Souza, *La Famille de Souza*, 254, 273.
[181] See Robert Smith, *The Lagos Consulate 1851–1861* (London, 1978).

evidently remained at Ouidah thereafter, dying there in 1858, and founded a family that still exists, in Ganvè quarter.[182] Another, Marcos Borges Ferras, initially stayed in Lagos, but was expelled on suspicion of continued slave-dealing in 1855 and also withdrew to Ouidah; in 1856 he returned to Bahia, where he was imprisoned for his earlier involvement in illegal slaving, but by 1863 he was back in Ouidah.[183] Augusto Amadie, Hungarian by birth but an honorary 'Brazilian' by employment, having formerly served as secretary to Domingos Martins in Ouidah, who had removed to Lagos in 1852, was forcibly deported from there in 1853; he went initially to Agoué, but also ended up in Ouidah, where he is attested by 1863.[184] Other Brazilians who moved from Lagos to Ouidah, although in these cases there is no explicit evidence that their relocation was connected with illegal slaving activities, were Angelo Custodio das Chagas, attested in Lagos in 1853 but established at Ouidah by 1863, who founded a family in Maro quarter;[185] and Joaquim de Cerqueira Lima, whose father had reportedly been 'the headman of Brazilian emigrants' at Lagos, but who by 1864 was resident in Ouidah and whose descendants live in Brazil quarter.[186]

Conversely, there seems to have been a reverse movement of freed slaves of Sierra Leonian origin from Ouidah to Lagos. At any rate, the community of Sierra Leonians reported by visitors to Ouidah in 1843–51 seems no longer to have existed by the mid-1850s, since the records of the British Methodist mission established in 1854 make no reference to it. Burton in 1864 noted explicitly that British subjects in Ouidah numbered only a dozen, and these were mostly Fante from Cape Coast.[187]

British intervention &
the end of the Brazilian slave trade, 1849–52

The British intervention at Lagos was part of a wider attack on the illegal slave trade in the Bight of Benin, which in its initial stages had in fact focused on Dahomey more than upon Lagos. The diplomatic exchanges had been initiated by Gezo, who enlisted the missionary Freeman in 1843 and the explorer Duncan in 1845 to transmit messages to the British authorities expressing his desire for closer relations, and in particular for the reoccupation of the English fort in Ouidah. (Duncan, in fact, understood Gezo to be offering to 'cede' Ouidah to the British,

---

[182] Verger, *Flux et reflux*, 578; J.S.G. Gramberg, *Schetsen van Afrikas Westkust* (Amsterdam, 1861), 156; Burton, *Mission*, i, 111; Reynier, 'Ouidah', 60.

[183] Verger, *Flux et reflux*, 435–6, 580–85; Burton, *Mission*, i, 74 n. One of the letters of dos Santos in 1863 (written from Godomey) is addressed to Marcos Borges Ferras at Ouidah, and the latter also witnessed the will of Antonio d'Almeida in 1864: dos Santos correspondence, no. 92 [1 Aug. 1863]; Verger, *Os libertos*, 124.

[184] Smith, *The Lagos Consulate*, 46–7; PP, Slave Trade 1853–4, Class A, enc. in no. 128, Journal of G.C. Phillips, 25 April 1853; Burton, *Mission*, i, 74 n.

[185] Verger, *Flux et reflux*, 578; Burton, *Mission*, i, 74, n.; Reynier, 'Ouidah', 45. Das Chagas wrote out Antonio d'Almeida's will for him in 1864.

[186] Burton, *Mission*, ii, 8–9; Reynier, 'Ouidah', 42.

[187] PP, Slave Trade 1864, Class B, no. 9, Consul Burton, 23 March 1864.

but it is clear from the context that he meant only the fort.)[188] The British government followed up these informal contacts with a series of official missions that attempted to negotiate a treaty abolishing slave exports from Dahomey, from 1847 onwards.[189] Gezo, however, although he accepted a treaty of 'friendship and commerce', which guaranteed 'free liberty of commerce' and 'complete protection and security' for British traders (5 April 1847), initially evaded pressure for an anti-slave trade treaty. Missions to Abomey in 1848 and 1850 (the latter jointly led by Forbes) were informed that the revenues derived from the slave trade were too great to be immediately given up and that, although 'legitimate' trade in palm oil and other agricultural produce was welcome it could not be expected to provide an adequate substitute, at least in the short term.

One significant, although temporary, by-product of these exchanges was the establishment of official British diplomatic representation in Dahomey, located in Ouidah. When the British government created a consulate for the Bights of Benin and Biafra, based in the island of Fernando Po, in 1849, it at the same time appointed John Duncan as vice-consul to Dahomey. Duncan arrived in Ouidah in August 1849, taking up residence in the English fort, but his tenure was brief, as he died in October of the same year. The vice-consulate then remained vacant until his successor, Louis Fraser, arrived in July 1851, and Fraser abandoned the post, following a series of disputes with the local authorities, in November 1852; he was then transferred to the newly opened consulate at Lagos, and the Ouidah vice-consulate lapsed. The Dahomian authorities clearly regarded the vice-consuls as occupying the fort on the same terms as its former governors in the eighteenth century; when Duncan visited the king on his arrival in 1849, he was informed that 'it will be necessary, holding office in his dominion, that I shall attend his annual Custom', which also implicitly involved the payment of 'presents'. In the fort, Duncan found his position contested by Hutton's local agent, who asserted the firm's prior rights of occupation, retaining the key to the fort and assigning the vice-consul to inferior accommodation.[190] When Fraser arrived in 1851, he too initially shared it with Hutton's agent, but at the beginning of 1852 Hutton found alternative premises, purchasing a house from Jacinto Rodrigues and leaving the vice-consul in sole possession of the fort.

The British involvement in turn provoked counter-moves by the French and the Portuguese, seeking to defend their own interests in Ouidah. A French mission to Dahomey in July 1851 negotiated a treaty that promised 'protection' and 'freedom' for French merchants in turn and, more concretely, reaffirmed Régis's right to command the labour of the inhabitants of the French quarter in Ouidah;[191] although of limited significance in itself, this treaty can be seen as the start of the

---

[188] Duncan, *Travels*, ii, 269. The citation of this supposed offer in support of the argument that Dahomey was reluctant to 'absorb' the town is misconceived: Polanyi, *Dahomey*, 132.

[189] Robin Law, 'An African response to abolition: Anglo-Dahomian negotiations on ending the slave trade, 1838–77', *S&A*, 16/3 (1995), 281–310.

[190] PP, Slave Trade 1849–50, Class B, no. 6, Duncan, 22 Sept. 1849; enc. 9 in no. 9, Forbes, Journal, 7 Oct. 1849.

[191] See Nardin, 'La reprise des relations'.

process which, 41 years later, would lead to the establishment of French rule over Ouidah. Later in 1851 the Portuguese authorities on the island of São Tomé also made contact with the Chacha Isidoro de Souza, who was formally appointed as governor of the Portuguese fort in Ouidah, with the status of lieutenant-colonel in the Portuguese army, and in April 1852 the governor of São Tomé visited Ouidah in person to confirm the appointment.[192]

Frustration at the refusal of Dahomey to give up the slave trade provoked a British naval blockade of Ouidah at the end of 1851, under pressure of which Gezo finally accepted a treaty abolishing the slave trade, on 13 January 1852. In fact, the blockade of 1851–2 and the consequent treaty were largely irrelevant, except as a symbol, since by this time the slave trade to Brazil had already come to an effective end. The critical developments had occurred in Brazil itself, rather than in Africa, with the British navy's adoption of a more aggressive policy of pursuing and arresting slave ships within Brazilian territorial waters from June 1850, under pressure of which the Brazilian government finally enacted effective legislation for the suppression of the slave-trade in September 1850. The effects were soon evident in Africa itself. In February 1851 a British naval officer calling at Ouidah was told by Hutton's agent there that 'the Slave Trade was in a most depressed state, no shipment having taken place for many months' and that 'the slave-merchants finding all efforts to get off slaves futile' were trading instead in palm oil. Vice-Consul Fraser in August 1851 was likewise assured that during the year the Portuguese 'had not bought one slave'.[193] This lack of demand evidently produced something of a glut of slaves in Dahomey, reflected in a fall in prices, which by 1851 had fallen to $40 per slave, half the level of the late 1840s (see Table 5.1). At Porto-Novo early in that year, slaves were reportedly offered for sale at only $7–8 each.[194]

Although Gezo's policy, in seeking to continue the slave trade in the face of British pressure but ultimately acceding to abolition under duress in 1852, is clear enough, the attitude of the Ouidah merchant community in this crisis is less easy to determine. John Yoder argued, mainly on the basis of debates at the Annual Customs of 1850 reported by Forbes, that the abolition of the slave trade became a matter of explicit disagreement within the Dahomian ruling elite, which divided into rival factions on the issue; within the Ouidah merchant community, he suggested that resident Brazilians, such as Martins and the de Souzas, supported defiance of Britain and continuation of the slave trade, whereas indigenous Dahomians who had gone into the palm-oil trade were willing to accede to British demands for its abolition.[195] It is doubtful, however, whether this reading of the debates at the 1850 Customs can be sustained. The issue explicitly discussed on that occasion was not the slave trade but whether Dahomey should launch its next

---

[192] Corrêa da Silva, *Viagem*, 81, 120; Sarmento, *Portugal no Dahomé*, 62.

[193] PP, Papers relative to Lagos, enc. 2 in no. 35: Lieutenant Drew, off Ouidah, 27 Feb. 1851; FO84/886, Fraser, Daily journal, 22 Aug. 1851.

[194] PP, Papers relative to Lagos, 1852, enc. 4 in no. 35, Captain Adams, 24 March 1851.

[195] John C. Yoder, 'Fly and Elephant Parties: political polarization in Dahomey 1840–70', *JAH*, 15 (1974), 417–32.

military campaign against Abeokuta, to the east, or against some less militarily formidable opponent; it is only by speculative implication, since Abeokuta was currently allied to Britain, that this can be interpreted as referring to the question of whether to accommodate British wishes more generally and hence over the slave trade in particular. It is also questionable whether the conflict of interest between Brazilian slave-traders and indigenous Dahomian oil traders which Yoder posits is plausible, since, as has been seen, both Brazilian and Dahomian merchants in the 1840s engaged in the slave and oil trades simultaneously; and individual Brazilian and Dahomian merchants were linked in business partnerships (as between Joaquim d'Almeida and Azanmado Houénou, for example) rather than the two groups confronting each other as discrete collective blocs. Conflicts between individual Brazilian and indigenous merchants certainly occurred (as between Houénou and de Souza) but reflected commercial rivalries rather than conflicting class interests or policy differences.

A number of statements on this issue by leading individuals in Ouidah are in fact recorded. Yovogan Dagba, the representative of the Dahomian state in Ouidah, speaking to Forbes in 1850, unsurprisingly reiterated the standard official line, that the revenues from the slave trade were too great to give up, dramatically illustrating the point by comparing the volume of a tumbler and a wine glass: 'If the King has been accustomed to give the full of this [tumbler], can he live to give the full of that [wine glass]? The tumbler is the slave, the wine-glass the palm-oil trade.' More interestingly (and in contradiction to Yoder's interpretation), the indigenous merchant Gnahoui, who served as interpreter for the British in the subsequent negotiations, but who was also a substantial slave-trader, remarked that 'he was working against his own interest in explaining matters to us, saying that the Slave Trade was sweet to him'.[196] However, Ouidah's natural opposition to discontinuing what remained a profitable trade in slaves had to be balanced against its equally rational desire to avoid an alienation of Britain that might prejudice the operation of trade in general. When Gezo formally rejected the British demand for the ending of the slave trade, Forbes noted that, while the generality of his 'ministers' showed their pleasure at the decision, the Yovogan alone 'could not disguise his anxiety, lest the refusal might lead his government into danger from the stoppage of trade'.[197]

More evidence is available on attitudes within the Brazilian community, and this conversely refutes the suggestion that they offered intransigent opposition to the British proposals. The leading merchant Martins told Forbes in 1850, before the final breakdown of the negotiations, that, if the British would pay him compensation to cover the cost of his tax payments to the king, 'he would stop the Slave Trade in the Bights; he would so increase the palm-oil trade, as to render it necessary to the King'. Early in 1851, he was reported to have declined to purchase slaves at Porto-Novo, even though they were offered very cheaply, and declared that 'he had come to the determination of having no more to do with them, owing

---

[196] PP, Slave Trade 1849–50, Class A, enc. 1 in no. 198, Forbes, Journal, 15 March 1850; 1850–1, Class A, enc. 2 in no. 220, Forbes, Journal, 4 July 1850.
[197] Forbes, *Dahomey*, ii, 189.

to the difficulties of the passage across to Brazil'.[198] In July 1851, when Vice-Consul Fraser arrived in Ouidah, Martins again told him that he was 'quite willing to sign a treaty on his own account against the slave trade, and also to assist the English government to put an end to it', while Antonio de Souza said that, if the British would allow him to ship a final 2,000 slaves, 'he would willingly enter into securities never again to aid or abet the same traffic, and would render all the assistance in his power to suppress it'.[199] While this clearly represented a recognition of reality rather than a moral conversion, it implied that the Ouidah merchant community could see a viable future for itself beyond the ending of the slave trade and was reconciled to this as inevitable even if unwelcome in the near future. During the blockade of 1851–2, Fraser believed that the Portuguese–Brazilian traders were in general in favour of the king conceding to British demands but also fearful of provoking retaliation from the Dahomian authorities. In a private conversation with Antonio de Souza and Jacinto Rodrigues, he found them 'frightened out of their wits, they fear the natives will murder them'; the former even asked to be taken under British protection. The Chacha Isidoro de Souza observed he was 'afraid to tell the King what he thinks of this blockade, as he says, if it turns out well, the King will call him his "dear friend", if the reverse he will take his life'. Although Martins did promise to persuade the King to sign the treaty, in the event he did not take any active part in the negotiations. All three de Souza brothers, Isidoro, Antonio and Ignacio, however, did accompany the British mission to the capital and witnessed the treaty signed in January 1852; Rodrigues, who spoke English, also went with them to serve as interpreter.[200]

From slaves to palm oil: transition embraced, 1852–7

In the years following the crisis of 1851–2, the slave trade out of Ouidah, now going solely to Cuba, remained at a low level, with only a handful of successful shipments. During 1853, although there were no reported shipments of slaves from Ouidah itself, a couple were made from near Agoué to the west; the British consul at Lagos reported that Gezo had 'strictly forbidden' the shipping of slaves from Ouidah, but that the slave-traders there were simply sending their slaves along the lagoon for embarkation further west.[201] During 1854, however, a number of shipments were made from Ouidah itself: during May three vessels were dispatched with around 1,700 slaves between them, and later in the year a French brig called the *Caesar* was purchased jointly by slave-dealers at Ouidah and Agoué, in order to ship a cargo of slaves from Ouidah for Cuba, though the British regarded this as 'a most reckless venture', since the ship was in a 'most unseaworthy and dangerous state'. However, all four of these vessels were subsequently seized by the authorities

[198] PP, Slave Trade 1849–50, Class A, enc. 3 in no. 198, Forbes, 6 April 1850; Papers relative to Lagos, enc. 4 in no. 35, Captain Adams, 24 March 1851.
[199] PRO, FO84/886, Fraser, Journal, 22 July 1851.
[200] PRO, FO84/886, Fraser, 23 Dec. 1851; Daily memoranda, 26–27 Dec. 1851; 'Facts relating to my second visit to Abomey', 1851–2.
[201] PP, Slave Trade 1853–4, Class B, no. 47, Campbell, Lagos, 31 Oct. 1853.

in Cuba, three before disembarking their slaves.[202] Further attempts to ship slaves during 1855–6 were thwarted by the British navy: in August 1855 a Spanish ship, the *Fernando Po*, was believed to be intending to take slaves at Ouidah, but was arrested before reaching there, and in January 1856 another suspected slaver was run ashore and destroyed at Cotonou.[203]

To what degree established Brazilian traders such as Martins were involved in these ventures is uncertain. Although the British understood that Martins was among those who purchased and shipped slaves in the *Caesar* in 1854, there was otherwise little circumstantial substance to their allegations of his continued involvement in slave-trading. The principal figure in the slave trade out of Ouidah in 1854–6 was a Spaniard called Domingo Mustich, whose chief establishments were at Agoué and Little Popo;[204] in 1854, he travelled as supercargo on the *Caesar* to Cuba and went on to Barcelona to organize the dispatch of further vessels from there (including the *Fernando Po*), before returning to Ouidah around the beginning of 1856.[205] In any case, the losses of ships and cargoes incurred quickly undermined enthusiasm for the attempt to continue the slave trade. At the end of 1854 it was reported that the slave-dealers in Ouidah had 'taken alarm' at these reverses and were 'now resuming the palm-oil trade', and in the following year that they were 'in a great state of despondency' at the loss of the *Fernando Po*.[206] Although there were rumours of subsequent shipments, these were not authenticated, and the commander of the British squadron in May 1857 stated that he '[did] not think any slaves have been shipped to windward [west] of Lagos for the last two years'.[207] In these circumstances, the price of slaves remained depressed: when the French negotiated with Gezo for the supply of slaves (under the guise of 'free emigrants') in 1857, the price agreed was only $50 per head.[208]

In the face of this eclipse of the slave trade, Gezo accepted the need to commit Dahomey completely to the palm-oil trade as an alternative source of income. He suspended the regular Dahomian military campaigns that had fed the slave trade, declaring to the French mission of 1856 that 'Peace is a good thing, it permits involvement in cultivation and trade'.[209] Although some of the established 'legitimate' traders, including the British firm of Hutton and the Hamburg merchant Diedrichsen, abandoned Ouidah for Lagos from 1852,[210] the trade at Ouidah also expanded. European visitors to Dahomey in the 1850s reported a great increase in

---

[202] PP, Slave Trade 1854–5, Class B, nos 17, 26, Campbell, Lagos, 12 Aug. and 1 Dec. 1854; 1855–6, no. 5, Campbell, Lagos, 2 June 1855.

[203] PP, Slave Trade 1855–6, Class B, nos 9, 28, Campbell, Lagos, 28 Aug. 1855, 6 Jan. 1856.

[204] Mustiche had engaged in illegal slaving at Popo already in the 1840s, but is not previously attested at Ouidah: Strickrodt, 'Afro-Brazilians'.

[205] PP, Slave Trade, 1854–5, Class B, no. 17, Campbell, Lagos, 12 Aug. 1854; 1855–6, Class B. nos 9, 28, Campbell, Lagos, 28 Aug. 1855, 1 Feb. 1856.

[206] PP, Slave Trade 1854–5, Class B, no. 26, Campbell, 1 Dec. 1854; 1855–6, Class B, no. 9, Campbell, 28 Aug. 1855.

[207] PP, Slave Trade 1857–8, Class A, no. 155, Commander Hope, 25 May 1857.

[208] Ibid., Class B, no. 25, Campbell, Lagos, 10 Aug. 1857.

[209] Vallon, 'Le royaume de Dahomey', 2/344.

[210] Newbury, *Western Slave Coast*, 57.

the production and export of palm oil. The French mission in 1856 noted that 'exports of palm oil are increasing each year', and 'the number of recently planted palm trees ... around nearly all the villages is incalculable'; the British missionary Freeman in the same year likewise had the impression of 'a great commercial change passing over and through Dahomey, the manufacture of palm oil is increasing to an enormous extent'.[211]

This perception of a substitution of the palm-oil trade for the slave trade was an oversimplification, in so far as a domestic market for slaves still existed: as Gezo himself told the British in 1856, although he had prohibited the export of slaves, 'he cannot interfere with the internal Slave Trade', a formula that enabled him to turn a blind eye to the sending of slaves from Ouidah along the lagoon for shipment elsewhere on the coast.[212] Indeed, given the labour-intensive character of the production and transport of palm oil and the fact that much of this labour was provided by slaves, this expansion of the palm-oil trade itself implied an increase in the domestic demand for slaves, albeit (at least to judge from the depressed prices noted earlier) not to a level sufficient to compensate for the loss of the overseas market. An expansion of the scale of slavery, presumably linked to the growth of palm oil production, seems to be reflected in a panic that gripped Ouidah, Godomey and other coastal towns in Dahomey in 1855, when an invasion was feared from the Yoruba state of Abeokuta, which was also alleged to have fomented 'an extensive conspiracy among the Anagoos [Yoruba] and other tribes of analogous origin, slaves to the Portuguese at Whydah, and to natives in other parts of the country'; the leaders of the supposed plot were arrested and carried off to Abomey.[213] Local tradition in Ouidah also recalls a plot to 'betray the town' by Yoruba slaves, who were liquidated ('lost') in punishment, which may relate to this incident, although the traditional account implicitly places it earlier, during the lifetime of the first de Souza.[214] The large-scale incorporation of slaves was also reflected in the growth of the size of the town. Estimates of its population during the 1850s range between 18,000 and 30,000, even the lowest of these figures – which is perhaps the most credible, as supplied by the informant most likely to be well informed, the missionary Freeman – being substantially higher than previous estimates (see Table 3.1). Such growth, reflecting the labour demands of the new economy of 'legitimate' commerce, was common to other towns of coastal western Africa at this period.[215]

At the same time, the Dahomian state sought to offset the loss of its revenues from the slave trade by asserting increased control over the expanding oil trade. In January 1852, after accepting the treaty for the abolition of the slave trade, Gezo raised the price of palm oil by 50 per cent (from $8 to $12 per measure) and also instituted a new duty of $4 per puncheon 'for rolling off the beach'. At the

[211] Vallon, 'Le royaume de Dahomey', 1/357; WMMS, Freeman, Porto-Novo, 2 April 1856.

[212] WMMS, Freeman, 2 April 1856.

[213] PP, Slave Trade 1855–6, enc. 5 in no. 10, McCoskry, 19 Aug. 1855.

[214] Gavoy, 'Note historique', 66.

[215] E.g. Luanda, whose population more than doubled (from 5,600 to 12,400): José C. Curto, 'The anatomy of a demographic explosion: Luanda, 1844–1850', *IJAHS*, 32 (1999), 381–405.

same time, it was announced that 'in future the King would monopolize the palm oil trade'; and in February it was reported that 'the King has taken possession of all the palm oil trees', sending agents 'to collect the fruits'.[216] It is doubtful whether this was intended to establish a royal monopoly of the oil trade on a permanent basis; more probably, this was a short-term emergency measure,[217] to meet the immediate fiscal crisis posed by the ending of the slave trade and perhaps also by the need to raise finance to redeem Dahomian captives taken in the defeat of an attack on Abeokuta in March 1851. Nevertheless, the 1850s were certainly marked by a higher level of state intervention in the palm-oil trade, including in particular the entry of the monarchy into the actual production of oil for export.

The kings of Dahomey had always maintained plantations, employing slave labour, around the capital Abomey, to provide food for the palace establishment, and these were now adapted and extended to produce palm oil for export. Standard accounts of royal palm-oil plantations in Dahomey, however, present a number of problems. The classic ethnography of Dahomey by Auguste Le Herissé refers to the kings settling large numbers of war captives on plantations around Ouidah to produce palm oil for export; however, this account is ambiguous, in that it also states that these royal oil plantations were managed by persons called *ahisinon*, which is the normal Dahomian term for the private merchants involved in the export trade.[218] References to royal palm-oil plantations in the contemporary accounts of the French mission in 1856 are similarly ambivalent:

> A certain number of individuals honoured with the title of king's merchants develop the immense estates which he has reserved to himself, sell the crops, and give him part of the profits ... [he has] vast plantations cultivated by his slaves, [whose crops] he sells through individuals who take the title *king's merchants*, and usually realize enormous profits in this trade.[219]

The term 'king's merchant' probably translates *ahisigan*, and the wording here also suggests that the reference is to private merchants in the Ouidah area; although technically such private merchants held their estates and slaves as gifts from the king, these were not 'royal' plantations in a strict sense. However, oil plantations under direct royal control were certainly also established. An important feature of the expansion of the oil trade in the 1850s was that the area devoted to oil palm cultivation was now extended geographically into the Dahomian heartland in the interior. Whereas earlier the production of palm oil for export appears to have been restricted to the area south of the Lama, the French missions of 1856–8 noted extensive oil-palm cultivation around Cana; and Burton in 1863 found the area between Cana and Abomey 'scattered with valuable plantations of the oil palm',

---

[216] PRO, FO84/893, T.G. Forbes to H.W. Bruce, 18 Jan. 1852; Forbes, Journal, 13 Jan. 1852; FO84/886, Fraser, 'Occurrences', 20 Jan. and 16 Feb. 1852.

[217] See Reid, 'Warrior Aristocrats', 299–301.

[218] Le Herissé, *L'Ancien Royaume*, 87, 90.

[219] Vallon, 'Le royaume de Dahomey', 1/343; Repin, 'Voyage', 100.

which he understood to belong to 'the King and his ministers'.[220] Some of the oil produced in the Abomey area was taken overland across the Lama for shipment from Ouidah, but the high cost of transport by human porterage over a distance of 100 km must have severely compromised the profitability of this option.[221] Alternatively and more cheaply, as will be seen below, it could be transported by canoe down the River Weme and across Lake Nokoué, to be shipped from Cotonou rather than Ouidah.

The entry of the monarchy into palm-oil production exacerbated the conflict of interest between it and the Ouidah merchant community, since they were now in direct competition in the supply of oil.[222] At the same time, royal taxation of private enterprise in the oil trade was racked up. The export duty of $4 per puncheon imposed in 1852 was presumably a tax levied on the foreign purchasers of the oil, distinct from and additional to that already levied on the Dahomian sellers (which was taken in the form of a share of the oil sold).[223] But taxation was also increased upon Dahomian subjects. The French missions in 1856–8 noted that the duties levied on the oil trade 'have become heavier and heavier, reaching both the producer in the interior, obliged to pass the royal customs-posts, and the purchaser at the coast'; the British consul at Lagos likewise observed in 1857 that although Ouidah and other coastal towns were now 'becoming enriched by the palm-oil trade', this was offset by 'the tyranny and exactions of the King of Dahomey, which are now, from the great reduction of his revenue, being acutely felt'.[224] The principal innovation in taxation in this period was the institution of a tax on the production, as well as the sale, of palm oil. Dahomian tradition recalls that Gezo adapted an existing tax on agricultural production, called the *kuzu*, which had earlier been levied on maize, millet and other food crops, to apply to palm oil, the transformation occurring 'at the time of the wars with Abeokuta', i.e. *c.* 1851. A new office, that of Kuzugan, was created to collect the new tax in Ouidah.[225] In the contemporary record, this tax on the oil harvest is first attested in the early 1860s.[226] The tax is said by tradition to have been based on a count of palm trees, and this is confirmed by Burton, who observed that palm trees north of Ouidah were 'numbered, with a view to revenue'.[227] Tradition indicates that the tax was levied at a rate of around one-third of estimated output (the same as on commercial incomes), the oil collected being sold on the king's account.[228]

These increases in regular taxation were accompanied by irregular exactions. Already in 1850, Forbes noted that merchants such as Adjovi, Gnahoui and

[220] Vallon, 'Le royaume de Dahomey', 1/353; PP, Slave Trade 1864, Class B, no. 9, Burton, 23 March 1864; Burton, *Mission*, i, 280.

[221] See Reid, 'Warrior aristocrats', 347–50.

[222] Bay, *Wives of the Leopard*, 281. Bay refers only to the Brazilians, but the argument applies equally to indigenous Dahomian merchants.

[223] Reid, 'Warrior aristocrats', 175–6.

[224] Vallon, 'Le royaume de Dahomey', 1/357; PP, Slave Trade 1857–8, Class B, no. 4, Campbell, 4 April 1857.

[225] Le Herissé, *L'Ancien royaume*, 86–7.

[226] Abbé Laffitte, *Le Dahomey* (Tours, 1874), 99. Laffitte was at Ouidah in 1861–4.

[227] Burton, *Mission*, i, 128.

[228] Herskovits, *Dahomey*, i, 114–15.

Houénou tried to conceal their wealth, in order not to attract the expropriatory attentions of the king.[229] The French mission in 1856 noted the wealth and importance of 'the king's merchants' who were engaged in the production of palm oil, but also that taxation of them was a principal source of royal revenue, including arbitrary exactions, sometimes disguised as 'loans'.[230] The Ouidah merchant community also continued to suffer rigorous enforcement of the royal inheritance tax. When Adjovi died, sometime during the 1850s, family tradition recalls that 'all his goods were plundered by the Dahomians', despite the family's attempts to conceal his wealth.[231] The harmonious relationship between the monarchy and the merchant community that had characterized the heyday of the illegal slave trade under the first de Souza came to an end in the new conditions of the palm-oil trade.

The British Methodist mission

The 1850s were also marked by the establishment of a British Methodist mission in Ouidah.[232] Gezo had requested the establishment of such a mission when Freeman first visited Dahomey in 1843, and had repeated the request on several occasions subsequently. The Methodists finally installed a resident missionary and opened a school at Ouidah in 1854 and then maintained their presence there until 1867. For most of this period, the resident missionary was an African from the Gold Coast, first Joseph Dawson (1854–6) and subsequently Peter Bernasko (1857–66). Also prominent in support of the mission was John Beecham, in origin a slave from Mahi who had been given to the mission (probably on Freeman's original visit in 1843), educated on the Gold Coast and returned to Dahomey, whom Gezo now employed as his intermediary with the Methodists.[233]

The strictly religious impact of the mission was minimal; in 1863/4 Burton found that its congregation numbered only twelve, who were mostly from the Gold Coast, with a total of 46 children enrolled in the school, who included a number of slaves who had been given as gifts by the king.[234] In part, the limited achievement of the mission was due to restrictions imposed by the Dahomian authorities, who explicitly envisaged the purpose of the Methodist presence as supplying religious and educational services to the existing 'English' community in Sogbadji ward, rather than evangelization of the population at large. In 1854 Gezo told Dawson, 'I give you the whole of the English Town & people to do all the good you can there for the present', and also held out the prospect of permitting the enrolment of children from the French and Portuguese quarters if these nations did not establish schools of their own. However, it was later made clear that this permission

[229] Forbes, *Dahomey*, i, 113.

[230] Vallon, 'Le royaume de Dahomey', 1/343; Repin, 'Voyage', 100.

[231] Reynier, 'Ouidah', 42, 47.

[232] Paul Ellingworth, '"As others see us": sidelights on the early history of Methodism in Ouidah', *Bulletin of the Society for African Church History*, 1 (1963), 13–17; 'As they saw themselves: more about the beginnings of Methodism in Ouidah', *Bulletin of the Society for African Church History*, 2 (1964), 35–41.

[233] WMMS, Freeman, Cape Coast, 20 July 1855; Burton, *Mission*, i, 122.

[234] Burton, *Mission*, 89–91.

extended only to the education of children of 'mulatto' families, rather than of Africans.[235] One leading Dahomian merchant, Gnahoui, did entrust three of his sons to the Methodists, to learn English, but these were sent for education in their mission at Little Popo rather than in Ouidah itself, presumably as a means of evading this restriction.[236] Moreover, by the 1850s there was no longer a Sierra Leonean community in Ouidah, such as formed the social basis of British Protestant missions elsewhere in the region, for example at Abeokuta and Lagos; the repatriate community in Ouidah, as has been seen, was Brazilian and therefore Roman Catholic in its religious allegiance.

Although the timing of the establishment of the Methodist mission was to some extent adventitious, it fitted in with Gezo's more general policy in the mid-1850s of promoting 'legitimate' trade as a substitute for the now languishing slave trade. The Dahomians evidently regarded the mission as an agency of the British government and expected it to promote British trade at Ouidah;[237] its semi-official status was underlined when in 1856, at Gezo's urging, it took over the former English fort, which had been vacant since the closing of the British vice-consulate in 1852.[238] These expectations of a revival of British trade were not realized, however. Although the mission itself did some trading in palm oil, this itself became a source of tension with the Dahomian authorities, who demanded that if the missionaries were to trade they should pay customs like other merchants.[239]

The beginnings of the decline of Ouidah and the rise of Cotonou

In aggregate value, the expansion of exports of palm oil (supplemented, from the mid-1860s, by palm kernels) on the face of it more than compensated for the decline of the slave trade. Figures compiled by Patrick Manning suggest that the combined value of slave and palm-produce exports from the Dahomey area in the 1860s had more than doubled since the 1840s (from £106,000 to £229,000 annually at current prices).[240] These figures relate to the wider area of colonial 'Dahomey' (modern Bénin) rather than to the kingdom of Dahomey alone, and may mask a shift of trade away from the latter towards Porto-Novo to the east; but whatever the precise share of Dahomey within the new palm-produce trade, it is difficult to believe that there was not an overall increase.

Nevertheless, European visitors to Ouidah in the 1860s described it as a town in visible decline. The British naval officer Wilmot, who had visited Ouidah in 1851/2 and returned in 1862/3, observed 'a great falling off in this place; twelve

---

[235] WMMS, Joseph Dawson, Ouidah, 23 Feb. 1855; William West, Cape Coast, 6 June 1859.

[236] They are said to have been educated 'in Togo': Obituary of Edouard David Gnahoui, in *La Voix du Dahomey*, no. 66, June 1932. Two of the brothers, Edouard David and Isaac Nahum Gnahoui were later patrons of the re-establishment of the Methodist church in Ouidah in the 1900s: Agbo, *Histoire*, 102.

[237] Paul Ellingworth, 'Christianity and politics in Dahomey, 1843–1867', *JAH*, 5 (1964), 209–20.

[238] WMMS, Freeman, Cape Coast, 14 Feb. and 15 May 1856.

[239] Vallon, 'Le royaume de Dahomey', 1/350–1.

[240] Manning, *Slavery, Colonialism* and *Economic Growth*, 332–3 (appendix II).

years ago it was in a flourishing condition, with many capital houses and merchants residing there; now, the houses are in ruins, and the trade small'. Burton in 1863/4 had a similar impression: 'Whydah is a ruined place, everything showing decay, and during the last three years it has changed much for the worse ... The place is temporarily ruined, and as dull as can be'; the reference to 'the last three years' suggests that he derived this view from the French Catholic mission, which had arrived in Ouidah in 1861.[241] The town's population was also in decline. Estimates in the early 1860s were generally lower than in the 1850s, between 12,000 and 15,000, and Burton reported explicitly that the Catholic mission believed that 'the population diminishes'.[242] Although this in part reflected emigration from the town resulting from political disaffection (as explained in the following chapter), it also supports the suggestion of economic decline.

The explanation for this apparent contradiction may be in part the lower profitability of the palm-produce trade. The merchant's commission on sales of palm oil was probably comparable to that on slaves, which in the 1840s was $16 out of a standard selling price of $80, or 20 per cent.[243] Given the higher cost of transport in the oil trade, however, it seems likely that net profits were lower. To the extent that Ouidah merchants had been able to move into the production as well as the marketing of palm oil, their income was presumably increased, but this was offset by the higher level of royal taxation during the same period. Moreover, the initially promising profitability of the palm-oil trade was compromised in the 1850s by a levelling off, if not an actual fall, in prices. But, even beyond this, it appears that much of the increased trade in palm oil from Dahomey in the 1850s and 1860s was in fact not passing through Ouidah. In estimates of palm-oil exports made by the British consul at Lagos in 1856–7, Ouidah is credited with only 2,500 tons annually, which, although two-thirds above the level of 1848, was hardly sufficient to compensate for the loss of slave exports.[244] A considerable proportion of the increased palm oil exports from Dahomey was now going from other ports to the east, on the shores of Lake Nokoué. Already in 1846, Godomey was described as 'a famous oil town', and Freeman in 1856, on a journey through the lagoons from Ouidah east to Porto-Novo, noted the expansion of the oil trade through Godomey and Cotonou, at both of which places factories formerly used in the slave trade had now been turned over to palm oil. He reported that 'several hundred thousand gallons' of oil had been shipped through these ports in the current season, while 'thousands upon thousands of gallons' could be seen stockpiled there.[245]

As seen in earlier chapters, both Godomey and Cotonou had originally been opened by the first de Souza, as bases for the illegal slave trade in the 1830s and 1840s, and they initially remained in the possession of the de Souza family after his

---

[241] PP, Despatches from Commodore Wilmot, no. 2, 10 Feb. 1863; Burton, *Mission*, i, 60, 115.

[242] Burton, *Mission*, i, 61. See chapter 3, Table 3.1.

[243] I have found no evidence relating specifically to Ouidah, but at Lagos in the 1850s the merchant was reported to receive 20%, the producer 80% of the selling price of palm oil: PP, Slave Trade 1855–6, Class B, no. 6, Campbell, Lagos, 2 June 1855.

[244] PP, Slave Trade 1856–7, Class B, enc. in no. 46, Report on the Trade of the Bight of Benin for the year 1856; 1858–9, Class B, enc. in no. 1, Report of the Trade of Lagos and the Bight of Benin for the year 1857.

[245] PRO, CO96/12, Hutton, Ouidah, 20 Dec. 1846; WMMS, Freeman, 2 April 1856.

death. In 1852 trade at Godomey and Cotonou was reported to be 'monopolized' by two of his sons, respectively Isidoro and Antonio.[246] Subsequently, however, the de Souzas lost control of these eastern ports: in 1856 Freeman found the factories at Godomey and Cotonou owned respectively by Nobre and Martins.[247] Nobre, as has been seen, had been a leading slave-trader at Lagos, who removed to Ouidah at the time of the British intervention there in 1851. After his death in 1858 other Brazilian traders were able to establish themselves in Godomey: Jacinto Rodrigues had a house there by 1859, where a British Methodist missionary lodged in transit from Badagry to Ouidah, and José dos Santos was also trading there by 1859.[248] The indigenous Dahomian merchant Azanmado Houénou also had a base in Godomey; the French Catholic missionary Borghero, passing through in 1862, found that some of his sons had a factory there, where he lodged.[249] As for Martins, his original establishment in 1846 had been at Sèmè (Porto-Novo) to the east; but by 1854 it was reported that he also had 'another establishment' at a place called 'Ape Vista', which (as seen earlier) was an alternative name for Cotonou.[250] At the time of Martins's death in 1864, it was noted that he 'had long been virtually king of Kutunun', although shortly before he died his monopoly was compromised when Glele gave permission for the French also to establish a factory there.[251]

Precise figures for the relative importance of the export trade of Ouidah, Godomey and Cotonou in the 1850s and 1860s are not available. The British consular reports of 1856–7 note that exports of oil from Porto-Novo and 'other ports between Badagry and Whydah', including Cotonou ('Appi Vista'), exceeded those through Ouidah: an estimated 4,000 tons in 1856, rising to 4,500 in 1857, but no detailed breakdown of the distribution of trade among these ports is offered. Another account of the 1850s, however, states that Martins was paying the king of Dahomey nearly $10,000 annually for the monopoly of the palm oil trade at 'Appi Vista';[252] if this refers to 'head-money', levied at the rate of one-third of income, it would imply a volume of around 1,400 tons of oil annually, over half the volume of exports at this time through Ouidah.[253]

There is also some uncertainty over the provenance of the palm oil exported through Godomey and Cotonou. The British Consul in 1859 asserted that the kingdom of Porto-Novo was supplying 'the whole of the palm oil' shipped not merely from 'Porto-Novo on the sea [Sèmè]' and 'Appi Vista', but also from Badagry

---

[246] PRO, FO2/7, Fraser, Commercial Report, enc. to Fraser, 15 May 1852.

[247] Freeman, 'West Africa', 489. The former is referred to only as 'Senr N.', but the details given (especially the reference to his having left Lagos in 1851) show that it was Nobre.

[248] WMMS, William West, Cape Coast, 6 June 1859; Reid, 'Warrior aristocrats', 421. Five of the letters in the dos Santos correspondence, nos 92–5 and 97, were written from Godomey, in July–Aug. 1863.

[249] Borghero, *Journal*, 108 [29 May 1862], giving the name as 'Couenou'.

[250] PP: Slave Trade 1854–5, Class B, no. 6, Campbell, 30 May 1854.

[251] Burton, *Mission*, i, 73.

[252] T.J. Hutchinson, *Impressions of Western Africa* (London, 1858), 71–2. Martins is not named, but the description of 'one of the oldest and most celebrated slave-dealing residents there' can only apply to him. This account places 'Appi Vista' west rather than east of Ouidah, evidently by miscopying.

[253] Assuming the price of oil to be $107 per ton and the broker's commission to be 20%, $30,000 dollars would represent the commission on about 1,400 tons.

to the east and Godomey to the west.[254] Godomey, however, from its geographical situation, must have derived its principal supply of palm oil from Dahomian territory, and Cotonou clearly also handled produce from Dahomey, as well as from Porto-Novo. The diversion of Dahomian oil exports to Godomey was probably due in part to the concentration of palm-oil plantations eastward of Ouidah, from where it was a shorter distance to shift produce for shipment from Godomey than from Ouidah. But oil was also delivered to Godomey by canoe, presumably from further north: Freeman described the landing there as 'crowded with canoes unlading palm oil'.[255] Even more clearly, the rise of Cotonou was due to its advantageous situation in relationship to water-borne transport across Lake Nokoué. In fact, produce could be delivered to Cotonou (and to Godomey) by canoe not only across Lake Nokoué, but also from the interior down the River Weme into the lake; Vice-Consul Fraser in 1851 learned that there was a 'deep waterway' connecting Cotonou to Cana.[256] Fraser noted that this route was 'kept secret', i.e. from Europeans, evidently for reasons of military security; it was indeed by the river that the French were to mount their invasion of Dahomey in 1892. But it was understood in the 1850s that slaves were brought from Dahomey to the coast by canoe down the River Weme,[257] so it is likely that, when commercial palm-oil production began in the Abomey area, some of it was likewise taken to the coast by this route. At Cotonou itself, moreover, a creek of the lake reached to within 100 metres of the seashore, thus minimizing the distance goods required to be transported overland to and from the beach.[258] This advantage would have become more critically important with the shift of the export trade from slaves to palm oil and kernels, whose greater bulk involved higher transport costs relative to their sale price at the coast.

It is clear, therefore, that the beginnings of the decline of Ouidah relative to Cotonou predated the establishment of French colonial rule and the construction of a wharf at the latter in the 1890s, which is commonly stressed as the principal factor in the rise of Cotonou, and were closely tied to the transition from the slave to the palm-oil trade. Having risen with the slave trade, the fortunes of Ouidah also declined with it.

---

[254] PP, Slave Trade 1859–69, Class B, no. 6, Campbell, 5 April 1859.

[255] Freeman, 'West Africa', 489.

[256] PRO, FO84/886, Fraser, Daily memoranda, 19 Nov. 1851; see also Journal, 2 Aug. 1851, reporting the existence of 'a creek which leads from Whydah to Egabomey [Abomey-Calavi?]', which afforded 'the quickest and best route to Abomey, and avoids the swamp [i.e. the Lama].'

[257] Letter of Samuel Crowther, Lagos, 10 Sept. 1856, in Hutchinson, Impressions, 271 (referring to the Opara, actually an affluent of the Weme).

[258] Tradition current later in the nineteenth century claimed that there had in fact formerly been a channel connecting the lagoon and the sea at Cotonou: Bouche, Sept ans, 8, 295 (citing 'les légendes et les chants populaires'). But contemporary evidence suggests that this can only have been an occasional occurrence, at times of exceptionally high water levels, as happened, for example, in 1804: King Hufon of Porto-Novo, 16 Nov. 1804, in Verger, Flux et reflux, 270 (not naming Cotonou, but presumed to relate to it). Hufon on this occasion asked the Portuguese to cut a canal from the lagoon to the sea, for military rather than commercial purposes (to present an obstacle to Dahomian troop movements). A channel was eventually cut by the French in 1885.

7

Dissension & Decline
Ouidah Under King Glele
1858–77

Although in the early 1850s Dahomey had appeared to be embracing the transition from the slave trade to that in palm oil with some success, later in the decade the oil trade began to run into difficulties. Most immediately, these were caused by a fall in the world price of palm oil. The price in the UK reached a peak of £48 per ton in 1854, but then declined, averaging only around £43 during the rest of the 1850s and falling below £40 in the 1860s.[1] How far this was reflected in prices paid on the African coast is unclear. As was seen in the previous chapter, the expansion of oil exports at Ouidah had been stimulated by a rise in prices to $8 per measure ($142 per ton) by 1852, and Gezo then decreed a further rise to $12 per measure ($213 per ton). By 1857, however, the price is quoted as 3 gallons to the dollar, or $6 per measure ($107 per ton) (see Table 6.1). On the face of it, therefore, prices were substantially lower from the mid-1850s; and in apparent confirmation, Burton in 1863/4 reported local complaints of 'commercial depression'.[2] Interpretation of these prices, however, is complicated by the depreciation of the local cowry currency, due to the importation of large quantities of the cheaper Zanzibar cowries from the 1840s onwards. Already in 1850, Forbes noted that, although the 'head' of 2,000 cowries still had a 'nominal' value of one dollar, actual silver dollars passed at between 2,400 and 2,600 cowries and cowries fell further to 5 heads for $3 (3,333 cowries to the dollar) in 1851, 2 heads (4,000) to the dollar by the beginning of 1852 and 2½ heads (5,000) by 1863/4.[3] This devaluation of cowries was reflected in an inflation of local prices: Burton in 1863/4

[1] Lynn, *Commerce and Economic Change*, 29, 112 (Tables 1.9, 5.2)

[2] Burton, *Mission*, i, 77.

[3] Forbes, *Dahomey*, i, 36; PRO, FO2/7, 'Commercial Report', enc. to Fraser, Fernando Po, 15 May 1852; FO84/886, bill of sale of a house from Jacinto Joaquim Rodrigues to Thomas Hutton, 21 Jan. 1852 [for 1,500 heads of cowries, or $750]; Burton, *Mission*, i, 143, n. The depreciation continued until the 1880s, by which time cowries had fallen to 20,000 to the dollar: for further documentation and analysis, see Robin Law, 'Cowries, gold and dollars: exchange rate instability and domestic price inflation in Dahomey in the eighteenth and nineteenth centuries', in Jane Guyer (ed.), *Money Matters* (London, 1994), 59–69.

reported that prices in the Ouidah market had doubled during the previous ten years.[4] It seems clear, in fact, that the prices given for palm oil down to 1852, although quoted in dollars, actually refer to payment in cowries, reckoned at the conventional rate of 2,000 to the dollar, and reflect, at least in large part, the declining value of cowries rather than a rise in the real price of oil, while the price of $6 per measure cited in 1857 was based on the contemporary exchange rate of 4,000 rather than the nominal rate of 2,000 cowries to the dollar, and was thus in fact identical with the price of '$12' proclaimed in 1852. Likewise, when in 1858 Gezo was again reported to have 'raised the price of palm oil', this too may have been an adjustment of the cowry price to take account of further depreciation.[5] Given that the price of oil in hard currency, as opposed to cowries, remained at around the same level down to the 1870s, it may be that the burden of the declining price of palm oil in world markets was absorbed by European purchasers rather than the African sellers.[6]

This is not to say, however, that the devaluation of cowries did not pose problems for African coastal merchants. The falling value of cowries must have tended to undermine the profits of the merchants who imported them and might now have to sell them on at a lower rate, and would also have operated to reduce the real value of debts outstanding to them from their local customers, if these were denominated in cowries (while they themselves could not settle their own debts to their European and American suppliers in this devalued currency). Moreover, it was not feasible to refuse to deal in cowries in the palm-oil trade, because of the involvement of large numbers of small producers who, as noted in the last chapter, were commonly paid in cowries. Domingos Martins in 1853–4, presumably in response to the depreciation of cowries, ordered large quantities of silver dollars from Britain, to exchange against palm oil, but found that 'as the natives who manufacture palm oil do not require specie … the supply of palm oil fell off'. It may be symptomatic of these difficult trading conditions that by 1859 Martins was rumoured to be 'on the verge of bankruptcy'.[7] It is also noteworthy that, unlike de Souza earlier, he did not succeed in passing on a substantial household to his heirs; although he did leave descendants in Ouidah (in Ganvè quarter), they were not especially prominent and in fact have been absorbed into the de Souza family.[8]

The revival of the slave trade, 1857–63

The attractiveness of the oil trade was further undermined by the reappearance of a viable alternative, with a revival of the slave trade. Around March 1857 reports

---

[4] Burton, *Mission*, i, 66.
[5] PP, Slave Trade 1858–9, Class A, no. 142, Rear-Admiral Sir F. Grey, Sierra Leone, 11 Feb. 1858.
[6] As also suggested at Lagos: Newbury, *Western Slave Coast*, 86–7.
[7] PP, Slave Trade 1854–5, Class B, no. 32, Campbell, Lagos, 7 Dec. 1855; 1859–60, Class B, no. 17, Campbell, Lagos, 7 Feb. 1859.
[8] See de Souza, *La Famille de Souza*, 254–8, for the family of a son of Martins, José Antonio Martins (surnamed Draye), whose son (born 1882) took the name Etienne Domingo de Souza.

reached the British consul at Lagos that 'the slave-dealers at Whydah had begun to purchase slaves largely, and were giving an increased price for them'; slaves were allegedly even being sent from Lagos to Porto-Novo, for sale on to Ouidah. This revived demand for slaves was also thought to account for a renewal of Dahomian military campaigns, with an attack on the Yoruba town of Ekpo, to the east, early in 1858. When Gezo died in November 1858, his son and successor Glele 'publicly proclaimed his intention to follow in the steps of his father, and to continue slave-hunts and the slave trade'.[9]

One factor in this revival of the slave trade was a French project for the recruitment of supposedly 'free emigrants' in Africa for the French West Indies, by the firm of Régis, which was in effect the revival of the slave trade under a cloak of legal pretence, the purchase of slaves being represented as their 'redemption' into liberty, prior to entering into supposedly voluntary contracts of indenture. The price stipulated in Régis's agreement with the Dahomian authorities, $50 per head, reflected the currently depressed state of the market for slaves. Although this plan caused considerable concern to the British, however, its practical effects as regards Ouidah specifically were negligible. When a steamship belonging to Régis finally arrived at Ouidah, in August 1857, intending to purchase 1,200 'free emigrants', it found that the project had been overtaken by a revival of the slave trade to Cuba, which pushed the price of slaves back up to a level with which Régis's agents could not compete; in the event it purchased only 40–50 slaves at Ouidah and went on instead to the Congo, where slaves could be obtained more cheaply. In March 1858, the British consul reported that 'the attempt to purchase slaves at Whydah as free emigrants has not yet been renewed by M. Régis, and, so long as the current value of slaves among the natives of this part of Africa continues so high as at present, it is not likely to be'. In early 1859 two steamships belonging to Régis again called at Ouidah hoping to purchase slaves, but negotiations conducted by the local French naval commander to give the French preference failed, and they again went on elsewhere.[10]

Much more significant in its impact on Ouidah was the revival of the slave trade to Cuba. This was associated not with the established Brazilian traders on the coast, such as Martins, but with a new company formed in Havana, called the 'Expedicion por Africa', whose ships were fitted out from the United States and sailed under US colours, in an attempt to secure some degree of protection from the British navy, which as yet had no legal authority to arrest US ships.[11] During 1857, this company sent five ships to the Bight of Benin for slaves. The first to arrive, the *Adams Gray* in April 1857, however, failed to obtain slaves at either Cotonou or Ouidah and left for the Congo instead (but was captured by the British navy before taking in any slaves). The reaction of the established traders in Dahomian ports was evidently unenthusiastic. At Cotonou, Martins declined to

---

[9] PP, Slave Trade 1857–8, Class B, no. 26, Campbell, Lagos, 31 Aug. 1857; 1858–9, Class B, nos 3, 17, Campbell, Lagos, 3 March 1858, 7 Feb. 1859.

[10] PP, Slave Trade 1857–8, Class B, nos 25, 35, Campbell, Lagos, 10 Aug. & 12 Oct. 1857; 1858–9, Class B, no. 5, Campbell, Lagos, 8 March 1858; 1859–60, Class B, no. 2, Campbell, Lagos, 4 March 1859.

[11] PP, Slave Trade 1858–9, Class A, no. 142, Grey, 11 Feb. 1858.

deal with the *Adams Gray*, advising it to try elsewhere since 'the Bight of Benin was now too closely watched'. The failure of traders at Ouidah to supply slaves to the same ship is explained, in different reports, as due to their hoping to be able to ship them instead on their own account for greater profit, or more simply because they were 'not ready'.[12] But a more critical factor may have been doubt about the profitability of the slave trade: two unnamed former slave-traders visiting Lagos at this time opined that, given that the *Adams Gray* was offering only $60–70 per slave, 'such trade ... is beneath their notice: the palm-oil trade is infinitely better'.[13]

Subsequent ships of the company, however, did succeed in obtaining slaves: in June 1857 one took in slaves at 'Praya Nova [New Beach]', a newly opened embarkation point five miles west of Ouidah, but succeeded in embarking only 70 before it was arrested by the British navy; and at the end of August another shipped 250–270 slaves from Ouidah beach but was then also captured.[14] Other embarkations from Ouidah were reported in September 1857, by two vessels apparently unconnected with the company, which together shipped over 400 slaves, these succeeding in evading capture.[15] During 1858 another ship was reported to have landed $25,000 in cash at Agoué in prepayment for a cargo of slaves, but was captured in May before taking any on board.[16] In January 1859 one ship intended to take slaves at Ouidah was taken by the British navy, but another succeeded in shipping 400 slaves, 200 each from Agoué and Ouidah; and in September three separate shipments totalling 1,300–1,400 slaves were made from Agoué and Porto-Seguro (though one of these was captured by the British).[17] During 1860, four recorded shipments of slaves were made from Ouidah, for a total of around 2,500 slaves. One of these, in May, was apparently the *Clotilde*, the ship on which Cudjo Lewis was transported, which delivered its slaves not to Cuba but to Alabama in the USA; another, in August, represented a significant technical innovation in the illegal slave trade (following the example of Régis), in the employment of a steam-powered ship, which embarked no fewer than 1,300 slaves in a single cargo.[18] During the first ten months of 1861, only a single shipment of slaves was recorded west of Keta, but there were further shipments in December 1861 and February 1862, the latter directly from Ouidah.[19] Although many of these shipments were made from ports west of Ouidah, most if not all of the slaves were thought to have originated

---

[12] PP, Slave Trade 1857–8, Class B, no. 8, Campbell, Lagos, 11 May 1857; Class A, enc. 2 in no. 166, Commander Burgess, Ouidah, 12 Aug. 1857.

[13] Ibid., Class B, no. 9, Campbell, Lagos, 11 May 1857.

[14] Ibid., Class A, enc. 1 in no. 159, Lieutenant Pike, 2 July 1857; Class B, no. 22, Campbell, Lagos, 5 Aug. 1857; Class A, enc. 2 in no. 166, Burgess, Ouidah, 12 Aug. 1857.

[15] Ibid., Class B no. 44, Campbell, Lagos, 3 Nov. 1857.

[16] PP, Slave Trade 1858–9, Class A. no. 133, Commodore Wise, 6 Aug. 1858.

[17] PP, Slave Trade 1859–60, Class A, enc. in no. 4, Extract from the *West African Herald*, 10 Feb. 1859; no. 95, Wise, Sierra Leone, 15 March 1859; no. 110, Wise, Cabinda, 16 May 1859; no. 150, Wise, Ascension, 23 Nov. 1859.

[18] PP, Slave Trade 1860, Class A, no. 57, Commodore Edmonstone, 2 Oct. 1860; Class B, nos 23–4, Acting Consul Hand, Lagos, 10 Sept. & 9 Oct. 1860. The *Clotilde* is not mentioned by name, but can be identified with 'a schooner under American colours' reported to have embarked 101 slaves on 11 May 1860.

[19] PP, Slave Trade 1862, Class A, enc. 1 in no. 82, Edmonstone, 7 Nov. 1861; enc. in no. 93, Commander Bedingfield, Lagos, 12 March 1862.

from there: as the British consul at Lagos observed at the beginning of 1862, 'Whydah alone is now to be looked upon as the slave-exporting station; shipments may occasionally be made at other places, but the slaves will in most cases be found to have been collected there.'[20]

The re-entry of Ouidah into the slave trade reflected not simply the renewed arrival of ships seeking slaves, but also the fact that this revived demand had the effect of bidding up prices to a point where the trade again became attractive: by August 1857, slaves were selling at Ouidah at $80 per head, a price that Régis's agents, who were then seeking to purchase 'free emigrants', could not match; and prices continued at this level into the early 1860s.[21] Nevertheless, it does not appear that this was sufficient to tempt the older-established traders such as Martins, back into slaving. Although Martins was from time to time accused by the British of involvement in the revived slave trade, and his death in January 1864 was assumed to be 'a sore blow ... to the slave interest at Whydah',[22] no clear evidence to this effect was ever cited; and Martins himself insisted in 1862 that 'he has given up the Slave Trade'.[23] The correspondence of José Francisco dos Santos in 1862–71 likewise shows him exporting palm oil, now to Europe as well as to Brazil, and kola nuts to Brazil; but does not contain any hint of involvement in the slave trade to Cuba. Among other leading former slave-traders of the older generation, Joaquim d'Almeida at Agoué had in any case died in 1857, and Nobre at Ouidah died in 1858.

The leading figures in the revived slave trade from 1857 onwards were newly arrived on the coast, or at least not previously prominent in trade at Ouidah. Some of them had personal and business links to Cuba and/or the USA, rather than to Brazil; and they mostly had their main bases not in Ouidah itself but at Agoué to the west. In 1857 the principal figure, described as the 'general agent for the slave trade at Whydah and the adjacent shipping ports', was Samuel da Costa Soares, who, although described as 'one of the ... old slave-traders', had not hitherto been sufficiently prominent to attract documentary notice. He was from metropolitan Portugal rather than Brazil, had links with Portuguese merchants resident in New York and was himself a naturalized US citizen, and his main base was at Agoué, rather than in Ouidah.[24] In 1859 slave ships sent to Ouidah were reported to be consigned to 'J.M. Carvalho' and 'Mr Baeta'.[25] The first of these is presumably identical with 'M.D. Joaquim Carvalho, called Breca', whose death on the coast was reported around the beginning of 1864 and who had been based at Grand-Popo earlier in the 1850s.[26] The second was João Gonzalves Baeta, already attested as

[20] Ibid., Class B, no. 7, Acting Consul McCoskry, Lagos, 7 Jan. 1862.
[21] PP, Slave Trade 1857–8, Class B, no. 25, Campbell, Lagos, 10 Aug. 1857; see Table 6.1.
[22] PP, Slave Trade 1864, Class B, no. 19, Consul Burton, Bonny River, 23 March 1864.
[23] PP, Slave Trade 1863, Class A, no. 91, Commodore Wilmot, off Lagos, Nov. 1862.
[24] PP Slave Trade 1857–8, Class B, no. 19, Campbell, Lagos, 27 July 1857; Turner, 'Les Brésiliens', 125–6.
[25] PP, Slave Trade 1859–60, Class B, enc. in no. 4, Extract from *West African Herald*, 10 Feb. 1859; Class A, nos 95, 117, Wise, Sierra Leone, 15 March, & off Congo, 9 June 1859.
[26] PP, Slave Trade 1864, Class B, no. 19, Burton, 23 March 1864; for his earlier activities, see Strickrodt, 'Afro-Brazilians'. But there was another Carvalho active in this period, Manoel Joaquim de Carvalho, whose activities were mainly centred at Porto-Novo: Newbury, *Western Slave Coast*, 64.

engaging in illegal slaving at Agoué earlier in the 1850s; he seems to have withdrawn from the business soon after, returning to Bahia (where he was one of the correspondents of dos Santos from 1862 onwards).[27] By the end of 1859, Agoué was the base of slave-traders called 'Maderes' and 'Swarey'.[28] Of these, the first was Francisco José de Medeiros, who was also Portuguese by nationality, in origin from Madeira, but resident for several years in Cuba; in the 1840s he had commanded an illegal slave-ship trading to Ouidah, but he is not attested at Agoué before 1859.[29] The second is apparently not the Samuel da Costa Soares of 1857, but a different man, João Suares Pereira, who was also Portuguese rather than Brazilian. He had a base at Ouidah, as well as at Agoué; he was described in 1864 as 'the principal [slave] dealer at Whydah'.[30] In 1867, after the slave trade to Cuba had come to an end, Suares Pereira and Medeiros were described as 'the last of the rich slave dealers'.[31]

Although primarily a response to changing market opportunities, in the revival of demand from Cuba, the renewal of the slave trade in the late 1850s also reflected internal political divisions within Dahomey.[32] Even at the height of enthusiasm for the new trade in palm oil, in the mid-1850s, there was apparently internal opposition to the new direction of Dahomian policy. The British Methodist missionary Freeman in 1854–5 had the impression that, whereas Gezo himself was favourable to the mission, others among the Dahomian chiefs were hostile, and, given the mission's identification with British influence and the promotion of 'legitimate' trade, he believed that these differences reflected divisions over commercial policy. In particular, he identified the Mehu as 'evidently in his secret heart opposed to improvements, and a staunch supporter of the Slave Trade', and the Yovogan of Ouidah also as 'entirely in the interests of the Slave Dealers there'. The French diplomatic mission that visited Dahomey in 1856 likewise noted the existence of a faction opposed to Gezo's policies: 'the old party discontented with Gezo's European tendencies', 'the party of resistance ... what would be called elsewhere, in Turkey for example, the old national party', which was led by the Mehu; and they also linked the Yovogan with him as having 'very little liking for the French, preferring the former slavers who heap them with presents'. Whereas the British Methodists had earlier regarded the heir apparent Badahun (the future King Glele) as favourable to them, however, the French in 1856 understood Badahun to be now in the 'national' faction.[33] Ultimately, the opposition attained such strength that it was able effectively to take over the government of Dahomey;

[27] Strickrodt, 'Afro-Brazilians'.

[28] PP, Slave Trade 1859–60, Class A, no. 158, Elphinstone, 21 Jan. 1860, with enc., Commander Bowen, Lagos, 21 Nov. 1859.

[29] For Medeiros, see Turner, 'Les Brésiliens', 126–7. He commanded the ship *Fortuna* from Havana, taken in the Bight of Benin in 1842: PP, Slave Trade 1842, Class A, no. 54.

[30] Burton, *Mission*, i, 74–5 n.; PP, Slave Trade 1864, Class A, no. 151, Wilmot, Ascension, 1 Dec. 1864.

[31] PP, Slave Trade 1867, Class A, no. 65, Commodore Hornby, Elephant Bay, 7 June 1867.

[32] Robin Law, 'The politics of commercial transition: factional conflict in Dahomey in the context of the ending of the Atlantic slave trade', *JAH*, 38 (1997), 213–33.

[33] WMMS, Freeman, Cape Coast, 12 March & 20 July 1855; Vallon, 'Le royaume de Dahomey', 1/341, 2/342; Repin, 'Voyage', 83.

a second French mission in 1858 described Gezo as 'only the shadow of his son and his Ministers', whose influence was blamed for growing hostility towards the French.[34] The implication is that the revival of the slave trade and of Dahomian militarism in 1857–8 represented the capture of the government by the conservative faction, rather than a change of mind on Gezo's own part. When Gezo died in 1858 these divisions were reflected in a disputed succession to the throne, the claim of his heir apparent being contested by a faction committed to the reforming policies of his father; Glele's succession thus represented, as Burton retrospectively observed, the triumph of the 'reactionary party'.[35]

The immediate issue in this internal opposition appears not to have been the promotion of the palm-oil trade as such, but rather the issue of human sacrifice, whose abolition Gezo proclaimed in 1853; but this renunciation of human sacrifice served to symbolize the abandonment of traditional Dahomian militarism and thus by implication of the slave trade, Dahomian military campaigns having historically supplied the captives who became both victims for sacrifice and commodities for export. This interpretation of factional divisions within the Dahomian ruling elite has been questioned by Edna Bay, who argues that the conflict over Glele's accession reflected an internal power struggle, rather than differences over commercial or foreign policy.[36] But these interpretations need not be regarded as contradictory, to the extent that policy differences would inevitably tend to crystallize around points of structural tension within the ruling establishment; and Bay's argument that the contemporary understanding that these disputes concerned the slave trade and human sacrifice represented merely a projection of British policy concerns does not account for the fact that the most explicit references to the existence of such factions occur in French rather than British sources.

The end of the Atlantic slave trade

In the event, the revival of the slave trade to Cuba proved short-lived. Renewed British diplomatic pressure on Dahomey to end its export of slaves, with missions to Glele at his capital by the commander of the local British naval squadron, Commodore Wilmot, in 1862–3 and by Consul Burton in 1863–4, was unsuccessful, the king merely insisting upon his need and intention to continue the slave trade. The British naval patrols had more impact, especially as their effectiveness was enhanced by the Anglo–US treaty of 1862, which finally conceded the right of search of American vessels, and thus ended the abuse of the US flag by illegal slave

---

[34] Protet, 20 May 1858, quoted by Soumonni, 'Trade and politics', 124–5. However, since by 1858 the French themselves were seeking to purchase slaves (under the guise of 'free emigrants'), their complaints may have related mainly to the Dahomian preference for selling slaves to Cuba (for higher prices).

[35] Francesco Borghero, 30 Sept. 1861, in 'Missions du Dahomey', *Annales de la Propagation de la Foi*, 25 (1862), 220; Burton, *Mission*, ii, 27.

[36] Bay, *Wives of the Leopard*, 263–73. Bay rejects the reports in 1856 of a split between Gezo and Badahun, and argues that the opposition to the latter's accession represented a struggle for control of the royal succession between the royal family and the mainly female palace organization.

ships.[37] Ouidah was subject to particular attention, Wilmot issuing instructions in 1863 that it was 'never to be left unguarded'.[38] But, as in the case of the ending of the Brazilian trade earlier, the ultimately decisive factor was the closing down of the Cuban market. This was partly a matter of pure economics, with a decline in the price of slaves in Cuba in the 1860s, which rendered importation from Africa no longer profitable; any prospect of a subsequent revival of the trade was killed by the belated enactment of more effective legislation to prevent illegal imports by the Spanish authorities in Cuba in 1867.[39]

The last trans-Atlantic shipment of slaves directly from Ouidah beach was on 20 March 1862, when the Spanish steamship *Noc d'Acqui* got away with 1,600 slaves for Cuba.[40] In October the same ship was back on the coast and a cargo of around 1,000 slaves was collected for it; but it found Ouidah so closely watched by the British navy that it was impossible to take on slaves there and instead they were sent along the lagoon for shipment from Agoué.[41] Following Wilmot's mission at the beginning of 1863, Glele was understood to have issued instructions that 'slaves, whether purchased from him or otherwise, are not to be shipped from the sea-board of his territory'; but as in the 1850s, this clearly did not preclude the sending of slaves along the lagoon from Ouidah for shipment elsewhere.[42] The last exportation of slaves for a trans-Atlantic market in which Ouidah was involved was on 10 October 1863, when another Spanish steamer, the *Ciceron*, shipped 960 slaves for Cuba from Godomey, though this cargo was confiscated by the Spanish authorities after delivery to Cuba. The slaves for this shipment were marched overland from Ouidah to Godomey; their passage east, under armed guard, was witnessed by the French Catholic missionary Borghero, who happened to be returning in the opposite direction, from a visit to Lagos and Badagry. According to Burton, who arrived in Ouidah a few weeks later, the successful embarkation was celebrated by those who had shipped the slaves with a banquet that lasted ten hours and was attended by 'legitimate' as well as slave-traders, who joined in 'pro-slavery toasts' along with the slavers.[43]

In fact, this celebration proved to be the swansong of the slave trade at Ouidah, since this was apparently the last shipment of slaves for Cuba from anywhere in the Bight of Benin. Although Glele, in negotiations with Burton at the beginning of 1864, still insisted that he would continue to sell slaves, his determination was irrelevant in the absence of ships to sell to. During 1864, Commodore Wilmot reported that in the Bight of Benin 'as far as I can learn, there has not been a

---

[37] The significance of the 1862 treaty is questioned by Eltis, *Economic Growth*, 210, who points out that no ships were actually condemned under its arrangements; however, it presumably operated as a deterrent.

[38] PP, Slave Trade 1864, Class A, no. 119, Wilmot, Sierra Leone, 31 Dec. 1863.

[39] For the argument that the Cuban trade 'died a market death', so that the 1867 legislation was significant only as a 'symbol', see Eltis, *Economic Growth*, 218–19.

[40] PP, Slave Trade 1862, Class B, no. 14, Consul Freeman, Lagos, 9 May 1862; WMMS, Henry Wharton, Cape Coast, 14 April 1862.

[41] PP, Slave Trade 1862, Class B, no. 25, Freeman, Lagos, 29 Oct. 1862; Borghero, *Journal*, 116–17 [20–21 Oct. 1862].

[42] PP, Slave Trade 1864, Class A, no. 119, Wilmot, Sierra Leone, 31 Dec. 1863.

[43] Ibid.; Borghero, *Journal*, 139 [9 Oct. 1863]; Burton, *Mission*, i, 115.

single shipment during the year', which he claimed was 'entirely attributable to the close blockade that has been established'; although the steamer *Ciceron* had reappeared on the coast west of Ouidah, off Porto-Seguro, in May, it had been unable to embark any slaves. The consequences for the slaves who had been assembled on the coast for shipment were not entirely positive, since there had been 'great mortality amongst them, from privations and disease of every kind'; of 2,000 reportedly collected for the *Ciceron* in May, no fewer than 800 had died by the end of the month. In 1865, Wilmot again reported that the slave trade from the Bights 'in consequence of the close blockade established and carried out, is virtually at an end. There has been no shipment of slaves from thence during the past year.'[44]

The local slave-traders had perhaps not yet given up hope, since in July 1864 João Suares Pereira travelled from Ouidah to London, by the steamer service from Lagos, in order to purchase ships, and intended if unsuccessful in England to proceed from there to New York for the same purpose; and the British understood (or assumed) that these ships were intended for use in the slave trade.[45] Presumably as a result of this mission, in the next year a ship called the *Dahomey*, owned by Pereira and Medeiros, sailed from New York via Lisbon to West Africa, arriving at Ouidah in December 1865. After some months' trading between Ouidah and places to the west, this vessel was arrested at Agoué in March 1866; but although the British claimed that over 600 slaves had been assembled at Agoué for shipment in the *Dahomey*, there was no conclusive evidence of its intention to ship slaves and it was eventually released.[46] After this, local hopes of a revival of the trade evidently evaporated. In 1867 Wilmot's successor as local British naval commander reported that 'The demand for slaves from Cuba has apparently ceased'; since the dispersal of the slaves collected for shipment in the *Dahomey* in the previous year, 'none, so far as we can hear, have been held in readiness for embarkation on that part of the coast'. Suares Pereira and Medeiros began dismantling their establishments at Agoué and shifting their business eastwards along the coast; as Medeiros explained to a British naval captain, 'The slave trade is finished for the present, so I am going into legal trade; your cruizers have not stopped it, but there is no demand from Cuba'.[47] Medeiros settled at Ouidah, founding a family that still survives today, in Sogbadji quarter.[48]

The ending of the export trade did not, of course, mean that the internal slave trade ended. In 1865 it was reported that 'the slave merchants who had collected a number for shipment are now selling them back to the natives, to work on their plantations'; one of their customers was the British Methodist mission in Ouidah, which 'redeemed' seven slaves at the end of 1864, at a cost of $60 each, a price that

[44] PP, Slave Trade 1864, Class A, no. 151, Wilmot, Ascension, 1 Dec. 1864; 1865, Class A, no. 83, Wilmot, Sierra Leone, 19 Dec. 1865.

[45] PP, Slave Trade 1864, Class A, no. 151, Wilmot, 1 Dec. 1864.

[46] PP, Slave Trade 1866, Class A, nos 37, 39, 43, case of the *Dahomey*; also no. 60, Hornby, Accra, 11 March 1866; 1867, Class A, no. 48, Hornby, Sierra Leone, 12 Feb. 1867.

[47] PP, Slave Trade 1867, Class A, no. 65, Hornby, Elephant Bay, 7 June 1867.

[48] Reynier, 'Ouidah', 67. This account says that Medeiros moved to Ouidah in 1863, but from contemporary sources it must have been a few years later. His residence there was noted in 1871: Skertchly, *Dahomey*, 67.

reflected the depressed state of the market.[49] In consequence, although its profit-ability was reduced, the gathering of slaves through Dahomian military operations continued, to supply the domestic market.

The revival of the produce trade

How the revival of the slave trade from 1857 affected the operation of the 'legiti-mate' trade in palm oil at Ouidah is unclear. British observers consistently reported that it disrupted the oil trade, but this may have represented only a projection of their a priori assumption of an incompatibility between the two trades, which has been seen to be ill-founded. When Gezo in 1858 raised the price of palm oil, although the British interpreted this as 'directly interfering with the legitimate traffic', this cannot logically have been its intended purpose.[50] The operations of the British naval squadron, however, inevitably created tensions with the Dahom-ian authorities: in October 1859, for example, the Yovogan interdicted the supply of provisions to British warships calling at Ouidah, although this ban was raised after a few weeks.[51] Moreover, Anglo-Dahomian relations were also strained in this period by British support of Abeokuta, which Glele was determined to attack (as he finally did, unsuccessfully, in 1864). In 1860, the British consul at Lagos threatened to destroy Ouidah and other coastal towns of Dahomey if any attack was made on Abeokuta, in response to which the Yovogan issued a warning at Ouidah that 'if the [British] Government do so, he would also kill all the English residents at this place'.[52] Glele was further angered by British attacks on Porto-Novo in 1861, which he regarded as an intrusion into his own sphere of influence.

At the beginning of 1861 it was reported that at Ouidah 'legal trade is com-pletely stopped', but, in fact, it appears to have been only specifically British traders who were placed under restraint, and in particular forbidden to communi-cate with the British naval squadron.[53] One British trader, Captain James Croft, in the service of the firm of King Brothers of Bristol, was arrested and fined by the local authorities for lending his boats to land a crew from a captured slaver.[54] In 1862, however, it was reported more generally that 'in the Kingdom of Dahomey agriculture is at a stand-still, and legitimate trade next to nothing', the explanation offered this time being that the mobilization of the population for military cam-paigns was diverting labour needed for agricultural production: 'the population of the villages is most scanty, and liable to be called out at any moment to go on some slave-hunting expedition'.[55] The disruption of palm-oil production by Glele's revival of militarism was to remain a recurrent complaint thereafter.

---

[49] *African Times*, 23 Sept. 1865, letter dated Grand-Popo, 29 July 1865; WMMS, West, Cape Coast, 9 Oct. 1866

[50] PP, Slave Trade 1858–9, Class A, no. 142, Grey, 11 Feb. 1858.

[51] PP, Slave Trade 1859–60, Class A, no. 158, Elphinstone, 21 Jan. 1860.

[52] WMMS, Bernasko, Ouidah, 31 Dec. 1860.

[53] PP, Slave Trade 1861, Class A, no. 62, Edmonstone, Ascension, 4 Jan. 1861.

[54] PP, 1865 Select Committee, § 5395–5401, James Croft.

[55] PP, Slave Trade 1862, Class B, no. 21, Freeman, Lagos, 1 July 1862.

Even before the ending of slave exports, however, the produce trade had revived. Wilmot in 1863 reported that the harassment of British traders by the Dahomian authorities had ceased, and 'the trade at Whydah has again been opened to a very considerable extent, and the King has given directions that all the produce of his country may be freely offered to merchants';[56] although Wilmot attributed this change of attitude to the influence of his own recent mission, it was more probably due to Glele's awareness of the declining scale and doubtful future of the slave trade and the consequent need to develop whatever alternative sources of revenue were available. Beyond this, the shift in Dahomian policy may also have reflected a changing balance of influence between the rival political factions in the capital. When in June 1863 a British merchant, William Craft, was received at Abomey by Glele, the latter assured him that 'there are no more hindrances between him and the English, because he has now put aside all rogue men'.[57] This may allude to events in May 1863, when the two leaders of the 'reactionary' faction, the Yovogan and the Mehu, had clashed with royal authority. First, the Yovogan was imprisoned and fined, for responding late to a summons to Abomey, the fact that the delay was due to illness not being regarded as sufficient excuse. Although the Yovogan's case was tried by the Mehu, as his overlord, the Mehu in turn shortly afterwards suffered an accusation from other chiefs and also had to pay a heavy fine.[58]

These improved conditions encouraged a newly formed British firm, the Company of African Merchants, to seek to develop a trade at Ouidah. They engaged Craft to act as their agent in Ouidah and he returned there at the beginning of 1864; in Ouidah, Glele granted him the house that had formerly belonged to Ignacio de Souza, at Kindji in Brazil quarter.[59] The company still had an agent in Ouidah in 1870;[60] but its factory was presumably abandoned soon after (the company itself going into liquidation in 1873). By 1868, another English firm, F. & A. Swanzy of the Gold Coast, also had an agent at Ouidah, who was able to take up residence in the English fort, which had been vacated by the Methodist mission in 1867.[61] During the same period, French trade at Ouidah was opened to greater competitiveness, with the breakup of the Régis monopoly and the formation of rival firms by former agents and associates of his, Daumas & Co. in 1866 and Cyprien Fabre two years later.[62] By the mid-1860s, exports of palm oil had recovered to levels comparable to those of the mid-1850s: Burton estimated exports from Ouidah as between 2,000 and 3,000 tons annually, while the trader Croft suggested 3,000 tons; the French merchant (and vice-consul) Béraud estimated it

[56] PP, Slave Trade 1864, Class A, no. 119, Wilmot, Sierra Leone, 13 Dec. 1863.

[57] WMMS, Bernasko, 5 June 1863.

[58] Borghero, 'Relation', in *Journal*, 256. Burton suggests that the Yovogan was punished for 'incivility to strangers': *Mission*, i, 211. But, although the fine followed soon after the Yovogan had himself fined the Roman Catholic mission in Ouidah (after the striking of the mission by lightning), Borghero does not connect the two incidents.

[59] PP, Slave Trade 1863, Class B, enc. in no. 38, Mr Fitzgerald to Foreign Secretary, 16 Dec. 1863; WMMS, Bernasko, Abomey, 30 Jan. & 3 June 1864; Burton, *Mission*, i, 92.

[60] PP, Slave Trade 1870, Class A, no. 56, Commodore Dowell, 6 March 1870.

[61] PP, Slave Trade 1869, Class A, no. 40, Dowell, 12 Jan. 1869; Skertchly, *Dahomey*, 46.

[62] Schnapper, *La Politique et le commerce français*, 193.

as between 2,300 and 2,700 tons.[63] From the mid-1860s, moreover, exports of palm oil were supplemented by those of palm kernels, also initially used mainly in the manufacture of soap, which were first reported as a significant item of trade in 1865.[64] By 1878, although palm-oil exports from Ouidah had fallen to only 500,000 gallons (between 1,500 and 1,600 tons) annually, this was now supplemented by exports of 2,500 tons of kernels; by value, kernel exports were equivalent to about two-thirds of those of oil.[65]

The organization of the African side of this trade was also undergoing some transformations in this period. Elsewhere on the coast, Martin Lynn has argued that the introduction of regular steamship services from Britain (beginning in 1852) facilitated the entry into the palm-oil trade of smaller-scale traders, on both the European and African sides of the trade, who could now hire cargo space on the steamers rather than needing to provide their own shipping. The trend was reinforced by the spread of the 'commission houses', which supplied goods to traders on the coast in return for selling their produce in Europe at a commission; those who exploited these new opportunities to enter the oil trade including not only Europeans but also many freed slaves from Sierra Leone.[66] It is doubtful, however, how far this process operated in Ouidah, which was not regularly visited by steamship services until the establishment of the French mail service in 1889; only occasional shipments were made by steamship from Ouidah in the 1870s, mainly by the British firm of Swanzy.[67] On the other hand, one of the leading new commission houses was the Company of African Merchants, which established a factory at Ouidah in 1864. Although there were no longer any significant numbers of Sierra Leoneans in Ouidah by the 1860s, a similar role could have been played by the Brazilian ex-slaves there.

That the steamship did have some impact on the conduct of trade at Ouidah is suggested by changes in the local system of taxation of trade. Lynn notes that elsewhere the earlier practice of charging ships for permission to trade according to their size became difficult to apply when a single steamer was carrying produce for a large number of different traders, and the practice was therefore replaced by a standard export duty on each puncheon of oil.[68] At Ouidah, an export duty of $4 per puncheon had already been imposed in 1852 and was additional to rather than in place of the payments demanded from each ship. The system of charging 'customs' according to the size of the ship (measured by its number of masts) was still operating there in the early 1870s when it was explicitly complained that this practice 'prevents anything like a small trade being transacted from a trading vessel, as the percentage would be too heavy'.[69] However, in 1875 it was noted that

---

[63] PP, 1865 Select Committee, § 2461, R.F. Burton; § 5541, James Croft; Béraud, 'Note', 385.

[64] PP, Slave Trade 1865, Class A, no. 83, Wilmot, Sierra Leone, 19 Dec. 1865; Reid, 'Warrior Aristocrats', 472.

[65] Serval, 'Rapport sur une mission au Dahomey', *RMC*, 59 (1878), 191. For comparative prices of oil and kernels, see Manning, *Slavery, Colonialism and Economic Growth*, 332–3 (Appendix 1).

[66] Lynn, *Commerce and Economic Change*, 115–16, 137–41, 155–9.

[67] Martin Lynn, personal communication, on the basis of Customs Bills of Entry (in PRO, CUST).

[68] Lynn, *Commerce and Economic Change*, 136.

[69] Swanzy, 'On the trade in Western Africa', 481.

there were various alternative methods of payment of duties at Ouidah; in addition to paying according to the number of masts of each ship, locally resident merchants could agree on a sum to be paid per annum, irrespective of how many vessels they received, while a further option was to pay a 2 per cent duty on goods landed.[70] From retrospective testimony, it appears that around this time the fixed payments were completely replaced by an import tax levied according to the value of goods imported, and at the same time payment in cowries was replaced by the taking of written vouchers for the value of the tax due, which were stored in the Yovogan's residence, to be redeemed against goods at the king's subsequent convenience.[71] The shift from cowries to payment in kind was probably due to the devaluation of cowries by the inflation that had occurred since the 1850s; but the change to *ad valorem* import duties might reflect the entry into the trade of steamships calling at Ouidah *en route* to and from Lagos, which were doing only a small part of their business there.

However, the changes that occurred in commercial organization in Ouidah seem to have followed a different pattern. James Croft, in his evidence to the British Parliamentary Select Committee on the West Coast of Africa in 1865, observed that the principal change in the operation of trade at Ouidah (and also Badagry) during the period of his experience, between 1851 and 1863, was that 'instead of trading with the natives, we have often to trade with Portuguese settlers in oil, now the slave trade is nearly done for'.[72] The implication is that former slave-traders were able to insert themselves as intermediaries between African suppliers and European purchasers of oil. In the longer run, however, the Brazilian merchants in Ouidah were not able to compete effectively with the European firms, with their greater capital resources, and survived only by becoming agents to the latter. An early example was Manoel Joaquim de Carvalho, who was serving as agent to the French firm of Régis at Porto-Novo by 1862–3 (when he played a prominent role in the negotiation of the first French protectorate over Porto-Novo).[73] In Ouidah, a Brazilian called J.C. Muniz evidently formed a similar partnership with the local Régis agent, Jules Lartigue; when the latter returned to France, he left Muniz to wind up his affairs – though when Muniz died in February 1863, leaving his own affairs in confusion, José dos Santos, who was one of his creditors, had to write to Lartigue in France to secure settlement.[74] In the following generation, the sons of leading Brazilian traders are to be found no longer as independent merchants but as subordinate agents of European firms. In the 1870s, for example, the son of dos Santos, Jacinto da Costa Santos, was serving as agent to the British firm of Swanzy.[75] Later, in the 1890s, after Swanzy's had withdrawn from the Ouidah trade

---

[70] PRO, FO84/1465, no. 83, Governor Strahan, Cape Coast, 22 Nov. 1875.

[71] Extraits des procès-verbaux du Conseil d'Administration de la Colonie du Dahomey, 17 & 25 Aug.1897, in Hélène d'Almeida-Topor, *Histoire économique du Dahomey* (Paris, 1995), ii, 277–8 (recording the change as having taken place about 20 years earlier).

[72] PP, 1865 Select Committee, § 5449–50.

[73] Newbury, *Western Slave Coast*, 64.

[74] Dos Santos correspondence, no. 88 [31 Jan. 1863]; also nos 97, 103 [26 July 1863, 3 May 1864, addressed to Lartigue].

[75] Foà, *Le Dahomey*, 33.

and sold its premises there to the German firm of Goedelt, a son of Francisco de Medeiros, Julio de Medeiros, likewise served as agent to the latter firm, while Georges Antonio de Souza (son of Antonio Kokou), worked for another German firm, Trangott-Sollmer.[76]

Ouidah versus Dahomey: conflict in the 1860s

The leader of the conservative opposition to Gezo, the Mehu, was the ultimate head of traders in Dahomey and overlord of Ouidah, and, as has been seen, European accounts of 1855–6 associate the Yovogan of Ouidah with him in this stance. It does not appear, however, that in this the Mehu and the Yovogan were speaking for the Ouidah merchant community as a whole. Although there is no evidence that the Ouidah merchant community, or any faction within it, played any direct role in the succession dispute of 1858, there is explicit evidence for disaffection in the town in the early years of Glele's reign. In 1860, the British consul at Lagos reported that the new king of Dahomey was 'much disliked at Whydah, his government being more intolerable than that of his father', and even suggested that 'at the present moment it would require but little to cause a revolt against the authority of Guelele'.[77] Although there may have been an element of wishful thinking in this assessment, it is supported by other testimony. The Methodist mission in 1861 also understood that Glele was 'now rendering himself hateful to many of his people', so that 'numbers of them are fleeing from his territory on the sea coast'.[78] Likewise Burton in 1864: 'The people of Whydah are worn out with wars and customs, and many of them are flying with their wives and families to the adjoining provinces'; he referred specifically to forty families who had recently fled from Ouidah to Porto-Novo to the east, lately brought under a French protectorate, 'as a land of liberty'.[79] This emigration from Ouidah, as well as the commercial decline noted earlier, evidently contributed to the fall in the town's population that Burton also reported.

The exodus from Ouidah noted by these observers involved in part runaway domestic slaves. The Methodist mission in 1861 suggested that their flight was motivated by fear of being seized for sacrifice in the funeral ceremonies for the late Gezo. More generally, with the revival of the slave trade to Cuba, they feared that they might now be sold for export. Already in 1858, before Gezo's death, it was reported that, since the revival of the slave trade at Ouidah, 'a considerable number' of slaves from there and other neighbouring towns had deserted their masters and made their way to Lagos to claim British protection: 'they all state as the cause of their desertion, the dread of being sold to the Spanish slave-dealers and carried away from their country'. Again, in 1860, a fugitive slave, whose owner was 'one of the Whydah dealers', turned up at Lagos, explaining that although 'he

---

76 Turner, 'Les Brésiliens', 303–5, 333.
77 PP, Slave Trade 1860, Class B, no. 8, Consul Brand, Lagos, 18 April 1860.
78 WMMS, Wharton, Cape Coast, 13 Aug. 1861.
79 PP, Slave Trade 1864, Class B, no. 19, Burton, 23 March 1864; Burton, *Mission*, ii, 85, n.

had been with his master several years ... from what he saw going on, he believed that it was intended to ship off all the old slaves as soon as possible, and for that reason he had made his escape'.[80]

But the disaffection in Ouidah clearly extended beyond slaves who feared sale into export or seizure for sacrifice, to include the population more generally and indeed the wealthy merchant class in particular. Glele's accession was marked by a spectacular clash with one of the leading merchant families of Ouidah, the de Souzas. The second Chacha, Isidoro Felix de Souza, had died in May 1858.[81] According to what Burton heard a few years later, Gezo initially appointed one of Isidoro's younger brothers, Antonio Kokou, to succeed him, but the latter soon provoked royal displeasure. As Burton was told, Antonio was 'a debauched man, rich, prodigal, and bigoted; he had thousands of armed and trained slaves; he built a swish house with rum instead of water, wishing to imitate the King, who for such purposes uses blood, and he threatened to compel Gezo perforce to become a Christian.'[82] Family tradition likewise recalls Antonio as a man of great bad temper, who maintained many soldiers. It also records his clash with royal authority, explaining that the de Souza family was under attack from the king, who was sending soldiers to break into their properties and seize family members for execution, including many of Antonio's brothers; and that Antonio organized his military retainers to defend the family.[83] The allusion to the execution of Antonio's brothers may conflate events that in fact occurred subsequently; but it is likely enough that the de Souza family was the subject of expropriatory attacks, including the seizure of family members, in the course of the levying of the royal inheritance tax on Isidoro's estate. Burton comments that '[Antonio's] career was short', which presumably means that he was dismissed by Gezo; at any rate, it does not appear that he was liquidated, since family tradition insists that he died naturally.[84] However, he evidently died soon afterwards.[85] According to Burton, the title of Chacha was then conferred on the third of the prominent de Souza sons, Ignacio, but he too did not last long. Probably in 1860 (and certainly after Glele's accession) he was accused of supplying information to the British anti-slaving squadron and 'mysteriously disappeared', and his property at Kindji was 'broken'; Burton in

---

[80] PP, Slave Trade 1858–9, Class B, no. 10, Campbell, Lagos, 27 March 1858; 1860, Class B, no. 8, Brand, Lagos, 18 April 1860.

[81] Corrêa da Silva, *Viagem*, 62, 83.

[82] Burton, *Mission*, i, 105–6.

[83] Fieldwork, Antonio Kokou Félix de Souza Adekpeti compound, 12 Dec. 2001; De Souza compound, Eusébio Frédérique de Souza, 12 Dec. 2001.

[84] De Souza, *La Famille de Souza*, 60, 110, says that Antonio was dismissed, but perhaps on the authority of Burton rather than of family tradition. Tradition among his descendants nowadays does not recall that he ever held the title of Chacha.

[85] De Souza, ibid., 60, suggests that Antonio Kokou lived until *c*. 1885, but on what basis is unclear. Burton in 1863/4 listed two Antonios among the surviving sons of the first de Souza, but one of these is distinguished by the surname 'Pito', and the second must be Antonio 'Agbakoun', who certainly survived until 1887. Burton also notes that 'the only grandson of any importance' was Kokou's son Antonio Francisco de Souza, which also implies that Kokou himself was already dead: *Mission*, i, 106, n. A recently repainted inscription in Antonio Kokou's burial chamber (seen in fieldwork, 12 Dec. 2001) gives the date of his death as 1854, which cannot be correct; perhaps it is a miscopying of '1859'?

1863 saw it still in ruins (and it was later, as has been seen, granted to the Company of African Merchants).[86] Precisely how Antonio's dismissal and the liquidation of Ignacio de Souza may have been connected with the disputes in the capital over the revival of the slave trade is unclear. The reported charges against Antonio suggest a direct challenge to royal authority, rather than differences over policy. However, that against Ignacio, identifying him with the British anti-slavery campaign, whether or not it was factually true, does by implication link his fall to the wider policy struggle.

According to a later account, in the crisis following Isidoro's death, Glele initially appointed another of the de Souza brothers, a second Antonio, this one surnamed 'Agbakoun', to the title of Chacha, but the appointment was annulled after protests from other traders at Ouidah, who complained that 'having never been to Brazil, he had no idea of the interests of the greater part of them'.[87] Presumably this abortive appointment followed the liquidation of Ignacio. Unlike the latter, however, Antonio Agbakoun was not liquidated but lived on until the 1880s. The title of Chacha was eventually given to another brother, Francisco 'Chico'. Unlike Agbakoun, this man had been to Brazil, having served as supercargo on the ship *Galliana*, owned by their brother Antonio Kokou, in a voyage from Bahia to West Africa in 1848/9, as noted in an earlier chapter, but otherwise had not attracted documentary notice. He had not previously been prominent in Ouidah and was living as a trader at Agoué prior to his appointment. The de Souza family at this point evidently went through considerable internal turmoil. A younger member of the family, Jeronimo Felix de Souza, who in 1861 presented himself at Elmina, the Dutch headquarters on the Gold Coast, for enlistment for service in the Dutch colonial army in Java, explained that he did so to escape 'maltreatment' on the part of his family, following the death of his parents.[88] Presumably, he was a son of Isidoro, Antonio or Ignacio. Wilmot in 1863 observed that 'the great families [*sic*] of De Souza are either dead or dispersed; those that remain are of small importance to what their fathers were'. Although the office of Chacha survived, it was now of little political or commercial significance, amounting to no more than the headship of the de Souza family. In 1860 it was reported that the office was 'little more than a name', and Burton in 1863/4 thought that the Chacha had 'little power'.[89]

The liquidation of the Chacha Ignacio de Souza was only the most dramatic of a series of clashes between Glele and members of the Ouidah merchant community. Other incidents involved indigenous rather than Brazilian merchants. The head of the Codjia family was arrested and his property confiscated shortly after Glele's accession: according to different accounts, either in revenge for a personal insult to Glele before his accession, because he had allegedly failed to pay his taxes in full or

[86] Burton, *Mission*, i, 91–2 (dating Ignacio's fall to 'four to five years ago', i.e. 1859/60), 106. Family tradition gives the date of his death as 1860: de Souza, *La Famille de Souza*, 150.

[87] Foà, *Le Dahomey*, 31.

[88] Larry Yarak, 'New sources for the study of Akan slavery and slave trade: Dutch military recruitment in the Gold Coast and Asante, 1831–72', in Robin Law (ed.), *Source Material for Studying the Slave Trade and the African Diaspora* (Stirling, 1997), 59, n. 70.

[89] PP, Despatches from Commodore Wilmot, no. 2, 10 Feb. 1863; Slave Trade 1860, Class B, no. 8, Brand, Lagos, 18 April 1860; Burton, *Mission*, i, 106.

simply because of the king's jealousy of his wealth. Although he was eventually released from prison, Codjia was relegated to his farm outside Ouidah and was only able to re-enter the city after the French conquest in 1892; presumably, this was not the Codjia who had been associated with the first Chacha but his successor as head of the family.[90] Toedji Hodonou (son of Dovonou) was also imprisoned, for reasons unspecified but probably in connection with a fine.[91] Tradition in the Dossou-Yovo family also recalls that the wealth accumulated by its founder Antonio Dossou-Yovo was seized by Glele.[92] Other substantial merchants of Ouidah abandoned the town in this period, the most prominent being Jacinto Rodrigues, who moved to Porto-Novo, according to family tradition in 1862, and remained in the latter town until his death in 1882.[93] Likewise Pedro Felix d'Almeida, probably also in the 1860s, moved back to Little Popo (his town of origin), following a dispute over payment of taxes.[94] Both these persons (or their families), however, continued to maintain households in Ouidah, which remain occupied by their descendants to the present.

Probably, as the cases of Codjia and Pedro d'Almeida suggest, the principal reason for disaffection in Ouidah was resentment over taxation, which was evidently being increased at this time. This was in part to meet the cost of the funeral ceremonies for the deceased King Gezo, to which wealthy Ouidah residents were required to contribute. At the end of 1858, the leading merchants from Ouidah and other Dahomian ports were summoned to the capital and required to bring both gifts of merchandise and victims to be offered as human sacrifices; the wealthiest of them, Domingos Martins, contributed 'large quantities of merchandise, rum, gunpowder, tobacco, &c.', as well as silverware and Havana cigars to be buried with the deceased monarch.[95] For the main ceremonies in 1860, Martins, the de Souzas and apparently José dos Santos were obliged to contribute further victims for sacrifice.[96] Increased expenditure was also being incurred in Glele's military expeditions and (after the Dahomian defeat at Abeokuta in 1864) to redeem Dahomian captives. In 1859, for example, on return from a campaign, Glele transmitted through the Yovogan a message to 'the White men, and merchants of Whydah' that they should 'go up and wash the King's hands, or, in other words, to go and congratulate him, and make him large presents to cover the expenses of the expedition', and again in 1862 'the people of Whydah and other adjacent towns' were ordered by the Yovogan 'to wash the king's hands', for which purpose about

---

[90] Hazoumé, *Le Pacte de sang*, 112–13; Bay, *Wives of the Leopard*, 236. Current family tradition claims it was the same man, but if he was still alive in 1892 this seems chronologically implausible: fieldwork, Codjia compound 13 June 1997.

[91] Reynier, 'Ouidah', 53. This clash is suppressed in current Hodonou family tradition, which maintains that the family's relations with Dahomian royalty were always friendly: fieldwork, Hodonou compound, 21 Sept. 2000.

[92] Fieldwork, Kokou compound, 9 Jan. 1996.

[93] Reynier, 'Ouidah', 45.

[94] Turner, 'Les Brésiliens', 109–10.

[95] PP, Slave Trade 1858–9, Class B, no. 17, Campbell, Lagos, 7 Feb. 1859.

[96] WMMS, Wharton, Cape Coast, 13 Oct. 1860, citing Bernasko, Abomey, 8 Aug. 1860, where 'Josey of Godomey' is probably José dos Santos.

4,000–5,000 heads of cowries were contributed.[97] But in the longer run, the increased taxation of this period also reflected the financial difficulties caused for the monarchy by the ending of slave exports: as was noted in 1866, 'The king is becoming daily more needy since the ending of the slave trade.'[98]

In addition to regular taxes and ad hoc levies, resentments were also generated by the operation of the inheritance tax. This was perhaps an especial grievance for the Brazilians, who subscribed to European notions of heritable property rights.[99] The property of Domingos Martins, for example, was seized for the king on his death in January 1864, the key to his house in Ouidah being appropriated by the Yovogan; officials were also sent to sequester his property at Cotonou, despite protests from the French authorities recently installed in Porto-Novo, seeking to act as protectors of Europeans and the security of their property.[100] The oppressive exaction of the royal inheritance duty in this period is also recalled in local tradition, in loaded language. At the death of Francisco de Medeiros in 1875, for example, family tradition recalls that his property was 'plundered by the Dahomians'; the explanation offered, that a 'caboceer' who was in debt to Medeiros and wished to destroy the accounts in which his debt was registered had falsely claimed that Medeiros had willed his goods to the king, suggests either misunderstanding or a retrospective attempt to deny the legitimacy of the royal right of inheritance.[101] On the death of the Chacha Francisco 'Chico' de Souza in 1880, likewise, the de Souza quarter in Ouidah was 'plundered', the blame in this instance being laid upon the heir apparent Kondo (the later King Behanzin), rather than Glele himself.[102] Ouidah also became notorious in this period for arbitrary seizures of property. It was a traditional prerogative of Dahomian kings to seize goods for the use of the palace, but this custom is said to have been 'nearly abolished' under Gezo. In 1861, however, Glele revived the practice, sending his agents into Ouidah to 'collect for the king everything which his envoys thought proper for his service', this official plundering continuing for the space of three weeks; many of the inhabitants sought to pre-empt confiscation by depositing their goods – 'provisions, brandy, cloth, pottery, etc.' – for safe keeping in the Portuguese fort, at this time occupied by the French Catholic mission, which it was assumed the royal agents would not violate. A similar official predatory visitation occurred in 1866.[103]

The effects of these fiscal exactions on the operation of trade at Ouidah are illustrated by the correspondence of José Francisco dos Santos during the 1860s. At the end of 1864, Glele forbade the sale of palm oil for Europeans, a prohibition maintained for at least 50 days, in order to buy all the oil himself (it is to be assumed, at low prices) in order to finance the redemption of captives taken in the defeat of the Dahomian army at Abeokuta. Dos Santos complained more generally

[97] WMMS, West, Cape Coast, 6 June 1859, 12 Aug. 1862.
[98] Fleuriot de Langle, 7 Oct. 1866, quoted in Schnapper, *La Politique et le commerce français*, 192, n. 1.
[99] Guézo, 'Commerce extérieur', 158.
[100] Burton, *Mission*, i, 73; Turner, 'Les Brésiliens', 227–8.
[101] Reynier, 'Ouidah', 67.
[102] Le Herissé, *L'Ancien Royaume*, 327, n. 1.
[103] Bouche, *Sept ans*, 186.

of the failure of the king to settle his debts: 'the King of Dahomey also sets out to be a thief! He buys and doesn't pay'; he owed dos Santos for tobacco from three separate shipments and also for some thousands of dollars' worth of cowries 'which I loaned him at Porto-Novo to redeem his prisoners and now he refuses to pay me'.[104] Likewise in the following decade, a British trader at Ouidah complained that 'The king's men occasionally seize all the palm oil brought to market and pay the owners a very low price in return.'[105] Beyond these narrowly fiscal issues, as noted earlier, it also appears that the revival of the slave trade and of Dahomian militarism under Glele had the effect of disrupting the palm-oil trade, since the mobilization of large numbers of men for military campaigns and for the cycle of ceremonies at Abomey withdrew labour from the agricultural sector. The ending of the trans-Atlantic slave trade did not mean the end of this problem, since Glele's military expeditions continued, bolstered in part by the continuing existence of a domestic market for the captives taken. The French vice-consul in 1866 still noted that the 'wars and continual ceremonies' of Glele were unpopular with his people, who were 'obliged to spend a large part of the year at the capital, ruining trade by making the exploitation of the palms almost impossible'.[106] Although reported in general terms, it is likely that these complaints reflect mainly the views of the merchant community in Ouidah.

Reorganization of the Ouidah administration

The eclipse of the power of the office of Chacha following the liquidation of Ignacio de Souza in 1860 was only one aspect of a far-reaching reorganization of the administration of Ouidah in Glele's early years. In 1860 it was reported that the king had appointed one of his close relatives at Ouidah 'to watch over and direct the proceedings of the Yer-vo-gar'.[107] Later accounts give this man's name as Chodaton.[108] According to tradition, he was a son of a brother of Gezo (and thus a grandson of King Agonglo). He is said to have been a trader in Ouidah before his elevation. His original name was Akodé; 'Chodaton' is a title or surname, meaning 'the king owns everything', evidently expressive of the purpose of his appointment, as an assertion of royal control in Ouidah.[109] The appointment of members of the royal family as deputies to leading officials was not entirely new but had been initiated under Glele's predecessor Gezo;[110] but the absence of any reference to

104 Dos Santos correspondence, no. 105 [19 Jan. 1865].
105 Swanzy, 'On the trade in Western Africa', 482.
106 Béraud, 'Note', 375–6; see also Serval, 'Rapport', 188.
107 PP, Slave Trade 1860, Class B, no. 8, Brand, Lagos, 18 April 1860.
108 In contemporary sources, e.g. 'Tchiudato', in Borghero, *Journal*, 55 [10 Oct. 1861], etc.; 'Schoundaton', in Laffitte, *Le Dahomé*, 93; 'Chudatorry', in PP, Slave Trade 1863, Class A, no. 91, Wilmot, Nov. 1862; 'Chyudaton', in Burton, *Mission*, i, 209.
109 Reynier, 'Ouidah', 48. Akodé may be identified with a 'Dahoman prince' who attended a religious service conducted by the missionary Freeman at the newly opened Methodist chapel in the English fort in 1856: WMMS, Freeman, Cape Coast, 15 May 1856.
110 Le Herissé, *L'Ancien Royaume*, 33; also Glélé, *Le Danxome*, 118, 142; Bay, *Wives of the Leopard*, 177–8.

such a royal deputy to the Yovogan in the abundant contemporary documentation for the 1840s and 1850s suggests that its extension to the Ouidah administration was an innovation. The purpose of the practice, as understood by Burton, was to 'neutralize' the officials inherited by Glele from his father without immediately dismissing them, 'by appointing as their aids younger men, of higher rank in the empire', in order to 'keep the elder in check'.[111] The fact that this practice was applied not only to officials who had opposed Glele's accession but also to his partisans, such as the Yovogan, implies that his intention was to avoid becoming the prisoner of the 'national' faction by reducing the influence of all officials in order to enhance effective royal power.

Gezo had also introduced (or perhaps elaborated) the appointment of women of the royal palace as counterparts (termed 'mothers') to senior officials.[112] Here again, although Forbes and other sources of the 1850s noted the existence of female counterparts to the Migan and Mehu and to senior military officers, there is no explicit evidence in contemporary sources for a 'mother of the Yovogan' (Yovogannon) under Gezo. Burton in 1863, however, records meeting a 'she-Yevogan', called Na Dude Agoa, who was one of Glele's wives, and this woman is also recalled (under the name Miagbe) in palace tradition;[113] here too, therefore, the extension of the system to Ouidah was probably an innovation of Glele. These female counterparts remained resident within the palace, where they served as intermediaries between the king and his officials. The system operated as a means of royal control over the latter, the women attending interviews between the king and the officials whom they shadowed and serving as a sort of oral archive of relevant information.[114]

Glele also around this time reorganized the Ouidah merchant community, raising one of the leading indigenous Dahomian merchants, Azanmado Houénou, to primacy of status within it. According to Ouidah tradition, as recorded by the French administrator Reynier in 1917, Glele on his accession to the throne 'raised Quénum to the rank of great caboceer and ahigan [i.e. *ahisigan*] (chief of the ahissinou), and in short gave him a preponderant position, and all the ahissinous of the kingdom were placed under his control'.[115] This wording is ambiguous, leaving unclear whether 'great caboceer' and *ahisigan* are alternative names for the same office, or represent two separate appointments, though, since (as seen in an earlier chapter) the rank of *ahisigan* was not unique to Houénou but was shared with other leading merchants (namely, Adjovi, Codjia, Gnahoui, and Hodonou), logic would suggest the latter, and this interpretation is supported by the contemporary evidence of Burton, who in 1864 described Houénou as 'before an akhi-gan, or "king's merchant", now promoted to the captaincy of all traders at Whydah'.[116] Quénum family tradition also distinguishes Azanmado Houénou's original

---

[111] Burton, *Mission*, i, 53.

[112] Bay, *Wives of the Leopard*, 239–41. Tradition claims that the system dates back to the reign of Tegbesu (1740–74), but it is not clearly documented in contemporary sources before the nineteenth century.

[113] Burton, *Mission*, i, 297, 366–7; Bay, *Wives of the Leopard*, 209.

[114] Herskovits, *Dahomey*, i, 110–11.

[115] Reynier, 'Ouidah', 63.

[116] Burton, *Mission*, ii, 126, n.

promotion to the rank of *ahisigan* from a subsequent commission for the 'reorganization' of trade in Dahomey, which placed all the *ahisinon* 'under [his] authority', but dates both appointments to the reign of Gezo rather than of Glele;[117] more probably, Houénou was made an *ahisigan* by Gezo but raised to the higher rank by Glele. A French missionary who met Houénou in 1861 describes him as 'minister of commerce', which may translate either the generic rank *ahisigan* or the higher office to which he was now appointed.[118]

The pre-eminence of Houénou was reinforced by the eclipse of the other four indigenous merchant families whose heads had shared the status of *ahisigan*. The banishment of Codjia and the imprisonment of Hodonou were noted above. The founder of the Adjovi family had died earlier, during Gezo's final years. To judge from the lack of reference to them in later contemporary sources, none of these families was able to maintain its wealth and standing into the following generation. The Gnahoui active in 1843–51 was probably also dead or no longer held his post as official interpreter for the English, since he is not mentioned in this capacity in the records of the British Methodist mission from 1854, or of the British government missions to Dahomey in the 1860s. One of his daughters was married to Glele, but this connection may predate the latter's accession.[119] A Gnahoui, perhaps his son, is mentioned incidentally in the records of the French Catholic mission in 1864, when one of his sons was among Dahomians taken prisoner in the unsuccessful attack on Abeokuta, and Father Borghero subsequently recognized the young man in captivity and arranged his redemption.[120] A younger member of the family, Edouard David Gnahoui, who had been educated by the British Methodist mission, served as interpreter to the British firm of Swanzy in the 1870s.[121] Otherwise, here too, the silence of the contemporary record suggests that the family's status was in eclipse. In contrast, when Azanmado Houénou died in 1866, he was succeeded in his rank of 'great caboceer and ahi[si]gan' and evidently also as head of all traders at Ouidah by his son Kpadonou Houénou.[122]

The precise nature of the office to which Azanmado Houénou was appointed and to which Kpadonou Houénou succeeded in 1866 is not made very clear in these accounts. According to family tradition, the elder Houénou became, at some point, the sole agent for royal trade: '[the King] entrusted only to Houénou, to the exclusion of any other intermediary, the captives which passed through Ouidah before their embarkation';[123] and this is corroborated by a contemporary report of 1871, which describes the younger Houénou as 'the king's agent', 'the agent of the king in all matters with white people'.[124] Effectively, therefore, he replaced the

---

[117] Quénum, *Les Ancêtres*, 61–3.

[118] Laffitte, *Le Dahomé*, 198–202.

[119] Bay, *Wives of the Leopard*, 212.

[120] Borghero, *Journal*, 159–60 [19 April 1864].

[121] Obituary of Edouard David Gnahoui, in *La Voix du Dahomey*, no. 66, June 1932.

[122] Reynier, 'Ouidah', 63. The dating of Azanmado's death to 1886 in Quénum, *Les Ancêtres*, 70, is clearly a misprint for '1866'.

[123] Quénum, *Les Ancêtres*, 61: actually referring to Houénou's position before his appointment to overall authority, when he merely had the rank of *ahisigan*, but this must be a confusion.

[124] Skertchly, *Dahomey*, 13.

Chacha as the king's commercial agent. The office also involved the collection and transmission of income tax from other traders: as the traditions recorded by Reynier about the elder Houénou recall, 'it was to him that [the *ahisinon*] paid their annual contributions, he himself added his own and passed the whole to the King'.[125] Between 1864 and 1871, the functions of the office were also extended to include the collection of taxes on the European trade, and in market transactions in Ouidah, which had earlier been the responsibility of the Yovogan and his subordinate officials: in 1871 it was noted that the younger Houénou 'inspects all ships' cargoes, and receives the customs duties' and was also serving as 'caboceer' of Zobé, the principal market of Ouidah, meaning presumably that he was responsible for the collection of sales taxes in it.[126] The authority of the office evidently extended over resident Brazilian traders as well as indigenous Dahomians: when in 1876 José da Costa Santos, then operating as agent to the English firm of Swanzy, was accused of misconduct, it was Houénou who conducted the resulting inquiry and imposed a fine upon Santos.[127] The office thus represented a greater concentration of formal authority, if not of effective political influence, than had hitherto existed within the Ouidah merchant community.

The politics of the appointment of Azanmado Houénou to this new position, beyond that it was evidently intended to supersede the now eclipsed Chacha, are unclear. Although the context of the factional divisions surrounding Glele's accession might seem to indicate that the elder Houénou would have been a partisan of the revival of the slave trade, as against the disgraced de Souzas, the example of the appointment of the Chodaton raises the possibility that it might equally have been a means of circumscribing the power of the Yovogan. However this may be, it is clear that in the longer run the Houénous had to accommodate to the reality of the eclipse of the slave trade and therefore the necessity of developing 'legitimate' trade to make up the lost revenues. The younger Houénou is credited by tradition with persuading Glele to develop the trade in palm-kernels, in association with the French merchant Béraud, and against the opposition of the Yovogan, who argued that the kernels were needed for the use of the army, in lighting fires; he is also said to have established extensive palm plantations, using the labour of the slaves who were now no longer exportable.[128] A British visitor in 1871 records visiting an oil plantation belonging to Houénou.[129]

Burton's account of Dahomian court ceremonial in 1863 shows that the Chodaton ranked second in the Ouidah hierarchy, after the Yovogan, and Houénou only third.[130] Whether formal precedence corresponded to the real distribution of power, however, is uncertain. Burton himself thought that the eclipse of the Chacha had left 'the whole authority of the place' concentrated in the hands of the Yovogan.[131] But he may have underestimated the power of Houénou, whom he

[125] Reynier, 'Ouidah', 63.
[126] Skertchly, *Dahomey*, 32, 45.
[127] Foà, *Le Dahomey*, 33–4.
[128] Reynier, 'Ouidah', 63–4.
[129] Skertchly, *Dahomey*, 23, 33–4.
[130] Burton, *Mission*, i, 209–10.
[131] Ibid., i, 106.

seems not to have met personally.[132] A treaty with France negotiated at Ouidah in 1868 was 'signed' by Yovogan Dagba and the Chodaton, but not by the younger Houénou, but this may mean only that the latter had no formal responsibility in political, as opposed to commercial, matters.[133] In any case, the effective power of Yovogan Dagba was presumably undermined by his advancing age. Dagba was still alive, although now 'a very old man', in 1871;[134] but he evidently died soon afterwards.[135] In 1871 Houénou was thought to be the principal power in Ouidah, exercising 'almost regal sway' within the town.[136] However this may be, it appears that the appointment of Chodaton and Houénou to these new positions of authority within Ouidah created tensions with the Yovogan Dagba. Local tradition records that Glele resolved these tensions by a division of responsibility among the Ouidah chiefs, placing Sogbadji quarter and the English fort under Houénou, Docomè and the Portuguese fort (and also Maro quarter) under the Yovogan and Ahouandjigo with the French fort under Chodaton.[137] Contemporary sources confirm that Chodaton was charged specifically with relations with the French: Burton in 1863/4 describes him as the 'landlord' of the French, and a French account of 1878 as having responsibility for 'the oversight of foreign trade and, in particular, the protection of the French'.[138] The Brazilian quarter is not mentioned in this administrative partition of Ouidah, perhaps because it remained under the authority of the Chacha.

The lower levels of the Ouidah administration were also reconstructed under Glele, although its detailed functioning is difficult to grasp. Burton names a number of subordinate 'caboceers' but without making clear their precise functions or their relations either with each other or with the three leading offices of the Yovogan, Chodaton and Houénou. The 'fourth caboceer of Whydah', ranking immediately after these three, was now Hechili; he was no longer, as in 1849–51, 'caboceer' of the English fort, but no indication of his current duties is given.[139] The office of Boya, who under Gezo had served as deputy to the Yovogan, is barely mentioned and was evidently now in eclipse; presumably because, on the death of Gezo's appointee Boya-Cissé, his heir, although inheriting his title, did not succeed

---

[132] Burton mentions Houénou three times. In a formal reception at Cana, he noted that Houénou ('Wenu') was represented by his 'place', he himself being absent. Subsequently, he twice saw Houénou ('Ukwenun', 'Kwenun') in processions, but does not record meeting him face to face: ibid., i, 209, 313 n.; ii, 126 n.

[133] Treaty of 19 May 1868, text in Aublet, La Guerre, 8–10.

[134] Skertchly, Dahomey, 51. Skertchly does not name the Yovogan, but observes that he 'was raised to the office of viceroy in the beginning of the reign of Gezu'.

[135] Family tradition dates his death to 1880: Dagba, La Collectivité familiale, 42. But according to other traditions he was succeeded as Yovogan by Zinhunmé and the latter in turn by Sèkloka: Agbo, Histoire, 56. Sèkloka was already in office by 12 May 1877, when he signed a treaty with Britain ('Sachloca, the Avogah of Dahomey'): text in PP, Treaty of Friendship, Commerce, and for the Suppression of the Slave Trade, between Her Majesty and the King of Dahomey (1878).

[136] Skertchly, Dahomey, 13.

[137] Reynier, 'Ouidah', 64, seemingly garbled; cf. Quénum, Les Ancêtres, 75, with n. 2; Dagba, La Collectivité familiale, 44, evidently derived from a different and more accurate version of the same text.

[138] Burton, Mission, i, 209; Serval, 'Rapport', 186.

[139] Burton, Mission, i, 368. The post of 'caboceer' of 'English Town' was now vacant: ibid., i, 65.

to his substantive office.[140] On Burton's arrival at Ouidah, in the absence of the most senior officials, he was formally greeted by officers called 'Nyan-kpe' and 'Ainadu', the former described as 'acting-viceroy for Gezo, the last king' and the latter as 'acting-viceroy for Gelele, the present king', which presumably means that they were deputizing respectively for the Yovogan and the Chodaton.[141] The first of these seems to represent Gnahouikpé, the name of a family in Fonsaramè that claims descent from a Dahomian official; although not mentioned in Forbes's account in 1849–50, he is documented in the records of the British vice-consulate in 1851–2, when he was understood to be 'next in authority' under the Boya, so perhaps he succeeded to the latter's position.[142] The second name 'Aïnadu' occurs later, among the signatories of a treaty with France in 1890, when he is described as 'treasurer' to the Ouidah administration.[143] Other officials from Ouidah observed by Burton taking a prominent role in ceremonial processions included Noudofinin, still listed as overseeing the Chacha's 'Brazil' quarter, and 'Nuage', described as a half-brother to Glele, and therefore presumably another of the royal counterparts appointed to shadow commoner officials.[144] Oddly, Burton does not mention the new office of Kuzugan, who collected the tax on palm-oil production – unless perhaps this was the position now held by Hechili. In the contemporary record, the Kuzugan is first mentioned in 1890, also among the signatories of the treaty with France, when he was 'acting as Yovogan' during a vacancy in the latter office.

The Christian missions under Glele, 1858–71

The shifting commercial and political context also affected the fortunes of Christian missionary enterprise in Ouidah. As seen earlier, a British Methodist mission had been established in Ouidah since 1854. The mission had always been treated by the Dahomian authorities as a medium of communication with the British state, rather than an independent religious agency, and it consequently suffered when Anglo-Dahomian relations deteriorated under Glele after 1858. In the first place, Glele's revival of Dahomian militarism and the slave trade affected attitudes towards the mission, which was identified with the reformist policies of the late Gezo. In 1859 Glele informed the head of the mission, Peter Bernasko, that he was aware that the Christian God 'forbids killing [i.e. human sacrifice], selling [i.e. slaves] and the worship of Fetish', and that therefore 'if my people be allowed to hear the word of God they will be changed and become cowards and they will not serve the Fetish with me neither will they go to war'; and he said that the mission would have to relinquish possession of the English fort in Ouidah so that it

---

[140] Burton mentions the Boya ('Bonyon') only as 'caboceer' of 'Portuguese Town', which may be copied from the earlier account of Forbes rather than reflecting current conditions: ibid., i, 65.

[141] Ibid., i, 52–3.

[142] Reynier, 'Ouidah', 53; PRO, FO84/886, Fraser, Journal, 23 July 1851 ['Nar-o-pay'].

[143] Treaty of 3 Oct. 1890, text in Aublet, La Guerre, 74–5.

[144] Burton, Mission, i, 208–9, giving the former title as 'Nulofren'; cf. i, 64, listing 'Nodofré' as 'caboceer' of 'Brazilian Town'.

might be made available for the use of merchants and other British visitors.[145] When later relations further soured over the issues of Abeokuta and Porto-Novo, threats were made against the mission: in 1860, when the Yovogan threatened to kill British residents at Ouidah in the event of a British attack on the town, he specified that 'the Missionary should be the first person', and recurrently during the following year Bernasko was warned that he would be 'lost' if the British should intervene to assist Abeokuta.[146] Conversely, the improvement of Anglo-Dahomian relations from 1862 ameliorated conditions for Bernasko, whose services as diplomatic intermediary were again required, as in the missions of Wilmot and Burton. However, when Wilmot pressed the king to allow freedom of access to the mission school, Glele reiterated the established policy that only 'any of the mulattoes can send their children', and he repeated to Burton his objection that 'when black men learn to read and write ... they could not be taken to war'.[147]

The position of the Methodists was undermined, however, by the arrival of the French Catholic mission in 1861, which led to the withdrawal from their school of children of Brazilian families in the town.[148] It was also weakened by the loss of the interpreter John Beecham, who was dismissed for taking a wife 'after the country fashion' and by 1865 was working in a secular school established by the merchant William Craft.[149] Bernasko himself came under increasing criticism from the mission itself, for alleged drunkenness and toleration of 'fetish' practices within the British fort (scandals retailed by Burton) and also for supposedly holding slaves (a misrepresentation of his having purchased slaves to 'redeem' them). He was eventually forced to resign in 1866, when he refused to obey an instruction to transfer to Winnebah on the Gold Coast. He remained in Ouidah thereafter, running a hotel for European sailors and according to the hostile testimony of one observer, this included supplying the services of his daughters as prostitutes.[150] There was clearly an element of racial prejudice in the criticism of Bernasko, the mission stating explicitly its desire to appoint a white missionary to the post instead. Ironically, the European who replaced him himself turned out to be an alcoholic, who absconded from Ouidah when his wife fell ill in 1867. He was not replaced, and the Methodist mission lapsed, to be revived only after the French colonial occupation.

The Roman Catholic church had also been represented in Ouidah since 1844, by the chaplains of the Portuguese fort, appointed from São Tomé. The priest appointed in 1859, Claudio Fernando de Lencastre, is alleged to have both alienated his congregation and fallen out with the Dahomian authorities; threatened with prosecution, he fled to Agoué but was caught and brought back to Ouidah.[151] At this point, however, in April 1861 a party of missionaries of the French Société des

---

145 WMMS, West, 10 Feb. 1860; Bernasko, Ouidah, 1 Oct. 1860.
146 WMMS, Bernasko, Ouidah, 31 Dec. 1860; Wharton, Cape Coast, 13 April 1861, citing Bernasko, Abomey, 28 March 1861; Bernasko, Ouidah, 1 Nov. 1861.
147 PP, Despatches from Commodore Wilmot, no. 1, 29 Jan. 1863; Burton, *Mission*, ii, 281.
148 WMMS, West, Cape Coast, 11 March 1863.
149 Ibid., 15 June 1865.
150 Skertchly, *Dahomey*, 16, 49.
151 Borghero, *Journal*, 45 [20 April 1861].

Missions Africaines of Lyon arrived in Ouidah.[152] Although these were also treated by the Dahomian authorities as representatives of the secular power of France and, like the British Methodists, they had little impact in terms of conversions, they were able to play a much more significant role in Ouidah society through their relationship with the substantial pre-existing Roman Catholic community represented by the Brazilian immigrants. By 1863 they had administered 208 baptisms and had 100 pupils enrolled in their school, with an average attendance of 70.[153] The missionaries found, in fact, that they had to use the Portuguese language to communicate with their congregation; on their first arrival, the head of the mission, Francesco Borghero (actually himself Italian), knowing no Portuguese, preached in Spanish in order to make himself understood;[154] and the mission school subsequently used Portuguese as its language of instruction. For present purposes, indeed, the brief history of the Catholic mission is principally of interest for the light it sheds on the internal workings of the Ouidah Brazilian community.

On arrival in Ouidah, the missionaries initially lodged in the Régis factory in the French fort, but within a short while they were able to take over the chapel in the Portuguese fort, in the process ousting the priest from São Tomé whom they found in possession. Their takeover of the fort was done with the consent of the Yovogan and also with support of at least a substantial element within the Brazilian community. Borghero's account in fact implies that he had the unanimous consent of the Brazilian community, who were allegedly disgusted at the immoral behaviour of the incumbent São Tomé priest.[155] It is noteworthy, however, that there is no reference to the Chacha, Francisco 'Chico' de Souza, playing any role in these transactions. The most active initial supporter of the French missionaries within the Brazilian community was João Pinheiro de Souza, surnamed Taparica, who loaned his slaves to repair the roof and windows of the chapel in the fort and supplied one of his slaves to act as interpreter;[156] Pinheiro de Souza was a Portuguese official, who had been appointed notary of the fort from São Tomé in 1852 but had latterly been effectively abandoned by the Portuguese authorities.[157] The mission was also backed by the leading trader Domingos Martins, who paid for restoration of the chapel doors and supplied palm oil for its lamps, and on a subsequent occasion paid for the repair of the roof.[158] Although some children of the de Souza family were initially recruited into the mission school, they were

---

[152] For the French Catholic mission in Ouidah, see esp. Jean Bonfils, *La Mission catholique en République du Bénin* (Paris, 1999), chs 3–5; also Christiane Roussé-Grosseau, *Mission catholique et choc des modèles culturels in Afrique: L'Exemple du Dahomey (1861–1928)* (Paris, 1992); Rosario Gordano, *Europei e Africani nel Dahomey e Porto-Novo: "Il periodo della ambiguità" (1850–1880)* (Turin, 2001), 61–94; and original documentation in Paul-Henry Dupuis, *Histoire de l'église du Bénin, t. I: Le Temps des sémeurs (1494–1901)* (Cotonou, [1998]).

[153] Borghero, 'Relation', in *Journal*, 265, 280.

[154] Borghero, *Journal*, 46 [21 April 1861].

[155] Ibid., 44–9 [20 April–10 May 1861].

[156] Ibid., 47 [2 &10 May 1861].

[157] Corrêa da Silva, *Viagem*, 81, 83–4.

[158] Borghero, *Journal*, 47 [7 May 1861], 134 [12 May 1863].

expelled in the following year for alleged involvement in theft, which must have further soured relations.[159]

As Burton noted, unlike the British Methodists, the French Catholics in Ouidah adopted an attitude of uncompromising hostility towards indigenous religious practices and consequently clashed recurrently with the local community.[160] An initial confrontation occurred in 1863, when the Portuguese fort was struck by lightning and Borghero attempted to prevent the priests of the thunder-god Hevioso from carrying out the necessary rites of propitiation and purification, but was arrested by the Yovogan and forced to pay a fine of $100.[161] In June of the same year the mission was involved in a further dispute, arising from their eviction of a python, sacred to the god Dangbe, which had entered its premises.[162] The position of the mission may also have been weakened by the death of its principal patron Domingos Martins in January 1864. More clearly, it suffered from a comeback in influence by the de Souza family, who were able to reassert their claim to control of the Portuguese fort. In April 1865 the Chacha Francisco 'Chico' de Souza made contact with the Portuguese authorities on São Tomé, whose governor made an official visit to Ouidah, where the French missionaries were evicted from the fort and the Chacha was formally invested with the office of its governor.[163] The French missionaries, however, retained the allegiance of a considerable section of the Brazilian community; a declaration in their support was signed by several other leading Brazilians, including José dos Santos, Marcos Borges Ferras and Angelo Custodio das Chagas.[164] Another Brazilian trader, Francisco Antonio Monteiro, granted the mission alternative premises within Ouidah, in Zomaï quarter.[165]

A final crisis occurred in 1871, when a child in the mission's care died and the mission head was arrested and fined by the Yovogan, in the face of which the mission was evacuated.[166] The head of the mission withdrew to Lagos and, when a separate Dahomian mission was created in 1874, its headquarters were at Agoué, rather than Ouidah. The Ouidah mission was re-established only a few years before the French colonial occupation, in 1884, under Father Alexandre Dorgère.[167]

The rise of Cotonou, continued

The 1860s were marked not only by the final ending of the trans-Atlantic slave trade but also by the beginnings of formal European imperialism in the area east of Ouidah, beginning with the British annexation of Lagos in 1861, followed by that

[159] Ibid., 48 [11–18 May 1861], 109 [30 May 1862].
[160] Burton, *Mission*, i, 70–1.
[161] Borghero, *Journal*, 130–2 [1–2 May 1863]; WMMS, Bernasko, Ouidah, 30 April 1863.
[162] Burton, *Mission*, i, 71.
[163] Corrêa da Silva, *Viagem*, *passim*; for a view from the French missionary side, see Dupuis, *Histoire de l'église du Bénin, t. I*, 121–6.
[164] Turner, 'Les Brésiliens', 195.
[165] Ibid., 195–6; Dupuis, *Histoire de l'église, t. I*, 127–8.
[166] Dupuis, *Histoire de l'église, t. I*, 180–82.
[167] See René F. Guilcher, *Au Dahomey avec le Père Dorgère* (Lyon, n.d.).

of Badagry in 1863. This provoked the French into counter-measures to defend their own position, with the appointment of a vice-consul for Ouidah and Porto-Novo (an office conferred on Régis's local agent) and the negotiation of a treaty of protectorate with Porto-Novo in February 1863.[168] The French interest in Porto-Novo also had the effect of focusing attention on the coastal port of Cotonou, control of which was necessary for access to the Porto-Novo market, and in July 1863 the vice-consul visited Abomey and obtained from Glele a verbal agreement to what the French understood as the 'cession' of Cotonou to France, but which Glele probably intended merely as permission for them to establish a trading post, in return for payment of $4,000 annually. Domingos Martins, who had hitherto enjoyed a monopoly of commerce at Cotonou, was understandably furious, commenting bitterly that 'he had learned these people too late', and some attributed his death in January 1864 to a fit of apoplexy brought on by the news.[169] Although the Porto-Novo protectorate was abandoned, in the face of local opposition, at the end of 1864, the claim to Cotonou was not given up. In May 1868 the French vice-consul negotiated a treaty with the Dahomian authorities at Ouidah confirming the cession of Cotonou, although the port was to remain under Dahomian administration until the French should establish effective occupation, which they made no immediate move to do.

In part, this focusing of French attention on Porto-Novo and hence also on Cotonou, rather than on Dahomey and Ouidah, reflected the relative political and military weakness of the former kingdom, which left it more readily susceptible to European influence. In particular, the French could play upon Porto-Novo's fears of the British, who had already carried out naval bombardments of the town in 1861, as well as of Dahomey. But it also reflected the fact that, with the shift from the slave trade to trade in palm produce, Porto-Novo, which was more favourably situated in relation to areas of palm oil production in the interior, was in fact becoming commercially more valuable than Dahomey.[170]

The rise of Cotonou was not, however, solely dependent on its role as an outlet for Porto-Novo. It acquired an additional importance as a side-effect of the British annexation of Lagos and the consequent imposition of increased import duties there, which led to the landing of goods destined for Lagos at Cotonou, from where they were taken east to Lagos by canoe through the lagoon in order to evade these duties.[171] Although goods landed at Cotonou had to pay customs duties to the Dahomian authorities there, these were lower than British duties at Lagos. Cotonou also, as noted in the last chapter, handled produce originating from within Dahomian territory to the north-west. The increasing importance of this trade is indicated by the opening of a new Dahomian port on the shore of Lake Nokoué which played a key role in the palm-produce trade, at Abomey-Calavi (or, in

[168] Schnapper, *La Politique et le commerce français*, 194–8; John D. Hargreaves, *Prelude to the Partition of West Africa* (London, 1963), 110–18.

[169] Burton, *Mission*, i, 72–3.

[170] Michel Videgla, 'Le royaume de Porto-Novo face à la politique abolitionniste des nations européennes de 1848 à 1882', in Law & Strickrodt, *Ports of the Slave Trade*, 135–52.

[171] Bouche, *Sept ans*, 295; Serval, 'Rapport', 193.

nineteenth-century sources, alternatively Abomey-Kpevi, 'Little Abomey'), north of Godomey. Abomey-Calavi is already attested as a centre of trade in the 1770s, when it was serving as a market for slaves brought from Oyo, presumably by the lagoons from Porto-Novo and Badagry. It reappears in the contemporary record in 1862, when the missionary Borghero, on a voyage by canoe back from Lagos, found the channel from Lake Nokoué to Godomey impassable and landed instead at Calavi.[172] In Borghero's time there were no European factories at Calavi, but another French missionary, Pierre Bouche, who spent two periods on the coast between 1866 and 1875, noted that the French had recently opened factories at Calavi and that, by the time he left the coast in 1875, it had grown in importance at the expense of Godomey; Quénum family tradition credits the establishment of the first French factory at Calavi to the second head of the family, Kpadonou Houénou, in 1871.[173] Whereas Godomey had its own roadstead at the seashore, Abomey-Calavi shipped its produce by canoe across Lake Nokoué to be exported through Cotonou.[174]

Bouche noted that Calavi served as an outlet for palm produce from the interior of Dahomey: 'the offices at Agbomé-Calavi intercept the goods coming from the north'.[175] To what extent use was made of water transport to deliver this produce to Calavi is unclear. In the 1860s the Weme waterway was still 'prohibited to whites', although at least one European did subsequently use this route, in 1874, going from Cana overland to the Weme and then by canoe downriver to Porto-Novo and Cotonou.[176] One report states that the Dahomians also prevented 'the local people' from navigating the river, but this perhaps means only that they prohibited merchants from independent coastal communities such as Porto-Novo from proceeding upriver.[177] The increased commercial prominence of Abomey-Calavi in the 1870s may reflect the growing importance in the supply of palm produce of the royal plantations in the Abomey area, relative to the privately owned farms south of the Lama; by 1871 a European visitor to Dahomey thought that 'the greater part of the oil exported' originated from the king's plantations.[178] Alternatively, it may have represented increased exploitation of the facility for cheaper transport by canoe down the Weme, in preference to the head-loading of produce overland to Ouidah.

The second British blockade of Ouidah, 1876/7

As was noted earlier, the ending of the slave trade to Cuba by the mid-1860s did not end the tensions between Ouidah and Dahomey. The divisions arising from Glele's accession persisted beyond the 1860s. It is likely that these continuing

[172] Borghero, *Journal*, 108 [29 May 1862].
[173] Bouche, *Sept ans*, 298; Quénum, *Les Ancêtres*, 73–5.
[174] Bouche, *Sept ans*, 295; Serval, 'Rapport', 192–3.
[175] Bouche, *Sept ans*, 298.
[176] Map of the Slave Coast, after Borghero (1865), reproduced in Newbury, *Western Slave Coast*, opp. 77; Buzon, 'Une visite à la cour du roi de Dahomey en 1874', *Revue politique et littéraire*, 51/24 (1893), 759.
[177] Béraud, 'Note', 374.
[178] Skertchly, *Dahomey*, 271.

tensions were reflected, as Patrick Manning has suggested, in conflict over the succession to Glele himself, which developed from the 1870s onwards.[179] Glele initially appointed one of his sons, called Ahanhanzo, as his heir apparent, but his claim was contested by another son, called Kondo, and when Ahanhanzo died prematurely, it was alleged that he had been poisoned (or killed by occult means) by Kondo. Kondo in turn was installed as heir apparent in 1876, and it was he who eventually succeeded Glele, under the name Behanzin, in 1889. There is some suggestion that Ahanhanzo was associated with a policy of relative friendliness towards European influence, while Kondo stood for more uncompromising resistance. Consistently with this hypothesis, Kpadonou Houénou, the head of the Ouidah merchant community, supported the claims of Ahanhanzo against Kondo.[180] More generally, Ouidah tradition systematically demonizes Kondo/Behanzin, who is depicted as consistently and virulently hostile not only towards the Houénous but towards the town in general.

The tensions that existed both within the Ouidah merchant community and between it and the Dahomian monarchy are illustrated by the story of the Anglo-Dahomian dispute of 1876–7, which provoked a second British naval blockade of Ouidah.[181] The confrontation with the British arose out of a minor intra-Dahomian quarrel. The Brazilian trader Jacinto da Costa Santos (son of José Francisco dos Santos, who had died five years earlier) gave offence to the newly installed heir apparent Kondo by refusing to sell a particular sort of cloth to him on the plea that stocks were exhausted, but a rival within the Brazilian merchant community, Julião Felix de Souza (brother of the Chacha and seemingly a more prominent trader), seized the opportunity to discredit Santos by alleging that supplies of the cloth were, in fact, available.[182] Glele charged Kpadonou Houénou, in his capacity as 'chief of traders' in Ouidah, to investigate the matter, and Houénou imposed a fine on Santos and seized his property to settle it. The British were drawn in because Santos was employed as agent by the British firm of Swanzy, whose local head, Henry Turnbull, protested that the property seized from Santos in fact belonged not to him but to the company. When he failed to obtain satisfaction, he threatened to invoke the support of the British naval squadron, and this in turn provoked his own arrest by the Ouidah authorities; he was manhandled, partly stripped and detained during a hot afternoon on a rubbish heap without his trousers. Turnbull then called in the local British naval commander to secure redress; the latter visited Ouidah in February 1876 and, in an irrregular and unprecedented usurpation of authority, imposed a fine of 500 large puncheons (250 tons) of palm oil on the Dahomian authorities. Glele, however, refused to pay and, in July 1876, the British instituted a blockade of the Dahomian coast in an attempt to enforce settlement. According to local tradition, the British also fired on the town on this occasion,

[179] Patrick Manning, 'Le Danhomè face aux contradictions économiques de l'ère impérialiste, 1858–1889', Colloque internationale sur on 'La Vie et l'Oeuvre du Roi Glélé', Abomey, Dec. 1989.

[180] Quénum, Les Ancêtres, 85.

[181] For which, see Catherine Coquery, 'Le blocus de Whydah (1876–1877) et la rivalité franco-anglaise au Dahomey', CEA, 7/25 (1962), 373–419; Hargreaves, Prelude, 201–7.

[182] Foà, Le Dahomey, 33.

although the contemporary sources refer only to threats of bombardment.[183] The blockade was maintained for ten months and was ended only when the French merchants in Ouidah, whose trade was being disrupted by the British action, offered to pay the fine on Glele's behalf. Under an agreement reached in May 1877 the fine was reduced to 400 puncheons of oil, of which the firms of Régis and Fabre paid a first instalment of 200 (but the remainder was never paid). A treaty was also signed with the Yovogan at Ouidah, but this merely reiterated and conflated the terms of the earlier Anglo–Dahomian treaties of 1847 (guaranteeing freedom of commerce) and 1852 (abolishing slave exports) and was clearly no more than a device to save the British government's face.

Although the episode was most obviously significant as a harbinger of the more aggressive European imperialism of the later nineteenth century and in exacerbating Anglo–French rivalry, it also served to bring to a head tensions between the Dahomian monarchy and the Ouidah merchant community. These were evident even in the early stages of the dispute, when the local Ouidah authorities, led by the Yovogan, were initially willing to pay the fine but were overruled by the king, who insisted upon defiance of the British.[184] In the aftermath of the blockade, Glele took punitive action against several members of the Ouidah merchant community whose actions during it he judged to have been disloyal, including both Brazilians and Dahomians, several of whom were summoned to Abomey and detained there.[185] Among the Brazilians subjected to varying periods of detention in the capital were Francisco Rodrigues da Silva and the Chacha's brother Julião de Souza.[186] The Chacha himself, Francisco Chico, although not called to Abomey, was held under house arrest in Ouidah for several days.[187] The most distinguished victim of the purge, however, was the indigenous merchant Kpadonou Houénou. Julião de Souza, when summoned to Abomey, contrived to turn Glele's wrath against Houénou, accusing him of conspiring with the British to place himself on the throne of Dahomey. Houénou in turn was called to Abomey to defend himself, but there found that the heir apparent Kondo also supported the accusation. He was imprisoned at Abomey, his property at Ouidah was confiscated and he himself died still in prison in 1887.[188]

Although the fall of Kpadonou Houénou was thus due in part to rivalries within the Ouidah merchant community and in particular represented the delayed revenge of the de Souzas against their rivals the Houénous, it also reflected the progressive alienation between that community and the Dahomian monarchy that had been evident since the 1860s. This alienation in turn, as has been seen, was in large part a consequence of tensions arising from the transition from the slave trade to

---

[183] Agbo, *Histoire*, 71–2; but cf. Reynier, 'Ouidah', 65, who says that the British fired only blanks. The bombardment is dated to 9 Oct. 1876; perhaps the traditions confuse the 1876–7 blockade with the shelling of Ouidah by a British warship in Oct. 1841, for which see Chapter 5.

[184] Reid, 'Warrior aristocrats', 480–82.

[185] Serval, 'Rapport', 191.

[186] Foà, *Le Dahomey*, 36.

[187] De Souza, *La Famille de Souza*, 61; cf. Le Herissé, *L'Ancien Royaume*, 327, n.

[188] Reynier, 'Ouidah', 65; Quénum, *Les Ancêtres*, 78–80.

'legitimate' trade in palm produce.[189] The principal interpretation of internal political problems within West African coastal societies arising from the commercial transition of the nineteenth century, by Hopkins, emphasized competition and conflict between existing rulers, who had dominated the slave trade, and small–scale farmers and petty traders, who were able to enter the new trade in palm produce.[190] In Dahomey, although small–scale enterprise played a significant role in 'legitimate' trade, the 'crisis of adaptation' took a different form, with the main challenge to royal authority coming from wealthy private merchants, who were now able to enter the production as well as the marketing of palm oil, in direct competition with the monarchy. It was also given a special character by the fact that in Dahomey the distinction between the state and the private sector broadly coincided with a geographical and political division, between the inland capital Abomey and the coastal commercial centre of Ouidah. Resentment in Ouidah at the rule of Dahomey, already recurrently visible during the period of the Atlantic slave trade, reached a critical level in the second half of the nineteenth century.

[189] For a somewhat different (but complementary rather than contradictory) interpretation, relating internal divisions in Dahomey to differing responses to the growth of European influence more generally, see Gordano, *Europei e Africani*, 95–140.

[190] Hopkins, *Economic History*, 143–7.

8

From Dahomian to French Rule

1878–92

The British blockade of Ouidah in 1876–7 was ineffective, indeed counter-productive, in terms of its declared objectives. The attempt to intimidate the Dahomian authorities had backfired; British prestige and influence in Dahomey were weakened rather than strengthened. In fact, the most obvious and immediate consequence of the blockade was the collapse of British trade at Ouidah. In the following year, it was noted that, although Turnbull, the agent of the firm of Swanzy who had provoked the British intervention, was still resident at Ouidah, he was doing little business, because local people were afraid to be associated with him.[1] A few years later, Swanzy sold its establishment in the English fort to a German firm, C. Goedelt of Hamburg; the transfer was announced in a letter from the German government to Glele in 1882.[2] Thereafter, British interest in Dahomey and Ouidah effectively ceased; subsequent attempts by Dahomey to elicit British intervention, as a counterweight to the growing threat of French imperialism, came to nothing.

The British intervention also had the effect of provoking French counter-measures to assert and protect their interests in the area.[3] In April 1878 a French officer, Paul Serval, visited Ouidah and obtained a new treaty confirming the cession of Cotonou to France. The status of this treaty, which, like that of 1868, was negotiated with the local authorities in Ouidah only, was doubtful, and it was later repudiated by Glele. But the matter was not yet put to the test, since the French, beyond stationing a Resident at Cotonou, took no immediate steps to establish effective occupation of the town, which remained under Dahomian administration. In relation to its European rivals, however, the French claim had been reasserted. The British responded by extending the territory of their own Lagos colony further westwards to occupy Kétonou, 15 km north-east of Cotonou,

---

[1] Serval, 'Rapport', 191.

[2] Bismarck to King Glele, 16 Jan. 1882, in Milan Kalous, 'Some correspondence between the German Empire and Dahomey in 1882–1892', *CEA*, 8/32 (1968), 635–6.

[3] See Newbury, *Western Slave Coast*, 104–5; Hargreaves, *Prelude*, 207–12.

thus threatening communication between Cotonou and Porto-Novo, in 1879.

This concentration of French interest on Cotonou reflected in part the relative weakness of Dahomian control there, but also its increasing commercial importance and the relative decline of Ouidah. Estimates of the volume of trade at Ouidah and other ports to the east made by Serval in 1878 illustrate the diversion of trade away from the older port.[4] Exports of palm oil from Ouidah were put at 500,000 gallons annually, i.e. between 1,500 and 1,600 tons, only around two-thirds of the level of the 1860s; though this was now supplemented by an additional trade in palm kernels of 2,500 tons annually. Of Dahomey's two ports on the western shore of Lake Nokoué, Godomey accounted for exports of 100,000 gallons of oil and 600 tons of kernels and Abomey-Calavi for 140,000 gallons and 600 tons. Total exports from Dahomey thus amounted to 740,000 gallons (2,300 tons) of oil and 3,700 tons of kernels, around a third of which was bypassing Ouidah. In comparison, Serval estimated French purchases from Porto-Novo at 670,000 gallons (around 2,000 tons) of oil and 2,000 tons of kernels annually. If it is assumed that the whole of French trade at Porto-Novo and Abomey-Calavi (but not that of Godomey) was passing through Cotonou, the latter was handling a total of 810,000 gallons (between 2,500 and 2,600 tons) of palm oil and 2,600 tons of kernels; its oil trade was therefore around two-thirds greater than that of Ouidah, though its trade in kernels was only marginally higher. This picture of the relative importance of the two ports is confirmed by figures given by Dahomian officials for the revenue received by the king from import duties at the time of the French conquest in the 1890s, estimated at £1,600 annually for Cotonou but only £1,000–1,200 for Ouidah.[5]

The commercial decline of Ouidah was compounded by the continuing pressure of the Dahomian monarchy, in its quest for revenue to support its military and ceremonial activities. Serval paints a picture of excessive and arbitrary impositions by royal officials, countered by systematic evasion from the local community. The tax-collectors 'now surround some houses, and seize the cattle, provisions and poultry; now they stop the goods on the streets and paths'. The inhabitants of Ouidah, when fetching goods from the European factories, posted lookouts on the roads to make sure that there were no royal officials about. Any attempt at resistance or expression of dissatisfaction was treated as rebellion, incurring arrest and confiscation of property or condemnation to military service, and any man of wealth was the object of denunciation, accusations being contrived in order to justify heavy fines. Serval also repeats the complaints heard since the 1860s, that Glele's regular military expeditions were undermining the trade in palm oil by diverting labour required for its production.[6]

These problems were presumably exacerbated by the declining profitability of the palm produce trade. The UK price of palm oil continued its long-term decline, from an average of £39 per ton in the 1860s to an all-time low of £19 in 1887–8;

---

[4]   Serval, 'Rapport', 191–4
[5]   Extrait des procès-verbaux du Conseil de l'Administration, 17 Aug. 1897, in d'Almeida-Topor, *Histoire économique*, ii, 277–8.
[6]   Serval, 'Rapport', 188.

that of kernels also fell, from around £15 to £11 per ton;[7] although it is unclear how completely European traders were able to pass on this price fall to their African suppliers, it seems certain that the incomes of the latter must have been severely reduced. The decline of the produce trade was, however, briefly offset by a final revival of the slave trade at Ouidah, which now took the form of the recruitment of supposedly free contract workers for the cocoa plantations on the island of São Tomé and later also for the German colony of Kamerun (Cameroun) and the 'Congo Free State' of the Belgian king Leopold. This revived overseas demand also raised prices once again to levels comparable to those during the heyday of the Atlantic trade: apparently $100 per (male) slave in 1889 and $80 in 1890–91.[8] Although trans-Atlantic shipments to the Americas had ended in the 1860s, therefore, the slave trade out of Ouidah did not come to a complete end until the French conquest in 1892.

Julião de Souza and the Portuguese protectorate 1883–7

The British blockade, or more precisely the actions taken by the Dahomian authorities in response to it, also affected the political situation within Ouidah, increasing disaffection among the local merchant community. At least one of the Brazilian merchants arrested after the blockade left the town soon after: Francisco Rodrigues da Silva, who had removed to Porto-Novo by 1880.[9] The most important consequence of the blockade, however, was the elimination of the leading indigenous merchant-official Kpadonou Houénou. With his removal, the influence of the Quénum family in Ouidah was broken. The family property was plundered by royal officials, and several members fled from the town; one of Kpadonou's sons in particular, Tovalou Quénum, moved to Porto-Novo, where he set up as a merchant and in time became closely associated with the French colonial authorities there. Kpadonou does not appear to have been replaced in his position as 'chief of traders' at Ouidah, which office therefore effectively lapsed. On his death in 1887, one of his brothers, called Tchéou, succeeded him as head of the family but not in his official rank of *ahisigan*. Tchéou's power was negligible; according to family tradition, 'he could not order anything, undertake anything, or exercise his authority in any way'. He resigned or was dismissed by Glele after only one year in office. Glele at first nominated one of his brothers, Kpossy-Gbely Azanmado Houénou, to succeed him, but the latter evaded the unwelcome burden by fleeing from Ouidah to Grand-Popo. Another brother, Atinzala Houénou, was appointed to the headship of the family, shortly before Glele's death in 1889.[10]

---

[7] Lynn, *Commerce and Economic Change*, 112, 121 (Tables 5.2, 5.10).

[8] Etienne Maigre, 'De Lagos au Dahomey', *Bulletin de la Société de Géographie de Marseille*, 14/1 (1890), 120 [£25]; Foà, *Le Dahomey*, 419 [£16/$80]; Aublet, *La Guerre*, 114, n. 1 [400 fr. for men, 250 for women]. It is assumed that the first of these prices is based on the conventional value of £1 = $4, whereas the second is explicitly based on the then current actual exchange rate of £1 = $5; also that, as earlier, $1 = 5 fr.

[9] Da Silva & da Silva, *Histoire de la famille*, 13–14.

[10] Reynier, 'Ouidah', 65; Quénum, *Les Ancêtres*, 80–87, 140–41.

From Dahomian to French Rule

With the eclipse of the Quénums, effective power in Ouidah passed back to other senior officials of the town. Serval in 1878 identified 'the first three authorities in the town' as the Yovogan, the Chodaton and the Chacha; the treaties with Britain in May 1877 and with France in April 1878 were 'signed' by the Yovogan and the Chodaton, the second being also witnessed by the Chacha, Francisco 'Chico' Felix de Souza.[11] The Yovogan at this time (named in the former treaty, though not in the latter) was Sékloka. Whether the Chodaton was still the man appointed in the 1860s, whose personal name was Akodé, is uncertain; at some point in the 1870s or 1880s the title passed, on Akodé's death, to one of his sons, called Ouidi.[12] The Chacha Francisco Chico died in 1880; his brother Julião Felix de Souza was chosen to succeed him, taking office formally in 1883.[13] Under Julião, a more energetic person and more substantial merchant than his predecessor, the de Souzas enjoyed a last brief flourishing of influence in Ouidah, which however once again brought down upon the family the disapproval of the Dahomian monarchy and occasioned its definitive downfall.

The context that enabled Julião de Souza to recover a predominant role in the politics of Ouidah was the growth of European imperialism in the early 1880s.[14] This was, of course, a global process, which extended beyond the West African coast; nevertheless, local factors played a significant role in motivating European expansion in this region, with the catastrophic fall in African produce prices in the 1880s exacerbating conflict between European purchasers and African suppliers and stimulating demands from the former for intervention to remove perceived obstacles to commercial development.[15] In the specific case of Dahomey, the militaristic and autocratic character of the monarchy was increasingly seen as strangling commercial enterprise; as European hopes for the reform of the Dahomian state, briefly raised under Gezo in the 1850s, faded, they gave way to demands for its destruction.[16] The process of European expansion, however, in the Bight of Benin as elsewhere, was complicated by intra-European rivalries, which African states regularly sought to exploit in defence of their sovereignty. To the east of Dahomey, the French protectorate over Porto-Novo was re-established in April 1883; British interest was effectively excluded from the area, as was formally recognized in a boundary agreement in 1889, whereby the British abandoned their westernmost outpost at Kétonou. To the west a French protectorate was proclaimed over Grand-Popo, Agoué and Little Popo in July. Further west, the Germans established their protectorate of 'Togo' in 1884; ensuing boundary negotiations left Agoué under French rule and Little Popo in German hands. Although this incipient European scramble for African territory left Dahomey – with the debatable exception of Cotonou – still intact, the geographical pattern of European acquisitions implicitly assigned that kingdom to the French sphere, restricting

---

[11] Serval, 'Rapport', 190; texts of treaties in PP, Treaty between Her Majesty and the King of Dahomey; Aublet, *La Guerre*, 10–12.

[12] Reynier, 'Ouidah', 48.

[13] Le Herissé, *L'Ancien Royaume*, 337, n. 1; Foà, *Le Dahomey*, 36.

[14] See Newbury, *Western Slave Coast*, 107–14; Hargreaves, *Prelude*, 294–301, 324–8.

[15] Hopkins, *Economic History*, 154–9.

[16] Reid, 'Warrior aristocrats', 511–12.

British and German territory to the east and west respectively. There was, however, a fourth European power with an established interest in Dahomey: Portugal, which had maintained its occupation of its fort in Ouidah since 1865. Portuguese interest in Ouidah was, moreover, reinforced at this point, as has been seen, by the project of recruiting contract labourers, in effect a revival of the slave trade, for São Tomé. Some in Dahomey therefore thought to consolidate links with Portugal as a means of fending off the French.

The de Souzas were the traditional intermediaries in dealings with Portugal, as expressed in the appointment of two earlier holders of the title of Chacha as governors of the Portuguese fort in Ouidah, Isidoro de Souza in 1851 and Francisco Chico in 1865. For the de Souzas, indeed, given their recently fraught relationship with the Dahomian monarchy, it seems likely that their cultivation of the Portuguese connection was conceived not only as a counterweight to French influence but also as a quest for external recognition and support as a means of securing protection against indigenous authority. Julião de Souza now made contact with the Portuguese authorities on São Tomé, whose governor visited Ouidah in August 1885, formally appointed Julião in turn as commander of the Portuguese fort in Ouidah and was taken by Julião for an audience with Glele in Abomey. Two treaties were signed, on 5 August and 13 September 1885, placing Dahomey under a Portuguese protectorate.[17] On this basis, the export of slaves to São Tomé was pursued, a total of 691 being supplied between August 1885 and November 1887.[18] However, Julião lost royal favour in May 1887, when he was summoned to Abomey and detained there; he died in prison shortly afterwards and was assumed to have been murdered on the king's orders. In the face of the loss of its local ally, Portugal officially abandoned its claimed protectorate over Dahomey at the end of 1887. The usual explanation for Glele's volte-face is that he had belatedly realized that the Portuguese treaty had compromised Dahomey's independence, the Chacha Julião having allegedly misrepresented its terms. This is supported by his declaration in a letter to the king of Portugal, 'I give my lands to no nation', although he also indicated that he was angry at the Chacha's failure to pay for slaves delivered, claiming an outstanding debt of $30,100.[19]

The internal political dimension of the episode of the Portuguese protectorate emerges incidentally in the contemporary records. As in the case of Kpadonou Houénou earlier, the heir apparent Kondo played a prominent role in the judgement and punishment of the Chacha, although this may have reflected Glele's advancing age and incapacity as much as Kondo's hostility to Ouidah or to European influence. Within Ouidah itself, Julião was initially supported in his policy not only by other members of the de Souza family but also by others within the Brazilian community. The first of the two protectorate treaties was also signed by

<hr />

[17] See esp. Joseph Adrien Djivo, 'Le roi Glélé et les européens: l'échec du protectorat portugais sur le Danhomè (1885–7)', *Cahiers du Centre de Recherches Africaines*, 8 (1994), 269–84; also Turner, 'Les Brésiliens', 246–60. For a contemporary Portuguese account, see Sarmento, *Portugal no Dahomé*.

[18] Djivo, 'Le roi Glélé', 278.

[19] Letter of Glele to King of Portugal, 16 July 1887, quoted ibid., 271, 279. The argument of Bay, *Wives of the Leopard*, 286–7, that the breach between Glele and the Chacha was commercial, rather than political, seems overstated.

Candido Joaquim Rodrigues, a son of Jacinto Rodrigues, and the second by Antonio Felix de Souza (presumably Julião's brother, surnamed 'Agbakoun'); and a letter in support of the Portuguese protectorate, written in response to French protests, in September 1885 was co-signed by, among others Rodrigues and Antonio de Souza, and also by Lino Felix de Souza (another brother of the Chacha) and Germano Julião de Souza (Julião's eldest son).[20] However, Candido Rodrigues subsequently shifted his ground and played a critical role in Julião's downfall. According to the testimony of a royal prince, one of Glele's sons, recorded 24 years later, it was Candido who denounced Julião for having allegedly misled the king about the contents of the treaty, and Julião's son Germano, in a letter written seven years later, concurs in blaming him for his father's death.[21] Julião's policy was also opposed throughout by the Yovogan (presumably this was still Sékloka), who warned Glele that the Chacha was selling the country to the Portuguese.[22] It may be that the Yovogan, as a party to the treaty of 1878 ceding Cotonou to the French, was championing the French connection.

The consequences of the Chacha's fall for the de Souza family were catastrophic; its property was seized and several other prominent members of the family summoned to Abomey, where some of them were also liquidated. His brother Antonio Agbakoun was officially cleared and released, but died two days after his return to Ouidah, provoking allegations that he had been poisoned by the king's agents.[23] The office of Chacha now passed to another of the de Souza brothers, Lino Felix de Souza, but he held office for only one year, dying in 1888.[24] Family tradition is divided over whether Lino died naturally or was killed by 'black magic', allegedly by rivals within the de Souza family rather than by the king. Thereafter, the position of Chacha lapsed, no successor being appointed until Norberto Francisco de Souza, a son of Francisco Chico, elected by the family under French rule in 1917; this interregnum is also explained in tradition as due to dissensions within the family.[25] Individual members of the de Souza family remained prominent in Ouidah, but the collective power of the family was broken. The leading role among the advisers to Glele's successor Behanzin now passed to their enemy Candido Rodrigues.

The French challenge

The episode of the abortive Portuguese protectorate over Dahomey was significant for the future of the country in two related ways. First, the Portuguese threat provoked the French into a more vigorous assertion of the rights they claimed in

---

[20] Turner, 'Les Brésiliens', 247, 249–50. I assume that the 'Joaquim Rodrigues' who signed the first treaty was, in fact, Candido, rather than (as does Turner) a different person, brother to Candido.

[21] Le Herissé, *L'Ancien Royaume*, 336–7; ANB, 1E14/6₁, letter of Germano Julião de Souza to Administrator n. d. [1894?].

[22] Turner, 'Les Brésiliens', 252, 257.

[23] Foà, *Le Dahomey*, 44; de Souza, *La Famille de Souza*, 56–7.

[24] De Souza, *La Famille de Souza*, 110, 172.

[25] Fieldwork, De Souza compound, Eusébio Frédérique de Souza, 12 Dec. 2001; Lino Felix de Souza compound, 5 Dec. 2001.

the area; the French flag was finally officially raised at Cotonou on 14 September 1885. The collapse of the Portuguese protectorate in 1887, on the other hand, left the field clear for the imposition of French influence. Within less than three years, Dahomey and France were at war over their disputed claims to possession of Cotonou.[26]

The issue was ultimately irresolvable by diplomacy, since there was no realistic prospect of Dahomey giving up sovereignty over Cotonou. Not only was any such territorial concession incompatible with the ideology of the Dahomian monarchy; Glele told the French, as he had earlier told the Portuguese, 'Absolutely no one, not even the king of Dahomey, ever gives his possessions to any other nation.'[27] At the same time, the growing commercial importance of Cotonou and the decline of Ouidah, noted earlier, meant that in any case the Dahomian monarchy simply could not afford to relinquish the revenues it received from taxing the trade at Cotonou.[28] At the beginning of 1889, the French proposed to establish a customs post at Cotonou, as they assumed they were entitled to do by the treaties of 1868 and 1878; but Glele in response sent a message of protest, insisting that he would not give up Cotonou and repudiating these treaties as signed without his authority. In an attempt to resolve the dispute, in November 1889 a senior French official, Jean Bayol, undertook a mission to Abomey, seeking to negotiate confirmation of the cession of Cotonou, but the heir apparent Kondo, speaking on his father's behalf, rejected the French demands. On his return to the coast, Bayol then provoked war by arresting the Dahomian officials at Cotonou, on 22 February 1890.

The Dahomian response to French pressure intersected with a struggle for the succession to the throne. Although Kondo had been designated heir apparent since 1876, his claim was disputed by one of his brothers, Sasse Koka; while Kondo identified himself with resistance to the French demands, his opponents supported compromise with them.[29] As in the earlier rivalry between Kondo and Ahanhanzo, Ouidah was identified with the opposition to Kondo. Towards the end of 1888 a Dahomian embassy was sent to the British authorities at Lagos in an abortive attempt to secure British support against the threat from the French. The mission explained that Kondo was engaged in a succession struggle with another prince (referring presumably to Sasse Koka), whose power base was in Ouidah and who was playing for French support. Kondo proposed in response to close the roads to Ouidah and open an alternative trade route to Kétonou, then still under British occupation.[30]

---

[26] For the origins and course of the French–Dahomey wars of 1890–94, see esp. Luc Garcia, *Le Royaume du Dahomé face à la pénétration coloniale (1875–1894)* (Paris, 1988); Boniface Obichere, *West African States and European Expansion* (New Haven, 1971), chs 3–4; Newbury, *Western Slave Coast*, 127–32; John D. Hargreaves, *West Africa Partitioned*, ii (London, 1985), ch.10.

[27] Letter of Glele to President of France, 12 May 1889, quoted in Luc Garcia, 'Archives et tradition orale: à propos d'une enquête sur la politique du royaume de Danhomé à la fin du 19e siècle', *CEA*, 61–2 (1976), 194–5.

[28] Newbury, *Western Slave Coast*, 126.

[29] See Bay, *Wives of the Leopard*, 274–7, 285–91. Bay again argues that the foreign policy issues were secondary to the internal power struggle.

[30] Ibid., 290–91.

When relations with the French deteriorated in the following year, this led to attacks on the elements in Ouidah who were identified with a policy of friendship with them. In his message of March 1889 repudiating the cession of Cotonou, Glele declared that he had executed the Yovogan and other officials who had signed the treaties of cession.[31] The Yovogan concerned was evidently Sékloka; the other officials executed on this occasion presumably included the Chodaton (probably Ouidi), who had also signed the 1878 treaty. The office of Yovogan was now conferred by Glele on Aguessi Dagba, who was a son of the earlier Yovogan Dagba. This man, however, seems to have held office only briefly, since he was succeeded by another incumbent, called Jagba, who is said to have been in office at the time of Glele's death at the end of 1889.[32] In the case of the title of Chodaton, local tradition recalls that after Ouidi's death (execution is not explicitly mentioned) Glele refused to appoint another son of the first holder Akodé to the post, but conferred it instead on a stranger to the family.[33] The dismissal or resignation of Tchéou as head of the Quénum family, which also occurred around this time, may also have been connected. These troubles evidently provoked a further exodus of disaffected elements from Ouidah: a contemporary report noted that 'most Dahomians, if they can escape from the kingdom with the certainty of never returning, are rushing to disappear', citing 'the desolate aspect of Whydah, which was once a large and well populated town, now in ruins and deserted', as evidence of local hostility to the monarchy.[34]

Glele died in December 1889, shortly after the departure of Bayol from Abomey, and was succeeded by Kondo, who now took the name Behanzin. Behanzin's succession was, however, challenged by the partisans of his brother Sasse Koka. Ouidah was evidently divided in its allegiance in this dispute. Tradition recalls that the Yovogan (i.e. Jagba) supported Behanzin.[35] However, a significant faction within the Ouidah merchant community backed his rival. According to a report by the interpreter to the Bayol mission, the faction opposed to his accession included two powerful figures within Ouidah, the Chodaton and 'a creole called Nicolas', both of whom, along with the other leading dissidents, were imprisoned and their property confiscated.[36] The latter is to be identified with the head of the d'Oliveira family of Ganvè quarter, who at this time was Gregori Nicolas d'Oliveira; local tradition in Ouidah confirms that he was imprisoned and his property confiscated by Behanzin, but explains this as a response to internal disputes within the family.[37] The consolidation of Behanzin's power was accordingly followed by a reassertion of royal authority in Ouidah. On his accession, he appointed partisans of his own to the administration there. He conferred the office of Yovogan on a man called

---

[31] Text in Cornevin, *Histoire*, 317–18; cf. Bay, *Wives of the Leopard*, 287.

[32] Agbo, *Histoire*, 57; Dagba, *La Collectivité familiale*, 49, 68. The latter omits Jagba, and claims that Aguessi Dagba was still alive at the time of Glele's death.

[33] Reynier, 'Ouidah', 48.

[34] Bertin, 'Renseignements', 398.

[35] Bay, *Wives of the Leopard*, 289.

[36] C.W. Newbury, 'A note on the Abomey Protectorate', *Africa* (London), 29 (1959), 148, n. 1; Bay, *Wives of the Leopard*, 288–9.

[37] Reynier, 'Ouidah', 59.

Nugbodohwe, recalled in local tradition as the last person to hold this position; this man had been diviner-adviser to Glele and is credited with having persuaded the latter to choose Kondo as his heir.[38] Whether the incumbent Yovogan Jagba was removed (despite his own support for Behanzin's succession) or happened opportunely to die at this point is not clear. Glele also restored the title of Chodaton to the family of its original holder, Akodé, appointing another of the latter's sons, called Zinzindohoué, to the position of 'caboceer' at Ouidah, seemingly succeeding to his father's post as deputy to the Yovogan.[39]

The war of 1890

The arrest of Dahomian officials in Cotonou by the French was regarded by Behanzin as *casus belli*, and on 4 March 1890 a Dahomian force attacked Cotonou but was beaten off. The French then went on to the offensive and pushed forces inland from Porto-Novo, which defeated the Dahomians at the battle of Atchoukpa, 20 April 1890. However, negotiations between France and Dahomey were then reopened. Initially, the French demanded not only confirmation of the cession of Cotonou but also to be allowed to establish military occupation of the French fort at Ouidah, but the latter was rejected by Behanzin. The agreement ultimately reached on 3 October 1890 accepted only French occupation of Cotonou in return, as originally agreed in 1863, for an annual payment of 20,000 francs ($4,000), which the French regarded as compensation for the surrender of territory but the Dahomians probably interpreted as tribute in acknowledgement of continuing Dahomian sovereignty.

It is doubtful whether there was much enthusiasm in Ouidah for the war. The Yovogan Nugbodohwe is said to have advised Behanzin against fighting the French, on the grounds that 'it was the whites who made the guns'.[40] Ouidah's role in the campaign of 1890 was limited. On 24 February, in retaliation for the arrest of Dahomian officials in Cotonou, the French residents in Ouidah, including the missionary Dorgère as well as several traders, were summoned to the Yovogan's residence and arrested, the message of summons being delivered by Candido Rodrigues; they were later taken to Abomey under the charge of the deputy Yovogan Zinzindohoué.[41] The Dahomian force that attacked Cotonou in March 1890 was commanded by the Caho, the head of the garrison of Ouidah;[42] but

---

[38] Ibid., 51; Agbo, *Histoire*, 57, 209; see Melville J. Herskovits & Frances S. Herskovits, *Dahomean Narrative* (Evanston, 1958), 375–6. Bay, *Wives of the Leopard*, 256, however, says that Nugboduhwe opposed Kondo's accession; but, if so, it is difficult to understand why he should have been given preferment by him.

[39] Glélé, *Le Danxome*, 143, says that Zinzindohoué was appointed by Behanzin as Yovogan; see also Garcia, *Le Royaume du Dahomé*, 141. But in the text of the treaty of 3 Oct. 1890, signed by Zinzindohoué, he is described merely as 'caboceer' and it is made clear that the office of Yovogan was then vacant: text in Aublet, *La Guerre*, 113–14.

[40] Herskovits & Herskovits, *Dahomean Narrative*, 376.

[41] Aublet, *La Guerre*, 33; Guilcher, *Au Dahomey*, 31–8. See also the account by another of the hostages, E. Chaudouin, *Trois mois de captivité au Dahomey* (Paris, 1891).

[42] Gavoy, 'Note historique', 67; see Le Herissé, *L'Ancien Royaume*, 338.

thereafter the Ouidah forces seem to have stayed on the defensive and to have been uninvolved in the subsequent fighting. In fact, the French did not seek to attack Ouidah by land, but on 29–30 April 1890 Ouidah was bombarded by French warships;[43] the episode was, memorably, witnessed by the British writer Joseph Conrad, then on his way by ship to take up employment in the Congo Free State, who in his famous anti–imperialist novel *Heart of Darkness* describes with irony the bombardment by the French ships of a supposed enemy on land whom they could not see, 'firing into a continent'.[44] The bombardment was, however, more effectively targeted than Conrad supposed. According to local tradition, it killed 120 people in the town.[45]

Ouidah played a more prominent role in the subsequent negotiations between the Dahomian and French authorities. In an initial move of conciliation, the French hostages were returned to Ouidah and released on 8 May. The Yovogan Nugbodohwe seems to have been made a scapegoat for the arrest of the hostages and was relieved of his post. At any rate, it was the Kuzugan of Ouidah who now sent to initiate negotiations with the French, the post of Yovogan being presumably vacant, and, in the following year, the 'former Yovogan', referring presumably to Nugbodohwe, was reported to have been executed for mistreating the French hostages.[46] The missionary Dorgère, one of the hostages earlier taken from Ouidah and now liberated, emerged as a mutually acceptable intermediary, and undertook a mission to Abomey to negotiate with Behanzin in August 1890; he was accompanied by the heads of the Dahomian administration in Ouidah, the Kuzugan and Zinzindohoué. The agreement of October 1890 was made at Ouidah and 'signed' for Dahomey by the Kuzugan ('acting as Yovogan'), the 'caboceer' Zinzindohoué and Aïnadu as 'treasurer of the agore', and witnessed by Candido Rodrigues and another Brazilian, Alexandre da Silva.[47]

There were continued tensions, however, between the Dahomian monarchy and the town of Ouidah. The exiled Tovalou Quénum at Porto-Novo had supplied provisions for the French forces and was reportedly on the French side at the battle of Atchoukpa; the Dahomian authorities responded by declaring him a traitor and placing a price on his head.[48] After the European hostages were liberated in May 1890, the Dahomians carried out mass arrests of members of Ouidah families who had connections with the French, including in particular relatives of the renegade Tovalou Quénum. The story is told by local historian Casimir Agbo, who as a child was among those taken, together with his mother and grandmother, the latter being a sister of Tovalou Quénum; according to him, over 1,000 persons were taken as hostages from Ouidah, many of whom died in captivity, the survivors being liberated only by the French conquest of Dahomey in 1892.[49] Another of those arrested on this occasion, and who died in prison, was Atinzala Houénou, head of the

[43] Aublet, *La Guerre*, 54.
[44] Joseph Conrad, *Heart of Darkness* (Penguin edn, Harmondsworth, 1983), 40–41.
[45] Agbo, *Histoire*, 73.
[46] Aublet, *La Guerre*, 56–8, 113–14.
[47] Text ibid., 74–5.
[48] Reynier, 'Ouidah', 65.
[49] Agbo, *Histoire*, 74–5.

Quénum family, who thus paid the price for his nephew's treason.[50] In the continuing Dahomian negotiations with the French after 1890 also, local officials in Ouidah continued to suffer as scapegoats for the shifts in Behanzin's policies. Around April 1891, for example, Behanzin was reported to have 'changed the Cussugan', for reasons unspecified;[51] and later in the same year, as has been seen, the former Yovogan Nugbodohwe was executed. The post of Yovogan seemingly remained vacant during 1892, negotiations with the French in that year being again conducted by the Kuzugan, now a man called Guedou.[52]

The loss of Cotonou, acknowledged in the treaty of October 1890, enhanced the importance for Behanzin of continued possession of Ouidah, which was now his only outlet to the sea. He depended on it for supplies of guns, needed to equip his army for what was seen as the inevitable second round of fighting with the French, the guns were obtained from German firms in exchange for slaves, sold under the guise of voluntary contract labourers. In this last flourishing of the slave trade from Ouidah between 1889–1891 a total of five shipments, totalling 1,365 slaves, were recorded.[53]

The French occupation, 1892

The peace of 1890 was probably never considered by either side as anything more than a truce, and fighting again broke out in March 1892. A French expedition was again mounted from Porto-Novo, commanded by General Alfred Dodds, and fought its way inland to the capital Abomey, which was occupied on 17 November 1892. The power of Dahomey was thus finally broken, although Behanzin himself remained at large for some time, surrendering to the French only on 25 January 1894.

Ouidah was again marginal to the campaign of 1892, although on 9 August the town was once more bombarded by French warships.[54] In fact, after the defeat of Behanzin Ouidah was peacefully negotiated into French rule. On 18 November General Dodds at Abomey issued a proclamation to 'the chiefs and inhabitants of Dahomey', guaranteeing security of their persons and property to those who accepted French 'protection', and promising that chiefs who made their submission would be continued in their positions but those who refused would be punished.[55] Among those who accepted this offer were the local authorities in Ouidah; when Dodds returned to Porto-Novo on 30 November, he received a message from Ouidah declaring the town's acceptance of French sovereignty and willingness to receive a French garrison.[56] It is not clear who sent this message; it

[50] Reynier, 'Ouidah', 65; Quénum, *Les Ancêtres*, 84.
[51] Aublet, *La Guerre*, 109.
[52] Ibid., 317; Garcia, *Le Royaume du Dahomé*, 234–5.
[53] Newbury, *Western Slave Coast*, 130, with n. 4.
[54] Aublet, *La Guerre*, 180; Agbo, *Histoire*, 75.
[55] Text in Aublet, *La Guerre*, 323–4.
[56] Agbo, *Histoire*, 144.

was certainly not the legal Dahomian authorities, the Kuzugan Guedou and Zinzindohoué, who were still with the king in the interior; the former, as has been seen, negotiated with the French on Behanzin's behalf in November 1892, while the latter was captured by the French only in the following year.[57] Possibly it was a senior member of the de Souza family who took the initiative.[58] On 2 December 1892, French troops arrived by sea to occupy Ouidah.[59] On the following day Dodds at Porto-Novo issued a decree deposing Behanzin and placing Dahomey under a French protectorate, and at the same time annexing Ouidah, together with the other towns of the coastal area of Dahomey – Savi, Avlékété, Godomey and Abomey-Calavi – to France.[60] The first French civilian administrator, Alexandre d'Albéca, arrived in Ouidah on 1 January 1893, formally inaugurating the colonial period in its history.[61]

The attitudes of the people of Ouidah towards their passage from Dahomian to French rule were doubtless ambivalent. Many of the male inhabitants fled into the surrounding bush on the arrival of the French troops, who found the town occupied mainly by women and children, but within a couple of months, as fears of French reprisals receded, they had mostly returned.[62] For many of those who had recently suffered in clashes with the Dahomian monarchy, such as the Quénum family, the overthrow of Dahomian rule was clearly welcome. The exiled (and recently outlawed) Tovalou Quénum was now able to return from Porto-Novo to Ouidah and to assume the headship of the family, to which he was formally elected in 1894.[63] Among those still resident in Ouidah, there were also some active collaborators with the French, notably the das Chagas family, close allies of the French Catholic mission, the younger generation of which now served as interpreters and scouts to the French army; Iancio das Chagas, in particular, the eldest son of Angelo Custodio das Chagas, served as spokesman for the French in negotiations with Behanzin in 1892–3.[64] However, many other leading members of the Ouidah merchant community had rallied to the Dahomian monarchy. A member of the Dossou-Yovo family, Henry Dossou-Yovo served during 1890 as adviser to Behanzin and was his emissary on missions to the British at Lagos; he remained loyal to him even in defeat, being charged with a final abortive peace mission to France on the king's behalf in 1893.[65] Among the Brazilians, Candido Rodrigues served throughout as Behanzin's secretary, interpreter and adviser; he too remained

[57] Garcia, *Le Royaume du Dahomé*, 231.

[58] Agbo, *Histoire*, 145, records that the French troops who occupied Ouidah were welcomed by 'the Chacha Lino', who was received in the French fort and exchanged toasts with their commander. But the Chacha Lino Felix de Souza had died in 1888 and his eldest son, Felix Lino, was at that time still with the king in the interior.

[59] Aublet, *La Guerre*, 329; Agbo, *Histoire*, 144.

[60] Text in Aublet, *La Guerre*, 332.

[61] Agbo, *Histoire*, 145–6.

[62] Aublet, *La Guerre*, 331, 333.

[63] Quénum, *Les Ancêtres*, 85, 90.

[64] Turner, 'Les Brésiliens', 321–2; Garcia, *Le Royaume du Dahomé*, 54, 236, 241; Aublet, *La Guerre*, 320.

[65] Le Herissé, *L'Ancien Royaume*, 339–40, 348; Hazoumé, *Le Pacte de sang*, 33; Hargreaves, *West Africa Partitioned*, ii, 165–6, 175, 177.

with Behanzin even after the fall of Abomey, when the king maintained his court at Atcherigbé to the north during 1893.[66] Julio de Medeiros (in his capacity as agent of the German firm of Goedelt) arranged the supply of munitions for the Dahomian war effort during 1890–91, although he does not seem to have taken any active role in the war of 1892.[67] Five other Brazilians were included along with Rodrigues among persons in Ouidah whom the French identified as supporters of Behanzin and whose property was in consequence declared confiscated in January 1893, including Alexandre da Silva and three members of the de Souza family, Georges (son of Antonio Kocou), Felix Lino (son of the late Chacha Lino) and Cyrille (another grandson of the first Chacha).[68] Da Silva, after serving as interpreter in the Franco-Dahomian negotiations in 1890, had remained in Behanzin's service as his secretary.[69] Georges de Souza had also assisted Rodrigues in approaches to German trading firms, to supply munitions to Dahomey;[70] while Cyrille and Félix Lino de Souza managed the Dahomian artillery during the campaign of 1892.[71]

There is room for debate, of course, as to whether (or how far) those who continued to serve Behanzin were motivated by loyalty to Dahomey or simply by fear of the reprisals that might otherwise be expected from the Dahomian government, as illustrated by the fate of the Chacha Julião de Souza earlier.[72] The attitude of some of them was clearly at best unenthusiastic. Tradition among descendants of Candido Rodrigues, for example, maintains that, far from being committed to resistance, he had advised Behanzin against fighting the French, predicting the probability of defeat.[73] Alexandre da Silva and Cyrille and Felix Lino de Souza, when they surrendered to the French in 1893, claimed that 'they had followed the king under duress'.[74] Behanzin, as has been seen, had harboured doubts of the loyalty of the Ouidah community, causing him to take hostages from the town in 1890, and this suspicion evidently continued to the end. During 1891, there were rumours that he had accused Rodrigues and Georges and Felix Lino de Souza of giving him 'bad advice' and they were said to be in fear for their lives.[75] According to tradition, in the final crisis of defeat in 1893 he denounced the Brazilian community more generally, disdaining to employ as his emissaries any of 'the mulattoes and indeed all the "men in jackets", descendants of blacks who returned from the land of the whites', because of their supposedly divided loyalties; for his final mission to France he chose instead the purely African (although culturally Brazilianized) Henry Dossou-Yovo.[76] He also continued to take reprisals against

---

[66] Garcia, *Le Royaume du Dahomé*, 239, refers to a letter written from Ouidah to Rodrigues at Atcherigbé, 23 March 1893.

[67] Turner, 'Les Brésiliens', 303–5.

[68] Ibid., 318–19, 325–6.

[69] Garcia, *Le Royaume du Dahomé*, 241.

[70] Turner, 'Les Brésiliens', 307, 333.

[71] Garcia, *Le Royaume du Dahomé*, 141, 185.

[72] As suggested by Turner, 'Les Brésiliens', 305–6.

[73] Ibid., 306.

[74] Garcia, *Le Royaume du Dahomé*, 227.

[75] Aublet, *La Guerre*, 114 (where 'Feliciano de Souza' is presumably a mistake for 'Felix Lino').

[76] Hazoumé, *Le Pacte de sang*, 32–3.

elements in Ouidah. At the end of 1893, when he carried out funeral ceremonies for his father Glele, those offered as human sacrifices were reported to have included 'numerous inhabitants of Whydah'.[77] One of those killed on this occasion was apparently Georges de Souza, who is recalled by family tradition to have been executed by the king. Family memory blames his execution on Candido Rodrigues, who is said to have falsely denounced him to the king for allegedly plotting a coup;[78] this perhaps alludes to plots to depose Behanzin in favour of his brother Goutchili, who was eventually enthroned (under the name Agoli-Agbo) by the French in January 1894.

What does not seem in doubt is that there was little feeling in Ouidah of regret at the downfall of Dahomey; from a local perspective, the French conquest represented, not the loss of independence, but the substitution of one foreign colonial regime for another.[79] Given the recent history of conflict between Ouidah and the Dahomian monarchy, moreover, there was a disposition to believe or hope that French rule might prove more benevolent. Immediately after the conquest, the French issued assurances to his former subjects in the coastal areas that 'Behanzin's despotic regime is over, they can cultivate, harvest and sell their produce without their profits being mostly taken away, as before';[80] and current tradition in Ouidah generally agrees that conditions were better under the French than under Dahomey, especially as regards the freedom to make (and more particularly, keep) money. There was clearly a widespread feeling of relief in Ouidah at the ending of Dahomian rule. Local tradition later claimed that Behanzin, on his accession in 1889, intended to send an army to destroy Ouidah and was diverted only by the French invasion of Dahomey. While probably not literally true, the story is metaphorically appropriate; for the people of Ouidah, French rule offered the prospect of liberation from what had been increasingly seen as the oppressive hand of Dahomey.[81]

Epilogue: Ouidah under French colonial rule

The expectations of the Ouidah merchant community that they stood to benefit from French rule were only partially realized. Hopes among leading families of recovering property confiscated by the Dahomian state were largely disappointed, although the head of the Adjovi family, Akanwanou Adjovi, sought to use the colonial courts to re-establish control over palm groves confiscated by King Gezo,

[77] Bay, *Wives of the Leopard*, 303–4.

[78] Fieldwork, De Souza compound, Eusébio Frédérique de Souza, 12 Dec. 2001; Antonio Kokou Felix de Souza Adekpeti compound, 12 Dec. 2001; cf. Bay, *Wives of the Leopard*, 352, n. 33.

[79] See the perception of continuity in anti-colonial struggle, '*Ils ont … lutté contre la domination des rois d'Abomey, contre le colonisateur français*', in the preface to [UGDO], *Les Voies de la renaissance de Ouidah*, 7–8, written by Emile Ologoudou.

[80] Aublet, *La Guerre*, 331.

[81] Karl-August, 'Pour une politique de recherche', 20; de Souza, *La Famille de Souza*, 57. In 1892 Behanzin did in fact initially encamp at Allada, prepared to march on Ouidah, but this was evidently for defensive purposes, in case the French should invade from that direction: Aublet, *La Guerre*, 235.

provoking a protracted legal battle from 1903 onwards. The control of family heads over lineage lands was also undermined. In a dispute between the de Souza family and some of its former slaves in 1902, the French authorities intervened, first to encourage the ex-slaves to demand wages in return for their work and then, when the family in response attempted to evict them from land which they occupied, to grant them legal title to it. Disputes between family heads and other leading family members also led to the partition of the Quénum family lands in 1910 and the Adjovi lands in 1928.[82]

More critical, however, was the economic and political marginalization of Ouidah during the colonial period.[83] Most obvious was the town's commercial decline relative to Cotonou to the east, a process that had already begun during the second half of the nineteenth century and which was indeed a principal reason for the French establishment at Cotonou; although, conversely, the early establishment of French colonial administration there also served to attract European trade away from Ouidah and other rival ports, a tendency that was already evident by the end of the 1880s.[84] The process was substantially accelerated from the 1890s. The key development was the construction of deep-water port facilities at Cotonou, beginning with a wharf, which permitted cargoes to be landed without needing to be carried through the dangerous surf and which became operational in 1893.[85] This was compounded by the construction of the railway from Cotonou to the interior from 1900, which facilitated the delivery of produce to the port. Although a branch railway line to Ouidah itself was built in 1903, this had the effect of further diverting trade to Cotonou, since now even produce from the Ouidah area itself could more conveniently be sent for shipping from Cotonou, rather than overland for embarkation from the beach to the south. Ouidah continued to function as an outlet for export trade for some time, as illustrated by the published reminiscences of the agent of an English firm (presumably John Walkden) who resided at Ouidah in 1925–7.[86] But the export trade through Ouidah had ceased altogether by the 1940s, and the French customs post on the beach was closed down. Members of Ouidah families therefore had to seek prosperity under French colonialism through migration elsewhere.

The town suffered a second economic marginalization in the 1970s, with the upgrading of the international coastal road from Cotonou west to Lomé, which involved the construction of a bypass to the north of the town. The historical centre of Ouidah was thus cut off from the flow of traffic; this has stimulated the migration of economic activity northwards towards the new road, including the construction of a new periodic market, called after the town's founder Kpase, which has now replaced Zobé as the town's main centre of commerce.

---

[82] Patrick Manning, 'L'affaire Adjovi: la bourgeoisie foncière au Dahomey face à l'administration', in Catherine Coquery-Vidrovitch (ed.), *Actes du colloque Entreprises et entrepreneurs en Afrique* (Paris, 1990), ii, 241–68; idem, *Slavery, Colonialism and Economic Growth*, 192, 198–202.

[83] B. Codo & S. Anignikin, 'Ouidah sous le régime colonial', in [UGDO], *Les Voies de la renaissance de Ouidah*, 103–14.

[84] Newbury, *Western Slave Coast*, 123–4.

[85] Subsequent improvements culminated in the opening of the modern deep-water port in 1965.

[86] Frank J. Quinn, *A Coaster's Letters from Dahomey* (n.p., 1928).

Politically also, Ouidah suffered marginalization in the colonial period. It was Porto-Novo rather than Ouidah that remained the seat of the French colonial administration. Ouidah under the French, as under Dahomey, served only as a centre of local administration, as capital of a *cercle*, which initially had nearly the same boundaries as the Dahomian province over which the Yovogan had ruled (though excluding Tori to the north). But, even at this local level, Ouidah's role was progressively eroded. Administrative arrangements decreed in 1896 separated Cotonou (with Godomey and Abomey-Calavi) from Ouidah, which now retained authority only over Savi and Avlékété. In a subsequent reorganization in 1934, Ouidah lost its autonomy and was included in the *cercle* of Cotonou, though following local protests this decision was reversed in 1938 and the *cercle* of Ouidah was restored.[87] When a further administrative reorganization in 1946 grouped the *cercles* into departments, Ouidah was included in the Department of Atlantique, now again subject to Cotonou as the departmental capital. The main importance which Ouidah retained under French rule (and to the present) was as the site of one of the principal garrisons of the national army, located on the west of the town.

Table 8.1 Population figures for southern Bénin towns

	1937	1947	1953	1972
Porto-Novo	27,016	29,925	29,144	105,518
Ouidah	12,818	12,881	13,289	16,107
Abomey	11,435	16,772	18,832	32,800
Cotonou	6,811	19,802	20,019	197,901

Source: Extracted from Mondjannagni, *Campagnes et villes*, 335 (Table 27).

In these circumstances, Ouidah experienced only modest population growth during the colonial period; in 1913 the town was estimated to have a population of 15,000;[88] the censuses taken under colonial rule recorded a lower figure, of under 13,000, in 1937, and minimal growth thereafter (see Table 8.1). In 1937 Ouidah had been the second largest town in the French colony, smaller only than the capital Porto-Novo, but narrowly exceeding the former Dahomian capital Abomey, which had still not recovered from its destruction in 1892 and its subsequent marginalization; but by 1947 Ouidah had already been overtaken by both Abomey and the port city of Cotonou, whose rapid development was on the way to making it the largest town in the country. Ouidah remains today only the fourth largest town in southern Benin and the sixth in the country as a whole, being now exeeded in population also by Parakou and Djougou, the leading towns in northern Bénin.

One sphere in which Ouidah remained pre-eminent was in European education. In 1895 the town once again became the official headquarters of the Roman Catholic Church and, when a territorial archdiocese was created for the colony of Dahomey in 1901, it was located at Ouidah, where a cathedral was constructed on

[87] Cornevin, *Histoire*, 410–12; Agbo, *Histoire*, 153–7.
[88] Gavoy, 'Note historique', 63.

the former site of the Yovogan's palace (consecrated in 1909). Ouidah remained the religious headquarters of the country until 1960, when the archbishopric was transferred to Cotonou.[89] Ouidah also became the location of the Roman Catholic seminary of Saint-Gall established in 1914, which played a key role in the growth of the Dahomian educated elite. Persons from or resident in Ouidah consequently played a prominent role in the francophone literary culture that developed in colonial Dahomey from the 1920s: for example, the pioneer African novelist, Félix Couchoro, born in Ouidah in 1900, whose first work *L'Esclave* was published in 1929.[90] Consequently also, members of Ouidah families were prominent in the early stages of the development of the anti-colonial nationalist movement during the 1920s and 1930s. Notable examples were Jean Adjovi, son of Akanwanou Adjovi (and his successor as head of the Adjovi family in 1914), who edited the early nationalist newspapers *Le Guide du Dahomey* and *La Voix du Dahomey* in the 1920s;[91] and, on an international stage, Marc Tovalou Quénum (son of the man who had assisted the French war effort against Dahomey in 1890–92), founder and president of the Ligue Universelle pour la Défense de la Race Noire, affiliated to Marcus Garvey's Universal Negro Improvement Association.[92] But Ouidah, given its small population, inevitably became more marginal in the more popular-based nationalism of the 1940s and 1950s.

Ouidah families have remained prominent in the ruling elite of Dahomey/Bénin since independence in 1960. Most obvious has been the continuing eminence of the de Souza family, which in particular has provided one head of state (General Paul-Emile de Souza, head of the military government that ruled the country in 1969–70) and a distinguished Cardinal of the Roman Catholic Church (Monseigneur Isidore de Souza), who also played a critical role, as President of the National Assembly, in the democratic revolution of 1990. Other Ouidah families have also been politically prominent: most recently, Idelphonse Lemon was a minister in the transitional democratic government headed by Nicéphore Soglo in 1990 (and a candidate in the presidential elections in 1991), and Désiré Vieyra (brother-in-law to Soglo) joined his government subsequently, while Séverin Adjovi was a member of the government formed by Mathieu Kérékou when he replaced Soglo as president in 1996. Another son of Ouidah, Léopold David-Gnahoui, was appointed Bénin's ambassador to Canada in 1996.

Of course, success in business, politics or the literary world has to be pursued in the wider world, so that although of Ouidah extraction, these scions of the town have generally left it to live elsewhere. However, relations with their ancestral homes in the town are maintained, especially in regard to ceremonies of commemoration

---

[89] For the Catholic Church in Ouidah, see Théophile Villaça, *La Basilique de Ouidah* (n.p. [Ouidah], 2000); Théodule Codo, 'Les oeuvres missionnaires dans la diffusion du Catholicisme à Ouidah 1861–1960' (Mémoire de maîtrise, UNB, 1992).

[90] This first work was published in France; but (although Couchoro himself had emigrated to Togo in 1939) his second and third novels, *Amour de féticheuse* (1941) and *Drame d'amour à Anécho* (1950), were actually published in Ouidah.

[91] Manning, *Slavery, Colonialism and Economic Growth*, 263–5, 269, 273–4.

[92] J. Ayodele Langley, *Pan-Africanism and Nationalism in West Africa, 1900–1945* (Oxford, 1973), 290–300.

of deceased members of the family. In effect, it has been suggested, Ouidah has tended to become 'a vast necropolis', in which the households of prominent families are maintained essentially as funeral shrines, with most of the active members of the family living elsewhere.[93]

The circumstance that persons of Ouidah extraction remain disproportionately represented among the bureaucratic and entrepreneurial elite has also facilitated in recent times the development of an organized concern to devise means of regeneration of the town, as articulated especially by a body called the Union Générale pour le Développement de Ouidah, which held its inaugural conference in the town in 1985.[94] This movement has been informed by an awareness of the town's illustrious past (as it was commonly perceived), which is seen not only as a source of inspiration but also a potential means of regeneration, through the development of Ouidah as a cultural and touristic centre, focusing on its historical role in the Atlantic slave trade and in the cultural interchanges between Africa and America which that trade engendered. This led to promotion of Ouidah as a potential centre for academic research on the slave trade and the African diaspora, with the organization of two major international conferences in the town: 'Ouidah '92' in January 1993, and the inaugural conference of the UNESCO 'Slave Route' project in September 1994.[95] This was conjoined to an attempt to promote 'cultural tourism' focused on monuments commemorating the slave trade, with the development especially of the 'slave route' from Ouidah to the beach as a site of memory. In the process, as has been seen, the town, or at least a substantial element among its inhabitants, has begun to come to terms with its earlier participation in the slave trade.

---

[93] Sinou & Agbo, *Ouidah*, 181.

[94] See the proceedings: [UGDO], *Les Voies de la renaissance de Ouidah*.

[95] For the latter, see Soumonni et al., *Le Bénin et la Route de l'esclave*; and proceedings of the conference published as Diène, *La Chaine et le lien*.

Sources & Bibliography

Oral sources in Ouidah

Adanle compound, Sogbadji quarter: Adanle Comlan, interviewed 11 Jan. 1996
Agbamou compound, Ahouandjigo quarter: Tobias Agbo, 11 Dec. 2001
Amoua family, Docomè quarter: Sebastien Amoua, museum guide, 11 Dec. 2001
Antonio Kokou Félix de Souza Adekpeti compound, Brazil quarter: Balbina de Souza, 12 Dec. 2001
Azilinon compound, Tové quarter: Azilinon (priest), Houngan (deputy chief priest), Da (head of family), and others, 14 Sept. 2000
Codjia compound, Brazil quarter: Codjia Agbanchénou Saturnin, 13 June 1997
Déhoué compound, Sogbadji quarter: family members, 9 Jan. 1996
De Souza compound, Brazil quarter: Prosper Norberto de Souza, 18 Jan. 1996, 5 Dec. 2001; Eulalie Dagba, 9 Dec. 2001; Eusébio Frédérique de Souza, 12 Dec. 2001
Dossou-Yovo compound, Tové quarter: family members, 11 Jan. 1996, 5 Dec. 2001
Fakanbi, Justin, local historian, Alafia quarter, 3 Dec. 2001
Gbeti compound, Sogbadji quarter: Gbeti Eugène, 9 Jan. 1996
Glehue Daho compound, Fonsaramè quarter: family members, 3 Dec. 2001
Hechili compound, Tové 2 quarter: Hechili Celestine, 13 June 1997
Hodonou compound, Hodonousaramè quarter: Tagnnin Agor, Tagnnin Candji, Tagnnin Hinhami and Tagnnin Ninhouénou, 21 Sept. 2000
Hounon compound, Sogbadji quarter: Daagbo Hounnon Houna Agbessi, 18 Jan. 1996
Kocou compound, Sogbadji quarter: Dagbo Kocou Dossou-Yovo Calliste, 9 Jan. 1996
Kpatenon compound, Docomè quarter: Kpatenon Akokpon Medjeron, 3 Dec. 2001
Lemon compound, Sogbadji quarter: Lemon Sika, 9 Jan. 1996
Lima compound, Brazil quarter: Léopoldine Lima, 9 Dec. 2001
Lino Felix de Souza compound, Brazil quarter: Odile David-Gnahoui, 5 Dec. 2001
Midjrokan compound, Sogbadji quarter: family members, 9 Jan. 1996
Zossoungbo compound, Sogbadji quarter: family members, 9 Jan. 1996
Zoungbodji village: Martin Cakanacou, 11 Dec. 2001

Sources & Bibliography
Archival sources

Bénin
Archives Nationales, Porto-Novo
1E14: Affaires politiques, Ouidah

France
Archives Nationales, Section d'Outre-Mer, Aix-en-Provence

Archives des Colonies
C6/25–27bis: Papers concerning Juda [Ouidah], Ardres [Porto-Novo], etc., 1712–1806

Dépôt des Fortifications des Colonies, Côtes d'Afrique
104: 'Relation du royaume de Judas en Guinée, de son gouvernement, des moeurs de ses habitans, de leur religion, et du négoce qui s'y fait', n.d. [*c*.1715].
111: 'Réflexions sur Juda par les Sieurs de Chenevert et abbé Bullet', 1 June 1776.

Bibliothèque Nationale, Paris
Fonds français, 24223: 'Journal du voiage de Guinée et Cayenne, par le Chevalier des Marchais Capitaine commandant la frégatte de la Compagnie des Indes, l'Expedition, pendant les années 1724, 1725 et 1726'

Spain
Bibliotheca Publica do Estado, Toledo, Spain
Collecçion de MSS Bornon-Lorenzo, 47: Basilio de Zamora, 'Cosmographia o descripcion del mundo' (1675)

Togo
Lawson family papers, Aného:
Le Grand Livre Lolamé [transcription supplied by Adam Jones]

United Kingdom
Public Record Office, London

Admiralty records
ADM55/11: Journal of Commander Hugh Clapperton, 1825–6

Chancery records
C113/276: Papers of James Phipps, Chief Merchant at Cape Coast Castle, correspondence with William Baillie and others at Ouidah

Colonial Office records
CO2: African Exploration
CO96: Gold Coast
CO147: Lagos

Sources & Bibliography

Foreign Office records
    FO2: Africa, Consular
    FO84: Slave Trade

Treasury records
    T70: Records of African Companies, 1663–1821

Wesleyan Methodist Missionary Society Archives, School of Oriental and African Studies, University of London

Correspondence, Gold Coast, 1854–67
T.B. Freeman, 'West Africa', typescript for book, *c*.1860

UK Parliamentary Papers

Copy of Despatches from the Lieutenant-Governor of the Gold Coast, giving an account of Missions to the King of Ashantee and Dohomey [*sic*], (1849)
Correspondence relating to the Slave Trade (1822–1870)
Despatches from Commodore Wilmot respecting his Visit to the King of Dahomey, in December 1862 and January 1863 (1863)
Papers relative to the Reduction of Lagos by Her Majesty's Forces (1852)
Report from the Select Committee on the Slave Trade (1848)
Report from the Select Committee on the State of the British Settlements on the Western Coast of Africa (1865)
Report from the Select Committee on the West Coast of Africa (1842)
Treaty of Friendship, Commerce, and for the Suppression of the Slave Trade, between Her Majesty and the King of Dahomey, signed at Whydah, May 12, 1877 (1878)

Published contemporary sources

Adams, John: *Remarks on the Country extending from Cape Palmas to the River Congo, with an appendix containing an account of the European trade with the West Coast of Africa* (London, 1823; repr. 1966)
Atkins, John: *A Voyage to Guinea, Brasil and the West Indies* (London, 1735; repr. 1970)
Aublet, Édouard: *La Guerre au Dahomey 1888–1893 d'après des documents officiels* (Paris, 1894)
Barbot, Jean: *Barbot on Guinea: The Writings of Jean Barbot on West Africa, 1678–1712*, ed. Paul Hair, Adam Jones & Robin Law, 2 vols (Hakluyt Society, London, 1992)
Béraud, Médard: 'Note sur le Dahomé', *Bulletin de la Société de Géographie*, 5th series, 12 (1866), 371–86
Bertin: 'Renseignements sur le royaume de Porto-Novo et le Dahomey', *RMC*, 106 (1890), 385–93.
Blancheley: 'Au Dahomey', 5 parts, *Les Missions catholiques*, 23 (1891), 534–7, 545–8, 562–4, 575–6, 587–8
Borghero, Francesco: *Journal de Francesco Borghero, premier missionnaire du Dahomey, 1861–1865*, ed. Renzo Mandirola & Yves Morel (Paris, 1997)
———: 'Missions du Dahomey', *Annales de la Propagation de la Foi*, 25 (1862), 209–35
Bosman, William: *A New and Accurate Description of the Coast of Guinea* (London, 1705; repr. 1967)

Sources & Bibliography

Bouche, Pierre: *Septs ans en Afrique occidentale: La Côte des Esclaves et le Dahomey* (Paris, 1885)

Bouet, Auguste: 'Le royaume de Dahomey', *L'Illustration*, 20 (1852), 3 parts, 31–42, 58–62, 71–4

Brue, [A.]: 'Voyage fait en 1843, dans le royaume de Dahomey', *RC*, 7 (1845), 55–68

Burton, Richard F.: *A Mission to Gelele, King of Dahome*, 2 vols (London, 1864)

Buzon: 'Une visite à la cour du roi de Dahomey en 1874', *Revue politique et littéraire: revue bleue*, 51/24 (1893), 751–9.

Chaudouin, E.: *Trois mois de captivité au Dahomey* (Paris, 1891)

Clapperton, Hugh: *Journal of a Second Expedition into the Interior of Africa from the Bight of Benin to Soccatoo* (London, 1829; repr. 1966)

Conneau, Theophilus: *A Slaver's Log Book, or 20 Years' Residence in Africa: The Original 1853 Manuscript*, ed. Mabel M. Smythe (London, 1977)

Corrêa da Silva, Carlos Eugenio: *Uma viagem ao estabelecimento portuguez de S. João Baptista de Ajudá na Costa da Mina em 1865* (Lisbon, 1866)

Cruickshank, Brodie: *Eighteen Years on the Gold Coast of Africa*, 2 vols (London, 1853; repr. 1966)

Dalzel, Archibald: *The History of Dahomy, An Inland Kingdom of Africa* (London, 1793; repr. 1967)

Damon: 'Relation du voyage d'Issyny fait en 1701 par le Chevalier Damon', in Paul Roussier (ed.), *L'Etablissement d'Issigny 1687–1702: Voyages de Ducasse, Tibierge et D'Amon à la Côte de Guinée* (Paris, 1935), 91–107.

Dapper, Olfert: *Naukeurige Beschrijvinge der Afrikaensche Gewesten* (Amsterdam, 1668; 2nd edn 1676)

Davenant, Charles: *The Political and Commercial Works of Charles d'Avenant* (London, 1771)

Delbée: 'Journal du voyage du Sieur Delbée, Commissaire general de la Marine, aux Isles, dans la coste de Guynée', in J. de Clodoré (ed.), *Relation de ce qui s'est passé dans les isles et terre-ferme de l'Amérique pendant la dernière guerre avec l'Angleterre et depuis en exécution du Traitté de Bréda* (Paris, 1671), ii, 347–558

De Monleon: 'Le Cap de Palmes, le Dahomé et l'Île du Prince en 1844', *RC*, 6 (1845), 62–82

de Naxara, Joseph: *Espejo mistico en que el hombre se mira prácticamente illustrado* (Madrid, 1672)

de Sandoval, Alonso: *Naturaleza, policia sagrada i profana, constumbres i ritos, disciplina i catechismo evangelico de todos Etiopes* (Seville, 1627)

Donnan, Elizabeth (ed.): *Documents Illustrative of the History of the Slave Trade to America*, 4 vols (Washington, 1930–5; repr. New York, 1969)

[dos Santos, José Francisco, correspondence of]: trans. Pierre Verger, 'Cent-douze letters de Alfaiate', in Pierre Verger *et al*: *Les Afro-américains* (Dakar, 1952), 53–99

Doublet, Jean: *Journal du corsaire Jean Doublet de Honfleur*, ed. Charles Bréard (Paris, 1883)

Du Casse: 'Relation du voyage de Guynée fait en 1687 sur la frégate "La Tempeste" par le Sieur Ducasse', in Paul Roussier (ed.), *L'Établissement d'Issigny 1687–1702: Voyages de Du Casse, Tibierge et Damon en Guynée* (Paris, 1935), 1–47

Duncan, John: *Travels in Western Africa in 1845 and 1846, comprising a Journey from Whydah, through the Kingdom of Dahomey, to Adofoodia, in the Interior*, 2 vols (London, 1847; repr. 1968)

Foà, Édouard: *Le Dahomey: Histoire – Géographie – Moeurs – Coutumes – Commerce – Industrie – Expéditions françaises (1891–1894)* (Paris, 1895)

Forbes, F.E.: *Dahomey and the Dahomans, being the Journals of two missions to the King of Dahomey, and residence at his capital, in the years 1849 and 1850*, 2 vols (London, 1851; repr. 1966)

Sources & Bibliography

Freeman, Thomas Birch: *Journal of Various Visits to the Kingdoms of Ashanti, Aku and Dahomi in Western Africa* (London, 1844; repr. 1968)

Gramberg, J.S.G.: *Schetsen van Afrikas Westkust* (Amsterdam, 1861)

Guillevin: 'Voyage dans l'intérieur du royaume de Dahomey', *Nouvelles annales de voyages, de la géographie et de l'archéologie*, 2 (1862), 257–99

Heintze, Beatrix (ed.): *Fontes para a história de Angola de seculo XVII* (2 vols, Wiesbaden, 1985–8)

Huntley, Sir Henry: *Seven Years' Service on the Slave Coast of Western Africa* (London, 1850)

Hutchinson, Thomas J.: *Impressions of Western Africa* (London, 1858; repr. 1970)

Isert, Paul Erdman: *Letters on West Africa and the Slave Trade: Paul Erdman Isert's* Journal to Guinea and the Caribbean Islands in Columbia *(1788)*, trans. Selena Axelrod Winsnes (British Academy, London, 1992)

Kalous, Milan: 'Some correspondence between the German Empire and Dahomey in 1882–1892', *CEA*, 8/32 (1968), 635–41

Labat, Jean-Baptiste: *Voyage du Chevalier des Marchais en Guinée, isles voisines et à Cayenne, fait en 1725, 1726 et 1727* (Paris, 1730; 2nd edn, Amsterdam, 1731)

Laffitte, Abbé: *Le Dahomé: Souvenirs de voyage et de mission* (Tours, 1874)

Lander, Richard: *Records of Captain Clapperton's Last Expedition to Africa*, 2 vols (London, 1830; repr. 1967)

Law, Robin: 'A neglected account of the Dahomian conquest of Whydah (1727): the "Relation de la guerre de Juda" of the Sieur Ringard of Nantes', *HA*, 15 (1988), 321–8

—— (ed.): *Correspondence from the Royal African Company's Factories at Offra and Whydah on the Slave Coast of West Africa in the Public Record Office, London, 1678–93* (Centre of African Studies, University of Edinburgh, 1990)

—— (ed.): *Correspondence of the Royal African Company's Chief Factors at Cabo Corso Castle with William's Fort, Whydah, and the Little Popo Factory, 1727–8: An Annotated Transcription of Ms. Francklin 1055/1 in the Bedfordshire County Record Office* (African Studies Program, University of Wisconsin-Madison, 1991)

—— (ed.): *Further Correspondence of the Royal African Company of England Relating to the "Slave Coast", 1681–1699: Selected Documents from Ms Rawlinson C.745–747 in the Bodleian Library, Oxford* (African Studies Program, University of Wisconsin-Madison, 1992)

—— (ed.): *The English in West Africa, 1681–1683: The Local Correspondence of the Royal African Company of England, 1681–1699, Part 1* (British Academy, London, 1997)

—— (ed.): *The English in West Africa, 1685–1688: The Local Correspondence of the Royal African Company of England, 1681–1699, Part 2* (British Academy, London, 2001)

[*Le Dahomet*, accounts of]: in Simone Berbain, *Le Comptoir français de Juda* (Paris, 1942), 99–125

M'Leod, John: *A Voyage to Africa, with some account of the manners and customs of the Dahomian people* (London, 1820; repr. 1971)

Maigre, Etienne: 'De Lagos au Dahomey, 10–20 juillet 1889', *Bulletin de la Société de Géographie de Marseille*, 14/1 (1890), 118–31

N****: *Voyages aux Côtes de Guinée et en Amérique* (Amsterdam, 1719)

Norris, Robert: *Memoirs of the Reign of Bossa Ahadee, King of Dahomy* (London, 1789; repr. 1968)

Peixoto, António da Costa: *Obra nova de lingua geral de Mina de António da Costa Peixoto*, ed. Luís Silveira & Edmundo Correia Lopes (Lisbon, 1945)

Phillips, Thomas: 'A Journal of a Voyage made in the Hannibal of London, Ann. 1693, 1694', in *Collection of Voyages and Travels*, ed. Awnsham Churchill & John Churchill (London,

1732), vi, 173–239

Pires, Vicente Ferreira: *Viagem de Africa em on reino de Dahomé*, ed. Clado Ribeiro de Lessa (São Paulo, 1957)

Plimpton, George (ed.): 'The Journal of an African slaver, 1789–1792', *Proceedings of the American Antiquarian Society*, ns, 39/2 (1930), 379–465

Pruneau de Pommegorge, [Joseph]: *Description de la Nigritie* (Amsterdam, 1789)

Quinn, Frank J.: *A Coaster's Letters from Dahomey, French West Africa* (n.p., 1928)

Repin, Dr: 'Voyage au Dahomey', *Le Tour du monde*, 1 (1863), 65–112

Ridgway, Archibald: 'Journal of a visit to Dahomey, or the Snake Country, in the months of March and April, 1847', 3 parts, *New Monthly Magazine*, 81 (1847), 187–98, 299–309, 406–14

Robertson, G.A.: *Notes on Africa, particularly those parts which are situated between Cape Verde and the River Congo* (London, 1819)

Sarmento, Augusto: *Portugal no Dahomé* (Lisbon, 1891)

Serval, [Paul]: 'Rapport sur une mission au Dahomey, *RMC*, 59 (1878), 186–95

Skertchly, J.A.: *Dahomey As It Is* (London, 1874)

Smith, William: *A New Voyage to Guinea* (London, 1744; repr. 1967)

Snelgrave, William: *A New Account of Some Parts of Guinea, and the Slave-Trade* (London, 1734; repr. 1971)

[*Swallow*, accounts of]: see Plimpton, George

Swanzy, [Alexander]: 'On the trade in Western Africa with and without British protection', *Journal of the Society of the Arts*, 22 (1874), 478–87

Vallon, A.: 'Le royaume de Dahomey', 2 parts, *RMC*, 1 (1860), 332–63; 2 (1861), 329–53

Van Dantzig, Albert: 'English Bosman and Dutch Bosman: a comparison of texts', Parts I–VIII, *HA*, 2 (1975), 185–216; 3 (1976), 91–126; 4 (1977), 247–73; 5 (1978), 225–56; 6 (1979), 265–85; 7 (1980), 281–91; 9 (1982), 285–302; 11 (1984), 307–29

—— (ed.): *The Dutch and the Guinea Coast 1674–1742: A Collection of Documents from the General State Archive at The Hague* (Ghana Academy of Arts and Sciences, Accra, 1978)

Newspapers

The African Times, London

Royal Gold Coast Gazette and Commercial Advertiser, Cape Coast, 1822–3

La Voix du Dahomey, no. 66 (June 1932): Obituary of Edouard David Gnahoui

Ex-slave memoirs

Baquaqua, Mahommah Gardo: *An Interesting Narrative: Biography of Mahommah G. Baquaqua, A Native of Zoogoo, in the Interior of Africa*, ed. Samuel Moore (Detroit, 1854)

Childers, James Saxon: 'From jungle to slavery – and freedom', *Birmingham News – Age - Herald*, 2 Dec. 1934

Hurston, Zora Neale: 'Cudjo's own story of the last African slaver', *Journal of Negro History*, 12 (1927), 648–63

Law, Robin & Paul E. Lovejoy (eds): *The Biography of Mahommah Gardo Baquaqua: His Passage from Slavery to Freedom in Africa and America* (Princeton, 2001)

Sources & Bibliography
Colonial surveys

Gavoy, [Marcel]: 'Note historique sur Ouidah par l'Administrateur Gavoy (1913)', *ED*, 13 (1955), 45–70
Reynier: 'Ouidah: organisation du commandement [1917]', *Mémoire du Bénin*, 2 (1993), 27–73

Local histories and pamphlets

Agbo, Casimir: *Histoire de Ouidah du XVe au XXe siècle* (Avignon, 1959)
Assogba, Romain-Philippe Ekanyé: *Le Musée d'histoire de Ouidah: Découverte de la Côte des Esclaves* (Cotonou, 1990)
Dagba, Léon-Pierre Ghézowounmè-Djomalia: *La Collectivité familiale Yovogan Hounnon Dagba de ses origines à nos jours* (Porto-Novo, 1982)
da Silva, Rodrigues & Christophe da Silva, *Histoire de la famille Rodrigues da Silva sur la Côte du Bénin* (Cotonou, 1992)
de Souza, Martine: *Regard sur Ouidah/A Bit of History* (Ouidah, 2000)
de Souza, Martine, & Mère Jah Evejah: *Bienvenue à Ouidah au Bénin/Welcome to Ouidah in Bénin* (Ouidah, n.d. [1998])
de Souza, Norberto Francisco: 'Contribution à l'histoire de la famille de Souza', *ED*, 13 (1955), 17–21
de Souza, Simone *La Famille de Souza du Bénin-Togo* (Cotonou, 1992)
Fakambi, Justin: *La Route des esclaves au Bénin (ex-Dahomey) dans une approche régionale* (Cotonou, n.d. [1992])
Hazoumé, Paul: 'Aperçu historique sur les origines de Ouidah', 6 parts, *La Reconnaissance africaine*, 6 parts, no. 4 (15 Oct. 1925), 7–8; no. 5 (19 Nov. 1925) 7–9; no. 7 (1 Dec. 1925), 8; no. 8 (18 Dec. 1925), 8; no. 10 (1 Feb. 1926), 8; no. 11 (15 Feb. 1926), 8
Mouléro, Thomas: 'Histoire et légendes des Djêkens', *ED*, ns, 3 (1964), 51–76
Quénum, Dominique Avimagbogbênou: *L'Histoire de Glexwe (Ouidah)* (Dakar, 1999)
Quénum, Faustin Possi-Berry: *Généalogie de la dynastie Houéhoun à la collectivité familiale Azanmado Houénou-Quénum* (Cotonou, 1993)
Quénum, Maximilien: *Les Ancêtres de la famille Quénum: histoire de leur temps* (Langres, 1981)
Quénum, Venance S.: *Ouidah, cité historique des "Houeda"* (Ouidah, [1982])
[UGDO]: *Les Voies de la renaissance de Ouidah: Almanach de Ouidah, Actes du pré-colloque ORIGINES tenu à Ouidah du 23 au 27 september 1985* (Caen, 1985)
Verger, Pierre & Clément da Cruz: *Musée historique de Ouidah* (Porto-Novo, 1969)
Villaça, Père Théophile: *La Basilique de Ouidah: Son histoire et ses premiers Pasteurs à partir de diverses sources* (n.p., [Ouidah] 2000)

Other published works

Adandé, Alexis B. (ed.): *Ouidah à travers ses fêtes et patrimoines familiaux* (Cotonou, 1995)
—— : 'Buried heritage, surface heritage: the Portuguese fort of São João Baptista de Ajudá', in Claude Daniel Ardouin & Emmanuel Arinza (eds), *Museums and History in West Africa* (Oxford, 2000), 127–31
Adandé, Joseph: 'Le *gelede* à Ouidah: mieux vaut tard que jamais', in Alexis Adandé (ed.), *Ouidah à travers ses fêtes et patrimoines familiaux* (Cotonou, 1995), 65–82

Sources & Bibliography

Adoukonou, Barthélémy: *Jalons pour une théologie africaine: essai d'une herméneutique chrétienne du vodun dahoméen*, 2 vols (Paris, 1980)

Akibode, I.:'De la traite à la colonisation', in Alain Sinou & Bernardin Agbo (eds), *Ouidah et son patrimoine* (Cotonou/Paris, 1991), 29–60.

Akindélé, A. & C. Aguessy: *Contribution à l'étude de l'histoire de l'ancien royaume de Porto-Novo* (Mémoires de l'IFAN no. 25, Dakar, 1953; repr. Amsterdam, 1968)

Akinjogbin, I.A.: *Dahomey and its Neighbours 1708–1818* (Cambridge, 1967)

Akyeampong, Emmanuel: "'*O pe tam won pe ba*'/"*You like cloth but you don't want children*": urbanization, individualism and gender relations in colonial Ghana, *c.* 1900–1939', in David M. Anderson & Richard Rathbone (eds), *Africa's Urban Past* (Oxford, 2000), 222–34

Anderson, David M. & Richard Rathbone (eds), *Africa's Urban Past* (Oxford, 2000)

Arnold, Rosemary: 'A port of trade: Whydah on the Guinea Coast', in Karl Polanyi, Conrad M. Arensberg & Harry W. Pearson (eds), *Trade and Market in the Early Empires* (New York, 1957), 154–76

——: 'Separation of trade and market: Great Market of Whydah', in Karl Polanyi, Conrad M. Arensberg & Harry W. Pearson (eds), *Trade and Market in the Early Empires* (New York, 1957), 177–87

Austen, Ralph A.: 'The moral economy of witchcraft: an essay in comparative history', in Jean Comaroff & John Comaroff (eds), *Modernity and its Malcontents: Ritual and Power in Post-colonial Africa* (Chicago, 1993), 89–110

——: 'Douala: slave trade and memory on the periphery of the Nigerian hinterland', in Robin Law & Silke Strickrodt (eds), *Ports of the Slave Trade (Bights of Benin and Biafra)* (Centre of Commonwealth Studies, University of Stirling, 1999), 71–83

——: 'The slave trade as history and memory: confrontations of slaving voyage documents and communal traditions', *WMQ*, 58 (2001), 229–44

Austen, Ralph A. & Jonathan Derrick: *Middlemen of the Cameroons Rivers: The Duala and their hinterland, c. 1600–c. 1960* (Cambridge, 1999)

Bailyn, Bernard: 'The idea of Atlantic history', *Itinerario*, 20/1 (1996), 38–44

Bay, Edna G.: *Wives of the Leopard: Gender, Politics and Culture in the Kingdom of Dahomey* (Charlottesville, 1998)

——: 'Protection, political exile, and the Atlantic slave-trade: history and collective memory in Dahomey, *S&A*, 22 (2001), 42–60

Berbain, Simone: *Le Comptoir français de Juda (Ouidah) au XVIIIe siècle* (Mémoires de l'IFAN no. 3, Paris, 1942; repr. Amsterdam, 1968)

Bethell, Leslie: *The Abolition of the Brazilian Slave Trade: Britain, Brazil and the Slave Trade Question 1807–1869* (Cambridge, 1970)

Blier, Suzanne Preston: *African Vodun: Art, Psychology and Power* (Chicago, 1995)

Boco, Pamphile: *Proverbes de la sagesse fon (Sud-Bénin)*, 4 vols (Cotonou, 1995–7, 2000)

Bonfils, Jean: *La Mission catholique en République du Bénin: Des origines à 1945* (Paris, 1999)

Brégand, Denise: *Commerce caravanier et relations sociales au Bénin: les Wangara du Borgou* (Paris, 1998)

Brown, Spencer H. 'Public health in Lagos, 1850–1900', *IJAHS*, 25 (1992), 337–60

Cafuri, Roberta: 'Silenzi della memoria: la tratta degli schiavi', *Africa* (Rome), 55/2 (2000), 244–60

Chatwin, Bruce: *The Viceroy of Ouidah* (London, 1980)

Clarence-Smith, William Gervase: 'The dynamics of the Atlantic slave trade', *Africa* (London), 64 (1994), 275–86

Clifford, Barry, with Paul Perry: *Expedition Whydah: The Story of the World's First Excavation*

of a Pirate Treasure Ship and the Man who Found Her (New York, 1999)

Codo, B., & S. Anignikin: 'Ouidah sous le régime colonial', in [UGDO], *Les Voies de la renaissance de Ouidah* (Caen, 1985), 103–14

Cohen, Abner: *Custom and Politics in Urban Africa: A Study of Hausa Migrants in Yoruba Towns* (London, 1969)

Conrad, Joseph: *Heart of Darkness* (Harmondsorth, 1983)

Coquery, Catherine: 'Le blocus de Whydah (1876–1877) et la rivalité franco-anglaise au Dahomey', *CEA*, 2/7 (1962), 373–419

Coquery-Vidrovitch, Catherine: 'De la traite des esclaves à l'exportation de l'huile de palme et des palmistes au Dahomey: XIXe siècle', in Claude Meillassoux (ed.), *The Development of Indigenous Trade and Markets in West Africa* (London, 1971), 107–23

Cornevin, Robert: *Histoire du Dahomey* (Paris, 1962)

Curto, José C.: 'The anatomy of a demographic explosion: Luanda, 1844–1850', *IJAHS*, 32 (1999), 381–405

d'Almeida-Topor, Hélène: *Histoire économique du Dahomey*, 2 vols (Paris, 1995)

da Cunha, M. & M.C. Cunha: *From Slave Quarters to Town Houses: Brazilian Architecture in Nigeria and the People's Republic of Benin* (São Paulo, 1985)

Dayan, Joan: *Haïti, History and the Gods* (Berkeley, 1998)

de Souza, Rachida Ayari: 'La danse de la mémoire: le *buriyan*', in Alexis Adandé (ed.), *Ouidah à travers ses fêtes et patrimoines familiaux* (Cotonou, 1995), 43–63

Diène, Doudou (ed.): *La Chaine et le lien: une vision de la traite négrière* (Paris, 1998)

Djivo, Joseph Adrien: 'Le roi Glélé et les européens: l'échec du protectorat portugais sur le Danhomé (1885–7)', *Cahiers du Centre de Recherches Africaines* (Paris), 8 (1994), 269–84

Dupuis, Père Paul-Henry: *Histoire de l'église du Bénin, Tome 1: Le Temps des sémeurs (1494–1901)* (Cotonou, [1998])

Ellingworth, Paul: '"As others see us": sidelights on the early history of Methodism in Ouidah', *Bulletin of the Society for African Church History*, 1 (1963), 13–17

——: '"As they saw themselves": more about the beginnings of Methodism in Ouidah', *Bulletin of the Society for African Church History*, 2 (1964), 35–41

——: 'Christianity and politics in Dahomey, 1843–1867', *JAH*, 5 (1964), 209–20

Eltis, David: *Economic Growth and the Ending of the Transatlantic Slave Trade* (New York, 1987)

——: 'Precolonial western Africa and the Atlantic economy', in Barbara L. Solow (ed.), *Slavery and the Rise of the Atlantic System* (Cambridge, 1991), 97–119

——: *The Rise of African Slavery in the Americas* (Cambridge, 2000)

Eltis, David, & David Richardson: 'West Africa and the Transatlantic slave trade: new evidence of long-run trends', *S&A*, 18 (1997), 16–35

Eltis, David, Paul E. Lovejoy & David Richardson: 'Slave-trading ports: towards an Atlantic-wide perspective', in Robin Law & Silke Strickrodt (eds), *Ports of the Slave Trade (Bights of Benin and Biafra)* (Centre of Commonwealth Studies, University of Stirling, 1999), 12–34

Elwert, Georg: *Wirtschaft und Herrschaft von 'Daxome' (Dahomey) in 18 Jahrhundert: Ökonomie des Sklavenraubs und Gesellschaftstruktur 1724–1818* (Munich, 1973)

Fall, K., B. Légonou-Fanou & F. Légonou: 'Typologie des cultes vodoun', in Alain Sinou & Bernardin Agbo (eds), *Ouidah et son patrimoine* (Paris/Cotonou 1991), 61–81

Feinberg, Harvey M.: *Africans and Europeans in West Africa: Elminans and Dutchmen on the Gold Coast during the Eighteenth Century* (Philadelphia, 1989)

Fuglestad, Finn: 'La questionnement du "port" de Ouidah (Côte des Esclaves)', in Oystein Rian, Finn Erhard Johannsen, Oystein Sorensen & Finn Fuglestad (eds), *Revolusjon og*

Sources & Bibliography

Resonnement: Festskrift til Kare Gonneson (Oslo, 1995), 125–36
Fyfe, Christopher: *A History of Sierra Leone* (London, 1962)
Garcia, Luc Messanvi: 'Archives et tradition orale: à propos d'une enquête sur la politique du royaume de Danhomé à la fin du 19e siècle', *CEA*, 61–2 (1976), 189–206
——: *Le Royaume du Dahomé face à la pénétration coloniale: Affrontements et incomprehension (1875–1894)* (Paris, 1988)
Gayibor, N.L.: *Le Genyi: un royaume oublié de la Côte de Guinée au temps de la traite des noirs* (Lomé, 1990)
Glélé, Maurice Ahanhanzo: *Le Danxome: Du pouvoir aja à la nation fon* (Paris, 1974)
Gordano, Rosario: *Europei e Africani nel Dahomey e Porto-Novo: "Il periodo delle ambiguità" (1850–1880)* (Turin, 2001)
Greene, Sandra E.: *Gender, Ethnicity and Social Change on the Upper Slave Coast: A History of the Anlo Ewe* (London, 1996)
Grivot, R.: 'La Pêche chez les Pedah du lac Ahémé', *BIFAN*, 11/1–2 (1949), 106–28
Guilcher, René F.: *Au Dahomey avec le Père Dorgère* (Lyon, n.d.)
Guran, Milton: *Agudás: os "brasileiros" do Benim* (Rio de Janeiro, 1999)
Hammond, R.J.: *Portugal and Africa, 1815–1910: A study in uneconomic imperialism* (Stanford, 1966)
Hargreaves, John D.: *Prelude to the Partition of West Africa* (London, 1963)
——: *West Africa Partitioned, Vol. I: The Loaded Pause, 1885–1889* (London, 1974); *Vol. II: The Elephants and the Grass* (London, 1985)
Harms, Robert: *The Diligent: A Voyage through the Worlds of the Slave Trade* (New York, 2002)
Hazoumé, Paul: *Le Pacte de sang au Dahomey* (Institut d'Ethnologie, Paris, 1937)
Henige, David: *Oral Historiography* (London, 1982)
Herbert, Eugenia W.: 'Smallpox inoculation in Africa', *JAH*, 16 (1975), 539–59
Herskovits, Melville J.: *Dahomey: an Ancient West African Kingdom*, 2 vols (New York, 1938)
Herskovits, Melville J. & Frances S. Herskovits: *Dahomean Narrative: a Cross-cultural Analysis* (Evanston, 1958)
Hogendorn, Jan. & Marion Johnson: *The Shell Money of the Slave Trade* (Cambridge, 1986)
Hopkins, A.G.: *An Economic History of West Africa* (London, 1973)
Iroko, Abiola Félix: 'Le sel marin de la Côte des Esclaves durant la période précoloniale', *Africa* (Rome), 46 (1981), 520–40
——: 'Le spectre de la mort à Cotonou des origines à nos jours: un essai d'histoire des mentalités', *Le Mois en Afrique*, 227–8 (Dec. 1984–Jan. 1985), 133–44
——: 'Cauris et esclaves en Afrique occidentale entre le XVe et le XIX siècle', in Serge Daget (ed.), *De la traite à l'esclavage* (2 vols, Nantes, 1988), i, 193–204
——: 'Les hommes et les incendies à la Côte des Esclaves durant la période précoloniale', *Africa* (Rome), 48 (1993), 396–423
——: *Les Hula du XIVe au XIXe siècle* (Cotonou, 2001)
Johnson, Marion: 'The ounce in eighteenth-century West African trade', *JAH*, 7 (1966), 197–214
——: 'The Atlantic slave trade and the economy of West Africa', in Roger Anstey & P.E.H. Hair (eds), *Liverpool, the African Slave Trade and Abolition* (Liverpool, 1976), 14–38
Jones, Adam: 'Litte Popo and Agoué at the end of the Atlantic Slave Trade: glimpses from the Lawson correspondence and other sources', in Robin Law & Silke Strickrodt (eds), *Ports of the Slave Trade (Bights of Benin and Biafra)* (Centre of Commonwealth Studies, University of Stirling, 1999), 122–34
Kaba, Lansiné: 'The Atlantic slave trade was *not* a "black-on-black holocaust"', *African Studies Review*, 44/1 (2001), 1–20

Kadja, Germain: 'Les communautés de base de Ouidah: leurs origines et leurs apports', in [UGDO], *Les Voies de la renaissance de Ouidah* (Caen, 1985), 49–60.

Karl-August, Emmanuel: 'Pour une politique de recherche historique sur Ouidah et sa région', in [UGDO], *Les Voies de la renaissance de Ouidah*, (Caen, 1985), 61–79

Kelly, Kenneth G.: 'Using historically informed archaeology: seventeenth and eighteenth century Hueda/European interactions on the coast of Bénin', *Journal of Archaeological Method and Theory*, 4 (1997), 353–66

Klein, Herbert S.: *The Atlantic Slave Trade* (Cambridge, 1999)

Knight, Franklin W. & Peggy K. Liss (eds): *Atlantic Port Cities: Economy, Culture and Society in the Atlantic World, 1650–1850* (Princeton, 1991)

Kopytoff, Jean Herskovits: *A Preface to Modern Nigeria: The 'Sierra Leonians' in Yoruba, 1830–1890* (Madison, 1965)

Krapf-Askari, Eva: *Yoruba Towns and Cities: An Enquiry into the Nature of Urban Social Phenomena* (Oxford, 1969)

Kreamer, Christine Mueller: 'Contested terrain: cultural negotiation and Ghana's Cape Coast Castle exhibition, "Crossroads of People, Crossroads of Trade"', in Ralph Austen (ed.), *The Atlantic Slave Trade in African and Diaspora Memory* (forthcoming, Durham, N.C.).

Langley, J. Ayodele: *Pan-Africanism and Nationalism in West Africa 1900–1945: A Study in Ideology and Social Classes* (Oxford, 1973)

Latham, A.J.H.: 'Witchcraft accusations and economic tension in pre-colonial Old Calabar', *JAH*, 13 (1972), 249–60

——: *Old Calabar 1600–1891: The Impact of the International Economy upon a Traditional Society* (Oxford, 1973)

Law, Robin: 'Royal monopoly and private enterprise in the Atlantic trade: the case of Dahomey', *JAH*, 18 (1977), 555–77

——: 'Towards a history of urbanization in pre-colonial Yorubaland', in Christopher Fyfe (ed.), *African Historical Demography* (Centre of African Studies, University of Edinburgh, 1977), 260–71

——: 'The career of Adele at Lagos and Badagry, *c*.1807–*c*.1837'. *JHSN*, 9/2 (1978), 35–59

——: 'Trade and politics behind the Slave Coast: the lagoon traffic and the rise of Lagos, 1500–1800', *JAH*, 24 (1983), 321–48

——: 'Islam in Dahomey: a case study of the introduction and influence of Islam in a peripheral area of West Africa', *Scottish Journal of Religious Studies*, 7/2 (1986), 95–122

——: 'Between the sea and the lagoons: the interaction of maritime and inland navigation on the pre-colonial Slave Coast', *CEA*, 29 (1989), 209–37

——: 'Slave-raiders and middlemen, monopolists and free-traders: the supply of slaves for the Atlantic trade in Dahomey, *c*.1715–1850', *JAH*, 30 (1989), 45–68

——: '"The common people were divided": monarchy, aristocracy and political factionalism in the kingdom of Whydah, 1671–1727', *IJAHS*, 23 (1990), 201–29

——: 'The gold trade of Whydah in the seventeenth and eighteenth centuries', in David Henige & T.C. McCaskie (eds), *West African Economic and Social History: Essays in Memory of Marion Johnson* (African Studies Program, University of Wisconsin-Madison, 1990), 105–18

——: 'Computing domestic prices in pre-colonial West Africa: a methodological exercise from the Slave Coast', *HA*, 18 (1991), 239–57

——: 'King Agaja of Dahomey, the Slave Trade, and the question of West African plantations: the mission of Bulfinch Lambe and Adomo Tomo to England, 1726–32', *Journal of Imperial and Commonwealth History*, 19 (1991), 137–63

Sources & Bibliography

———: *The Slave Coast of West Africa, 1550–1750: The impact of the Atlantic Slave Trade on an African society* (Oxford, 1991)

———: 'Posthumous questions for Karl Polanyi: price inflation in pre-colonial Dahomey', *JAH*, 33 (1992), 387–420

———: 'Warfare on the West African Slave Coast, 1650–1850', in R. Brian Ferguson & Neil L. Whitehead (eds): *War in the Tribal Zone: Expanding States and Indigenous Warfare* (Santa Fé, 1992), 103–26

———: 'Cowries, gold and dollars: exchange rate instability and domestic price inflation in Dahomey in the eighteenth and nineteenth centuries', in Jane I. Guyer (ed.), *Money Matters: Instability, Values and Social Payments in the Modern History of West African Communities* (London, 1994), 53–73

———: '"Here is no resisting the country": the realities of power in Afro-European relations on the West African "Slave Coast"', *Itinerario*, 18 (1994), 50–64

———: 'A lagoonside port on the eighteenth-century Slave Coast: the early history of Badagri', *CJAS*, 28 (1994), 35–59

———: 'On pawning and enslavement for debt in the pre-colonial Slave Coast', in Toyin Falola & Paul E. Lovejoy (eds), *Pawnship in Africa: Debt bondage in Historical Perspective* (Boulder, Colorado, 1994), 55–69

———: 'An African response to abolition: Anglo-Dahomian negotiations on ending the slave trade, 1838–77', *S&A*, 16 (1995), 281–310

——— (ed.): *From Slave Trade to 'Legitimate' Commerce: The Commercial Transition in Nine-teenth-century West Africa* (Cambridge, 1995)

———: '"Legitimate" trade and gender relations in Yorubaland and Dahomey', in Robin Law (ed.), *From Slave Trade to 'Legitimate' Commerce: The Commercial Transition in Nine-teenth-century West Africa* (Cambridge, 1995), 195–214

———: *The Kingdom of Allada* (Research School CNWS, Leiden, 1997)

———: 'The politics of commercial transition: factional conflict in Dahomey in the context of the ending of the Atlantic slave trade', *JAH*, 38 (1997), 213–33

———: 'Finance and credit in pre-colonial Dahomey', in Endre Stiansen & Jane I. Guyer (eds), *Currencies, Credit and Culture: African Financial Institutions in Historical Perspective* (Uppsala, 1999), 15–37

———: 'The origins and evolution of the merchant community in Ouidah', in Robin Law & Silke Strickrodt (eds), *Ports of the Slave Trade (Bights of Benin and Biafra)* (Centre of Commonwealth Studies, University of Stirling, 1999), 55–70

———: 'Ouidah: a pre-colonial urban centre in coastal West Africa, 1727–1892', in David M. Anderson & Richard Rathbone (eds), *Africa's Urban Past* (Oxford, 2000), 85–97

———: 'A carreira de Francisco Félix de Souza na África Ocidental (1800–1849)', *Topoi: Revista da História* (Rio de Janeiro), 2 (2001), 9–39

———: 'The evolution of the Brazilian community in Ouidah', *S&A*, 22/1 (2001), 22–41

———: 'The port of Ouidah in the Atlantic community, 17th to 19th centuries, in Horst Pietschmann (ed.), *Atlantic History: History of the Atlantic System 1580–1830, Papers pre-sented an at International Conference, held 28 August–1 September, 1999, in Hamburg, orga-nized by the Department of History, University of Hamburg* (Göttingen, 2002), 349–64

———: 'Legal and illegal enslavement in West Africa, in the context of the Atlantic slave trade', in Toyin Falola (ed.), *Ghana in Africa and the World: Essays in Honor of Adu Boahen* (Trent NJ, 2003), 513–33

———: 'Memory, oblivion and return in commemoration of the Atlantic slave trade in Ouidah, Republic of Bénin', in Ralph Austen (ed.), *The Atlantic Slave Trade in African and Diaspora Memory* (forthcoming, Durham, N.C.)

Law, Robin, & Kristin Mann: 'West Africa in the Atlantic community: the case of the Slave Coast', *WMQ*, 56/2 (1999), 307–34

Law, Robin, & Silke Strickrodt (eds): *Ports of the Slave Trade (Bights of Benin and Biafra)* (Centre of Commonwealth Studies, University of Stirling, 1999)

Le Herissé, A.: *L'Ancien Royaume du Dahomey: moeurs, religion, histoire* (Paris, 1911)

Levtzion, Nehemiah: *Muslims and Chiefs in West Africa: A Study of Islam in the Middle Volta Basin in the Pre-colonial Period* (Oxford, 1968)

Lindsay, Lisa A.: '"To return to the bosom of their fatherland": Brazilian immigrants in nineteenth-century Lagos', *S&A*, 15 (1994), 22–50

Lloyd, Christopher: *The Navy and the Slave Trade* (London, 1949)

Lombard, Jacques: 'Cotonou, ville africaine', *ED*, 10 (1953)

Lovejoy, Paul E.: 'Polanyi's "ports of trade": Salaga and Kano in the nineteenth century', *CJAS*, 16 (1982), 245–77

——: *Transformations in Slavery: A history of slavery in Africa* (Cambridge, 1983)

Lovejoy, Paul E. & David Richardson: 'Trust, pawnship and Atlantic history: the institutional foundations of the Old Calabar slave trade', *American Historical Review*, 102 (1999), 333–55

——: 'The business of slaving: pawnship in western Africa, *c.* 1600–1810', *JAH*, 41 (2001), 67–89

Lynn, Martin: *Commerce and Economic Change in West Africa: The Palm Oil Trade in the Nineteenth Century* (Cambridge, 1997)

Mabogunje, A.L.: *Urbanization in Nigeria* (London, 1968)

MacGaffey, Wyatt: 'The West in Congolese experience', in Philip D. Curtin (ed.), *Africa and the West: Intellectual Responses to European Culture* (Madison, 1972), 49–74

Manning, Patrick: 'The slave trade in the Bight of Benin, 1640–1890', in Henry A. Gemery & Jan S. Hogendorn (eds), *The Uncommon Market: Essays in the Economic History of the Atlantic Slave Trade* (New York, 1979), 107–41

——: *Slavery, Colonialism and Economic Growth in Dahomey, 1640–1960* (Cambridge, 1982)

——: 'L'affaire Adjovi: la bourgeoisie foncière au Dahomey face à l'administration', in Catherine Coquery-Vidrovitch (ed.), *Actes du colloque Entreprises et entrepreneurs en Afrique* (Paris, 1990), ii, 241–68

——: *Slavery and African Life: Occidental, Oriental and African Slave Trades* (Cambridge, 1990)

Martin, Susan: 'Slaves, Igbo women and palm oil in the nineteenth century', in Robin Law (ed.), *From Slave Trade to 'Legitimate' Commerce: The Commercial Transition in Nineteenth-century West Africa* (Cambridge, 1995), 172–94

Marty, P.: 'Etudes sur l'Islam au Dahomey, Livre 1: Le Bas Dahomey', 2 parts, *Revue du monde musulman*, 60 (1925), 109–88; 61 (1926), 75–146

Merlo, Christian: 'Hiérarchie fétichiste de Ouidah (Inventaire ethnographique, démographique et statistique des fétiches de la ville de Ouidah, Dahomey)', *BIFAN*, Série B, 2/1–2 (1940), 1–84

Merlo, Christian & Pierre Vidaud: 'Dangbe et le peuplement houeda', in François de Medeiros (ed.), *Peuples du Golfe du Bénin: Aja-Ewé (Colloque de Cotonou)* (Paris, 1984), 269–304

Métraux, Alfred: *Le Vaudou haïtien* (Paris, 1958)

Mondjannagni, Alfred Comlan: *Campagnes et villes au sud de la République Populaire du Bénin* (Paris, 1977)

Montilus, Guérin: *Dieux en diaspora: les loa haïtiens et les vaudou du royaume d'Allada (Bénin)* (Niamey, 1988)

293

Sources & Bibliography

Murray, David R.: *Odious Commerce: Britain, Spain and the Abolition of the Cuban Slave Trade* (Cambridge, 1980)

Nardin, Jean-Claude: 'La reprise des relations franco-dahoméennes au XIXe siècle: la mission d'Auguste Bouet à la cour d'Abomey', *CEA*, 7/25 (1967), 51–126

Newbury, C.W.: 'A note on the Abomey protectorate', *Africa* (London), 29 (1959), 146–55

——: *The Western Slave Coast and its Rulers: European Trade and Administration among the Yoruba and Adja-Speaking Peoples of South-western Nigeria, Southern Dahomey and Togo* (Oxford, 1961)

Nicolau Parés, Luís: 'Transformations of the sea and thunder voduns in the Gbe-speaking area and the Bahian Jeje Candomblé', in José C. Curto & Renée Soulodre-La France (eds), *Africa in the Americas: Interconnections during the Slave Trade* (New Brunswick, N.J., 2003).

Nwanunobi, C. Onyeka: 'Incendiarism and other fires in nineteenth-century Lagos (1863–1886)', *Africa* (London), 60/1 (1990), 111–20

Obichere, Boniface I.: *West African States and European Expansion: The Dahomey–Niger Hinterland, 1885–1898* (New Haven, 1971)

Oyesakin, Adefioye: 'Preliminary notes on Zangbeto: the masked vigilante group among the Ogu in Badagry', in G.O. Ogunremi, M.O. Opeleye & Siyan Oyeweso (eds), *Badagry* (Ibadan, 1994), 165–73

Parker, John: *Making the Town: Ga State and Society in Early Colonial Accra* (Oxford, 2000)

Patterson, K. David: 'A note on slave exports from the Costa da Mina, 1760–1770', *BIFAN*, série B, 33/2 (1971), 249–56

Peel, J.D.Y.: 'Urbanization and urban history in West Africa', *JAH*, 21 (1980), 269–77

Peukert, Werner: *Der atlantische Sklavenhandel von Dahomey 1740–1797: Wirtschaftsanthropologie und Sozialgeschichte* (Wiesbaden, 1978)

Polanyi, Karl: 'Sortings and "ounce trade" in the West African slave trade', *JAH*, 5 (1964), 154–69

——, with Abraham Rotstein: *Dahomey and the Slave Trade: An Analysis of an Archaic Economy* (Seattle, 1966)

Price, Jacob: 'Summation: the American panorama of Atlantic port cities', in Franklin W. Knight & Peggy K. Liss (eds): *Atlantic Port Cities: Economy, Culture and Society in the Atlantic World, 1650–1850* (Princeton, 1991), 262–76

Quénum, Maximilien: *Au pays des Fons: us et coutumes du Dahomey* (3rd edn, Paris, 1983)

Randsborg, Klavs, with Obarè Bagodo, Thomas Roland, Richard Sogan, Gérard Tognimassou & Souayibou Varissou: 'Subterranean structures: archaeology in Bénin, West Africa', *Acta Archeologica* (Copenhagen), 69 (1998), 209–27

Reis, João José: *Slave Rebellion in Brazil: The Muslim Uprising of 1835 in Bahia*, trans. Arthur Brakel (Baltimore, 1993)

Rivallain, Josette: 'Le sel dans les villages côtiers et lagunaires du Bas Dahomey', *Annales de l'Université d'Abidjan*, série I (Histoire), 8 (1980), 81–127

Rosenthal, Judy: *Possession, Ecstasy and Law in Ewe Voodoo* (Charlottesville, 1998)

Ross, David A.: 'The career of Domingo Martinez in the Bight of Benin, 1833–64', *JAH*, 6 (1965), 79–90

——: 'The first Chacha of Whydah: Francisco Felix de Souza', *Odu*, ns, 2 (1969), 19–28

——: 'The Dahomean middleman system, 1727–c. 1818', *JAH*, 28 (1987), 357–75

Roussé-Grosseau, Christiane: *Mission catholique et choc des modèles culturels en Afrique: L'Exemple du Dahomey (1861–1928)* (Paris, 1992)

Ryder, A.F.C.: 'The re-establishment of Portuguese factories on the Costa da Mina to the mid-eighteenth century', *JHSN*, 1/3 (1958), 157–83

Sources & Bibliography

Sarracino, Rodolfo: *Los que volvieron a Africa* (Havana, 1988)

Schnapper, Bernard: *La Politique et le commerce français dans le Golfe de Guinée de 1838 à 1871* (Paris, 1961)

Shaw, Rosalind: *Memories of the slave trade: Ritual and the Historical Imagination in Sierra Leone* (Chicago, 2002)

Singleton, Thereza A.: 'The slave trade remembered on the former Gold and Slave Coasts', *S&A*, 20 (1999), 150–69

Sinou, Alain: *Le Comptoir de Ouidah, une ville africaine singulière* (Paris, 1995)

Sinou, Alain & Bernardin Agbo (eds): *Ouidah et son patrimoine* (Paris/Cotonou: ORSTOM/ SERHAU, 1991)

Smith, Robert S.: *The Lagos Consulate 1851–1861* (London, 1978)

Soglo, Gilles: 'Notes sur la traite des esclaves à Glexwe (Ouidah)', in Elisée Soumonni, Bellarmin C. Codo & Joseph Adandé (eds), *Le Bénin et la Route de l'esclave* (Comité National pour le Bénin du projet La Route de l'esclave, Cotonou, 1994), 66–9

Soumonni, E.A.: 'Dahomean economic policy under Ghezo, 1818–1858: a reconsideration', *JHSN*, 10/2 (1980), 1–11

——: 'The compatibility of the slave and palm oil trades in Dahomey, 1818–1858', in Robin Law (ed.), *From Slave Trade to 'Legitimate' Commerce: The Commercial Transition in Nineteenth-century West Africa* (Cambridge, 1995), 78–92

——: 'The administration of a port of the slave trade: Ouidah in the nineteenth century', in Robin Law & Silke Strickrodt (eds), *Ports of the Slave Trade (Bights of Benin and Biafra)* (Centre of Commonwealth Studies, University of Stirling, 1999), 48–54

Soumonni, Elisée, Bellarmin C. Codo & Joseph Adandé (eds): *Le Bénin et la Route de l'esclave* (Comité National pour le Bénin du Projet La Route de l'esclave, Cotonou, [1994]).

Strickrodt, Silke: 'Afro-Brazilians of the western Slave Coast', in José C. Curto and Paul E. Lovejoy (eds), *Enslaving Connections: Western Africa and Brazil during the Era of Slavery* (Amherst, N.Y., 2003), 213–44

Sutherland, Peter: 'In memory of the slaves: an African view of the Diaspora in the Americas', in Jean Muteba Rahier (ed.), *Representations of Blackness and the Performance of Identities* (Westport, 1999), 195–211

Sy, Moussa Oumar: 'Le Dahomey: le coup d'état de 1818', *Folia Orientalia*, 6 (1964), 205–38

Thornton, John K.: *Africa and Africans in the Making of the Atlantic World, 1400–1680* (Cambridge, 1992)

Tidjani-Serpos, Nouréini & Patrick Écoutin: *Ouidah, La Route des esclaves/ Ouidah, The Slave Route* (Ministère de la Culture et des Communications, Cotonou, n.d.)

Verger, Pierre: *Flux et reflux de la traite des nègres entre le Golfe de Bénin et Bahia de Todos os Santos du XVIIe au XIXe siècle* (Paris, 1968)

——: *Os libertos: sete caminhos na liberdade de escravos da Bahia no século XIX* (Salvador, Bahia, 1992)

Verger, Pierre et al.: *Les Afro-américains* (Dakar, 1952)

Videgla, Michel: 'Le royaume de Porto-Novo face à la politique abolitionniste des nations européennes de 1848 à 1882', in Robin Law & Silke Strickrodt (eds), *Ports of the Slave Trade (Bights of Benin and Biafra)* (Centre of Commonwealth Studies, University of Stirling, 1999), 135–52

Vignondé, Jean-Norbert, 'Esclaves et esclavage dans la parémologie fon du Bénin', in Doudou Diène (ed.), *La Chaîne et le lien: une vision de la traite négrière* (UNESCO, Paris, 1998), 345–54

Wendl, Tobias: 'The Tchamba cult among the Mina in Togo', in Heike Behrend & Ute Luig (eds), *Spirit Possession: Modernity and power in Africa* (Oxford, 1999), 111–23

Sources & Bibliography

Williams, Gomer: *History of the Liverpool Privateers and Letters of Marque, with an account of the Liverpool slave trade* (London, 1897; repr. 1966)

Yarak, Larry W.: 'New sources for the study of Akan slavery and the slave trade: Dutch military recruitment in the Gold Coast and Asante, 1831–72', in Robin Law (ed.), *Source Material for Studying the Slave Trade and the African Diaspora* (Centre of Commonwealth Studies, University of Stirling, 1997), 35–60

Yoder, John C.: 'Fly and Elephant Parties: political polarization in Dahomey 1840–70', *JAH*, 15 (1974), 417–32

Unpublished items

Anignikin, Sylvain C., with Marthe B. Anignikin: 'Etude sur l'évolution historique, sociale et spatiale de la ville d'Abomey', Ministère de l'Equipement et des Transports, République Populaire du Bénin, 1986

Barnes, Sandra T.: 'The organization of cultural diversity in pre-colonial coastal communities of West Africa', Annual Meeting of the African Studies Association, 1991

Brown, Spencer H.: 'A history of the people of Lagos, 1852–1886', PhD thesis, Northwestern University, 1964

Codo, Théodule: 'Les oeuvres missionnaires dans la diffusion du Catholicisme: Ouidah 1861–1960', Mémoire de maîtrise, UNB, 1992

Guézo, Anselme: 'Commerce extérieur et évolution économique au Dahomey: Danxome (1818–1878)', Mémoire de maîtrise, UNB, 1978

Hargreaves, Susan M.: 'The political economy of nineteenth-century Bonny: a study of power, authority, legitimacy and ideology in a Delta trading community from 1790–1914', PhD thesis, University of Birmingham, 1987

Houssou, B.F.: 'Histoire et civilisation: le Zangbeto à Xogbonu (Porto-Novo) des origines à nos jours', Mémoire de maîtrise, UNB, 1985

Kelly, Kenneth G.: 'Transformations and continuity in Savi, a West African trade town: an archaeological investigation of culture change on the coast of Bénin during the 17th and 18th centuries', PhD thesis, University of California at Los Angeles, 1995

Manning, Patrick: 'Le Danhomè face aux contradictions économiques de l'ère impérialiste, 1858–1889', Colloque internationale sur 'La Vie et l'Oeuvre du Roi Glélé', Abomey, Dec. 1989

Reid, John: 'Warrior aristocrats in crisis: the political effects of the transition from the slave trade to palm oil commerce in the nineteenth-century kingdom of Dahomey', PhD thesis, University of Stirling, 1986

Robertson, Natalie Suzette: 'The African ancestry of the founders of Africatown, Alabama', PhD thesis, University of Iowa, 1996

Ross, David A.: 'The autonomous kingdom of Dahomey, 1818–1894', PhD thesis, University of London, 1967

Soglo, Gilles Raoul: 'Les Xweda: de la formation du royaume de Sayi (Saxe) à la dispersion, XVe–XVIIIe siècle', Mémoire de maîtrise, UNB, 1994/5

Sorensen-Gilmour, Caroline: 'Badagry, 1784–1863: The political and commercial history of a pre-colonial lagoonside commnity in south-west Nigeria', PhD thesis, University of Stirling, 1995

Soumonni, E.A.: 'Trade and politics in Dahomey, with particular reference to the house of Régis, 1841–1892', PhD thesis, University of Ife, 1983

Strickrodt, Silke: 'Afro-European trade relations on the western Slave Coast, 16th to 19th

centuries', PhD thesis, University of Stirling, 2003

Tettekpoe, Ayélé Marlène: 'Portée socio-historique des louanges familiales au Bénin (cas de la famille de Souza de Ouidah)', Mémoire de maîtrise, UNB, 1988–9.

Turner, Jerry Michael: 'Les Brésiliens: the impact of former Brazilian slaves upon Dahomey', PhD thesis, Boston University, 1975

Wariboko, W.E.: 'New Calabar and the forces of change, c.1850–1945', PhD thesis, University of Birmingham, 1991

Index

Index

Index

Index

Index